Central and East European Politics

Changes and Challenges

Fifth Edition

EDITED BY

ZSUZSA CSERGŐ
Queen's University

DAINA S. EGLITIS
George Washington University

PAULA M. PICKERING
William & Mary

ROWMAN & LITTLEFIELD
Lanham • Boulder • New York • London

Senior Executive Acquisitions Editor: Susan McEachern
Assistant Editor: Katelyn Turner
Sales and Marketing Inquiries: textbooks@rowman.com

Credits and acknowledgments for material borrowed from other sources, and reproduced with permission, appear on the appropriate pages within the text.

Published by Rowman & Littlefield
An imprint of The Rowman & Littlefield Publishing Group, Inc.
4501 Forbes Boulevard, Suite 200, Lanham, Maryland 20706
www.rowman.com

86-90 Paul Street, London EC2A 4NE

British Library Cataloguing in Publication Information Available

Library of Congress Cataloging-in-Publication Data

Names: Csergo, Zsuzsa, editor. | Eglitis, Daina Stukuls, editor. | Pickering, Paula M. (Paula May), 1966– editor.
Title: Central and East European politics : changes and challenges / edited by Zsuzsa Csergő, Daina S. Eglitis, Paula M. Pickering.
Description: Fifth edition. | Lanham, Maryland : Rowman & Littlefield, 2021. | Includes bibliographical references and index.
Identifiers: LCCN 2021005841 (print) | LCCN 2021005842 (ebook) | ISBN 9781538142790 (cloth) | ISBN 9781538142806 (paperback) | ISBN 9781538142813 (epub)
Subjects: LCSH: Europe, Eastern—Politics and government—1989– | Europe, Central—Politics and government—1989– | Post-communism—Europe, Eastern. | Post-communism—Europe, Central. | Democracy—Europe, Eastern. | Democracy—Europe, Central. | European Union—Europe, Eastern. | European Union—Europe, Central.
Classification: LCC DJK51 .C437 2021 (print) | LCC DJK51 (ebook) | DDC 947.0009/049—dc23
LC record available at https://lccn.loc.gov/2021005841
LC ebook record available at https://lccn.loc.gov/2021005842

Contents

Illustrations

Figures

Maps

Photos

Tables

Acknowledgments

All books are the product of many minds and many hands, and we would like to recognize our colleagues, contributing authors, editors, assistants, friends, and family who have been instrumental in the completion of this book.

We would like to acknowledge our contributors, both old and new. We are grateful to the terrific authors of chapters published in past editions who came back for this edition, and we welcome and recognize the outstanding new contributors who have enriched this book with new topics and perspectives.

As the editors of the fifth edition of *Central and East European Politics*, we are the inheritors of a significant legacy passed down from the book's original editors, Sharon L. Wolchik and Jane Leftwich Curry. Sharon and Jane's seminal work in educating generations of scholars and students about the politics of the region has informed and inspired our own work. We are honored that they entrusted us to carry this book forward. We would like to add that all three of us are Sharon's academic progeny: she has taught and mentored each of us (formally or informally), and we aspire to continue her legacy as researchers, educators, and mentors.

We are grateful for the support and guidance of Rowman & Littlefield's executive editor, Susan McEachern, and assistant editor, Katelyn Turner. We would also like to thank George Washington University student Heather Harper for her support with photo research and final chapter preparation, as well as Varsha Venkatasubramanian, doctoral student in history at the University of California Berkeley, for her work on the index. We appreciate the careful work of Elwood Mills on the book's maps and that of contributor Kevin Deegan-Krause on many of the book's figures.

We recognize that no work comes without sacrifices of time and commitment to other responsibilities, and we are grateful for the support of our families. Paula thanks in particular Steve Menzies for his love and support, for carefully listening to her mull over research problems, and for improving her writing. Daina offers special thanks to her husband, Joseph Burke, whose patience with every new and old project and pursuit is unmatched. Zsuzsa is grateful to Gábor, Eszter, and Daniel for creating the loving and unfailingly supportive family environment that enables and inspires her work.

We would also like to acknowledge the scholars who have mentored us and shaped our thinking about Central and East Europe. Paula is indebted to Zvi Gitelman, John Fine, and Val Bunce for challenging her to conduct research more rigorously and in depth, for their steadfast support, and for serving as inspirations in their commitment to helping others understand Central and East Europe. Daina thanks the many scholars and friends who have so kindly and consistently supported her work on the region, in particular Michael D. Kennedy, Sharon L. Wolchik, and Vita Zelče. Zsuzsa is thankful to Sharon L. Wolchik, Zora Bútorova, and Irina Culic for setting the example of balance, courage, and integrity in researching, writing, and teaching about difficult and divisive subjects. We would also like to thank our students, from whom we always learn.

It is also important to recognize the significant contributions of academic area studies centers in educating and supporting scholars of this region. We have been beneficiaries of the University of Michigan's Center for Russian and East European Studies; George Washington University's Institute for European, Russian, and Eurasian Studies; and the Center for Southeast European Studies at the University of Graz. Finally, we want to acknowledge the international scholarly associations that have contributed to our professional development, as well as to that of others who study and teach about Central and East Europe within and outside that region—including many authors of this book. Key among these are the Association for Slavic, East European, and Eurasian Studies (ASEEES), the Association for the Study of Nationalities (ASN), and the Association for the Advancement of Baltic Studies (AABS). The understanding of political developments in any setting, let alone a large and diverse geographic region, is made possible only through the work of many generations of scholars. They contribute approaches and methodologies, while challenging, complementing, and supporting each other to move the field forward.

Part I

INTRODUCTION

CHAPTER 1

Central and East Europe

TURBULENT HISTORIES, DRAMATIC TRANSFORMATIONS, AND TWENTY-FIRST-CENTURY CHALLENGES

Zsuzsa Csergő, Daina S. Eglitis, and Paula M. Pickering

The second decade of the twenty-first century in Central and East Europe has been characterized by significant paradoxes. Consider a few recent events. In May 2020, demonstrators in Budapest, Hungary, took to the streets to protest legislation that took rights away from sexual minorities.[1] Several months later, in September 2020, thousands of demonstrators formed a human chain from the Hungarian parliament to the University of Theatre and Film Arts in defense of the autonomy of the university and other educational and cultural institutions, and for the freedom of artistic expression.[2] In October 2020, in neighboring Poland, massive protests known as the "Women's Strike" reemerged across the country, demonstrating against legislation limiting women's reproductive freedom. The act, adopted by a right-wing populist government controlled by the Law and Justice party, further tightened an already restrictive anti-abortion law.[3]

Numerous European institutions, including the European Parliament, have regularly criticized these governments' antidemocratic policies during the 2010s. By November 2020, in the middle of the global coronavirus pandemic, the conflict escalated to a European Union–wide crisis, as the governments of Hungary and Poland allied against the rest of the European Union (EU) and vetoed the EU's seven-year budget, delaying its COVID-19 recovery plan. The reason for the veto was that the plan linked the distribution of funds to rule-of-law requirements in an effort to hold member states accountable for violating the EU's democratic norms, which both Poland and Hungary have done.[4]

These developments seem paradoxical against the backdrop of these countries' post-1989 histories. After all, when communism began collapsing in Central and East Europe three decades ago after half a century in the Soviet-dominated communist bloc, the Hungarian and Polish governments were in the forefront of liberalization and Europeanization. They enthusiastically embraced the principles of *liberal democracy*, which formed the core of the European integration process. As the name suggests, liberal democracy emphasizes freedoms. Its scope is broader than that of *electoral democracy*, which focuses on the procedural aspects of democratic government. In an electoral democracy, the emphasis is on ensuring that governments emerge through competitive, regular, free, and fair elections—and that voters have opportunities and institutions available to challenge or question the acts of governments between elections. Beyond these procedural requirements for electing a government and hold-ing it accountable, liberal democracy pursues constitutionally guaranteed civil liberties, as well as a strong rule of law, in order to provide protection against potential excesses of executive power or majoritarian rule. In most established democracies, including the majority of member states of the European Union, liberal democracy is the dominant principle.

The illiberal policies introduced by governments to eliminate civil rights and insti-tutions that could provide protection from excessive state power run counter to this principle. Thus, the "illiberal turn" currently unfolding in some countries in the region (including other former front-runners of liberalization, such as the Czech Republic) is viewed as part of the political landscape of "democratic backsliding."[5]

At the same time, manifestations of democratic consolidation are also present in the region. While in some countries, women's reproductive autonomy has come under threat and the leadership of the state is almost exclusively in men's hands,[6] in October 2020, Lithuania's newly elected center-right coalition government brought together three par-ties, all of which are led by women.[7] This was a historic first, though Lithuania—like its Baltic neighbors Latvia and Estonia—has also had a woman president in the postcom-munist period. Estonia also gained its first woman prime minister in January 2021, after the resignation of her predecessor in response to a corruption investigation involving his party. Estonia remains a positive example of democratic transparency in a region where both communist- and postcommunist-era corruption eroded public trust in government. Estonia ranks well above the European Union average in the international transparency index, which measures perceived levels of public sector corruption. It scores high for its independent institutions, transparency of electoral financing, and openness of gov-ernment, much of which functions on a digital platform that also enables convenient e-voting for citizens.[8] Anticorruption forces have also strengthened in Slovakia, when mass protests against the murder of a journalist investigating ties between the government and organized crime in 2018 helped bring about the resignation of the prime minister and interior minister and fueled the election of an antigraft president and, in 2020, a new government.[9]

A key goal of this book is to illuminate contemporary politics in Central and East Europe and to provide insights into regional paradoxes, as well as past accomplish-ments, current developments, and future challenges. Importantly, the politics of the early twenty-first century are products not only of our moment or of the current choices politicians and citizens make. The past shapes the present in significant ways in this region. The history of interethnic relations, clashing interpretations of the past, and enduring alliances and threats are among the social forces that influence governance, regional relations, and social group interactions in these states. As we prepare to embark on our collective journey through Central and East Europe, this chapter offers a broad overview of major historical events, including the fall of empires, rise of new states, two world wars, experiences with communism, and the evolution of postcommunism in the region. As you read, take time to consider the questions at the end of each section that invite you to recognize the political significance of the time period covered for your understanding of current political developments in these fascinating countries and this dynamic part of the world.

Photo 1.1. Kersti Kaljulaid became president of Estonia in 2016. She is the first woman president.

The Decline of Empires, World War I, and the Interwar Period

The twentieth century in Central and East Europe witnessed the dramatic decline of empires, two brutal world wars, economic devastation and depression, and loss of human life on a scale that is difficult to comprehend. It also gave rise to new nations with ambitions of independence and democracy, flourishing civil societies, and populations with deep resilience and a commitment to preserving their history, language, and culture.

The early years of the twentieth century were dominated by the empires that birthed many of the region's states: the Russian Empire in the east, Austria-Hungary and Germany in the west and center, and the Ottoman Empire in the south.[10] As imperial subjects, the populations of Central and East Europe had little political or economic autonomy, and both they and the territories where they resided were exploited by powerful rulers for their labor and resources. They did, however, have local cultures and languages and a developed or evolving sense of nationhood and aspirations for independence.

The Russian Empire, which dated back to 1721, stretched across a vast Eurasian space and included the Baltic territories (now Latvia, Lithuania, and Estonia), eastern Poland,

Map 1.1.   Central and East Europe Today

and a part of Ukraine. Private ownership of agricultural land was uncommon among the peasant populations of this region, and they labored with few prospects for better lives. Imperial authorities also practiced aggressive Russification.[11] Small groups of intellectuals, educated in the exclusive universities of the empire, and a handful of local cultural figures fostered a growing sense of national identity among the Baltic peoples. Poles, for their part, retained a sense of nationhood from a distant past, when Poland had existed as a state and even, in the form of the Polish-Lithuanian Empire, as a regional power. Poles resisted Russian control with underground organizations and periodic uprisings. The Russian Empire formally came to an end on March 15, 1917, when Tsar Nicholas II abdicated the throne and ended the Romanov dynasty. A provisional government took his place but survived only briefly, collapsing in the face of the Bolshevik (communist) insurrections that triggered a civil conflict and, eventually, the establishment of the communist Union of Soviet Socialist Republics (USSR) in 1922.[12]

The Austro-Hungarian Empire, which was established in 1867 as a dual monarchy uniting the Austrian Empire and the Kingdom of Hungary, included the current territories of Austria, Hungary, the Czech Republic, Slovakia, Croatia, Slovenia, parts of Serbia and Poland, a western territory of Ukraine, and, later, Bosnia-Herzegovina. Ruled from Vienna and Budapest, the empire was a significant regional power. The populations that inhabited its space had diverse experiences of imperial rule. For example, the areas ruled from Vienna (Austria) experienced significant industrial development and some autonomy in local governance. By contrast, Hungarian-ruled territories, including Slovakia and Croatia, experienced little economic development, had limited local autonomy, and were subject to pressure for linguistic assimilation (that is, adoption of the Hungarian language). The empire ended in 1918: having been on the losing side of World War I and unable to satisfy the demands of its constituent ethnic groups for autonomy, the Austro-Hungarian Empire dissolved. Its lands came to comprise new or revived states, including new, multiethnic Yugoslavia and Czechoslovakia.[13]

The longest-lasting empire in the region was the Ottoman Empire. Established in about 1299, it included the territories of what would later come to be Serbia, Montenegro, Macedonia, Bulgaria, Bosnia-Herzegovina, Albania, and parts of Romania and Croatia. The Ottomans did not allow political autonomy, though they did tolerate religious minority communities. The empire's "millet system" provided significant nonterritorial autonomy to communities that did not belong to the dominant Islamic religion. Economic development in the territories was minimal, and the empire, particularly in the latter part of its existence, was riven by corruption. It progressively lost land. In 1878, the Congress of Berlin declared the independence of Serbia, Bulgaria, and Romania. During the Balkan Wars that followed in 1912 and 1913, the Ottoman Empire lost nearly all of its European territories. The empire came to a formal end in 1922. Its legatee state, Turkey, came into being in 1923.[14]

Finally, the Kingdom of Prussia, which was part of the German Empire, existed from 1701 to 1918. While its largest legatee is the country of Germany, its territories encompassed parts of what would later become Poland, Lithuania, the Czech Republic, and Denmark. Some of its territories were also absorbed by Russia after its dissolution.[15]

As is clear from these brief histories, the age of empires, which denied the peoples of Central and East Europe self-rule, was coming to an end in the early twentieth century. This era would give birth to a multitude of smaller states, both new (such as the Baltic countries of Latvia, Lithuania, and Estonia; Czechoslovakia; and Yugoslavia) and revived (such as Poland), but not before the region had experienced the terror and tumult of World War I.

World War I began in 1914 after the assassination of Archduke Franz Ferdinand in Sarajevo (a city in Bosnia-Herzegovina) by a Serbian who wanted Bosnia-Herzegovina,

Map 1.2. Central and East Europe, 1914

which was still part of the Austro-Hungarian Empire, to become part of Serbia. On one side of the war were the Central powers, which included Germany, Austria-Hungary, Bulgaria, and the Ottoman Empire. On the other were the Allied powers: Great Britain, France, Italy, the Russian Empire, Romania, Japan, and the United States. The war was brutal: the advent of new military technologies and trench warfare brought dramatic suffering across Eurasia.

The triumph of the Allied powers finally came in 1918. While the end of the war was welcomed across the continent, it also signaled significant political and territorial shifts, some of which would sow the seeds of later conflicts. The Treaty of Versailles created borders for a new Europe, answering a call by US president Woodrow Wilson for national determination for the peoples of Europe. As empires fell, states were born or reborn. Some of these states, such as Latvia, Lithuania, and Estonia, which emerged largely from the Russian Empire, were governed by titular ethnic groups, though the states themselves had significant minority populations. Poland and Romania emerged as states patched together from the territories of multiple broken empires. Hungary became an independent though truncated state. As a loser in the war, it was deprived of significant swaths of territory inhabited by ethnic Hungarians, which would be a source of discontent for decades. Bulgaria, a Central power, also lost territory. Other states emerged that were an amalgamation of ethnic groups: Czechoslovakia and Yugoslavia had no titular ethnicity; Czechoslovaks and Yugoslavians existed only as political creations. At the same time, their creation had the support of many local leaders, who were responding in part to strategic conditions that favored the territorial security of more diverse, expansive states.

The early postwar period in Central and East Europe brought hope that democracy could take root, though democratic development faced some formidable obstacles, including devastated postwar economies and massive population losses due to conflict and refugee movements. Most newly created states incorporated large ethnic minority populations, and the hardships of the postwar economic recovery exacerbated ethnic tensions over the nation-building policies adopted in new state centers, which impacted minority populations in significant ways, including language rights and access to political and economic power.

The newly independent Baltic countries ambitiously established the constitutional and institutional building blocks of parliamentary democracies with universal suffrage (including for women), equality before the law, and guarantees of minority rights. They also undertook massive land reform: land that had been concentrated in the hands of Baltic German estates for generations was transferred to peasants, many of whom were members of the titular ethnic groups and had worked the soil for decades but had never owned land. While economies remained largely agricultural, land reform brought some stability and prosperity to the new states. Political and economic progress, however, were short-lived: parliamentary systems intentionally created with a weak executive branch paradoxically led to legislatures populated by a multitude of small parties and consequently weak governments. In 1926, Lithuanian democracy succumbed to an authoritarian presidential regime (note that in this text, we use the term *regime* interchangeably with the term *system of government*). Estonian and Latvian democracies lasted through 1934 but could not survive the worsening economic conditions of a global depression and the rising tide of authoritarianism in Europe.[16]

Poland established a parliamentary democracy in 1919. It lasted until 1926, when József Piłsudski seized power over a fractious Sejm (parliament), though he allowed the Sejm to continue to exist, in name at least. In 1935, a new constitution was adopted and Piłsudski died. Poland, following the regional pattern, took a turn toward harsher authoritarian rule, including the persecution of perceived internal enemies, which lasted until the country was attacked and occupied by Germany and then the USSR in 1939.[17]

The first government of Czechoslovakia sought to build a democratic republic governed from its new capital in Prague. This government undertook economic and land reforms to build prosperity, but the success of these efforts was derailed in part by the worldwide depression. As in other parts of the region, one consequence of the economic downturn was heightened ethnic tension. In the case of Czechoslovakia, disaffection was particularly acute among ethnic Germans living in the Sudetenland region, near the German border, though Slovaks and Hungarians were also unhappy with their lack of access to political power, which was concentrated in the hands of ethnic Czechs. Among the German population, sympathy grew for the Nazi Party. Despite its efforts to enlist allies like France to resist German territorial aspirations, Czechoslovakia lost this border area in 1938, when the Munich Agreement, which recognized German control of the Sudetenland, was signed by Germany, Britain, and France.[18]

The Kingdom of Yugoslavia was born in 1918, comprised of myriad ethnic groups with diverse histories, languages, and religious orientations, but under a Serbian-dominated unitary state. Like so many of its regional neighbors, Yugoslavia began its political life with efforts at representative governance but eventually dissolved into authoritarianism, economic decline, and growing ethnic discord. In 1941, the country was occupied and divided up by the Axis powers. Neighboring Albania, which succeeded in maintaining its territorial integrity and independence at the end of World War I in spite of efforts of larger powers to partition it, was under parliamentary rule through 1928, when a coup led to the proclamation of a monarchy.[19]

Genuine democratic rule was largely elusive in Hungary, even in the early postwar period. In 1920, the National Constituent Assembly, elected for the purpose of determining the new government's future, opted for a monarchy. While not overtly a dictatorship until 1932, power in the 1920s was largely concentrated in the hands of a landed aristocracy that limited the political voice of other constituencies. Romania and Bulgaria followed a similar path, though the monarchy had already existed for many years: efforts at democratic governance were weak and were further derailed by economic instability and ethnic tensions that grew through the 1930s. All of these countries would also see the rise of extremist parties and movements, particularly right-wing groups, which embraced anti-Semitism and leaned hard toward Nazi sympathies.

Thus, the governments of states created from the three large empires that collapsed during World War I were keen to establish national sovereignty, but they were unable to resolve the massive challenges of this period, which ultimately became a short "interwar period," soon followed by another devastating world war.

The new and renewed states of the Central and East European region shared some key features in this period: most countries sought to build practices and institutions of democratic government, but none successfully navigated the shoals of a worldwide economic depression, growing authoritarianism in powerful West European states like

Germany and Italy, and tensions between ethnic communities that were rendered more acute by nationalist politics and policies that discriminated against minority populations. Between 1939 and 1941, all would become actors in the bloody and brutal drama of World War II, some siding with the Axis powers, some with the Allies, and some broken by occupation and partition that split their political and military loyalties.

The fall of the previous century's dominant imperial powers, the devastation of World War I, and the experience of interwar efforts at political and economic self-governance as independent states left significant legacies for these regional states, some of which are present today.

As you read this text, consider the following questions:

- What were and are the key catalysts of interethnic tensions in Central and East Europe? What are their roots in history? What are their contemporary manifestations?
- How does the interwar period feature in the politics and social memory of the Baltic countries, Poland, Romania, and Hungary? How has it manifested in the politics, social memory, and conflicts in the states of former Yugoslavia?
- What are the similarities and differences between the development and fate of democratic governance in the interwar period and the postcommunist period in Central and East Europe?

World War II and the Holocaust in Central and East Europe

World War II wrought mass destruction across the Eurasian continent. Central and East Europe experienced significant and long-lasting devastation in the form of military and civilian casualties; genocide of Jewish, Roma, and other marginalized populations at the hands of the Nazis; economic catastrophe; near-complete destruction of cities and towns; the mass exodus of refugees, many of whom would never return; and the loss of political autonomy and, in some cases, independent statehood. The legacies of World War II live on today in the form of demographic consequences, as well as memory conflicts between and within some countries over who were victims and who were villains in the war.

The events that precipitated World War II took place over the course of several years. The first events of what would become a massive continental conflagration were the result of diplomatic acquiescence to Nazi Germany's demands for territory rather than an outcome of military conflict. In October 1938, Germany occupied the Sudetenland, a part of the country of Czechoslovakia that the German government claimed was a historical home of ethnic Germans. The shared sentiment of the Western powers that ceded the Sudetenland to Germany was that it would quell German ambitions and maintain peace on the continent, a belief that would prove to be catastrophically wrong.

In August 1939, the foreign ministers of Germany and the Soviet Union signed the Molotov-Ribbentrop nonaggression pact, a document that foresaw mutual territorial respect between the two powers but also contained a secret protocol that divided parts of Central and East Europe into spheres of influence. This provision foresaw the division of the Baltic countries, Poland, Finland, and Romania between Germany and the USSR. On September 1, 1939, Germany attacked Poland, and on September 17, the Soviet Union launched its invasion of Poland. By 1941, the war spread eastward: on June 22, 1941, Germany launched a surprise attack on the USSR, violating the Molotov-Ribbentrop Pact and opening the eastern front of World War II, which would see nearly four brutal years of war.

While the Soviet Union fought with the Allies against Nazi Germany, some of the countries of the region allied themselves with the Axis powers, which included Germany and Italy. Bulgaria, Hungary, and Romania fought on the side of the Axis. Alliances, however, were complicated in the region. Germany and Italy took advantage of extremist factions of minorities unhappy with their political rights in interwar states to create "puppet states" in Slovakia and Croatia. Other countries, including Poland, the Czech Republic, most of Yugoslavia, western Ukraine, and the Baltic states were occupied by Germany and thus comprised strategic territories from which Germany could launch attacks and recruit soldiers.

The German occupation of Central and East Europe also signaled an even deadlier phase of the Holocaust, as Nazi Germany and local collaborators murdered large proportions of the Jewish populations of occupied states and used their territories to establish the concentration camps that would last through the end of the war and see the killing of millions of Jews, Roma and Sinti, and prisoners of war from across the European continent.

Germany's occupation of Poland in September 1939 resulted in a mass movement of refugees, both Jewish and non-Jewish, eastward. Refugees hoped that the Polish army would halt the German advance. Instead, the Soviets moved in from the west, and about three hundred thousand Jewish refugees ended up in Soviet-occupied territories. Rather than finding safety, however, many were arrested by Soviet authorities and deported to Siberia, accused of being political threats to the state. Still others fled the Soviets, ending up in Hungary, Romania, or Lithuania, where most would lose their lives to German forces and their local collaborators.[20]

Poland was home to the first ghettos established by Nazi Germany. The largest ghetto in Nazi-occupied territory was the Warsaw ghetto, created in October 1940, which at its peak held over four hundred thousand Jews in a 1.3-square-mile space. The Nazis ordered Jews into ghettos they created as a means for authorities to segregate and persecute them. Ghettos, which were established in the poorest parts of many cities and towns, were generally enclosed by a fence or wall and physically separated Jews from non-Jews. Living conditions in the ghettos were dire, with shortages of food, medicine, and clothing. The risk of violence was ever present.[21]

After Germany attacked the USSR, more ghettos were constructed in the occupied territories of the Baltic states, Ukraine, Belorussia, and western Russia. Among the largest ghettos in this area were Minsk, Lviv, Vilnius, and Kaunas. An expansive ghetto was also created in Riga, the capital city of Latvia, where Jews had been about 10 percent of the population in the mid-1930s. Shortly after German occupation, an estimated thirty thousand Jews from Riga and surrounding areas were crowded into the Moscow district of the city, a working-class area without the capacity to house so many residents. While the ghetto would last until December 1943, most of the Latvian Jews who populated the ghetto in the first months of its existence were murdered before the end of 1941.

Map 1.3. Axis and Allies in World War II, December 1941

Photo 1.2. The Warsaw ghetto in Poland was the largest Nazi ghetto in German-occupied Central and East Europe. This photo shows the surrender of Polish Jews after an uprising in the ghetto there. (Unknown author, Wikimedia Commons)

In two mass killings that took place on November 30 and December 8–9, 1941, German forces and local collaborators shot an estimated twenty-six thousand Latvian Jews in the Rumbula forest. Almost immediately, their place in the Riga ghetto was occupied by West European Jews deported by Nazi authorities from their homes in Germany, Austria, and Czechoslovakia.[22] Notably, ghettos were never established in Germany or the German-occupied states of Western Europe.

The Holocaust in the occupied territories of the Soviet Union is sometimes referred to as a "Holocaust by bullets"[23] because Jewish communities in, for example, the Baltic territories were largely wiped out in mass shooting actions like the one at Rumbula forest, where over twenty-five thousand Latvian Jews were murdered in just two days. Of the estimated seventy thousand Jews who were in Latvia when the German occupation began at the end of June 1940, only a few hundred remained alive in that territory at the end of the war. Their numbers rose in the postwar years as several thousand Jews returned from concentration camps where they had been held prisoner and from the Soviet interior, where some had lived in exile during the war or had served in the Soviet army.[24]

Millions of European Jews perished in the Nazi concentration camps, many of which were established on German-occupied territory in Poland. In Auschwitz-Birkenau, a death camp near the city of Kraków, an estimated 1.1 million prisoners were murdered, including Jews, Soviet prisoners of war, and Roma and Sinti people. Among the last to be deported before war's end were the Jews of Hungary, who had survived through the spring of 1944, when the Hungarian government, an ally of Nazi Germany, sent over 440,000 of them to Auschwitz-Birkenau. Death camps like Treblinka, Sobibor, and Belzec, also located in occupied Polish territory, comprised other pieces of the machinery of genocide that killed Jews and other perceived enemies of the Nazis in gas chambers and through sickness, starvation, and overwork.[25]

Altogether, the loss of Jewish communities across the space of Central and East Europe, where they had comprised a historically rooted and robust proportion of the population, was dramatic. In Latvia, Lithuania, and Romania, over 90 percent of the Jewish population was killed in the Holocaust. In the 1930s, Poland was home of the largest Jewish population in Europe with about 3.3 million Jews, comprising 10 percent of the population. Most of this population died in the ghettos of Warsaw, Kraków, and other cities, or in the death camps. The Nazis targeted other communities for destruction as well: the US Holocaust Memorial Museum estimates that about a quarter of Europe's Roma population, which lived across a wide swath of states, was killed.[26]

The momentum of the war on the eastern front had shifted by the late summer of 1943, and leaders from the United States, Britain, and the Soviet Union began to plan for the defeat of Germany and the restoration of European states and societies. Decisions made by the Allied nations would prove fateful for Central and East Europe: at the Yalta Conference, held in February 1945, US president Franklin D. Roosevelt, British prime minister Winston Churchill, and Soviet premier Joseph Stalin agreed that Germany and the city of Berlin would be divided into four occupation zones controlled by the United States, Britain, France, and the Soviets. At Yalta, Stalin declared that Polish territory annexed by the USSR in 1939 would not be returned (it subsequently became part of Soviet Ukraine, albeit after years of resistance).

In a decision with profound political consequences, the United States and Britain also acceded to Stalin's demand that future governments in the Central and East European states adjacent to the Soviet Union be "friendly" to the Soviet regime. This essentially established a buffer zone around the USSR. In exchange, Stalin agreed to permit free elections in the territories liberated from Nazi occupation, including Czechoslovakia, Hungary, Romania, Bulgaria, and Poland. With the exception of nominally competitive elections that took place in Hungary in 1945 and Czechoslovakia in 1946, the free elections foreseen in the Yalta agreement did not come to pass, and communist governments, backed by Soviet military might, were installed across the region. Communist regimes would largely remain in power until the signal events of 1989, when mass social movements for change that had been building through the 1980s replaced communism with democratic governments in most countries.[27]

The Baltic countries, which had been independent in the interwar period, lost their political autonomy entirely and were incorporated into the USSR. Significantly, this chapter of the war has remained a source of controversy and tension in contemporary Baltic politics and relations with Russia, the key legatee of the cult of World War II that was prevalent in the USSR. Specifically, as the Soviet army pushed Nazi German forces westward over the course of 1944 and early 1945, it took control of territories, like those of the Baltic countries, that had been occupied by the Nazis since 1941. From the Soviet perspective, this constituted *liberation* of the Baltics, as those territories had indeed been freed from German control. From the perspective of many ethnic Latvians, Lithuanian, and Estonians, however, the Soviet seizure of the space and institutions of the Baltics constituted *occupation*, as one occupation would be replaced by another and the Baltics would unwillingly become republics of the USSR until they reestablished independence in 1991.

The path followed by the territories of Albania and Yugoslavia at war's end differed from that of other states in the region. In Albania, Yugoslav fighters with Western support ousted German forces, and a provisional communist government, which would last for decades, was established in 1944. Most of Yugoslavia's own territory was liberated not by the Soviet army but by Josip Broz Tito and the partisans he led in battle against German occupiers and extremist Croat and Serb groups. Tito received support from Western allies in his fight. Domestic forces largely established a communist state in Yugoslavia. Tito created a multinational federation under one-party rule that attempted to address conflicts that plagued the Serbian-dominated interwar Yugoslavia. This effort was increasingly challenged after his death in 1980.

World War II and the Holocaust left a significant mark on the states, territories, and populations of Central and East Europe. This includes a legacy of violence, destruction, societal transformation, and the coerced adoption of Communist Party rule that lingers in contemporary relations and politics.

As you read this text, consider the following questions:

- What are the dominant national narratives of World War II in the region? How do they differ across and even within countries?
- How is the Holocaust characterized and memorialized, particularly in countries that lost most of their Jewish communities during the German occupation?
- What is the significance of World War II and the Holocaust in contemporary political debates and discussions? Thinking more broadly, how do conflicting narratives of history create challenges for multiethnic communities seeking to build democratic institutions?

Communist Rule in Central and East Europe

The one-party communist rule that was imposed on Central and East Europe at the end of World War II profoundly transformed the political, economic, and social systems of the region. The problems of interwar governments and the horrific human and physical destruction of World War II left the peoples of the region craving change—and normalcy. The Soviet role in World War II and the Western allies' unwillingness to stop the USSR from creating a buffer zone out of Central and East Europe ensured that the communist vision of change won out.[28] This vision, however, presented fundamental issues of legitimacy. *Legitimacy* means not simply authority (or capacity) to rule but the right to rule. In democratic systems, governments gain legitimacy through regular, free, and fair elections. Communist parties established governing authority relatively quickly in war-devastated Central and East Europe with Soviet support, but their legitimacy (that is, their right to rule) was weak from the start and steadily diminished.

The efforts to impose a system based on the USSR's Marxist-Leninist ideology were met with substantial resistance, particularly in Poland, the Baltic states, western Ukraine, and Romania. Other than in Yugoslavia and Albania, where the Partisans who had fought the fascists' occupation established Communist Party rule in territories they liberated during the war, Soviet-backed communists forcibly eliminated opposition in order to capture power in World War II's aftermath. In the Baltic states, after deporting tens of thousands of Estonian, Lithuanian, and Latvian citizens in 1941, the Soviets deported in 1949 an additional one hundred thousand rural residents who resisted collectiviza-tion and sent in Russian-speaking populations to take over key political, military, and economic roles. Even in Czechoslovakia, where the Communist Party won a substantial proportion of the vote in the first postwar election, authorities in Moscow rejected the sharing of power with other parties. Instead, the Communist Party began in 1948 decisive efforts to eliminate political opponents.

The Soviet blueprint for the region was characterized by Communist Party control over not just politics and the military and security services, but also over the economic and social systems. This included one-party rule by the Communist Party, state owner-ship of the means of production, state-directed industrialization, and party control over information and social organizations. These features were enforced internally by Soviet secret police and Soviet-trained security forces and from outside by the Soviet-controlled military alliance of the Warsaw Pact and an economic union called the Council for Mutual Economic Assistance (Comecon). The former intervened to overturn reformers in the region, while the latter dictated economic development and trade relations within the bloc's nontransferrable ruble zone. Membership in the Communist Party was required for any significant economic or social mobility, which was realized through the party's *nomenklatura* system of lists of citizens deemed loyal to the cause.

Communist rule across the region manifested in a variety of ways. Even Communist Party leaders admitted that they were unable to establish *communism*, a political and economic system whose ultimate goal was the elimination of private property and the state and the eventual creation of a system of self-organized, self-managed communal life. Instead, *state socialism*, constructed as a hierarchical structure with one-party control over politics and the state, as well as state domination of the means of production and social groups, is a term that many scholars consider a more accurate description of the systems Central and East European communist parties actually developed.[29] This book uses both terms—communist and state socialist—to describe political and economic systems set up by communist parties in the region. In terms of differences across countries, Yugoslavia and Poland abandoned collectivization of agriculture after the policy provoked significant resistance there. In addition, Yugoslavia adopted a "self-management" economic model that injected some market mechanisms into a socialist economic system, decentralized economic planning, and gave more control to managers and a semblance of control to workers.

Efforts by the communist parties to control all social organizations was a failure in, for instance, the case of the Catholic Church in Poland, which retained a degree of autonomy, but social control, particularly in the early postwar years, was strict across the region. Yugoslavia was something of an exception. After breaking with Stalin in 1948, Tito's Yugoslavia allowed for a society more open than any other country run by the

Communist Party. This was a part of the Yugoslav Communist Party's improvisation, which arguably was afforded by the greater legitimacy the Yugoslav Communist Party enjoyed, largely based on its victory in World War II, compared to the other communist parties in the region.[30] This constant political improvisation included efforts to manage its diverse ethnic groups through genuine decentralization of power to an ethnic-based federal system and to republic-specific communist parties, as well as "power sharing" within one-party rule.[31] It also included freedom to travel outside Yugoslavia's borders and participation in the global Nonaligned Movement, which eschewed membership in either of the Cold War military blocs.

Communist parties in the countries of Central and East Europe suffered significant legitimacy crises. The weaker their popular support was, the more repressive the parties became of any source of opposition, which in turn reinforced popular resentment against communism. During Stalin's rule, real or imagined resistance to communist rule was met with brutal force. The most devastating example was in 1933 when Soviet authorities responded to resistance to collectivization in Ukraine with an artificial famine that claimed an estimated 3.3 to 3.9 million lives.[32]

After Stalin's death in 1953, Nikita Khrushchev's denunciation of Stalin's use of terror had a destabilizing effect on communist regimes in Central and East Europe that had relied heavily on backing from the Soviet Union rather than acceptance by their own citizens. Significantly, efforts at reform came from within the party as well. For instance, perceiving a window for reform, elements within the Hungarian Communist Party led by Imre Nagy in 1956 proposed implementing multiparty elections and condemned the Warsaw Pact. These efforts resulted in invasion by Warsaw Pact troops and Nagy's execution.

In response to legitimacy challenges in the post-Stalin period, Central and East European governments developed a variety of control strategies, a number of which used coercion but did not rely on naked use of force, to at least gain quiescence of their populations. Anthropologist Katherine Verdery labels these "sticks and carrots," as surveillance and socialist paternalism, respectively. Surveillance against ordinary citizens was exercised by internal police, who conducted the most extensive operations in East Germany and Romania. Romania's infamous Securitate thoroughly penetrated society, creating an atmosphere of fear and pervasive threat.[33] Central and East European leaders who resisted the relaxation of controls included Romania's Nicolae Ceauşescu and Albania's Enver Hoxha. Even though these leaders developed economic relationships with some non-Comecon states—Romania with the West and Albania with China—they maintained repressive controls over their societies.

In addition to the stick of surveillance, the Communist Party also deployed the carrot of the socialist social contract. The Communist Party pledged to provide for the population's basic needs in exchange for their acceptance of one-party rule. Delivered through state-owned enterprises, this unwritten contract included pensions and state-subsidized housing and basic goods, as well as free education, health care, and child care. When Communist Party officials feared popular unrest, they ramped up efforts to fulfill their end of the socialist social contract.[34] As long as the party could reasonably uphold its side of the contract, many citizens accepted the situation, even if they lamented circumscribed opportunities for free assembly, travel, and political voice. Indeed, many came to expect the social benefits provided by communist states. Hungary's "goulash communism," under which some market experimentation was infused into the state socialist economic system, allowed the Communist Party to deliver previously scarce consumer goods to citizens. Hungarian leader János Kádár famously proclaimed that "those who are not against us are with us," which categorized quiescence as acceptance.

Communist parties' claims to legitimacy were significantly rooted in economic achievements. It was a huge blow when communist parties failed to deliver on their claim to build an economic system that gave genuine power to workers and met citizens' basic needs. These failures were vividly clear to all citizens through their daily lives. For example, workers toiled in factories or other jobs while their Communist Party bosses, who often had less expertise, enjoyed privileges not accessible to ordinary workers. Meanwhile, citizens scoured shops for an increasing number of goods in short supply. These failures generated even greater anger when contrasted to lies relentlessly propagated through state-controlled media and workers' and social organizations about ever-increasing economic gains and worker power.[35]

After initial economic advancements from rapid postwar industrialization, the centrally planned economies of Central and East Europe began to falter. This was due to the center being unable to plan the interactions of myriad economic forces, and because the information used to build economic plans was often based on lies about, among other things, raw materials and productivity. In contrast to the supposed iron grip that communist parties exerted over economic and social life in Central and East Europe, even ordinary workers used a range of strategies to adapt to or engage in small but repeated acts of survival, resistance, and even sabotage against the state and its enterprises.[36] Managers learned that central planners gave targets for production that they could not meet because the inputs they needed often did not arrive in time or were not of the right quality or quantity. As a result, managers "bargained their plans," demanding more investment and input than needed and keeping any extra material for bartering or personal use.[37] Workers were in on the bargaining through their practice of "we pretend to work and you pretend to pay us" and through the skimming of materials for the informal economy, which was needed to procure goods that the formal economy could not provide. These dynamics led the Hungarian economist János Kornai to label state-run socialist economies "economies of shortages."[38] Five-year plans were repeatedly rewritten, and Sisyphean "campaigns" to fix shortages in one area generated shortages in other areas.

There was a profound lack of incentives for efficiency or innovation. Instead of supporting improvements, communist parties regularly bailed out unproductive enterprises (except in Yugoslavia). Rather than focusing on authentic economic growth, economic priorities were put on contributing to Soviet power, maintaining full employment, and, to a lesser extent, producing consumer goods that could be redistributed by the state to citizens at subsidized prices. The socialist social contract and state socialist economic practices put a deep strain on the economies of Central and East Europe, which in the 1970s became increasingly unable to keep up their end of the contract. Bloated bureaucracies in which party officials engaged in corruption, blatantly contradicting the party's promises of ruling on behalf of workers and ensuring social mobility, compounded the problems confronting the region's governments.

As you read this text, consider the following questions:

Communism was forced everywhere except YSl & Albania
– 1956 crackdown in Hungary
– Stick (surveillance) and carrots (social programs) to keep people in line
– Warsaw Pact, Comecon
– economic plans were bad

- What are the legacies of the state socialist experience on political culture—for example, on citizens' expectations of government support?
- How might different collective memories of Communist Party rule influence the types of transitional justice mechanisms adopted after the end of one-party rule?
- How did differences in the ways communist regimes governed influence political reforms after the end of one-party rule?

Glasnost, Social Movements, and Social Change

Communist governments in Central and East Europe confronted various forms of dissent. *Within-system* dissent refers to efforts to reform the state socialist system, while *system rejective* dissent indicates efforts to throw out the existing system and establish a different one.[39] Until Soviet Communist Party leader Mikhail Gorbachev ascended to power in 1985, dissent was much harder for the Baltic and Ukrainian populations that were part of the Soviet Union, where social control was more strident than in many neighboring states.

An early example of within-system dissent was top Yugoslav Communist Party official and Partisan hero Milovan Đilas, who was jailed for publicly criticizing top party officials for corruption that created a "new class" of privileged party functionaries, thus betraying the communist cause. After the brutal Warsaw Pact repression of the Hungarian Revolution in 1956, Alexander Dubček led reformers within the Czechoslovak Communist Party to propose more modest reforms of the state socialist system that included competition within one-party elections but excluded condemnation of the Warsaw Pact.[40] Because Soviet Communist Party leader Leonid Brezhnev and conservative leaders in Central and East Europe still regarded these reforms as a threat to Soviet control over the bloc, the Warsaw Pact invaded Czechoslovakia—though Romania refused to participate—to repress it, remove reformers, and impose hard-line communist leaders.

Poland experienced a number of large workers' strikes and demonstrations in response to price increases and economic problems in 1956, 1970, and 1976, which were violently put down by the Polish communist government. To assist protesting workers arrested in 1976, oppositionists formed the Workers' Defense Committee (KOR), which published underground information on the Communist Party's violations of rights. KOR's efforts reached dissidents in other parts of the region. Inspired partly by KOR and exploiting the hypocrisy of the USSR and Soviet bloc leaders' signing of the Helsinki Final Act that became law in 1977, which included commitments to human rights, Václav Havel and other Czechoslovak dissidents formed Charter 77.

These anticommunist dissents came to embrace a bottom-up approach to dissent, seeking to bring down communism. The leaders of Charter 77 and their Polish allies advocated a civil society–based approach to transforming society, which they believed would ultimately topple one-party rule. Havel urged citizens to stop "living within a lie" and complying publicly with Communist Party dictates they did not genuinely believe in for the sake of getting by.[41] This targeted a widespread social schizophrenia[42] in which citizens did in public what the party expected of them to avoid repercussions while voicing genuine feelings of criticism only within a small private circle of those they trusted. The next step, the dissidents believed, was to create "parallel structures" in society that could generate independent ideas and action. These movements called upon citizens to take risks. They were most successful and extensive in Poland, where dissidents formed independent discussion groups, an independent trade union, and groups associated with the Catholic Church, which was buoyed by the ascent of the first ethnically Polish pope, John Paul II.

Confronting ongoing strikes of shipyard workers led by Lech Wałęsa, the formation of KOR, and Poland's large debt to Western lenders, the Polish Communist Party in 1980 acceded to striking workers' demands, including the legalization of Solidarity, an independent trade union that would genuinely represent workers. Solidarity, which had more than ten million members by 1981, was a dramatic defeat for the Communist Party, which had built its legitimacy in part on the image of being a party of workers. Solidarity's growing power to disrupt the economy, mobilize society, and pressure the Polish Communist Party alarmed conservative party officials. To head off invasion by Warsaw Pact troops (which had happened in Czechoslovakia and Hungary during periods of reform), Polish general Wojciech Jaruzelski imposed martial law in December 1981. He declared Solidarity illegal, arrested many of its leaders, and ordered military officers to supervise factories, schools, media, and government offices.

The Soviet Communist Party's approach to the Eastern bloc—and to policies within the USSR itself—changed dramatically after Mikhail Gorbachev became general secretary of the Communist Party. Concerned about mounting economic problems, the burden of propping up flailing Central and East European economies, and the bloated and opportunistic party bureaucracy, Gorbachev launched reforms of economic restructuring (perestroika) and societal openness (glasnost). These initiatives were intended to reform—not replace—the communist governments and institutions in the region. Gorbachev described them as representing both a "revolution from above"—recognizing the party's role—and a "revolution from below," which would involve citizen efforts to support reforms, call out corruption, and increase economic efficiency.[43] Glasnost opened space in the media and in society for independent initiatives. Some of the first independent groups in the USSR were environmental groups in Ukraine and the Baltics that protested the party's role in and response to the Chernobyl nuclear catastrophe in Ukraine and questioned the safety of other nuclear power plants. Significantly, glasnost was unable to contain the ideas and actions it enabled: there was no limiting it to within-system dissent. Instead, new citizen initiatives, suppressed for decades, spilled over into system rejective dissent, which faced opposition from conservative party leaders and bureaucrats seeking to maintain their power. While dissent challenged one-party rule and communist claims to political legitimacy, visions of what should come next varied, ranging from liberal democracy to ethnically exclusive nation-states.

By the late 1980s, a number of political and economic forces culminated in the stunningly rapid collapse of one-party rule in Central and East Europe. One long-brewing crisis that accumulated problems was the persistent stagnation of state socialist economies, many of which were unable to deliver on fundamental Communist Party promises to meet basic citizen needs. This crisis interacted with crises of legitimacy, both among Communist Party elites who no longer believed in their party's ideology and among significant segments of ordinary citizens, who could easily see that the system was not working.[44] At a time when socially modern populations—ironically, a significant achievement of communist policies of urbanization and mass education—were demanding more from their governments, communist political and economic institutions were unable to respond. In this environment of crisis and thirst for change, the media, long a reliable vehicle of state propaganda, became harder to control, and civil society leaders presented democratic alternatives to those at the top and the bottom who were disgruntled with Communist Party rule.

These forces of change interacted with the catalyst for the collapse of one-party rule in Central and East Europe: Gorbachev's reforms and his unwillingness to use force to prop up party leaders unable to address crises within their own countries. Facing significant challenges to their rule, Polish and Hungarian communists decided to negotiate an end to their sole grip on power through roundtable negotiations with elements of the civic opposition. In Poland's historic, months-long roundtable process, Catholic Church leaders facilitated talks between Solidarity and the Polish Communist Party. This led to semi-free elections in June 1989 that Solidarity overwhelmingly won.

Participants in the Hungarian roundtable discussions agreed to free elections by mid-1989. In May of that year, Hungary opened its border with Austria, a noncommunist country, a move that attracted thousands of East Germans seeking to leave the country. Large public protests occurred throughout East Germany in October, with arrests only driving more people into the streets. A confused announcement by the East German party leadership's press spokesman on November 9 that private trips abroad could be requested prompted hundreds of thousands to gather at the Berlin Wall, where overwhelmed border guards allowed people to cross to the West.[45] These conditions allowed the German people to dismantle the wall that had artificially separated Central and East Europe from its West European neighbors.

As protest tactics diffused across Central and East Europe in the late 1980s, people who cautiously began to join them became more emboldened by visible action and the apparent unwillingness of authorities to use force against them. One of the startling aspects of the fall of communist rule was the rapidity with which it happened. Both Communist Party leaders and citizens were seemingly unaware of the breadth and depth of discontent. A system that appeared strong was revealed to be structurally weak, broken by grave problems with legitimacy, Soviet inaction against dissent, and ever-growing protests. Citizens used to hiding their real views and to being uncertain of the views of their coworkers and neighbors saw opportunities to express and act upon them, resulting in mass mobilization.[46] This occurred even in Czechoslovakia, where civil society groups were small and Communist Party officials were dug in. Three weeks of protests initially led by university students mushroomed into a general strike in late November 1989, forcing the resignation of the Communist Party leadership, the parliament's renunciation of the leading role of the Communist Party, and the selection of Prague Spring reformer Alexander Dubček and playwright Václav Havel as new political leaders.

Opposition forces, including embryonic civil society groups, were weaker in Bulgaria and Romania. In contrast to Yugoslavia, Bulgarian and Romanian leaders had chosen to try to compel ethnic minorities—Turks and Macedonians in Bulgaria, Hungarians in Romania—to assimilate. The expulsion of three hundred thousand

Turks unwilling to Bulgarize their names weakened potential opposition from among this minority. Romania's 1.7-million-strong Hungarian minority remained more resilient, despite decades of repressive policies designed by the government to gradually eliminate institutions of cultural reproduction (e.g., minority schools and cultural institutions).[47] The collapse of the Ceauşescu regime in December 1989 was triggered by a public demonstration to prevent the forced relocation of a Hungarian Reformed minister from Timişoara, a historically multiethnic city in the western part of Romania's Transylvania province. This bold act of public resistance started on December 16 and grew from a small "human chain" to a major demonstration of about a thousand participants from different ethnic backgrounds. To crush the resistance, Ceauşescu sent in the army and approved the use of violence, which led to significant civilian casualties. A general strike followed, which signaled to the Romanian military and a group of Communist Party elites that the nepotistic and megalomaniac rule of Ceauşescu needed to end. Ceauşescu and his wife were executed by a firing squad in late December. No such violence was needed for Communist Party members to change their party leadership in Bulgaria. Without widespread opposition, factions within Bulgarian, Romanian, and Albanian communist parties deposed their leaders, maintained control over state institutions, and recast their parties as "reformed," allowing them to survive later multiparty elections.

The collapse of one-party rule in Yugoslavia, which had always been different, came later and was tragically violent. There, divergent republican Communist Party positions

Photo 1.3.   On August 23, 1989, an estimated two million Baltic inhabitants joined hands across the three Soviet republics of Estonia, Latvia, and Lithuania to showcase a popular desire for independence. (Kusurija, Wikimedia Commons)

on political and economic reform overlapped with ethnic differences. Wealthier Slovenia and Croatia advocated democratic and market reforms and sovereignty. Serbia opposed these reforms, and multiethnic Bosnia-Herzegovina and Macedonia sought an elusive compromise. Alternatives to the communists advocated exclusive nationalist visions of new political systems and territory and channeled grievances about governance failures against ethnic "others" rather than working to build inclusive, civic-based democratic systems. These conscious policies contributed to the violent disintegration of one-party rule and the country beginning in late June 1991.

In the Baltic republics, which had been incorporated illegally into the Soviet Union in 1940, the key item on the opposition agenda was independence. Early protests against the communist government were small and focused on less politically charged issues, including protection of the environment. The end of Soviet rule and communism came later in the Baltics than it did in neighboring states like Poland, Hungary, and Czechoslovakia. For the Baltic countries, independence—and the opportunity to establish democratic governance—arrived in late summer 1991 with the collapse of the USSR.[48] Ukraine, where reform-minded communists agreed with democratic activists about the desirability of independence, soon followed. By the end of 1991, the Soviet Union, once a powerful empire, had splintered into fifteen new countries.

While reading this text, consider the following questions:

- How did the roles played by civil society in the collapse of one-party rule affect multiparty elections and the building of democratic institutions in the region?
- How did discontent with economic conditions, lack of political freedom, Communist Party corruption, and nationalism influence the dynamics of transition away from one-party rule?
- How might different narratives of who and what institutions are most responsible for repression during communism affect current debates about transitional justice?

Opportunities, Challenges, and Actors in Postcommunist Transformations

The collapse of repressive communist regimes was greeted with overwhelming popular support across Central and East Europe. The three generations who lived through communist rule in this region experienced major parts of their lives deprived of basic freedoms. Those who questioned decisions made by state authorities, let alone mobilized to reform existing one-party structures, were silenced and punished. Two generations grew up without the freedom to learn about other forms of government. The end of these regimes created hope across the region that democratic "social contracts" could emerge to empower postcommunist societies to move forward to a better future. A historic transformation began in the early 1990s against the backdrop of this hope.

The strength of popular support provided unprecedented legitimacy to the first democratically elected governments to design and lead the transformation. But the popular mandate for change was coupled with enormous responsibility. The changes these postcommunist governments made in state and economic structures, and in regional and international relationships, would lay down the paths on which societies could move forward. Given the strength of domestic and international support for democratization in this region, the conditions looked favorable in the early 1990s; but the challenges were significant, and the learning curve was steep.

Competitive multiparty elections were introduced as a necessary first step toward democratization. But the unavoidable volatility and divisiveness of party development and electoral competition made coherence and continuity in institutional design in state centers and policy implementation on the ground difficult. Moreover, elected political actors faced a new kind of limitation for which experiences under one-party rule provided no guidance: they became replaceable in subsequent elections. *Governmental account-ability* had to be learned. For the first time in the lives of most people in the region, the possibility arose that "the people" might indeed become the source of "popular sovereignty." That is, while governments might represent them and work in their service, citizens could question decisions, express different interests, and hold elected officials accountable. Long-term vision had to be balanced with short-term electoral requirements, and fundamental decisions about the building blocks of democracy were up for grabs in political competition.

Conflicting Hopes

The challenges facing postcommunist societies were as great as the opportunities offered by the end of the Cold War in Europe. Deep sources of tension underpinned the desires that motivated support for the transformation. One was the tension between longing for democracy and for ethnically conceived national self-determination in societies with multiethnic populations. Another was the tension between the desire to move forward, away from the communist past, and strong interest in the past, in talking about collective memory and looking at the past (particularly the interwar period) as a source of justification for major political decisions. The third was the tension underlying the goal of achieving self-determination while joining a transnational framework, the European Union, which established a set of challenging conditions for membership. Exploring these tensions will help us to understand the energy behind the historic transformations that began in the early 1990s, the difficulties countries and populations faced, and the achievements and disappointments they experienced along the way.

In the early 1990s, the idea of national self-determination mobilized support for regime change as powerfully as the idea of democracy. Demands for national sovereignty had been expressed already before 1990—in anti-Soviet uprisings (in Hungary and Poland in the 1950s, Czechoslovakia in 1968, and the Polish Solidarity movement in the 1980s) and in claims for increased autonomy for "titular" cultures in the substate republics in Czechoslovakia, the Soviet Union, and Yugoslavia. The "Singing Revolution" in the Baltics in the mid- to late 1980s also provided powerful illustrations of how national sentiments can reinforce democracy movements that seek peaceful regime change.[49] Across Central and East Europe, national self-determination was envisioned as a way to empower people to govern themselves as Estonians, Poles, Slovaks, Hungarians,

Romanians, Bulgarians, Croats, Serbs, Macedonians, Albanians, Ukrainians, and so on, rather than as embodiments of the culturally nondescript socialist human being prescribed by "scientific socialism." In a world designed according to the principle of national self-determination, every nation would have its own state in which people could define their own government. Many supporters of democratization saw the end of the Cold War as an opportunity to achieve that goal. From this perspective, it is not surprising that the collapse of repressive regimes contributed to the disintegration of all ethnofederal states in the region (the Soviet Union, Czechoslovakia, and Yugoslavia).

In principle, nationalism and democracy can work well together. By some accounts, nationalism and democracy were born together as part of an ideology that expanded political membership and promised equal rights to people beyond class barriers.[50] Demands for national independence are typically justified in terms of rightful sovereignty claims by people who have lived under external rule. Such claims became major drivers of decolonialization movements during the twentieth century. In Central and East Europe, too, most of the population experienced some form of external rule before 1990. Despite the internationalist ideology of Soviet-style communism and the initial intent of ethnofederal states in the region to create broad nonethnic identifications ("Soviets," "Czechoslovaks," and "Yugoslavs"), states reinforced ethnic conceptions of national belonging and ethnic hierarchies. "The Russians" were seen as colonizers in non-Russian republics and across the Soviet bloc, "the Serbs" as dominant across Yugoslavia, and the "the Czechs" as the dominant partners in Czechoslovakia. Ethnic shorthand expressions appeared not only in everyday stereotyping but also in official narratives of victimhood, and they were effectively instrumentalized by post-1990 nationalists to justify ethnic majoritarian state building.

Yet the evolution of state-society relations in the region reveals the difficulties of achieving both ethnically conceived national self-determination and democracy in multiethnic states. Most post-1990 state borders did not create a match between national and state boundaries. Ethnofederations fell apart along their substate administrative borders, which had rarely aligned neatly with ethnic boundaries. Where the mismatch was significant, independence claims encountered obstacles. State dismemberment and new state formation became much smoother in some places than others, and differences in ethnic demography and international support help to explain the variation. Where independence declarations generated no serious domestic challenge *and* were backed by strong international consensus and substantive support (such as access to NATO and EU membership), successor states had a much better chance of achieving the stability required for democratization. The Czechoslovak federation was arguably the only candidate for easy divorce. It required separation between only two republics (compared to six in Yugoslavia and fifteen in the Soviet Union), and there was no significant mismatch between the ethnic and territorial border separating these republics. The new states were immediately recognized and lined up for membership in NATO and the EU. Although Slovakia incorporated a large territorialized Hungarian national minority along the Hungarian border (at the time, over 10 percent of the population), this minority organized democratically and presented moderate rights claims to the new state center. The conditions for smooth dissolution were much less favorable in the other two ethnofederations, where independent statehood still has not completely materialized in several successor states.

Comparative scholars of democratization have identified the resolution of the "stateness problem" as a precondition for successful regime change.[51] Among post-Soviet states, the Baltic states had the most favorable conditions for achieving this precondition. Although Estonia and Latvia incorporated large Russophone populations, these minorities did not challenge independence, and the post-Soviet government of Boris Yeltsin in Moscow did not pursue irredentist claims but accepted these countries' shift to the West. Influential international actors had already strongly advocated for these states' independence during the Soviet period, and their integration into NATO and the EU began shortly after 1991. For other post-Soviet states in Europe, conditions for independent statehood and democratization were less favorable. The Russian state center was reluctant to let Belarus and Ukraine go, and it backed the secessionist groups in Moldova that established a "de facto" state in Transnistria. These conflicts have continued since the Soviet collapse, undermining statehood and democratic consolidation. In Ukraine, Russian interference triggered mass demonstrations in 2004 and 2014, fostered the Russian annexation of Crimea in 2014, and continues to fuel a war in eastern Ukraine.

The fragility of statehood also remains a challenge in parts of the former Yugoslavia. Over twenty-five years after the 1995 Dayton Peace Accords that ended the war in Bosnia-Herzegovina, the survival of this confederation depends on active international engagement. The relationship between Serbia and Kosovo has not been resolved, and

Photo 1.4. After the collapse of the Soviet Union in 1991, Russia has sought to retain influence over its former republics, including the Baltic countries and Ukraine. The Russian annexation of Crimea in 2014 set off armed conflict with Ukraine. In this 2017 photo, a Ukrainian soldier stands on a tank in Mariupol. (Volodya Senkiv, Shutterstock)

without Serbian recognition, Kosovo remains a disputed territory vulnerable to internal and external conflict. International recognition of Macedonia's independence came only after a name change to North Macedonia in 2019, which satisfied external challengers in Greece while fueling nationalist resentments domestically.

Struggles over sovereignty were not confined to disintegrating federations. States that continued within preexisting boundaries also faced obstacles in matching ethnic nationalism with democratization. Post-1990 Bulgarian nation builders faced challenges from a large Turkish minority, and their Romanian counterparts had to negotiate with a politically resourceful Hungarian minority party. Poland had no significant ethnic minority populations in 1990, but its governments engaged in divisive memory politics in an effort to create a coherent Polish national historiography for the post-1990 state against the backdrop of earlier border shifts and the ethnic cleansing that led to Poland's post–World War II geographic location and ethnic demography. Thus, although national self-determination appeared to be a stable match for democratization at the beginning of the 1990s, its realization across the region occurred along a logic reminiscent of what earlier generations in the region had experienced, involving ethnic "othering" and conflict that undermined inclusive notions of democratic citizenship.

Another tension underlying post-1990 state and regime transformations was the desire to move away from the past—from the Soviet Union, the Soviet bloc, the "Czechoslovak" and "Yugoslav" identities, etc.—while focusing on the past to "tell the truth" about the previous regime and to look for historical precedents to justify the right to post-1990 statehood. The call for uncovering the past after the end of a repressive regime was not unique to postcommunism. Often labeled "transitional justice," such processes had taken place elsewhere, such as in post–World War II West Germany, postapartheid South Africa, and several postauthoritarian South American and Southern European societies. In Central and East Europe, the usual tensions generated by the search for transitional justice were compounded by the reemergence of conflicting collective memories about the precommunist past. For reasons discussed earlier, these historical narratives involved competing narratives of victimhood, and the politics of memory became a divisive feature of state and nation building in many parts of the region.

A consequential dimension of memory politics was the search for historical precedent to justify the right to statehood. For instance, Czech elites identified the interwar Czechoslovak Republic as a precedent to emphasize the democratic character of the state created by the Czech founders. Though interwar Czechoslovakia was a dualist state built for Czechs and Slovaks, the framers of Slovakia traced the origin of their new state back to a ninth-century Slavic empire to claim a continuous right to statehood. Baltic leaders "restored" interwar statehood. The consequences of these state justifications varied widely. In Estonia and Latvia, state restoration was used to justify the political disenfranchisement of Russian-speakers who had arrived during the Soviet period. Lithuanian elites chose a different path, arguing for restoration but granting citizenship to all post-Soviet inhabitants, though the country's Russian-speaking population was far smaller than that of Latvia and Estonia and the decision had less political significance.

Memory politics can have short-term benefits for dominant political actors, but it can also generate long-term negative consequences for the interethnic trust and social solidarity necessary for sustainable democratic government. Failure to recognize the complexity of historical memory and to uncover and acknowledge local responsibilities for crimes committed in the name of ethnicity and nationhood can reinforce ethnic entitlement and undermine empathy for ethnic "others." Simplified interpretations of the state socialist period also had major consequences, for instance on gender relations after 1990. The discourse about how "token women" achieved "undeserved" positions in communist party structures was used to justify the exclusion of women from decision making in the post-1990 transformation.

A third important tension underlying postcommunist transformation was the conflict between desiring state sovereignty (for reasons discussed earlier) and joining an integrating transnational European framework that required states to give up significant elements of sovereignty. The European framework provided a safe environment for the major institutional and social changes that began in 1990. It also provided a democratic ideology and well-established institutional models for designing constitutions, parliamentary and electoral systems, and market economies. The EU's "Eastern Enlargement" project offered material resources to help these societies overcome the unavoidable economic difficulties associated with massive restructuring. Moreover, EU conditionality provided some protection for domestic leaders in relation to their electorates: European actors could "take the blame" when governments had to introduce unpopular policies required by membership conditionality. In the process, the EU and postcommunist Central and East Europe mutually reshaped each other. The EU itself was created only in 1992, in anticipation of challenges Europe was expected to face after the end of the Cold War—as regimes were collapsing and independent states were emerging from dissolving federations. The Eastern Enlargement project took shape immediately, ushering in European-level activities of unprecedented intensity and consequence. The Copenhagen criteria adopted in 1993 laid down conditions for EU membership, emphasizing democracy and marketization and specifying minority protection. Other European partner institutions, primarily the Council of Europe and the Organization for Security and Co-operation in Europe, were engaged in coordinated activities to develop a strategy for incentivizing and shaping democratization in the region. European organizations were also actively engaged in helping to end the wars in the former Yugoslavia.

Although external involvement was broadly supported and the changes were led by elected elites across the region, these processes reveal an element of continuity in regional politics—namely that domestic political actors with a historic opportunity to create new social contracts did so, yet again, on the basis of models borrowed (and to some extent imposed) from abroad and implemented under external oversight. It was under these conditions that Central and East European governments and societies had to fulfill the hopes of a great postcommunist transformation. Both the expectations and the challenges were enormous.

Unequal Conditions

People in different parts of Central and East Europe were not equally situated on a shared trajectory toward successful democratization. On the one hand, all new governments faced similar challenges in moving away from state socialism, and all adopted political and economic institutions from the same small set of existing (Western) models. On the other hand, no government was starting anew with a blank slate. Differences in institutional legacies, ethnic demography, and geopolitical conditions (primarily in relation to the EU and Russia) mattered.

On the political dimension of transformation, lessons from earlier examples of democratization (for instance, in Southern Europe and Latin America) provided some guidance. On the economic dimension, a comparative perspective offered little help. A repressive state socialist regime, where most of the economy is state owned and state controlled, is very different from a repressive capitalist regime. The shift from state socialism required large-scale privatization. For economies that had been tied to the Soviet Union (either as part of the Soviet state or part of the Soviet bloc), opening to the global market presented another set of structural challenges. Regardless of the speed and sequencing, whether governments opted for "gradualism" or "shock therapy," the restructuring triggered economic recession. To recover quickly and move forward with the transformation, governments had to multitask in new ways, and there were no analogies in other regions to learn from. The Chinese experience with marketization was too dissimilar to be adopted, because the Chinese state began the process as an overwhelmingly agriculture-based society, and privatization and economic globalization in China took place within a one-party system. In Central and East Europe, privatization, Europeanization, and globalization unfolded simultaneously with the elimination of one-party rule and the introduction of political competition. The expression "rebuilding the ship at sea" captures the enormity of these challenges.[52]

Although support for democratic and capitalist institutions and practices was strong, conditions and resources for the transformation varied significantly across the region. As discussed earlier, state stability was a major issue in many parts of the region. Where states were weaker and unable to provide for social needs, informal structures were strengthened (e.g., the "oligarchs" and patronage structures in Ukraine). These informal structures created alternative sources of power, outside formal political institutions populated by elected leaders and representatives and those appointed by them. Although democratic consolidation requires strong nongovernmental institutions, the kinds of informal institutions that were strengthened in weak post-Soviet states were not those described in the civil society and democratization literature. Rather, they were clientelistic networks that undermined democratic institutions.

The availability of political actors who could engage effectively in new institution building also varied across the region. Lack of experience was a problem everywhere, but elite continuity could also become an obstacle. Many leaders of change were "reformed" members of the former regime. In Bulgaria and Romania, where elite continuity was significant through "reformed" communists winning the first multiparty elections, these politicians delayed deep democratic reforms, contributing to delays in EU accession. In contrast, the first president of the Czech Republic, Václav Havel, a former dissident of international stature, became a visible and inspiring example for new democratic leadership. Yet even with new elites and favorable conditions, building a market democracy proved difficult in the Czech state as well. The gap between the enthusiasm for market democracy and the preparedness for making this tremendous change was great across the region. The learning curve was steeper in states emerging from harsher dictatorships (for instance, East Germany, Czechoslovakia, Bulgaria, and Romania). Even in societies formerly ruled by "hard-liners," however, East German society gained advantages through German unification. Societies with more developed informal markets (such as the "shadow economies" in Hungary and Poland) were better prepared for post-1990 economic marketization.

Yet the advantages of pre-1990 experience could be damaged by conflicts triggered by state collapse. The former Yugoslavia, for instance, had been outside the Soviet bloc and had the strongest ties to the West before 1990, which could have turned its successor states into front-runners of European integration and democratization. Only Slovenia remained on that path, however, benefiting from conditions that helped to avoid the wars of Yugoslav succession and becoming the only post-Yugoslav state to gain EU membership in 2004. For most people in the former Yugoslavia, the "transition" their politicians led became synonymous with devastating wars that hijacked democratization for a long time.

Europeanization

European integration had a major impact on regional trajectories after 1990. The states that joined the European integration project received normative and substantive support for democratization and marketization. Substantive support for democracy building and economic reform helped to speed up the process of regime change and economic recovery after the initial postcommunist recession. The normative dimension of Europeanization was also significant. The primary motivation behind the EU's Eastern Enlargement was to ensure regional peace through economic interdependence and democratization. Central and East European societies were undergoing transformations that created previously unexperienced freedoms (of expression, mobility, etc.) but also generated new insecurities (for instance, status changes for large segments of the population, loss of job security, and widening gaps in income and wealth). Under these conditions, EU membership conditionality incentivized peaceful and democratic ways of dealing with conflict, and European actors actively facilitated peaceful negotiations. Although the influences of Europeanization have been complex and there are many critical voices among scholars who study them, there is broad agreement in the literature that EU conditionality helped to facilitate peaceful transformation and democratization.

Most of Central and East Europe was able to avoid the violence that characterized the collapse of authoritarian regimes and their aftermath in many regions.[53] EU membership helped to soften (or "virtualize") borders, which facilitated mobility and learning for populations that had been divided for decades by the "Iron Curtain" established during the Cold War. It also made cross-border cultural and social relations easier for members of "divided nations." The expression "return to Europe" captures this dimension of the post-1990 transformations. European institutions (for example, the European Parliament and the European Court of Human Rights) created possibilities for social actors to articulate interests, build transnational alliances for shared interests, and hold governments accountable. EU conditionality also helped to moderate the effects of marketization by reinforcing norms of equity (for instance, against gender and age discrimination in the labor market) and monitoring corruption. Once states gained membership in the EU, however, EU institutions lost the leverage of conditionality, and many achievements of democratization became vulnerable to domestic political power games. The Fidesz-led government in Hungary since 2010 and the PiS-led government in Poland since 2015 have used populist nationalism to attack the liberal democratic state and dramatically weaken obstacles to their continued hold on power. Developments in other parts of the region suggest that democratic consolidation was not solid in Central and East Europe at the time of the "big bang" enlargement of the EU. The socioeconomic costs of the transformation weakened the resilience of these societies against European crises, such as the 2008–2009 financial crisis and the refugee crisis since the mid-2010s.

The Agency of Political Actors

Democracy is an interactive process between state and society, and it is always a "work in progress" that requires continuous commitment on the part of political actors and ordinary citizens. There is ongoing debate among comparative political scientists about what explains continuities and changes in political regimes, what makes democracy work, and what makes it vulnerable to degradation or collapse. Some scholars argue that institutional legacies and structural conditions (such as geopolitical location, ethnic demography, and economic development) are the most formative. Others emphasize the significance of *agency*, arguing that the actions of people who make political decisions or choose between parties and institutions to support and populate make a major difference in shaping trajectories of political development.

Postcommunist transformation demonstrates that structural conditions and agency interact in creating and sustaining democratic government. Beyond democratic institutions, democracy requires political actors capable and willing to engage in the kind of political competition that enables peaceful contestation over conflicting social interests without undermining social solidarity. During the historic transformation that began in the early 1990s, it mattered who the dominant decision makers were and what approaches they chose. But political agency involves not only those decision makers who are the most visible actors in governments and parliaments. Less visible actors also play a significant role. Democratic government is not possible without the participation of "intermediary" elites (for instance, mayors, school directors, media leaders, and civil society activists) and ordinary citizens, who make choices about voting, consumption of media, which institutions to support, whether and when to join public demonstrations, and so on. All of these actors and their engagement have been necessary for the accomplishments of the last three decades, though political decision makers bear heavier responsibility for both successes and failures.

Three decades after the beginning of the great transformation, democracy in Central and East Europe appears to be fragile. Former front-runners of democratic consolidation have become leaders of democratic backsliding. An important lesson from these decades is that democracy cannot survive without a complex array of formal governmental and intermediary institutions that are populated and maintained by actors committed to democratic processes and norms and supported by a regional environment favorable to democracy.

As you read this text, consider the following questions:

1. What were some major challenges that governments of the region faced in their efforts to create new "social contracts" after communism? To what extent were they successful in realizing their goals?
2. What has been the role of the European Union in shaping the political trajectories of Central and East European states? Might this role change in the future?
3. What are key threats to the stability and preservation of democratic practices and institutions in the region? What are key political, economic, and social forces that function to support the continuation of democratic practices and institutions in the region?

Notes

1. Suyin Haynes, "Hungary's Parliament Votes to End Legal Recognition of Transgender People. Activists Fear 'Devastating' Consequences," *Time*, May 19, 2020, https://time.com/583 8804/hungary-gender-recognition-vote-transgender.

2. "Hungary: Protesters Tally against University 'Takeover' in Budapest," *BBC News*, September 7, 2020, https://www.bbc.com/news/world-europe-54052182.

3. Vanessa Gera and Monika Scislowska, "Polish President Elected to 2nd Term after Harsh Campaign," *Global News*, July 13, 2020, https://globalnews.ca/news/7171856/poland-election -results.

4. Vlagyiszlav Makszimov, "EP Condemns Hungary and Poland's Controversial Coronavirus Moves," *Euractiv*, April 17, 2020, https://www.euractiv.com/section/justice-home-affairs/news/ep -condemns-hungarys-and-polands-controversial-coronavirus-moves.

5. Sean Hanley and Milada Anna Vachudova, "Understanding the Illiberal Turn: Democratic Backsliding in the Czech Republic," *East European Politics* 34, no. 3 (2018): 276–96.

6. "Orbán's Cabinet: Here Are the 13 Men and 1 Woman Who Will Be Running Hungary for the Next Four Years," *Hungary Today*, May 18, 2018, https://hungarytoday.hu/orbans-cabinet -here-are-the-13-men-and-1-woman-who-will-be-running-hungary-for-the-next-four-years.

7. Agnia Grigas, "Lithuania's New Government: Women-Led Coalition Wins Confidence in Difficult Times," Atlantic Council, last modified October 30, 2020, https://www.atlanticcouncil .org/blogs/new-atlanticist/lithuanias-new-government-women-led-coalition-wins-confidence-in-d ifficult-times.

8. "CPI 2019: Western Europe & European Union," Transparency International, January 23, 2020, https://www.transparency.org/en/news/cpi-western-europe-and-eu.

9. "Slovakia's National Council 2020 Elections," Inter-Parliamentary Union Parline database, accessed December 10, 2020, https://data.ipu.org/node/155/elections?chamber_id=13526.

10. For reference, instructors and students may wish to use the "Europe in Year 1900" map at https://www.euratlas.net/history/europe/1900/index.html.

11. Russification refers to the cultural and linguistic assimilation of non-Russian communities into Russian culture and language. Russification may be voluntary or coerced. The Russification practiced by the Russian Empire and, later, the government of the Soviet Union was largely coercive. On this subject, see Edward C. Thaden, ed., *Russification in the Baltic Provinces and Finland, 1855–1914* (Princeton, NJ: Princeton University Press, 2014).

12. Richard A. Pipes, *A Concise History of the Russian Revolution* (New York: Vintage, 2011).

13. John W. Mason, *The Dissolution of the Austro-Hungarian Empire, 1867–1918* (New York: Routledge, 2014).

14. Alexander Lyon Macfie, *The End of the Ottoman Empire, 1908–1923* (New York: Routledge, 2014).

15. Christopher M. Clark, *Iron Kingdom: The Rise and Downfall of Prussia, 1600–1947* (Cambridge, MA: Harvard University Press, 2006).

16. Andres Kasekamp, *A History of the Baltic States* (New York: Macmillan International Higher Education, 2017).

17. Norman Davies, *God's Playground: A History of Poland*, vol. 2, *1795 to the Present* (New York: Oxford University Press, 2005).

18. Patrick Crowhurst, *A History of Czechoslovakia between the Wars: From Versailles to Hitler's Invasion* (New York: Bloomsbury, 2015).

19. Marie-Janin Calic, *History of Yugoslavia* (West Lafayette, IN: Purdue University Press, 2018).

20. Sara Bender, *The Jews of Bialystok during World War II and the Holocaust* (Lebanon, NH: University Press of New England, 2008).

21. Dan Michman, *The Emergence of Jewish Ghettos during the Holocaust* (Cambridge: Cambridge University Press, 2011).

22. Andrej Angrick and Peter Klein, *The "Final Solution" in Riga: Exploitation and Annihilation, 1941–1944* (New York: Berghahn Books, 2009).

23. Father Patrick Desbois, *The Holocaust by Bullets: A Priest's Journey to Uncover the Truth behind the Murder of 1.5 Million Jews* (New York: St. Martin's, 2008).

24. Daina S. Eglitis and Didzis Bērziņš, "Mortal Threat: Latvian Jews at the Dawn of Nazi Occupation," *Nationalities Papers* 46, no. 6 (2018): 1063–80.

25. Nikolaus Wachsmann, *KL: A History of the Nazi Concentration Camps* (New York: Farrar, Strauss & Giroux, 2016).

26. This is the estimate given by the US Holocaust Memorial Museum in the online *Holocaust Encyclopedia*. See https://encyclopedia.ushmm.org/content/en/article/genocide-of-european-roma-gypsies-1939-1945.

27. Anne Applebaum, *Iron Curtain: The Crushing of Eastern Europe, 1944–56* (New York: Penguin, 2012).

28. Joseph Rothschild and Nancy Wingfield, "The Communists Come to Power," in *Return to Diversity: A Political History of East Central Europe since WWII* (Oxford: Oxford University Press, 2008), 122.

29. Joni Lovenduski and Jean Woodall, *Politics and Society in Eastern Europe* (Bloomington: Indiana University Press, 1987), 2.

30. Bogdan Denitch, "Violence and Social Change in the Yugoslav Revolution," *Comparative Politics* 8, no. 3 (1976): 465–78.

31. Dennison Rusinow, *The Yugoslav Experiment, 1948–1974* (Berkeley, CA: University of California Press, 1988).

32. Iuliia Mendel, "85 Years Later, Ukraine Marks Famine That Killed Millions," *New York Times*, November 24, 2018.

33. Gale Stokes, *The Walls Came Tumbling Down* (Oxford: Oxford University Press, 1993), 57.

34. Linda J. Cook and Martin K. Dimitrov, "The Contract Revisited: Evidence from Communist and State Capitalist Economies," *Europe-Asia Studies* 69, no. 1 (2017): 1–24.

35. Michael Burawoy, *Manufacturing Consent: Changes in the Labor Process under Monopoly Capitalism* (Chicago: University of Chicago Press, 1982).

36. Istvan Rev, "The Advantages of Being Atomized," *Dissent* 34 (1987): 335–49; Katherine Verdery, *What Was Socialism, and What Comes Next?* (Princeton, NJ: Princeton University Press, 1996).

37. Verdery, *What Was Socialism, and What Comes Next?*, 21.

38. János Kornai, *The Socialist System: The Political Economy of Communism* (Princeton, NJ: Princeton University Press, 1992).

39. Tony Judt, "The Dilemmas of Dissidence: The Politics of Opposition in East-Central Europe," *East European Politics & Societies* 2, no. 2 (1988): 185–240.

40. Robin Allison Remington, *Winter in Prague: Documents on Czechoslovak Communism in Crisis* (Cambridge: MIT Press, 1969).

41. Václav Havel, "The Power of the Powerless," in *The Power of the Powerless*, ed. John Keane (Armonk, NY: M. E. Sharpe, 1985), 31.

42. Verdery, *What Was Socialism, and What Comes Next?*, 94.

43. Mikhail Gorbachev, *Perestroika* (New York: Harper and Row, 1987).

44. Daniel Chirot, "What Happened in East Central Europe in 1989?," in *The Revolutions of 1989: Rewriting Histories*, ed. Vladimir Tismaneanu, 19–40 (New York: Routledge, 1999).

45. Guenter Schabowski, "Guenter Schabowski's Press Conference in the GDR International Press Center," *Making the History of 1989*, Item No. 449, accessed December 9, 2020, https://chnm.gmu.edu/1989/items/show/449.

46. Timur Kuran, "The East European Revolution of 1989: Is It Surprising That We Were Surprised?," *American Economic Review* 81, no. 2 (1991): 121–25.

47. Tamás Kiss et al., eds., *Unequal Accommodation of Minority Rights: Hungarians in Transylvania* (Cham, Switzerland: Palgrave Macmillan, 2018), https://www.palgrave.com/it/book/9783319788920.

48. Kristian Gerner and Stefan Hedlund, *The Baltic States and the End of the Soviet Empire* (New York: Routledge, 2018).

49. Anatol Lieven, *The Baltic Revolution: Estonia, Latvia, Lithuania and the Path to Independence* (New Haven, CT: Yale University Press, 1994).

50. Liah Greenfeld, *Nationalism: Five Roads to Modernity* (Cambridge, MA: Harvard University Press, 1992); Eric J. Hobsbawm, *Nations and Nationalism since 1780* (Cambridge: Cambridge University Press, 1992).

51. Juan J. Linz and Alfred Stepan, *Problems of Democratic Transition and Consolidation: Southern Europe, South America, and Post-Communist Europe* (Baltimore, MD: Johns Hopkins University Press, 1996).

52. Jon Elster, Claus Offe, and Ulrich Preuss, *Institutional Design in Post-Communist Societies: Rebuilding the Ship at Sea* (Cambridge: Cambridge University Press, 1998).

53. Jack L. Snyder, *From Voting to Violence: Democratization and Nationalist Conflict* (New York: Norton, 2000).

Part II

POLICIES AND ISSUES

CHAPTER 2

Liberal, Fascist, and Communist Legacies

Jeffrey S. Kopstein

During World War II, Soviet ruler Joseph Stalin remarked in a conversation with the visiting Yugoslav communist partisan leader Milovan Djilas that even though the tide had been turned against the Nazis, it was time to think about the future of Europe. "This war is not as in the past," he said. "Whoever occupies a territory also imposes on it his own social system. Everyone imposes his own system as far as his army has power to do so. It cannot be otherwise."[1] True to his word, the Soviet dictator imposed his country's system on Central and East Europe after 1945. The countries covered in this book began their post-1989 journeys from a common starting point. All experienced decades of communist rule. Communism did not destroy the cultural, ethnic, and linguistic distinctiveness of this exceptionally large and diverse geographical territory extending from Berlin to Vladivostok, from the Baltic to the Black Sea, nor did it do away with centuries of imperial and national pasts of over two dozen countries. Communism did, however, create a distinctive institutional order that was recognizable to the outsider. No matter where one lived or visited in the communist world, one encountered a common ideology, set of economic policies, and political institutions that made these countries instantly identifiable and in some ways defines them as distinctively "East" European. Communism also bequeathed to the societies political, economic, and social legacies that deeply influence virtually every aspect of life more than thirty years after its disappearance.

This chapter focuses on communism's legacy in contemporary Central and East Europe. When scholars of the region speak of a "legacy," they refer to the profound impact on the contemporary order of ideas and institutions that have long since faded away. More than thirty years after communism's collapse in 1989, politics in the region continue to be shaped by the long-term impact of communism's political ideology and institutions. Among the many areas of political life influenced by the legacy of communism, scholars have highlighted contemporary voting behavior, trust in politicians and fellow citizens, popular attitudes toward ethnic minorities, and economic and social policy. In some countries, such as Hungary and Poland, the main political cleavages continue to reflect the long-term impact of the communist experience.

How, then, did communism matter? What exactly are its legacies? Pinpointing these are tricky. Communist rule was authoritarian and often violent but never monochromatic. It encountered a set of countries with diverse historical experiences, and these precommunist experiences frequently shaped the nature of communist rule itself. In other words, precommunist legacies influenced the nature of communist rule in Central and East Europe, which in turn conditioned the politics we see today. In fact, during the twentieth century, the region became an ideological and institutional laboratory for every major ideology and institutional order.

Perhaps even more so than communism itself, students of the region have consistently identified two interrelated characteristics of the region that for more than a century have defined it as an object of analysis. The first feature is the difficulty the countries have encountered in creating a stable institutional order amid economically backward societies, a problem they share with much of the developing world. The second feature characteristic of the region is the importation of institutional models from abroad developed in different social settings and under different circumstances. In roughly chronological order, the countries of Central and East Europe experienced failed liberal democracy (1900–1930), right-wing or fascist dictatorship (1930–1945), Soviet-style communism (1945–1989), and after 1989 a second attempt at liberal democracy. Of course, such a periodization is problematic and misses some important variations in the region. It nevertheless captures much of the reality.

Present-day rulers and ordinary people look back on each of these periods as a reservoir of memories (both positive and negative) and possibilities for action. With the exception of the present period, the outcome of which is not yet known, scholars have maintained that each of these orders failed due to the relative economic backwardness of the region and the corruption of the original institutional design in the face of local resistance or circumstances. Each of these previous orders paved the way for what ultimately became communism in Central and East Europe. Let us turn first to the region's first encounter with liberalism and democracy.

Failed Liberalism, 1918–1930

Before World War I, most of the present-day countries of Central and East Europe were part of either the Habsburg, German, Russian, or Ottoman Empire. Some, such as Poland and Yugoslavia, were divided among several. But even before the collapse of the imperial orders and the emergence of independent states at the end of World War I, liberal institutions had been adopted throughout much of the region. Constitutions with grandiose declarations of universal rights and freedoms were widely adapted from Western Europe. The Bulgarian constitution of 1879 drew heavily on Belgium's 1831 charter and was considered highly progressive for its time. Architectural replicas of English and French parliamentary and presidential buildings marked the landscape of national capitals. The grand neo-Gothic style of Hungary's parliament, completed in 1906, received its inspiration from London's House of Parliament. After the war, the new postimperial states implemented, on paper at any rate, broad constitutional guarantees of freedom of speech and assembly, parliamentary government, near universal male suffrage, and judicial independence.

The elites of these poor countries focused on the West. They traveled to London and Paris and often returned to look upon their own countries as poor and backward,

Photo 2.1. The grand neo-Gothic Hungarian parliament building, completed in 1906, was an architectural metaphor of Western-oriented liberal democratic ideas predominant across Central and East Europe at the time. (Mike/NG, Shutterstock)

either resolving to change things or sinking into a depressed state. In a classically humorous observation from the nineteenth century, the Pole Jan Dombrowski is said to have "vowed to die for his fatherland any day, as long as he could spend his remaining days in Paris rather than in the backwater of his own sprawling estates."[2] Economic advancement and political liberalism became the watchwords of the faith in "progress" throughout the region.

Nothing better attests to the dominance of Western culture in the imagination of Central and East Europe than the adoption of liberal democratic institutions. In the interwar period, only Russia failed to do so. These institutions were seen as the "entry ticket" to the club of civilized nations. Economic backwardness would be overcome by integrating the economies of these new countries into the broader markets dominated by Western Europe and North America. The rights of ethnic minorities, arguably the thorniest issue in the region, would be guaranteed through national legislation and a series of treaties and documents drawn up by the League of Nations immediately after the war.

The problem with this institutional design was that liberalism was not homegrown. Instead it had been adopted to emulate the West rather than as a response to industrialization and the growth of capitalism.[3] Whereas in Western Europe economic development had preceded the expansion of bureaucracies that grew in response to demand for regulation over expanding domestic markets, in the Central and East European region this sequence was reversed. National bureaucracies developed in anticipation of rather than in reaction to increased societal complexity and industrial growth. They tended to be overstaffed, inefficient, and corrupt. This was not true everywhere—in the relatively wealthy Czech Lands, state administrative rectitude compared favorably with that of Germany and France—but in the poorer countries of the region, economically distressed rural elites bloated the public payroll. Although the Czech Lands, due to the particularities of Habsburg imperial economic policy, possessed a native middle class, in most of the other countries of the region, such as Poland, Hungary, and Romania, entrepreneurial functions were dominated by ethnic minorities: Jews, Greeks, and Germans.

Whereas in most of Western Europe the task of creating a unified national subject had mostly been completed by the end of World War I, at this time the new states in Central and East Europe still had formidable tasks of nation building ahead of them. Czechoslovakia, Poland, and Romania possessed huge minority populations—Germans and Hungarians in Czechoslovakia; Ukrainians, Jews, Germans, and Belarusians in Poland; Hungarians, Germans, and Jews in Romania—plus multiple other smaller ethnic groups (including millions of uncounted Roma) scattered in these and other countries, leaving open the question of their status in newly founded states. Treaties and constitutions guaranteed equality among ethnic groups, but in reality the ethnic majorities of each country considered the state their "own"—Poland for Poles, Romania for Romanians, Hungary for Hungarians, and even Czechoslovakia for the Czechs and Slovaks—and instituted a set of policies to benefit primarily themselves.[4] Credit and tax policies favored ethnic majorities. One might expect that in economically under-developed countries the main political cleavage would be between the "rich" and the "poor," but, in fact, ethnicity divided these societies as much as differences in wealth, and this fact exercised a profound impact on mass politics. Even as this situation began to change in the 1920s as native entrepreneurs grew in numbers, an ethnic division of labor remained in place, and political careers in state employment remained the preserve of the dominant national groups.

Bloated Central and East European states could only be sustained, and economic development policies pursued, by extracting resources from an already poor peasantry, whether they lived on large latifundia in Poland or Hungary or on small dwarf holdings in Romania. Economic chaos in Germany following World War I and disruptions to trade created by the presence of new national borders that divided previously unified imperial markets combined to slow growth. Cities could not absorb the huge number of poor and seasonally employed peasants. Land reform, the initial answer to rural poverty, was largely abandoned or watered down in Poland and Hungary in the 1920s or used as a tool of interethnic equalization or advantage in Czechoslovakia and Poland.[5] Even where implemented, as in Romania, it often created unproductive subsistence holdings whose largely illiterate inhabitants continued to live in squalor.[6]

Such difficult economic and social circumstances conspired to render liberal democracy extraordinarily precarious throughout Central and East Europe. Landless peasants, marginalized ethnic minorities, and the sporadically employed could easily be mobilized into radical, antiliberal politics. Political control and "democracy" could therefore only be maintained through electoral corruption, "managed" elections in which certain parties were not allowed to compete (for example, the communists in Hungary, Poland, and Romania), or quasi-military dictatorships (as in Poland and Lithuania after 1926 under the tutelage of Marshal Józef Piłsudski and Antanas Smetona, respectively).[7]

In most places, liberal democracy never really got off the ground or foundered after one or two elections. Only Czechoslovakia managed to sustain genuine liberal democracy through the 1930s, and the reasons are instructive. The Czech Lands within the country were highly industrialized, with a native middle class and a relatively efficient bureaucracy. An informal agreement among the five dominant parties, the so-called *pětka*, kept the worst fights off the parliamentary floor. However, even this otherwise stable country had several close calls with authoritarianism. The large and restive German minorities in the "Sudetenland" and Hungarians in the Slovak lands challenged the dominance of Czechs and Slovaks.[8] The Slovaks themselves, in search of greater autonomy or additional resources from the wealthier Czechs, frequently voted for authoritarian parties, such as the Slovak Populists under the leadership of the Catholic priest Andrej Hlinka.

Even if corrupted, though, liberalism was not abandoned altogether. Elites rigged elections in many districts and most countries at various times, but competing political parties continued to operate freely for the most part. The case of Poland is instructive. Following independence, Poland held its first free and fair election in 1922, in which more than twenty parties competed for seats in the national parliament, the Sejm, under proportional representation rules. The result was a victory for the nationalist right, which formed a government that froze out the representatives of the 35 percent of the population who were ethnically non-Polish (primarily Ukrainians, Jews, Germans, and Belarusians). But, having gained power, Poland's right-wing parties were unable to form a stable government, since the majority Poles were themselves divided along right-left lines. The ensuing political chaos lasted until May 1926 when the military staged a coup d'état under the leadership of Marshal Józef Piłsudski, Poland's military hero who had spectacularly rebuffed an invading Soviet army in 1920. Piłsudski, though an authoritarian at heart, wanted to rule through parliament and decided to hold one more free and fair election after the coup, in 1928, so that his tellingly named pro-government party, the Non-Party Bloc for Cooperation for the Government, could gain a parliamentary majority. The campaign and vote proceeded fairly (with a modicum of fraud in the multiethnic eastern provinces), the best evidence being the fact that, even with a great deal of government support, the pro-government party failed to gain a majority.[9] In Hungary and Romania, vestiges of liberal restraint were maintained by right-wing authoritarian but traditionalist elites against fascist competitors well into the 1930s. The police and other state officials sometimes violated rights to free speech, political assembly, and even property, but courts frequently reversed such acts of arbitrariness. Public discourse and debate were raucous and often impolite but continued to exist, and the press remained lively.

Not until the rise of the Nazi dictatorship in Germany and the availability of an alternative to the Anglo-American world order did the elites of Central and East Europe unhitch themselves completely from their liberal (and quasi-democratic) moorings. Even here, however, there were crucial differences among the countries. Czechs, and to a lesser degree Poles, resisted right-wing radicalism because their territory was the immediate object of German revisionist claims, and they hoped for support from their patrons in Britain and France. Hungary, Romania, and the Slovak lands, on the other hand, all succumbed to fascist dictatorships, hoping to benefit from Nazi power or at least be spared the more unbearable forms of discrimination that were starting to take shape in the "new European order."

Fascism, 1930–1945

There is very little agreement among scholars about the causes or social roots of fascism. They are clearer on what it is. Fascists believed in racial and ethnic hierarchy, the use of force in pursuit of restoring traditional orders or constructing new ones, a zero-sum competition between national and ethnic groups, and, above all, a violent reckoning with the legal restraints of liberalism and the egalitarianism of socialism. Some argue that it is a form of psychological and nationalist escape into irrationalism that is inherent in modernity.[10] Others maintain that it is an attempt by the middle and lower middle classes to protect their wealth and property rights in the face of economic downturns and socialist threats.[11] Still others hold that it is in fact a radical form of developmental dictatorship that appears quite regularly in industrializing societies.[12] In the case of Central and East Europe, the main appeal of fascism lay in the potential, through an alliance with Germany and Italy, to cast aside liberal democratic restraints in the pursuit of border revisions abroad and turning the tables against ethnic minorities at home.

By 1933, Adolf Hitler had come to power in Germany, crushed or co-opted the country's institutions, stepped away from remaining obligations to the League of Nations before quitting it altogether, and formed an alliance with Benito Mussolini's fascist Italy. Germany had long considered Central and East Europe its backyard, and under Hitler it set about deconstructing the fragile interstate order crafted by the victorious powers after World War I. Economic historians continue to debate whether the German economic and trade offensive of the 1930s under Hitler was a net gain or loss for the region. In the short run, it appears to have had a positive effect, or at least was perceived to have had one among Central and East European elites. The design was a simple one and in some ways resembled arrangements that the Soviets later instituted in the region. Central and East European agricultural goods and raw materials would supply the German military buildup.[13] In return, the countries of the region received credits against which they could buy German industrial goods. Of course, in the long run these credits were all but worthless, and the onset of World War II in the East ensured that the Nazis would never repay the debts they incurred in the 1930s. Yet the modest recovery of the region's economies during the early Nazi years could not help but draw these countries more firmly into the German sphere of influence.[14]

Regional elites hoped that Germany and Italy would accept their Eastern neighbors as junior partners as long as their institutional and legal orders mirrored those of their masters. Thus, local Hitlers and Mussolinis came to power in several countries in the 1930s, and even where they did not, they waited in the wings for the day when German or Italian armies could install them at the top of the local political pyramid. Of course the ideological design of the right and its subsequent institutional expressions were far less elaborate and well articulated than the liberal one. This was so not only because it was much newer but also because most ideologies of the right were explicitly anti-procedural and anti-organizational. They called for national purity, honor, dignity, and, most tantalizingly, the possibility of national glory. For the most part the "little dictators" of 1930s Central and East Europe did not share Hitler's racial fantasies, since Nazi ideology had little good to say about the non-Germanic (especially the Slavic) peoples of the area, but they did use the opportunity to free themselves from parliamentary and other liberal restraints in pursuit of economic development, regional power, and, above all, ethnic advantage.[15]

On this last point, ethnic minorities in many countries of the region had been uneasily tolerated and frequently discriminated against during the interwar period. But they still had recourse to parliamentary representatives and courts, and sometimes even international institutions such as the League of Nations, in pursuit of their communal interests. The more levelheaded, technocratic, and conservative authoritarian/right-wing governments of the 1930s, who still considered their task to be national "development," in many places took the "gloves" off in their struggle with national minorities. They taxed and expropriated their national minorities; drove them out of high-prestige professions such as medicine, law, and journalism; and did not discourage emigration. But even when paying lip service to the "achievements" of Nazi Germany, they failed to implement the full Nazi design. Fascist parties such as the Iron Guard in Romania, the Arrow Cross in Hungary, and the Falange in Poland, who were eager for a final, violent reckoning, especially with their large Jewish populations, were all suppressed, sometimes violently. Minority policies in the 1930s were not yet murderous, but they were now blatantly one sided, in some cases tolerating violence emanating from civil society.

As in the earlier liberal era, political elites corrupted the pure German and Italian model in an attempt to turn it to their own purposes. Nevertheless, the conflict between the developmentalist conservative technocratic right, which favored a nonpolitical dictatorship and still called the shots in the 1930s, and the fascist zealots who gained the upper hand in the 1940s and favored an ideological party-dictatorship that more closely

Photo 2.2. The Legionary Movement in Bucharest, Romania. The Iron Guard, a political party formed by this movement's paramilitary, led a totalitarian fascist regime between September 1940 and February 1941. (Unknown author, Wikimedia Commons)

resembled the Nazi German model was never fully resolved in any country of the region until the onset of the war in the East in 1939.

With the outbreak of hostilities in the East in September 1939, the scales tilted in favor of the fascist zealots. An important indicator of these differences can be seen in the changing fate of the region's Jews. Anti-Jewish laws had been on the books in several countries of the region since the mid-1930s (and in Hungary from as early as 1920), but in most places they were ignored or poorly enforced. By the late 1930s, often under German pressure but sometimes voluntarily and with a good deal of enthusiasm (as in Poland, Hungary, and Romania), they were implemented assiduously. It is nevertheless important to distinguish between the institutionalized discrimination of the 1930s and the historical "revenge" against the Jews that was exacted in horrific form by the Germans and their local Central and East European helpers on the fascist right during World War II. From the standpoint of "development," the organized massacre of the Jews that occurred during World War II marks clearly the difference between the corrupted developmentalist model of the 1930s and the antidevelopmentalist bacchanalia of the 1940s. The conservative authoritarian Hungarian ruler Miklós Horthy, for example, who had been an admiral in the Habsburg navy before becoming regent for a monarchy that no longer existed, was undoubtedly an anti-Semite of the traditionalist sort (even if he continued to play cards with selected wealthy Jewish friends), but he protected his country's Jews from German depredations for much of the war and preferred his prime ministers to be competent managers. His aristocratic prejudices bore little resemblance to the murderous fantasies of the leader of the Arrow Cross Party (the Hungarian Nazis), Ferenc Szálasi, whom the Nazis installed in power in 1944 and who eagerly collaborated in the murder of the country's Jews.[16]

Whereas interwar liberalism had failed in the region because it could neither overcome the backwardness of the region nor adapt its institutional order to the constraints of scarcity, the fascist order failed because it did not really have an institutional response to backwardness at all. Instead, it retreated into the psychological appeal of glory inherent in war, the pleasure of feeling superior to one's "inferiors," or the potential for looting the wealth of one's neighbors and historical enemies. Although it probably did not appear as such to most Central and East European elites in the early 1930s, by the end of the war it must have been clear that fascism ultimately had little to do with development at all.

The legacies of failed prewar liberalism and wartime fascism have left an important imprint on the political imagination of contemporary Central and East Europe. Citizens throughout the region continue to debate the pluses and minuses of both eras, some viewing them as a lost opportunity or golden age and others as nightmares never to be repeated. The recurring and heated disputes over museums and national monuments reflect the depth of feeling about these pasts. Whether it is Hungary's Admiral Miklós Horthy, who preserved the country's sovereignty and to some extent protected the country's Jews, but who also sided with Germany in the war to regain territory lost to Hungary's neighbors after World War I; Poland's Marshal Piłsudski, who took power by force in Poland but remained tolerant toward the country's minorities and permitted a modicum of political freedom; or Czechoslovakia's President Tomáš Garrigue Masaryk, who embodied the country's commitment to democracy and moderation even while the policies of various Czech governments discriminated against local Germans and Hungarians, the leaders of the liberal and antiliberal past do not provide easy and uncontroversial role models for emulation. The past today remains hotly contested throughout the region.] time of contradictions and complexity

Communism: From Marx to Lenin

What was communism and what legacies did it bequeath to Central and East Europe? As with the failed liberal and fascist orders, the original sources, ideas, and institutions of communism are to be found outside the region. The core idea for communism sprang from the fertile mind of the nineteenth-century German social theorist and journalist Karl Marx, who like many others around him sought to understand the profound changes taking place throughout Europe, especially the dislocations and injustices produced by industrialization, urbanization, the collapse of traditional monarchies, and the rise of liberal democracies. Marx maintained that all societies are divided between the ruling classes who control the means of production and the exploited majority who do not. The type of rule in each society reflects the interests of the ruling class. Feudal societies ruled by nobilities preferred monarchies. In Marx's lifetime, most of these older feudal and monarchical orders had already been overthrown (as in the French Revolution in 1789) or were being challenged by new urban classes, the capitalists (sometimes labeled the "bourgeoisie") who owned the new industrial and commercial means of production and the industrial workers (the proletariat) who labored for wages. The new order would be based on the rule of law, markets, individual rights, and democratic citizenship, which included the right to vote. Marx admired these new rights, but he also saw them as deceptive because the bourgeoisie exploited the proletariat just as ruthlessly as the nobility had exploited the peasantry. Capitalism generated unprecedented riches, but the new resources were distributed highly unevenly and workers continued to live in miserable conditions throughout Western Europe. Seen correctly, Marx argued, the new "rights" and ideals that inspired them were a trick, a mask for the genuine source of power, an "ideology" designed to deceive the exploited workers. Just as Christianity had fooled peasants in feudal societies into believing their poverty would be rewarded with entry into heaven in the afterlife, so too did the idea of rights and elections trick workers into thinking they were free and exercised power. Ultimately, Marx argued, workers would come to understand the sources of their misery and would overthrow the capitalists and their phony liberal democratic order in a revolution and institute a new order, "socialism" or "communism,"[17] one of fundamental equality in which the workers themselves would own the means of production and rule over themselves.[18]

Marx's vision captivated the imagination of many Europeans. A society in which one could "hunt in the morning, fish in the afternoon, and criticize in the evening, without ever being a hunter, a fisherman, or a critic" (as Marx described communism), sounded utopian, but his analysis of capitalist society was powerful. The idea of equal rights did not seem to mean much in societies of gigantic material inequalities—what did freedom mean if it was merely the freedom to be homeless and malnourished?—and the idea of socialism/communism was compelling. But when Marx died in 1883, he left a lot of questions unanswered. The most important one was, how would this new society come about?

Marx saw human history in materialist and developmental terms. Feudalism led to capitalism, which would ultimately be overthrown in favor of socialism/communism. Each stage was necessary to the development of the next. Within feudal society, capitalism was born, and the seeds of socialism and communism would germinate within capitalist society. But when and where would the communist revolution occur? It seemed reasonable that since the revolution would occur in capitalist societies, one could expect it to occur first in the most advanced countries: Germany, France, or England. But would it happen spontaneously, without leadership? Could the workers be counted on to make the revolution themselves? And what would happen to the poorer countries of Central and East Europe where capitalism had yet to develop?

Subsequent "Marxists" (those who considered themselves followers of Marx's ideas) throughout Europe disagreed among themselves on the answers to these questions even during Marx's lifetime. Marxist political parties (mostly calling themselves "Social Democrats") formed to capture power in national elections, but did not the very idea of a party staffed by professional politicians seem to contradict the placement of industrial workers as the key dramatis personae of history?[19]

Nowhere were these ambiguities and contradictions more obvious than in Russia. Marxist ideas had taken root there, too, but Russia at the beginning of the twentieth century was not an advanced capitalist and democratic country with a large industrial working class. It was instead mostly made up of illiterate peasants and ruled by an autocratic monarch and nobility unconstrained by a constitution. It was in many ways more feudal than capitalist. How could a working-class revolution occur without a large industrial working class? Some Russian Marxists believed Russia had to wait for "necessary historical developments," that is, for capitalism to develop first. Vladimir Lenin, the leader of the "Bolshevik" branch of the Russian Social Democrats, disagreed and maintained that other Marxists had dangerously misunderstood Marx and especially Russian conditions. First, he argued, workers would never make a revolution on their own. They were corruptible and could be bought off with higher wages, so they had to be led by a professional party that understood the "laws" of history. Second, such a party in Russian conditions had to be conspiratorial and staffed by true believers, by full-time fanatical revolutionaries. Otherwise the authorities would quickly arrest and imprison its leaders. Third, he maintained that Russia had already been rushing through capitalism and that socialism and the working class could in any case be cultivated after the revolution. Finally, on the question of communism, Lenin argued that rule after the revolution would be a "dictatorship of the proletariat" and would cast aside the conventional restraints and institutions of liberal democracy. Revolutionaries were not normal politicians, and a revolutionary party was not a normal party competing for votes against other political parties in elections. This vision of revolutionary strategy and rule, one determined by Russia's specific conditions, was to have a decisive impact on what communism became.

Stalinism and the Origins of Communist Institutions

In 1924, Lenin, like Marx, died before the ambiguities in his ideas could be resolved. Communists had seized power in 1917 amid the chaos of World War I and by 1922 had formed the Soviet Union from conquered neighboring territory in Central Asia, the Caucasus, and Ukraine. They established a one-party dictatorship and vanquished counterrevolutionary forces in a civil war. But what would communism actually look like? The Soviet Union remained a poor agricultural country in a world of powerful and hostile states. The Bolshevik leaders violently disagreed among themselves about the best way forward, each side accusing the other of misunderstanding Marx and Lenin and betraying the revolution. Some wanted to march forward and conquer the rest of the world; others believed revolutions would occur in the more developed Western countries; still others counseled gradualism both domestically and abroad. The winner of the internal infighting was Joseph Stalin, and it was under his long rule (1928–1953) that the main features of communism took shape and were exported to Central and Eastern Europe after World War II. Stalin believed the Soviet Union could survive even without a revolution in the heartland of Europe and that it could become the core of a new international communist order. But he also maintained that it could do so only with a crash program of industrialization and modernization.

A speech Stalin gave to industrial managers in 1931 captured the essence of his thought:

> One feature of the history of old Russia was the continual beatings she suffered because of her backwardness. She was beaten by the Mongol Khans. She was beaten by the Turkish beys. She was beaten by the Swedish feudal lords. She was beaten by the Polish and Lithuanian gentry. She was beaten by the British and French capitalists. She was beaten by the Japanese barons. All beat her because of her backwardness, military backwardness, political backwardness, industrial backwardness, agricultural backwardness. They beat her because to do so was profitable and could be done with impunity. . . . In the past we had no fatherland, nor could we have one. But now that we have overthrown capitalism and power is in our hands, in the hands of the people, we have a fatherland, and we will defend its independence.[20]

Much of this speech does not sound very "Marxist" and seems to fit neatly into conventional, "realist" views of state: weak states need to become powerful or they will be conquered by the strong. Scholars disagree on whether Stalin believed this because he wanted to create a rich country at home or a powerful country capable of exporting revolution abroad. The truth is probably a combination of both, but either way Stalin's dictatorship became one that focused on catching up with the West. The method would be mobilization of resources from the agricultural economy through brute force to produce the rudiments of industrial growth. Forcibly requisitioned grain was sold abroad, and entire factories were purchased from the West, such as the giant steel complex in Magnitogorsk.[21] Millions of peasants died of starvation, but the end result was an industrial society with a powerful military. This was the model of the 1930s, and it worked well enough to survive the war and defeat Nazi Germany in the 1940s.

When scholars discuss the legacies of communism in Central and East Europe, they primarily refer to the policies and institutions first developed under Stalin in the Soviet Union during the 1930s. The Stalinist model exported to the region in 1945 was characterized by some key economic, social, and political features. In the economy, private property and markets were almost completely eliminated in favor of a "planned" or command economy, with state control of prices, banks, communication, and transportation. The party pursued ambitious goals of economic development to build up heavy industry and the military. Agriculture was collectivized, and the powers of the party and secret police were extended throughout the countryside.[22] Foreign trade fell completely into the hands of the state, and a policy of self-sufficiency was pursued to break any bonds of dependency on the capitalist world.

Socially, the party launched huge modernization programs to eliminate illiteracy and institute public health measures as a means of ensuring a skilled workforce and army. Lower classes tended to be favored, and anyone with ties to the older "bourgeois" order, especially technical specialists and army officers, found themselves disadvantaged or in peril of losing their positions and sometimes their lives as scapegoats for unworkable economic plans. The state strictly controlled rents, extended pensions to all workers, eliminated tuition for schools and universities, and provided free medical care. Women, who had largely been excluded from many fields before the communist era, took up positions throughout the economy and enjoyed important new reproductive rights.[23] These social measures, taken together, were popular and constituted the core of what became "actually existing" socialism and communism.

Politically, Soviet leaders created a dual hierarchy of Communist Party and state bureaucratic organs at virtually every level of society to ensure that central directives were followed and the plans of the Communist Party were met. Propaganda departments spread the official communist ideology ("Marxism-Leninism") throughout society through mandatory classes in schools; censorship of books, movies, and art; and the careful curation of museums. Networks of informers reported to a ruthless secret police (the NKVD, the precursor of the KGB), which had virtually unlimited powers of arrest, detention, and punishment. Communist Party members themselves faced strict surveillance and were among the first to be punished for failure to meet economic plans or deviation from official views in meetings or even casual conversation. During the late 1930s, many thousands of party officials from the top to the bottom of the communist hierarchy were executed during the "Great Purge," accused of being "enemies of the people." At the same time, leading party and state officials were granted better living conditions that included privileged access to apartments, food, consumer goods, and travel. Taken together, these measures produced a mixture of enthusiasm, fear, and interest, which the party harnessed to the goals of building communism.

Communist parties outside of the Soviet Union attracted little support. Following the Russian Revolution in 1917, communists in Central and East Europe considered launching revolutions in their own countries. For a brief period after World War I, from March until August 1919, as the Habsburg and Hungarian armies disintegrated, the Hungarian communists under Béla Kun managed to seize power and declare their own Soviet republic. Communist rule was unpopular, especially in the countryside. It quickly became known for its inefficiency and violence against targeted enemies. Lenin's Bolsheviks in Russia intended to link up with Kun's forces by invading Hungary through Romania, but having suffered setbacks in Ukraine during their own civil war, the promised Soviet invasion never occurred. By August, Romanian forces had captured Budapest and Kun had fled, first to Austria and from there to Moscow, where he was ultimately executed during the great purges of the 1930s. Back in Hungary, rightist forces, nominally under the command of Admiral Horthy, exacted brutal revenge against the erstwhile communist elite.

Having failed to gain power anywhere in Central or East Europe outside of the Soviet Union after World War I, communist parties throughout the region tended to be small and made up of tiny groups of devoted fanatics who subordinated their national organizations to the Comintern (the Communist International), a Soviet-controlled organization with offices in Moscow. To the extent that industrial workers voted for left-wing parties, they tended to support reformist Social Democrats who pushed for higher wages and better working conditions rather than revolution. Ironically, because they envisioned solidarities based on class rather than nation or race, it was among national minorities, the losers of ethnic politics in interwar Central and East Europe—Hungarians in Slovakia, Belarusians in Poland, and Jews in Romania—that communist parties attracted a modicum of members and a respectable number of votes, but such alliances only confirmed the conviction among majority elites that the communists represented "foreign" interests rather than those of the "nation."[24] When communists took power after World War II, they had few allies.

During World War II, some communists in Central and East Europe stayed in their homelands and fought underground battles against the Nazis, risking imprisonment and death at the hands of the gestapo. Others made their way to the West. The East German playwright Bertold Brecht, for example, spent the war in Hollywood, as did his friend, composer Hanns Eisler, who went on to compose East Germany's national anthem after returning following the war. The vast majority of leading communists, however, fled to the Soviet Union. There they prepared their return along with the victorious Soviet army. The end of the war, as Stalin predicted, provided the opportunity to bring communism to the countries of Central and East Europe, but rather than through revolution, it was introduced by the power of Soviet tanks.

Making Sense of Actually Existing Communism

Although Western scholarly debates on the nature of communism were often influenced by the seminal work of local Central and East European dissidents such as Milovan Djilas in Yugoslavia, Václav Havel in Czechoslovakia, György Konrád and Iván Szelényi in Hungary, and Alexander Solzhenytsin in the Soviet Union, the political restrictions of Soviet-type rule in the region meant that the study of the region under communism mostly took place abroad.

Two schools of thought dominated analysis of communism: totalitarianism and modernization theory. The totalitarian school was inspired by the writings of Hannah Arendt and Carl Friedrich.[25] Its adherents argued that despite doctrinal differences between Nazi Germany and the communist Soviet Union, they had so much in common that it made sense to group the two dictatorships together as essentially the same. For one thing, both professed an ideology of earthly salvation and were prepared to cast aside conventional moral restraints and deploy unlimited violence in pursuit of their higher goals. For another, both orders destroyed existing civic and personal attachments for the purposes of creating a single locus of devotion. And while the Nazis placed the "leader" at the center of their ideology and the communists the highlighted importance of the Communist Party, in practice both devolved into personal dictatorships. The Nazis believed in hierarchy and the communists in equality, but these ideological differences exercised a minute impact on political and even social organization. However, most important, these theorists told us, the unprecedented capacity for social control inherent in modern political technologies and bureaucratic organizations render totalitarian orders exceedingly difficult to change.

Students of Central and East Europe in the 1950s had little difficulty finding proof of totalitarian parties with instrumental views of their own societies. Private property was expropriated, and with the arrival of Soviet troops in 1944–1945, liberal freedoms failed to reemerge after the liberation from Nazi Germany, or they were abolished in steps that culminated with the onset of the Cold War in 1948. Under careful Soviet tutelage, secret police forces intimidated and subjugated entire societies. The stories of secret police tactics are chilling: children taken away from parents, informers recruited with blackmail, interrogations of suspected opponents involving threats and torture lasting for days. In one report from Hungary, the Communist Party secretary in a factory delivers a short speech in which he praises "Comrade Stalin," at which point everyone rises in applause. In the corner sits a secret police informer watching the crowd carefully. Who, he wants to know, stops clapping first? There you have your "enemy of the people." How could one be safe under such circumstances? Who could be trusted? The party-state was a fickle and dangerous leviathan that demanded more than obedience; it demanded complete devotion.

At first, communists retained the veneer of liberal democratic institutions: parliaments, judiciaries, and civil services. Stalin remained cautious regarding the intentions and resolve of his erstwhile Western allies. The trappings of national sovereignty were kept in place. Little by little, however, all of this was whittled away.[26] Within three years, communists controlled every bureaucracy in the region. Social Democratic parties were forcibly amalgamated with the communists, and other parties were banned or turned into tame "satellite" parties. Communist parties and their secret police forces "managed" or rigged elections, or they simply falsified the results, as in Poland in 1946. Where this did not happen, as in Czechoslovakia in 1948, the Communist Party simply took power in a military takeover. Rounds of "purges" were responsible for the arrest and torture of thousands of real and imagined foes. Similar to the Soviet Union of the 1930s, between 1948 and 1952, the "little Stalins" of Hungary, Bulgaria, and Czechoslovakia staged trials of "traitors" from among the highest ranks of their own communist parties, all of whom confessed under duress to having worked for Western intelligence services throughout their long careers as revolutionaries. In some cases, such as in the trial of Paul Merkur in East Germany and Rudolf Slánský in Czechoslovakia, anti-Semitic stereotypes reemerge in these trials, with the defendants accused of having worked for "Zionists," "the American Jewish Joint Distribution Committee," or "world Jewry."[27] With these "show trials," communist leaders sought to eliminate any national "deviations" from the Soviet line emanating from Moscow.

Everywhere the Soviet army occupied, local Communist Party leaders replicated the Soviet experience. Private farms were collectivized, and large and eventually medium-sized businesses were nationalized. The party eliminated market economies and introduced

Soviet-style economic planning, even in countries with preexisting industrial development such as Czechoslovakia and East Germany (which formally separated from West Germany in 1949), and also in Romania and Bulgaria, into which virtually every part of the new Stalinist steel factories had to be imported. Local circumstances were largely ignored. National churches saw their role in education and public life greatly diminished and in politics all but eliminated.

The cultural orientation of these countries shifted overnight from the West to the East. Russian-language instruction became mandatory in schools, library shelves groaned under the weight of imported Soviet books, and Soviet standards permeated everything from music instruction to filmmaking to scientific patents to city planning. As the East German slogan put it, "To learn from the Soviets means learning to win!" The legacy of the forced domestic adoption of external policies would be a long-lasting one.

The Nobel Prize–winning writer and poet Czesław Miłosz, who had worked as a diplomat for a short time in communist Poland and eventually defected to the West in 1951, described in his book *The Captive Mind* both the allure of Stalinism for intellectuals and the myriad ways in which people resisted it in their private lives. The work was banned in Poland but read widely underground and appeared in English in 1953. According to Miłosz, intellectuals understood the difference between the ideology of the communists and the reality of rule, but they made small and large compromises in their daily lives, sometimes collaborating but mostly avoiding direct conflict with the regime and escaping into a private existence. The same intellectuals who denounced Western literature in print would often savor it in private. This led to a dual existence.

> It is expressed in that unconscious longing for strangeness which is channeled toward controlled amusements like theater, film, and folk festivals, but also into various forms of escapism. Writers burrow into ancient texts, comment on and re-edit ancient authors. They write children's books so that their fancy may have slightly freer play. Many choose university careers because research into literary history offers a safe pretext for plunging into the past and for converse with works of great aesthetic value. The number of translators of former prose and poetry multiplies. Painters seek an outlet for their interest in illustrations for children's books, where the choice of gaudy colors can be justified by an appeal to the naïve imaginations of children. Stage managers, doing their duty by presenting bad contemporary works, endeavor to introduce in their repertoires the plays of Lope de Vega or Shakespeare—that is, those of their plays that are approved by the center.[28]

The intelligentsia played a cat-and-mouse game with the communist regime. Sometimes they enthusiastically engaged, other times they feigned compliance, and on occasion they risked everything by resisting.

Theories of totalitarianism did not dispute that the communist parties found inspiration in the ideals of Marxism, which saw a future of equality and harmony after capitalism. But whatever the "humanistic" inspiration of the original Marxist ideal, it had been lost in the murderous drive to overcome economic backwardness and in pursuit of world revolution. The result, these theories maintained, was a nightmare of modern tyranny that resisted all fundamental change.

Modernization theorists took this response to backwardness as their point of departure. Although not questioning the characterization of communism as dictatorial and essentially antiliberal, scholars inspired by modernization theory in the 1960s began to challenge the totalitarian school's interpretation of the *dynamics* of communism, that is, how it would change over time.[29] Modernization theory maintained that even accounting for broad ideological differences, all societies that industrialize, urbanize, and educate their populations face the same kinds of pressures and will most likely have similar kinds of politics. Furthermore, over time, the functional prerequisites of modern societies produce a convergence in cognitive orientations toward power, politics, administration, and justice. Again, studying Central and East Europe after Stalin's death in 1953, scholars had little trouble finding proof of what they were seeking. The Soviet leadership and its Central and East European counterparts appeared to espouse a more pragmatic, less "ideological" approach to the problems of their own societies. Scholarly focus shifted away from revolutionary terror to the everyday needs of real people: housing, education, consumer goods, and leisure. No longer, modernization theorists pointed out, were shortcomings seen as the dirty work of "wreckers," "saboteurs," "counterrevolutionaries," and "enemies of the people" but rather as problems to be dealt with and overcome through the "scientific technical revolution" and sensible policies. Marxism-Leninism, the official ideology of communist Central and East Europe, would not be cast aside completely, but in such highly industrialized counties as East Germany and Czechoslovakia, the clash between a mobilizational dictatorship and the prerequisites of industrial modernity would most likely be resolved in favor of the latter.

Modernization theorists agreed that communists were not democrats, but they maintained that many of their policies produced the same modern and urbanized societies found in the West. Ultimately, they believed, things would change. Indeed, in the decades following Stalin's death, Central and East European culture and literature came into its own. Czech, Hungarian, and Polish cinema produced important and popular films. Directors such as Miloš Forman (Czechoslovakia), István Szabó (Hungary), and Andrzej Wajda (Poland) were celebrated internationally. Forman's *The Fireman's Ball* (1967), for example, portrays the leadership of a volunteer fire department in a small town in Czechoslovakia that decides to supplement its annual ball with a beauty pageant, a raffle, and the gift of a ceremonial axe to their retired fire chief who is suffering from terminal cancer. The beauty pageant is quickly corrupted, the items in the raffle mysteriously disappear from the table one by one, and the axe, too, is ultimately stolen. Meanwhile, a fire breaks out in town, which the firefighters are unable to extinguish. It did not require too much imagination to see this film as a send-up of the pervasive corruption and inefficiency within the communist order. Even in otherwise tightly controlled East Germany, writers such as Stefan Heym and Christa Wolf received prizes for their work from all over the world. What could not be written about in communist newspapers or discussed on television often appeared in their novels and short stories.

Communist leaders were obsessed with meeting the consumer expectations of their people because they knew that nothing could destabilize their rule faster than unmet needs. They kept careful track of housing supply and demand, seasonal changes of fashion, automobile production, and the possibilities for tourism. This last point, travel, was an especially sore one because the authorities feared that those who traveled to the West might return with subversive ideas or not return at all. For that reason, tourism was tightly controlled and was directed mainly into other communist countries. Whereas West Germans vacationed in Paris and Mallorca, East Germans went to Hungary and Bulgaria. These were modern societies but with strict limitations.[30]

Notwithstanding their important insights, in some respects both the totalitarian and modernization approaches got it wrong. Contrary to the expectations of the totalitarian school, the communist world did change, but it did not change in a direction predicted by modernization theory. Rather than a leadership increasingly infused with a rational-technical and pragmatic spirit that would adopt practical policies that worked regardless of ideology, Soviet-style institutions throughout the region produced economic stagnation and corruption. Concerning economic dynamism, the key error of the modernization theorists was to confuse Soviet-style industrialization with capitalist economic development. No Soviet or Central and East European economic theorist ever devised a nonmarket and postmobilizational model of economic growth. In fact, once they were permitted to write with greater candor, economists in Yugoslavia, Poland, and especially Hungary articulated quite convincing accounts of why these economies would never generate growth based on greater allocative efficiency that could respond to rapid changes in taste.[31]

On the question of corruption, in the absence of some mechanism for ensuring the circulation of elites, the end of Stalinist secret police terror simply turned public offices into private sinecures. Barrington Moore articulated such a possibility already in 1954, and his insight became a full-blown model of "neotraditionalism" in Ken Jowitt's work of the 1980s.[32] Jowitt explained the decay of communist rule by the party's inability to articulate a new, postmobilizational "combat task" that would have provided a yardstick against which to judge bureaucratic rectitude. Increasingly communism resembled rule in the developing countries of Latin America and Africa more than the Western capitalist countries they sought to displace.

Others, mainly Western but also Eastern economists, devised related models based on organizational, as opposed to ideological, features of communist political economy, which they argued was in essence a gigantic "rent-seeking" (that is, corruption) machine designed to move resources from ordinary people to communist elites, factory directors, and central planning bureaucracies.[33] The dissonance between the official egalitarian ideology and the way outcomes turned out on the ground were apparent to all. In East Berlin, limousines ferried top Politburo members back and forth to their compound in the leafy suburb of Wandlitz, with its nicely appointed houses and stores filled with Western consumer goods. High party officials in Bulgaria and Czechoslovakia enjoyed hunting on well-stocked game preserves, while the Communist Party leader of Romania, Nicolae Ceaușescu, built himself a white palace in downtown Bucharest.

The Soviet Bloc

If Stalinist political and economic institutions constituted a crucial legacy of communism, a further legacy was subordination to the Soviet Union. The Soviet empire in Central and East Europe first took shape in the 1940s. Unlike in the Soviet Union itself, which had been cobbled together between 1922 and 1940 into a single multinational state, Stalin took great pains to preserve the appearance of national autonomy. Even so, as his remarks to Djilas quoted at the beginning of this chapter show, Stalin wanted a bloc of communist states that would support the Soviet Union economically, militarily, and diplomatically. He expected American-dominated Western Europe to be capitalist and liberal democratic, but Central and East Europe would be different. Communism in the region after World War II began essentially as a colonial operation in which local elites were controlled by Soviet supervisors, political direction stemmed from the Soviet embassy, and resources were extracted through trade agreements that favored the Soviets. The countries of the region were integrated into Soviet-led security and economic structures, the Warsaw Treaty Organization (known as the Warsaw Pact) and the Council for Mutual Economic Assistance (CMEA).[34]

As in the interwar liberal and then fascist periods, however, local conditions conspired to alter the original institutional design. After Stalin's death in March 1953, the states of the bloc began to move in their own directions in search of domestic legitimacy. The dilemma for East European elites was that, in order to gain some measure of local support, policy had to be dictated by local circumstances. In 1956, the Polish leadership decollectivized agriculture. During the 1960s, Czechoslovakia and East Germany experimented with decentralized economic planning. Later, Poland and especially Hungary introduced significant economic reforms allowing for markets and private small enterprise. In every country of the region, concessions were made to local nationalisms and religious traditions. Romanians celebrated their "Daco-Roman" heritage; East Germans marked the anniversary of Martin Luther's initiation of the Protestant Reformation (but gave it a specifically Marxist twist); Czechs marked their own Christian reformer, Jan Hus; Bulgarians were permitted to Slavicize their Muslim minority. Above all, the Catholic Church in Poland regained a great measure of the social power it had lost in the first decade of communism.

These local variants of communism, however, always threatened to exceed the bounds of what the Soviets might allow. The Soviets wanted a cohesive group of states—Western analysts sometimes called these states "satellites"—that could serve as the base of the communist world. Disputes flared up even while Stalin was alive. Yugoslavia under the leadership of Josip Broz Tito resisted subordination to Soviet leadership and as a result was unceremoniously expelled in 1948 from the Soviet-dominated international communist movement (redubbed the "Cominform" after World War II). Both Yugoslavia and Albania, never fully occupied by the Soviet army, rejected the Soviet model, the former maintaining that the Stalinist regime was too strict and bureaucratic, the latter that it was not strict or pure enough. Before Stalin's death, suspected "Titoites"—those who wanted their countries to pursue their own brand of communism—were arrested, tried, and shot throughout Central and East Europe.

Stalin's successor, Nikita Khrushchev, called for reconciliation with Tito (who considered himself a good communist) on the grounds of there being "many roads to socialism"; he also called for increasing living standards and ending police terror. Such a move, however, raised difficult questions for the Stalinist rulers of Central and East Europe who had supported every small twist and turn in Soviet domestic and foreign policy. What would be the limits of autonomy? Did every country have to resemble a small version of the Soviet Union? Could the Polish or Hungarian communist parties, for example, follow Yugoslavia and construct their own model of socialism/communism? Could they also call for Soviet soldiers to leave their countries and return to the Soviet Union? None of these questions received a firm answer in the years after Stalin's death in March 1953. Chaos ensued.

In fact, the history of the Soviet bloc was largely one of rebellion. In 1953 in East Germany, 1956 in Hungary, 1968 in Czechoslovakia, and 1980 in Poland, local Communist Party leaders made concessions to local sentiment by making significant institutional changes. In June 1953, two months after Stalin's death, East German workers marched for higher wages and against price increases for basic goods, but they ultimately wanted unification with West Germany. In fall 1956, Hungarians came out into the streets demanding an end to secret police terror, but the revolt quickly escalated, with the local Stalinist leadership resigning and the new communist reformist leaders offering to leave the Soviet bloc. During the "Prague Spring" in 1968, the Czechoslovak reform communists called for "socialism with a human face," but they soon lost control of the narrative as well as the situation on the ground. In Poland in 1980–1981, workers first organized an independent trade union, dubbed "Solidarity," in the shipyards of Gdańsk, but the strikes and demonstrations associated with worker demands quickly engulfed the entire country and threatened communist rule—Solidarity was much more than a trade union. In each instance, these changes led to a weakening of Communist Party control, a

Photo 2.3. A tank in Prague during the military invasion of Czechoslovakia in 1968. The Soviet Union led the invasion suppressing the socialist reform movement there and restoring Soviet hegemony in the region. (František Dostál / Wikimedia)

threat to Soviet hegemony in the country, mass street protests, and ultimately a military crackdown and restoration of Communist Party rule. Attempts to specify clear limits on local autonomy—such as the "Brezhnev doctrine" (named after the Soviet leader at the time, Leonid Brezhnev) put forward after the Soviet invasion of Czechoslovakia in 1968 that stipulated that Communist Party rule and membership in the Warsaw Pact could not be abandoned—only highlighted the sense that communist rule had been externally imposed and lacked domestic legitimacy.

Notwithstanding repeated campaigns to impose ideological and institutional uniformity, by the 1980s different models of communism had emerged among the Central and East European countries. These variations were the product of the "raw material" the communists had at hand (the "precommunist legacies") as they reconstructed their countries after World War II. In Czechoslovakia and East Germany, countries with large industrial working classes and a precommunist tradition of administrative professionalism and rectitude, leaders such as Erich Honecker and Gustáv Husák trumpeted their countries' commitment to scientific rationality and bureaucratic efficiency. These regimes were dictatorial but for the most part not corrupt. In Hungary, Poland, and Yugoslavia, communist leaders attempt to reconcile with strong national sentiments by permitting markets and easing up on the strictures of central planning in the hope of meeting consumer demand. All three countries permitted some travel to the West, loosened communist control over cultural and intellectual life, and even (in the case of Yugoslavia) permitted their citizens to live abroad and send money home to relatives and friends. Differences in incomes grew. In all three cases, the atmosphere became looser and palpably freer. In Bulgaria and Romania, by contrast, countries with poorly developed traditions of administrative efficiency and the rule of law, authority evolved in a neopatrimonial direction in which a few families and clans dominated public life, the Zhivkovs in Bulgaria and the Ceaușescus in Romania. In both countries, the national leaders were cast as "fathers" of the nation, traditional rulers in the mold of other strongmen from their nations' histories. All of these variations on the communist theme, however, never exceeded certain bounds. Communist parties continued to play the "leading role," Marxism-Leninism remained the official ideology, and subordination to the Soviet Union in foreign policy went unchallenged.

In foreign policy, perhaps the most "deviant" of the countries within the Soviet bloc was Romania. Although deeply authoritarian at home, in 1968 Romania's leader, Nicolae Ceaușescu, denounced the Soviet invasion of Czechoslovakia to reinstall orthodox Communist Party rule and refused his country's military participation with Warsaw Pact forces. In addition, Romania was the only country in the bloc to retain diplomatic relations with Israel throughout the Cold War and (for a tidy sum of money paid for each person) permitted its Jews to emigrate to Israel. It retained its membership in the Warsaw Pact and continued to coordinate military and intelligence matters with its Soviet allies, but it also carved out a sphere of autonomy.

Communist trade relations bequeathed to Central and East Europe their own legacy: a complete reorientation away from the West and toward the Soviet Union. After 1945, trade initially favored the Soviets. East Germany's economy in particular became a source of reparations to the Soviet Union for World War II, both in the form of dismantled factories and running production. Even without the burden of reparations, the Soviets forced other countries to alter their economic structures to accommodate Soviet domestic and military needs. The big benefit appeared to be the ability to purchase Soviet oil and gas at subsidized prices. This began to change in the 1970s as global prices for hydrocarbons spiked and the Soviets wanted to divert their production to Western markets. During the 1970s and 1980s, the relationship of economic exploitation between the Soviet Union and Central and East Europe was reversed, with the former subsidizing the latter and shielding it from the full effect of the dramatic increase in world oil prices.[35] Even with these subsidies, rising consumer demands could not be met, and throughout the region, governments borrowed from Western banks to purchase consumer goods in the West in order to maintain domestic peace. The debt load to Western governments and financial institutions soared and, in the case of Hungary and Poland, became unserviceable. The debts could only be repaid through austerity and deferred maintenance on infrastructure. In an attempt to retain autonomy and service its loans from Western banks and private creditors, Romania took the route of austerity. Prices for basic goods were increased several times, and real incomes shrank. Rationing for basic foodstuffs that had been eliminated in the 1950s was reintroduced in 1981, and periodic power cuts left apartments cold in the winter. It became the only communist country to begin to suffer from chronic food shortages and malnutrition. Other countries in the region deferred maintenance and begged their Soviet patrons for increased subsidies and their Western creditors for easier terms.

By the mid-1980s, roads were decaying, buildings went unpainted and unrepaired, and the urban landscape of classically European cities such as Budapest, Prague, and (East) Berlin looked increasingly drab. Although incomes had risen considerably over the forty years of communist rule and almost nobody went homeless, hungry, or without basic medical care and education, the relative disparities between West European living standards and those in Central and East European had never been greater. Despite decades of murderous effort to define an appealing alternative to capitalist modernity, the communist bloc had failed.

Civil Society, Resistance, and 1989

Communist countries were ideological and mobilizational dictatorships. For this reason, they also bred resistance. In many cases, resistance was passive. Ordinary people frequently ignored the official ideology and constructed private lives that minimized the intrusions of heavy-handed communist officials. Václav Havel, the Czech playwright and dissident, spoke of "living in truth," by which he meant living with a measure of dignity, as if the communist rulers were not even there.[36] Of course, this was not entirely possible. Havel himself went to prison for involvement in oppositional activity. Even so, art, literature, and music evolved into pockets of self-expression and personal freedom.

Beyond passive resistance, religious groups, environmental organizations, informal sports clubs, and educational associations challenged the dominance of the Communist Party. For the most part, they did not do so openly or with great fanfare—this was too risky—but increasingly social organization slipped the bonds of official control. Political scientists term this associational life outside of the state "civil society." Secret police informers never ceased to penetrate these groups and write reports (the East German secret police, known as the Stasi, accumulated almost seventy miles of files on citizens between 1950 and 1989), but increasingly there were simply too many groups to suppress.

Although communists sought to destroy civil society and replace it with their own official organizations—with everything from youth leagues to sports clubs—once secret police terror diminished after 1953, associational life came roaring back in many countries of the region. Each of the rebellions against Soviet domination—East Germany in 1953, Hungary and Poland in 1956, Czechoslovakia in 1968, and Poland in 1980–1981—involved civic organization and protest, the mobilization of civil society against the Communist Party–dominated state, which could only be put down with renewed secret police repression. Even when they did not directly challenge the state, these organizations were poised to do so when the time was right. In the meantime, they slowly but surely chipped away at the power and authority of communist parties everywhere in Central and East Europe. By the 1980s, the rulers of some countries, such as Hungary and Poland, permitted a great deal of civic association, while in others, such as Czechoslovakia and East Germany, artists and writers were sometimes harassed, fired from their jobs, or forced to emigrate, and in Bulgaria and Romania, secret police forces continued to mistreat and imprison those who insisted on organizing outside of official channels.

Civil society groups shared a common goal of maximizing their autonomy from communist government control, but they did not always share a common ideology. One crucial divide among them concerned nationalism and liberalism. Parts of civil society reflected traditional or rural orientations. These groups criticized communist governments for undermining religion, altering and modernizing gender relations, and generally undermining respect for traditional social norms. They tended to be nationalist and hark back to the positive experiences of the precommunist era. Other groups, however, focused on cities, modernity, and the liberal freedoms embodied in the West. Their criticism of Communist Party rule focused on individual rights and political freedom. They tended to be cosmopolitan and liberal rather than nationalist. The legacy of these rival orientations in civil society under communist rule carried over into the postcommunist era, with many of the players reemerging into nationalist or liberal politics after 1989.

Central and East European civil society found its moment in 1989 when the Soviet Union under Mikhail Gorbachev withdrew its support for its client regimes in the region. The Brezhnev doctrine was declared null and void, and the Central and East European communist parties were on their own. This move immediately destabilized all of these regimes, because ordinary citizens understood that communist parties could no longer count on military intervention from abroad to shore up their rule. Already in Poland, the underground opposition printed newspapers and even broadcast on radio, receiving help in doing so from the CIA and the Vatican. In the summer of 1989, Hungary opened its border to the West, and immediately thousands of East German citizens vacationing there used the opportunity to cross into Austria and from there to West Germany. Other East Germans, ones visiting Prague, stormed the West German embassy and demanded free transit to the West; their demands were ultimately met. This was the beginning of the end. By the fall, Communist Party rule was crumbling everywhere in the face of popular demand.

How communism fell depended in large measure on civil society. In Hungary and Poland, where civil society was well developed, communist leaders could identify potential negotiating partners and extricate themselves from power, mostly with carefully managed elections. Power shifted peacefully, almost seamlessly. Where the opposition was less organized and civic life remained weaker, such as in Czechoslovakia and East Germany, communist leaders only sought out intermediaries once massive street demonstrations against communist rule forced them to do so. In Bulgaria and Romania, where civil society barely existed or had been ruthlessly crushed in the decades running up to 1989, the regime lacked any counterpart with which to negotiate, and street demonstrations turned violent. In Romania this violence culminated in the speedy trial and execution of Communist Party leader Nicolae Ceauşescu on Christmas Day.

Communism's Mixed Legacies in Central and East Europe

As noted at the beginning of this chapter, part of what defines Central and East Europe as a region is that for the past century it has been mostly a "system taker" rather than a "system maker." That is, every political order has been externally inspired or imposed rather than internally cultivated. Each order failed in the face of economic backwardness and local corruption of the original design. The initial adoption of liberal democracy at the end of the imperial era and the first post–World War I years failed virtually everywhere in the face of these two constraints. Fascism, too, came from abroad, but beyond settling interethnic rivalries with genocidal violence, it never developed a compelling and appealing approach to economic and political development. Communism did not do much better. Incomes grew everywhere after 1945, but the disparities in wealth between the two halves of the continent did not shrink under communism and even grew. The sense of it being imposed from abroad never waned.

One important legacy in Central and East Europe of so many imported and failed institutional orders and ideologies is a general cynicism about every order. Whereas North Americans and West Europeans mostly attach an intrinsic worth to liberal democracy regardless of its economic performance, Central and East Europeans, because of the long history of institutional mimicry, view the post-1989 attempt at liberal democracy as one more imported model to emulate, one that may or may not work, rather than as an institutional tradition to be valued for its own sake. Except for Czechoslovakia, no country in the region had a history of successful and stable liberal democracy that it could claim as its own, as a tradition on which to look back proudly.

As the most recent of these imports, communism bequeathed to the region a set of legacies more immediate and palpable, and probably more enduring, than either prewar liberal democracy or wartime fascism. In the initial years after communism, most scholars viewed these legacies as uniformly "bad."[37] In the economy, inefficient and decayed state-owned factories had to be privatized and rebuilt. Without a preexisting class of investors or even a merchant middle class, however, who would own and control these new factories? How can one build capitalism without capitalists? What would keep the basic industries and housing stock of the countries from falling into the hands of insiders or corrupt bureaucrats? As we will see in subsequent chapters of this book, no "perfect" method of privatization and marketization that would prevent corruption and insider trading could be devised. Collective farms were to be broken up, but who would get to buy the land? Agonizing choices had to be made about whether it made more sense to retain the expertise and experience of communist economic officials or to import an entirely new managerial and ownership class from the West. Especially in those countries that had not experimented with markets at all, capitalism would have to be built from scratch.

In 1989, communist parties lost their monopoly of power, but the legacy of communist dictatorship left a panoply of political dilemmas. Perhaps most worrying in countries with such a weak tradition of democratic rule was whether this would be the hour of the "colonels" rather than the citizenry or the politicians. That is, might Poland, for example, be subject to a military takeover after 1989 in the same way it had been in 1926 under Piłsudski after four chaotic years of democracy? Would Yugoslavia, a country that had been ripped apart in ethnic war during World War II, be subject again to even stronger nationalist centrifugal forces? As it happened, the former did not occur—in Poland the colonels have so far been no-shows—but Yugoslavia did descend into a bloody civil war. The point is that the demise of Communist Party rule created an atmosphere of extreme uncertainty, and nobody knew what would fill the void.

What about the secret police forces that had kept the communist parties in power? What would happen to the thousands of secret police officials and stool pigeons who had informed on their neighbors and friends? Should they be exposed and lose their citizenship rights even though they were operating "within the law" under communism? Civil society reemerged under communism, but decades of secret police repression left a legacy of distrust among ordinary people that could not easily be overcome. The same applied to the institutions of the judiciary. Were judges who had been educated and appointed by communists and had put dissidents in prison appropriate members of courts in a democratic society? The legacies of communism's organs of state power continue to plague the countries of postcommunist Europe today.

Communism's legacy made the construction of democracy difficult. It is one thing to announce free and fair elections, but who would run in these elections? The key players in democratic politics are political parties. Under communism, however, normal political parties that competed in elections for parliamentary seats did not exist. How could they be fielded overnight, and what would be the principle of their organization? Notwithstanding their precipitous decline in popularity, did communist parties not have an unfair organizational advantage here, too? They still held control over buildings, newspapers, and the apparatus of public life that in 1989 no other group really possessed. The legacy of communism in Central and East Europe continues today to structure party competition and foster political resentment. Many Communist Party members resigned in 1989, but a huge number did not, and clever reformist elites could "transform" themselves into electorally competitive left-wing parties. In Hungary and Poland where this happened, perhaps the most important political cleavage continues to be the dispute over the communist past.

Of course, one can also identify "positive" legacies of communism. Recall the "modernization" school of Central and East European studies. Regional communist regimes were certainly dictatorships with Stalinist command economies, but they were more than that. In the name of competing with the West, communist regimes also educated their populations and eliminated illiteracy, instituted universal and free medical care, ensured that everyone had adequate housing, outlawed racial discrimination, and created a general rough-and-ready equality among the citizenry.

This last point is a controversial one and is perhaps easily misunderstood. Democratic citizenship does not require equality of material condition—although if too few people control too much wealth, that can be a problem—but it does entail a recognition that one's fellow citizens are equals in status. The societies of Central and East Europe in the first half of the twentieth century were ones of deep and abiding inequality—the sort of "clubbish" inequality that even money does not easily overcome—and that made democracy a tenuous proposition. Communism did not completely eliminate these inequalities, but in matters of relations between people it bequeathed to the postcommunist societies not only more material equality than ever before in their histories but societies of far less social deference to one's "betters." In this sense, although the communist rulers of Central and East Europe did not intend to do so, their policies of social modernization may have partially paved the way for the democratic breakthrough in 1989.

Even these "positive" legacies, however, could not overcome the impediments posed to democratic stability by a system that disappeared more than thirty years ago. The consensus of most scholars is that communism bequeathed to the postcommunist countries a set of economic, social, and political legacies that have made the construction of liberal democracy more difficult than it otherwise might have been. More than three decades after the fall of the Berlin Wall, communism's shadow still looms large over the region.

Can these legacies be overcome? The historical record indicates caution. The European Union's (EU's) Eastern Enlargement project that got underway shortly after communism's demise in 1989 perpetuated the long-term pattern of these countries as system takers rather than system makers. Theoretically the postcommunist elites had the opportunity for the first time to carve out an independent path during the 1990s when great power aggression was temporarily illegitimate on the continent. But they chose not to do so. The developmentalist imperative that had influenced the adoption of previous orders in the region remained as alluring as ever. Having regained sovereignty in 1989, the elites of Central and East Europe chose to hand much of it back over to the European Union in the hope of joining the club of the prosperous in the West. This sort of breathless desire to move up the hierarchy of nations by importing (and then corrupting) ideas and institutions from abroad has driven politics in the region for over a century. Seen this way, the EU era in contemporary Central and East Europe may reflect as much historical continuity as it does change.

Study Questions

1. How and why did liberal and fascist rule in Central and East Europe before 1945 differ from the original designs imported from the West?
2. What was the essence of communism? Was it a strategy for world revolution, a model of tyranny, or a path to industrialization?

3. What were the main sources of instability in the Soviet bloc?

4. How did the experience with so many different social orders in the twentieth century influence the fate of liberal democracy in Central and East Europe in the decades after 1989?

5. What are the key legacies of communism in Central and East Europe?

Suggested Readings

Arendt, Hannah. *The Origins of Totalitarianism*. New York: Harcourt, Brace, Jovanovich, 1973.

Berend, Ivan. *Decades of Crisis: Central and Eastern Europe before World War II*. Berkeley: University of California Press, 1998.

Brzezinski, Zbigniew K. *The Soviet Bloc: Unity and Conflict*. Cambridge, MA: Harvard University Press, 1967.

Connelly, John. *From Peoples into Nations: A History of Eastern Europe*. Princeton, NJ: Princeton University Press, 2020.

Fitzpatrick, Sheila. *The Russian Revolution*. Oxford: Oxford University Press, 2017.

Janos, Andrew C. *The Politics of Backwardness in Hungary, 1825–1945*. Princeton, NJ: Princeton University Press, 1982.

Kopstein, Jeffrey S. *The Politics of Economic Decline in East Germany, 1945–1989*. Chapel Hill: University of North Carolina Press, 1997.

Polonsky, Antony. *The Little Dictators: The History of Eastern Europe since 1918*. London: Routledge and Kegan Paul, 1975.

Viola, Lynne, ed. *Contending with Stalinism: Soviet Power and Popular Resistance in the 1930s*. Ithaca, NY: Cornell University Press, 2002.

Notes

1. Milovan Djilas, *Conversations with Stalin* (New York: Harcourt, Brace and World, 1962), 119.

2. Andrew Janos, "The Politics of Backwardness in Continental Europe, 1780–1945," *World Politics* 41, no. 3 (April 1989): 37.

3. Andrew Janos, *East-Central Europe in the Modern World: The Small States of the Borderlands from Pre- to Postcommunism* (Stanford, CA: Stanford University Press, 2000).

4. Tara Zahra, *Kidnapped Souls: National Indifference and the Battle for Children in the Bohemian Lands, 1900–1948* (Ithaca, NY: Cornell University Press, 2008); Jeremy King, *Budweisers into Czechs and Germans: A Local History of Bohemian Politics, 1848–1948* (Princeton, NJ: Princeton University Press, 2002).

5. Hugh Seton-Watson, *Eastern Europe between the Wars, 1918–1941* (Cambridge: Cambridge University Press, 1946).

6. George D. Jackson Jr., *Comintern and Peasant in Eastern Europe, 1919–1930* (New York: Columbia University Press, 1966); Henry L. Roberts, *Rumania: Political Problems of an Agrarian State* (New York: Archon Books, 1969).

7. Antony Polonsky, *Politics in Independent Poland: The Crisis of Constitutional Government* (Oxford: Oxford University Press, 1972).

8. Elizabeth Wiskemann, *Germans and Czechs: A Study of the Struggles in the Historic Provinces of Bohemia and Moravia* (Oxford: Oxford University Press, 1938).

9. Jeffrey S. Kopstein and Jason Wittenberg, "Who Voted Communist? Reconsidering the Social Bases of Radicalism in Interwar Poland," *Slavic Review* 62, no. 1 (Spring 2003): 87–109.

10. Hannah Arendt, *The Origins of Totalitarianism* (New York: Harcourt, Brace, Jovanovich, 1973).

11. Seymour Martin Lipset, *Political Man: The Social Bases of Politics* (New York: Doubleday, 1960); Gregory M. Luebbert, *Liberalism, Fascism, or Social Democracy: Social Classes and the Political Origins of Regimes in Interwar Europe* (Oxford: Oxford University Press, 1991).

12. James A. Gregor, *Interpretations of Fascism* (New Brunswick: Transaction Publishers, 1997).

13. Ivan Berend, *Decades of Crisis: Central and Eastern Europe before World War II* (Berkeley: University of California Press, 1998).

14. Albert O. Hirschmann, *National Power and the Structure of Foreign Trade* (Berkeley: University of California Press, 1945).

15. Antony Polonsky, *The Little Dictators: The History of Eastern Europe since 1918* (London: Routledge and Kegan Paul, 1975).

16. Andrew C. Janos, *The Politics of Backwardness in Hungary, 1825–1945* (Princeton, NJ: Princeton University Press, 1982).

17. Marx tended to use these terms interchangeably. Later followers of Marx, however, who offered new interpretations of his texts considered "socialism" a lower stage of development than "communism."

18. Shlomo Avineri, *The Social and Political Thought of Karl Marx* (Cambridge: Cambridge University Press, 1968).

19. Robert C. Tucker, *The Marxian Revolutionary Idea* (New York: Norton, 1969).

20. Joseph V. Stalin, *Problems of Leninism* (Moscow: Foreign Languages Publishing House, 1953).

21. Stephen Kotkin, *Magnetic Mountain: Stalinism as a Civilization* (Berkeley: University of California Press, 1997).

22. Lynne Viola, *Contending with Stalinism: Soviet Power and Popular Resistance in the 1930s* (Ithaca, NY: Cornell University Press, 2002).

23. Sheila Fitzpatrick, *The Russian Revolution* (Oxford: Oxford University Press, 2017).

24. Jeffrey S. Kopstein and Jason Wittenberg, "Between National Identity and State Loyalty: Electoral Behavior in Interwar Poland," *POLIN: Studies in Polish Jewry* 24 (2011): 171–85.

25. Arendt, *The Origins of Totalitarianism*; Carl J. Friedrich and Zbigniew K. Brzezinski, *Totalitarian Dictatorship and Autocracy* (Cambridge, MA: Cambridge University Press, 1965).

26. Hugh Seton-Watson, *The East European Revolution* (New York: Praeger, 1956).

27. Jeffrey Herf, *Divided Memory: The Nazi Past in the Two Germanys* (Cambridge, MA: Harvard University Press, 1997).

28. Czeslaw Miłosz, *The Captive Mind* (New York: Vintage, 1990), 76.

29. Jerry F. Hough, *The Soviet Union and Social Science Theory* (Cambridge, MA: Harvard University Press, 2014).

30. Jeffrey S. Kopstein, *The Politics of Economic Decline in East Germany, 1945–1989* (Chapel Hill: University of North Carolina Press, 1997).

31. Janos Kornai, *The Socialist System* (Princeton, NJ: Princeton University Press, 1992).

32. Barrington Moore Jr., *USSR: Terror and Progress* (Cambridge, MA: Harvard University Press, 1954); Ken Jowitt, *New World Disorder: The Leninist Extinction* (Berkeley: University of California Press, 1992).

33. Jan Winiecki, *The Distorted World of Soviet-Type Economies* (London: Routledge, 2013).

34. Zbigniew K. Brzezinski, *The Soviet Bloc: Unity and Conflict* (Cambridge, MA: Harvard University Press, 1967).

35. Ellen Comisso, "State Structures, Political Processes, and Collective Choice in CMEA States," *International Organization* 40, no. 2 (1986): 195–238.

36. Václav Havel, *The Power of the Powerless* (London: Routledge, 1985).

37. Jowitt, *New World Disorder.*

CHAPTER 3

Nationalism and Its Challenges to Democratic Governance

Zsuzsa Csergő and Jason Wittenberg

One of the most iconic images from the period of the fall of communism is the waving of national flags with the hammer and sickle removed. The symbolism of this is highly significant. It was meant to demonstrate that communism, for all its hegemonic pretensions and corrosive effects, never succeeded in eliminating the ties of history, culture, and identity that bind a nation together. Despite decades of repression and communist propaganda, the nation survived. It also signaled that the nation was to be a source of political legitimacy going forward. It is impossible to understand contemporary Central and East European politics without accounting for nationalism.

This chapter evaluates the challenges nationalism poses to democratic governance in Central and East Europe. This region is not the only place where nationalism is often at odds with democracy. Wherever political elites design nationalist strategies, the process reveals the sources of tension rooted in the Janus-faced character of nationalism: as with other political ideologies, nationalism is forward looking in that it articulates a vision of the future but backward looking in that nationalist strategies almost always purport to turn to the past for self-definition.[1] When nationalists claim self-government rights for "the nation" on a "national" territory or "homeland," they usually offer a certain interpretation of history to justify these claims. Historical evidence is less important than the degree to which such historiography can foster a sense of shared history and purpose. To express this idea, "national myth" is the term most often used to describe national stories.

Some national myths are more successful than others in accommodating cultural and linguistic diversity. The so-called civic type of nationalism, which builds community on shared political traditions and beliefs in a common creed, is potentially more inclusive than ethnic nationalism, which requires members of the nation to share a common language and culture and relies on a particular combination of cultural markers (such as language, race, or religion) and practices (such as holidays and customs around food and marriage). In many instances, the national myth contains stories about ethnic competition over territory, invoking memories of past ethnic dominance and subordination, which continue to influence current state- and nation-building processes. Yet not all ethnic groups engage in national competition. A key difference between ethnic and national groups is that although ethnic groups aim to reproduce particular cultures, only national groups claim self-government rights on a particular territory.[2]

Central and East Europe (CEE) is a particularly interesting place to study national-ism. First, it reveals that the popular appeal of nationalism does not necessarily diminish with the introduction of liberal capitalist democracy and membership in a transnational institutional sphere, such as the European Union (EU). Rather, nationalism can thrive under democratization, marketization, and regionalization. Although the economic and political path out of communism proved bumpy, overall postcommunist CEE has expe-rienced robust economic growth and enjoyed multiparty democratic systems. Virtually all countries became members of the EU or are lined up to join. Yet not only did nationalism not decline, but in some cases it strengthened over time. Second, the study of nationalism in CEE helps us identify key conditions under which ethnic nationalism can be effec-tively used (like low-hanging fruit) by political leaders and elites interested in taking and maintaining control over societies, undermining democratic institutions, and weakening societies' ability to hold governments accountable.

State centers around the world have been engaged in nation building since the emergence and global spread of the territorial nation-state model. This model promotes the pursuit of congruence between the territorial and cultural boundaries of a nation.[3] In Europe, this pursuit in earlier centuries involved aggressive efforts to "right-size" the state by changing territorial boundaries to include external ethnic kin, assimilating inter-nal "others," eliminating nonconforming groups to "purify" the nation, or encouraging them to repatriate to other countries.[4] Such methods caused brutal ethnic cleansings dur-ing World War II and forced population movements thereafter. But by the 1950s, such means of nation-state creation became unacceptable in the Western part of the continent. The primary motivation behind the post–World War II Europeanization process was to create incentives for sustainable peace through economic interdependence and increased social interaction across territorial borders. As the communist regimes began collapsing in CEE, the same interest in regional peace and security motivated the creation of the European Union in 1992 and its "Eastern Expansion" to postcommunist states. Yet a review of the political developments of the last three decades shows that the appeal of nationalism coexists with interest in democratic government across the continent, and the experiences of CEE have revealed key reasons why the relationship between nationalism and democracy remains fraught with tension.

Studying CEE also provides valuable insights into the questions of what makes societies vulnerable to ethnic nationalism, and how the instrumentalization of ethnic nationalism by political elites in turn undermines the ability of social actors to resist authoritarian control. There is a long-standing debate over whether a fully democratic ("civic") nationalism devoid of ethnic politics can be achieved. Influential political theo-rists point out that no state is completely ethnically "neutral."[5] Even countries tradition-ally described as textbook cases of "civic nationalism," such as Britain, France, and the United States, reveal significant similarities to "ethnic nationalism." In all these countries, schools, churches, the media, the military, and various other state and private or public institutions privilege a dominant ethnic culture (language, narratives about history and homeland, literature, music, etc.) to create and perpetuate a unified national canon that is rooted in a dominant ethnicity.[6] Others argue that democratic governments have the power to choose between more or less "ethnicized" forms of government.[7] Differences in those choices are manifested in the ways that states institutionalize or work toward mitigating the advantages and disadvantages associated with ethnic belonging (and similar socially constructed distinctions, such as race or caste) that are embedded in institutions of power and in the bundle of institutions and policies that create or hinder opportunities for people in a state—such as systems of education, employment, and housing.

In the pages that follow, we provide a brief overview of the evolution of nationalism in CEE prior to the 1990s. We then consider the implications of the politics of ethnic demography for democratic governance in postcommunist CEE. We divide the roughly three decades since communism collapsed into two periods. In the first, we discuss how national majorities and minorities struggled, sometimes violently, to assert their rights in their new postcommunist political systems. For most countries, this period lasted roughly until the country entered the EU as a democratic state. In the second, we consider what might (unartfully) be termed the post-postcommunist period, in which the liberal state is under attack and nationalism manifests as populism, especially in states that three decades earlier were front-runners in "Europeanization" and the institutionalization of liberal democracy in the region.

Nationalism before Democratic Competition

Across CEE, the legacies of the previous decades and the challenges of the post-1990 period that followed made societies vulnerable to *ethnic* nationalism. Societies in this region have experienced border changes three times within three generations: at the ends of World War I, World War II, and the Cold War. Most of the time, border changes were associated with devastation: war, mass violence, and forced population movements (that is, expulsions, ethnic cleansing, or flight from states in which another ethnic group claimed "titular" rights). This was the norm in 1918 and 1945 and during the collapse of the Yugoslav state in the 1990s. After each border change, large parts of societies became traumatized. Successful nation building requires a broadly shared narrative of nationhood, and the conflicting collective memories of victimization in this region have made the creation of such shared national narratives extremely difficult. The appeal of particular national narratives, however, remains alive, and part of the reason is that narratives of collective memory offer a sense of rootedness for individuals and social groups that undergo dramatic political and socioeconomic changes like those experienced in CEE.

It was not coincidental that the most ambitious efforts by state centers to replace competing national narratives with an internationalist ideology were made by the communist elites that assumed power with Soviet help after World War II. This conflict provided an unprecedented display of the devastation that ethnic nationalism can cause. The first generation of communist leaders, itself disproportionately from minority backgrounds, introduced an internationalist political discourse to counter nationalist ideology. The idea was to transcend differences in ethnicity and race by introducing a supranational identity that would bind the constituent ethnic groups together in one nation. The three ethnofederations—the Soviet Union, Czechoslovakia, and Yugoslavia—are the clearest examples of this. All three countries tried to bridge ethnic differences by creating "federal" identities—Soviet, Czechoslovak, and Yugoslav—to which any citizen, in principle, could belong. In the Soviet Union, the most successful, this involved creating a unifying

Soviet culture rooted in the Russification of the language of school instruction and promoting the dominance of Russian cultural production across the vast territory of the federation. But even though communism provided leaders with unprecedented power to conduct "social engineering," none of these regimes succeeded in creating homogeneity in societies where multiple groups had earlier competed for national rights. Nationalism never really disappeared under communism. It only took different forms.

Despite an initial emphasis on internationalism, in practice nationalism remained a key organizing principle during the communist period.[8] The three ethnofederations are again instructive. In the Soviet Union, the constituent republics recognized a "titular nationality" that was numerically predominant in that republic. For example, there was an Estonian Soviet Socialist Republic (SSR), a Latvian SSR, and a Lithuanian SSR. The borders of all three roughly corresponded to the borders of independent Estonia, Latvia, and Lithuania during the interwar period. Other ethnicities, such as Jewish, were also recognized. Every Soviet citizen was required to choose the ethnicity of one of their parents to list on their ID card.[9] This ethnofederal model was replicated in Czechoslovakia and Yugoslavia. In Czechoslovakia, Czechs and Slovaks were equivalents of "titular" nationalities with separate territories, while Hungarians, Roma, and Jews were treated as ethnic categories with more limited rights.

Yugoslavia, like the Soviet Union, was organized into ethnic republics. Over time the republics succeeded in gaining substantially more autonomy from the federal government in Belgrade. Though all but Yugoslavia were limited in the realm of foreign affairs by their subservience to the Soviet Union, CEE countries pursued their own brand of nationalism in the realm of domestic politics. The post–World War II Czechoslovak government, for instance, declared ethnic Germans and Hungarians collectively guilty of having contributed to Hitler's destruction of Czechoslovakia and gained Soviet approval for the expulsion of these ethnic groups from the country. Based on the Beneš decrees (named for the state's president, Eduard Beneš), Czechoslovakia expelled the overwhelming majority of ethnic Germans to Germany and a large percentage of the Hungarian population, including much of the Hungarian educated class, to Hungary.[10] Those who remained in the state were denied citizenship rights until 1948. Despite such a drastic policy to achieve an ethnic balance favoring Czechoslovakia's two titular groups, a significant number of Hungarians remained in the Slovak part of Czechoslovakia. Throughout the communist decades, they were subject to economic, cultural, and educational policies that severely restricted their ability to reproduce their culture or improve their socioeconomic status. The relationship between the Czechs and the Slovaks was also tense from the beginning of cohabitation. Initial notions of a unified Czechoslovak identity were soon replaced by efforts to loosen Prague's control over the Slovak part of the land in a federative structure that better represented national interests.

Compared to Czechoslovakia, the post–World War II Romanian communist government adopted more minority-friendly policies. Because the ethnic Hungarian party was instrumental in the communist takeover in Romania, Hungarian minority leaders gained Moscow's support in achieving full citizenship rights, participation in the government, and the right to maintain cultural and educational institutions. The same Soviet government that in Czechoslovakia gave full support to President Beneš's policies to expel German and Hungarian minorities facilitated the establishment of regional autonomy for

Hungarians in Romania's Transylvania region in 1952. Although this autonomous region was short-lived, the first communist-dominated Romanian government was much better disposed toward minorities overall than was the Beneš government in Czechoslovakia.[11] As the influence of ethnic Hungarian leaders in the Communist Party weakened, however, the government launched a nationalizing strategy that severely weakened the political status and social structure of the Hungarian community in Transylvania. Beginning in the mid-1960s, the government of Nicolae Ceauşescu launched a ruthless strategy to consolidate a centralized unitary nation-state. Ethnic Germans were offered incentives to emigrate to West Germany, and Hungarians were subjected to administrative, economic, and educational policies aimed at their assimilation.

The popular appeal of nationalism is illustrated by the anti-regime movements that emerged in the region after the communist takeover. The failed Hungarian national uprising of 1956 sought to free Hungary from the Soviet orbit and establish national self-determination. The idea of different national roads to socialism was picked up by reformists in Czechoslovakia, who in 1968 attempted to establish an independent Czechoslovak "socialism with a human face." As in Hungary, the attempt was quashed by Soviet troops. Nationalism also featured in the anti-Soviet Solidarity movement in Poland, which ultimately played a key role in the collapse of Polish communism. In Romania, Ceauşescu's efforts to assimilate the Hungarian minority to Romanian culture produced a backlash. Ethnic Hungarians played a significant role in the collapse of the Ceauşescu regime in December 1989.[12]

In the Soviet Union, the liberalizing reforms introduced by Gorbachev in the mid-1980s opened possibilities for anti-regime movements among the non-Russian republics. This opportunity was seized in the Baltic states, where nationalist groups organized demonstrations for self-determination. The "Singing Revolution" galvanized voices that rejected Russification and reclaimed national sovereignty through language reforms and a reassertion of Baltic cultures. In the former Yugoslavia, mobilization by the more prosperous Croats and Slovenes against Serbian dominance had begun earlier, after Tito's death in 1980. These nationalist goals had been inadvertently encouraged by an ethnic power-sharing system created within one-party rule, entrenched in the 1974 constitution that devolved power to ethnically defined republics.

Once the communist regimes began collapsing in 1989, all three ethnofederations fell apart along nationalist lines. This is understandable. As detailed above, these states had been organized along ethnic lines that formed the basis for nationalist opposition to the federal system. Ethnonationalism manifested itself powerfully in claims for independence and rearrangement of political borders across the region. In contrast to the border changes that followed the First and Second World Wars, however, the rearrangement at the end of the Cold War was peaceful across the former Soviet bloc (i.e., the Soviet Union and its regional allies). Ethnic nationalism generated war only in the former Yugoslavia. By the mid-1990s, the political map of postcommunist CEE included twelve newly created or recreated states, with only five states continuing within the same borders. The leaders of all states chose ethnically majoritarian systems, yet the postcommunist governments faced major challenges in satisfying desires to build liberal capitalist democracies in majoritarian nation-states. Moreover, most of these governments were asserting national sovereignty while simultaneously demonstrating keen interest in joining a transnational institution (the European Union) that required them to give up significant elements of sovereignty. The way governments addressed these conflicting challenges revealed the continuing salience of ethnic nationalism. Efforts to design and implement democratic "social contracts" during the three decades of transformation were shaped significantly by patterns of ethnic demography. But it was not ethnic demography itself that "caused" democratic governance to succeed or fail in some place at some time. Rather, it was the *politics* of ethnic demography, in other words, the way political actors employed ethnicity in designing and implementing political and economic systems, that shaped the relationship between nationalism and democracy in each case.

Asserting National Sovereignty

The collapse of communist regimes across the region made self-government tangible, and the majority and minority groups that articulated competing notions of self-government rights were national groups that defined "nation" on the basis of ethnic markers—most commonly language and culture, and in some cases religion. But the states emerging from the post–Cold War rearrangement do not fulfill the nationalist longing for congruence between the boundaries of state and "nation." Although CEE states became ethnically majoritarian, most still incorporate sizable ethnic minority populations and include at least one "national" minority population that has organized to claim self-government rights. As majority political actors in state centers designed institutions for their version of national sovereignty, the presence of such minorities was often framed as a threat to state stability and national security. This "securitization" of the presence of ethnic minority populations became predominant in newly created or reconstituted states. Securitization became especially "acute" in relation to minorities that had potentially activist kin-states in the region—that is, states in which their ethnic kin compose a titular majority. Due to the frequency of border changes and reversals of ethnic hierarchies in this region, most sizable minority populations have kin-states. Among the ethnic minorities targeted as sources of "threat to the nation," Jews and Roma are exceptions in that they have no kin-states in the neighborhood that might be suspected of separatist goals.

Differences in ethnic demography create different challenges for majoritarian nationalists in state centers that aim for "national" congruence. Most CEE states include a *titular* nationality (e.g., Romanians in Romania or Estonians in Estonia) plus other national minorities that seek some degree of political self-determination (e.g., ethnic Hungarians in Romania, ethnic Russians in Estonia, ethnic Albanians in North Macedonia). Some states have no sizable national minorities that claim self-government (e.g., the Czech Republic, Hungary, Poland). But nationalism in some of these states (e.g., Hungary, Poland) is complicated by the presence of sizable ethnic kin populations in neighboring countries. It adds to the complexity of this "mismatch" between territorial and cultural notions of nationhood that many states in the region are both home states and kin-states. Romania, for instance, is the home state of a sizable Hungarian minority (in absolute numbers one of the largest national minorities in the region), and it also conducts kin-state politics in relation to ethnic Romanians in Moldova. Serbia also has an important Hungarian minority and yet conducts kin-state politics with Serb co-ethnics in Croatia

Table 3.1. Significant Internal and External Minorities in Central and East Europe

Country	Significant internal minority (>2% of population)	Significant external ethnic kin (>2% of home state population)
Bulgaria	Turks 8.8	—
Estonia	Russians 25.5	—
Hungary	—	Slovakia 8.5, Romania 6.1, Serbia 3.5
Latvia	Russians 26.9, Belarusians 3.3, Ukrainians 2.2, Poles 2.2	—
Lithuania	Poles 6.6, Russians 5.8	—
Poland	Lithuanians 6.1, Latvians 2.4	—
Romania	Hungarians 6.1	Moldova 6.9
Slovakia	Hungarians 8.5	—

Note: Countries are listed in the first column. The second column identifies national minorities that make up more than 2 percent of the country's population. The third column identifies countries that contain greater than 2 percent of the members of the nation in column 1. For example, the fourth row indicates that Hungary has no internal minorities that comprise greater than 2 percent of the population but that Slovakia's population has 8.5 percent Hungarians, Romania's has 6.1 percent Hungarians, and Serbia has 3.5 percent Hungarians.

and Bosnia-Herzegovina. The only state in the region that is more or less "right-sized" from the perspective of ethnic nationalism is the Czech Republic, where the vast majority of citizens are ethnic Czechs, and the small number of minorities (e.g., Jews and Roma) present no national claims. These demographic realities are summarized in table 3.1.

Ethnonationalism and the Collapse of Multinational States

The nationalist movements that pursued state formation emerged in the three multinational federations: Czechoslovakia, the Soviet Union, and Yugoslavia. Although each of these dissolving federal states was ethnically diverse, only a limited number of groups defined themselves in national terms and claimed rights to national self-government. In each case, the titular groups of substate administrative units were most likely to claim such rights. These were Serbs, Slovenians, Macedonians, Montenegrins, and Croatians in former Yugoslavia; Czechs and Slovaks in former Czechoslovakia; and Estonians, Latvians, and Lithuanians in the former Soviet Union. Those engaged in state formation had to answer the following questions: What would be the physical boundaries of the successor states? What would "the nation" mean within those boundaries? Who belonged to the new political community and under what terms? And what should happen to those who did not belong? In all cases, the political elites who led the movements for national independence played an important role in shaping the debates about these questions. In Czechoslovakia and the Soviet Union, nationalist claims and territorial changes were managed peacefully and even democratically. In Yugoslavia, however, democratic forms of parliamentary debate and party competition were unable to contain national conflicts, and these conflicts escalated into devastating wars.

The difference between the peaceful breakups of Czechoslovakia and the Soviet Union and the violent breakup of Yugoslavia demonstrates the political importance of elite choices. It is tempting to dismiss the peaceful Czechoslovak "Velvet Divorce" that led to the Czech Republic and Slovakia as a lucky fluke. After all, the Beneš decrees after World War II had "right-sized" the Czech Lands by expelling the formerly influential German minority and reducing the number of Hungarians in the Slovak lands. Czechs and Slovaks dwelled largely in the Czech and Slovak parts of the federation, respectively, and neither group had significant territorial claims against the other. Moreover, the Hungarian minority in the Slovak part of the state, a historic minority with competing homeland claims in the southern region of Slovakia, did not challenge the Slovaks' right to independence. The circumstances were thus ideal for a peaceful parting of the ways. Yet the creation of independent Czech and Slovak states was an outcome negotiated among the political leaders of the two parts of the federation, with only limited public support.[13] This was not the case with Russians in the Soviet Union and Serbs in Yugoslavia, both of whom benefited from being a dominant group and had substantial ethnic diasporas in other republics of their respective federations. The difference between the Soviet and Yugoslav breakups can be attributed to the decision of the Soviet elites to peacefully dissolve the Soviet Union, whereas the Yugoslav elite—dominated by Serbians—decided to hold things together by force.

Independence and State Building in the Baltic States

The Baltic states' journey to independent statehood occurred without significant border disputes and largely reproduced the territorial boundaries that these states had before their forcible annexation to the Soviet Union in 1940. An important factor in the absence of territorial disputes was that, although ethnic Russians were closely associated with Soviet federal power structures, the Russian-speaking population in the Baltic republics overwhelmingly comprised relatively recent settlers whom the native population viewed as colonizers. As the formerly dominant ethnic group in the Soviet Union, the Russians remaining in the Baltic states stood to lose the most at independence. Yet they articulated no systematic challenge to Baltic aspirations for independence. The new states, with their prospects for European integration, offered better socioeconomic conditions than neighboring Russia.

Nonetheless, Baltic statehood did involve a great deal of political rancor. Although Estonians, Latvians, and Lithuanians were formally titular ethnicities in their respective republics during the Soviet occupation, the share and status of these ethnic groups had decreased dramatically during the Soviet period due to large-scale deportation campaigns aimed against the native population, the emigration of great numbers of Baltic peoples to the West, and the massive influx of Russian-speakers. During the Soviet occupation, Russian became the predominant language in the public domain, especially in urban centers.

The relationship between Russian and the titular national languages during the Soviet era remained that of one-sided bilingualism despite language legislation adopted in the final years of Soviet political reform that aimed at "emancipating" the Baltic languages.

Non-Russians had to be fluent in Russian in order to function fully and advance socio-economically, but Russian-speakers were not learning the languages of the republics in which they resided.[14] The notion that the Russian presence represented "illegal occupation" would become a significant building block in strategies of state reconstruction (see chapter 14).

[handwritten margin note: mass deportations, language policies, Russians as colonizers]

Democratization Derailed: Nationalism in the Balkans

In former Yugoslavia, the substate borders of the republics did not coincide with people's mental maps of "historic homelands." Consequently, national self-determination became a vehemently contested idea, as multiple national groups living in a mixed demographic pattern claimed the same territory as "their own," and each group turned to a different national myth and conflicting interpretation of past relations of dominance and subordination, sacrifice and victimization.

Serbs and Croats comprised the majority of the state's population and the overwhelming majority in the largest republics—Serbia (including its autonomous provinces, Kosovo and Vojvodina), Croatia, and Bosnia-Herzegovina. Approximately 24 percent of Serbs lived outside the Republic of Serbia, and 22 percent of Croats lived outside Croatia. Tensions between Serbs and Croats influenced interethnic relations throughout Yugoslavia. Montenegrins generally identified with Serbs, and Muslims lived intermixed with Serbs and Croats. Only Slovenia and Macedonia, with very small Serbian and Croatian populations, avoided the Serbian-Croatian competition.[15] In such a context, successive unilateral declarations of independence by nationalist elites contributed to a cycle of conflict that marked the entire decade of the 1990s and caused devastation and horror not seen in Europe since World War II.

In Yugoslav republics where majority and minority political elites advanced competing and mutually incompatible claims for the same "national homeland," these claims mobilized large-scale support among extremists and demobilized liberals and moderates in the population, enabling the outbreak of violent conflict.[16] The Serb Democratic Party in the Krajina region of Croatia, for instance, immediately challenged the emerging Croatian movement for an independent state by demanding administrative and cultural autonomy for the Serb-majority region. Unable to achieve this goal immediately, the leaders of the four Serb-controlled areas declared the formation of the Serb Autonomous Region of Krajina in January 1991 and added in March of that year that this region would "dissociate" from an independent Croatia and remain within Yugoslavia. This exacerbated already existing distrust and helped trigger a devastating war in Croatia. The government of Croatia on one side and the Serbian-dominated Yugoslav state presidency, as well as local Serb authorities, on the other employed armed forces to achieve their goals. The war ended in 1995 with the help of US and European mediation, but only after brutal destruction in Croatian cities and villages, great suffering among the civilian population, and ethnic cleansing on both sides that resulted in the displacement of more than half a million people. Today, the Serbian minority represents only slightly more than 4 percent of Croatia's population.

Competition over national sovereignty became particularly vicious in Bosnia-Herzegovina, a republic in which three groups began their armed fight for an acceptable state design in April 1992. The Party of Democratic Action, representing the plurality Muslim population, advocated an independent and unitary Bosnia-Herzegovina, with no internal territorial division along national lines. The Serb Democratic Party first rejected separation from Yugoslavia and then, after boycotting a referendum in which citizens voted in favor of independence, fought for a separate state in the Serb-populated areas. They did so with the support of the Yugoslav army and in the hope of future reunification with other Serbian-inhabited territories of (former) Yugoslavia. Bosnia's Croatian Democratic Union allied itself with the Muslim party against the Bosnian Serbs but also staged its own secessionist attempt in Herzegovina from 1993 to 1994, supported by Croatia. This conflict was resolved only through strong international pressure, which led to the formation of a Muslim-Croat federation. The war over the fate of Bosnia-Herzegovina lasted from 1992 to 1995, forcibly displaced 2.5 million people, and involved the engagement of the Serbian and Croatian militaries as well as NATO forces.

The Dayton Peace Accords, reached through international mediation in 1995, created a loose confederation that holds the Muslim-Croat federation and the Serb republic in the common state of Bosnia and Herzegovina, dividing the Muslim-Croat federation into separate national cantons and allowing the Bosnian Croats to maintain a close link with the Croatian state. It also imposed rigid ethnic power-sharing arrangements at these levels of governance. The main political parties representing the Serb population have continued to articulate desires for an independent state (see chapter 18).

An externally negotiated arrangement helped to prevent the escalation of ethnic violence in the former Yugoslav Republic of Macedonia. In 1991, as the conflict in Croatia was turning into a war, Macedonian leaders declared independence after a referendum demonstrated overwhelming popular support (96 percent in a voter turnout of 76 percent). A new constitution was adopted in November 1991 to establish parliamentary democracy in an independent Macedonian republic. The leaders of this new state, however, faced significant challenges both internally from a large Albanian minority population and externally from Greece, which opposed naming the state Macedonia, which is also the name of Greece's largest administrative region. The UN admitted the new state in 1993 under the provisional name of "the former Yugoslav Republic of Macedonia." The first democratically elected government of this new state began major institutional transformations and nation building under difficult conditions, against the backdrop of nationalist wars in its neighborhood and continuing objections from Greece to the assertion of an independent "Macedonian" nationhood.

Although internal conflict led to a military conflict with Albanian paramilitaries, this conflict did not escalate into another post-Yugoslav war. International mediation involving European and US actors helped to resolve the conflict quickly through the so-called Ohrid Framework Agreement signed in August 2001. In this framework, the constitution was amended to guarantee Albanian minority members equitable political representation similar to power-sharing arrangements, including the ability to veto legislation in parliament, decentralization and the redrawing of municipal boundaries, and institutional rights to enable minority cultural reproduction and peaceful coexistence in a shared state.

The Ohrid Agreement helped to prevent further violence, but the legitimacy of this externally negotiated framework became a major source of internal political conflict. Majoritarian nationalists in opposition (converging in the Internal Macedonian Revolutionary Organization–Democratic Party for Macedonian National Unity, or VMRO-DPMNE) sought internal electoral support and external allies to undermine the multiethnic political coalition (sustained by the Social Democrats) that was working to implement it. Since 2001, the conflict between the VMRO-DPMNE and the Social Democrats has shaped the politics of this new state. The nationalist coalition won the 2006 parliamentary elections, and VMRO-DPMNE leader Nikola Gruevski began to instrumentalize popular interest in majoritarian Macedonian nation building in a large segment of the population. This government invested a great deal of public resources into the articulation of a nationalist discourse about the greatness of an ethnic Macedonian nation, which according to this discourse is a continuation of the kingdom of Alexander the Great, who also features in the Greek nationalist canon. The Greek veto in 2008 against Macedonia's EU accession generated popular resentment and greatly facilitated the Gruevski government's success in expanding its nationalist electoral base. The government fueled these sentiments through large-scale investments aimed at changing physical spaces to reflect this ancient ethnic Macedonian nationalist account. For instance, it raised an eight-story-tall statue of Alexander the Great on Macedonia Square. Meanwhile, Gruevski's party changed legislation and captured key institutions of the state in a direction that shifted the country's political development from democratic consolidation to gradual autocratization. This shift fueled intra-ethnic political friction within the majority and further complicated relations between the majority Macedonian and Albanian minority populations. A multiethnic coalition government formed by Social Democrats in late 2016 resumed democratic politics and negotiated with Greece a change in the country's name to North Macedonia, unblocking the EU accession process. In the year of the name change (2019), however, the Bulgarian government took over Greece's role in threatening to block the country's EU accession—this time over the question of whether Macedonians can write their own history books or must adopt the Bulgarian narrative, according to which they are a segment of an ethnic Bulgarian nation created in the ninth century.[17]

There is a postscript involving postconflict Serbia: the issue is Kosovo, a region that features prominently in the Serbian national myth. Before 1989, Kosovo was an autonomous part of the Serbian republic of Yugoslavia but had a majority ethnic Albanian population. In 1989, Slobodan Milošević revoked Kosovo's autonomy. As a result, the Albanians in this province were systematically excluded from institutions of political and economic power, and their means of cultural reproduction (such as education in the Albanian language) were virtually eliminated from state-sponsored institutions. When the opportunity for democratization presented itself, Albanian members of the Kosovo Assembly articulated the Kosovar Albanians' right to national self-determination as early as 1990. In September 1991, they organized a referendum in which an overwhelming majority of Kosovars (99.8 percent) voted for independence.

After significant efforts to achieve independence through peaceful civil disobedience and the gradual construction of a "parallel state" (e.g., parallel institutions of education and health care), the National Movement for the Liberation of Kosovo (KLA) became

Photo 3.1. The eight-story-high statue of Alexander the Great on Macedonia Square in Skopje was erected during the Gruevski government and unveiled on September 8, 2011, on the twenty-year anniversary of the country's independence referendum from Yugoslavia. (Ognen Vangelov)

impatient with this strategy and began a series of violent attacks against Serbs (police officers and civilians) in Kosovo. Serbian authorities responded with a massive offensive in July 1998, forcing the KLA to withdraw into the hills. The Serbs then began a ruthless and systematic process of ethnic cleansing, which resulted in approximately seven hundred thousand ethnic Albanian civilians from Kosovo being expelled from their villages and forced to flee to Albania or Macedonia. Despite international intervention, including two months of massive NATO bombings against military and industrial targets also in Serbia, the Serbian government refused to agree to an independent Kosovo. When Serb forces finally agreed in a June 1999 peace agreement to withdraw from Kosovo, the agreement guaranteed the continued territorial integrity of Yugoslavia (Serbia-Montenegro), including the province of Kosovo, which has been under UN administration since 1999. However, following the collapse of internationally facilitated negotiations between Serbian and Kosovar leaders over the final status of Kosovo and the publication of a UN report calling for the independence of the former Serbian province[18] (albeit under international supervision), the Kosovo Assembly adopted a unilateral proclamation of independence on February 17, 2008. Swiftly recognized· by the United States and several EU member states, Kosovo's independence remains challenged by Serbia. Tensions over the border have decreased following an EU-brokered deal in April 2013 that recognized Serb majority areas of Kosovo as autonomous at the municipal level. Yet Kosovo suffers from weak state capacity and remains under considerable international supervision.[19]

Broader Influence of External Actors

The influence of international actors was not limited to peacekeeping in the former Yugoslavia. The EU accession process was very important in moderating the demands of both majority nationalists and minority groups. It incentivized peaceful contestation over violence and set norms for minority protection that governments at least had to pretend to respect if they wanted to become EU members. The "Copenhagen criteria" for EU accession, adopted by the European Council in 1993, included a requirement that states guarantee "respect for and protection of minorities."[20] During the first round of the EU's "Eastern Enlargement," which lasted until the accession of ten CEE countries to the EU from 2004 to 2007, European organizations had an unprecedented degree of influence on political decision making in candidate states. The term "EU conditionality" is widely used for the bundle of tools European actors employed to ensure that the institutions, policies, and practices in aspiring member states became compatible with EU norms. EU actors worked together with other European institutions to achieve this goal. In the domain of minority protection, the EU's main partner institutions were the Council of Europe (CoE) and the High Commissioner on National Minorities (HCNM), an organ of the Organization for Security and Co-operation in Europe (OSCE). The HCNM, mandated to work for interethnic peace and security by identifying ethnic conflict and actively seeking to resolve tensions that might endanger peace, became the most visible European actor engaged in persuading governments to adopt, ratify, and implement European norms of minority protection. These norms were set forth in a number of documents that were adopted by European institutions in the 1990s, reflecting how the transformations taking place in CEE, and the needs for interethnic peace in that region, impacted the development of European minority rights law.

The 1990s have often been described as "the decade of minority protection" in Europe due to the high degree of consensus on Europe-wide norms, reflected in an unusually high level of activism in drafting and adopting European documents. Among these, the 1992 European Charter of Regional and Minority Languages (ECRML) and the 1995 Framework Convention for National Minorities (FCNM) are considered the most significant, and the FCNM became an informally accepted precondition for EU accession. OSCE recommendations also became important building blocks of an emerging European minority rights regime, including the 2008 Bolzano/Bozen Recommendations on National Minorities in Inter-State Relations, which focus on peaceful cross-border relations between kin-states and external kin populations.[21] The *Europeanization* process, which means both the enlargement of the EU and the diffusion of European norms and practices, also expanded opportunities for minority actors to find new arenas and build alliances externally, in both kin-states and in the European Parliament, for minority activism. Transnational activism, however, also complicated minority actors' ability to forge domestic alliances with majority actors in their home states, where nationalist parties routinely framed minority activism as a threat to state stability.[22]

Varieties of Nationalism

Thus, ethnic nationalism was a significant aspect of political development across the region during the period of postcommunist transformations from the 1990s to the first wave of EU accessions in 2004–2007. It coincided with a strong desire to join western transnational institutions, both the security community (NATO) and the European Union. The ability of governments to lead states into these institutions became a source of popular support and governmental legitimacy. At the same time, nationalism remained an effective political strategy across the continent as differently situated political actors pursued competing national interests. The typology in table 3.2 provides four categories for analyzing and comparing these nationalist strategies: traditional, substate, trans-sovereign, and protectionist.

Traditional nationalism aims to achieve and maintain a territorially sovereign and culturally homogeneous nation-state. In other words, this is mainstream majoritarian nationalism, which seeks coherence between political and cultural boundaries in an independent state. *Substate nationalism* is the political strategy of groups that define their nationhood as culturally different from the state's mainstream culture but do not claim an independent state (through secession). Instead, they claim some form of institutionalized self-government, typically either territorial or cultural autonomy, that enables them to maintain and reproduce that culture. Throughout Europe, these groups organize on behalf of "homeland communities" that have a lengthy history (and associated historiography, geography, literature, art, etc.) linking them to the territory in the state within which they reside. *Trans-sovereign nationalism* is a type of nationalism that does not pursue a traditional nation-state through border changes or the repatriation of ethnic kin but instead aims to sustain common cultural "nationhood" across existing state borders.[23] "Divided nationhood" is a term used in the literature for describing

Table 3.2.   Typology of Nationalist Political Strategies That Coexist in the European Union

Type of nationalism	Main objective	View EU as alliance of
Traditional	Ensure congruence of political and cultural boundaries	States
Substate	Strengthen political representation for homeland vis-à-vis state	Nations
Trans-sovereign	Create institutions to link nation across state boundaries	Nations
Protectionist	Protect national culture in face of immigration/ social change	States

Source: Zsuzsa Csergő and James M. Goldgeier, "Nationalist Strategies and European Integration," *Perspectives on Politics* 2, no. 1 (2004): 23.

situations where populations with a shared sense of national belonging, together with associated collective memories and cultural repertoires, have been territorially separated by shifting borders.[24] Such situations exist in many parts of the world, including Latino communities that straddle the border between Mexico and the United States; indigenous peoples living in territories divided across states in North and South America; Kurds living in neighboring territories divided across Iraq, Syria, and Turkey; and Russians living in former Soviet states. Most ethnic and national minorities in CEE live in such situations. *Protectionist nationalism* focuses on preserving a purportedly established national culture and protecting it from newcomers who might introduce unwelcome changes. This type of nationalism involves strategies that keep ethnic "others" from entering the "national" space and usually favors immigration policies that differentiate between co-ethnic and other categories of potential entrants. Protectionist nationalism has been more prevalent in immigrant recipient countries but has also emerged as a significant element of nationalist political discourse in CEE in the context of the so-called European refugee crisis of the 2010s.

In practice, these options coexist in most states in various combinations at various times, and they can be at times competing and at other times complementary to each other. For instance, a state center can engage in traditional (majoritarian) nationalism in relation to internal minorities (adopting policies and funding institutions that ensure the dominance of the majority culture), practice trans-sovereign nationalism in relation to an external "kin" minority (engaging in activities that support "kin" minority cultures outside the state), and also practice protectionist nationalism in relation to refugees or migrants who attempt to enter the state (adopting harsh anti-migration discourse and policies). A national minority political organization can engage in substate nationalism in relation to the home state center (asking for policies and institutions that ensure the continuity of minority culture), and the same organization can also engage in trans-sovereign nationalism in relation to a kin-state, while simultaneously also joining mainstream (majority) actors in protectionist nationalism in relation to refugees or migrants. Political developments in CEE since 1990 have revealed that all these types of nationalism can coexist with an interest in belonging to a transnational framework founded on the principles of democracy and multiculturalism such as the European Union. The next section discusses two types of nationalism that became predominant in CEE during the first period of the post-1990 transformations, highlighting how the politics of ethnic demography complicated democratization goals and contributed to diverse paths and outcomes.

Majoritarian Nationalism and Its Internal Challenges

The collapse of the multinational federations might have been expected to bring about greater congruence in the region between state and ethnic borders, but it did not work out that way. Of the ten new CEE states that emerged from these federations—the Czech Republic and Slovakia (from Czechoslovakia); Estonia, Latvia, and Lithuania (from the Soviet Union); and Bosnia-Herzegovina, Croatia, the Republic of North Macedonia, Slovenia, and the newly reconstituted Federal Republic of Yugoslavia consisting of Serbia and Montenegro (from Yugoslavia)—all but the Czech Republic resembled Bulgaria and Romania as states where there is a mismatch between territorial and ethnic borders. Majoritarian nationalism had to contend with national minorities that sought some form of group rights and participation in the new democratic governments.

This situation created its own challenges for democracy even as most of these countries were democratizing in preparation for possible entry into the European Union. First, at least during the first decade or so of postcommunism, majoritarian nationalists in state centers sought to exclude minorities (as well as their potential allies in the majority opposition) from political power. Minority representatives were not invited to join governing coalitions that decided on the fundamentals of state reconstruction and regime change, nor were they consulted in a meaningful way about legislation that affected minority populations. Minority inclusion in governmental decision making became institutionalized only in the three post-Yugoslav states where external actors directly intervened in state design to end or prevent major interethnic violence (in Bosnia-Herzegovina, North Macedonia, and Kosovo).

Second, although all potential entrants to the European Union recognized the individual rights of minority group members to speak their languages and engage in their cultural practices, there was an intense (though peaceful) struggle over what, if any, *group* rights minorities should have. The difference between individual rights and group rights is subtle but crucial. No minority individual in postcommunist CEE was prevented by the government from speaking their mother tongue, eating their native cuisine, or engaging in their cultural practices. Instead the fight was over what official status, if any, minority culture should have. The main issue was the primary cultural marker, language. Do minorities have a right to be educated in their own language? Do minorities have a right to interact with government—the post office, the courts, local officials—in their own languages, or must they use the majority language? Should markings in public spaces be only in the majority language or in both majority and minority languages? There were fights over everything that had to do with asserting majoritarian dominance in areas of sovereignty and cultural reproduction.[25]

Third, what in most countries would be considered purely domestic matters, such as administrative territorial reorganizations, sometimes escalated into international political issues due to increased international attention to interethnic conflict in post–Cold War Europe. Minority parties and advocacy groups, too small to effect change on their own and unable to find support among majority parties for institutional accommodation or policy change, used the opportunities provided by democratization and regional realignment toward NATO and the EU. They appealed to external actors in kin-states, European institutions, the United States, or the UN to influence domestic legislation. Transnational lobbying helped to prevent the escalation of conflict and resulted in more accommodative minority policies in several instances, even in the case of Russian minorities in Estonia and Latvia that were largely disenfranchised and seen as "fifth columns" of a kin-state unbound by Western transnational institutions.

The struggle between majorities and minorities was perhaps sharpest in the Baltic states. After 1991, there was a strong sense among Baltic populations that democratization should bring national justice. Baltic governments thus adopted harsh policies to establish national dominance over the institutions of the new states. To start, each of the three Baltic governments adopted citizenship and language policies that established the dominance of the titular language in the state. The politics of ethnic demography became apparent in these policies, as new governments made efforts to incentivize Russians to leave and to prevent those who remained from participating in the design of new political systems. These strategies were most aggressive in Latvia, where the ratio of the Russophone population compared to the native population was the highest, and most moderate in Lithuania, where the ratio of the Russian minority was the lowest. In Lithuania, with some exceptions, residents who had lived in the republic before 1991 could obtain citizenship simply by applying. In Estonia and Latvia, only citizens of the interwar Estonian and Latvian states before Soviet annexation in 1940 and their descendants had an automatic right to citizenship. Citizenship laws required other residents to pass a language proficiency test in order to become citizens of the reestablished states, even though during the Soviet era hardly any Russian school taught Estonian or Latvian. As a result, roughly a third of the population of Estonia and Latvia was excluded from citizenship.[26] Citizenship laws also disadvantaged ethnic Russians in public sector employment and the distribution of resources. The 1991 Latvian privatization law, for instance, excluded noncitizens. In Estonia, property restitution similarly discriminated against Russians.[27]

Despite these exclusionary minority policies, majoritarian nation building in the post-Soviet Baltic states did not trigger the kinds of conflict that devastated large parts of the former Yugoslavia during the same period. The peaceful resolution of the so-called alien crisis in Estonia illustrates the contrast. Russian activists, in response to the Aliens Act adopted in 1993, which reinforced fears of expulsion among Estonia's Russophone population, claimed territorial autonomy in the northeastern region of Estonia, where Russian-speakers (Russophones) compose local majorities. Although the Russian government advocated for the rights of Russophones in former Soviet states and escalated the conflict rhetorically, the Yeltsin government was more interested in regional peace than in the reassertion of Russian geopolitical power. Substantial European involvement (by the OSCE's HCNM), combined with NATO and US involvement, helped to deescalate the crisis. Most Russophones remained excluded from citizenship for a long time, but the Estonian government agreed to moderate naturalization requirements and accelerate the implementation of naturalization laws. Estonia also enabled permanent residents to vote (if not run for office) in local elections, which provided Russian minority members a higher degree of participation rights than those enjoyed by their counterparts in Latvia.

At the same time, "returning to Europe" and obtaining protection from future Russian reannexation by joining the EU were inextricable parts of the pursuit of national sovereignty in this region.[28] Employing the powerful leverage that these motivations provided, European institutions—especially the OSCE's HCNM, the CoE, and the EU—applied strong pressure on the Baltic governments to adopt more inclusive citizenship laws and more pluralistic educational and language policies that complied with "European norms."[29] After 1998, the Estonian and Latvian governments began adopting amendments to their citizenship laws that made the naturalization of "nonhistoric" minorities easier. International pressure was less successful in influencing them to liberalize their language policies. Language legislation in both states continued to reflect a nationalist state-building strategy, although in most cases restrictions were moderately implemented.[30] In Latvia, a new bilingual curriculum introduced in 2002 and 2003 required that minority-language schools teach certain subjects exclusively in Latvian.

In Estonia, a 2007 education reform introduced similar requirements. In both states, policies that mandate the exclusive use of the majority language in subjects considered significant for the reproduction of national cultures, such as history and music, reinforced fears among Russophones that majorities intend to erase Russian culture from these states.[31]

Compared to other minorities of similar "size," the challenge that Russophones presented to these reconstituted states after the collapse of the Soviet Union was relatively weak. Rather than demanding self-government (like Serbs in Croatia), let alone secession and unification with Russia (like Transnistrians in Moldova), Russophone political actors in the Baltics simply contested the exclusionary aspects of citizenship and language laws and occasionally lobbied external actors to pressure these governments to adopt more minority-friendly policies. The weakness of shared Russian "ethnic" identification and the absence of experience with minority politics both played a role. Regardless of when they settled in their current homelands, most Russians were new minorities that had yet to learn how to be a minority, that is, how to articulate and negotiate minority claims under the post-Soviet states in which they found themselves after the breakup. Moreover, speaking the Russian language did not signify ethnic or national identity in these states in the same way that language was the primary marker of Latvian, Estonian, or Lithuanian identity. The Russophone population included people of different ethnicities who had switched to Russian as the language of advancement to higher status. Consequently, no commonly shared national myth existed among Russophones in the Baltic states that could have become the grounds for national sovereignty claims.[32] State-minority relations remained peaceful, and Russophone minority actors continued to pursue claims for minority integration through electoral politics, relying particularly on their strength in the local governments of major cities.[33] The situation of these Russophone minorities differed significantly from that of Russians living as a large regionally concentrated population in eastern Ukraine—a large post-Soviet state with a unique set of historical and contemporary links to Russia and the European Union (see chapter 19).

The Polish minority in Lithuania was a continuing minority, a "homeland community" with historic ties to the Vilnius region, which had been in the core of the Polish-Lithuanian Commonwealth and became a contested territory repeatedly in the context of various redrawings of borders in this region. A large ratio of Poles (including most of the educated class) migrated from Vilnius to Poland after World War II, and Vilnius became populated mostly by ethnic Lithuanians and Russophones. The majority of Poles today live in rural areas around Vilnius. During the Soviet period, they were exposed to decades of Russification in local schools. Despite their relative socioeconomic weakness, however, their strength as an ethnic community (with an institutional legacy in their current homeland and a Polish ethnonational narrative) protected them from the possibility of disenfranchisement and facilitated Polish collective action at the time of the Lithuanian "re"-independence movement. Polish minority actors were the first to create a political party in post-Soviet Lithuania, and they articulated a stronger challenge to the Lithuanian nation-state project than Russophones, including a claim for territorial self-government in the region where a high ratio of Lithuania's Poles remain territorially concentrated. These claims were "tamed" with external facilitation, including consensual politicians in the Polish kin-state center, who helped compel Lithuania's majoritarian nation builders to adopt more minority-friendly policies than their Estonian and Latvian counterparts, at least in the first part of the 1990s.

In Slovakia, the key question was how a Slovak "nation-state" could materialize on a territory that incorporated a relatively large, geographically concentrated, and politically well-organized historic Hungarian community. During the first period of independence, from 1992 to 1998, the Slovak political parties in power, under the leadership of Prime Minister Vladimír Mečiar, opted for traditional nationalist policies.[34] In an attempt to suppress minority claims for substate institutional autonomy, these policies were aimed at establishing Slovak majority control over all institutions of government and cultural reproduction. Restrictive language legislation adopted in 1995 was designed to strengthen the status of the Slovak literary standard against dialects and to exclude minority languages from the spheres considered most important for the reproduction of national cultures: local government, territorial markings, the media, and the educational system. Hungarian minority parties forcefully challenged these policies and pressed for a pluralist Slovak state. Employing the methods of party competition and parliamentary debate, Hungarian minority political elites asked that Slovakia's historic Hungarian minority be recognized as a state-constituting entity. To guarantee the reproduction of Hungarian minority culture in Slovakia, they demanded substate forms of autonomy, at various times emphasizing either the cultural, educational, or territorial aspects of self-government. Despite internal debates among Hungarian parties about the best institutional forms, they agreed on the importance of language rights and claimed the right to use the Hungarian language in the southern region of Slovakia in all public spheres and the educational system.

Majority-minority debates over these questions marked the first decade of democratization in Slovakia. The Mečiar government's policies of increasing centralized control over society also created sharp divisions within the Slovak majority. Based on their agreement about the necessity of moving Slovakia away from a recentralizing authoritarian regime, the Slovak and Hungarian parties in opposition eventually formed a strategic electoral alliance that defeated the Mečiar government in the 1998 parliamentary elections. Although vehement debates about minority self-government and language equality continued, the prospect of European integration provided incentives for peaceful negotiation. While preserving the predominance of the majority language throughout the country, policies gradually expanded minority-language rights in ways that satisfied the main aspirations that minority parties articulated from the beginning of the 1990s. The controversies over restrictive amendments to the Slovak language law adopted in 2009, however, revealed the limits of EU influence in the post–EU accession period, when membership conditionality can no longer constrain majority policy. Since then, electoral and party politics remain the primary form of minority mobilization. Deepening intra-minority fragmentation in the 2010s resulted in loss of representation for Hungarians in the 2020 Slovak parliament, creating new challenges for this large minority population.

Similar contestations in Romania provide a useful comparative perspective on how ethnic majoritarian nation building featured in the postcommunist transformation of a state that continued within its pre-1989 borders. Romania's new constitution adopted an ethnic concept of Romanian nationhood, and Romanian became the only official language. Laws on public administration and education were in some ways more restrictive of minority-language rights than their precedents during the Ceauşescu dictatorship. These restrictions mobilized the Hungarian minority electorate to lend overwhelming support for the minority political organization that emerged in December 1989 to represent Romania's 1.6 million Hungarian population. Much in keeping with developments in Slovakia, the prospects of NATO and EU membership contributed to majority willingness to accommodate claims. But accommodation occurred only gradually, as an outcome of strategic negotiations between moderate majority parties and the Hungarian umbrella party in the state center.[35] Although Romania was considered a "laggard" in democratic consolidation and EU accession (admitted together with Bulgaria in 2007), post-accession Romanian governments remained more supportive of minority-friendly policies than their Slovak counterparts. In both states, the question of whether minority parties can hold their electorates together and navigate in volatile political environments remains open.[36]

The Trans-Sovereign Nationalism of Kin-States

In addition to majoritarian nationalism, trans-sovereign nationalism also gained significance in the region during this period, revealing the continuing impact of the legacies of shifting borders and ethnic hierarchies described earlier. Since the beginning of postcommunist restructuring, a growing interest emerged in kin-states to develop cross-border relations with external kin populations. The constitutions of several states, including Albania, Croatia, Hungary, and North Macedonia, contain commitments to care for the well-being of kin living abroad. Many governments, such as in Bulgaria, Croatia, Hungary, Poland, Romania, Russia, Serbia, Slovenia, and Slovakia, adopted legislation to provide benefits to ethnic kin living abroad. Although the constitutional clauses and benefit laws adopted in kin-states differ in their specific content (ranging from cultural and economic benefits to nonresidential citizenship), their common characteristic is that they support the preservation of a shared national identity and foster a relationship between a kin-state and those outside its borders who define themselves in some sense as co-nationals.[37]

The Hungarian state's nation-building strategy after 1990 is a robust example of trans-sovereign nationalism in the region. Close to three million ethnic Hungarians live in Hungary's neighboring states. In an integrated Europe, they compose one of the largest historically settled minority groups. Meanwhile, the population of Hungary has declined steadily since the 1980s, from over 10.7 million people to just under 10 million as of 2011. After 1990, the democratically elected leaders of Hungary were keen on strengthening ties with Hungarians living in neighboring states, but they were aware that territorial revisionism was an unacceptable proposition if they wanted to join an integrated Europe. Instead of pressing for border changes, they created a network of institutions that link Hungarians living in neighboring countries to Hungary while encouraging them to remain "in their homeland" and, in effect, withstand assimilation where they reside. To complement these cross-border institutions, the Hungarian government expressed support both for EU membership for Hungary and its neighbors and for Hungarian minority demands for local and institutional autonomy in their home states. According to the logic of these policies, if Hungary and all its neighbors became EU members and the EU provided a supranational, decentralized structure for strong regional institutions, then Hungarians could live as though no political borders separated them.

Although the "virtualization of borders" appeared attractive to many Hungarians, the idea found little appeal among majority political parties in neighboring countries. Seven states neighboring Hungary include ethnic Hungarian populations, and five of these states were newly established after the collapse of communist federations. As discussed earlier in this chapter, the majority national elites in both newly created and consolidating national states were deeply reluctant to weaken their sovereignty and accommodate multiple nation-building processes in their territories. Thus, Hungarian efforts to unilaterally "virtualize" borders triggered tensions between Hungary and its neighbors, particularly those engaged in establishing newly gained independence. The adoption in June 2001 of the Law Concerning Hungarians Living in Neighboring Countries (commonly known as the Hungarian Status Law)—which defined all ethnic Hungarians as part of the same cultural nation and on this basis offered a number of educational, cultural, and even economic benefits to those living in neighboring states—triggered significant attention from policy makers in the region, European institution officials, and scholars of nationalism.[38] The governments of Romania and Slovakia, the two states with the largest Hungarian populations, expressed concern that the legislation weakened their exclusive sovereignty over ethnic Hungarian citizens and discriminated against majority nationals in neighboring countries. Although these neighboring governments themselves had adopted similar policies toward their own ethnic kin abroad, controversy over the Hungarian Status Law brought Hungary's relations with these neighbors to a dangerous low point. The fact that all these governments were keenly interested in EU membership eventually helped them compromise. Hungary signed a bilateral agreement with Romania and altered the language of the law in response to European pressure in 2003. Yet the controversy over the Hungarian Status Law foreshadowed the challenges of reconciling European integration with the continuing power of divergent and competing national aspirations. By the end of the 2000s, trans-sovereign nationalism became "normalized" as part of the set of nationalist strategies described earlier, employed in varying combinations by state centers and substate political actors.

Although less coherent than the Hungarian kin-state's policies, the Polish government has also solidified its engagement with external ethnic kin populations after EU accession. The "Karta Polaka" or "Pole's Card" was introduced in 2007. Individuals who can demonstrate their Polish origin and can speak Polish are eligible to receive one. The cardholder receives prerogatives not available to ordinary visitors to Poland, such as a reduced waiting period to apply for permanent residency, exemption from having to apply for a work permit, reduced fares on public transportation, and free admission to state museums. The Polish Senate has institutionalized government support for Polish minority institutions abroad through the Ministry of Foreign Affairs. This funding plays a major role in sustaining Polish minority institutions (e.g., schools, cultural and social organizations).

Democracy and Its Discontents

The entry of most CEE states into the EU beginning in 2004 was a watershed for the region. It rewarded a decade and a half or more of often painful efforts to transform the formerly communist states into free market liberal democracies that respect individual freedoms and human rights, a precondition for EU entry. It recognized the region's rightful place in "Europe" after nearly half a century of separation behind the Iron Curtain. CEE populations were overwhelmingly in favor of joining the EU and taking advantage of opportunities for travel and work. For the first time ever, Europe was free and undivided.

At the same time, however, EU membership loosened constraints on the behavior of parties, elites, and governments in the region. In the relationship between nationalism and democracy, EU membership brought some unforeseen changes. If liberal democracy had to gain primacy during the pre-EU accession period, then once EU membership was achieved by a large number of CEE states in the wave of the EU's Eastern Enlargement project (2004–2007), the commitment to liberal democracy weakened and nationalism evolved and strengthened. Democratic commitments weakened due to a confluence of factors. First, those commitments were probably never as deep as they were made to appear during the period of EU conditionality. Although all CEE states made the requisite reforms to create liberal democratic market economies, normative commitments to the resulting institutions remained weaker. Unlike in more established democracies, *liberal* democracy was not viewed as the only possible game in town. Second, after accession, Brussels moved on to other problems, such as corruption, and lost interest in overseeing further political developments in the domain of minority protection beyond funding to help the Roma population. Third, even if Brussels had maintained its oversight, the penalties to CEE for deviating from liberal democracy were considerably fewer post-accession than pre-accession. The West European political elites who created and initially sustained the EU were so convinced of the superiority of liberal democracy that they neglected to incorporate a formal procedure for ejecting countries that no longer met EU standards. The penalties for deviation are not trivial; they include freezing a member state's voting privileges and withholding funds to assist economic development. But even these require unanimous approval from all the other member states and fall well short of the loss of membership. In practice the weakness of EU institutions in enforcing the democratic norms they advocated during the pre-accession period became visible, signaling to political actors in the rest of the region that less democracy and more nationalism were in fact acceptable, so long as states maintained peace in the region.

Two international crises gave nationalists (and other opponents of liberal democracy) throughout the region further ammunition with which to advance their agendas. The first was the global financial crisis of 2008–2009. The most obvious effect of this was that it put a halt to several years of sustained economic growth and caused great hardship throughout the region. Mass conflation of democracy with prosperity meant that nationalists and other critics of the economic and political reforms could effectively attack incumbent politicians and claim that they had been right all along about the dangers of adopting Western-style systems. In countries with mature capitalist systems, people generally accept the reality of periodic economic contractions and the difficulties that go with them. There is little mass demand for a radical overhaul of the system. That is not the case in CEE. When market capitalism was introduced after 1989, mass publics in the region imagined that once the tribulations of the transition were over, their countries would eventually become as rich and democratic as Germany or Sweden. Like true believers who are mugged by reality, the financial crisis disabused people of this illusion. This made populations more open to radical solutions.

The second crisis was the mass influx of refugees fleeing conflict and hardship in the Middle East and beyond in 2015. The overwhelming majority of refugees sought asylum in Germany, Sweden, and elsewhere in Western Europe. Many CEE (and also West European) political elites nonetheless were able to instrumentalize the crisis. They encouraged popular anti-migrant sentiment with inflammatory rhetoric and attempted to position themselves as defenders of "Christian national traditions" against foreign Muslim "invaders." They could do this for three reasons. First, although the migrants did not intend to stay in CEE, many traversed through it to reach their destinations. The sight of thousands of migrants crossing borders made the perceived threat concrete rather than merely theoretical. Second, the EU wanted its member states to share the burden of settling the migrants, so quotas were instituted. The obligations of CEE were relatively small (in the low thousands of migrants), but elite opposition was able to portray this as a Brussels diktat that went against the will of the people. Third, these countries had very limited experience with immigration. Migration had been a normal feature of life in the region for centuries before communism, resulting in a multiethnic demography that became forcibly altered by the violence of the Holocaust and forced population movements during and after World War II. During the communist period, these countries were sources of out-migration, a trend that accelerated after the collapse of communism (see chapter 6). Lack of experience with immigrant integration remains a significant legacy of communism in CEE, and it makes these societies highly vulnerable to protectionist nationalism.

Protectionist nationalism, espoused on both the left and right sides of the political spectrum, differs in important ways from the ethnic nationalism we have thus far discussed. First and foremost, it redefines the "enemy" from being the local politicized national minority group (e.g., ethnic Hungarians in Slovakia or ethnic Poles in Lithuania) to non-Europeans of a different religion, as well as their liberal allies at home, in the EU, and elsewhere. Second, the "threat" is no longer the challenge to majority cultural dominance from minority autonomy but instead the attack on "Christian-national traditions" posed by Muslims. The migrant crisis is a prime example of how politics can make strange bedfellows. On one side of the debate stood nationalists from across CEE, who are normally at loggerheads with each other, and a minority of other politicians who thought opposition to migrants was a winning political strategy. On the other side stood their largely liberal and left-wing opponents, Brussels, and other proponents of liberal policies, such as the Hungarian-American Jewish philanthropist George Soros.

In sum, political elites in CEE exploited the confluence of forces buffeting liberal democracy in the region—the loss of EU interest in and ability to significantly sanction undemocratic government behavior post-accession, a financial crisis that shook popular confidence in the market system and liberal democracy itself, and a migrant crisis that brought (or at least threatened to bring) thousands of foreigners into these countries. The result has been increased nationalism and democratic backsliding, though in varying degrees across the region.

The front-runners in this process have been Hungary and to a lesser extent Poland. Although in these countries there are no significant internal national minorities to target,

Photo 3.2. Protestors against refugees and immigrants in Warsaw, Poland, organized by the National Radical Camp and Korwin party in April 2016. (Wiola Wiaderek, Shutterstock)

leaders in both countries have nonetheless invoked a "threat to nation" discourse, where the "threat" is "liberalism" and its supporters, broadly understood, rather than neighboring ethnic groups. Both the Fidesz party since 2010 in Hungary and the PiS party since 2015 in Poland have sought to overturn the hegemony of the postcommunist liberal state, which in their view has weakened national identity and thwarted the popular will. The details of their attacks on the liberal democratic state, which have put them both at odds not just with the EU and other international institutions but also with their own liberal and leftist oppositions, can be found in the Poland and Hungary country chapters (chapters 11 and 13, respectively). Here we focus on the nationalist component.

There are three aspects to the nationalist attack on the liberal state. One is liberalism's perceived disdain for conservative values and national traditions. Postcommunist liberal freedoms brought not just the right to speak one's mind and travel but also sexual minority rights, wide access to abortion, and multiculturalism. These are anathema to those who seek to preserve ethnic nationhood and traditional values. For example, Fidesz and PiS are both opposed to same-sex marriage, child adoption by same-sex couples, and sexual minority rights generally. Politicians from both parties have attacked such minorities in order to win conservative votes. In Poland, where the Roman Catholic Church is a conservative bulwark, PiS and others have demonized sexual minorities as "pedophiles," "sodomites," and a "threat to the nation."[39] In Hungary, Fidesz changed the constitution to outlaw same-sex marriage and establish the family as the basis of the nation. It forbade the ability of transgender people to change the sex listed on their birth certificates. Prominent Fidesz politicians and their allies have expressed opposition to pride parades and various other LGBTQIA movements, have likened adoption by same-sex couples to pedophilia, and in one case openly admitted to being homophobic.[40]

The second is liberalism's fondness for free markets, which immiserate many and ignore national borders. In the quarter century separating the collapse of communism and entry into the EU, the primacy of neoliberal economics across the political spectrum meant that macroeconomic stability came at the expense of social welfare. Governments privatized state-owned businesses, often to foreign interests, or in the case of Hungary, to parties close to Prime Minister Viktor Orbán. This cronyism and concomitant corruption have led some to refer to Hungary as a "mafia state."[41] These businesses then cut their costs by throwing people out of work, thus increasing unemployment. Governments cut public services such as mass transportation and health care to balance budgets. Meanwhile, inflation has eroded the standard of living for pensioners and those in low-skilled jobs. Both Fidesz and PiS responded by intervening in the market. Fidesz has sought to regain state control over the economy by, among other things, instituting discriminatory taxes on foreign-owned businesses and restricting foreign investment in so-called strategic sectors, such as energy, finance, transportation, and agriculture. Fidesz has been zealous in regulating businesses, such as taxi service and the sale of tobacco, for the "national interest," and it favors "nation-friendly" policies such as financial incentives to boost Hungary's low birthrate. In Poland, PiS has sought to remedy the ills of the market system with generous welfare benefits. Poland lacks the economic cronyism of Hungary but is no less concerned with fostering national solidarity. Policies include generous cash subsidies for families that have children and annual bonuses for pensioners, along with a promise to increase the minimum wage.

Finally, nationalists attack the liberal state by removing, or at least attempting to remove, impediments to the ability of the ruling party to implement public policy. One of the distinguishing features of the liberal state introduced after 1989 was the separation of powers. Rather than investing all political power in one institution (as had been the case under communism), reformers spread power over several institutions, such as an elected legislature, an executive branch, and especially an independent and impartial judiciary with the power to declare government actions unconstitutional. The idea, of course, was to put limits on the power of a transitory parliamentary majority or executive to implement illiberal and antidemocratic measures. All would be held accountable by a free press. These rules worked fine for Fidesz and PiS when they were out of power. For example, while the Hungarian Socialist Party was still in power, the current Hungarian prime minister, Viktor Orbán, famously referred to the constitution as a "shield" to protect the people. But once in power, Fidesz and PiS saw both the judiciary and the press as obstacles to achieving their illiberal policy preferences.

After its landslide victory in the 2010 national parliamentary elections, Fidesz was gifted with a supermajority in parliament, giving it the power to change even the constitution without opposition consent. The party used this power with vigor. It successfully packed the Constitutional Court with partisans and ultimately wrote and ratified a new constitution. It muzzled the opposition through administrative chicanery. It denied opposition platforms advertising and broadcasting licenses. It instituted fines for publishing "biased" news, where a Fidesz-controlled commission was charged with determining such bias. Ultimately, Fidesz-friendly outlets dominated TV, radio, and newspaper sources. In Poland, the PiS government after 2015 enjoyed an absolute majority in the parliament and sought to copy the Fidesz example by creating a "Budapest on the Vistula." However, PiS's parliamentary majority, while sufficient to pass ordinary laws, was insufficient to legally rewrite the rules of the game, as Fidesz had in Hungary. Consequently, opposition to PiS's illegal efforts to intimidate and neuter the judiciary has been more successful than in Hungary. Whereas in Hungary Fidesz's changes will endure even should it lose a future election, in Poland, PiS's changes can still be undone if a different party comes to power.

With the judiciary and press effectively out of the way, Fidesz set about implementing its nationalist vision, branding itself as a "savior of the nation" and trailblazer of "illiberal democracy" in Europe. The popular appeal of exclusivist ethnic nationalism was already apparent in the strong showing of the vehemently xenophobic Movement for a Better Hungary (Jobbik) in the 2009 European Parliament elections, as well as in this party's increasing success among the Hungarian electorate (obtaining parliamentary seats for the first time in the 2010 elections and gaining 20 percent of the votes in 2014). A series of acts adopted by the Orbán government after 2010 codified this ethnic understanding of the nation. An amendment to the citizenship law made it easier for ethnic Hungarians living abroad to become Hungarian citizens and gain nonresident voting rights. The new Hungarian constitution adopted in 2011 included provisions that made members of Hungary's large Roma minority more vulnerable to discrimination. After 2015, the government successfully instrumentalized the Syrian refugee crisis to brand itself as the defender of the nation and of European Christianity. In the same spirit, a set of laws adopted in 2017 undermined those nongovernmental organizations

Photo 3.3. Thousands protested in Budapest on April 12, 2017, against legislation targeting civil society organizations and the Central European University. Demonstrators on Heroes' Square formed a heart around the word "civil," signaling the centrality of nongovernmental actors in protecting democracy. (Drone Media Studio, Shutterstock)

and institutions that represent and encourage critical attitudes about ethnic exclusivism and populist nationalism (e.g., the Central European University of Budapest and human rights nongovernmental organizations).[42]

Notwithstanding the close relationship between nationalism and democratic backsliding in Hungary and Poland, nationalism is neither a necessary nor sufficient cause of such backsliding. In Slovakia and the Baltic states, for example, restrictive minority policies continued (actually worsening in the case of Slovakia[43]) after EU accession, but no nationalist party has achieved the electoral success of Fidesz in Hungary or PiS in Poland, and there has been less of a challenge to the liberal democratic state. In the Czech Republic, on the other hand, there has been a notable centralization of power under President Andrej Babiš, but without an accompanying discourse on Czech nationalism.[44]

We conclude our discussion with Estonia and Latvia, where ethnic Russians constitute substantial minorities and the post–EU accession period has been a double-edged sword. On the one hand, once NATO and EU membership had been achieved, these countries, like others in CEE, were freer to turn to less minority-friendly strategies. On the other hand, neighboring Russia's hands-off strategy in the years leading up to the Baltic states' NATO and EU memberships began to give way to a more aggressive posture in defense of ethnic Russian minorities. The 2014 invasion of Ukraine drove home President Vladimir Putin's willingness to intervene outside Russia's borders. He seized Crimea, which was majority ethnic Russian, and ultimately presided over a rigged election that resulted in Russia annexing the territory. Estonia and Latvia (and Lithuania, which has far fewer ethnic Russians) feared that they, too, were vulnerable. Russian ethnic minorities were not just a matter of domestic politics but acquired a security dimension. The Baltic response has been to pursue nation-building policies under increased NATO protection. Since the Crimea annexation, NATO has deployed soldiers, weapons, and other equipment in the Baltic states to deter any potential Russian aggression. All three states have continued to restrict Russian-language rights and have instituted policies to limit and control the ability of Russophone minorities to gain effective political representation and maintain their culture. Yet differences in the policies adopted toward Russophones since the 2014 Crimea crisis reflect higher degrees of "securitization" in Latvia and greater willingness to accommodate in Estonia, indicating that political actors in state centers have significant power to choose between minority exclusion and accommodation (see chapter 9).[45]

Continuing Tensions between Nationalism and Democratic Governance

Tensions between ethnic nationalism and democracy continue to shape politics in CEE in important ways. Ethnic conceptions of political nationhood remain dominant despite a mismatch between ethnic and political boundaries, creating a continuing source of conflict over the criteria for who belongs in a state and under what terms. Members of majority ethnic populations whose understandings align with dominant nationalist ideologies have a different perspective on the democratic performance of their states than members of permanent minority populations. The continuing divisiveness of ethnopolitics reveals how deeply the legacies of the region's modern history influence the strength and sustainability of democracy today.

The contemporary political map of this region was created through postwar rearrangements involving shifts in state borders and ethnic hierarchies. CEE societies have lived under externally designed regimes that were either imposed (as was communist one-party rule) or adopted by local elites (as was liberal capitalism after 1990). Along the way, competing national aspirations emerged as powerful sources of political mobilization. It was against this backdrop that the end of state socialism triggered the collapse of ethnonational federations and that postcommunist states institutionalized ethnic nation building. Contrary to the situation after World War II, however, post-1990 international norms did not allow for the physical removal of ethnic "others." Instead, the EU developed an Eastern Enlargement project to incentivize CEE governments to democratize and adopt inclusive policies toward minorities. Longing for Western recognition and European membership, however, did not replace the appeal of ethnic nationalism—even if much of the region avoided the devastating wars that broke out in the former Yugoslavia, which in some cases derailed democratization for over a decade.

Thirty years after the beginning of historic state and regime transformations, the unrealized hopes of liberal democracy and EU integration make CEE societies vulnerable to political entrepreneurs who use ethnic nationalism to reinforce insecurities and weaken resistance to authoritarian rule. Developments across Europe in the 2010s, such as the strengthening of racist and nativist discourse, ethnic justifications behind Russia's annexation of Crimea and support for secessionists in eastern Ukraine, the securitization of the presence of Russophones in the Baltic states, and the xenophobic nationalism used by populist political leaders that "lead" democratic backsliding in countries that were former front-runners of democratization are among the most conspicuous manifestations of the way the politics of ethnic demography can undermine democratic governance.

Support for the EU remains strong, and formal democratic structures are in place in much of CEE; but their meanings and applications vary across the region. Moreover, understandings about the scope of democracy diverge within states, in some cases creating deep political cleavages that weaken societies. Moving forward, the challenge for people in CEE is to build more broadly legitimate forms of democracy that can generate interethnic solidarity, and strengthen the sphere of social organizations that can help to hold governments accountable, while also accommodating the complex matrix of nation-building aspirations that characterize this ethnically diverse region.

Study Questions

1. Explain the "Janus-faced" character of nationalism and the way it has influenced postcommunist democratic development in Central and East European countries. In what ways can we say that nation-building policies have been both forward looking and, at the same time, turned to the past?
2. Bearing in mind the significance of preexisting institutions, national composition, and the choices made by political elites, what seems to set apart the violent ethnic politics of the former Yugoslavia from the largely peaceful evolution of majority-minority conflicts in the rest of Central and East Europe?
3. Most ethnic minorities in Central and East Europe have kin-states in the region, and most governments have enacted legislation to extend various kinds of benefits to ethnic kin living abroad. Discuss the reasons why kin-state nationalism is controversial in this region and how it affects the evolution of democratic government and European integration.
4. Democratization and entry into the European Union were supposed to decrease the salience of nationalist competition in Central and East Europe, yet they seem to have had the opposite effect in some countries. What explains this apparent paradox?
5. Liberal democratic backsliding is occurring in many Central and East European countries, but the hardest hit are Hungary and Poland, two relatively prosperous countries that were at the forefront of market and democratic reform in the years after the collapse of communism. How does nationalism figure into this puzzling outcome?

Suggested Readings

Bunce, Valerie. "Peaceful versus Violent State Dismemberment." *Politics and Society* 27, no. 2 (1999): 217–37.
Cramsey, Sarah A., and Jason Wittenberg. "Timing Is Everything: Changing Norms of Minority Rights and the Making of a Polish Nation-State." *Comparative Political Studies* 49, no. 11 (2016): 1480–512.

Csergo, Zsuzsa. *Talk of the Nation: Language and Conflict in Romania and Slovakia*. Ithaca, NY: Cornell University Press, 2007.

Enyedi, Zsolt. "Right-Wing Authoritarian Innovations in Central and Eastern Europe." *East European Politics* 36, no. 3 (2020): 363–77.

Gagnon, V. P., Jr. *The Myth of Ethnic War: Serbia and Croatia in the 1990s*. Ithaca, NY: Cornell University Press, 2004.

King, Charles. *Extreme Politics: Nationalism, Violence, and the End of Eastern Europe*. Oxford: Oxford University Press, 2010.

Schulze, Jennie L. *Strategic Frames: Europe, Russia, and Minority Inclusion in Estonia and Latvia*. Pittsburgh, PA: University of Pittsburgh Press, 2017.

Vachudova, Milada Anna. "Ethnopopulism and Democratic Backsliding in Central Europe." *East European Politics* 36, no. 3 (2020): 318–40.

Websites

The Association for the Study of Nationalities: https://nationalities.org/virtual-asn
Freedom House: https://freedomhouse.org/report/nations-transit
The European Center for Minority Issues: https://www.ecmi.de
Radio Free Europe/Radio Liberty: https://www.rferl.org

Notes

1. Tom Nairn, "The Modern Janus," in *The Break-Up of Britain: Crisis and Neo-nationalism*, ed. Tom Nairn (London: New Left Books, 1977).

2. For a political self-determination theory of territory, see Margaret Moore, *A Political Theory of Territory* (New York: Oxford University Press, 2015).

3. Ernst Gellner, *Nations and Nationalism* (Ithaca, NY: Cornell University Press, 1983), 1; Andreas Wimmer, *Waves of War: Nationalism, State Formation, and Ethnic Exclusion in the Modern World* (Cambridge: Cambridge University Press, 2012).

4. Brendan O'Leary, Ian S. Lustick, and Thomas Callaghy, eds., *Right-Sizing the State: The Politics of Moving Borders* (Oxford: Oxford University Press, 2002).

5. Will Kymlicka, *Multicultural Citizenship: A Liberal Theory of Minority Rights* (New York: Oxford University Press, 1995).

6. Taras Kuzio, "The Myth of the Civic State: A Critical Survey of Hans Kohn's Framework for Understanding Nationalism," *Ethnic and Racial Studies* 25, no. 1 (2002): 20–39.

7. Alan Patten, *Equal Recognition: The Moral Foundations of Minority Rights* (Woodstock, UK: Oxford University Press, 2014).

8. Valerie Bunce, *Subversive Institutions: The Design and the Destruction of Socialism and the State* (Cambridge: Cambridge University Press, 1999).

9. Rogers Brubaker, *Nationalism Reframed: Nationhood and the National Question in the New Europe* (Cambridge: Cambridge University Press, 1996).

10. Vojtech Mastny, "The Beneš Thesis: A Design for the Liquidation of National Minorities, Introduction," in *The Hungarians: A Divided Nation*, ed. Stephen Borsody, 231–43 (New Haven, CT: Yale Center for International and Area Studies, 1988).

11. Bennett Kovrig, "Peacemaking after World War II," in *The Hungarians: A Divided Nation*, ed. Stephen Borsody, 69–88 (New Haven, CT: Yale Center for International and Area Studies, 1988).

12. Peter Siani-Davies, *The Romanian Revolution of December 1989* (Ithaca, NY: Cornell University Press, 2007).

13. Sharon Wolchik, "The Politics of Transition and the Break-Up of Czechoslovakia," in *The End of Czechoslovakia*, ed. Jiri Musil, 240–41 (Budapest: Central European University Press, 1995); Abby Innes, "Breakup of Czechoslovakia: The Impact of Party Development on the Separation of the State," *East European Politics and Societies* 11, no. 3 (Fall 1997): 393.

14. Rasma Karklins, *Ethnopolitics and Transition to Democracy* (Washington, DC: Woodrow Wilson Center Press and Johns Hopkins University Press, 1994), 151–52.

15. Aleksa Djilas, "Fear Thy Neighbor: The Breakup of Yugoslavia," in *Nationalism and Nationalities in the New Europe*, ed. Charles Kupchan et al. (Ithaca, NY: Cornell University Press, 1995), 88.

16. Chip Gagnon, *The Myth of Ethnic War: Serbia and Croatia in the 1990s* (Ithaca, NY: Cornell University Press, 2004).

17. Edward P. Joseph and Ognen Vangelov, "The Age-Old Struggle for Narrative," *The American Interest*, June 18, 2020; see also Georgi Gotev, Sarantis Michalopoulos, and Zeljko Trkanjec, "Bulgaria Spells Out Conditions for Unblocking North Macedonia's EU Path," *Euractiv*, November 18, 2020.

18. United Nations, *The Comprehensive Proposal for Kosovo Status Settlement* (New York: United Nations Office of the Special Envoy for Kosovo, March 26, 2007).

19. For different scholarly perspectives, see the special issue titled "Self-Determination after Kosovo," *Europe-Asia Studies* 65, no. 5 (July 2013).

20. "Presidency Conclusions. Copenhagen European Council—21–22 June 1993," European Council, accessed August 30, 2020, https://www.europarl.europa.eu/enlargement/ec/pdf/cop_e n.pdf.

21. Organization for Security and Co-operation in Europe, *The Bolzano/Bozen Recommendations on National Minorities in Inter-State Relations* (The Hague: Organization for Security and Co-operation in Europe, 2008), https://www.osce.org/hcnm/bolzano-bozen-recommendations.

22. Zsuzsa Csergő, Ognen Vangelov, and Balázs Vizi, "Minority Inclusion in Central and Eastern Europe: Changes and Continuities in the European Framework," *Intersections: East European Journal of Society and Policies* 3, no. 4 (2017): 5–16; Myra Waterbury, "National Minorities in an Era of Externalization: Kin-State Citizenship, European Integration, and Ethnic Hungarian Minority Politics," *Problems of Post-Communism* 64, no. 5 (2017): 228–41.

23. Zsuzsa Csergo and James M. Goldgeier, "Nationalist Strategies and European Integration," *Perspectives on Politics* 2, no. 1 (March 2004): 26.

24. Myra Waterbury, "Populist Nationalism and the Challenges of Divided Nationhood: The Politics of Migration, Mobility, and Demography in Post-2010 Hungary," *East European Politics and Societies* 34, no. 4 (November 2020): 962–83; Tristan J. Mabry, John McGarry, Margaret Moore, and Brendan O'Leary, eds., *Divided Nations and European Integration* (Philadelphia: University of Pennsylvania Press, 2013).

25. Zsuzsa Csergo, *Talk of the Nation: Language and Conflict in Romania and Slovakia* (Ithaca, NY: Cornell University Press, 2007).

26. Graham Smith et al., *Nation-Building in the Post-Soviet Borderlands: The Politics of National Identities* (Cambridge: Cambridge University Press, 1998), 94.

27. Julie Bernier, "Nationalism in Transition: Nationalizing Impulses and International Counterweights in Latvia and Estonia," in *Minority Nationalism and the Changing International Order*, ed. Michael Keating and John McGarry (Oxford: Oxford University Press, 2001), 346.

28. Rawi Abdelal, *National Purpose in the World Economy* (Ithaca, NY: Cornell University Press, 2001); David J. Smith, "Minority Rights, Multiculturalism and EU Enlargement: The Case of Estonia," *Journal on Ethnopolitics and Minority Issues in Europe* 14, no. 4 (2015): 79–113; Zsuzsa

Csergő and Ada Regelmann, eds., "Europeanization and Minority Political Action in Central and Eastern Europe," special issue published in *Problems of Post-Communism* 64, no. 5 (2017).

29. Judith Kelley, *Ethnic Politics in Europe: The Power of Norms and Incentives* (Princeton, NJ: Princeton University Press, 2004). For a more skeptical view of the power of this leverage, see Bernd Rechel, ed., *Minority Rights in Central and Eastern Europe* (London: Routledge, 2009).

30. Rasma Karklins, "Ethnic Integration and School Policies in Latvia," *Nationalities Papers* 26, no. 2 (1998): 284.

31. Ojarrs Kalnins, "Latvia: The Language of Coexistence," *Transitions Online*, last modified September 1, 2004, http://www.to.cz/TOL/home; Gerli Nimmerfeldt, "Integration of Second Generation Russians in Estonia: Country Report on TIES Survey in Estonia," *Studies of Transition States and Societies* 1, no. 1 (2009): 25–35; Tatjana Bulajeva and Gabrielle Hogan-Brun, "Language and Education Orientations in Lithuania: A Cross-Baltic Perspective Post–EU Accession," in *Multilingualism in Post-Soviet Countries*, ed. Aneta Pavlenko, 122–48 (Toronto: Multilingual Matters, 2008).

32. Zsuzsa Csergő and James M. Goldgeier, "Kin-State Activism in Hungary, Romania, and Russia: The Politics of Ethnic Demography," in Mabry, *Divided Nations and European Integration*, 89–126.

33. Licia Cianetti, "Representing Minorities in the City: Education Policies and Minority Incorporation in the Capital Cities of Estonia and Latvia," *Nationalities Papers* 42, no. 6 (2014): 981–1001.

34. The main driver of exclusivist policies was the Slovak National Party, which exerted pressure on the main governing party, Movement for a Democratic Slovakia. Tim Haughton, "Vladimír Mečiar and His Role in the 1994–1998 Slovak Coalition Government," *Europe-Asia Studies* 54, no. 8 (2002): 1319–38.

35. Csergo, *Talk of the Nation*.

36. Tamás Kiss and István Székely, "Shifting Linkages in Ethnic Mobilization: The Case of RMDSZ and the Hungarians in Transylvania," *Nationalities Papers* 44, no. 4 (2016): 591–610.

37. Szabolcs Pogonyi, *Extra-Territorial Ethnic Politics, Discourses and Identities in Hungary* (Basingstoke, UK: Palgrave Macmillan, 2017).

38. Zoltán Kántor et al., eds., *The Hungarian Status Law: Nation Building and/or Minority Protection* (Sapporo, Japan: Slavic Research Center, 2004); Myra Waterbury, *Between State and Nation: Diaspora Politics and Kin-State Nationalism in Hungary* (Basingstoke, UK: Palgrave Macmillan, 2010).

39. See Dariusz Kalan, "In Poland's Upcoming Election, the Law and Justice Party [PiS] Is Demonizing the LGBT Community to Win," *Foreign Policy*, October 9, 2019, https://foreign policy.com/2019/10/09/poland-pis-demonizing-lgbt-community-win-upcoming-elections.

40. See Felix Schlagwein, "Viktor Orban Expands Hungary's Anti-LGBTQ+ Measures," *Deutsche Welle*, May 21, 2020, https://www.dw.com/en/viktor-orban-expands-hungarys-anti-lgb tq-measures/a-53526969.

41. See Bálint Magyar, *Post-Communist Mafia State: The Case of Hungary* (Budapest: Central European University Press, 2016).

42. András L. Pap, *Democratic Decline in Hungary: Law and Society in an Illiberal Democracy* (Abingdon, UK: Taylor & Francis, 2017).

43. A 2009 language law in Slovakia is interpreted by its opponents as seeking to relegate Hungarian and other minority languages to the private sphere. It concerned the ethnic Hungarian community and caused tensions between Bratislava and Budapest.

44. See Sean Hanley and Milada Anna Vachudova, "Understanding the Illiberal Turn: Democratic Backsliding in the Czech Republic," *East European Politics* 34, no. 3 (2018): 276–96.

45. Jennie L. Schulze, *Strategic Frames: Europe, Russia, and Minority Inclusion in Estonia and Latvia* (Pittsburgh, PA: University of Pittsburgh Press, 2018).

CHAPTER 4

Civil Society and Political Parties

GROWTH AND CHANGE IN THE ORGANIZATIONS LINKING PEOPLE AND POWER

Kevin Deegan-Krause

Communism fell and democracy rose because of complex geopolitical interactions and powerful structural forces. Amid the turmoil, small groups of thoughtful, committed citizens brought about big changes. Fledgling civil society organizations and political parties promoted democratic values and built new institutions that helped prevent a return to dictatorship. If we want to understand how Central and East Europe has changed and what we might expect for its future, we need to look not only at the big questions of constitutions, markets, and national identity but also to the concrete and local experience of civil society and political parties. This chapter will set down basic definitions for civil society and political parties, consider the difference between the two, and then discuss how they developed in Central and East Europe, especially with regard to laws, values, organizations, and their impact on society.

What We Mean by Civil Society and Political Parties

Civil society and political parties are different, but they are similar enough to share a chapter because together they inhabit the same "in-between" space. *Civil society* in particular is often defined by what it is not. It is not the family, the state, or the market but rather a sphere of activity located between these in which "institutions, organizations and individuals . . . associate voluntarily to advance common interests."[1] More recent and specific definitions recast this negative space into a positive set of values. Roberto Foa and Gregorz Ekiert define civil society as

> the realm of organized social life that is open, voluntary, self-generating, at least partially self-supporting, autonomous from the state, and bound by a legal order or set of shared rules [and which] involves citizens acting collectively in a public sphere to express their interests, passions, preferences, and ideas, to exchange information, to achieve collective goals, to make demands on the state, to improve the structure and functioning of the state, and to hold state officials accountable.[2]

Civil society organization is the generic term for any institutional unit of civil society, and this includes all those interest groups, service organizations, clubs, think tanks, foundations, churches, and any other institution that fits the definition's requirements of being voluntary, independent, and oriented toward public, collective goals.

Parties are not quite the same as civil society organizations. It is tempting to try to identify them by their names, but not all of them use the *party* label and not everything with the label is a party. One of the most widely used definitions sets up two criteria: a party is an "institution that (a) seeks influence in a state, often by attempting to occupy positions in government, and (b) usually consists of more than a single interest in the society and so to some degree attempts to 'aggregate interests.'"[3] The lines between civil society organizations and parties are sometimes blurry, but the general rule is that while parties seek "influence from within the government," civil society organizations work from outside. In addition, parties are more likely to take a "comprehensive view of the public interest and political agenda," while civil society organizations may focus more narrowly on a few specific agenda items.[4] Because political parties cooperate and compete directly with one another, we often speak of them as part of a broader entity, a "political party system," with its own internal rules and norms that govern how parties interact, what issues they fight about, and where they stand on the political spectrum.

Understanding Civil Society in Central and East Europe

How Civil Society Developed in a Chaotic Region

Civil society in Central and East Europe faced widespread destructive pressure under communism, but when that pressure lifted, civil society organizations rapidly emerged to play an important role in the postcommunist period. The development of civil society has not been smooth, however. The mid-1990s were a time of particularly difficult adaptation, and civil society organizations in the southern part of the region faced the most severe challenges.

The seizure of power by communist parties in the late 1940s did profound damage in Central and East Europe, but civil society's problems in the region actually began much earlier. Professional associations, discussion circles, charitable societies, and other groups began to flourish in industrialized cities such as Prague and Budapest in the late 1800s, but they were much slower to develop in the countryside and in countries to the south and east. Further growth was made more difficult both by the economic crises of the 1920s and 1930s, which starved civil society of resources, and by the emergence of authoritarian leaders who saw civil society as a threat to their rule and tried to suppress its activity. When communist parties took over after World War II, they also attacked independent civil society but from a different direction. Communists were willing to allow clubs and associations—and even to help build them—but only on the condition that they became completely dependent on the state. Communist parties in the region actively used what remained of civil society as "transmission belts" for mobilizing support (or at least the appearance of support) for government efforts, and they made major efforts to create a "dense network of large associations" while at the same time ensuring that these were "tightly controlled by the party-state."[5]

At the same time, another type of organization began to emerge beneath the surface to resist communist rule, a type that Michael Bernhard refers to as "insurgent civil society."[6] Dissidents who rejected the overwhelming power of the communist regimes began to work together to organize their opposition even though they faced the constant risk of political persecution and legal prosecution. Most of these organizations remained fragmented and hidden from view, except in rare instances when (as in Poland) they could find protection from other institutions such as trade unions or the Catholic Church or when (as in Czechoslovakia) leaders of dissident organizations openly accepted imprisonment as the price of speaking out. Yet, whenever pressure from above eased—as it did in Hungary in 1956, in Czechoslovakia in 1968, in Poland in the late 1970s, and across the region in the late 1980s—organizations such as these showed a strong capacity to organize, and they quickly mobilized marches and other acts of public opposition, along with newspapers, informal schools, and help for the families of those who were fired or jailed.

As communism weakened and the Soviet Union withdrew support from communist governments in Central and East Europe, an independent civil society again began to emerge through a variety of pathways: the increased strength of independent dissident groups, the increased independence of formerly state-run groups, and the creation of many wholly new civil society organizations. In the northern and western countries of the region, these organizational networks played critical roles in pushing some governments into negotiations and others out of office. In the south of the region, significant activity by civil society organizations also helped to end the communist monopoly in Yugoslavia, but much of that effort became bound up in ethnic conflicts over which groups would control the state.

As a vibrant and voluntary alternative to the tired and oppressive state apparatus of communism, civil society played a key role in these democratic transitions, but popular enthusiasm eventually waned. When the most skillful activists turned their attention to parliament and the government and smaller, less-connected organizations saw their resources dry up, many skeptics feared that civil society simply could not overcome the destructive historical legacies of suppression by interwar dictators followed by subservience under communist rule. History was not destiny, however, and instead of wasting away, civil society organizations adapted to the new circumstances with new goals and new forms of organization. Much of civil society made an awkward and difficult transition from its "insurgent" type to an "institutionalized" type that worked to "enhance and support democratic institutions" in the broader political system.[7]

Measuring Civil Society across Time and Space

How can we assess the state of civil society? The region of Central and East Europe is diverse and rapidly changing, and there are simply not many tools for making good comparisons. Of the available measures, one of the best is the Varieties of Democracy (V-Dem) project that asks scholars to estimate the strength of civil society for every year, past and present. Figure 4.1 summarizes the views of experts about whether civil society enjoyed "autonomy from the state" and whether citizens could "freely and actively pursue their political and civic goals, however conceived." In every country in the region, the autonomy of civil society rose sharply from extremely low levels in the late 1980s to higher levels in the early 1990s and then remained fairly strong.[8]

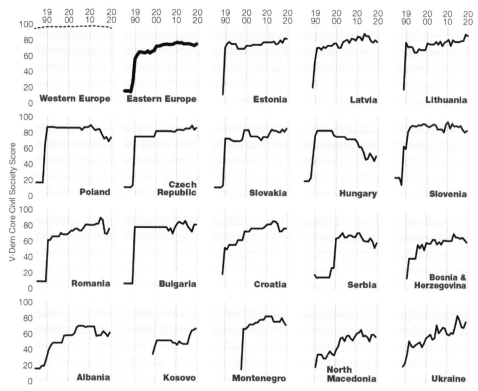

Figure 4.1. Overall Strength of Civil Society over Time. (Kevin Deegan-Krause). *Data Source:* V-Dem 2020.

A closer look at individual countries, however, shows some significant variation. The data show two fairly distinct regional patterns and a few variations. In the northern and western countries of the region (especially in the eight countries that entered the European Union [EU] in 2004), the graphs show that civil society followed an almost identical pattern, strengthening rapidly from exceptionally weak civil society under communism and then remaining relatively strong in subsequent decades. In the south and east, the graphs show much more variation, with some repeating the pattern above—especially in Romania and Bulgaria—and others experiencing more gradual climbs and lower peaks. While most countries in the region remained close to the levels they reached in the late 1990s, Hungary, Serbia, and North Macedonia[9] have shown noticeable declines. Even with the drop, however, they have stayed well above their mid-1980s levels (unlike countries to the east, such as Russia, whose civil society experienced the same initial rise but by 2016 had fallen back to the levels of the late communist era).

Dimensions of Civil Society Growth and Change

These broad, all-purpose measurements are useful for making big comparisons, but they do not tell the whole story because civil society can succeed or fail in many different ways. Helmut Anheier and Lisa Carlson argue that civil society has multiple dimensions.

Their "civil society diamond" breaks down the analysis of civil society into four different categories:

- *Space:* What is the legal and political space within the larger regulatory environment in which civil society operates; and what laws and policies enable or inhibit its development?
- *Values:* What values underlie civil society; what values, norms, and attitudes does it represent and propagate; how inclusive and exclusive are they; and what areas of consensus and dissent emerge?
- *Structure:* How large is civil society in terms of institutions, organizations, networks, and individuals; what are its component parts; and what resources does it command?
- *Impact:* What is the contribution of civil society to specific social, economic, and political problems?[10]

Space: What Institutions Shape Civil Society?

All organizations work within broader frameworks of rules and resources that they cannot completely control. The "in-between" nature of civil society makes it especially dependent on decisions that are made somewhere else, whether by families, firms, or especially governments. But the relationship with government is complicated. Civil society is at risk if government does too much or too little. On the one hand, civil society needs government restraint because governments that become too intrusive in their regulation (either accidentally or intentionally) can undermine the positive efforts of civil society organizations, scare off memberships, and threaten their essential independence.[11] On the other hand, civil society organizations cannot function without some degree of public order or formal legal status that allows them to protect their organizational identity, oversee membership, and manage accountability and finances. Many civil society organizations, furthermore, depend on government for financial support, either directly through subsidies or indirectly through tax codes that promote voluntary donations. The suppression and even criminalization of civil society during the fascist and communist eras demonstrate the dangers of too much government, while the chaos of some countries in the early postcommunist era demonstrates the risk of too little. Like free markets, civil society *needs* government to enforce the rule of law.

Some countries in Central and East Europe in the postcommunist era have found it more difficult than others to maintain this complicated equilibrium. Since the mid-1990s, the United States Agency for International Development (USAID) has issued annual reports on civil society's "legal environment," with special attention to questions about how well governments register, tax, regulate, and respect the independence of civil society organizations. The results follow familiar regional patterns: the legal environments in most countries in the north and west of this region have consistently received high marks as "supportive," while most countries in the south and east of the region received the lower assessment of "evolving" because of problems such as administrative harassment, fines, and deliberate refusal to register new organizations. Positive change continued in the 2010s as many countries began to enact more streamlined rules on tax exemptions, donations, and accounting procedures, but improvement nevertheless remained slow.[12] A few countries actually saw a sharp decline, especially Hungary, whose once widely praised nonprofit legal environment descended into "an atmosphere of intimidation" with the rise of Viktor Orbán's self-proclaimed model of "illiberal democracy." The civil society atmosphere in Hungary is now characterized by "accusatory statements by the government" and "ongoing administrative harassment," such as police raids on organizations distributing civil society–related grants from the Norwegian government.[13]

Values: What Are Civil Society's Motivations?

Even a supportive legal structure will not produce a strong civil society if a society's underlying values do not contribute to individuals volunteering the time, money, and effort that civic efforts require. Under these circumstances, even a high degree of government support may not produce positive results if the values nurtured by civil society organizations are too sharply at odds with one another or with the fundamental values of democracy.

The first question for a successful civil society is whether anyone cares. Other spheres of action—governments, firms, and families—have carrots and sticks that allow them to exert leverage and get what they want; but civil society organizations have no sticks to force cooperation, and their carrots are in short supply because of the famous "free rider" problem that allows some people to stand by and take advantage of the social benefits produced by the civic engagement of others.

In the last years of communism, the incentives won out, and large parts of the populations of many countries demonstrated the core values that sustain civil society. At first, only a courageous few risked severe punishments to organize into groups and take small-scale actions. They typed multiple copies of forbidden texts, organized small discussions and events, and even mounted legal defenses of others facing prison, as the Workers' Defense Committee (KOR) did after the 1970s strikes in Poland and the civil rights advocacy group Charter 77 did in Czechoslovakia. As organized groups got stronger and sensed a lack of resolution from the communist governments in the 1980s, ever-larger numbers turned out for collective protests and introduced an independent spirit into once-subservient communist-era associations. Many of the leaders of these efforts came from the earlier opposition groups: Lech Wałęsa, the shipyard worker who became head of the Solidarity organization and movement in Poland, had been in the KOR, and Václav Havel, the playwright who helped lead mass demonstrations in Prague in November 1989, had spent years in prison for his activity as a spokesperson for Charter 77.

After communism's fall, many of the leaders of dissident groups and civil society organizations went on to prominent government positions—Wałęsa and Havel became the presidents of their respective countries—but at the grassroots level, the victory was less obvious. As early public enthusiasm for demonstrations waned, it became increasingly apparent that the everyday experience of the communist era could inhibit the habits and values necessary for a thriving postcommunist civil society. According to Marc Morjé Howard, communism's tendency to force people into supportive organizations and then label those activities as "voluntary" not only poisoned the idea of "voluntary associations" that is at the heart of civil society but also produced a low level of generalized trust in society as a whole and encouraged the narrow relationships of trust based on the close-knit "private and informal networks" that people built for self-protection. The predominance of these inward-focused social relationships combined with the economic slumps and political crises of postcommunism to produce a deep dissatisfaction that encouraged many people to "withdraw even further from public activities."[14]

More recent evidence, however, indicates that instead of withdrawing completely, many people in the region shifted their civil society participation to other, less obvious activities and gradually developed a civil society ethos. Foa and Ekiert have found that, although the level of many civil society behaviors in Central and East Europe falls considerably below those of Western Europe, the gap is narrowing.[15] Small-scale studies and local opinion polls show that the idea of "volunteering" is losing some of the stigma of the communist era and that some segments of the population have also begun to adopt West European patterns of charitable giving and philanthropy.[16]

The values of civic engagement, however, can do more harm than good if citizens are engaged in the pursuit of destructive goals. Bernhard contrasts the democracy-building organizations of "institutionalized civil society" with those of "uncivil society," which "lack a principled commitment to democracy and are willing to play fast and loose with its rules."[17] Simone Chambers and Jeffrey Kopstein mince no words when they confront the problem of "bad civil society," by which they mean groups that embody the civil society ideals of voluntary mutual engagement among individuals but in the service of "hate and bigotry."[18] Ugliness, of course, is in the eye of the beholder, and fears about the violence of football fan clubs such as the Czech Ultra Sparta, the intolerance of conservative religious organizations such as the Polish nonprofit Radio Maryja, or the nationalism of patriotic organizations such as the Croatian Disabled Homeland War Veterans Association exist alongside fears about the danger to the social order posed by what others see as morally corrosive gay pride parades or the "antipatriotic cosmopolitanism" of organizations funded by Hungarian billionaire George Soros. In reality, though, the potential sources of "uncivil society" in Central and East Europe represent a relatively small share of the sector as a whole. Far from the extremes, most civil society organizations in East and West alike act to help the needy, solve practical problems, and engage together on hobbies and areas of mutual interest.

Structure: What Are Civil Society's Capacities?

Even the apparently simplest goals of civil society organizations—providing opportunities for people with similar goals or interests to interact—can often benefit from some degree of formal organization, which may include formal names, bylaws, membership lists, and regular physical or virtual space. How these are structured can have a huge impact on whether people can use civil society to reach their goals. Along with its review of legal frameworks, USAID has also evaluated civil society based on measures of membership, management, fund-raising, training, and partnerships with other sectors, along with the transparency and accountability of civil society organizations.[19] These show rapid growth in the capacity of Central and East European civil society in the early 1990s, followed by a long period of overall stability. During this stable period, however, big changes were happening under the surface. A three-decade analysis of Poland, conducted by Grzegorz

Ekiert, Jan Kubik, and Michal Wenzel, found that the submissive associations of the communist era faced major challenges caused by both the loss of state resources and the acquisition of a new and unfamiliar independence. Many formerly communist-led unions, associations, and organizations either simply collapsed or limped along with inherited memberships and little sense of direction. At the same time, new professional associations, unions, and clubs emerged as fresh-thinking alternatives to communist-era groups, and other groups emerged to meet needs that had not existed under communism, such as campaign watchdog organizations, chambers of commerce, and homeless shelters. In the process, civil society's "center of gravity shifted from the large, membership-based, formal organizations, such as trade unions and professional associations (mostly inherited from the old regime), to a highly diverse sector of small, professionalized nongovernmental organizations (NGOs) that rely on voluntary involvement and public as well as private funding."[20] In Poland's case, for example, there are "tens of thousands" of "small organizations run by professional staffs that rely on public funding, fundraising, and volunteers" and "focus on a wide range of local and national issues and initiatives."[21] Poland is not unique. Countries across the region exhibit similar patterns, with the most effective associations of the old regime being "complemented by the dynamic growth of new organizations," together creating "a diverse, competitive, and balanced associational sphere."[22]

Along with this organizational transition came new patterns of economic impact and funding. Although civil society plays a significant role in serving people's needs and stabilizing the political system, it remains a relatively small part of the economy. A 2013 study by Johns Hopkins University found that the nonprofit sector in the Czech Republic, for example, accounted for just under 2 percent of all jobs and economic activity, though the direct impact was slightly larger when adjusted to include volunteers, and the indirect, nonmonetary effects were even more significant.[23] Because civil society organizations did their work with relatively few financial resources, wealthy outside institutions could, by devoting only a tiny fraction of their own resources, have an outsized impact on the organization and direction of civil society. During the 1990s and early 2000s, the EU and the United States, together with private philanthropists such as George Soros, funded hundreds of consultants and contributed hundreds of millions of dollars to strengthen civil society organizations in the hopes of helping to consolidate democracy. Although these efforts appear to have played a big role in creating the basic infrastructure for civil society, there were limits. Critics argue that this funding failed to achieve many of its goals because recipients were concentrated in a relatively thin layer of elite nonprofits with international connections rather than among local-level organizations with more members but fewer connections.[24] This dependence on outside sources may help to explain a small convergence of civil society capacities across the region in the 2000s when special funding programs for soon-to-be EU member states began to dry up and outside donors focused their efforts on the more vulnerable democracies of the south and east.

Finally, it is important to note that existing alongside the formal nonprofit organizations of civil society, there was also a wide variety of informal, horizontally organized movements in the region that did not establish permanent structures but nevertheless helped shape societal and political outcomes at pivotal moments. Taking inspiration from the loosely structured movements that emerged to help overthrow communist rule and from subsequent people's movements elsewhere in the world, nearly every country in Central and East Europe has seen at least one large series of demonstrations, from marches in Poland against tighter abortion restrictions to the mass demonstrations against corruption in North Macedonia that took on the label "colorful revolution."[25] Many of these have not achieved their goals, but others played instrumental roles in reversing unpopular policy initiatives, forcing new elections, and even stopping government violations of democratic norms.

Impact: How Does Civil Society Shape Its Surroundings?

The impact of civil society depends on the combination of the rules that govern it, the values that shape it, and the organizational capacity of its organizations. A recent report by the World Economic Forum offered a long list of tasks that civil society organizations perform in any society: "watchdog" over public institutions, "advocate" for awareness of social issues, "service provider" to meet societal needs, "expert" to provide well-crafted solutions, and "capacity builder" and "incubator" to make future efforts possible, as well as "representative," "champion," and "definer of standards" to identify voices that otherwise go unheard and bring them into existing systems of governance.[26] To what extent does civil society in Central and East Europe actually fulfill these roles?

During the late stages of communism, dissidents' insurgent civil society excelled in the role of champion of the people against the regime. In the absence of rival parties or opposition newspapers, the small and vulnerable civil society organizations were representatives of the society and its concerns by talking and writing as openly as they could about societal problems including everything from corruption to industrial pollution, as well the quality and availability of vegetables. As democratically elected governments emerged in the early stages of postcommunism, much of civil society added watchdog functions. Over time, much of the watchdog role shifted to political parties that sought to keep one another in check, but institutionalized civil society continued to advocate for policies that did not have any strong political representation of their own and also began to respond directly to public needs. As a result they became increasingly involved in providing services, even if they often lacked the funding to really solve the problems they were addressing.

The surveys by USAID measure the impact of civil society on two main dimensions. It defines *advocacy* as the ability of organizations to "communicate their messages through the media to the broader public, articulate their demands to government officials, and monitor government actions to ensure accountability," and it defines *service provision* as "the range of goods and services that [civil society organizations] provide and how responsive these are to community needs and priorities."[27] Civil society organizations across the region rank higher for their advocacy than for their service provision. This is understandable because civil society groups generally have relatively few resources, and it is usually more expensive to provide services than to advocate. Furthermore, even with foreign support, civil society organizations usually cannot afford to provide wide-reaching services without assistance from the domestic government. The barriers to advocacy, by contrast, are more uneven and depend heavily on how governments treat civil society. The biggest barrier to their efforts is actually simple disinterest by political leaders who do not see any personal or political benefit in supporting civil society efforts. In more extreme cases, however, governments frame civil society as the enemy. Hungarian prime minister Viktor Orbán, for example, claimed that policy advocates from civil society organizations "are being paid by foreigners" who use this access to government "to apply influence on Hungarian political life."[28] Orbán subsequently escalated tensions with a law whose administrative procedures limited the Hungarian campus of the Central European University, a social science–oriented institution based in Budapest and funded by Hungarian refugee and human rights advocate George Soros. In response, some organizations have tried to get around these barriers by turning to more public forms of protest. Hungarian civil society has responded not only with significant demonstrations but also with numerous smaller efforts that range from serious investigations of corruption by government officials to successful GoFundMe.com campaigns for creating parodies of government anti-immigrant billboards, with sardonic pro-immigration messages such as "Come to Hungary, *we've* got jobs in London."

In these instances, many civil society organizations may reorient their efforts toward the explicit defense of democracy. These efforts—which Bernhard describes as "firewall civil society"[29]—aim to protect against "democratic backsliding" led by opponents in uncivil society and in government itself. Firewall efforts come in many forms, from the systematic efforts of established NGOs to maintain freedom of the press and monitor

Photo 4.1. Members of a Bosnian civil society organization work with William & Mary students in borrowed space to plan a summer camp for local youth. Much of the labor of civil society in the region involves hard work with limited resources, eased somewhat by benefits of shared effort and common values. (Paula M. Pickering)

government corruption to the loud and sometimes chaotic demonstrations of the sort exemplified by the Polish antiabortion marches and North Macedonian anticorruption demonstrations mentioned above. Furthermore, as the case of Hungary illustrates, even the concerted efforts of a firewall civil society can do only so much to check the efforts of a government that has both the desire and the parliamentary votes necessary to undermine democratic accountability. But the absence of victory does not mean total defeat, and even if civil society is not the make-or-break factor in preventing the return to dictatorship, it is still important because it reinforces support for the everyday work of democratic institutions, it builds connections among citizens that may later help with mobilization, and it helps to secure the well-being of those who are hit hardest by political and economic decline.

Indeed, the true impact of civil society—the full expression of its values and its capacity—is often only apparent when these organizations find themselves under pressure. Attempts by the governments of Slovakia, Croatia, and Serbia to impose or extend authoritarian rule in the mid-1990s led to strong and effective responses by civil society organizations, revealing strengths that had been honed under four decades of resistance to communism combined with new tactics learned from around the world. Working independently of political parties (though accepting European and American financial and technical assistance), these organizations produced "rock the vote" tours and sought to boost turnout with a campaign built around the slogan "It's not all the same to me." They built a network of election monitors to watch for manipulation of ballots and let the government know that they were prepared with both legal challenges and civil disobedience efforts in case any manipulation was discovered. While these efforts probably could not have succeeded without an equally effective campaign of cooperation by parties in the political opposition, they certainly helped to increase the new, more democratic government's majority and gave it political breathing room in its first years of operation. These efforts also provide one of the earliest examples of Central and East European civil society as an international influence in its own right, since leaders from Slovakia helped advise their counterparts in Croatia the following year, and representatives of both groups went on to advise civil society organizations in Serbia in 2000 and in Georgia and Ukraine in the early 2000s. In some countries—especially Russia and some other former Soviet republics—firewall civil society has been unable to stop the emergence of authoritarian regimes and has transformed itself yet again into new variants of the insurgent civil society that helped bring about democratic change in the first place.

Understanding Political Parties in Central and East Europe

If it was civil society that raised the curtain on democracy in Central and East Europe, it was political parties that stole the show.[30] Civil society organizations moved to the margins, and in most countries of the region they transformed into a solid, stable sector of service providers and advocates. Political parties jumped to the center of the political stage, transformed to keep up with changing circumstances, and then transformed again and again to keep up

Photo 4.2. Election billboard from Slovakia's 2012 election by a new political party, Ordinary People and Independent Personalities, featuring the party's leader, Igor Matovič. The billboard shows the party slogan, "Together let's stop politicians from stealing Slovakia," and a background reference to the anticorruption investigation code-named "Gorilla." (Tim Haughton)

with opponents who were changing too. In the process, Central and East Europe produced complex party systems with many parties and rapid shifts in names and membership, as well as in their ideological goals and methods of organization. Many of those parties built themselves in traditional ways, around economic and cultural issues and ties to specific voting groups, but others burst in with new ideas and new ways of organizing.

How Political Parties Developed in a Chaotic Region

Central and East Europe lacked party competition between 1948 and 1989, but it certainly never lacked political parties. In every country of the region, a single, dominant Communist Party controlled every political institution, and though there were periodic elections, voters usually faced the choice of voting for the sole Communist Party–approved candidate on the ballot or risking party disapproval (or worse) by failing to vote or by making the ballot invalid with an X across the page or writing "No" next to candidates' names. In some cases, voters had a "choice" between candidates from the Communist Party and those of other parties that identified with specific groups while remaining fully loyal to the Communist Party. The Polish Peasant Party, for example, offered the illusion of choice in rural areas where Poland's ruling Communist Party had less appeal.

The communist monopoly on power ended by the early 1990s, but communist parties did not. In most countries of the region, the successors of the various communist parties proved resilient. Some broke into multiple parts, and most were pushed out of office in the first years after 1989. However, some actually managed to stay in governing coalitions, and others returned to power in coalitions at the next election through a combination of internal reform (usually marked by a name change to "Socialist," "Reform," or "Labor"), strong organization, and voters' desire for economic protection. Since they began with a huge membership base and still retained some member loyalty, most were successful in combining these with other inherited resources—including funds, facilities, and bureaucratic connections—into strong results in the early competitive elections.

Competing against the former communists in these elections were parties representing all of the various forces that had previously opposed communist rule: those who favored freer markets or sought more civil liberties, those with strong religious belief or ethnic identity, and those seeking specific policies such as stronger ecological protections, larger pensions, or higher farm supports (or even more particular interests such as the Czech Republic's "Independent Erotic Initiative" and "Friends of Beer"). In some countries, these extremely disparate forces managed to band together into one or more large anticommunist movements. In others, they found cooperation more difficult. Although all of the anticommunist movements ultimately splintered into many parts, some of the fragments went on to become strong parties in their own right. Many of these new parties took as their models the kinds of parties found in Western Europe. These include liberal parties supporting free markets, Christian democratic parties supporting moral values, ethnic parties seeking cultural rights, and new or revived social democratic parties (without ties to communist successor parties) supporting moderate redistribution of wealth and income.

Yet many other parties did not easily fit into traditional Western European party families but possessed well-known leaders who could attract votes. During the 1990s, some of these leader-driven parties (often allied with nationalist groups) sought to stifle competition and return to one-party rule. Croatia's Franjo Tuđman, Serbia's Slobodan Milošević, Slovakia's Vladimír Mečiar, and Ukraine's Leonid Kuchma all used their executive powers to defeat or undermine (or sometimes kill) political opponents who threatened to hold them accountable. To varying degrees, these leaders were even willing to retain power by manipulating elections themselves. However, through a combination of illness, political miscalculation, and popular counterpressure, none of the four succeeded in bending the political system fully to his will (in contrast to their counterparts in Russia and Belarus).

By the mid-2000s, nearly every country in Central and East Europe had developed a reasonably robust political party system in which entities recognizable as political parties actively competed fairly over jobs, taxes, minority rights, and other predictable and often mundane issues. The emergence of regularized party competition did not necessarily produce stable party systems, however, and the 2000s and 2010s brought significant disruptions by new political parties that capitalized on public dissatisfaction with politics and the apparent corruption of the newly entrenched postcommunist leaders. Often led by celebrities from nonpolitical backgrounds (including an ex-king, the manager of a supermarket chain, several investigative journalists, some reality TV stars, and a surprising number of singer-songwriters), these parties promised cleaner government based on new ways of thinking ("neither left nor right but forward"). However, they usually found it difficult to deliver on these promises and faced their own outsider challenges in the elections that followed. Parties such as Positive Slovenia (the supermarket manager), Lithuania's Party of National Resurrection (the game show host), the Czech Republic's Public Affairs (the journalist), and the National Movement of Simeon the II (the king) rose quickly and then disappeared without a trace one or two election cycles later, leaving room for another new party in its place.

Measuring Political Parties across Time and Space

The challenges of assessing parties are different from those of assessing civil society. On the one hand, gathering statistics on individual parties is easier because governments keep specific lists of what counts as a party, and when parties compete they use common currencies of votes and seats. On the other hand, there is no easy way to judge the overall health of a party system. The number of parties and the speed of change provide two good starting points because there are dangers on *both* sides: too many parties can be as dangerous as too few, and too little change can be as destructive as too much.

Fragmentation: How Many Parties?

There is no way to determine the ideal number of parties in a political party system. Meaningful competition requires at least two parties. Every additional party increases the diversity of options but also makes it more difficult to cobble together a coalition that can agree on who will run the government and what policies it will pursue and lock in by the vote of a parliamentary majority. Figure 4.2 shows the sizes of political party systems in Central and East Europe using a mathematical formula designed to deal with the problem of how to count parties with vastly different sizes, especially tiny parties.[31] A measure of less than 2.0 on this scale suggests that one party is significantly larger than all the rest combined, indicating a tightly limited party system. A measure of more than 6.0 indicates a party system with so many parties that cooperation becomes difficult. The figure shows that the average in Central and East Europe has declined from the high end of the normal range in the early 1990s to a middle position that is now in line with political party systems in Western Europe.

Unlike the graphs for civil society strength, the graphs of fragmentation do not show any clear geographic patterns. Slightly larger party systems were more common in the north, particularly in the Baltic countries of Estonia, Latvia, and Lithuania, which tended to hover between five and six parties, with below-average levels of fragmentation more common in the south and east of the region. The biggest exception is Bosnia-Herzegovina, where the constitution separates voting along ethnic lines and multiple parties can compete successfully for support within each of the three major ethnic groups. Only a few countries fell below the 2.0 threshold that protects against one-party dominance, and it was rare for any single party to command a majority of the seats in parliament. Some of these single-party-dominant periods were short-lived, such as Bulgaria and Lithuania during the mid-1990s and Slovakia in the early 2010s. Though a few other countries have seen longer-term one-party dominance, especially Montenegro, where the

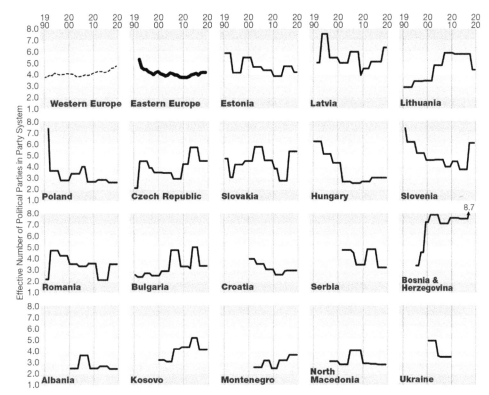

Figure 4.2.   Size of Party Systems in Central and East Europe over Time. (Kevin Deegan-Krause). *Data Source:* Fernando Casal Bértoa, *Who Governs in Europe and Beyond,* 2020.

Party of Democratic Socialism dominated over other parties between 1992 and 2000 and nearly always controlled a parliamentary majority, and Hungary, where Viktor Orbán's party Fidesz gained a two-thirds majority in parliament in 2010 against a fragmented opposition and then reshaped the political system to build in substantial advantages that contributed to its victories in 2014 and 2018.

Volatility: How Much Change?

The first decade of democracy in any country is often a time of extreme change in political party systems as voters and politicians try various options before deciding to settle down. Central and East Europe experienced similar early instability but never actually came to rest. Party volatility is measured here by changes in every party's vote share from one election to the next. Like fragmentation, volatility has "danger zones" at both the high and low ends. Constant change means that voters and politicians cannot make intelligent guesses about what will happen next and therefore cannot make long-term plans. Infrequent change gives parties little incentive to listen to voters.

Volatility in Central and East Europe started high and has remained high. Even the relatively conservative measurements used in figure 4.3 show that about one-third of all voters changed their minds from one election to the next, resulting in a volatility of about

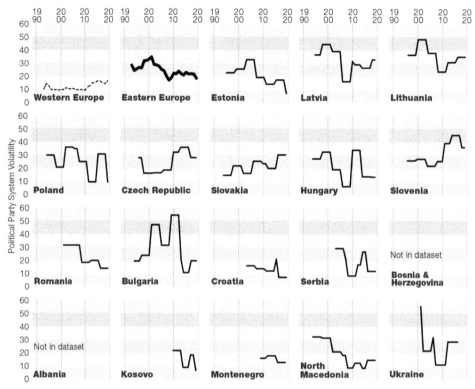

Figure 4.3. Volatility of Party Systems in Central and East Europe over Time. (Kevin Deegan-Krause). *Data Source:* Fernando Casal Bértoa, *Who Governs in Europe and Beyond,* 2020.

30 percent during the first postcommunist decade. This was three times as high as in Western Europe during the same period. Volatility dropped to around 20 percent in the second postcommunist decade with one-fifth of all voters changing their minds. Then, instead of declining further toward traditionally low West European levels, it began to rise again in the mid-2000s and remained high in the 2010s. (West European volatility also rose substantially in this later period, suggesting a general increase in the rate of change over and above regional differences.)

Higher volatility levels emerged in the northern and western countries than in the south and east (though even in those countries the level of change was well above West European levels). Part of the explanation lies in the fragility of political parties themselves. Without long-standing social identities and deep voter loyalties, parties in Eastern and Central Europe are more vulnerable to economic problems and corruption scandals, and their death opens space for new parties with even shallower roots. In some countries, such as Slovakia and Latvia, the cycles of party replacement have followed a slow but constant churn. In other countries, such as Hungary, the Czech Republic, Bulgaria, and Slovenia, periods of stability have alternated with massive earthquake elections. Some parties suffered self-inflicted wounds, such as the leaked recording of a Hungarian prime minister's profanity-filled admission that "we lied morning, noon and night"; the revelations in

Poland of top politicians' conversations in expensive restaurants about their planned luxury vacations and contemptuous comments about voters; and the police anticorruption raid on the office of the Czech prime minister. In other countries, the changes reflected the hope for a better alternative, as was the case with the return of Bulgaria's former king as a possible savior and the emergence in Slovenia of a wave of new parties run by nonpolitical outsiders.

Dimensions of Political Party Growth and Change

As with civil society, these broad measurements only scratch the surface. A deeper understanding of parties can use the same categories as the analysis of civil society, but the questions are different: How are parties regulated? How do they compete? How are they organized? And how do they govern?

Space: What Institutions Shape Political Parties?

Democracies depend on elections, and since political parties are the main actors in the electoral process, they are subject to a significant amount of regulation. As in other regions of the world, the countries of Central and East Europe have regulations that impose particular rules on parties regarding their formal registration (often requiring a petition with a minimum number of signatures), their names (preventing new parties from adopting the same or similar names or acronyms), and how they interact with their members (imposing requirements that party leaders submit to periodic election by party members). Government involvement is especially strong in the area of campaigns and their methods of finance. Almost every country in the region requires full disclosure of donations and places limits on what individuals and organizations can donate; they also prevent or limit what foreign organizations can give as well as how much parties can spend. In return, nearly all countries provide free media time for campaign advertisements, and most provide a public subsidy (in some countries as much as ten dollars for each vote a party receives over a certain threshold).[32] Lawmakers justify these rules and subsidies as part of an effort to reduce the dependence of parties on hidden private interests; but the enforcement of disclosure requirements in many countries often depends on what party is in power, and the generous subsidies to victorious parties are seen by many as an attempt to create a cartel of in-parties designed to exclude emerging rivals.[33]

Of all laws related to parties, by far the most important is the choice of an electoral system, the rules that determine how votes are translated into seats in parliament. Except for presidential elections, where there can only be one winner, the winner-take-all system of voting for individual candidates is extremely rare in Central and East Europe (even in the region's presidential voting systems, the winner is not simply the one with more votes than anybody else; if no presidential candidate wins an outright majority of 50 percent plus one vote, then the top two candidates must face each other in a second round of voting held several weeks later). Instead of winner-take-all, countries in Central and East Europe opted for proportional representation systems in which voters cast ballots for political parties rather than individuals, and the share of seats in parliament are allotted to match the party's share of the vote. (Only the parliaments of Lithuania and Hungary have consistently used winner-take-all systems to elect individual candidates from single-member districts, and even these countries also use proportional representation to elect a significant share of the seats in parliament). If proportional representation often fails to produce exactly proportional results, it is because most systems also try to reduce fragmentation by imposing a "vote threshold" that prevents a party from getting any seats at all unless its overall vote share exceeds a certain threshold (usually about 5 percent). When many smaller parties win votes but do not cross the threshold, the result can help to magnify the gains of larger parties. In Poland in 2015, for example, the threshold excluded five parties that together had received a total of nearly 16 percent of the overall vote. The seats that might have gone to these parties went instead to above-the-threshold parties. In this way Law and Justice saw its 37.8 percent share of the vote transformed into 51.1 percent of all seats in parliament.

Because electoral laws and electoral systems define the gateway to political power, they can be tempting targets for political manipulation. During the first decade of postcommunism, leaders in Slovakia, Croatia, and Serbia made significant changes in electoral laws: raising the level of the threshold, changing the ability of parties to band together in coalitions, and reducing the proportionality of the system to block rivals and limit the representation of ethnic minorities. Furthermore, they tended to make changes just before elections in order to knock opposition parties off balance. These manipulations were often successful, though in the long run they sometimes strengthened political oppositions by forcing them to unify their efforts. In subsequent decades, such electoral system manipulations have been less blatant, but parties in power continue to adjust the legal rules of party competition for their own benefit, especially in countries to the east and south, such as Ukraine, Albania, Montenegro, and North Macedonia, which score lower on measurements of integrity of the electoral process, especially because of problems with government use of state media, voters excluded from election rolls, and opaque party finance. Hungary faced particular scrutiny after 2010 for increasing the share of seats from winner-take-all districts and manipulating district boundaries in those districts (a phenomenon known in the United States as gerrymandering), as well as for electoral regulations that impeded the efforts of opposition parties and new entrants.[34]

Values: What Do Political Parties Fight About?

The only value that political parties in a democracy can be expected to agree on is the value of democracy itself (and even that is not a certainty). Fighting about how to create a better future is what parties do, and the party system is the main realm in which parties communicate their appeals to voters. Those visions take different forms depending on the preferences of the party. For clarity, political scientists group them into three main categories of appeals: charisma, clientelism, and program.

While *charisma* is notoriously resistant to a precise definition, it is found when individual leaders successfully argue that they (and they alone) have answers that satisfy their voters' deepest desires or resolve their greatest fears. Since charismatic parties depend on a personal connection between voters and the party leader, they often downplay political ideology and the specifics of how to solve the problem and instead emphasize the leader's ability to get things done. Many of these parties even bear the leader's name: "Palikot's Movement" and "Kukiz '15" in Poland, the "People's Party of Dan Diaconescu" in Romania, the "Homeland Movement of Miroslav Škoro" in Croatia, and many others.

The concept of clientelism refers to direct transfers of resources between parties and supporters, ranging from cash for votes to jobs for supporters to subsidies for particularly supportive regions, industries, or neighborhoods. Of course nearly all parties use public policy in one way or another to benefit their existing supporters and woo new ones (Poland's pro-Catholic PiS offers subsidies to larger families, for example), but in the most clientelist systems, the trade-off is even more direct and exclusive. Research by Herbert Kitschelt finds that parties in the south and east of the region have used the most clientelism, but even the less clientelist countries (those in the north and west of the region) used such tactics more than the Western Europe average (though not much more than in Greece, Italy, Portugal, and Spain).[35] Parties in the north and west tend to rely more on hidden "wholesale" clientelism at the national level in which firms receive lucrative government contracts in exchange for hidden cash payments that parties use to pay for expensive election campaigns. Parties in the south and east used these tactics too, but they also engaged more frequently in "retail" clientelism at the local level, such as the use of local community services to encourage turnout among favorable voting groups reported in Bulgaria and Romania and even the individual cash-for-votes transactions identified in analyses of Ukrainian elections.

While charisma and clientelism are important for specific parties, the strongest sources of overall competition still occur on the basis of political program (referred to in some countries as "party platform"). Some early observers expected that precommunist and communist legacies would sentence the region to unproductive struggles over personalities and payments, but many parties across the region quickly adopted specific policy positions and began to compete along internationally recognizable issue dimensions. Several common dimensions of competition began to emerge quite early in almost every country in the region:

- *Economics:* Emerging parties immediately clashed over whether markets or the government would exert the dominant influence over economic activity. The battles took many forms: whether to lower taxes to attract investment or raise taxes to provide more public services in education and health care; whether to focus on the well-being of pensioners or opportunities for students; whether to keep industries under government control or raise revenue by privatizing them to the highest bidder; and whether those bids must come from domestic buyers or from wealthier foreign investors with less commitment to the country's well-being. Social democratic and socialist parties across the region (including some Communist Party successors) were the most frequent promoters of government intervention in the economy, facing off against pro-market parties that used labels such as "civic," "free," or "liberal" (in the classical, small-government sense of the word).
- *Culture:* Clashes over cultural values varied from country to country to a greater degree than economic questions, but the cultural issues tended to revolve around respect for norms of religion and moral authority on issues such as abortion, homosexuality, and restoration of church property previously confiscated by communists. These values,

championed by parties with labels such as "Christian" or "People's," were initially stronger in countries with Roman Catholic traditions such as Poland and Slovenia, but similar emphasis has subsequently also emerged in parties in the Baltics and Romania and other countries across the region. In some countries, parties emerged on the opposite end of this dimension, with calls for a free choice of lifestyle and morals. In the absence of strong interest in ecological questions, it is on these questions of cultural freedom that the region's green parties often focused their efforts.

- *Ethnicity:* Most countries in Central and East Europe have a sizeable ethnic minority with a distinct language and culture. Minority groups in these countries are almost invariably created of one or more political parties that sought more rights and resources for the group.[36] The ethnic dimension sometimes also encouraged conflicts among parties of the ethnic majority about whether to demand majority dominance or to adopt a more conciliatory stance toward the minority. Nearly every country in the region produced at least one sizeable party that went beyond affirmation of the majority ethnic group to call for strong limitations on the rights of minority ethnic groups because of their alleged secessionist tendencies or criminality. Extreme-right parties also emphasize external threats to their ethnic group, such as a flood of migrants, a loss of ethnic identity due to globalization or EU rules, or mistreatment of people from the same ethnic group living in neighboring countries. These extreme-right parties accuse other parties of being complacent—or even complicit—in the ethnic group's destruction. Although such extreme-right parties ("nationalist" constitutes yet another meaning of "right" in the region) have appeared across the region—from "Attack" in Bulgaria to "All for Latvia!"—their direct role in politics has rarely been pivotal except in Serbia, Croatia, and Bosnia-Herzegovina in the 1990s. However, larger parties with slightly more diluted ethnic majoritarianism have led recent governments in Poland, Slovakia, Hungary, Croatia, and Serbia.

Party competition on these three dimensions has come to be almost as important in Central and East Europe as in Western Europe, and recent research finds that the amount of voting based on programmatic positions in the East is rising to approach levels in the West.[37] In other ways, however, Central and East European competition is different. Whereas in Western democracies, a preference for higher taxes and spending usually aligns with a more open approach to cultural issues, this connection has been almost wholly absent in Central and East European countries such as Slovakia. It has actually been reversed in others such as Hungary, Poland, Romania, and Bulgaria, where those who want more government involvement in the economy may also seek a much stronger government role in affirming morals and national identity. This variation, in turn, has blurred the region's common political labels so that a party that supports more welfare spending and opposes gay marriage might call itself either "left" (as in Slovakia) or "right" (as in Poland and Hungary).[38]

Furthermore, although economic, cultural, and ethnic issues played the most important role, parties also fought about issues that have been far less common in Western Europe or have manifested themselves in different ways:

- *Democracy:* Nearly all parties in the region have claimed to support "democracy," but parties have still sometimes disagreed about what the term means. Some see democracy as entirely consistent with significant power in the firm hand of a charismatic leader who can put restrictions on rival branches of government, opposition parties, or public protest in order to preserve a higher goal such as public order, national unity, or moral cultural values. Such conflicts led to near collapses of democracy in Slovakia, Croatia, and Serbia in the 1990s and Ukraine in the 2000s. Related conflicts have persisted in various forms in Montenegro, North Macedonia, Hungary, and Poland, where governments have taken steps to weaken or subordinate potential sources of accountability such as courts, oversight agencies, and the mass media. The conflicts in Hungary and Poland are particularly worrisome because these countries, once exemplars of democracy in the region, have begun to see a political sorting of the population into those who are willing to tolerate a firmer political hand and those who are not. As long as advocates of the strong hand hold a parliamentary majority capable of constitutional change, the democratic system remains at risk.

- *Corruption:* The use of state resources for private gain has become a major issue in Central and East European politics, but corruption does not follow the ordinary rules of issue competition. Parties in power cannot easily defend the corruption that may have happened on their watch (and few parties that have served in government have avoided major corruption scandals). So they try instead to talk about their experience or redirect public attention to other issues where they can make stronger claims. On the other side stand antiestablishment parties—often newly created, with assertive, clever marketing and celebrity leaders from outside the political realm—that identify corruption as the single most important issue and argue that there is no difference between any of the existing parties, all of which should be replaced.

The debates over democracy and corruption are closely related to the often-used but rarely clear idea of *populism*. The subject is difficult to discuss because populism has developed many overlapping and contradictory meanings over recent decades and often becomes a slur used to describe the unexpected success of an opponent (we are "popu*lar*" but they are "popu*list*"). If populism still has any meaning, it involves the sweeping rejection of elites on behalf of virtuous ordinary people.[39] Extreme-right parties in particular often attack the entire political class as insufficiently committed to the majority ethnic group, and they can be appropriately labeled as populist, but not all parties that use populist messages can be considered extreme right. The antielite and anticorruption messages of populism do not necessarily require attacks on immigrants or minorities. Many new parties in Central and East Europe call for a thorough housecleaning but do not offer many details on policy positions, something that is readily apparent even in the new parties' names: "For Latvia from the Heart," "Party of National Resurrection" (Lithuania), "Alliance of Dissatisfied Citizens" (Czech Republic), "Ordinary People" (Slovakia), "Positive Slovenia," "Bridge" (Croatia), "Save Romania Union," and "No Such State" (Bulgaria).[40] Populist messages, however, often jump quickly from new parties to even newer ones, because these parties have unusually short life spans. The closer these parties get to power, the more fragile they become, since once in office they often prove to be just as corrupt as the parties they railed against, leaving them little to campaign on in the next election. Unless they shift their emphasis to one of the other programmatic issues, they find it hard to keep voters.

Structure: How Do Parties Organize and Build Relationships with Voters?

Relationships between parties and voters depend not only on parties' issue positions but also on how parties organize themselves to draw in potential supporters. As with civil society, the organizational structures in Central and East European parties are somewhat weaker than those of Western Europe, but the lower average levels of membership and member activity conceal wide variation. Parties in Central and East Europe follow every possible organizational style, from the deep, extensive organization of former communist parties (carried over from when they were in power) to the ephemeral webs of social media and celebrity marketing that characterize some newer party efforts. These organizational methods are not all created equal. The lightweight celebrity and social media method offers a recipe for short-term electoral success, but this usually only works once or twice, and according to a long-term study by Margit Tavits, a party's long-term survival and sustained influence is still greatest if it has a more traditional organization with paid employees, office space, and frequent membership activities.[41] Some new parties have begun to understand the advantages of organization "on the ground" but have then found that they cannot build such structures without diverting their already strained human and financial resources away from the difficult work of becoming an effective party in parliament or government. Many of these parties pay the price in the next election and find themselves replaced by even newer parties that then face the same dilemma.[42]

Even parties that have succeeded in establishing deeper societal roots have not necessarily followed expected patterns. Traditional ideas of "class" voting—laborers voting for left-wing parties, for example—have remained weak since the fall of communism despite increasing social inequalities, but parties have found other ties that can connect them to social groups. Ethnic voting patterns in particular are so strong that nearly all members of minority populations vote for ethnically defined parties such as the "Democratic Union for Integration" supported by ethnic Albanians in North Macedonia, the "Movement for Rights and Freedoms" supported by ethnic Turks in Bulgaria, and various parties supported by ethnic Hungarians in Romania and Slovakia and by ethnic Russians in the Baltics. Religious patterns also shape party support (especially in Roman Catholic countries) because frequent churchgoers give strong support to parties with clear positions on cultural morality, but many of the parties embracing the "Christian Democratic" label have declined in importance as the religious share of the population has declined. Major differences in party choice have also emerged between younger city dwellers with high education and potential for advancement who support parties such as Slovakia's "Freedom and Solidarity" or Slovenia's "Party of the Modern Center" versus older voters in the countryside with fewer opportunities who support parties such as Poland's "Law and Justice" and the Croatian Democratic Union.

Of course many citizens in the region do not become voters at all. Whether in elections for local governments, national legislatures, or the European Parliament, the countries of Central and East Europe tend to fall in the bottom half of Europe's voter turnout rankings. Voter mobilization remains weak in part because the region has produced few political parties with strong organization, and only a small fraction of these have established robust ties with social groups. Having lived through the political fabrications of the late communist era and seen politicians enrich themselves in the early democratic era, many voters became skeptical of the entire political system and tended to stay away from politics (though they were occasionally lured back for a charismatic outsider who later proved to be just as tarnished as the rest).

Impact: How Do Political Parties Turn Values and Votes into Policy?

The main way that parties shape their surroundings is by winning elections and using their power to determine government policy. The question of where to focus their electoral efforts is made easier by the fact that almost all the constitutions of the region create centralized, parliamentary systems of government. This means that political power in the region rests mainly in national-level legislatures and in prime ministers and cabinets that are chosen by the parliament and that serve only as long as they can maintain parliamentary support.[43] Furthermore, since proportional representation means that few parties win majorities in parliament, prime ministers are usually forced to depend on coalitions of several parties that have agreed to work together. The impact of a party thus depends in part on its ability to work with other parties while at the same time maintaining its own internal unity.

Coalitions are difficult work, and finding appropriate partners for long-run cooperation is difficult. Most of the region's coalitions have shared values on at least one of the major dimensions, whether economic, cultural, or national, while differing on others. No combination is easy, but some governments have found common cause or pliant partners that received support for specific issues: in Hungary, for example, the nominally left-leaning Hungarian Socialist Party could agree with the culturally liberal Free Democrats on morality issues (and some economic ones), while in Poland the pro-market Civic Platform was willing to accept some of the rural agricultural priorities of the Polish Peasants' Party. The lure of power has even brought bitter enemies into the same government, such as the decision of the Slovak National Party to join with the Bridge party of ethnic Hungarians in Slovakia. These combinations face constant challenges. Voters often punish parties for their willingness to make compromises: both the Slovak National Party and Bridge, for example, shrank to half their previous size in the election after their coalition. Furthermore, political events and shifts in the importance of political issues can often put stress on coalition relationships, as can scandals and other factors such as the illness or death of a party leader. Governments in the region last on average only about two years before a crisis in cooperation among parties leads to a new prime minister, a new coalition, or new elections that shuffle the parliament and cause the whole process of coalition building to start over again.[44]

Civil Society and Political Parties Looking Forward

Communism in Central and East Europe lasted four decades. Postcommunism is rapidly approaching the same age. Whether it lives longer than its predecessor will depend in no small part on the functioning of civil society and political parties. At the moment, those two intertwined sectors look moderately healthy in most of the region. Civil society organizations and parties have not slavishly imitated their counterparts in Western Europe, not in form, density, or strength, but in most cases, they bear a fair resemblance to the institutions of those countries around the world that have succeeded in keeping democracy alive.

But that does not mean there is no reason for concern. Some of the dangers are immediately familiar, most notably the Hungarian example of what happens when one organization—in this case a political party—becomes both strong and ambitious enough to force its rivals in the party system and civil society into submission. Even firewall civil society and determined opposition parties may not be enough to prevent the return of chaos or autocracy (especially when democracy is actively undermined by powerful foreign interests such as Russia). However, strong civil society and robust party competition are still the best hope for democracy.

Other challenges stem not from the region's history or geography but from new social and economic trends in a rapidly changing world. Civil societies and parties reemerged in Central and East Europe just as the world was rushing to an entirely new model of communication and organization that was both more flexible and more fragile. In older democracies, these innovations faced inertia from well-entrenched organizations, but in Central and East Europe, the fall of communism meant that strong institutions had little time to emerge. The resulting loose organization of civil society and rapid turnover of political parties may not pose an immediate threat to democracy. However, the region must figure out how to ensure stability and plan for the future despite the existence of organizations that themselves do not expect to survive the next funding cycle or the next election. Although these organizational decisions by civil society groups and political parties lack the drama of 1989's revolutions, they will nevertheless be critical in determining whether (and in what form) democracy in Central and East Europe survives into its fifth decade.

Study Questions

1. What functions do civil society and political parties have in common? How are they different?
2. How have civil society organizations changed from their role under communist rule to their role in the political change of the 1990s to their role in today's democracy?
3. How do civil society organizations differ geographically across Central and East Europe? Which countries stand out as different from their neighbors, and what is different about them?
4. How do electoral laws and electoral systems shape what political parties are like in Central and East Europe?
5. What kinds of value conflicts shape the competition among political parties in Central and East Europe? How do these differ from (or resemble) the competition in your own country?

Suggested Readings

Anheier, Helmut K., and Lisa Carlson. *The Civil Society Diamond: A Primer.* CIVICUS: World Alliance for Citizen Participation, 2001. http://www.civicus.org/view/media/CDMethodologyPrimer2.pdf.

Berglund, Sten, Joakim Ekman, Kevin Deegan-Krause, and Terje Knutsen. *The Handbook of Political Change in Eastern Europe.* 3rd ed. Cheltenham, UK: Edward Elgar, 2013.

Bernhard, Michael. "What Do We Know about Civil Society and Regime Change Thirty Years after 1989?" *East European Politics*, Early view, 2020. https://www.tandfonline.com/doi/full/10.1080/21599165.2020.1787160.

Ekiert, Grzegorz, Jan Kubik, and Michal Wenzel. "Civil Society and Three Dimensions of Inequality in Post-1989 Poland." *Comparative Politics* 49 (April 2017): 331–50.

Foa, Roberto Stefan, and Grzegorz Ekiert. "The Weakness of Postcommunist Civil Society Reassessed." *European Journal of Political Research* 56 (2017): 419–39.

Haughton, Tim, and Kevin Deegan-Krause. *The New Party Challenge: Changing Cycles of Party Birth and Death in Central Europe and Beyond.* Oxford: Oxford University Press, 2020.

Howard, Marc Morjé. *The Weakness of Civil Society in Post-Communist Europe.* Cambridge: Cambridge University Press, 2003.

Mudde, Cas, and Cristobal Rovira Kaltwasser. *Populism: A Very Short Introduction.* Oxford: Oxford University Press, 2017.

Post, Robert C., and Nancy L. Rosenblum, eds. *Civil Society and Government.* Princeton, NJ: Princeton University Press, 2001.

United States Agency for International Development (USAID). *The 2019 Civil Society Organization Sustainability Index for Central and Eastern Europe and Eurasia.* 23rd ed. 2015. https://www.fhi360.org/sites/default/files/media/documents/resource-csosi-2019-report-europe-eurasia.pdf.

Ware, Alan. *Political Parties and Party Systems.* Oxford: Oxford University Press, 1996.

Websites

Varieties of Democracy (V-Dem) Project: https://www.v-dem.net
Party Systems and Governments Observatory: https://whogoverns.eu
Political Data Yearbook Interactive: http://www.politicaldatayearbook.com

Notes

1. Helmut K. Anheier and Lisa Carlson, *The Civil Society Diamond: A Primer*, CIVICUS: World Alliance for Citizen Participation, 2001, 3, http://www.civicus.org/view/media/CDMethodologyPrimer2.pdf.

2. Roberto Stefan Foa and Grzegorz Ekiert, "The Weakness of Post-Communist Civil Society Reassessed," *European Journal of Political Research* 56 (2017): 421.

3. Alan Ware, *Political Parties and Party Systems* (Oxford: Oxford University Press, 1996), 5.

4. Nancy L. Rosenblum, "Primus Inter Pares: Political Parties and Civil Society," *Chicago Kent Law Review* 75, no. 2 (2000): 493–529, http://scholarship.kentlaw.iit.edu/cklawreview/vol75/iss2/9.

5. Grzegorz Ekiert, Jan Kubik, and Michal Wenzel, "Civil Society and Three Dimensions of Inequality in Post-1989 Poland," *Comparative Politics* 49 (April 2017): 335.

6. See Michael Bernhard, "What Do We Know about Civil Society and Regime Change Thirty Years after 1989?," *East European Politics*, Early view, 2020, 1.

7. Bernhard, "What Do We Know?," 5.

8. See Michael Coppedge et al., "V-Dem [Country-Year/Country-Date] Dataset v7.1," Varieties of Democracy (V-Dem) Project, 2017. Measurements conducted by the international

nongovernmental organization Civicus and the United States Agency for International Development (USAID) tell similar stories.

9. In a UN-negotiated agreement with Greece, the Republic of Macedonia agreed in June 2018 to change its name to the Republic of North Macedonia.

10. Anheir and Carlson, *The Civil Society Diamond*, 6.

11. See Robert C. Post and Nancy L. Rosenblum, eds., *Civil Society and Government* (Princeton, NJ: Princeton University Press, 2001), 8–12.

12. United States Agency for International Development (USAID), *The 2015 CSO Sustainability Index for Central and East Europe and Eurasia*, 2015, https://www.usaid.gov/sites/default/files/doc uments/1861/Europe_Eurasia_CSOSIReport_2015_Update8-29-16.pdf.

13. János Kornai, "Hungary's U-Turn," *Capitalism and Society* 10, no. 1 (2015): 6, http://kor nai-janos.hu/Kornai2015-Hungarys_U-turn.pdf.

14. Marc Morjé Howard, *The Weakness of Civil Society in Post-Communist Europe* (Cambridge: Cambridge University Press, 2003), 10.

15. Ekiert, Kubik, and Wenzel, "Inequality in Post-1989 Poland," 339.

16. Ekiert, Kubik, and Wenzel, "Inequality in Post-1989 Poland," 339.

17. Bernhard, "What Do We Know?," 1.

18. Simone Chambers and Jeffrey Kopstein, "Bad Civil Society," *Political Theory* 29, no. 6 (2001): 844.

19. USAID, *The 2015 CSO Sustainability Index*.

20. Ekiert, Kubik, and Wenzel, "Inequality in Post-1989 Poland," 334.

21. Ekiert, Kubik, and Wenzel, "Inequality in Post-1989 Poland," 333.

22. Ekiert, Kubik, and Wenzel, "Inequality in Post-1989 Poland," 335.

23. Lester M. Salamon, S. Wojciech Sokolowski, Megan A. Haddock, and Helen S. Tice, *The State of Global Civil Society and Volunteering* (Baltimore, MD: Johns Hopkins University Center for Civil Society Studies, 2013), 2–3.

24. Christine Mahoney and Michael J. Beckstrand, "Following the Money: European Union Funding of Civil Society Organizations," *Journal of Common Market Studies* 49, no. 6 (2011): 1339.

25. Gazela Pudar Draško, Irena Fiket, and Jelena Vasiljević, "Big Dreams and Small Steps: Comparative Perspectives on Social Movements' Struggle for Democracy in Serbia and North Macedonia," *Southeast European and Black Sea Studies* 20, no. 1 (2020): 199–219.

26. World Economic Forum, *The Future Role of Civil Society, 2013*, 9, http://www3.weforum .org/docs/WEF_FutureRoleCivilSociety_Report_2013.pdf.

27. USAID, *The 2015 CSO Sustainability Index*.

28. Viktor Orbán, "Prime Minister Viktor Orbán's Speech at the 25th Bálványos Summer Free University and Student Camp," website of the Hungarian Government, 2015, http://www .kormany.hu/en/the-prime-minister/the-prime-minister-s-speeches/prime-ministerviktor-orban-s -speech-at-the-25th-balvanyos-summer-free-university-and-student-camp.

29. Bernhard, "What Do We Know?," 16.

30. Much of the work in this section derives from a chapter written by the author with Zsolt Enyedi on "Voters and Parties in Eastern Europe" for Adam Fagan and Petr Kopecký, eds., *The Routledge Handbook of East European Politics* (London: Routledge, 2017).

31. Fragmentation is tied to the number of parties, but it is not just of a matter of counting the number of parties on the ballot. The formula for fragmentation weighs both the number and size of parties so that a few big parties will register low fragmentation while many small parties will register high fragmentation, and a mix will register a level in between.

32. Marijn van Klingeren, Margarita Orozco, Joost van Spanje, and Claes de Vreese, "Party Financing and Referendum Campaigns in EU States, European Parliament Directorate-General

for Internal Policies," http://www.europarl.europa.eu/RegData/etudes/STUD/2015/519217/IPO L_ STU(2015)519217_ EN.pdf.

33. Fernando Casal Bértoa and Ingrid van Biezen, eds., *The Regulation of Post-Communist Party Politics* (London: Routledge, 2018).

34. Pippa Norris and Max Grömping, "Populist Threats to Electoral Integrity: The Year in Elections 2016–2017," Electoral Integrity Project, 31–35, https://www.electoralintegrityproject .com/data.

35. Herbert Kitschelt, "Clientelism and Party Competition" (lecture delivered at Central European University, March 8, 2017), https://sites.duke.edu/democracylinkage/files/2014/12/2.5 .Kitschelt.pdf.

36. Some countries such as Poland, Croatia, Romania, Slovenia, and Serbia formally reserve a small number of seats for representatives of small ethnic minorities that otherwise might not be able to pass the parliamentary threshold, though these often side with the parliamentary majority in the hope of gaining tangible benefits for the group.

37. Robert Rohrschneider and Stephen Whitefield, *The Strain of Representation* (Cambridge: Cambridge University Press, 2012).

38. Jan Rovny and Erica Edwards, "Struggle over Dimensionality: Party Competition in Western and Eastern Europe," *East European Politics & Societies* 26, no. 1 (2012): 56–74.

39. Cas Mudde and Cristobal Rovira Kaltwasser, *Populism: A Very Short Introduction* (Oxford: Oxford University Press, 2017).

40. A similar phenomenon has subsequently had a profound effect on political competition in Italy (the Five Star Movement), Spain (We Can and Citizens), Greece (The River), and France, as well as in Asia, Latin America, and the United States.

41. Margit Tavits, *Post-Communist Democracies and Party Organization* (New York: Cambridge University Press, 2013).

42. Tim Haughton and Kevin Deegan-Krause, "Hurricane Season: Systems of Instability in Central and East European Party Politics," *Eastern European Politics and Societies* 29, no. 1 (2005): 61–80.

43. Although many countries in the region have popularly elected presidents, most of those presidents have relatively weak positions in the overall political system.

44. Courtney Ryals Conrad and Sona N. Golder, "Measuring Government Duration and Stability in Central Eastern European Democracies," *European Journal of Political Research* 49 (2010): 119–50.

CHAPTER 5

Economic Reforms and Trends

Sharon Fisher

The economies of Central and East Europe have experienced dramatic changes since the fall of communism, bringing considerable benefits to the countries' populations. While most of the region's citizens were unable to travel freely under communism, today they can study, work, and take holidays outside of their own countries with few limitations. Change has also been apparent on the enterprise front. In 1989, most firms in the region were state run, and the reliance on trade with the Soviet bloc meant that even countries that avoided shortages of goods had a limited selection of products for sale. Today, private shops are flooded with goods from around the world, and no one has to stand in line to buy basic necessities.

Despite progress in many areas, not everyone has gained from the shift to capitalism. While full employment was a key component of the communist system, the changes have brought job losses and uncertainty, with a disproportionate impact on older, less educated, and less flexible workers. Although entry to the European Union (EU) has triggered improvements in many areas, the region's economies are still well below the EU average in terms of gross domestic product (GDP) per capita levels. The crises that have hit Europe and the world since 2008 (the global economic crisis, the Eurozone debt drama, and the COVID-19 pandemic) have brought further hardship.

The eight countries that joined the EU in May 2004 (Poland, Czechia, Hungary, Slovakia, Slovenia, Estonia, Latvia, and Lithuania) are viewed as Central and East Europe's most advanced economies. All eight have reported significant economic growth since 1990 and have surpassed GDP per capita levels seen in West Europe's weakest economy (Greece). Several have overcome Portugal. The economic challenges facing these countries tend to be similar to those in Western Europe, as they struggle to improve international competitiveness and promote sustainable long-term growth amid aging and declining populations. Nevertheless, there have been significant societal consequences, and progress has not been as rapid as policy makers and populations had hoped at the time of EU accession. Job losses, reduction in welfare supports, and low pensions have contributed to rising poverty among certain segments of the population as the "losers" of the transition struggle to adjust. Even among the eight leading countries, major differences remain in terms of economic development and income levels.

Further behind the 2004 EU entrants are the countries that joined in 2007–2013 (Bulgaria, Romania, and Croatia), the six Western Balkan economies (Serbia, Montenegro, Albania, North Macedonia, Bosnia and Herzegovina, and Kosovo), and Ukraine. These countries have been slower and less consistent in implementing economic reforms, which were often introduced under pressure from outside actors such as the International Monetary Fund (IMF) or the EU. As a result, EU integration has moved ahead at a slower pace, and most have struggled with high rates of unemployment and poverty. Several of the laggards are still viewed as lacking a functioning market economy, which is a key requirement for EU membership. Meeting that goal requires a liberalization of prices and trade, the removal of significant barriers to market entry and exit, regulation and enforcement of property rights, macroeconomic stability (including inflation and sustainable public finances and external accounts), a well-developed financial sector, and a broad consensus on the essentials of economic policy.

In much of the region, the path toward market economies has not been a linear one. Some countries previously seen as behind have caught up, while others once viewed as leaders have slipped backward. The latter tendency has been especially pronounced amid the wave of populism that has struck since the 2008–2009 global financial crisis. Appealing to those who have suffered amid the postcommunist transition, illiberal governments have pushed forward economic policies aimed at shoring up support among their base, without regard for the broader population. Euroskepticism has grown, and external actors such as Russia and China have moved in to increase their influence in the region, particularly in the Western Balkans, but also in EU member states such as Hungary.

Throughout Central and East Europe, the economies continue to carry vestiges of the past. Wages tend to be considerably lower than in West Europe, helping to boost foreign direct investment (FDI), but at the same time triggering disillusion among the local population. Most countries in the region are still plagued by high levels of corruption, which is also a remnant of the communist past. Low salaries and living standards, limited opportunities for personal and professional development, and weak rule of law have contributed to high rates of external migration in much of Central and East Europe, damaging the region's long-term growth prospects.

Looking Back

In order to make sense of the similarities and differences across Central and East Europe today, it is helpful to look back to understand how these economic systems have evolved since the fall of communism in the period between 1989 and 1991. After all, transforming the region's economies was probably the most complicated aspect of the transition process. When the reforms began, there was no single model for how new market economies should be constructed. The postcommunist transitions were unprecedented in the scope of the changes required. Unlike the transitions in Latin America and elsewhere in the world, there was no foundational market economy on which to build. The existing centrally planned economies had to be dismantled as capitalist institutions and practices were developed. Reforms often happened in a rather haphazard way, and most knowledge of the transition process was formed after the fact. Across the region, advisers from organizations such as the IMF provided technical assistance to devise macroeconomic stabilization programs based largely on methods that were applied in developing countries. Even as governments implemented these programs, it was unclear how effective they would be.

There were significant variations in the transition path taken by Central and East European countries, both in the early years of the shift from communism and more recently. Some countries (for example, the Czech Republic) gained international recognition for certain reforms (such as privatization) but were laggards in other areas (such as banking reform). Some that initially appeared to be on a rapid path toward a market economy eventually slowed down (most notably, Slovenia), while the opposite occurred in other cases (such as Slovakia). In most countries, foreign observers perceived the success of reforms much differently than the domestic population did, and reformist politicians often suffered in elections, triggering interruptions in the reform process.

Why were some countries faster than others in shifting toward a market economy? Studies have shown that initial conditions were one of the most important factors in determining the economic success of individual countries.[1] Some countries had a head start in the transition, having begun reforms prior to 1989, as the communist economic system began to falter. Indeed, Hungary introduced limited market reforms through its so-called goulash communism in 1968, giving enterprises more autonomy and liberalizing prices on certain goods. In Poland, after several failed attempts, market reforms similar to those in Hungary were begun a final time in 1982. The Yugoslav regime—which was already more liberal and less plan oriented than other countries in the region—also introduced extensive market-oriented reforms in the late 1980s. Although the other Yugoslav successor countries were set back on the transition path by the wars of the 1990s, Slovenia was able to move ahead. Most other regimes in Central and East Europe were reluctant to make any significant changes to economic policy during the communist era, even after Mikhail Gorbachev launched partial reforms in the USSR during the late 1980s. Indeed, Czechoslovakia, East Germany, Bulgaria, Romania, and Albania maintained a hard-line economic stance until the fall of communism in 1989.

Even among the countries that launched reforms prior to 1989, most of the region was in poor economic shape by the end of the communist era amid falling output, profound shortages of consumer goods, accelerating inflation rates, widening current-account and budget deficits, and rising foreign debt. During the last years of the communist era, the only relative "success stories" were Hungary and Czechoslovakia. Czechoslovakia managed to steer clear of major imbalances despite the hard-line approach of its communist system. Meanwhile, Hungary had transformed itself into a socialist market economy while maintaining some degree of economic balance, although foreign debt did rise substantially. Both countries avoided the debilitating shortages that plagued other economies in the region.[2]

In addition to initial conditions, geography has also played a crucial role. The region's more successful reformers were generally those with close proximity to Western markets, benefiting from historical traditions and the ease of trade and investment ties with the EU. Geographic proximity made it easier to attract FDI and turn from trade with the former Soviet Union to West Europe. Czechia, which borders both Germany and Austria, has a strong historical manufacturing tradition, an advantage that has remained clear up to the present. Meanwhile, despite being substantially behind the Central European countries at the end of the communist era, the three Baltic states benefited in the transition period from cooperation with their Nordic neighbors. On the other hand, the countries that were further from Western markets often had a more difficult economic transition, especially when they experienced the bulk of their industrialization during the communist era, with production aimed at the Soviet bloc.

The policy approach of the first postcommunist governments served as another key factor determining the success or failure of the economic transition. According to the European Bank for Reconstruction and Development, the presence of a noncommunist government in the initial transition period is strongly correlated with the character of reforms in subsequent years.[3] Communists or former communists initially remained in control in Bulgaria, Romania, Ukraine, and Albania but were ousted in Poland, Hungary, Czechoslovakia, and the three Baltic states. As a result, reforms were considerably faster in the latter countries in the early 1990s, making it unsurprising that they were in the first wave of countries to join the EU in 2004.

Frequent changes in government, often brought on by popular dissatisfaction with how the economic reforms worked, contributed to a lack of continuity in the reform process throughout the region. Nevertheless, once the initial pace was set, successive governments generally continued with the reform process, even when left-wing parties came to power, as occurred in Poland in 1993 and Hungary in 1994. By the middle to late 1990s, prospects for EU accession also helped push countries along on the reform path, at least in Central Europe.

This chapter provides an account of key aspects of the transformations that Central and East European countries underwent to create market economies after the collapse of communism and the challenges they are facing today. Many elements of this evolution have been shared across the region, yet the trajectories have diverged due to differences in both structural conditions (including domestic characteristics and geopolitical position) and the decisions that specific political elites made in these countries. In looking at the transition path, this chapter starts by discussing *macroeconomic stabilization* programs, which are monetary and fiscal policies aimed at reducing volatility and paving the way for the initial recovery. These were followed by *structural reforms*, aimed at building the institutions needed to sustain the market economy and promote long-term growth. Next comes a discussion of *European integration*, the lure of which provided a key impetus during the transformation process that other developing regions of the world have lacked. The EU's importance cannot be overestimated, offering much-needed investment and development assistance, export markets, and reform incentives. During the communist

Table 5.1. Key Aspects of Postcommunist Economic Transformation

Macroeconomic stabilization	Structural reforms	European integration
Price liberalization	Privatization	Attracting FDI
Restricting monetary policy	"Right-sizing" government	Adopting the euro
Balancing fiscal budgets	Taxation reform	
Currency convertibility and exchange rate regimes	Pension reform	
Foreign trade liberalization	Labor market reform	

era, most Central and East European countries were part of the Soviet-dominated Council for Mutual Economic Assistance (CMEA) trading bloc, and EU demand was especially important as exports to the Soviet Union collapsed. The chapter concludes with a brief look at the how the crises that have hit Europe since 2008 have impacted the economies of Central and Eastern Europe, followed by current challenges facing the region, such as poverty, corruption, and aging populations.

Macroeconomic Stabilization

The key debates on macroeconomic stabilization focused not on what needed to be done but rather on how to sequence and pace the reforms. In terms of speed, reformers were divided into proponents of "shock therapy" (advocated in Poland) versus "gradualism" (an approach taken in countries such as Ukraine). The gradualists argued for relatively lax monetary and fiscal policies and a slower transfer of assets from the state to the private sector, with the aim of protecting the population from the social consequences of reforms. With time, it became clear that none of the countries that consistently advocated a gradual approach were successful reformers. Indeed, the speed and effectiveness of the initial macroeconomic stabilization process set the countries on a differentiated path that closely corresponded with the speed of European integration.

The issue of reform sequencing also provoked controversy. Some policy makers argued that sufficient competition and proper market institutions were needed before prices were liberalized. Otherwise, firms with a monopoly in a particular industry could raise prices well above costs, hurting domestic consumers. In the stabilization package, there was also considerable debate over the extent of the currency devaluation and how much interest rates should be shifted. Devaluation helped to improve external trade balances, allowing for international stabilization. Nonetheless, it also raised the price of imports of consumer and industrial goods, thereby contributing to higher inflation. The small- or medium-sized open economies in Central and East Europe were particularly vulnerable to these cross-pressures. Even countries like Czechoslovakia, which had relatively stable and positive initial macroeconomic conditions at the outset, had to deal with the inflationary impact of price liberalization and the effects of the collapse of trade with the USSR.

In the transition process, it is important to distinguish between first- and second-stage macroeconomic stabilization programs. The first stage occurred from 1990 to 1993 during the early part of the postcommunist transition. Some countries that started out well later showed signs of imbalance and had to implement second-stage programs. This happened in Hungary in 1995 with the Bokros Plan, as well as in the Czech Republic (1997–1999), Slovakia (1998–2000), and Poland (2001). The justification for second-stage stabilization programs differed depending on the country, resulting in the implementation of a variety of structural reforms.[4]

Price Liberalization

Price liberalization was one of the key elements of the macroeconomic stabilization programs. Under communism, prices were regulated, and fixed prices at both the wholesale and retail levels meant that open inflation was never a problem. Economic policy involved central planning, with a focus on quantity rather than on quality or profit. The pricing system encouraged an intentional lowering of quality by producers and contributed to shortages of consumer goods. Without market pricing, it was difficult for central planners to determine the relative value of different goods and services, meaning that many products that were valued by consumers were underproduced.

Among the countries that launched reforms before 1989, only Hungary broadly liberalized prices under the communist regime. Elsewhere in Central Europe, the "big bang" approach to price liberalization was used after the fall of communism. Poland took the lead in January 1990, and Czechoslovakia followed a year later. When "big bangs" happened, market forces took hold, allowing prices of consumer durables and nonfood items to be set according to supply and demand. Buyers demand less of a particular good as prices increase, while shortages disappear since higher prices trigger a rise in supply. Politicians and consumers were often reluctant to give up fixed prices on essentials such as food (particularly bread and meat) and gasoline because such a step would impoverish a population that expected economic gains under the new capitalist system. In the end, many governments dropped price controls only because of their inability to continue providing subsidies. In most Central and East European countries, rents, public transport, and utilities remained under state control throughout the 1990s and even into the first decade of the twenty-first century. Prices were often set below the real costs because price hikes were seen as politically risky.

Price liberalization caused inflation to surge throughout Central and East Europe in the initial transition years. Most countries experienced triple- or quadruple-digit price growth after the fall of communism, wiping out savings and putting pressure on consumers. Those increases were largely a result of filling out the imbalances from the previous regime, particularly where countries printed money to cover budgetary expenditures. The former Czechoslovakia, where the state maintained a balanced budget under communism, had the smallest increase in inflation following the launch of price liberalization, and inflation never reached triple digits. In contrast, countries such as Ukraine and rump Yugoslavia, where macroeconomic stabilization programs initially failed, suffered from hyperinflation.

Several key lessons regarding price liberalization can be drawn from the region's postcommunist transitions. First, populations willingly accepted price deregulation when it was accompanied by a change in the system. In fact, nowhere in the region did price liberalizations stir widespread protest.[5] Second, the initial liberalization had to be as comprehensive as possible. Any additional deregulation of prices proved to be extremely complicated, spurring passionate public debates and broad opposition. Finally, high levels of inflation are incompatible with economic growth. Countries that did not experience hyperinflation were able to moderate their declines in GDP during the early transition years. In contrast, Ukraine and Serbia have ranked among the region's weakest performers in terms of economic growth since 1990.

Restricting Monetary Policy

The liberalization of prices in Central and East Europe usually involved higher increases in inflation than were initially expected. This inflation resulted in demands for the region's

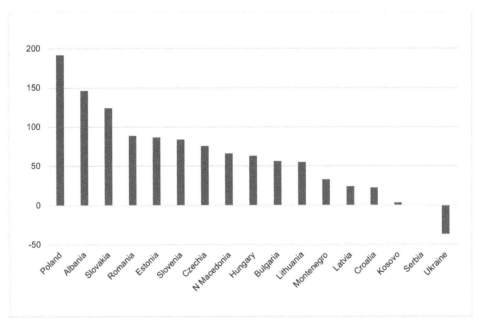

Figure 5.1.   Cumulative GDP Growth in Central and East Europe. (Sharon Fisher). *Source:* United Nations 2020.

central banks to loosen monetary policy through lower interest rates. Many countries in the region, in fact, maintained low interest rates in the initial transition years. This discouraged savings and contributed to a low level of trust in local currencies. Although this negatively affected average citizens, it benefited politically connected individuals because they could obtain loans at low real interest rates.

With the aim of keeping inflation down, monetary authorities eventually shifted from expanding the money supply to restricting it. Their policies involved, instead, a slow growth in the money supply, even a negative growth in real terms. These policies were also accompanied by large increases in interest rates to make them higher than the rate of inflation. In Bulgaria, for example, the policy interest rate reached as high as 300 percent. This policy of high interest rates discouraged domestic borrowing and encouraged saving and investment. Perhaps more important was the impact high interest rates had in reducing risky lending practices. In each country's transition, monetary authorities had to find a balance between the two extremes of high versus low interest rates to support economic growth. Since the mid-2010s, policy interest rates have been low in most Central European and Western Balkan countries, but Ukraine has been forced to keep rates elevated due to stubbornly high inflation.

Balancing Fiscal Budgets

While monetary policy is controlled by central banks, fiscal policy is the main tool used by governments to influence economic conditions. Because the printing of money provides a key source of financing for budget deficits, fiscal policy is closely linked to monetary policy as an important element in stabilizing economies undergoing transformation. The persistence of fiscal imbalances poses serious risks for the sustainability of long-term economic growth because it triggers higher inflation rates. Thus, a first step in the macroeconomic stabilization programs in Central and Eastern Europe was a dramatic reduction of fiscal deficits so that revenues and expenses in the state budget became more balanced. By reducing state expenditures and increasing revenues, the new elites sought to ensure that fiscal reforms would provide the necessary funds to sustain a radical stabilization program. Fiscal responsibility became a top criterion for receiving IMF financing and other credits from international financial markets. Governments in the region struggled to balance the demands of their constituents with the austere fiscal targets required by international financial institutions.

Initially, fiscal deficits were driven largely by high expenditures associated with the oversized public sector and the collapse of revenues due to production declines in the restructuring process. On the expenditure side, the first step transitional governments took was to eliminate consumer price subsidies, especially for basic food products. The second step involved cutting subsidies for state enterprises. This step proved much more difficult to implement because it contributed to higher levels of unemployment. As firms sought profitability, they typically laid off workers. Pressures for more state expenditures emerged through public demands for higher social spending in the form of social welfare programs and pensions. Most countries in the region maintained enterprise subsidies throughout the 1990s in at least a few key but inefficient sectors, including agriculture, mining, and energy. Eventually, direct subsidies were frequently replaced by indirect subsidies, with state companies getting cheap credits from state-owned banks.

Taxes typically provide the bulk of budget revenues, and an entirely new system was necessary as the economic transformation process moved forward. During the communist era, a "turnover tax" was utilized on a discretionary basis. Goods considered socially necessary were subsidized by negative tax rates. Under the new system, personal income and consumption taxes accounted for a larger share of total tax revenues, thereby taking the burden off enterprises and helping them maintain competitiveness. The first step was to replace the turnover tax with the value-added tax (VAT), a consumption tax levied at each stage of production based on the value added to the product at that stage, where the final consumer ultimately bears the tax burden. In the new system, VAT rates were typically around 20 percent, often with lower rates for necessities such as food and medicine.

The second important element in reforming the revenue side of the budget was the establishment of personal income taxes. Under communism, personal income taxes were insignificant. In the transition period, three alternative models were used: a social democratic approach with high progressive income taxes that went up to more than 50 percent of gross income for the wealthiest citizens (Hungary and Ukraine), a standard model with a progressive system taxing individuals between 12 and 40 percent of their income (Czechoslovakia), and the Baltic model (Estonia, Latvia) with a flat personal income tax—the same percentage for everyone.

The third step involved the establishment of a corporate tax system that was legislated rather than being subject to negotiations between managers and their government supervisors, as it had been during the communist era. Most countries initially chose to impose a flat profit tax of 30 to 35 percent.[6]

Another major concern of the transition countries was the need for an efficient and effective collection system. After all, since "taxes" were not really a part of the communist-era economy, there was no real infrastructure for tax collection and enforcement. Under communism, taxes were automatically transferred to the budget through the state-owned banking system. In the new regimes, there was a need for institutions, people, and funds to manage the new tax system. Most of the Central and East European countries were relatively successful in establishing a strong, relatively unitary revenue service. The countries of the Commonwealth of Independent States (CIS), which encompassed most of the post-Soviet countries, had more problems. In most cases, the introduction of the VAT proved successful in boosting revenue collection. With regard to personal income tax, the Baltic approach proved by far the most successful in terms of revenue collection because it was simple and easy to enforce. The progressive tax systems found elsewhere merely encouraged underreporting and avoidance. Second-stage tax reforms are discussed later in this chapter.

Currency Convertibility and Exchange Rate Regimes

Currency convertibility and the unification of exchange rates were important prerequisites for foreign trade liberalization. Because domestic prices were regulated nationally, communist regimes had no link between domestic and foreign prices. As a result, currencies were not convertible for international payments. An overvalued domestic currency provided little reason to export goods outside the region as long as countries did not have debts they needed to repay to foreign creditors. By the end of the communist era, some 60 to 75 percent of trade was conducted with other members of the CMEA trading bloc, and many of the goods produced were not competitive in the West.

Most former communist countries immediately adopted a fully convertible current account, allowing for trade in goods and services. In contrast, convertibility was introduced only gradually on capital accounts, which govern the transfer of financial assets. The Baltic states emerged in the forefront of the reforms aimed at bringing capital account convertibility.[7]

In regulating currencies, policy makers began the transition with an initial devaluation that accompanied the introduction of a stabilization program. While two or more different exchange rates had existed in communist systems, including the official and black market rates, this could not happen in economies that were joining the world economy. Thus a single, official exchange rate had to be established. The devaluation was introduced to improve trade imbalances by making imports more expensive and exports cheaper. After the initial devaluation, governments adopted one of four types of exchange rate regime: floating rates (in which the currency floats freely without intervention from the central bank), pegged rates (where the currency's value is fixed against that of another currency or basket of currencies to provide a nominal anchor), crawling pegs (a pegged exchange rate regime where the reference value is shifted at preestablished times), and currency boards (in which foreign exchange reserves are used to back the currency). While floating exchange rates gave countries more flexibility on the monetary policy front, some countries preferred currency boards or pegs. Over time, some countries switched from one approach to another, and managed floats (with occasional interventions when the currency shifts too rapidly) have been especially popular. Since 2007, five countries from the region have formally joined the Eurozone, as discussed further below.

Foreign Trade Liberalization

During the communist era, foreign trade was regulated by the CMEA trading bloc, established by the Soviet Union, Bulgaria, Czechoslovakia, Hungary, Poland, and Romania in 1949. The CMEA was formed in response to the US Marshall Plan's offer of economic aid to some of these countries (which the Soviet Union insisted they refuse). Within the CMEA (also known as Comecon), a system of international specialization was laid out so that different goods were produced in different parts of the region to meet Soviet needs (and also those of the bloc as a whole), particularly in the military sector. This policy ensured that no state could stand alone economically. It did not work like a common market; instead trade was negotiated and conducted bilaterally, with oversight by the Soviet Union.

The CMEA system was disbanded in January 1991. At that time, the USSR began demanding payment for raw materials in Western currencies and at world market prices. Thus the USSR signaled that it was no longer willing to subsidize the rest of the region by exporting hard goods and importing soft goods in exchange for political loyalty. Similarly, the Central and East European countries were no longer willing to accept political domination in exchange for Soviet subsidies. While many analysts initially thought that the CMEA's demise would significantly increase trade within the region by removing many of the impediments associated with the old structures, the opposite occurred. The collapse of demand in the Soviet Union caused sharp declines in exports.

For the Central and East European countries, the postcommunist transition required a major redirection of trade. These transitional economies needed to find export products that would be competitive on world markets in order to service their debts. Trade liberalization was carried out through a shift to tariffs, accompanied by reductions in tariff rates. This was reflected in the abolition of the many administrative restrictions on the import and export of industrial products from the old system. That shift had the advantage of making trade regulation more transparent and compatible with the General Agreement on Tariffs and Trade (GATT) and later the World Trade Organization (WTO). Trade liberalization began in manufacturing and gradually shifted to sensitive areas such as services and agricultural trade. The Central European countries and Estonia initially had the most success in the first phase of liberalization, introducing tariffs and reducing tariff rates in 1990 through 1991.

Trade liberalization was important for several reasons. Opening domestic markets to imported products from the West helped satisfy consumption-starved citizens. Moreover, trade liberalization pushed countries forward in their structural adjustment; given the small size of the domestic markets, competition in most countries could only happen from imports. External economic relationships also contributed to stabilizing the economy by forcing domestic inflation into line with international rates. Soviet/Russian trade with Central and Eastern Europe declined precipitously in 1990 and never recovered, as the region found new partners in Western Europe.

Transition Recessions and Recoveries

All Central and East European economies experienced steep recessions during the initial period of postcommunist restructuring, with declines in GDP ranging from about 15 to 70 percent between 1989 and 1993. As mentioned above, the countries that recovered most quickly from the recession generally had favorable initial conditions and managed to get inflation under control quickly. Poland was the first to begin to recover (1992), followed by the rest of Central Europe in 1993 through 1994. Poland, in 1996, was the first to reach its 1989 level of GDP, with Slovenia and Slovakia not far behind.

The countries that faced special difficulties with stabilization were those struggling the most with the legacies of the old system. Many of the countries in Central and East Europe were new, established in the early 1990s after the collapse of the USSR, Yugoslavia, and Czechoslovakia. They grappled simultaneously with state- and nation-building concerns and defining and defending their borders. As a result, economic reform was often not their top priority. Many had no previous experience with macroeconomic management. Problems also arose from having been part of dysfunctional currency areas, such as the ruble (former USSR) and dinar (former Yugoslavia) zones. In Ukraine, as in other former Soviet countries, the initial use of the ruble was a major impediment to macroeconomic stabilization and a significant cause of inflation, as each country in the ruble zone had an incentive to pursue expansionary macroeconomic policies because some of the resulting inflation would be exported to other countries in the region. Ukraine experienced one of the most serious transition recessions in the entire Central and East European region. Its economy did not begin to experience GDP growth until 2000 and remained below 1990 levels in 2019, before falling further in 2020 amid the COVID-19 pandemic.

It must be emphasized that it is difficult to compare pre- and post-transition GDP given the different ways of using statistics and the deliberate falsification or omission of unfavorable data under the old regime. GDP statistics exaggerated the true decline in economic welfare that occurred during the transition. In the communist system, output levels were often overreported for the sake of plan fulfillment. On the other hand, once the transition began, enterprises faced incentives to underreport in order to avoid taxes and divert output to the gray economy. Another factor was the so-called forced substitution practice: the lack of substitutes gave buyers little choice but to purchase goods available under the old system that were not really desired. After the transition began, better substitutes were often imported, reducing GDP but at the same time increasing consumer welfare.

As with GDP data, official measures of inflation exaggerated the declines in economic welfare associated with postcommunist inflation. Price liberalization only made explicit the hidden inflationary pressures that had existed in the previous system. The higher prices that resulted from liberalization reduced households' real income on paper, but they also allowed households to purchase whatever they could afford without having to wait in line or endure forced substitution. This trade-off—higher prices and lower real incomes in exchange for less waiting and forced substitution—benefited some people and rendered others worse off. It did not, however, connote automatic impoverishment. Moreover, the higher prices that occurred after liberalization were a partial reflection of the higher product quality that resulted from price liberalization and the creation of a buyer's market.

Structural Reforms

The achievement of macroeconomic stabilization paved the way for the launch of structural reforms, creating an institutional framework conducive to the development of a market economy. In centrally planned economies, all means of production, transportation, and financial intermediation had been owned by the state. The lack of competition and emphasis on quantity over quality meant that firms had few incentives to produce high-quality goods. Long-term investment was limited. Moreover, in planned economies, no consideration was given to profitability. Firms were often grossly overstaffed, with employees working at half capacity because of shortages of inputs for production.

The path toward building capitalist economies involved removing barriers to private business. Governments had to develop commercial, labor, and tax codes that provided the basis for the creation of new businesses while also paving the way for privatization. Banking regulation and supervision were also critical.

Fiscal reform played a double role in the transformation process of the former socialist countries. In addition to being a key element in the stabilization efforts, it was also part of the structural adjustment program as governments transformed the social welfare system.

Privatization

"Collective ownership," or nationalization of the means of production, was a key element of communist economic policy. Private ownership of land and the means of production were abolished without compensation, while lower classes benefited from social promotion. Agriculture was collectivized with the installation of communist rule. Only in Yugoslavia and Poland was private farming allowed.

Privatization was a crucial aspect of the restructuring process because, most significantly, it improved the efficiency of resource allocation and contributed to stronger budget constraints on enterprises. Private firms divested themselves of unprofitable sectors and laid off excess employees. Privatization also had positive spillover effects throughout the economy. It helped spur the development of the entrepreneurial spirit. Moreover, receipts from privatized enterprises improved the state's fiscal position as it struggled with reforms. Finally, although the privatization process itself was often plagued by corruption, the sale of state-owned firms eventually contributed to a reduction in the power of government policy makers by establishing new, private owners.

The privatization process across Central and East Europe began through the sale of small-scale enterprises, typically through auctions, direct sales, or giveaways, or through restitution schemes that returned properties to their precommunist owners. Restitution was also used with respect to land and housing. While Hungary and Poland had allowed for small private businesses in the 1980s, in hard-line regimes such as Czechoslovakia, 99 percent of the economy remained in state hands up until the fall of communism. Despite these very different starting points, small-scale privatization was accomplished with relative ease and was close to completion within one to two years in most countries.

The sale of state-owned companies became more complicated when countries began selling off medium- and large-scale enterprises. Privatization agencies were created to choose which firms should be sold and to establish the rules and regulations for the sales. The main methods used were manager-employee buyouts (MEBOs), voucher schemes, direct sales, initial public offerings (IPOs), and public tenders.

Privatization through MEBOs involved selling the enterprise to the current management and employees at discounted prices or sometimes simply transferring ownership without a cash payment. That is why the approach is often referred to as an "insider" model. While MEBOs are relatively quick, simple, and popular with the workers, they are also inefficient. Use of the MEBO method slowed the restructuring of the enterprise's management and operations, required continued state support given the dearth of funds employees and managers had for investment, failed to bring in the required market expertise, and left the state with little or no monetary compensation for the sale of the enterprise. Slovenia is the only country from the Central and East European region that had real success in using the MEBO approach, probably because its economy was already well integrated with Western Europe when the transition started.

The voucher or coupon method involved the transfer of shares in state-owned companies to citizens. In this method, citizens are given coupons for nominal sums (or sometimes for free). They trade these coupons for shares in firms or investment funds. The main advantages of the coupon method have been its speed, relative ease of administration, and equitability. In Central and East European countries, coupon privatization was presented as a way of garnering public support to continue market reforms by turning citizens into shareholders. Nonetheless, like the MEBOs, coupon programs failed to bring in the funds needed for enterprise restructuring. Another downside was that the diffusion of ownership translated into weak corporate governance, which, narrowly defined, refers to the relationship between a company and its shareholders. Both the coupon and MEBO methods allowed for the transfer of property in capital-starved economies, but state budgets did not benefit from the temporary boost in revenues that privatization can bring. The coupon method was first launched in Czechoslovakia in 1992 and later copied in other countries before eventually falling out of favor. A major flaw of the Czech program was that the government failed to first create an adequate legal and institutional framework. Insufficient regulation allowed for high levels of abuse, including insider trading and asset stripping. Moreover, because most shares were put in investment funds—many of which were controlled by Czech banks that remained in state hands—corporate governance was absent, unemployment remained unnaturally low, and the banking system ended up in shambles, providing a key trigger for the country's second-stage stabilization program.

IPOs, which involve issuing stock on securities markets at a predetermined price, are viewed by many market analysts as the most transparent way of selling off state corporations. That method can also reap large revenues for the government. However, IPOs were seldom used in the Central and East European region because of the lack of developed financial markets in the transitioning countries.

Direct sales and public tenders were among the most common forms of privatization in Central and East Europe. These were usually managed by the state privatization agency. In theory, direct sales go to the highest bidder. However, in practice, corruption can be rampant in direct sales due to the lack of transparency, with companies sold cheaply to political allies. Unlike direct sales, public tenders are based not on the level of privatization proceeds but rather on the premise of achieving the highest long-term economic growth potential. Thus, sales are negotiated with buyers who must present a business plan that takes into account such factors as employment, investment, and performance guarantees. These schemes require that the enterprises for sale be attractive enough to find investors willing to make a long-term commitment. The tender method is more difficult in the short term because negotiations can take a long time and revenues from the sales are generally not as high as in the case of direct sales. Another downside is that the rules for the tender are set at the discretion of state officials. Nonetheless, the short-term disadvantages are typically more than offset by the long-term benefits. The public tender method has been viewed as the most successful privatization method in Central and East Europe.

Privatization strategies varied considerably across the region, and some countries that started with coupon privatization, direct sales, or MEBOs were eventually forced to change course. Hungary was one country that had early success with its privatization program, focusing first on creating an institutional and legal framework for the new capitalist system and addressing the problem of limited domestic capital by beginning early with sales to foreign investors. The country stuck to traditional methods such as public tenders and IPOs, largely avoiding experimentation with alternative forms such as voucher schemes, restitution, and employee buyouts. Most of Hungary's lucrative state properties had been sold off by 1997, many of which went to foreign investors. This allowed deep restructuring to take place comparatively quickly, as the replacement of socialist-era managers removed a key obstacle that could obstruct market-oriented reforms. Through 1997, Hungary was the regional leader in attracting FDI.

Government Reform

While the initial macroeconomic stabilization efforts included tax reform and a dismantling of enterprise and price subsidies, subsequent structural reform programs aimed to adapt the public sector to the needs of a capitalist economy. Social policy is one of the most difficult aspects of the reform process, as such changes are extremely unpopular politically. The four Visegrad countries (Poland, Hungary, the Czech Republic, and Slovakia) inherited very comprehensive social safety nets from the communist period, featuring such perks as free health care, free education through graduate school, extensive paid maternity leave for women, and full pensions, even if no contributions had been made. Under communism, central government tax revenues averaged about 50 percent of GDP and reached as high as 61 percent in Czechoslovakia in 1989.[8] The Central European countries were considered premature welfare states, with social security benefit levels found in countries with much higher per capita GDPs. Many of the communist-era policies were maintained during the 1990s. By contrast, the CIS countries generally had underdeveloped welfare states during the transition period given their difficult budgetary constraints.

Policy makers faced several dilemmas in determining the extent of fiscal reform needed in the postcommunist era. First of all, there was no "optimal" size for government in established Western economies. Indeed, data from the Organisation for Economic Co-operation and Development (OECD) indicate that general government spending in 2019 accounted for about 25 percent of GDP in Ireland versus 56 percent in France. Second, the public sector experienced severe shocks during the transition. As declines in GDP and fiscal pressures reduced funding for social welfare programs, issues of poverty and inequality became more urgent. Fiscal reform does not necessarily mean cutting the size of the public sector. While the state's declining role is crucial with regard to enterprise development, it must expand in other areas such as regulatory activities (including antitrust, securities, and bankruptcy mechanisms), unemployment insurance, and other labor market policies.

During the transition, states faced the challenge of taking on more social welfare functions while at the same time reducing budget deficits. In practice, this was especially complicated since people were accustomed to relying on the welfare state. In the early transition years, governments set up generous unemployment schemes, with long payment periods and covering a large share of former salaries. Benefits also applied to new entrants to the labor market. As unemployment rates rose, however, the generosity of the schemes declined. Although public sectors decreased in size substantially in the early years of the transition, they remained large: budget revenues accounted for 42 to 47 percent of GDP in Central Europe by 1995.[9]

Countries adopted a variety of approaches to fiscal reform. Radical reformers such as Czechoslovakia, Estonia, and Latvia started early with balanced budget targets. The record shows that this was a wise decision, as delayed attempts at balancing were unsuccessful in Poland, Hungary, and Lithuania. In the latter cases, the habit of generous social spending was difficult to break for political reasons. Despite a favorable starting point in the Czech Republic and Slovakia, fiscal deficits surged in those countries during the latter part of the 1990s, partly due to the soft-budget constraints related to off-budget funds. The official state budget deficit reached about 1 to 2 percent of GDP in the Czech Republic during 1997 and 1998; however, the hidden deficit was almost three times that size.[10] As in the Czech Republic, rapid fiscal expansion (including large infrastructure projects and state guarantees for bank loans) put Slovakia on the verge of economic collapse by 1998, serving as a trigger for the country's second-stage stabilization program.

In carrying out reforms, a key concern was to better target the benefits provided to reach the people who needed them the most. Much of the traditional safety net was regressive, with the bulk of the subsidies going to those who were already relatively well-off. For example, across-the-board subsidies for household electricity and natural gas were especially beneficial for people with large homes, while those with smaller dwellings received less. Thus, one way of addressing this imbalance was to raise household electricity prices to market levels while providing subsidies for lower-income people.

Another key question relates to which agencies and levels of government should be charged with administering benefits. Two conflicting principles exist in this regard. First, if policies are made by national governments, statewide standards are established. Thus, a country avoids the situation in which regions compete for business by lowering taxation rates and providing fewer benefits. At the same time, however, putting policy making in the hands of regional or local governments may help promote experimentation and provide more accountability. There is no single standard in the EU; France embodies the first option and Germany the latter approach. Several of the new EU member states, including Poland and Slovakia, have implemented administrative reforms aimed at achieving decentralization.

Fiscal reforms became especially important as privatization wrapped up. In the early years of the transition period, some governments used privatization revenues to finance more spending, helping to compensate for the gap between domestic savings and private investment needs. As the countries approached the end of the transition, however, the international financial community discouraged such practices and called on countries to use privatization revenues to pay off government debts.

Taxation Reform

One key aspect of fiscal reform involved taxation rates. Slovakia was a regional leader in introducing a taxation system that was both simple and attractive to investors. In the aftermath of the country's second-stage stabilization program, Slovakia's tax reforms took effect in January 2004, just months before the country's EU entry. Whereas Estonia introduced a flat income tax in the early years of its transition, spurring several other countries to follow suit, Slovakia became the first to adopt that approach at a more advanced stage of reforms. The country's taxation changes applied not only to individuals but also to corporations, all at a flat rate of 19 percent. Moreover, Slovakia's VAT rate was unified at 19 percent, while the government canceled the inheritance, dividends, real estate transfers, and gift taxes.

There are several justifications for introducing more competitive taxation policies. First of all, initial transfers from the EU budget were considerably lower with the 2004 enlargement round than in the case of countries such as Portugal and Greece. Thus, the new member states had to rely on other factors to spur development with the aim of catching up with richer EU countries. Strong investment flows are seen as a prerequisite for the more rapid GDP growth needed to help countries reach the income levels of Western Europe. Once in the EU, however, member states are limited in the kinds of incentives they can offer to investors. Many of the perks provided by Hungary to attract FDI in the 1990s are no longer permitted. Moreover, some countries have struggled to attract investments that are not based on low wages alone, given that salaries are rising as the region becomes increasingly integrated with the West. Thus, fiscal reform provided a relatively simple way for these countries to bring in more investment.

Another justification for tax reform was the need to reduce budget deficits below the 3 percent of GDP Maastricht limit required for Eurozone entry, while also providing a basis for healthy medium- and long-term economic growth. If budget deficits are not brought under control, macroeconomic balance could be threatened, particularly once privatization revenues run out. Despite initial doubts about Slovakia's flat tax, the impact on public finances was surprisingly positive, as the new system helped to reduce tax evasion and thereby boosted revenues.

In the older EU countries, the so-called European social model, characterized by strong labor unions and the need for consensus in social dialogue, can complicate reforms. In contrast, the new member states have often found it easier to implement sweeping changes. Slovakia's 2004 taxation reforms met with very little formal protest.

Slovakia's tax changes triggered reform efforts elsewhere in Europe. In 2004, Poland's corporate income tax rate was reduced to the same level as in Slovakia, while the rate in Hungary was brought down to just 16 percent. The Czech Republic began to gradually lower its corporate income tax rate starting in 2004, reaching 19 percent by 2010. Initial reactions from countries such as Germany and France to tax reforms in the new member states were not positive, and Slovakia and other so-called neoliberal states were accused of "tax dumping." Some older member states called for the harmonization of taxation rates within the EU to prevent firms from moving eastward to benefit from more advantageous conditions. However, the prospect of harmonization proved challenging, and countries like Austria and Germany were forced to substantially reduce corporate tax rates to maintain competitiveness with their eastern neighbors. The tax changes in Central Europe and the Baltic states also inspired EU hopefuls in the Balkans and elsewhere. Serbia imposed a flat corporate tax rate of just 10 percent in August 2004, which at the time was the lowest rate in Europe. Montenegro went one notch lower in January 2006 with a 9 percent rate. A number of countries in the region adopted a flat tax on personal income as well. Nevertheless, several countries—including Slovakia, the Czech Republic, and Montenegro—were forced to abandon their flat tax in an effort to bring budgets into balance following the 2008–2009 global financial crisis, introducing higher tax rates for wealthier residents.

Pension Reform

The pension system has been a key concern of policy makers in the realm of social welfare reform, particularly in countries such as Hungary, where the aging population would have resulted in a fiscal meltdown if reforms were not implemented. Pension reforms generally include raising the retirement age, taxing working pensioners, shifting the formulas by which pensions are indexed, and moving toward a system based on employee contributions. International organizations such as the World Bank urged Central and East European countries to privatize their pension systems, in line with the models developed by Chile and other Latin American countries. Thus, countries were encouraged to shift from a pay-as-you-go system, where today's workers pay the benefits for current retirees, to one with personal accounts. The new approach is often referred to as a "three-pillar system," with the first pillar consisting of a downsized pay-as-you-go scheme and the second pillar comprising personal accounts. The third pillar is optional and refers to voluntary private savings accounts. The new approach to pensions was intended to encourage savings while at the same time improving the long-term health of state finances.[11]

Hungary and Poland were the first countries in the Central and East European region to pursue pension reform along the Chilean model, transforming their pension systems in 1998 and 1999, respectively. Latvia (2001), Bulgaria, Croatia, and Estonia (all 2002), Macedonia (2003), Lithuania (2004), Slovakia (2005), Romania (2008), and the Czech Republic (2013) followed, with variations from country to country. The costs of switching from one system to another were quite large. Nonetheless, privatization revenues provided a good source of funding, helping to make the reforms socially acceptable by avoiding large hikes in taxation rates. Participation in the new pension system was generally mandatory for new workers but optional for older citizens. Initially the personal accounts were more popular than expected among older workers, signaling distrust in the old system and expectations of higher yields from private funds.[12]

By the early 2010s, the three-pillar pension systems had fallen out of favor in some countries due to the poor performance of retirement funds during the 2008–2009 global financial crisis and subsequent economic challenges. Several governments reduced the level of funds going into personal accounts. The Czech Republic's pension reforms were remarkably short-lived, and the system was quickly dismantled when a new government took over in 2014. Nevertheless, the most dramatic backtracking occurred in Hungary, where the pension system was effectively renationalized in 2011, twelve years after its initial launch. Poland has gradually followed suit since 2014, approving a bill in March 2021 that would fully dismantle the second pillar in summer 2021. While Hungary accompanied its shift back to a pay-as-you-go system with an increase in the retirement age due to rising life expectancy, Poland's Law and Order (PiS) party moved in the opposite direction in October 2017, reversing the retirement age hikes put in place by its predecessor. Although Poland introduced a new employee-based pension system in 2019, participation rates have been far lower than the government expected, indicating that pressures on the public pension system will remain high.

Labor Market Reform

The communist system offered full employment. Governments introduced identity cards, and each citizen was required to have a place of employment or prove that he or she was legitimately out of the labor force. Those who did not work were considered "parasites." Factories were built in areas with high levels of joblessness, and collective farms and large enterprises helped to absorb residual unemployment. The maintenance of full employment meant that many workers received wages in excess of their contribution to their firms' revenues. Thus, the full-employment policy functioned as a disguised form of unemployment compensation.

A key aspect of the postcommunist transition was to transfer employment from the public to the private sector. In a market economy, companies locate plants where they can maximize profits, not reduce unemployment. Access to transport, electric power, and raw materials is a crucial factor and often more important than labor costs. Delivery times and transport costs are also key, so manufacturers often prefer to have plants closer to clients and markets. Thus, growth has been concentrated near big cities or Western borders. Large plants in out-of-the-way locations are frequently loss makers.

All of the countries in the region witnessed a rise in unemployment during the early years of the transition. In certain respects, the emergence of unemployment can be seen as a healthy development, a sign of the rationalization of production and employment. Enterprises had incentives to shed redundant workers as they faced firmer budget constraints, particularly in industries with declining competitiveness. Meanwhile, farms shed labor as agricultural subsidies fell. Still, the increase in unemployment was much greater in some countries than in others. In Central and Eastern Europe, layoffs were much more common during the 1990s than in the CIS, where less restructuring took place.

During the 1990s, governments fought the layoffs without much success. They did make it more difficult for companies to cut their workforces, however, by imposing high severance pay requirements along the West European model. Financial pressures forced enterprises to utilize other mechanisms to reduce labor costs, such as early retirement schemes and wage arrears, with the latter especially prevalent in the CIS countries. In an effort to deal with rising unemployment rates, some governments introduced active labor market policies such as public works projects, job retraining programs, and employment subsidies, especially for the unskilled population. Active labor market policies were often mixed with passive policies such as changes in taxation laws and regulations governing the hiring and firing of employees.

While active labor market programs are not always effective in the long run, cutting high payroll taxes and approving legislation that makes it easier for companies to hire and fire workers have had a more substantial impact on job growth. Also important are changes in the jobless benefits system aimed at encouraging the unemployed to find work, as benefits are sometimes set too high in relation to the minimum wage. Deregulation of rents can help encourage labor mobility, as can improvements in the banking sector that allow for the growth of mortgage lending.

Some countries have tried to use FDI as a way to bring down unemployment rates. Nonetheless, much of the FDI in the region was initially related to privatization. Foreign investors who buy existing firms do not always provide more jobs. Governments often require that investors agree to keep employment at a certain level; however, eventually the workforce has to be cut to raise productivity. Greenfield investment—which entails the construction of a new plant—is much more beneficial in terms of job creation, but luring investors is tough given the stiff competition among countries. Although some investors were attracted by the region's low wages, there was little to stop those firms from moving farther eastward once salaries edged closer to West European levels, especially if wage growth was not matched by increased productivity.

Hungary is one Central and East European country that achieved substantial success in using FDI as a job-creation policy. After reaching double digits between 1992 and 1995, Hungarian unemployment rates fell to around 6 percent from 2000 to 2004. That reduction occurred thanks partly to government incentives for foreign investors, especially those who invested in regions with high levels of unemployment, such as eastern Hungary. By 2000, Hungary was experiencing labor shortages in certain areas, as the country's population had been declining since 1980.

The development of small and medium enterprises represents another way to reduce unemployment. Nevertheless, many countries in the region were delayed in developing legal frameworks conducive to substantial growth of small business. Moreover, the slow development of the lending market also hindered progress, as banks were hesitant to lend to small enterprises because there was little recourse if they did not pay their debts, especially given the weak judicial systems. In contrast, mortgages were a safer bet for banks since property could be used as collateral.

Since the postcommunist transition began, unemployment rates in Central Europe and the Baltic states have rarely reached as high as 20 percent (see table 5.2), although divergent demographics have contributed to wide variations in jobless rates among countries. In Poland and Slovakia, populations with a lower median age meant that

Table 5.2.   Unemployment Rates for Central and East European States, 1998–2019 (Percentage)

Country	1998	2003	2008	2013	2019
Czechia	6.5	7.8	4.4	7.0	2.0
Poland	10.2	19.8	7.1	10.3	3.3
Hungary	8.7	5.8	7.8	10.2	3.4
Romania	6.3	7.7	5.6	7.1	3.9
Bulgaria	12.2	13.7	5.6	13.0	4.2
Estonia	9.2	10.4	5.5	8.6	4.4
Slovenia	7.4	6.7	4.4	10.1	4.5
Slovakia	12.7	17.7	9.6	14.2	5.8
Lithuania	13.2	12.4	5.8	11.8	6.3
Latvia	14.0	11.6	7.7	11.9	6.3
Croatia	17.2	14.1	8.6	17.4	6.7
Ukraine	5.6	9.1	6.4	7.3	8.2
Serbia	12.2	14.6	13.6	22.1	10.4
Albania	16.7	15.2	12.8	16.4	12.0
Montenegro	18.5	30.7	16.8	19.5	15.1
Bosnia and Herzegovina	—	26.5	23.4	27.5	15.7
North Macedonia	34.5	36.7	33.8	29.0	17.3
Kosovo	—	49.7	47.5	30.0	25.7

Source: Eurostat, IHS Markit.

unemployment rates were considerably higher than in Hungary during the first decades of the postcommunist transition, particularly among young adults. Nevertheless, since 2017, Poland's unemployment rates have ranked among the lowest in the region, partly due to government policies that have reduced labor market participation among women (due to child subsidies) and older people (due to a reduction of the retirement age), further exacerbated by external migration. Disparities among regions within countries have been substantial since poorly functioning housing markets limited labor mobility.

In general, Balkan countries have experienced much higher jobless rates than those in Central Europe, often reaching or exceeding 30 percent. That was partly a result of the wars of the 1990s and low levels of FDI. Kosovo, which declared independence from Serbia in February 2008, has faced some of the region's highest unemployment rates, surpassing 50 percent of the labor force in 2001 and 2002 before falling to about 26 percent by 2019. While unemployment levels in the Balkans have been unbearably steep, jobless rates are thought to be considerably lower in reality because of the strong informal economy in those countries. Still, long-term unemployment remains a serious challenge for policy makers in the Balkan region, where jobless rates remained in the double digits in 2019. In most countries, unemployment increased further in 2020 due to the COVID-19 crisis.

European Integration

In Central Europe and the Baltics, the goal of gaining full EU membership served as a top priority, helping to push forward economic reforms at a pace not typically seen in other transition regions. Countries started by developing new market-friendly institutions to promote economic integration within the region and gain access to preferential trading arrangements through the EU and other international organizations such as the General Agreement on Tariffs and Trade/World Trade Organization. These agreements served to boost exports and consolidate the opening of markets. Hungary, Poland, and Czechoslovakia established the Central European Free Trade Agreement (CEFTA) in 1992 with the aim of testing regional cooperation prior to EU integration. CEFTA was soon enlarged to include other countries from the region and continues to exist today, consisting of six Western Balkan countries and Moldova. By the mid-1990s, most Central European and Baltic countries had signed association agreements with the EU. Eight countries from the region took the final step in international economic integration and became full EU members in May 2004, followed by Bulgaria and Romania in January 2007 and Croatia in July 2013.

The integration path of the Western Balkans and Ukraine has been more complicated. Ukraine initially tied itself to Russia by joining the CIS in 1991. Although the country left the CIS following Russia's annexation of Crimea in 2014, Ukraine is part of the EU's European Neighbourhood Policy and is not currently viewed as a potential candidate for full membership. The Western Balkan countries, on the other hand, are potential candidates. Accession negotiations were opened with Montenegro (in June 2012) and Serbia (in January 2014), but progress has been much slower than was the case in Central Europe. In March 2020, the European Commission approved the start of accession negotiations with North Macedonia and Albania. Bosnia and Kosovo remain further behind.

Thanks to EU integration, Central and East European countries have dramatically reoriented their trade since the fall of communism. The EU accounted for more than half of 2019 exports for all but three countries (Kosovo, Montenegro, Ukraine). Among the region's EU member states, the share of goods exports going to the EU ranges from 55 percent in Lithuania to 80 percent in Slovakia. Despite Russia's efforts to expand its influence in the region, that country's share of exports reached 5 percent or more in only five countries (Latvia, Lithuania, Ukraine, Estonia, and Serbia). Moreover, Russia's importance as an energy source has also decreased significantly as the cutoff of natural gas supplies to much of the region during Russia's January 2009 price dispute with Ukraine highlighted the need for diversification. China's share of the region's exports is even smaller than Russia's, and only Ukraine has more than 5 percent of its exports going to China.

Attracting Foreign Direct Investment

European integration has gone hand in hand with an increase in FDI. There are many advantages to investing in Central and East Europe, including much lower labor costs than in Western Europe, rapid liberalization of foreign trade, proximity to Western markets (resulting in low transportation costs), and high levels of technical education. Nevertheless, transition economies are, in certain respects, risky for foreign investors. Labor regulations and taxes are frequently complex and subject to rapid change, depending on the whims of policy makers. Relatively high levels of corruption and insider trading exist, and many countries in the region have experienced serious problems with corporate governance, as company managers have often felt little responsibility to shareholders. Company registration has also been difficult, with barriers to small business and smaller-scale investors. Privatization negotiations have frequently been long and difficult, with significant political interference. Meanwhile, bankruptcy procedures have been complicated by an inadequate justice system. Finally, exchange rate volatility has added substantial risk.

During the 1990s, most of the FDI in the region went to Poland, Hungary, and the Czech Republic, which at the time were viewed as front-runners in the EU accession process. As it became clear that additional countries would be included in the first wave of the EU enlargement process, FDI also rose rapidly elsewhere. Investors in the new EU member states have the advantage of operating in the same legal and regulatory environment as their main markets. Moreover, EU membership is generally seen as a guarantee of a certain degree of political stability as well as the existence of enforceable contracts, should problems occur. More risky countries require higher returns to make the investment worthwhile, but inflows to the Western Balkans have also strengthened considerably, as investors seek opportunities to gain market access and reduce production costs.[13]

In some Central and East European countries, privatization deals involving foreign investors were initially unpopular as people feared that their governments were "selling out." That was particularly true when firms in certain strategic sectors were sold. While some countries (including Slovakia) initially had a nationalist approach to privatization, aiming to keep companies in domestic hands, the local owners often lacked the skills or incentive to run the firms in an effective manner. Countries that initially favored domestic over foreign buyers tended to have higher current-account deficits, which had to be financed by foreign borrowing rather than inflows of FDI.

Experience has shown that Central and East European countries have benefited considerably from foreign capital inflows, which have brought modern technologies, know-how, new forms of management, and an altogether different corporate culture, while also speeding up company restructuring and improving overall competitiveness. Foreign investment can also help to boost production and exports and improve a country's access to global markets, thereby preparing for the shock of full EU membership. Indeed, foreign-owned companies have often had much stronger export sales than domestic ones, particularly during the early transition years.

Much of the FDI in Central and East Europe was initially concentrated in a few manufacturing branches, such as automobiles and automotive components, electronics, food processing (particularly soft drinks, beer, dairy products, and sweets), tobacco, and construction materials. Investments in retail trade were also significant. From the mid-1990s, states began selling their shares in the strategic utilities, telecom, and banking sectors, with foreign investors often gaining significant stakes. FDI in the banking sector has been especially important, bringing in more competition, a greater variety of products, and higher levels of expertise.

Adopting the Euro

The eleven Central and East European countries that acceded to the EU between 2004 and 2013 are all expected to eventually join the Economic and Monetary Union (EMU), meaning that they will use the euro as their national currency. Advantages of Eurozone entry include reduced exchange rate risks, lower interest rates, and the elimination of transaction costs associated with maintaining a national currency, as well as access to the European Central Bank's stimulus measures in times of crisis. Eurozone membership can also make countries more attractive to investors.

In order to join the Eurozone, EU countries must first meet the criteria on inflation, interest rates, fiscal deficits, national debt, and exchange rate stability laid out in the EU's 1992 Maastricht Treaty. Inflation must fall below the "reference value," with the rate of consumer price inflation not exceeding the average in the three best-performing EU member states by more than 1.5 percentage points. Likewise, average nominal long-term interest rates must be no higher than 2 percentage points above the three best-performing member states. The general government budget deficit must be less than 3 percent of GDP, while public debt must be below 60 percent of GDP. Prior to entering the Eurozone, each country must join the Exchange Rate Mechanism II (ERM II), which serves as an EMU waiting room. On entry to the ERM II, a country pegs its currency to the euro, keeping the exchange rate within 15 percent of its central rate. A country must remain in the ERM II for two years without a currency devaluation before it may adopt the euro. The public debt criterion is somewhat flexible, as countries with debt over the 60 percent limit have been accepted into the Eurozone in the past, so long as the overall share was declining.

Three of Central and East Europe's EU member states (Estonia, Slovenia, and Lithuania) entered the ERM II in June 2004. All three countries initially hoped to adopt the euro in 2007, which was the earliest possible date for the new member states. Nonetheless, only Slovenia was given approval by the European Commission to join the EMU in 2007, as both Estonia and Lithuania were delayed by inflation rates above the Maastricht limit. Having joined the ERM II almost one year after its Baltic neighbors (in May 2005), Latvia initially expected to join the Eurozone in 2008. However, as in Estonia and Lithuania, stubbornly high inflation delayed EMU membership for Latvia. Inflation was a particular challenge in the Baltic states because the currency pegs did not allow for exchange rate fluctuations, meaning that real appreciation had to occur through inflation.

At the time of EU accession, the four Visegrad countries all had problems that would prevent them from adopting the euro in the near term. Public finances were seen as the biggest obstacle for Poland, Hungary, the Czech Republic, and Slovakia. Rising to the challenge, Slovakia launched fiscal reforms between 2003 and 2005 and joined the ERM II in November 2005. Although the change in government following the June 2006 parliamentary elections presented some risks with regard to both fiscal policy and inflation, Slovakia's adoption of the euro occurred on schedule in January 2009.

Slovakia's Eurozone entry happened just in time, as the global financial crisis would have set the country off course in 2009, particularly on the fiscal front. As budget deficits surged in 2009, most of the new EU member states outside the Eurozone were expected to experience further delays in EMU entry. Already in 2008, several of the new member states had deficits that were above the 3 percent of GDP Maastricht limit. Estonia was the only new member state to keep its deficit below the Maastricht limit in 2009, and the country adopted the euro in January 2011. Latvia made great strides in reducing its budget gap after the 2008–2009 crisis and won approval to join the common currency zone in January 2014. Lithuania adopted the euro in 2015. By 2021, no additional Central and East European countries had adopted the euro, although Croatia and Bulgaria joined the ERM II in July 2020.

Among the four remaining EU member states (Poland, Hungary, the Czech Republic, and Romania), the political will to adopt the common currency has diminished. While it makes sense for small countries such as the Baltic states to accede to the Eurozone as soon as possible, larger EU members have been more hesitant, preferring to maintain a national currency as long as possible in order to have more control over domestic economic policy. Although the currency instability that was associated with the 2008–2009 global crisis made some skeptics in the larger countries more amenable to rapid EMU entry, sentiment shifted away again during the subsequent Eurozone debt drama. In the Western Balkans, two countries (Montenegro and Kosovo) unilaterally adopted the euro as the national currency, with the potential to complicate eventual EU accession.

The Onset of Crisis

Thanks to the impact of second-stage stabilization programs, compounded with the positive effects of EU integration, the average GDP in Central Europe and the Balkans surged by some 6 to 7 percent annually between 2004 and 2007. Strong GDP growth was accompanied by a sharp drop in unemployment rates in most of the new EU member states and candidate countries. By 2007, rising labor shortages were viewed as one of the main challenges facing the more advanced countries of the region.

In many Central and East European countries, the rapid GDP growth of the mid-2000s was accompanied by rising external imbalances. This occurred as EU enlargement eased access to credit. Generally, a current-account deficit of more than 5 percent of GDP is seen as unsustainable. A current-account gap (stemming from imbalances on the goods, services, income, or current transfers accounts) must be compensated for by inflows of foreign direct and portfolio investment or long- and short-term foreign loans. If supported by inflows of FDI rather than by foreign borrowing, high current-account deficits were not seen as overly worrying. Indeed, Estonia's current-account gap reached about 9 to 15 percent of GDP between 2002 and 2007, a time when economic growth was strong, inflation was low, and budget balances were in surplus. Nonetheless, large external deficits raise a country's vulnerability amid a global downturn, especially since FDI inflows may decline as global companies scale back their investments, while tightening credit makes it harder for countries to finance external debt. Partly due to the need to finance large current-account deficits, the three Baltic states were among the hardest-hit countries during the global financial crisis of 2008–2009. The three countries were further impacted by the fact that currency boards or pegs prevented them from adjusting exchange rates.

In Central Europe, where current-account deficits tended to be lower than in the Baltic states, the first signs of recession emerged in the final months of 2008, as falling demand in Western Europe contributed to sharp declines in industrial output and exports. Falling remittances from citizens working abroad deprived countries of another key source of foreign-currency earnings, with especially negative implications for the Western Balkans. By early 2009, unemployment rates were rising across the region, and many analysts warned of imminent catastrophe. In an effort to avoid default, six countries in the region (Bosnia, Hungary, Latvia, Romania, Serbia, and Ukraine) sought stand-by arrangements with the IMF. The EU also stepped in to help remedy the situation, and Slovenia and Slovakia benefited from Eurozone membership.

Most Central and East European countries experienced sharp declines in GDP during 2009, in many cases the largest drops since the early 1990s. Poland, Albania, and Kosovo were the only countries in Europe to avoid recession in 2009. Whereas Poland's large domestic market and flexible exchange rate helped to shield the country from troubles elsewhere, Kosovo and Albania avoided recession due to their relative economic isolation.

Fiscal deficits soared as countries introduced anti-crisis measures. As the economies began to recover, austerity measures were introduced in an effort to reduce public debt and bring budgets back into balance. As discussed above, these fiscal pressures led some countries in Central and East Europe to cancel the flat tax and raise rates on corporate taxes and VAT. Pension reforms also frequently fell victim to the fiscal difficulties around the region, with personal accounts falling out of favor.

Just as a recovery from the global crisis was underway in the region, a new set of economic challenges emerged as a sovereign debt crisis that began in Greece spread through several other Eurozone member states. Slovenia was the only country in Central and Eastern Europe to experience the Eurozone debt crisis directly, as deteriorating bank assets due to a rapidly rising level of nonperforming loans led to calls for an EU bailout in 2013. Still, the government was reluctant to turn toward the Eurozone for help and instead drew up plans to recapitalize the sector and transfer nonperforming assets to a bad bank, much like in Slovakia and the Czech Republic during the second-stage stabilization process of the late 1990s. In December 2013, three Slovenian banks were bailed out, and a fourth requested recapitalization in April 2014.

Indirect and secondary effects of the Eurozone debt crisis were felt across Central and East Europe. Countries with strong economic links to Italy and Greece saw reduced revenues from exports, workers' remittances, and investment. By 2012 and 2013, the crisis had widened and deepened, pulling much of Europe into a double-dip recession. In Central and Eastern Europe, deteriorating export performance was matched by weak consumer confidence and investment. The situation was further exacerbated by the need to cut budget deficits and public debt following the upward surge in 2009. Otherwise healthy economies such as the Czech Republic were punished by the government's enthusiasm for fiscal austerity, pulling the country into a long-running recession. Other countries in the region managed to find a balance between austerity and growth, but even these economies saw a sharp slowdown. Croatia, Latvia, and Slovenia took a decade to return to the level of GDP seen before the 2008–2009 financial crisis, recovering in 2017–2019. Meanwhile, by 2019, Ukraine's economy was still well below the level seen in 2008, impacted partly by the country's military conflict with Russia.

After several more years of relative calm, the world was struck by the COVID-19 pandemic in early 2020. As West European countries such as Italy were hit hard, most countries of Central and Eastern Europe were quick to introduce lockdowns and border restrictions, helping to avoid a rapid spread of the disease during the first wave. Nevertheless, these lockdowns triggered a dramatic decline in GDP, and the impact was especially severe in countries that are heavily reliant on tourism, such as Montenegro and Croatia. Central and East Europe was less adept at managing the second wave of the virus, triggering new lockdowns in late 2020 and early 2021. As the COVID-19 crisis drags on, company bankruptcies and job losses are expected to heighten, with negative implications for household consumption and investment into 2021. The upswing in spending during the COVID-19 crisis may trigger a further round of tax reforms, although most countries will be cautious about shifting to austerity too quickly.

The economic turmoil that has struck Europe since 2008 has required considerable attention on the part of EU policy makers, further exacerbated by the 2015 migrant crisis and the United Kingdom's decision to leave the union. As a result, the EU has become more inward looking, shifting focus away from democracy promotion and enlargement, despite a continued desire to keep the Western Balkans in its sphere of economic and political influence. This has dampened prospects for that region's European integration, which has been painfully slow and is also complicated by a less compliant approach on the part of local policy makers in meeting EU requirements than was the case for the Central European and Baltic countries. The approval of the EU's budget and COVID-19 recovery fund in late 2020 provoked further controversy, as Hungary and Poland threatened to block the legislation due to disagreement with efforts to tie future funding to rule of law. The democratic backsliding of those two countries has made EU officials even more hesitant about future enlargement prospects.

Moving Forward

Some ten to twelve years after the transition began, the more advanced countries of Central and East Europe had completed the vast majority of their postcommunist economic reforms. That was particularly true in the case of the eight states that joined the EU in May 2004. As the postcommunist transition neared completion, the leading economies shifted their focus instead to issues also facing their counterparts in Western Europe and elsewhere in the world. At the same time, the Central and East European countries have to deal with the emergence of poverty, growing disparities in income, and demographic challenges. Other key concerns include fighting corruption and securing international competitiveness, allowing for a continued convergence of incomes with the wealthier West European economies.

Dealing with Poverty and Demographic Challenges

Countries of Central and East Europe began the transition with among the lowest levels of income inequality in the world; however, that situation has changed dramatically. Eurostat data shows that by 2019 Romania, Latvia, Bulgaria, and Lithuania had the highest risk of poverty or social exclusion rates in the entire EU. Still, other EU member states from the region ranked among the best performers, including the Czech Republic, Slovakia, Hungary, and Slovenia. While high inflation impoverishes society as a whole, stabilization programs can harm certain groups, particularly those living on fixed incomes or reliant on the state for transfers. The incidence of poverty also appears to be associated with high jobless rates, particularly when combined with states' increasing frugality in providing unemployment benefits. The loss of a stable income is the main cause of poverty throughout the region.[14] In terms of demographic groups, poverty is generally found more frequently among citizens with low levels of education and skills, those living in rural areas, those with large families, and women, children, and the elderly.

Although poverty and inequality have emerged as a key problem in some CIS countries, they are generally less severe in Central and East Europe than in other transitional societies. That may be partly due to the high levels of literacy in the postcommunist world, the close proximity to Western Europe, and better-targeted social benefits. Some citizens supplement their incomes with household garden plots and occasional employment; others work in the informal economy. Many urban families depend on relatives in the countryside for certain agricultural goods. Populations in countries such as Albania have survived mainly thanks to foreign assistance and workers' remittances, as citizens move to Greece and Italy in search of work, sending their earnings back home to their families. Despite rising poverty levels in the 1990s, purchases of consumer durables also increased significantly in many countries, partly due to the declining prices of such goods relative to salaries.

Poverty levels may stop growing or even decline once a country's economy strengthens; however, certain groups have continued to suffer. The situation is particularly severe among Roma, whose share of the total population varies from less than 1 percent in Poland to nearly 10 percent in Slovakia. In absolute terms Romania has by far the biggest

Photo 5.1. Elder poverty has been a particular challenge for the states of Central and East Europe. Widespread elder poverty is largely an outcome of weak social safety nets and the erosion of individual savings during periods of economic crisis in the region. (wjarek, Shutterstock)

Romani population, at an estimated 1.8 million. Throughout the region, Roma generally have lower levels of education than the rest of the population. For example, an estimated one million Romanian Roma are illiterate. They frequently face racial discrimination in hiring, resulting in much higher jobless rates than the rest of the population. Moreover, the housing of Roma is often poor and sometimes lacks electricity and running water.[15] Although efforts have been made by various governments and international institutions to alleviate poverty among Roma, the obstacles are great and progress has been slow.

Another unwelcome consequence of the transition has been an aging and declining population. These problems have arisen as the populations have become more Westernized and better educated, further compounded by high rates of external migration (see figure 5.2). EU membership allows for the free movement of labor, which has triggered a brain drain from Central and East Europe since 2004, especially among young, educated people who speak foreign languages. The Western Balkans have also experienced high rates of emigration, and Russia's 2014 annexation of Crimea triggered large-scale departures from Ukraine. While external migration has had a positive impact on unemployment rates, shortages of skilled labor present serious challenges for businesses. External migration is likely to continue across the region until economic opportunities and wages converge with those in more developed countries, indicating that policy makers need to take action to boost birthrates, attract immigrants, or bring emigrants back home. Many countries in the region have a difficult time achieving the latter goals due to language barriers, low wages, and comparatively poor living conditions. The only Central and East European countries that have experienced population growth since 1989 are Czechia, Slovenia, Slovakia, North Macedonia, and Montenegro, although in Czechia's case, that growth has been due mainly to favorable rates of net migration. In contrast, a number

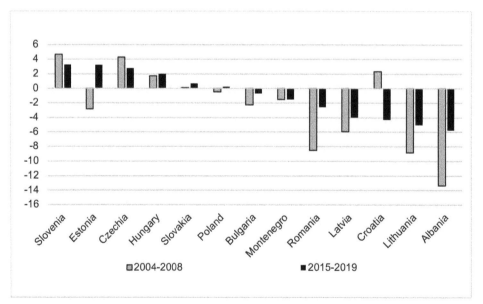

Figure 5.2. Net Migration Rates in Central and East Europe. (Sharon Fisher). *Source:* Eurostat 2020.

of countries have recorded double-digit population declines, including the three Baltic states, Romania, Bulgaria, Bosnia, Ukraine, Albania, and Croatia.

Fighting Corruption

Corruption has remained a key challenge for Central and East Europe throughout the postcommunist era. Under communism, citizens relied on their personal connections to obtain goods and services, and corruption was rampant. Although socialism was supposed to create individuals committed to the common good, most people were focused primarily on providing for their families.

The legacy of communism has meant that corruption remains a major problem throughout most of the region, impeding the efficient functioning of public institutions and failing to ensure a level playing field for companies. Countries with the greatest challenges tend to be those where state capture has occurred, with informal economic groups led by local oligarchs creating strong systems of political patronage and influencing the new formal market rules. For instance, the chapter in this volume dealing with Ukraine discusses how corruption features in the country's current economic system. In the case of Bulgaria and Romania, a delay in EU accession was linked to this phenomenon.

Transparency International's 2020 Corruption Perceptions Index puts Estonia in first place in the region, with one of the best rankings globally (in 17th place). Other EU member states are much further behind, ranging from 35th (Slovenia and Lithuania) to 69th (Hungary, Romania, and Bulgaria). Among the Western Balkan countries, Montenegro ranks first (at 67), while North Macedonia and Bosnia are last (at 111). Ukraine was ranked 117th place globally, one of the lowest in Europe. A number of countries (particularly Hungary) have seen a deterioration in their rankings since 2004.

Estonia's relative success in reducing corruption stems partly from its position as a global leader in e-government, helping to prevent bribery by removing the middleman. Elsewhere in the region, there have been some hopeful signs that change is on the way. In Slovakia, mass protests in 2017 against corruption were broadly ignored by the government, but the February 2018 murder of a journalist (along with his fiancée) who was investigating high-level corruption cases forced the prime minister's resignation. Presidential and parliamentary elections in 2019 and 2020 brought in fresh faces with an anticorruption agenda, leading to the approval of wide-ranging judicial reforms in December 2020.

Boosting International Competitiveness

Central and East Europe's postcommunist growth model (based on plentiful, cheap labor) is coming to an end. Countries at lower income levels can converge with richer EU member states rather easily through increased investment, given the capital scarcity in postcommunist economies. However, at higher income levels, convergence becomes more challenging, as they compete with innovative economies that benefit from quality education and highly skilled labor, a favorable institutional environment, and well-developed infrastructure. Across much of the region, convergence progress has slowed markedly since the global financial crisis.

Looking ahead, further convergence will require structural reforms aimed at raising efficiency and productivity, boosting labor market participation, and reducing the skills mismatch. Some reforms (such as changes to the education system) may take years to bear fruit. Nevertheless, the delayed impact does not decrease the importance of this step, as good skills will be essential in attracting investments and raising innovative capacity amid technological change and a declining and aging labor force. As the low-wage advantage begins to fade, adequate investment in research and development can spark innovation, serving as one of the key drivers of productivity and convergence. The Central and East European countries with the highest GDP per capita levels in 2019 (the Czech Republic, Slovenia, and Estonia) also have the highest innovative capacity, making them rather well positioned for faster growth.

As a whole, Central and East European countries benefit from the fact that they tend to be smaller, more flexible, and more reform oriented than their Western European counterparts. They also have much lower public debt-to-GDP ratios on average. By the end of 2019, three EU member states from the region had debt above the 60 percent of GDP Maastricht limit (Croatia, Hungary, and Slovenia), but all of them were below the EU average (at 78 percent). Still, the COVID-19 crisis has brought considerable uncertainty, triggering an upswing in debt across the region. Some countries were backsliding on the reform front well before the pandemic.

Looking Ahead

Despite their common experience with communism, the countries of Central and East Europe currently face more differences than similarities on the economic front. The differences are especially stark when comparing the region's EU member states to those outside the EU, as the Western Balkans and Ukraine continue to face considerable economic challenges to reform. With some exceptions based on proximity and historic ties (such as Bosnia and Croatia), bilateral trade and investment between the region's EU and non-EU members is limited. Instead, economic ties tend to be focused on development assistance, as the EU members act as donors and advisers with the aim of helping the region move forward more rapidly on the path toward economic reform and European integration.

Even among the region's EU member states, differences in the economic policy approach have grown. While Eurozone and ERM II members tend to be committed to European integration, Euroskepticism is rising in other countries (particularly Poland and Hungary). In terms of spending, some governments have prioritized long-term growth and innovation, while others (such as Poland) have focused expenditures on social programs aimed at reducing inequality and boosting the middle class while also raising support for the ruling PiS. Going forward, strategic alliances among postcommunist countries may become increasingly rare as policy priorities and economic outlooks continue to diverge and common historical experience fades into the background.

Study Questions

1. Which countries in Central and East Europe have had the most successful economic transitions? Have there been any surprises?
2. Privatization took many forms in Central and Eastern Europe. Which methods were the most successful in ensuring stable growth and employment?
3. The prospect of EU integration has been a driving force of economic development and reform in Central and East Europe. Do the countries of the region have any real alternatives to EU membership, such as closer ties with Russia?
4. Why have some countries in Central and East Europe been eager to adopt the euro as quickly as possible, while others have been hesitant?
5. Which Central and East European countries were hit hardest by the crises of 2008–2020? Which countries remain most vulnerable to future crises?

Suggested Readings

Aåslund, Anders. *Building Capitalism: The Transformation of the Former Soviet Bloc*. Cambridge: Cambridge University Press, 2002.

Connolly, Richard. "The Determinants of the Economic Crisis in Post-Socialist Europe." *Europe-Asia Studies* 64, no. 1 (2012): 35–67.

Ekiert, Grzegorz, and Stephen E. Hanson, eds. *Capitalism and Democracy in Central and Eastern Europe*. Cambridge: Cambridge University Press, 2006.

European Bank for Reconstruction and Development (EBRD). *Transition Report 2020–21: The State Strikes Back*. London: EBRD, 2020.

Keereman, Filip, and Istvan Szekely, eds. *Five Years of an Enlarged EU: A Positive Sum Game*. Berlin: Springer, 2010.

Medve-Bálint, Gergő. "The Role of the EU in Shaping FDI Flows to East Central Europe." *Journal of Common Market Studies* 52, no. 1 (January 1, 2014).

Orenstein, Mitchell A., and Bojan Bugarič. "Work, Family, Fatherland: The Political Economy of Populism in Central and Eastern Europe." *Journal of European Public Policy*, September 2020.

World Bank. *Transition: The First Ten Years*. Washington, DC: World Bank, 2002.

Websites

Eurostat: http://epp.eurostat.ec.europa.eu

European Bank for Reconstruction and Development (EBRD): https://www.ebrd.com

EU Enlargement and Neighbourhood Policy: https://ec.europa.eu/neighbourhood-enlargement

bne Intellinews: https://www.intellinews.com

V4 Revue: http://visegradrevue.eu

Notes

1. See World Bank, *Transition: The First Ten Years* (Washington, DC: World Bank, 2002), 11–21.

2. For more on the communist economic system and its collapse, see Anders Aåslund, *Building Capitalism: The Transformation of the Former Soviet Bloc* (Cambridge: Cambridge University Press, 2002), 20–70.

3. European Bank for Reconstruction and Development (EBRD), *Transition Report 2000: Employment, Skills and Transition* (London: EBRD, 2000), 18–19.

4. Slovakia's second-stage stabilization policies and their causes are discussed in Katarína Mathernová and Juraj Renčko, "'Reformology': The Case of Slovakia," *Orbis* 50, no. 4 (Fall 2006): 629–40.

5. The first three lessons are noted by Anders Aåslund. See Aåslund, *Building Capitalism*, 167–68.

6. See Aåslund, *Building Capitalism*, 227–32.

7. Aåslund, *Building Capitalism*, 171.

8. Aåslund, *Building Capitalism*, 222.

9. See EBRD, *Transition Report 2000*, 55, 69.

10. World Bank, *Transition*, 53.

11. World Bank, *Transition*, 81–83; Aåslund, *Building Capitalism*, 344–45.

12. World Bank, *EU-8 Quarterly Economic Report* (April 2005).

13. International Monetary Fund, "Foreign Direct Investment in New Member States of the EU and Western Balkans: Taking Stock and Assessing Prospects" (IMF Working Paper, no. 18, August 2018).

14. EBRD, *Transition Report 2000*, 106.

15. Arno Tanner, "The Roma of Eastern Europe: Still Searching for Inclusion," Migration Policy Institute, last modified May 1, 2005, https://www.migrationpolicy.org/article/roma-eastern-europe-still-searching-inclusion.

CHAPTER 6

Demography and Migration

Daina S. Eglitis and Michelle Kelso

In 1985, Margaret Atwood published her highly acclaimed novel *The Handmaid's Tale* about a dystopian society where fertility was controlled by the ruling regime to combat a decline in birthrates. Atwood's work was influenced in part by communist Romania's abortion and contraception ban.[1] From 1966 to 1989, Romanian women's fertility was treated as an affair of the state, which sought to mandate the number of children women were to bear, forbade almost all pregnancy terminations, banned contraceptives, and even policed women's wombs at their workplaces to check for pregnancy. While births initially increased, they soon declined as women learned to navigate the restrictions. Women's strategies to work around the restrictions, including illegal abortions performed in dangerous conditions, often had horrific consequences for women, including prison sentences, medical complications from botched procedures, and sterility. Romanian women were also at substantial risk of death during pregnancy and childbirth: during these years, the country had the highest maternal mortality rates in Europe. Unwanted children were another consequence of harsh pro-natalist policies in Romania.[2]

The 1989 anticommunist revolutions that swept the region brought freedom for Romanian women and families from the total control of the state. The legalization of abortion was the first legislation passed in the newly declared Romanian democracy, indicating how oppressive and despised the communist government's control of reproductive freedoms had been. In 1990, foreign journalists traveling to Romania uncovered the horrors of state institutions warehousing an estimated two hundred thousand children. The shocking images of children with shorn heads and skeletal bodies, dressed in rags, and living in unimaginable squalor stunned the world. Decades later, Atwood called the Romanian regime horrible, its impact on women and children not escaping her critical attention.[3] Romania's draconian effort to increase births offers a ghastly example of a state's failed efforts to control women's fertility.

Romania's extreme and coercive pro-natalism was unique in the region during the communist era, and it has not been repeated in Romania or other states of the region in the years since communism's end. However, some of the conditions that fostered its development, including acute concern about population decline, remain present in the region. While most countries are using benefits like generous parental leave and child welfare payments to entice families to have more children, some governments in Central and East Europe have also opted for restrictions on women's control of their fertility.

The goal of this chapter is to explore population trends in the region over the past several decades. These trends are significant in Central and East Europe because, as this chapter will show, they have an influence on politics and policies ranging from reproductive rights to migration and social welfare policies. They also have both short- and long-term effects on the economies and labor markets of these countries.

While there is notable variation across the region, four demographic trends are broadly characteristic. First, population counts have fallen since the end of communism, with losses attributable to a combination of low rates of natural increase, with deaths outpacing births, and significant labor migration, particularly among young adults, to West European countries. Second, marriage rates have dropped across the region since the end of communism, though there have been recent rises and, notably, many of the functions of marriage may have been replaced by cohabiting partnerships, which are widely seen as less restrictive and more "modern." Third, populations are aging as a result of fewer children being born and, in some countries, significant out-migration of young adults. The median age across the region has been on the rise. This has potentially significant repercussions for national economies as labor force participation rates fall and the ratio of workers to retirees declines, creating challenges for funding social benefits like pensions and health care. Fourth, since the enlargement of the European Union (EU), migration from East to West has dramatically increased, bringing economic and social changes to both sending and receiving states. While the countries of Central and East Europe have largely fallen into the category of sending states, the massive influx in recent years of refugees and asylum seekers from the Global South, specifically from the Middle East and Africa, has affected the region, its policies, and its politics, with many Central and East European governments resisting efforts by the European Union to shelter new migrants in their countries.

In this chapter, we examine these trends and consider their political significance for the region and its people.

Demographic Trends in Central and East Europe

Demographers study populations by looking at key indicators, such as the number of babies born, the number of deaths recorded, and the migration of people into and out of a country. A spectrum of internal and external factors influences those phenomena, including government policies, economic and political conditions, and overall quality-of-life perceptions. A key population indicator is a country's replacement rate, which is measured by the *total fertility rate* (TFR). To ensure population replacement, the TFR needs to be 2.1, meaning that each parent replaces him- or herself in the next generation; the figure is slightly greater than two because some children die before they reach reproductive age. A figure below replacement rate can provoke anxiety over a country's growth and future. Many Western countries have below replacement-rate fertility. For example, in 2020, Italy and Spain's TFR was 1.2, while Germany had a TFR of 1.6, and Sweden and France had TFRs of 1.8.[4]

One way to increase population size is through more births. Another is through immigration. The countries named above are all receiver states for significant numbers of immigrants, who may come for work, to reunite with family, as refugees, or for a variety of other reasons. Thus the population of Sweden has climbed from 8.5 million in 1990 to about 10.4 million in 2020. A quarter of the country's population is composed of immigrants. Over the same period, France's population climbed from 58 million to nearly 65 million. Like these receiver states, the countries of Central and East Europe have below replacement-rate fertility: in 2020, Estonia had a TFR of 1.7 and Latvia and Lithuania had TFRs of 1.6. Some of the lowest rates in the region are found further south, in the countries of Hungary (1.5); Croatia, Romania, and Poland (1.4); and Ukraine (1.3).[5] Unlike their Western neighbors, however, the countries of Central and East Europe are typically sending rather than receiving states. That is, their populations are more likely to be emigrating to other countries than receiving migrants.

Without significant immigration, populations with low rates of natural increase will over time take a downward turn. The *rate of natural increase* is the difference between the number of live births and deaths that take place in a given year, divided by the midyear population, multiplied by a factor of one thousand. This statistic clusters around zero in every country in the region: while in 2020 it was slightly above zero in Poland (0.1 percent), it was -0.3 percent in Romania; -0.4 percent in Latvia, Croatia, and Hungary; -0.6 percent in Ukraine; and -0.7 percent in Bulgaria. Another way of looking at this is to examine the *crude birthrate* and *crude death rate*. In Latvia, the crude birthrate was ten, and the crude death rate was fourteen. In Romania, the crude birthrate was eleven, while

Photo 6.1. In many Central and East European countries, fertility is low and one-child families are common. (Maria Sbytova, Shutterstock)

the crude death rate was fourteen.[6] When the number of deaths exceeds the number of births, the natural rate of increase drops below zero.

The low fertility trend in the region is not a new development. Unlike the United States, the Soviet Union and the countries of Central and East Europe did not experience a baby boom after World War II. The population losses over the course of the war were dramatic, and millions of men, women, and children died at or near the war fronts, perished from hunger or lack of necessities, never returned from Soviet concentration camps in Siberia, were murdered in the Holocaust, or fled the region as refugees, never to return. While practices of family formation and fertility slowly normalized in the postwar period, dramatic losses of young men in particular meant that many young widows would never have (more) children, and with a diminished marital pool, fewer women would marry and give birth to children at all.

By 1950, however, most countries in the region had reached above replacement-rate fertility, with Estonia posting a TFR of 2.4 and Poland a TFR of 3.7. Just over a decade later, however, the countries of the region would experience a "convergence" at around (or below) replacement-rate fertility, becoming the lowest-fertility region in the world. The European states of the communist bloc settled into a pattern of early marriage and childbearing, with an average number of two children. Conditions across the countries shared important similarities, including nearly full employment of working-age women, relatively high rates of divorce, chronic shortages of consumer goods and living space, poor access to quality birth control, and high rates of abortion, particularly in the Soviet territories, where, by some estimates, the average number of lifetime abortions may have been as high as three or four in the 1980s.[7]

Low and falling birthrates caused concern and consternation among political leaders and led to measures to try to stimulate childbearing that ranged from benign to draconian. Pro-natalist policies like generous maternity leave and inexpensive or free access to nurseries providing care for young children were instituted across the USSR and Hungary, among others.[8] In Romania, as noted in the chapter opener, efforts to boost fertility were cruel and coercive. Overall, the situation in the region remained largely static through the late 1980s, which brought a small uptick in births in countries including the Baltics and the Czech Republic, but also major political, social, and economic upheaval as long-standing communist governments and institutions collapsed.

In the period following the fall of communist regimes and the creation or restoration of democratic and free-market institutions, the region experienced steep declines in marriage and a fall in fertility that coincided with a rise in nonmarital births.[9] Marriage rates have not maintained a consistent trajectory in the postcommunist period, falling in many states and then recovering. In Latvia, for instance, the crude marriage rate (that is, the rate per one thousand population) was 9.8 in 1980 and a decade later remained high at 8.9. It slipped precipitously in the years after communism's end, dropping to 3.9 in 2000. By 2018, however, it had rebounded to 6.8. Divorces also fell—and then rose again—over this same period.[10]

Nonmarital births rose rapidly after the end of communism, though the manifestations of this phenomenon have varied across the region. In Bulgaria, for instance, the proportion of births outside of legal marriage has grown dramatically since 1970, when it was just 8.5 percent of all births. In 1990, the rate was 12.4 percent. It rose to 38.4

percent in 2000, 54.1 percent in 2010, and 58.9 percent in 2017. A similar pattern can be seen in Latvia: from 1970, when the proportion was 11.4 percent, the figure rose to 16.9 percent in 1990, 40.4 percent in 2000, and 44.4 percent in 2010. The rate turned down slightly in 2017, dropping back to 40.4 percent. Increases have taken place across the region, though the magnitude varies. Poland has experienced the least significant increase, rising from 5.0 percent to 6.2 percent to 12.1 percent in 1970, 1990, and 2000, respectively. However, in 2017, nearly a quarter of births were outside of marriage, a historic high for the predominantly Catholic country.[11]

These figures represent a variety of societal shifts, including changes in the perception of what constitutes a family. In many countries, couples choose cohabitation. A child may reside with both parents and could still be categorized as a nonmarital birth. At the same time, changing norms have brought widespread acceptance of single parenthood, and some women (and men) are raising children outside of a committed partnership.[12]

The relationship between increased nonmarital births and the fertility rate is complex. As we have seen, the total fertility rate remains lower across the region than it was during the communist period. Over the same period, marriages have declined overall, and cohabitation has risen. Demographers take an interest in the question of whether, while marital and cohabiting partnerships serve similar functions, the probability of a second birth is higher in registered marriages. Some research suggests that the pattern differs in West and East European countries: that is, while in West European states like France, fertility within marriage is higher than in nonmarital partnerships, in countries like Estonia, Romania, and Bulgaria, there is no difference. Declines in fertility, then, may be driven by factors other than the regional decline in marriage.[13]

Researchers have advanced a number of explanations for the postcommunist fertility decline in the region. Some reasons are country specific: for instance, Romania experienced an abrupt fall in fertility as the strict limitations on reproductive freedom that characterized the Romanian communist state under Nicolae Ceauşescu were lifted.[14] A similar "collapse" in fertility rates was seen in East Germany, though research suggests that the precipitating factors were linked closely to the abrupt political and economic transition experienced there when the formerly communist state merged with West Germany: it has been described as a "rational reaction to the new institutional and economic environment after the unification, bringing about an introduction of the new currency, new laws, massive economic restructuring, huge unemployment, but also new opportunities literally overnight."[15] The dramatic economic changes experienced in Central and East Europe in the years following the collapse of communist rule manifested in both growing wealth and rising poverty, and in a widening gap between the two. As unemployment rose and currency changes and banking crises eviscerated the wealth of some citizens, poverty and the pervasive uncertainties of the economic environment also shaped family decisions about childbearing, and the use of contraception and abortion to control fertility grew.[16]

Another theory used to explain the fall of fertility after the end of communism focuses less on changes in laws and the structure of the economy than on shifts in norms and ideas about family and fertility. That is, together with changes in attitudes about marriage and its desirability, necessity, or modernity, attitudes about parenthood—and the opportunity costs associated with bearing and rearing children—also changed. While the postcommunist transition created significant economic and social displacement, it also brought new opportunities for education, travel, and occupational mobility that some young adults may have been disinclined to forgo in order to start a family.[17]

While the fertility "shock" of the immediate postcommunist period has given way in these countries to a small recovery in fertility rates, they remain largely below replacement-rate fertility. As we will see further along in the chapter, this has fostered new efforts by national governments to incentivize—or control—fertility.

Aging and the Welfare State in Central and East Europe

Among the key consequences of demographic trends described in this chapter is the aging of populations, or what some researchers call "the greying of Europe."[18] In countries where the TFR is below a replacement rate of 2.1 and the immigration of working-age people is low, more people will be concentrated at the end of the life cycle. This in turn can have substantial economic effects, particularly in terms of funding social welfare programs such as national retirement supports and publicly funded health care. An aging population can also affect family roles and resources since caring for the elderly has long been culturally accepted in the region as a family responsibility, and private elder-care homes are, in any case, few and costly. Caretaking duties often fall to women, who may also be shouldering paid work and child-care responsibilities. Overall, few countries in the region seem prepared to tackle the major economic, social, and cultural implications of aging populations, which range from maintaining high economic productivity and raising sufficient tax revenues to support government institutions and social welfare programs, to providing gerontological health services, to ensuring the integration of the elderly into communal environments.

Of foremost concern among these modern welfare states, which endeavor to provide protective social policies such as health and pension programs, is meeting their obligations to pay public pensions, on which the majority of the elderly in the region depend to meet their basic needs. Many current retirees spent the majority of their productive years in communist systems, in which private pensions and individual retirement savings were unusual or nonexistent. Postcommunist legatee states have largely maintained the commitment to fund these pensions.[19] With decades of low fertility in the region, a declining number of young adults enter the labor force in each subsequent generation, thus reducing the number of people contributing to the tax base upon which governments draw for their social welfare payments. To illustrate this, demographers highlight a figure called the *dependency ratio*. The dependency ratio is an age-population ratio of those typically outside the labor force (for example, children fourteen and under and adults sixty-five and older) and those who are in the productive labor force (that is, those who fall into the years in between). The dependency ratio illuminates how much of the population is in the productive labor force and, by extension, how many working people are available to maintain a tax base that can support, among other things, pensions, insurance, and other welfare programs that ensure the well-being of those who are not yet in or no longer in the workforce.[20]

Recent European Union data on the *old-age dependency ratio*, which specifically looks at the level of support available to older populations (sixty-five years and up) by working-age populations (fifteen to sixty-four years of age), highlights the rapidity of change in this ratio. According to the data, just over twenty years ago, the ratio of working-age adults to seniors in the EU was 5:1, ten years ago it was 4:1, and in 2017 it was just under 30 percent—which means a ratio of 3:1.[21] Consider the case of Latvia, where the dependency ratio is higher than the EU average. In Latvia, the proportion of the population under fifteen years of age is 16 percent, while the proportion of those sixty-five and older is 20 percent. Similarly, in Romania, the figures are 18 percent and 20 percent, respectively, and in Bulgaria they are 14 percent and 21 percent. The significance of these figures is that they show a higher number of people in the older age group, which is near or in retirement, while a smaller group is anticipated to age into the working population.[22] At the same time, it is important to note that many older adults continue to work: public pensions in many countries are low, and some older adults have spent time working in the large informal economies of the region, which does not count toward public benefits as work in the formal sector does. As such, paid work remains a key means of household support. In the three Baltic countries of Latvia, Lithuania, and Estonia, labor force participation remains high and above the EU average for older adults, particularly women.[23] Work, however, is not only an important means of supporting oneself or one's family: it is also a source of interaction and status. As a Bulgarian economist noted about his country, "Retiring in Bulgaria equals impoverishment and loss of economic and social status—therefore, those who can continue to work even after retiring."[24]

As noted above, in Romania, nearly 20 percent of the population is over the age of sixty-five. By 2050, this figure is expected to rise to 30 percent, and in the absence of significant shifts in current trends, Romania's population will continue to age, adding strains to public welfare programs. Romania is poorly prepared to tackle the needs of its elderly as demands increase on its pension and health-care systems. Among EU countries, Romania has consistently spent the least of any state on health care over the past twenty years, allocating just 5.2 percent of GDP to this sector as of 2017.[25] This is lower than 2017 European and EU averages, 9.4 percent and 9.9 percent, respectively.[26]

Romania's elderly face income poverty, social exclusion, and inadequate living conditions, lagging behind their EU counterparts, though others in the region face similar situations: in Bulgaria in 2014, for instance, fully 58 percent of the sixty-five and older population were at risk of poverty and social exclusion.[27] A 2015 study on the quality of life of the elderly in Romania found that income needs are pressing for seniors and that the "expenses renounced most frequently are those relating to food [for instance, consumption of meat and meat products]."[28] In 2015, one in four Romanians experienced severe material deprivation, which the elderly suffered more deeply.[29] Older Romanians are more likely than the rest of the population to be rural dwellers, a population that is more vulnerable to poverty. One study found that the elderly in rural areas face serious problems: 88 percent experience harsh living conditions, 72 percent have problems with food supply, and 68 percent reported being lonely and isolated.[30]

The sixty-five and over population in Central and East Europe is heavily female. In fact, among those over age sixty-five, the number of women is more than double that of men. In 2018, the largest gender imbalances were in the Baltic countries. In Latvia, for instance, there were "more than two women aged 65 years or more for every man of the same age."[31] For women who are single and over sixty-five, the risk of poverty in Latvia has consistently held at about 74 or 75 percent.[32] The overrepresentation of women in the elder population represents a particular challenge to the social welfare systems of Central

Photo 6.2.   The median age of populations in Central and East Europe has risen as birth rates have remained low and emigration of young adults from many states has been high. Countries like Ukraine (shown) have large populations of older adults. (meunierd, Shutterstock)

and East Europe. As one study of the financial standing of elderly households noted, female earners over the course of their working lives receive lower earnings, and their pension contributions are set at a correspondingly lower level, resulting in lower pension capital, which is used as a basis for the calculation of pension benefits.[33]

The populations of Central and East Europe are aging as life spans expand and fewer babies are born. At the same time, the challenges this region faces differ somewhat from those faced by its Western neighbors like Germany, Sweden, and France, which also have aging populations. A key difference between the regions, which will be discussed in greater detail later in the chapter, is that Central and East European states have been losing population, particularly young adults, to emigration, while European countries to the west have largely been receiver states of economic migrants from Central and East Europe, as well as refugees and asylum seekers from the Middle East and Africa. Whether the region will open its doors to migrant populations from the Global South, which tend to be younger than the median, in order to bring in workers to support productive economies and aging populations is a question that will be examined ahead.

The Politics of Population

Many governments in Central and East Europe are profoundly concerned with demographic indicators that show population decline. Their concerns are shared by some

Western and Southern European countries as well. On January 25, 2020, the British magazine *The Economist* noted that, "after years of nagging from eastern member states, the topic [of population decline] was placed on the European Council's strategic agenda for the next five years. For the first time, the issue of demography has its own dedicated commissioner in Brussels, who will look at ways to make life easier for families. Natalism, where the state tries to increase the birth rate, is back."[34] Natalism—or pro-natalism—entails the development of policies and practices that encourage people to bear children, preferably more children than they might otherwise have chosen to have. Recall from earlier in the chapter that pro-natalism was a state priority in many communist Central and East European states in the 1960s and 1970s, when fertility rates took a downward turn. As populations decline and existential fears rise, pro-natalism is again on the agenda.

Pro-natalist policies and practices can be broadly categorized into those that are based on incentives and those that are based on coercion and limitation of choices. In the remainder of this section, we will examine the cases of Hungary, Poland, Latvia, and Romania and consider the balance of the two in these countries in 2020.

Over the past decade, some Central and East European states have introduced pro-natalist policies to incentivize higher birthrates. Perhaps the most controversial effort to combat fertility decline is that of Hungary's far-right President Viktor Orbán, whose government unveiled in July 2019 the "Family Protection Action Plan," which was touted to promote "procreation over immigration."[35] Like many of the countries of the region, Hungary has lost population as the rate of natural increase remains below zero and many members of the working-age population and families have migrated westward to better job opportunities and wages in the European Union. Orbán notably declared, "We do not want our color, traditions, and national culture to be mixed with those of others. We do not want to be a diverse country." While other states such as Sweden and the UK have relied on migration to boost their populations, Orbán's extremist government has consistently promoted xenophobic nationalism. The Orbán plan entails an array of financial incentives to spur procreation that benefit mainly middle-class Hungarian women. It includes a lifelong tax waiver for women having four or more children and preferential housing loans for women with at least two children. Subsidized minivans, free fertility treatments, and cash are also on offer.[36]

At the same time, Orbán's government allows limited access to abortion, legal in Hungary since 1953, in an effort to build practical and political obstacles to the realization of this right. In 2011, the Hungarian parliament inserted a "personhood" amendment into the country's constitution that foresaw legal recognition of fetuses. Further, only surgical abortion is legal in the country; a doctor must confirm the pregnancy, and women must complete two mandatory counseling sessions no less than three days apart. Politically, the Hungarian pro-natalist agenda mixes positive financial incentives that may benefit women and families with severe limits on their reproductive choices. This is interwoven with a nationalist xenophobia that forecloses the option of utilizing migration to increase the size of the population and labor pool. Orbán has been among the regional leaders most opposed to accepting migrants, largely refugees and asylum seekers from the Middle East and Africa, as permanent residents. He has called migration "surrender," saying that Hungary's goal is to add "Hungarian children."[37]

Poland has a pro-natalist profile similar to that of Hungary. It has a total fertility rate similar to that of Hungary and an anti-immigrant stance that has rejected efforts by the European Union to bring migrants from outside Europe to Poland despite significant population losses to labor migration westward. Poland provides significant financial incentives to families with children and offers generous maternity leave and somewhat less generous paternity leave.[38] It also has one of the most generous child support policies in Europe: since 2019, the "Family 500+" program has offered five hundred zloty monthly per child under eighteen. While the long-term effect on fertility behavior is unclear, the payment has contributed to a decline in child poverty, and one observer has suggested that the policy is succeeding in its aims: "Poland's increase in births in 2017 does seem to have coincided with a large increase in higher-parity births (note that in 2019, Poland expanded the 500+ program to include firstborn children)."[39]

Like Hungary, Poland has stringent laws on access to abortion, though Poland's laws date back further and are tied closely to the influence of the Catholic Church rather than political expediency. The church, which played a key role in the anticommunist movement, has continued to exercise significant influence on politicians and policy making. Poland's abortion law allows for termination only when a fetus is malformed, when the health or life of the mother is in danger, or in the case of rape or incest. Even in these instances, however, medical professionals may evoke a "conscientious objection" clause. The law was tightened in 2017, when emergency contraception was made accessible only with a prescription. In 2018, an estimated one thousand abortions were carried out in Poland, but a women's rights activist estimated that the number of women seeking legal abortions abroad may be as much as fifteen times higher.[40]

Latvia, which has seen significant population decline as a result of negative natural growth rates and substantial migration of young workers to other EU countries, has also pursued a pro-natalist agenda, though it has to this point been focused on incentives rather than social control. Latvia provides parents a generous infant support payment through eighteen months of age and a modest child welfare payment through age fifteen, or up to twenty if the child is in full-time education. It also offers lengthy parental leave for mothers and fathers.[41] Notably, in Latvia, pro-natalist incentives have not been spawned primarily by right-wing conservative political movements, as in Hungary and Poland. While conservative movements continue to embrace traditional ideas about gender roles and families, policies providing for family supports have largely been embraced across the political spectrum of Latvian-dominated parties. Latvia is home to a substantial Russian-speaking minority, and the fear of decline among the titular minority has held together an ideologically diverse political coalition that backs generous family supports to encourage childbearing. At the same time, limits on reproductive choice have gotten little traction, and abortion restrictions like those enacted in Poland and Hungary do not have a popular constituency or broad political support.

Like its neighbors, Romania has continued to experience declining births after the end of communism, and its total fertility rate has consistently been among the lowest in the world. In 2010, the government enacted paid leave policies to encourage more births. Romanian policies come in two key forms: maternity leave and child-rearing leave, each having particular conditions based on the number of months worked in the prior year or years. The law even mandates leave: mothers are obligated to take forty-two days' leave after a child's birth, and fathers are required to take five days. Women can take eighteen weeks' paid leave, up to half of which may be used during pregnancy. Once maternity leave ends, either parent that meets the eligibility requirements can take paid leave to care for the child. Notably, however, the law only assists parents who were in the workforce for a set time period prior to their child's birth. In 2016, parental leave became more financially generous, granting either parent 85 percent of their average net income salary, awarded until the child reaches age two or three in cases of disability.[42] The law, popular among voters, has been criticized by some politicians for being too generous; however, as in Poland, there is data to suggest that it may be fostering a small rise in fertility: in 2019, the TFR rose to 1.6, the highest it has been since 1992. Although many of the same conditions that contributed to previous low rates continue to exist, including a deficit of child-care options for families and expensive housing, the increase suggests that the law may have modestly achieved its goal.

Due to Romania's traumatic history with fertility control, there has been little political will to adopt restrictive legislation on women's fertility choices, including access to abortion, which remains legal up to fourteen weeks for all women, and up to twenty-three weeks for medical reasons. Doctors can opt not to perform abortions through conscience-based refusal, which as of 2017 was becoming more widespread among hospital practitioners.[43] In the period after communism, Romanian women underwent some of the highest rates of abortion in the world, with an estimated 50 percent of women having had at least one termination. By 1992, abortion rates peaked at 117 terminations per thousand women before steadily declining over the next two decades.[44] Family planning was slow to take hold in the population, but improvements in access have contributed to a significant reduction in abortions.

An examination of pro-natalist policies reveals a spectrum of approaches. On the one hand, some policies have positive benefits for women and families, particularly when they provide substantive financial resources to support the well-being of children, providing money that may help keep families out of poverty, and when they encourage not only maternal but also paternal paid leave that gives parents an opportunity to raise children in their first months or year of life without fear of losing a job or income. At the same time, pro-natalist policies are often tied to efforts to restrict women's reproductive choices, a direction in regional politics that seeks to bring private fertility decisions into the realm of the state and its ideological goals, recalling, if not precisely repeating, the coercive and oppressive practices of communist Romania.

Population Loss: Westward Migration from Central and East Europe

Researchers often categorize factors that influence migration into two categories: "push" and "pull" factors.[45] Push factors are motivators in the home country that cause people to leave, such as wars and natural disasters; persecutions that may be political, social, cultural, or religious; and economic disparities and struggles. Pull factors are those found in the destination country that appeal to the migrant, such as a large community of compatriots already established there, which can make the transition easier, better lifestyle and work opportunities, and greater political and cultural freedoms. The massive migration after 1989 from east to west, particularly in the period following EU accession, can best be understood as an amalgamation of powerful push and pull factors. Population emigration is an important issue in the region, not least because, in combination with the stagnant or negative natural growth rates, it has contributed to significant population change and loss.

In January 2018, *Politico* published an article titled "Latvia: A Disappearing Nation." As discussed earlier in this chapter, populations in the Baltic countries, and indeed across the region, have largely experienced negative natural growth rates, with death rates exceeding birthrates. The "disappearance" of population is not, however, only a result of below replacement-rate fertility. Population loss in Central and East Europe, particularly since the beginning of the new millennium, has been heavily driven by East-to-West migration, as Latvians, Poles, Romanians, Bulgarians, and others have flocked to the Western states of the European Union in search of new economic and educational opportunities. As the aforementioned article notes, "since joining the [EU] bloc, nearly a fifth of [Latvia] has left to work in more affluent nations: The U.K., Ireland, Germany."[46]

Latvia and its Baltic neighbors, Lithuania and Estonia, have experienced substantial population loss. Some migration took place prior to EU accession in 2004, but the pace picked up considerably afterward and was exacerbated by the economic crisis that began in 2008 and brought a dramatic drop in economic growth rates and a massive rise in unemployment across the Baltics. While migration slowed in the aftermath of the crisis, the key catalysts driving it have remained: a sharp gap between wages and prices that is acute for less-educated workers, a perceived inadequacy of health-care access and social supports, and the pursuit of higher wages in the West. By one estimate, in 2019 about 20 percent of Latvian nationals were living abroad, as were 17 percent of Lithuanian and 15 percent of Estonian nationals. Population losses to emigration are accelerating the rise of the median age in countries like the Baltics, where most migrants are of working age: by one estimate, by 2030 about half of Latvia's population will be over fifty years of age.[47]

Poland, with a population of about thirty-eight million, is a much larger state than any of the Baltics (who together have a population that is just a little over six million). Poland has historically been a sending state: Polish migration westward has a long history, and communities of Polish migrants and their descendants can be found in Western Europe, Canada, Australia, the United States, and numerous other countries.[48] During the communist period, when migration into and out of Soviet bloc countries was strictly limited, small numbers of Poles left the country. As in neighboring states, however, postcommunism and, in particular, EU accession opened the door to rapid and robust emigration westward. After Poland's 2004 accession to the EU enabled labor migration to the United Kingdom, Ireland, and Sweden—which was shortly followed by a lifting of immigration restrictions in countries like Norway and the Netherlands—young Poles streamed out of the country to take advantage of opportunities in sectors like construction and hospitality. From 2004 to 2006, the number of leavers doubled, reaching nearly forty-seven thousand. While that was the peak, the figure continued to be high in subsequent years. At the end of 2009, the number of Polish-born residents in the United Kingdom was over half a million. As of 2015, the estimate of Poles residing in other EU member states was between 1.3 and 2 million.[49]

Romania, too, has experienced massive labor migration, which began after 1989, increasing substantially once the country joined the EU in 2007. To understand present migration, a cursory look at post–World War II migration history is essential, not only because it was unique to the region but also because ties created during communism continue to function as pull factors in migration patterns. Communist Romania was theoretically a closed country; that is, it was difficult to enter or leave. Legal migration was nearly impossible for most citizens, with few exceptions, which included family reunifications. The unusual part of Romania's migration history came after 1950, when out-migration was permitted for two groups: ethnic Germans and Jews. Although the Romanian state center viewed all sizable ethnic minorities as untrustworthy (i.e., potentially disloyal to the state), the Soviet leadership sanctioned only the "repatriation" of ethnic Germans and Jews. (By contrast, the Soviets pressured the Romanian state to create a territorial autonomy arrangement for the largest historic minority, ethnic Hungarians, which lasted from 1952 to 1960.) Ethnic Germans were scapegoated for Romania's wartime World War II losses (Romania had been a Nazi ally until 1944, when it switched sides), and Jews due to long-standing anti-Semitism. Both ethnic Germans and Jews suffered persecution by the Romanian state, the former being deported in large numbers after World War II to Siberian labor camps by the new communist regime as a form of war reparations, the latter brutally persecuted by Romania's fascist regime during the war.[50]

Following World War II, German and Jewish populations decreased due to territorial losses, forced population transfers of ethnic Germans, and the Holocaust. The postwar transition from an open market to a communist-run economy was chaotic, creating disruptions in agriculture and industry. As such, communist Romania found itself continually short of cash. One means employed by the state to bring foreign currency into the treasury was the "sale" of unwanted ethnic groups to mother states under the guise of repatriation or family reunification. Sometimes out-migration agreements were brokered for cash per head, and at other times for goods and services the Romanian state needed. Begun in the 1950s, the practice intensified under the regime of Nicolae Ceaușescu, who in 1982 announced that he would pay down all of Romania's international debt. The country owed over $11 billion to Western banks. Ceaușescu and his advisers ramped up "selling" Jews to Israel and ethnic Germans to West Germany. In exchange for granting exit visas, Romania received cash payments for individuals based on their level of education and occupation. This practice continued through the end of communist rule.

For ethnic Romanians, migration was almost impossible until 1989, and citizens lived in a system in which the state exercised nearly full control over their lives, which was a key push factor for those wanting to leave. Clandestine border crossings or defections while traveling abroad were mainstays for illegal migration. Travel during communism was strictly monitored by the regime since Romanians going abroad had the best chance of defecting. To ensure return compliance, Romanians traveling or working abroad went alone, without their families, who remained behind under the surveillance of the much-feared Securitate, or secret police.

Once communism fell, the flow of Romanian migrants was transformed: the economic struggles of postcommunism replaced an oppressive state as a push factor driving migration. During the 1990s, Romanians migrated to the United States, Canada, and

Hungary, among other destinations, such as Israel and Germany. The countries were attractive for the economic opportunities they offered; for the last two, a pull factor included previous emigration that had fostered Romanian-speaking networks.

While admission to the EU grants free right of movement to its citizens, Romanian and Bulgarian workers were placed in a transition period in all but ten member states. Notably, Romania and Bulgaria joined the European Union in 2007, three years after Poland and the Baltic countries, which contributed to a large labor migration of workers from east to west. Fearing that a new wave of labor migrants might flood in, some EU states wanted to avoid a backlash against the new member citizens while protecting their labor markets and social welfare programs. As a result, rules were imposed that restricted Romanians and Bulgarians from working in certain countries for a set period of time. Some British leaders were particularly worried about "an invasion" of Romanian and Bulgarian workers, and in 2013, a year before restrictions were to be lifted, they raised the alarm that the UK might even have to defy EU laws to keep out Balkan migrants.[51]

Between 2006 and 2009, Italy and Spain were the top receiving countries, accounting for 85 percent of Romanian migration. In recent years, Germany has become the primary destination country, with the UK being the second (2012–2016). Belgium, the Netherlands, and Denmark remain in the top ten destinations for Romanian émigrés in the EU, though since Brexit there has been a dip in the number of Romanians working in the UK.[52]

When Romania began negotiations with the EU, receiving destinations changed. A decade after the end of communism, an estimated 20 percent of its working-age population was abroad, and the migration flow has drastically affected the country's domestic labor market, leaving shortages in critical areas like medicine and technology, as well as construction and manufacturing. Between 2000 and 2016, Romania ranked as a top origin country among all countries in the number of migrants leaving for Organisation for Economic Co-operation and Development (OECD) countries, which include several EU member states. In 2016, Romania ranked in the top five global sending states, together with China, Syria, India, and Poland.[53] While the majority of Romanians depart seeking better educational and employment opportunities abroad, they also leave to escape a government system marred by pervasive corruption.

In Romania, as in other sending states, the significant loss of working-age residents has exacted a toll on the workforce, which in certain sectors experiences continuous and widening shortages. Fewer workers also means less money coming into the state treasury through income taxes, which affects the country's ability to pay pensions and for public goods like health care and education. Emigration has also resulted in a "brain drain," creating a shortage of expertise: in 2020, Romania had a shortage of forty thousand doctors.[54] The field of family medicine, on which the health-care system is based, has seen a 25 percent decline in doctors.[55] An estimated fifty thousand nurses have left. The pull to Western Europe is not only higher salaries but also better working conditions that exclude the corrupt practices such as bribes that plague the Romanian health system. Skilled workers have also left in droves, with an estimated shortage of five hundred thousand laborers, particularly in the areas of construction, heavy industry, and car manufacturing.[56]

Bulgaria is among the European Union's poorest countries. Its losses have also been among the steepest. Figures on Bulgarians leaving, their destination, and the duration of their time working or studying abroad are imprecise, but information can be gleaned from statistics that receiver states provide on those who come there to live and work. By one estimate, in the year before Bulgaria joined the EU (2007), Germany recorded about eight thousand arrivals from Bulgaria. In the year after EU accession, the figure rose to twenty thousand. Altogether, about sixty thousand Bulgarians a year may be leaving for other EU member countries.[57]

The story of migration from Central and East Europe is a complicated one. On the one hand, many residents have left for western EU states. On the other hand, internal migration is also an issue of concern. For example, while Latvia has lost a significant proportion of its population to emigration, its capital city, Riga, has recently experienced growth after a lengthy period of decline. The starkest population losses are in small cities and towns, which offer the fewest opportunities for education and mobility and the poorest wages: many young adults who cannot or choose not to go abroad are opting to move to Riga to improve their options.[58] In Romania, rural areas are also losing population, and though the destination of internal migrants has been more varied, a key pull factor has been the robust employment opportunities in more urban areas. In December 2019, for instance, the capital city, Bucharest, and the surrounding county of Ilfov had an unemployment rate of only 1.1 percent, while the region nearest to the capital, South Muntenia, had a higher unemployment rate at 3.4 percent—providing an incentive for job seekers to move to the Bucharest area.[59]

Some of the countries of former Yugoslavia have also experienced substantial population loss. A decade of war in the region, which stretched from 1991 to 2001, had already created regional challenges, including human losses to conflict and refugee flight, economic devastation, and enduring tension between ethnic communities. While European Union accession offered new opportunities and expanded institutional support and security for member states from the Balkans (Slovenia joined in 2004 and Croatia in 2013; the other states are candidates for membership), it also increased the risk of population migration to more prosperous EU countries. For example, Croatia lost about 5 percent of its population to EU migration between 2013 and 2017.[60]

While the exodus of workers from East to West has been well documented since 1989, it is more difficult to determine reverse migration, returning from West to back to East, due to freedom of movement within the European Union. Migration is not static: that is, when workers go abroad, they may leave permanently, temporarily, or seasonally, or they may go back and forth between their home and host countries for many years, which is often referred to as circular or repeat migration. For this reason, pinpointing migration flows can be challenging, as a small amount of data must be pieced together from different EU and country sources. Research on Central and East European reverse migration, however, indicates that few migrants have returned to their home countries. Research suggests that a key predictor of return migration is the home economy and may also include factors such as political climate and policies.[61] Among those that return after living abroad, gender and education differences exist. For instance, more men return home than women, and those returning often have higher of levels education than the regional median, except for Romanians, where returnees have lower levels of education.[62]

Recent developments such as Brexit and COVID-19 may shift some migration dynamics within the European Union. For example, Latvia and Lithuania, which have policies in place to maintain a link to their diasporas and to encourage return migration, have seen a slight growth in returnees. This can be attributed in part to challenges created for Central and East European labor migrants by Brexit, the United Kingdom's withdrawal from the European Union, which was decided in a national referendum in 2016 but whose implementation has been somewhat chaotic. Neighboring Estonia stands out in the region for its small positive net migration; this has been driven less by return migration, however, than by Estonia's concentrated effort to brand itself as a "digital republic" and to attract expatriate digital workers from across the globe to take advantage of its "e-residency" for living and working in the country.[63]

Nationalism and the Challenge of Global Migration

In the previous section of this chapter, we focused on the issue of migration within the European Union, specifically the movement of Central and East Europeans seeking work and opportunities in EU states like Ireland, Germany, Sweden, and the (formerly an EU member state) United Kingdom. In this section, we turn to contemporary issues of immigration in Central and East Europe. In particular, we examine the events, politics, and practices of regional states during the 2015–2016 period when over a million refugees and asylum seekers from the Middle East and Africa arrived in Europe.

The mass arrival of migrants from conflict-riven states like Syria, Iraq, and Afghanistan and from economically struggling countries like Senegal, Nigeria, and Pakistan created a humanitarian and political crisis that exposed fear and xenophobia within European countries and tensions between them over responsibility and care of the new arrivals. Paradoxically perhaps, it was the Central and East European countries that had been significant "sending" states of western-bound economic migrants for over a decade that were particularly resistant to accepting migrants fleeing war and poverty.

Historical legacies may give us some insight into the region's resistance to newcomers. Central and East Europe was historically a diverse region ethnically and religiously; recall from the introductory chapter (chapter 1) that most states were once part of large, multiethnic empires. As an aspect of economic development and urbanization, the mixing of different ethnicities was a normal part of social life in the region. However, the experience of the interwar period, to which many in Central and East Europe today look with nostalgia, was characterized by smaller and more ethnically exclusive states. As well, in the decades that followed World War II, authoritarian control of the region sometimes resulted in forced population movements, as well as intentional efforts on the part of communist authorities to reengineer the demographics of some areas. For instance, in the Baltic countries, which were part of the Soviet Union from 1940 through 1991 (except for the period spent under Nazi occupation between 1941 and 1944), the Soviet government sought to change local populations by bringing in large numbers of Russian-speaking migrant workers from other parts of the Soviet Union. These new migrants did not speak local languages and largely did not choose to learn them. Their presence was widely resented by the Baltic populations because they took up scarce resources, including apartments, and were seen as part of an effort to "Russify" the Baltic republics.[64] The regional experiences of the last century have largely not lent themselves to a solid foundation for cultural acceptance and integration of immigrants. As we will see below, right-wing political parties in several countries in the region have sought to take advantage of population fears, stoking xenophobia and hatred of outsiders.

Unlike its North and West European neighbors, the Central and East European region has not emerged as a desired destination for refugees and asylum seekers (who will be referred to in this section also as migrants) from the Middle East and Africa. At the same time, the mass movement of refugees and asylum seekers, particularly that which took place in 2015 and 2016, has had a significant impact on political practices and narratives, particularly in countries such as Hungary and Serbia that functioned as transit points for migrants moving westward.

Many migrants from the Global South took a path through Europe, transiting across the countries of former Yugoslavia, including Serbia and Macedonia. While Serbia, a country with aspirations to join the European Union, initially followed EU guidelines on registration and treatment of entering migrants, the volume of arrivals fostered public discontent and fears that the migrants were a security and financial threat (though costs were largely borne by nongovernmental organizations or the EU). Attitudes and practices became increasingly punitive. As the crisis evolved, waves of migrants became trapped in camps and reception areas staged in border areas that were fenced and guarded to halt the flow. While conditions in these government-controlled areas were poor, the state of migrants outside of them was even more dire, as many were living on the streets or in warehouses around train stations in city centers.[65]

In Hungary in the summer of 2015, an estimated 390,000 asylum seekers passed across the Serbian-Hungarian border. Many of them made their way to Budapest in hopes of boarding trains at Keleti station to travel to Germany. The government of Hungary, under Orbán and the Fidesz party, did not approach the arrival of hungry and tired masses as a humanitarian issue; rather, they framed the presence of the migrants as a "Muslim invasion" that threatened national security, societal cohesion, and the Christian identity of Hungary. Significantly, while very few of the asylum seekers ended up remaining in Hungary, their transit has endured as a legacy of fear and xenophobia exploited by the dominant national party.[66]

The Orbán government has fought immigration from countries to the south with both physical and political barriers. At the height of refugee and asylum seeker movements to Europe, Hungary raised barbed-wire fences on the border to deter entrants. To further discourage passage, it criminalized crossing, damaging, or obstructing construction of the fence; between late 2015 and early 2016, over 2,300 people were punished for this transgression.[67] The government also involved private citizens, hiring several thousand "border hunters" to reinforce the estimated ten thousand police and soldiers patrolling the border. The "border hunters" were trained for six months and armed.[68]

Hungarian government policies on the provision of asylum have been restrictive and unwelcoming. Orbán's government resisted the European Union's efforts at "burden sharing," specifically, the policy of distributing asylum seekers across EU states in order to reduce the responsibility borne by both first-entry countries like Italy and Greece and the countries that many asylum seekers sought to reach, such as Sweden and Germany. Under the plan of shared responsibility, the EU asked Hungary to accept just under

Photo 6.3. In some countries, the rise in refugees and asylum seekers from the Middle East and Africa that began around 2015 resulted in political backlash, including a rise in xenophobic policies and practices. In this photo, refugees wait to cross the Croatian-Serbian border. (BalkansCat, Shutterstock)

1,300 refugees from Syria, Iraq, and Eritrea, a request that Orbán rejected with the assertion that the mostly Muslim group would destroy Hungary's Christian identity and culture.[69]

Though the politics of immigration have been outwardly less xenophobic in some other regional states, acceptance of asylum seekers and refugees has been elusive even among Central and East European countries with a history of willingness to accede to EU mandates (and a history of migration among their own populations). The Baltic countries of Latvia, Lithuania, and Estonia, for instance, were asked in a 2015 plan to accept a total of 1,679 migrants from the Middle East and North Africa. In spite of their declining population numbers and shrinking labor pool, the Baltic countries showed little willingness to take anywhere close to these numbers: the unpopularity of the plan among the Baltic publics shaped the lack of action by governments on the issue. In 2018, for instance, the government of Latvia granted just twenty-three approvals for refugee status to would-be migrants. For their part, however, migrants have also shown little inclination to stay in the Baltics, opting when possible to move westward to wealthier European countries with larger migrant populations offering more robust social networks and economic opportunities.[70]

By contrast to most of its neighbors, Romania has increased the number of migrants received. In 2017, Romania received 4,820 asylum application requests, the largest number it had received in fourteen years.[71] The year prior, it had only 1,886 applications. While not in the Schengen Area, Romania has been viewed as a transit-only state on migrant routes.[72] In 2015, Romania resisted the EU-imposed quota system. It has, however, continued to accept refugees in increasing numbers, becoming the most welcoming state in the region. In 2016–2017, it had accepted 56 percent of resettled foreigners in the region, above Slovenia's 19 percent (the second highest in the region), and well above Bulgaria (5 percent), Croatia (6 percent), and Poland (0 percent).[73] In 2019, the number of asylum seekers decreased to 2,592.[74] The majority of migrants seeking asylum are from Syria, Iraq, Afghanistan, and Algeria. Notably, public attitudes are not anti-Muslim, most likely because Romania does not have either populist or extremist political parties. Under communism, Romania enjoyed good relations with several Muslim countries and has had pockets of migrants from Syrian, Iraqi, Egyptian, and Palestinian communities settled for decades, in addition to its own small Muslim minority that includes Tartars as well as Turks.[75] In 2016, Romania's majority-ruling political party nominated a Muslim woman for prime minister, which was notable as she was both the first woman and the first Muslim to receive a nomination to head the government—notably, however, the nomination was rejected by Romania's president.

Interestingly, attitudinal data on whether people have a favorable or unfavorable opinion of Muslim settlement "in their country" shows a relationship to the number of Muslims in the country.[76] While not specifically tied to the migrant crisis of 2015–2016, Central and East European countries with very few Muslims (migrants or otherwise) show more unfavorable opinions than West European states with significantly larger populations. For example, while Polish and Lithuanian respondents indicated high unfavorable figures (66 percent and 56 percent, respectively), 28 percent of Swedish and 24 percent of German respondents had unfavorable opinions. While those figures are still high, they suggest that intolerance is fostered by unfamiliarity. Bulgaria, in contrast, has the highest favorable opinion in the region at 69 percent, most likely due to its historical Muslim population, which is composed largely of Turkish migrants and their descendants.[77]

The number of asylum seekers and refugees entering Europe from the Middle East and Africa has declined significantly from a peak of over one million in 2015.[78] An April 2016 deal between the EU and Turkey (which is not an EU member state) reduced the flow of migrants northward, particularly across the Aegean Sea. The deal sought to reduce pressure on Greece, which was the key entry point into Europe from the Aegean, by promising Turkey about €6 billion, as well as an expedited process of visa liberalization for travel into the EU. The number of arrivals fell to about 170,000 in 2017 and 115,000 in 2018. The figure dropped precipitously with the onset of the COVID-19 pandemic, though the arrival of migrants continues: as of the end of June 2020, about twenty-eight thousand asylum seekers had arrived via the Mediterranean Sea or over land, with most new arrivals entering through Greece, Italy, or Spain.[79]

Controversies over how to manage and distribute migrants across the EU have outlasted the apex of the migrant crisis. The issue has been exploited by illiberal parties and politicians across the bloc, including in Hungary, Italy, and Sweden. Europe has witnessed a rise of anti-immigrant and xenophobic politics in both national governing bodies and the elected European Parliament. The twenty-six-member Schengen Area, which enables free passage across borders in most of Europe, may also be under threat as transit and destination states seek to limit the movement of migrants into their territory.[80]

Demography, Migration, and the Central and East European Future

The events of the twentieth century, including two world wars, the Holocaust, and the Cold War, resulted in dramatic demographic shifts across the Eurasian continent. Central and East Europe experienced considerable losses of population, property, and productivity to conflict and genocide, and the legacy of the twentieth century is one that continues to resonate in the region, shaping, among other things, the politics and policies of family, fertility, and migration.

The twenty-first century offers new challenges to the region. As you will see in this text, these challenges manifest in a variety of forms: economic crises, the decline of democratic institutions and the rise of xenophobic nationalism in some states, the resurgent military threat from neighboring Russia, pervasive and persistent corruption in the public and private sectors, and new public health challenges in the form of the COVID-19 pandemic. Demography is woven into many of the challenges of the twenty-first century, and existential fears stemming from decades of declining population growth and increasing population loss to westward migration, as you learned in this chapter, make themselves visible in other societal spheres.

The countries of Central and East Europe constitute the majority of states classified by a recent article as the "fastest-shrinking countries in the world." The list includes Poland, Hungary, Latvia, Lithuania, Estonia, Romania, and Albania, among others.[81] At the top of the list is Bulgaria, which, if current trends continue, is estimated to lose 23 percent of its population by 2050, dropping from a population of 7.2 million to 5.2 million.[82] Population loss of this magnitude—and even of smaller magnitude—has present and potential implications for family formation, economic growth, political life, and military readiness, among others. Significantly, worsening conditions in these spheres will only strengthen the push factors that have already driven many young Central and East Europeans westward, particularly since European Union accession.

The postcommunist challenges of emigration exist beside the newer issue of immigration and the aspirations of migrants from the Global South to escape conflict and economic deprivation and to find shelter and opportunities in Europe. To this point, the countries of Central and East Europe have not been destinations with a strong pull for migrants from the Middle East and Africa: the relatively weaker economies and thinner social networks have deterred most from seeking refuge there. Several years of growing resistance to new migration in Western and Northern European states like Germany, France, and Sweden, however, may increase pressure on Central and East European countries, particularly member states of the EU, to accept and integrate new migrants. Their willingness to accede to requests—or demands—to open their doors to refugees and asylum seekers may depend on political factors, including the influence of extreme nationalism and xenophobia, and economic factors, including the dire need for workers in sectors of the labor market that are struggling to fill positions.

Will population losses slow before the most dire predictions about decline are reached? Will the governments of Central and East Europe succeed in enticing working-age adults who left for opportunities in the Western states of the EU to return to their home countries? Will they also welcome new citizens from the Global South? The answers to these questions will shape the region as we move forward into the twenty-first century.

Study Questions

1. Central and East European countries in the postcommunist period have been characterized by significant population loss. What key factors explain declining populations in the region? What distinguishes the countries of this region from Western and Northern Europe, where populations continue to grow even as birthrates remain low?
2. What challenges will rapid aging bring to the region?
3. What is pro-natalism? How have pro-natalist policies and practices manifested in the Central and East European region in the communist and postcommunist period? How might pro-natalist practices support or harm women's bodily and economic autonomy?
4. Describe patterns of migration in the Central and East European region. What have been key catalysts of population emigration from, in particular, European Union countries in Central and East Europe to Western and Northern Europe? What issues of emigration, in particular from the Middle East and Africa, have regional states encountered and how have they dealt with them?
5. How is population demography *political*? That is, where and how do we see it in political narratives and debates? Are there cases outside of East and Central Europe that you would compare to its demographic politics?

Suggested Readings

Corselli-Nordblad, Louise, and Andrea Gereoffy. "Marriage and Birth Statistics—New Ways of Living Together in the EU: Statistics Explained (2015)." Eurostat. Last modified August 29, 2018. https://ec.europa.eu/eurostat/statistics-explained/pdfscache/42059.pdf.

European Parliamentary Research Service. "Demographic Outlook for the European Union 2020." Last modified March 2020. https://population-europe.eu/books-and-reports/demographic-outlook-european-union-2020.

Gatrell, Peter. *The Unsettling of Europe: The Great Migration, 1945 to the Present*. London: Penguin UK, 2019.

Kostanick, Huey L. *Population and Migration Trends in Eastern Europe*. New York: Routledge, 2019.

Kučera, Tomas, Olga V. Kucerova, Oksana B. Opara, and Eberhard Schaich, eds. *New Demographic Faces of Europe: The Changing Population Dynamics in Countries of Central and Eastern Europe*. New York: Springer Science & Business Media, 2012.

Petrova, Tsveta, and Tomasz Inglot, eds. "Special Cluster Issue on Politics and Current Challenges of Demography in Central and Eastern Europe." *East European Politics and Societies* 34, no. 4 (May 2020). https://doi.org/10.1177%2F0888325420905886.

Smith, Stephen. *The Scramble for Europe: Young Africa on Its Way to the Old Continent*. Hoboken, NJ: Wiley, 2019.

Websites

Eurostat, "Population: Demography, Population Projections, Census, Asylum & Migration—Overview": https://ec.europa.eu/eurostat/web/population/overview

Migration Policy Institute: https://www.migrationpolicy.org/regions/europe

Population Research Bureau: https://www.prb.org

United Nations High Commissioner for Refugees (UNHCR), "Desperate Journeys: Refugees and Migrants Arriving in Europe and at Europe's Borders, January–December 2018": https://www.unhcr.org/desperatejourneys

Notes

1. "Margaret Atwood on the Real-Life Events That Inspired *The Handmaid's Tale* and *The Testaments*," Penguin UK, September 1, 2020, https://www.penguin.co.uk/articles/2019/sep/margaret-atwood-handmaids-tale-testaments-real-life-inspiration.html.

2. Gail Kligman, *The Politics of Duplicity: Controlling Reproduction in Ceausescu's Romania* (Berkeley: University of California Press, 1998); Gail Kligman, "Abortion and International Adoption in Post-Ceausescu Romania," *Feminist Studies* 18, no. 2 (1992): 405–19.

3. Andrea González-Ramírez, "Author of The Handmaid's Tale Says Anti-Abortion Laws Are 'A Form of Slavery,'" *Refinery 29*, June 5, 2017, https://www.refinery29.com/en-us/2017/06/157505/margaret-atwood-anti-abortion-bill-texas-slavery.

4. Population Research Bureau (PRB), *2020 Population Data Sheet*, https://www.prb.org/2020-world-population-data-sheet.

5. PRB, *2020 Population Data Sheet*.

6. PRB, *2020 Population Data Sheet*.

7. Alexandre Avdeev, Alain Blum, and Irina Troitskaya, "The History of Abortion Statistics in Russia and the USSR from 1900 to 1991," *Population: An English Selection* 7 (1995): 39–66; Tomáš Sobotka, "Fertility in Central and Eastern Europe after 1989: Collapse and Gradual Recovery," *Historical Social Research/Historische Sozialforschung* 36, no. 2 (2011): 246–96; Tomáš Sobotka, "Ten Years of Rapid Fertility Changes in the European Post-Communist Countries," *Population Research Centre Working Paper Series* 1 (2002), http://citeseerx.ist.psu.edu/viewdoc/download?doi=10.1.1.464.1996&rep=rep1&type=pdf.

8. Tomas Frejka, Stuart Gietel-Basten, Liga Abolina, Liili Abuladze, Svitlina Aksyonova, AnĎelko Akrap, Ekaterina Antipova, et al., "Fertility and Family Policies in Central and Eastern Europe after 1990," *Comparative Population Studies* 41, no. 1 (2016): 3–56.

9. Sobotka, "Fertility in Central and Eastern Europe," 246–96; Daina S. Eglitis, "Cultures of Gender and the Changing Latvian Family in Early Post-Communism," *Journal of Baltic Studies* 41, no. 2 (2010): 151–76.

10. Marina A. Adler, "Social Change and Declines in Marriage and Fertility in Eastern Germany," *Journal of Marriage and the Family* 59, no. 1 (February 1997): 37–49; Eglitis, "Cultures of Gender and the Changing Latvian Family," 151–76; Barbara Łobodzińska, ed., *Family, Women, and Employment in Central-Eastern Europe* (Westport, CT: Greenwood, 1995), 112.

11. "Share of Live Births outside Marriage," Eurostat, accessed October 10, 2020, https://ec.europa.eu/eurostat/databrowser/view/tps00018/default/table?lang=en.

12. Arland Thornton and Dimiter Philipov, "Sweeping Changes in Marriage, Cohabitation and Childbearing in Central and Eastern Europe: New Insights from the Developmental Idealism Framework," *European Journal of Population/Revue européenne de Démographie* 25, no. 2 (2009): 123–56.

13. Brienna Perelli-Harris, "How Similar Are Cohabiting and Married Parents? Second Conception Risks by Union Type in the United States and across Europe," *European Journal of Population* 30, no. 4 (2014): 437–64.

14. Cristina Bradatan and Glenn Firebaugh, "History, Population Policies, and Fertility Decline in Eastern Europe: A Case Study," *Journal of Family History* 32, no. 2 (2007): 179–92.

15. Sobotka, "Fertility in Central and Eastern Europe," 261.

16. Elwood Carlson and Megumi Omeri, "Fertility Regulation in a Declining State Socialist Economy: Bulgaria, 1976–1995," *International Family Planning Perspectives* 24, no. 4 (December 1998): 184–87; Dimiter Philipov and Hans-Peter Kohler, "Tempo Effects in the Fertility Decline in Eastern Europe: Evidence from Bulgaria, the Czech Republic, Hungary, Poland, and Russia," *European Journal of Population* 17 (2001): 37–60.

17. Jan M. Hoem and Dora Kostova, "Early Traces of the Second Demographic Transition in Bulgaria: A Joint Analysis of Marital and Non-marital Union Formation, 1960–2004," *Population Studies* 62 (2008): 259–71; Jan M. Hoem, Dora Kostova, Aiva Jasilioniene, and Cornelia Mureşan, "Traces of the Second Demographic Transition in Four Selected Countries in Central and Eastern Europe: Union Formation as a Demographic Manifestation," *European Journal of Population* 25 (2009): 239–55.

18. Jon L. C. Dall, "Medicine in Europe: The Greying of Europe," *BMJ* 309, no. 6964 (1994): 1282–85.

19. "Pension Reforms in the Large Accession Countries," Euractiv, last modified January 29, 2010, https://www.euractiv.com/section/enlargement/opinion/pension-reforms-in-the-large-accession-countries.

20. Marta Borda and Patrycja Kowalczyk-Rólczyńska, "Evaluation of Elderly Households' Financial Standing in Central and Eastern European Countries," *Post-Communist Economies* 30, no. 5 (2018): 1–16.

21. "Record High Old Age Dependency Ratio in the EU," Eurostat, last modified May 8, 2018, https://ec.europa.eu/eurostat/web/products-eurostat-news/-/DDN-20180508-1.

22. "2020 World Population Data Sheet," Population Research Bureau, accessed September 15, 2020, https://www.prb.org/2020-world-population-data-sheet.

23. "The Active Aging Challenge: For Longer Working Lives in Latvia," World Bank, last modified 2014, http://pubdocs.worldbank.org/en/205791443642635843/WB-Latvia-Active-Aging-Report.pdf.

24. Francesco Martino, "Elderly Bulgarians: The Lost Generation," *Observatorio balcani e caucaso transeuropa* 15 (February 2016), https://www.balcanicaucaso.org/eng/Areas/Bulgaria/Elderly-Bulgarians-the-lost-generation-167744#:~:text=Poverty%20and%20old%20age&text=According%20to%20the%20study%2C%2051,with%208%25%20in%20extreme%20poverty.

25. Cristina Tomescu, "The Development of Social Policies in Health," *Journal of Community Positive Practices* 19, no. 3 (2019): 23–33.

26. "Healthcare Expenditure Statistics," Eurostat, accessed August 15, 2020, https://ec.europa.eu/eurostat/statistics-explained/index.php/Healthcare_expenditure_statistics.

27. Simona I. Bodogai and Stephen J. Cutler, "Aging in Romania: Research and Public Policy," *Gerontologist* 54, no. 2 (2013): 147–52.

28. Gabriel Stanila, "The Quality of Life of the Elderly in Romania," *Journal of Community Positive Practices* 2 (2015): 26.

29. Cecilia Irina Rabonțu and Amalia Venera Todoruț, "The Effects of Ageing Population on the Economy and on Service Activities in Romania," *International Conference Knowledge-Based Organization* 24, no. 2 (2018): 88–97.

30. Agnes Neményi, "Demographic Ageing in Romania—General and Specific Consequences on the Rural Population and the Relation to International Migration," in *Population Ageing in Central and Eastern Europe*, ed. Andreas Hoff, 151–68 (New York: Routledge, 2011).

31. Eurostat, *Ageing Europe: Looking at the Lives of Older People in the EU, 2019 Edition* (Luxembourg: Publications Office of the European Union, 2019), https://ec.europa.eu/eurostat/documents/3217494/10166544/KS-02-19%E2%80%91681-EN-N.pdf/c701972f-6b4e-b432-57d2-91898ca94893.

32. "People at Risk of Poverty or Social Exclusion in Latvia in 2018," Central Statistical Bureau of Latvia, last modified January 16, 2020, https://www.csb.gov.lv/en/statistics/statistics-by-theme/social-conditions/poverty/search-in-theme/399-people-risk-poverty-and-social-exclusion.

33. Marta Borda and Patrycja Kowalczyk-Rólczyńska, "Evaluation of Elderly Households' Financial Standing in Central and Eastern European Countries," *Post-Communist Economies* 30, no. 5 (2018): 637.

34. "The New Natalism," *Economist*, January 25, 2020, 45.

35. Eszter Zimanyi, "Family B/Orders: Hungary's Campaign for the 'Family Protection Action Plan,'" *Feminist Media Studies* 20, no. 2 (2020): 305–9.

36. Jon Werthheim, "Subsidies for Minivans: Hungarian Government Paying Citizens to Start Families, but Only the 'Right' Kinds of Families," CBS News, July 19, 2020, https://www.cbsnews.com/news/hungary-paying-citizens-to-have-babies-60-minutes-2020-07-19.

37. Patrick Kingsley, "Orban Encourages Mothers in Hungary to Have 4 or More Babies," *New York Times*, February 11, 2019, https://www.nytimes.com/2019/02/11/world/europe/orban-hungary-babies-mothers-population-immigration.html.

38. Center for Economic Analysis, "FROGEE Policy Brief 1: Insights from Poland," CEA Policy Brief Series, December 2019, https://freepolicybriefs.org/wp-content/uploads/2019/12/frogee-policy-brief-1-pl-eng.pdf.

39. Lyman Stone, "Pro-natal Policies Work, but They Come with a Hefty Price Tag," IFS, March 5, 2020, https://ifstudies.org/blog/pro-natal-policies-work-but-they-come-with-a-hefty-price-tag.

40. Jessica Bateman and Marta Kasztelan, "In Poland, Abortion Access Worsens amid Pandemic," *Foreign Policy*, May 1, 2020, https://foreignpolicy.com/2020/05/01/poland-abortion-access-worsens-coronavirus-pandemic.

41. Lev Kvovskiy, Nicolas Gavoille, Anna Pluta, and Anna Zasova, "FROGEE Policy Brief 1: Insights from Latvia," December 2019, https://freepolicybriefs.org/wp-content/uploads/2019/12/frogee-policy-brief-1-lv-eng.pdf.

42. Monica Georgiadis, "Romania: Reforms to Child-Raising Leave and Indemnity," *Lexology*, April 27, 2016, https://www.lexology.com/library/detail.aspx?g=a3d2da39-df3f-4afb-9ffc-907f27c25108.

43. Lina Vdovii and Michael Bird, "Over 30 Percent of Hospitals in Romania Are Refusing Legal Abortions," *Black Sea*, July 11, 2019, https://theblacksea.eu/stories/quarter-hospitals-romania-are-refusing-legal-abortions.

44. Charles F. Westoff, "Recent Trends in Abortion and Contraception in 12 Countries," *DHS Analytical Studies* 8 (February 2005): 14.

45. Klaus F. Zimmermann, "European Migration: Push and Pull," *World Bank Economic Review* 8, no. 1 (1994): 313–42; E. Sylvester Vizi, "Reversing the Brain Drain from Eastern European Countries: The 'Push' and 'Pull' Factors," *Technology in Society* 15, no. 1 (1993): 101–9.

46. Gordon F. Sander, "Latvia, a Disappearing Nation," *Politico*, January 7, 2018, https://www.politico.eu/article/latvia-a-disappearing-nation-migration-population-decline.

47. Ieva Birka, "Can Return Migration Revitalize the Baltics? Estonia, Latvia, and Lithuania Engage Their Diasporas, with Mixed Results," Migration Policy Institute, last modified June 6, 2019, https://www.migrationpolicy.org/article/can-return-migration-revitalize-baltics-estonia-latvia-and-lithuania-engage-their-diasporas.

48. Krystyna Iglicka and Magdalena Ziolek-Skrzypczak, "EU Membership Highlights Poland's Migration Challenges," Migration Policy Institute, last modified July 17, 2019, https://www.mig rationpolicy.org/article/eu-membership-highlights-polands-migration-challenges.

49. Bart Bachman, "Diminishing Solidarity: Polish Attitudes toward the European Migration and Refugee Crisis," Migration Policy Institute, last modified March 2, 2017, https://www.mig rationpolicy.org/article/diminishing-solidarity-polish-attitudes-toward-european-migration-and-refugee-crisis.

50. Tuvia Friling, Radu Ioanid, and Mihail E. Ionescu, *Final Report of the International Commission on the Holocaust in Romania* (Bucharest: Polirom, 2005).

51. "'Sharp Rise' in Bulgarian and Romanian Workers in UK," Channel 4 News, August 15, 2013, https://www.channel4.com/news/immigrants-romania-bulgaria-workers-eu-migration -watch.

52. Organisation for Economic Co operation and Development (OECD), *Talent Abroad: A Review of Romanian Emigrants* (Paris: OECD Publishing, 2019).

53. OECD, *Talent Abroad*.

54. Diana Salceanu, "Romania Is Fighting the Coronavirus Epidemic with a Shortage of Doctors Mounting to 40,000," *Romania Journal*, March 24, 2020, https://www.romaniajourna l.ro/society-people/romania-is-fighting-the-coronavirus-epidemic-with-a-shortage-of-doctors-mou nting-to-40000.

55. Boryana Dzhambazova and Claudia Ciobanu, "Medical Exodus Leaves Romania, Bulgaria in Pain," *Deutsche Welle*, July 2, 2018, https://www.dw.com/en/medical-exodus-leaves-romania -bulgaria-in-pain/a-44487178.

56. "Romania Facing Shortage of Industrial Workers," Associated Press, May 12, 2015, https ://www.manufacturing.net/labor/news/13065096/romania-facing-shortage-of-industrial-workers.

57. Denise Hruby, "How to Slow Down the World's Fastest-Shrinking Country," BBC, September 30, 2019, https://www.bbc.com/worklife/article/20190913-how-to-slow-down-the -worlds-fastest-shrinking-country.

58. Sander, "Latvia, a Disappearing Nation."

59. "Romanian Unemployment Rate by Region," Statista, last modified November 29, 2020, https://www.statista.com/statistics/1177858/romania-unemployment-rate-by-region.

60. Anja Vladisavljevic, "One-Way Ticket: Croatia's Growing Emigration Crisis," *Balkan Insight*, January 8, 2019, https://balkaninsight.com/2019/01/08/one-way-ticket-croatia-s-gro wing-emigration-crisis-12-21-2018.

61. Reiner Martin and Radu Dragos, "Return Migration: The Experience of Eastern Europe," *International Migration* 50, no. 6 (December 2012): 109–28.

62. OECD, *Talent Abroad*.

63. Birka, "Can Return Migration Revitalize the Baltics?"

64. Daina S. Eglitis, *Imagining the Nation: History, Modernity, and Revolution in Latvia* (University Park: Penn State University Press, 2002).

65. Alice Greider, "Outsourcing Migration Management: The Role of the Western Balkans in the European Refugee Crisis," Migration Policy Institute, last modified August 25, 2020, https ://www.migrationpolicy.org/article/outsourcing-migration-management-western-balkans-europes -refugee-crisis.

66. Elżbieta M. Goździak, "Using Fear of the 'Other,' Orbán Reshapes Migration Policy in a Hungary Built on Cultural Diversity," Migration Policy Institute, last modified April 16, 2020, https://www.migrationpolicy.org/article/orban-reshapes-migration-policy-hungary.

67. Goździak, "Using Fear of the 'Other.'"

68. Nick Thorpe, "Migrant Crisis: Hungary Police Recruit 'Border-Hunters,'" BBC, September 2, 2016, https://www.bbc.com/news/world-europe-37259857.

69. Thorpe, "Migrant Crisis."

70. Birka, "Can Return Migration Revitalize the Baltics?"

71. Andrei Schwartz and Bogdan Neagu, "Refugees at the EU Borders—Status Update from Romania," *Euractiv*, April 30, 2018, https://www.euractiv.com/section/justice-home-affairs/interv iew/refugees-at-the-eu-borders-status-update-from-romania.

72. Oana Vasile and Armenia Androniceanu, "An Overview of the Romanian Asylum Policies," *Sustainability* 10, no. 5 (2018): 1461.

73. Vasile and Androniceanu, "An Overview of the Romanian Asylum Policies."

74. "2019 Statistical Data on Migrants and Refugees in Romania," European Commission, last modified February 18, 2020, https://ec.europa.eu/migrant-integration/news/2019-statistical-data -on-migrants-and-refugees-in-romania.

75. Maxim Edwards, "Romania, a Beacon of Coexistence for Muslims in Eastern Europe," Al Jazeera, August 20, 2019, https://www.aljazeera.com/features/2019/08/20/romania-a-beacon-of -coexistence-for-muslims-in-eastern-europe.

76. Bachman, "Diminishing Solidarity."

77. Richard Wike, Jacob Poushter, Laura Silver, Kat Devlin, Janell Fetterolf, Alexandra Castillo, and Christine Huang, "Views on Minority Groups across Europe," Pew Research Center, last modified July 14, 2020, https://www.pewresearch.org/global/2019/10/14/minority-groups.

78. Alice Greider, "Outsourcing Migration Management: The Role of the Western Balkans in the European Refugee Crisis," Migration Policy Institute, last modified August 25, 2020, https ://www.migrationpolicy.org/article/outsourcing-migration-management-western-balkans-europes -refugee-crisis.

79. "Operational Portal: Mediterranean Situation," United Nations High Commissioner for Refugees (UNHCR), https://data2.unhcr.org/en/situations/mediterranean.

80. Nikolai Atanassov, Costica Dumbrava, Maria-Margarita Mentzelopoulou, and Anja Radjenovic, *EU Asylum, Borders and External Cooperation on Migration: Recent Developments*, European Union, May 2018, https://www.europarl.europa.eu/RegData/etudes/IDAN/2018/621 878/EPRS_IDA(2018)621878_EN.pdf.

81. Andy Kiersz and Madison Hoff, "The 20 Fastest-Shrinking Countries in the World," *Business Insider*, July 16, 2020, https://www.businessinsider.com/the-fastest-shrinking-countries-in -the-world-declining-populations#7-croatia-the-population-is-projected-to-drop-from-41-million -in-2020-to-34-million-in-2050-an-180-decline-14.

82. Charles Lane, "Eastern Europe Is Headed toward a Demographic Crisis," *Washington Post*, November 11, 2019, https://www.washingtonpost.com/opinions/global-opinions/the-incredible -shrinking-nations-of-eastern-europe/2019/11/11/fd777326-04a6-11ea-b17d-8b867891d39d_ story.html.

CHAPTER 7

Transitional Justice and Memory

Eva-Clarita Pettai and Vello Pettai

For the past thirty years, the Central and East European region has been associated with stirring phenomena like dynamic popular protests, democratization, and the rebirth of national identities. These phenomena came about, however, because of preceding periods of severe political and social repression that in the case of Central and East Europe lasted some five decades, and in Ukraine more than seven decades. Although this oppression went through several phases and had variations from country to country, it encompassed not only restrictions on free speech, association, and travel but also more horrific human rights violations such as widespread surveillance, indiscriminate arrest, mass deportation, and summary killing. Moreover, much of what happened was kept secret, known only through individual recollections and family stories. While liberation between 1989 and 1991 was an exhilarating event for all of these peoples, it came with hard questions about how to deal with this past: Who should be held to account? How should victims be acknowledged? How should individual countries remember this era? As each society struggled with these questions, it soon became apparent that the periods of Nazi and communist rule in the region had not been a mere hiatus in an otherwise continuous and peaceful state development; for many, it was experienced as a national ordeal that would mark the identity and politics of these peoples for decades to come.

The process of reckoning with past regime abuse and people's suffering is usually referred to as "transitional justice." Postcommunism is only one of three broad contexts in which this increasingly global phenomenon has occurred: it has also followed authoritarian/military regimes (such as in Argentina and South Korea) and civil wars (such as in Sierra Leone and Sri Lanka).[1] What is particular about the crimes and abuses of communist rule is that they were more all pervasive and wide ranging than those in other regimes. Therefore, while Central and East Europeans could draw on certain transitional justice lessons from other countries, they also had to deal with specific communist-era legacies, such as dismantling extensive secret police networks and returning thousands of buildings and other forms of property that had been nationalized by the communist authorities. Moreover, many of the crimes and atrocities committed during World War II and the Nazi occupation, as well as the immediate postwar period, had not been sufficiently reckoned with due to ideological bias and restraints. Therefore, in many of these countries, these "historical" crimes and periods of repression had to be dealt with at the same time.

Finally, while transitional justice was strongly focused on "righting the wrongs" of the preceding regimes, it also had a forward-looking commitment to rebuilding democratic values, rule of law, and societal trust that would help to undergird the region's return to the Western world.

Yet all of these similarities notwithstanding, the countries of Central and East Europe have varied considerably in terms of not only the timing and scope of transitional justice measures adopted by the new governments but also the levels of political controversy that have accompanied these policies. Some countries like the Czech Republic were early and aggressive implementers of transitional justice, while others, such as Bulgaria, have been late and halting. Some countries, like Poland, have seen recurring waves of political debate over the need for such policies, while others, like Estonia, seem almost to have "closed the books" on these matters. In any case, none of the regional states has been able to avoid dealing with the past, as Poland's first postcommunist prime minister put it, by "drawing a thick line" and simply moving forward.

Moreover, as more time has elapsed since the collapse of communism, the question of how to deal with the past has gradually shifted from being an immediate issue of what to do with the remnants of the old system to a process of forming a common national memory of those troubled times. The oppressors of the former regime and their victims are no longer alive, or they are not as prominent in these societies as they once were. Transitional justice has also often been overtaken by new dimensions and challenges of political and social life, such as European Union (EU) membership, socioeconomic development, and a resurgent Russia. Debate about the Nazi and communist eras has frequently shifted toward how this past should be remembered and commemorated, depicted and framed, taught and communicated. This phenomenon is called the "politics of memory." Unlike transitional justice, which focuses on specific individuals or groups defined as victims or perpetrators of past crimes and abuses, the politics of memory looks at society as a whole and at the mechanisms and means by which actors propagate and enforce a certain "correct" version of history and of remembrance, thereby crafting particular historical identities for the longer term. Yet here, too, there are many national differences, in terms of not only how historiography has evolved but also how politicians have tried to instrumentalize commemorative events, institute certain national memorial days, and sometimes even adopt formal laws on how the past should be represented and remembered in the public sphere. Indeed, in the past decade, history and memory were particularly high on the political agenda of right-wing populist and neoauthoritarian leaders across Central and East Europe.

Different Dimensions of Postcommunist Transitional Justice

We begin our chapter by taking a closer look at transitional justice and laying out two important frameworks for analyzing this phenomenon. The first takes a time perspective and examines not only how quickly or slowly new democratic governments in Central and East Europe adopted certain transitional justice measures but also how far back in time the regime abuses were that these measures sought to rectify. The second framework involves understanding the range of specific transitional justice measures countries could adopt. Here the issues concern the degree to which countries deal with both perpetrators and victims of past regime abuse, as well as the legal level at which these measures are implemented.

When new democratic governments come to power, often one of their first priorities is to deal with the immediate aftermath of the prior regime.[2] This is not easy, however, since the necessary criminal procedures or laws for prosecuting offenses like human rights violations will not have existed under the legal codes left over from the nondemocratic era. In this respect, new democracies always face a dilemma. Either they can implement quick but perhaps also arbitrary justice (by banning, say, all former Communist Party members from politics regardless of what they did in that role) and thereby undermine the principles of rule of law, which democracy itself stands for, or they can take time to pass new legal frameworks, but in so doing they may lose momentum in the process as a whole (as certain suspects flee into exile or disappear into obscurity). Much will depend on the strength of the new democratic governments themselves. Where democratic leaders are in a strong position politically, they can adopt a number of transitional justice policies quickly. Where former rulers were able to negotiate their departure from power and remain active in political life, progress on transitional justice may be slower. Several electoral cycles may be needed before political forces committed to dealing with the past can (re)gain power and begin to adopt relevant measures. In these cases, we often speak of "late," "delayed," "second-wave," or "post-transitional" justice.

In Central and East Europe, the Velvet Revolution in Czechoslovakia allowed new leaders to push for speedy adoption of laws that not only purged the civil service of former communists but also offered rehabilitation and compensation to political prisoners under the former regime. Although Czechoslovakia later broke up through the "Velvet Divorce," the Czech Republic continued the implementation of these steadfast policies (while Slovakia did not). Albania was also a case of quick action on transitional justice under the Democratic Party elected in 1992. The new government moved swiftly to replace former communist officials with its own loyalists. It also passed legislation seeking to bar ex-communists from standing for future elected office. However, because many of these measures began to be used for partisan purposes, the Democratic Party soon became unpopular. The ex-communist Socialist Party was returned to office in 1997, and transitional justice essentially stopped.

In Lithuania, Hungary, and Poland, another combination ensued, as ex-communists were able to return to power within just a few years of the transition and thereby stall transitional justice measures relatively quickly. At the same time, right-wing forces were able to reestablish control later on and thereafter undertake what was mentioned above as delayed transitional justice. Conservative parties in Lithuania, for example, regained control of the government in 1996 and then began a series of truth and justice initiatives lasting for many years. In Poland, the rise to power of the Law and Justice (PiS) party in 2005 also opened up a new wave of transitional justice, including a more aggressive policy preventing former secret police employees from working in the public sector.[3] Bulgaria, Romania, and Ukraine, meanwhile, represented cases where ex-communist parties remained relatively strong throughout the 1990s (even when in the opposition), and as a result transitional justice remained weak all around.

Another dimension of time important for studying transitional justice relates to the fact that communist rule in Central and East Europe lasted for more than four decades, and in Ukraine more than seven. The consequence of this was that in some countries it was easier for politicians to address regime abuses that were further back in time than to confront those where perpetrators may have still been active in society.[4] Establishing historical commissions to look into the 1956 uprising in Hungary, the 1941 Stalinist deportations in Latvia, or the 1932–1933 Holodomor famine in Ukraine—even if it named specific persons involved—was politically a less audacious act of seeking justice than trying to put late communist officials on trial or establish expensive reparations programs for former regime victims. Morally speaking, both types of justice were important, especially in terms of understanding the whole communist era. However, when we want to understand why some countries addressed certain regime abuses and not others, we can see that some issues were politically more costly to tackle than others.

Indeed, the two temporal dimensions mentioned here were often intertwined. When new democratic governments did not have the political muscle to directly confront former communist leaders, they could focus on dealing with historical instances of repression. Likewise, when left-wing governments were in power and they had little interest in dwelling too much on the immediate past, they could still demonstrate a degree of bona fides regarding transitional justice by sponsoring measures that addressed decades-old injustices without fear of undermining their own political legitimacy. Sometimes governments could come to power many years after democracy had been established and then seek to take on tough transitional justice issues like putting an ex-communist leader on trial, as Poland did against former army general and Communist Party leader Wojciech Jaruzelski and the former interior minister of the People's Republic Czesław Kiszczak. But when this combination of dimensions (late but aggressive transitional justice) took place, the relevance of the act was often diminished, since the leaders were likely to be old and the charges more difficult to sustain.

A second overarching framework for comparing transitional justice processes in Central and East Europe involves scrutinizing the breadth of different measures that are undertaken. When governments abuse their power or repress their citizens, justice should in theory encompass both punishing the perpetrators and acknowledging the victims. In reality, however, it may be the case that the latter is easier than the former. Offering compensation or rehabilitation to a former deportee is often simpler to carry out than proving the legal culpability of the secret police official who ordered the deportation. This means that one aspect of studying transitional justice concerns looking at how much countries are able to deal with one or the other side of this same coin.[5]

Furthermore, even when a country addresses both perpetrators and victims, it may do so at three key levels of policy. On the one hand, classical transitional justice begins with enacting *criminal-judicial* legislation that would allow for the prosecution and trial of former regime officials responsible for human rights violations. Likewise, however, it is important to recognize that criminal-judicial legislation can also pertain to victims, in the sense of reversing erstwhile convictions imposed during show trials or politically motivated prosecutions. This is known as rehabilitation. A step lower in terms of policy are *administrative-political* measures that can deprive perpetrators of certain political rights or privileges while restoring or according such benefits to victims. Again, these tracks need not take place at the same time, but they both involve mid-level policy measures that will often be enacted by law but can also be implemented through administrative decisions. Lastly, certain truth and justice measures can be seen as having purely *symbolic-representational* value in terms of shaming perpetrators or acknowledging the suffering of victims. As such, they would appear to have the least consequence. However, for individual perpetrators or victims, these can still be important, as when a perpetrator's professional career may be damaged by having been exposed as a onetime secret informant or a victim's feeling of dignity is restored when he or she is able to gain access to surveillance files compiled by the security services or participate in official ceremonies commemorating past suffering.

In the sections that follow, we will show examples of all of these policy variants of transitional justice. However, we will also try to show where different time dimensions manifested themselves. That is, we will see how some of these types of action were taken early on following the collapse of communism and others were sometimes pursued years later. Likewise, we will observe that certain policy measures were more prevalent toward more historical injustices, while others pertained mainly to more recent communist repression.

Criminal-Judicial Justice: Prosecutions and Rehabilitations

Few Romanians alive during the collapse of communism will ever forget what they felt when they heard in December 1989 that their country's ruler, Nicolae Ceaușescu, and his wife Elena had been tried and summarily executed barely three days after they fled from power. This was an example of immediate criminal justice vis-à-vis a former repressive leader, akin to what one might imagine happens stereotypically when a society tired of being subjugated by a ruthless dictator rises up for revenge. Needless to say, the trial conducted for the Ceaușescus was not a formal court procedure. After he and his wife were caught, they were "tried" by their military captors and put before a firing squad. This illustrates one of the first challenges that many postcommunist countries faced when they tried to criminally prosecute former leaders: what law should or could be applied toward communist-era repression so that it would not be considered retroactive or post hoc justice? How could evidence be gathered for such culpability, how should such trials or procedures take place, and what should constitute proper punishment if an accused person were found guilty?

New leaders in three countries in the region, the former East Germany, Poland, and Bulgaria, actively sought to put prominent communist officials on trial; however, their strategies in this regard were slightly different. Both Germany and Poland sought to build cases against former party leaders Erich Honecker and Wojciech Jaruzelski, respectively, that centered on their role in ordering the direct killing of civilians. In Honecker's case, it involved his responsibility for issuing a policy to shoot people trying to cross the border to West Germany surreptitiously. For Jaruzelski, it concerned a command to open fire on workers striking in 1970 at the Gdańsk shipyards. Ultimately, however, both of these trials failed, not only because of the defendants' delaying tactics and their advanced age by the mid-1990s but also precisely because it was difficult to prove culpability so high up in the chain of command. The case against the longtime head of Bulgaria's Communist Party, Todor Zhivkov, was for a more banal offense of misappropriating state funds. In his case (along with a number of other defendants in the trial), the prosecution was more successful, and multiyear prison terms were handed down because these were provable offenses. The only successful prosecutions for actual political repression were of mid- and lower-level officials such as border guards or security personnel, who were tried and found guilty of manslaughter in specific incidents. Officials in Germany carried out more than five hundred such prosecutions, while in the Czech Republic the number was around fifty.[6]

In Hungary, a different challenge emerged when, during the early 1990s, authorities attempted to render justice for a more distant crime, seeking criminal charges against those who had been involved in the killing during the 1956 revolution—about forty years earlier. The Hungarian parliament repeatedly passed legislation enabling the relevant prosecutions to begin; however, each time the Hungarian Constitutional Court issued rulings declaring such amendments illegal, as they overrode the statute of limitations that existed for manslaughter under Hungarian law.[7] Eventually the court acknowledged that the statute of limitations would not apply if repressions during the 1956 uprising constituted a war crime or a crime against humanity, since these notions derived from international law. This opened up a new legal avenue for prosecutors, and a number of

Photo 7.1. General Wojciech Jaruzelski, president of Poland in 1989 and 1990 and former head of the Polish military, was tried for attacks on demonstrators during the Gdańsk protests in the 1970s. His trial spanned nearly a decade and then was dropped in 2013 due to his age and poor health. (Adam Chelstokski, FORUM)

trials were launched, including against Béla Biszku, a top-ranking communist official from 1956 who had publicly asserted that the reprisals had been justified.

In Romania, which was the only country in the region to have experienced significant violence during the democratic revolution of 1989–1990, two series of trials were carried out against individuals responsible for the violence. From the start, these trials reflected partisan politics: while the earlier trials, still under the government of the National Salvation Front (NSF), had focused on former Communist Party leaders and former security police officers, the second round of trials included army generals from the ranks of the NSF. A third series of trials commenced in 2016, this time encompassing the NSF leader Ion Iliescu, who was indicted for crimes against humanity in connection with his involvement in the violent crackdown against the demonstrations in 1989.[8] Romanian courts also heard some cases regarding more temporally distant crimes. The most public of these was against former prison guard Alexandru Vişinescu, who in 2015 was found guilty of crimes against humanity committed in his capacity as commander of the Râmnicu Sărat prison from 1956 to 1963.

The proposition that communist-era repression in many cases constituted a full-scale crime against humanity without any statute of limitations became a prevalent legal approach in the Baltic states as well. For these countries, the motivation was even more acute, since repression during the 1940s had included multiple waves of mass deportations, most notably in 1941 and 1949. During those years, more than 180,000 people had been herded into cattle cars and forced to resettle in remote areas of Siberia or were sent into the Gulag, a system of prison camps. Countless individuals died along the way, while even more perished later amid the harsh labor and living conditions. Many of the responsible agents of the Soviet secret police at the time, the NKVD, were still alive in the 1990s. The parliaments in Estonia, Latvia, and Lithuania therefore reworked their criminal codes in order to lay out statutes against not only war crimes and crimes against humanity but also genocide. They used these provisions to begin several hundred investigations (particularly in Lithuania), which resulted in nearly sixty convictions. However, as in several other countries, many of the accused died during trial proceedings, or they were given suspended sentences because of their advanced age.

Judicial authorities were also heavily involved in the process of rehabilitating victims of communist-era repression. Laws clearing individuals of conviction for politically motivated crimes were passed across the region as soon as democracy was reestablished. One example was Czechoslovakia, where barely six months after the Velvet Revolution parliament adopted a rehabilitation law that invalidated a wide range of convictions that had been carried out against dissidents and other opponents of the regime based on specific, political offenses listed in criminal law. It sufficed to simply rescind these statutes and annul all convictions issued on their basis in order to carry out rehabilitation. At the same time, other cases were more ambiguous, such as when people had participated in some anti-regime demonstration but were convicted for "hooliganism." These cases often needed to be reexamined before rehabilitation could be granted. Lastly, many countries (such as the Baltic states) adopted laws that went further back in time in order to deal with the victims of Stalinist repression during the 1940s and 1950s. In these instances, prior convictions were also readily overturned because they had often been handed down by extrajudicial tribunals. Nevertheless, there were also rehabilitated individuals who

Photo 7.2. This photo shows a corridor with prison cells in the basement of the former KGB headquarters in Vilnius, Lithuania. Today the site is a museum. (Sergio Delle Vedove, Shutterstock)

had actually been involved in crimes. Thus, in Lithuania, officials were forced to rescind rehabilitation for several dozen individuals after it came out that although these people had been tried for anti-Soviet activity in the late 1940s, they had also been linked to the repression and killing of Jews during the Nazi occupation of the Baltics in World War II.

Political-Administrative Truth and Justice: Lustration and Compensation

Transitional justice in Central and East Europe has most often been associated with lustration, or the process of investigating, exposing, removing, and possibly sanctioning individuals for different degrees of communist-era abuses that did not involve formal criminal offenses. In reality, this phenomenon involved three separate policy dimensions that centered on particular areas of inquiry. First, what level of prior participation in the regime would be seen as warranting lustration? Second, what precise administrative sanction would be imposed for that involvement? And third, how should the government organize the screening of existing state employees, as well as the vetting of future employees?[9]

Regarding the first dimension, most countries concentrated their attention on those who had most directly been responsible for repression: full-time agents and employees of the former security services. Therefore, some form of screening and vetting legislation targeting these people was adopted at some point in almost every country of the region. Closely related to this category, however, were the thousands of informants and collaborators of the secret police, whom most countries also sought to subject to lustration in some way. Yet here the verification process was not so easy, since it was never clear whether operative files from the secret services (often seized after the democratic transition) could be trusted to determine someone's degree of involvement given that agents of the police may have tried to embellish their successes within the system. This kind of ambiguity often gave pause for thought in some countries such as Estonia, where informants of the Soviet KGB were never actively pursued even though lustration legislation allowed for this. Meanwhile, other countries such as Albania cast their net in a different direction and included as subject to lustration all those who had been members of the Politburo and Central Committee of the former Communist Party, as well as communist-era parliamentary deputies and presidents of the Supreme Court.[10] In other words, a number of ex officio positions from the past regime could be included within the circle of lustration, irrespective of what they had actually done in office.

On the second question of determining appropriate sanctions, most countries began with a ban on employment in the civil service (especially for former secret police agents). In some countries, the notion of civil service was extended beyond simple administrative positions to include not only the courts but also high-level management positions in state-owned companies (Czech Republic) or university positions (Poland). This implied a maximum effort to keep former regime individuals out of the democratic state. Moreover, Lithuania sought to bar these people from working in many areas of the private sector, such as banking, detective services, or the legal profession. Although this 1999 version of the country's lustration law would eventually be overturned by the European Court of Human Rights (ECHR), it did lead in the very beginning to many private firms firing individuals alleged to have been involved with the Soviet KGB.

Another level of more formalized noncriminal sanctioning of former regime officials was adopted in Latvia, which after 1996 screened all candidate lists for parliamentary and local elections and authorized the central electoral commission to make public the names of all those who had been listed in leftover KGB files. Moreover, if a court had formally proven that person's collaboration with the Soviet security forces, they could be removed from the electoral list. In other words, the country effectively denied former agents their right to stand for public office, which the European Court of Human Rights upheld in the initial term but declared to be a violation of European human rights law in 2008.

To deal with this entire process of personnel review (the third important policy dimension), countries in the region established a variety of administrative offices and procedures. The Czech Republic had perhaps the most rigorous system, requiring individuals seeking to retain or obtain employment in the public sector to request a formal lustration certificate from a special section of the Ministry of Interior tasked with reviewing available files from the former secret police, the StB. In this respect, the burden of proof was put

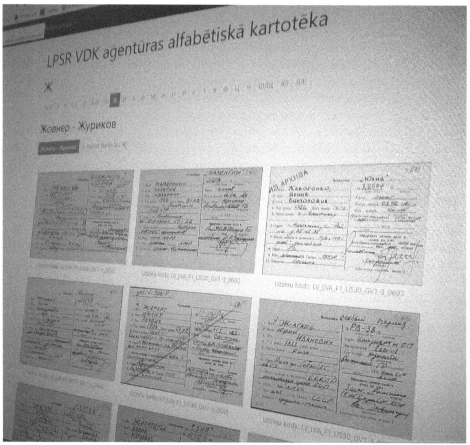

Photo 7.3. Latvia opened its archive of files left behind by the Soviet KGB to the public in 2018. The personal file cards of former agents and informers were even published online. (Eva-Clarita Pettai)

on each individual to directly vindicate themselves before being allowed into the system. Poland and Hungary enacted milder procedures, both in terms of limiting the scope of government posts under review to high-ranked elected officials (and not all civil servants), as well as by making the screening process less onerous. For example, under Poland's 1997 legislation, individuals were required to sign a declaration disclosing any prior collaboration with the old regime. Thus, in theory, one could admit collaboration and in so doing be exonerated and free to seek high elected office. If one lied on one's declaration, a special court could review the evidence and reveal the person's name in public. However, these proceedings were generally conducted behind closed doors, and this quickly became a battle cry among conservatives for a more rigorous lustration procedure. Lastly, Estonia took one of the most liberal approaches, specifying that current and future state employees sign an "oath of conscience" that they had not engaged in communist-era repression. Moreover, these documents would remain simply on file unless they were specifically contested by another individual or prosecutor. In this respect, the Estonian system presumed that individuals were telling the truth before they were scrutinized (and not the other way around). This process came to an end relatively quickly (December 2000) instead of being extended in duration as in the Czech Republic.

These diverse approaches engendered various levels of criticism for being either too lax or too severe.[11] Moreover, when particularly respected politicians were brought down by these provisions (such as Juris Bojārs in Latvia, a onetime prominent member of the Latvian independence movement, but also an ex-major in the KGB), it became obvious that cleaning out the skeletons in the closet would be tricky. Yet, beyond these formal procedures and their attempts to adhere to some degree of rule of law, the phenomenon of "informal lustration" also flared in each postcommunist country as politicians traded accusations of alleged collaboration by their opponents, and the news media amplified these debates as well as provided fodder of its own through investigative reporting and public speculation. This was the cross-fire to which two prime ministers in Poland (Jan Olszewski and Józef Oleksy) would be subjected during the first half of the 1990s and before Poland would even have a lustration law. In Bulgaria and Romania, this frenzy accelerated in the 2000s partly as a response to insufficient lustration policies being passed in the first place.[12] In Romania, debates about both the misdeeds of the Securitate and insufficient postcommunist lustration flared up again as late as 2019, when former president Traian Băsescu was found guilty for having collaborated with the communist secret political police while a student during the 1970s. The ensuing public debates revealed still-existing divisions among political elites about how to remember the communist past and its "impact on post-communist Romanian democracy and rule of law."[13]

The politicization and instrumentalization of lustration controversies also illustrates why (in contrast to many other transitional justice measures) these policies have most often been subject to a ratcheting up or a tightening many years after democracy is consolidated. In other words, a time dimension is clearly evident in this domain, such that many analysts have spoken of "late lustration" when examining, for example, how both Romania and Poland tried to tighten their policies in 2006.[14] These kinds of shifts have also made explaining lustration a complicated affair. While structural issues such as type of democratic transition may have mattered in the initial term, there have also been many wildcards in play when one considers how sensationalist media revelations can have unforeseen consequences for public opinion or political posturing. These waves of controversy have also been criticized for undermining one of the key objectives of transitional justice: to rebuild trust in society and the new democratic system.

Turning to the victim side of political-administrative transitional justice, it is perhaps no surprise that countries that decided to legally rehabilitate victims of repression also often worked out additional administrative forms of reparation, including granting those individuals monetary compensation and/or other social privileges. Ideally, this type of transitional justice involved adopting formal legislation that would accord certain individuals special legal status as "repressed persons" and make them eligible for particular benefits. Lithuania adopted such a law in 1997 specifying no less than three dozen types of repression or persecution individuals may have suffered during either the Soviet or Nazi occupations from 1939 to 1991 and making all of them entitled to special standing.

In terms of monetary compensation, former political prisoners in the Czech Republic, for example, received a base payment of roughly $83 per month of incarceration under the communist regime, while in Bulgaria those who had been held in labor camps or imprisoned could receive up to $1,060 per month of detention, as would former prisoners in Romania.[15] Meanwhile, in some countries like Poland, interesting dividing lines emerged on temporal grounds. The country's original 1991 compensation law limited benefits to those who had suffered from 1944 to 1956, thereby making the measure largely a more historical one. Many members of the Polish Senate objected to this restriction, saying that it would marginalize suffering that had happened after the end of the Stalinist terror. At the same time, a number of more recent victims of repression (especially those who had been imprisoned during the period of martial law after 1980) believed that compensation for them would cast in a disparaging light the pro-democracy struggle they had waged simply out of their convictions. Moreover, many politicians born out of the Solidarity movement were uneasy about making themselves personally eligible for such benefits. Expansion of the compensation policy in Poland therefore remained a thorny issue for many years.

In the Baltic states, the focus was overwhelmingly on measures to compensate suffering for victims of the 1940s deportations. All three countries tailored their pension systems and even some privatization processes to count time spent in Siberia as part of a victim's years of gainful employment. Lithuania also paid such victims direct compensation, although this raised certain ambiguities because it was the Soviet authorities who had deported these people; therefore, some found it questionable that the new Lithuanian state should take on this burden instead of the Russian Federation as the USSR's successor state.[16]

A further administrative type of restorative justice for victims involved the restitution of any property taken away by the communist authorities. Sometimes this concerned political prisoners or deportees who had had their homes or other property seized by the communist state. For these victims, the process of restitution was relatively easy. However, a much broader form of this policy involved the restitution of property that had been nationalized by the communists, usually during the beginning of their regime. Here the question was whether, and if so in what manner, all of these former owners and their descendants should get back their property. Moreover, property had to be differentiated into at least five forms: agricultural land, dwellings and buildings, nonphysical property such as stocks, property that had been demolished or destroyed during war, and church or religious community property. Concerning agricultural land, restitution processes generally proceeded smoothly, since in most Central and East European countries (with the exception of Poland), agriculture had been collectivized, and this meant that all arable land was in state hands. In most instances, it was not difficult to review whatever land records existed prior to nationalization and to develop procedures for return of this land, even if in the short term it went to smallholders and was counterproductive from the perspective of developing a strong agricultural sector.[17]

More controversial was the policy of returning houses and apartment buildings to former owners, especially if those dwellings now had new tenants, and people would suddenly become renters not to the state but to private owners.[18] Not only would this process require years of bureaucratic effort (verifying former ownership claims and negotiating among often multiple claimants and their descendants) but also in social terms so-called forced renters could be pressured to leave these homes so that restituted owners could undertake renovations or develop their properties for more profitable gain. In theory, this kind of housing transformation was supposed to help revive private real estate and make it more productive (especially in downtown urban areas). However, in reality it came at the cost of considerable social disruption. In many cases municipal authorities lacked alternative housing for forced renters. Controversies also flared over whether émigrés would be allowed to get back property abandoned decades earlier; in Estonia and Latvia they would, while in the Czech Republic and Lithuania they would not. Politically the issue would remain charged for many years.

This was one reason why some governments, including Lithuania, Hungary, and Poland, opted for more restrictive rules, such as offering claimants only compensation, especially if the prior dwelling, commercial enterprise, or land had since been substantially changed or privatized. In legal terms, this was justified as still constituting justice, since property rights were construed as meaning a right to a certain value or good, not an absolute right to a particular object. Restitution could therefore also take the form of privatization vouchers or other certificates, which could be used for the purchase of alternative property. Lastly, property restitution policy shifted over time as different governments attempted to either speed up or slow down these processes depending on their political persuasion. At the same time, the courts often stepped in to maintain some consistency in the process. Hence, Lithuania's courts stymied conservatives' attempts to expand restitution efforts in the late 1990s, while Estonian courts often sided with former owners even after lawmakers in that country sought to curtail some of the restitution provisions.

A final area of contention concerned religious property. In many countries, officials had to negotiate extensively with religious organizations concerning the return of not only buildings but also agricultural lands and other property. The restitution of Jewish property that had been seized or abandoned during the Holocaust was also very complicated, as that had not been returned or compensated by the subsequent communist authorities. Many Central and East European countries were reluctant to take on these claims, arguing that in most instances the individual claimants—often decedents of the original owners, who had either fled or were murdered during the Holocaust—were no longer citizens or residents of these countries and were therefore ineligible under existing law.

Furthermore, many governments demurred on recognizing Jewish community property, especially if it pertained to social welfare establishments like hospitals or schools. Lastly, acknowledging Jewish claims in cities like Warsaw, Vilnius, or Riga promised to open up large swaths of property to either restitution or expensive compensation. A number of international associations such as the World Jewish Restitution Organization put pressure on governments to resolve these issues. In 2011, Lithuania passed a special law on "goodwill compensation," allocating over $50 million over a ten-year period to a special restorative fund. Efforts to pass similar legislation in Latvia and Poland have failed.

Symbolic-Representational Justice: Truth Seeking and Recognition

A final cluster of transitional justice measures represents those actions that are seemingly of mere symbolic value in that they do not impose tangible punishment on perpetrators, nor do they offer reparations to victims. However, they play a substantive role in determining society's overall understanding of its past, or they contribute to individual truth revelation, healing, and/or reconciliation. Again, we can divide these measures in terms of their focus on perpetrators and victims, though often measures in this field will cover both groups.

Almost all countries in Central and East Europe have adopted parliamentary or other official declarations condemning their prior communist regime.[19] For example, in 1991 the Czechoslovak Federal Assembly issued a statement on the 1948–1989 period of "nonfreedom," in which it characterized its former government as having systematically violated human rights and its own laws. This stance was reaffirmed in 1993 after the Velvet Divorce, when Czech legislators adopted a new "Act on the Illegality of the Communist Regime and Resistance to It." In that document, the parliament specifically listed ways in which the regime had suppressed people's free will, violated human rights, restricted property rights, and committed other crimes and abuses. Moreover, the act asserted that "those who implemented the Communist regime as officials, organizers, and agitators in the political and ideological sphere, are fully responsible for the[se] crimes." Later a group of opposition MPs contested the act in the Czech Constitutional Court, claiming that the act established an illegal principle of collective guilt vis-à-vis former communists. Interestingly, the court rejected the appeal, saying, "The constitutional foundation of a democratic State does not deny the Parliament the right to express its will as well as its moral and political viewpoint by means which it considers suitable and reasonable within the confines of general legal principles."[20]

Some years later, the Slovak parliament passed a similar resolution decrying the "immorality and illegality of the communist system," while Bulgaria denounced its erstwhile Communist Party for (among other things) "purposefully and deliberately ruining the values of European civilization, . . . the moral and economic decline of the State, . . . [and] employing permanent terror against people who disagree with the system of ruling."[21] At the same time, a statement denouncing the role of the Slovenian Communist Party in sustaining the former Yugoslav regime failed to pass the Slovenian parliament in late 1997.[22]

In the Baltic states, such declarations have been even more poignant, as they have generally blamed a specific country, the Soviet Union, for these nations' communist-era suffering. In this respect, the Balts have largely externalized their condemnation of communist rule onto the USSR—and by implication the Russian Federation as the successor state to that onetime occupier. As the Latvian parliament declared in 1996,

> throughout the occupation, the Soviet Union conducted a targeted genocide against the Latvian people. . . . The occupation regime killed innocent people, carried out several mass deportations and other repressive policies, cruelly punished those, who with or without arms fought for the restoration of Latvian independence, and unlawfully expropriated Latvian citizens without compensation and suppressed freedom of expression.[23]

In many instances (such as the Czech Republic), political declarations have also sought to laud resistance fighters and dissidents against the regime or have otherwise drawn attention to the victims alongside condemning the perpetrators. Sometimes these declarations have also been the start of rehabilitation procedures as described earlier.

Still another approach to clarifying perpetrators and victims in the national psyche is through various forms of truth revelation by investigative commissions and other bodies. Although no country in postcommunist Europe established the kind of public truth commission pioneered famously in postapartheid South Africa, many countries began the process by convening special parliamentary commissions to study individual periods of repression, such as Poland during the 1981 military crackdown, Hungary in 1956, and Czechoslovakia in 1968.[24] More systematic examinations of regime abuse were conducted in Germany by two special Bundestag Enquête Commissions, and a comparable multiyear inquiry was conducted by the Slovenian parliament in the early 1990s.

Even more broadly, a number of countries appointed commissions made up of historians, cultural figures, and other prominent individuals in order to examine the crimes and legacies of these regimes in societal terms. Such historical expert commissions were established in Estonia, Latvia, Lithuania, and later Romania and Moldova.[25] In Estonia, the State Commission for the Examination of Repressive Policies Carried Out during the Occupations was launched in March 1992, barely six months after the reestablishment of independence.[26] It was one of the longest-standing government bodies, operating until 2005. While its focus was mostly historical (looking into the "crimes of genocide" committed by the Nazi and Soviet regimes), one of its lasting legacies was to publish extensive lists of the victims of Soviet deportations during the 1940s. A second group of historical commissions was created in the Baltic states during the late 1990s, when external pressure from international Jewish organizations and the United States succeeded in getting the countries to establish new truth bodies (mostly composed of historians) that would investigate both the Holocaust and Soviet repression in these states. Although each of the Baltic commissions would be distinctive in terms of its composition and its operating style, they all considerably advanced international historical knowledge about the wartime and postwar years. They also did not shy away from recording acts of local collaboration in crimes, including naming the perpetrators.[27]

By contrast, the Presidential Commission for the Analysis of the Communist Dictatorship in Romania was established much later (in 2006) and was intended to be a more political body aimed at discrediting the former Ceaușescu regime in the face of repeated returns to power by ex-communist parties during the 1990s and early 2000s.

Photo 7.4. The Memorial to the Victims of Communism stands in the yard of Sighetu Prison in Maramureş, Romania. (Pictor Picture Company, Shutterstock)

The commission's final report constituted an extensive investigation into the inner workings of both the erstwhile secret police, the Securitate, and the Communist Party, arriving at the conclusion that in many respects the regime had committed "genocide." Nevertheless, the public impact of the commission and its report was limited, with few of its recommendations ever implemented.[28] Far more successful in this respect was the 2003–2004 International Commission on the Holocaust in Romania, led by Elie Wiesel. Its final report contributed to much more public awareness, including the creation of a Holocaust commemoration day.

In many ways, the most direct pathway to truth revelation came through the opening of former regime archives, both in relation to former wrongdoers and their victims. The most innocuous version of this approach was to allow individuals to see whatever information the former secret services had collected on them. This was often of importance to those who had been repressed, arrested, or deported. While the names of former security agents or other related individuals would usually be blacked out, it was still possible for citizens to discover what the regime had once thought about them or what measures had been undertaken against them. The pioneer in this kind of openness was Germany, where the Stasi-Unterlagenbehörde organized free access to almost all of the former GDR's secret files for anyone interested in viewing them.

At the same time, any kind of transparency in terms of former secret archives often became a stark public contradiction when insufficient systems had been put in place for lustration. A case in point was Slovenia, where lawmakers failed to pass lustration legislation in 1997, and just a few years later a Slovene diplomat, Dušan Lajovic, made public on the internet a database of more than one million files from the Slovene branch of the Yugoslav secret police, the UDBA. Yet, because the files were simply a listing of all individuals who had ever come under the agency's purview (including common criminals), it was impossible to tell whether any person named in the files had a more specific or suspect relationship to the UDBA. In any case, names of prominent members from almost all of Slovenia's political parties turned up in the database, and this prompted an archetypal round of finger-pointing among the politicians. However, what is relevant here is the phenomenon of mass release of archival documents. A similar episode occurred in Poland when in February 2005 journalist Bronisław Wildstein released online a list of 240,000 people allegedly linked to the former secret services. Meanwhile, in some cases state authorities tried to control the process themselves. In 2014, the Lithuanian Genocide and Resistance Research Center published on its website historical files from the Lithuanian KGB dating back to the 1940s and 1950s. A year later, the new post-Maidan government in Ukraine opened the country's KGB archives. In 2018, legislators in Latvia decided to finally make available a stash of KGB documents (mostly file cards with names, code names, and recruitment dates of former agents and informers, but also some reports and other records) recovered in 1991. The digital publication of the file cards (and the exposure of names) had no consequences in terms of politicians suddenly being outed, as these figures had long been revealed through earlier vetting regulations. Its symbolic meaning lay more in the fact that a number of late-Soviet cultural figures, academics, and writers appeared in the files. A new wave of questioning, accusation, and explanation took place that was still ongoing in 2020 and could change the way Latvian society remembers the "national awakening" (*atmoda*) in the late 1980s.[29]

A related question, of course, was who was taking care of the files and what kinds of government agencies would be charged with examining the communist past. Special institutions emerged in this context, some solely focused on preserving and researching the files, as in the case of Latvia and the former East Germany, others with far greater competencies, for example in Poland, Lithuania, the Czech Republic, Slovakia, Albania, and Ukraine. In recent years, scholars have begun to comparatively analyze these "memory institutes," as they are often called, and have recognized that many are extremely broad in their functions and tasks.[30] Not only are many involved with facilitating access to files and organizing commemorative activities, but they may also be called upon to verify lustration processes, certify rehabilitation claims, or provide prosecutors with archival evidence for criminal trials against communist-era officials. The Institute of National Remembrance in Poland, known under its Polish abbreviation IPN, is a vivid example, with departments not only for historical research and national education but also for vetting government officials and for "the prosecution of crimes against the Polish nation." It has more than a dozen regional offices and delegations, totaling more than one thousand employees. Likewise, in Lithuania, the Genocide and Resistance Research Center is involved in all aspects of transitional justice and memory work. Meanwhile, almost all the countries of the region have prominent museums portraying the history of the communist period, including the House of Terror in Budapest, the Occupation Museum in Riga, and the Sighet museum in Romania.

It is therefore no surprise that commemorative efforts increased, particularly during the 2000s, as the process of dealing with the communist past began to shift from direct transitional justice policies and measures targeting individual perpetrators or victims to a much wider and often more diffuse process of national memory construction. To be sure, memory debates were present in the region as early as the 1990s, while controversies over certain politicians' or other public figures' communist pasts continued to arise, as the Latvian case demonstrated. However, the broad proportion of these two phenomena—transitional justice and the politics of memory—has slowly begun to lean toward the latter.

Social Memory, Master Narratives, and "Memory Wars": New and Old Battlegrounds

Memory is a term whose use has grown exponentially in the social sciences over the last two decades. However, it can be deceptive in the sense that it no longer tends to mean only what individuals actually remember but also what groups or entire nations see as their history and heritage, or how they perceive themselves in historical terms. It is therefore often difficult to pin down what is studied under "memory" and, by extension, the "politics of memory." For our purposes, we examine this phenomenon as it relates to transitional justice. In many respects, the two are mutually constituent: the kinds of truth and justice measures that a nation seeks depend on how people view the past repression of a regime. In a sense, memory molds transitional justice. If the regime is seen as having been soft (as is often said of Hungary), less transitional justice will be needed. At the same time, transitional justice measures can also begin to craft national memory, for instance, when lustration laws begin to reveal just how many people were involved with the old system, or when expert commissions are tasked with not only determining who did what to whom but also drafting an official narrative of a certain past event and making recommendations as to how these should be remembered in public. Even courts can be part of national memory constructions when they issue verdicts in relation to former regime perpetrators and thereby hand down a kind of judicially certified version of repression history.

In this section we examine how transitional justice and memory are often intertwined. We look at how memory issues were already present at the beginning of the democratic transitions but also at how they have grown in importance as the communist era has itself become more distant history. Measures that are, formally speaking, part of transitional justice increasingly have an effect on crafting historical understandings as well, in particular for younger generations who have had less or no personal experience under the communist regime. The thirtieth anniversary of the collapse of communism in 2019 was accompanied by robust public debates about the time of regime change and its legacy for society.[31] As the transition period of the 1990s is fading into history, issues of transitional justice undertaken during those early years are themselves becoming subject to memory contestation.

When we go back to the heady days of 1989, we see that memory was already very much at the forefront of the democratic revolutions, accentuating a wide array of other grievances against the regimes with respect to failed economic performance, environmental devastation, and social alienation. Long-neglected or silenced experiences of the early communist period, including occupation, mass arrests, extrajudicial executions, deportations, and show trials, poured into the open and stoked the rejection of the communist regimes once liberalization occurred in the mid-1980s. In Poland, stories about the mass shooting of Polish officers by the Soviets in Katyn during World War II had been part of family narratives and later dissident political activities ever since the 1970s. In the Baltic states, details slowly emerged about the scope and significance of having lost independent statehood in 1940 and then being subjected to Stalinist mass deportations to Siberia. For Czechoslovakia, the fateful dates of 1938 (when the Czech Lands where annexed by Nazi Germany), 1948 (when the Communist Party took over power in Czechoslovakia), and 1968 (when efforts at liberalization were crushed by communist authorities) became rallying cries of the Velvet Revolution and served as an important empowerment for those calling for change.

Yet historical memory also emerged as a divisive element in these turbulent times of regime change. The most ominous case was the former Yugoslavia where a former Chetnik commander and war criminal, General Dragoljub Mihailović, was rehabilitated and where the ideas and symbolism of the Serbian Chetnik and Croatian Ustasha extreme-right organizations of the 1930s and 1940s experienced a revival and provided nationalists with "weapons of destruction" to fuel already simmering interethnic tensions in the region.[32] Likewise, reemergent memories of interethnic violence and forced resettlement after border shifts between, for example, Poland and Lithuania and Ukraine, had potentially destructive power.

The question of how to remember the history of a twentieth century that had been in an ideological straightjacket for decades was thus crucial and highly political in the postcommunist processes of democratization and state building. Through public commemoration, the rewriting of textbooks, the renaming of spaces and streets, the removal of Soviet-era monuments, the creation of new museums, and numerous other acts, these countries sought to reclaim power over their recent history. The outcome of this process was generally a past reframed into one of national victimization and oppression. On the one hand, this narrative served an important political purpose of providing a sense of unity in times of economic hardship and political instability. It helped to heal some of the social atomization that the communist regime had promoted, and it developed a sense of purpose as the countries faced a new era of rebuilding. At the same time, it often swung the pendulum of national memory very starkly in a nationalist direction, to the chagrin of not only minority groups in these countries but also more broadly in Europe and internationally.

One of the most blatant memory tools at the disposal of states was to adopt laws criminalizing the denial, justification, or gross trivialization of certain historical events. Such "denial laws" exist in many Western European countries since the 1980s in relation to the Holocaust. After 1990, some Central and East European states implemented similar denial laws, yet complemented them with provisions that banned the denial of rather vaguely defined "Stalinist" or "communist crimes." Hence, Poland incorporated within its 1998 law establishing the IPN a provision allowing up to three years of imprisonment for "anyone who publicly and contrary to the facts denies" communist or Nazi crimes (Article 55). The Czech Republic issued a similar law in 2001, as did Slovenia, Latvia, and Lithuania. In addition, some countries (Lithuania, Poland, Hungary, Romania, and Ukraine) have sought to ban the public display of communist symbols such as the hammer and sickle (alongside the swastika).[33]

Increasingly, governments in the region have expanded their efforts to govern public memory and to restrict public historical speech by way of criminal law beyond the denial of Nazi and Soviet crimes. A 2018 amendment to Article 55 of the IPN law, for example, declared anyone publicly claiming that Poles were "responsible or co-responsible for Nazi crimes" liable for up to three years in prison. (After protests, mostly from outside Poland, this new provision was dropped, yet the option to pursue legal action still remains.[34]) In 2015, the Ukrainian parliament passed a set of so-called decommunization laws, among them Law No. 314-VIII, "On the Legal Status and Honoring the Memory of Fighters for Ukraine's Independence in the Twentieth Century," which declared "unlawful" any public denial of the heroic struggles of national freedom fighters, including the controversial Organization of Ukrainian Nationalists (OUN) and its military arm, the Ukrainian Insurgent Army (UPA). Other than the denial laws, this new set of "memory laws" no longer aims for the protection of former victims and minorities against hate speech but instead at protecting the majority nation against critical historical inquiry and debate—in particular with regard to historical cases of collaboration in the Holocaust. Interestingly, it is often the national memory institutes mentioned earlier that emerge as the most ardent "memory warriors,"[35] advocating (and even drafting) such memory legislation or instigating judicial investigations.

Another element worth noting in relation to memory processes is that they have not always been top-down or imposed by government. Nonstate actors have also been instrumental in fostering public memorialization of the entire communist era as criminal. In the Baltic states, especially in Lithuania, former deportees and repressed people constituted a strong voice in the national-conservative political camp, seeking to advance a staunch anticommunist narrative of national suffering and heroism through education and other public activities. Moreover, one such nonofficial activity involved organizing international public tribunals that would feature legal experts from different countries who would reexamine the crimes committed by the regimes and evaluate communist ideology from a legal perspective. The first such tribunal took place in Vilnius in 2000, organized by civil society organizations and supported by several public figures, resulting in a "judgment" that would condemn communism as a criminal doctrine responsible for, among other things, genocide and crimes against humanity. A similar citizen tribunal was held in 2006 in Cluj, Romania. Although these bodies lacked any formal legal standing, they sought to use the terminology of international criminal and humanitarian law in order to influence national narratives of the communist regime.[36]

Delving into the past has not meant only revealing communist regime crimes; it has also shed light on the mass killing of Jews and other minorities during the war in a region that Timothy Snyder would later term the "bloodlands" of Europe. Already in the early 1990s, the emerging master narratives of national victimhood and the overarching tendency in public commemoration and historical writing to externalize responsibility for any past wrongdoing clashed with tales of local collaboration with Nazi perpetrators, of locally initiated anti-Jewish pogroms, and of killing squads involved in the mass shooting of civilians, especially Jews. In some cases, the realization of long-neglected historical truths about local complicity in the extermination of Jewish life in the region gave rise to often painful and at times ugly public debates and national introspection. During the first decades, accusations of national governments' reluctance to confront these issues came mostly from outside, for example, from the Simon Wiesenthal Center, an international Holocaust research institution. These complaints provoked resistance among local populations, and the ensuing public debates and political rhetoric revealed many still-existing antisemitic myths and stereotypes. The 2001 publication of Jan Gross's book *Neighbors*, about the killing of Jews in Jedwabne by their Polish neighbors, arguably marked a watershed among both scholars and the interested public toward uncomfortable questions regarding local behavior during the German occupation.[37] Yet it also provoked resistance among those who saw themselves as the first victims of Nazi rule and who reject any notion of co-responsibility in Nazi crimes.

In the Baltic states, the investigation of local involvement in Nazi crimes often seemed to feed into the Soviet-era narrative of "fascist collaborators" in Estonia, Latvia, and Lithuania and was often picked up by Russian officials who tried to discredit the young democracies and aspiring EU members in the eyes of the West. Moreover, the exclusive focus on Holocaust history and memory was perceived by many politicians and intellectuals in the region as, at best, ignorant and, at worst, negligent of the suffering that had been inflicted on their countries by Stalin. Scholars of European and transnational memory have thus come to talk of "memory wars" and of "battleground Europe," at the center of which they see the history and memory of the Holocaust and the Gulag pitted against each other in an unfortunate competition of collective victimhood that held little value for advancing knowledge and awareness about the history of World War II and its aftermath of state violence.[38]

With the enlargement of the European Union and the direct incorporation of Central and East Europe into European politics in 2004, memory disputes reached the pan-European level. Again, it was the national memory institutes that had been involved in transitional justice, along with a number of related history museums, that teamed up into a novel set of memory agents that would begin appearing at EU-sponsored conferences and hearings, lobbying for European parliamentarians to acknowledge the criminal character of the communist regimes.[39] In particular, Baltic, but also Hungarian and Polish, members of the European Parliament (EP) were at the forefront of lobbying their colleagues to pass legislation or adopt resolutions that would condemn communism and call for European-wide commemoration. Eventually the EP adopted a pair of resolutions in which the crimes of Stalinism were condemned and remembrance pledged. The latter included the creation of a "European Day of Remembrance for Victims of Stalinism and Nazism" on August 23, the day of the signing of the Molotov-Ribbentrop Pact in 1939 that divided up East Europe between Nazi Germany and the Soviet Union.[40]

The European Union has also financed a number of projects and transnational networks related to commemoration and research, such as the Platform of European Memory and Conscience and the European Network Remembrance and Solidarity, the main aim of which is to raise awareness of the crimes of both totalitarian regimes in Europe.[41] The success of transnational memory activism by these organizations bore fruit when the European Parliament passed yet another resolution "on the importance of European remembrance" in September 2019, in which it condemned "in strongest terms" the mass crimes committed by communist regimes and called on all member states to "carry out moral assessments and conduct legal inquiries into the crimes of Stalinism."[42]

A second memory-related phenomenon that seemed to kick in around the 2000s was a more anthropologically laden notion of communist nostalgia. The concept gained currency in political science, as scholars sought to explain how ex-communist parties in many countries were returning to power in open elections. Later, it became an explanation for the rise of populist parties, with the conclusion being that voters were looking for a return to the social equality and order they remembered from before the transition to market capitalism in the 1990s. Among other social scientists (in particular, social anthropologists), the study of nostalgia was embedded in the notion of post-socialism and examined memories of past everyday life. Especially among older age cohorts as well as in countries that had experienced more liberal forms of communist rule, such as the former Yugoslavia and Hungary, a sense that "not everything was bad during socialism" seemed to exist. Yet, as numerous studies of this phenomenon have pointed out, it is in fact rarely the case that people yearn for a return of the old communist system as such; rather, it has been an expression of their dissatisfaction with existing socioeconomic conditions and the perceived lack of socioeconomic equality in society. In this sense, nostalgia is but a label referring to what Mitja Velikonja has called "retrospective utopia"—a notion of a better life that is as much a projection into the past as it is into the future.[43]

Lastly, with time elapsing since the end of communism and the establishment of democratic rule, the memories of that particular period have themselves become an object of contestation. In some countries, the contrasting narratives of that period continue to have a strong hold on the political landscape, as populist leaders on the right try to frame the negotiated transitions of the late 1980s, for example in Hungary and Poland, as a betrayal of the nation by the liberal elites of that time. Thus, the 2005 campaign by PiS for a new lustration law as well as the more recent efforts to carry out "judicial reforms" both built on a narrative of liberal political elites as corrupted by former communists, who continued after 1989 to sit in the judiciary or ministries and thus rule the country. In Romania, memories of the 1989 overthrow of Ceaușescu and the subsequent takeover by a second tier of communist elites remain contested and reappear in the political discourse especially during elections. Hence, the way in which 1989/1991 is being publicly remembered tells us a lot about not only party-political cleavages but also deeper cultural and structural undercurrents that define social and political life in this part of the world.

Politics in most of the countries that experienced peaceful revolutions in 1989 and 1991 is extremely polarized, or "fractured," as political elites seem to be split along seemingly irreconcilable narratives of the not so distant past.[44] Indeed, much of the populist rhetoric of the so-called illiberal leaders in the region (such as Poland's Jarosław Kaczyński, Hungary's Viktor Orbán, and Slovakia's Robert Fico) seeks to frame 1989 as an "incomplete revolution" and the subsequent transition period as marked by the betrayal of the nations by the liberal, cosmopolitan elites of the early 1990s.[45] Such narrative constructions clearly feed on a growing antagonism between the new liberal and internationally mobile elites and those who were less fortunate in benefiting from the neoliberal reforms and European integration of the past decades, or who have had difficulties adjusting to the challenges of global markets, digitalization, and urbanization and need a target for their grievances. The past, whether distant or more recent, seems to be a pliable entity in the hands of populist leaders trying to reframe their countries in new anticommunist, antielite, antiliberal, and anti-EU terms.

Conclusion

Studying politics in Central and East Europe involves examining multiple, successive layers of political development and change. The post-1945 period of communist rule is of course an essential starting point, but so are the subsequent regime transitions, the institutionalization of democratic politics, the challenges of European Union accession, and now in some cases the dangers of democratic backsliding. Transitional justice and memory politics fit into this landscape as accompanying processes aimed at establishing an understanding of what happened during communist rule, as well as what to do about it afterward. The two phenomena begin with an overarching aspiration to bring some kind of "truth" and "justice" to this repressive past. This is why these two terms are frequently used as synonyms for everything that had to do with coming to terms with the past. However, it is clear that these two goals are at best very ambiguous, if not subjective. No matter how hard societies may try to work out different degrees of accountability and develop adequate forms of reparation, there will be uncertainty about whether the full truth has been established or justice really achieved. This explains why transitional justice can also be a protracted and recurring political issue. There will probably not be a moment where all people agree that these two processes have been completed and that the books on the past can be closed. Rather, these issues remain unresolved, available for attachment to other political and economic grievances, as we saw with the discussion of communist nostalgia, or when making sense of the rise of illiberal leaders in Hungary or Poland. Truth and justice are inherently slippery phenomena, as they are largely in the eye of the beholder. As political analysts, we can at best try and sort out the different dimensions of this wide-ranging process. However, full explanations are difficult to come by given the way truth and justice interrelate and interact with other political strategies and societal issues.

Given that some countries have clearly engaged in greater degrees of transitional justice and memory politics than others, scholars have offered different accounts as to why this might be so.[46] Some point to differing communist-era historical legacies with regard to regime legitimacy as one explanatory variable. Thus, in some cases, like Hungary or ex-Yugoslavia, the regimes had already introduced economic reforms that allowed for certain freedoms long before the 1980s. In other cases, such as Poland or even Soviet Lithuania, local communist elites managed to pursue successful "national communist" strategies, thereby making it seem that the communist period had perhaps not been so divisive as to warrant extensive transitional justice.

A second explanatory level looks at how more conciliatory modes of regime transition led to differing degrees of justice seeking in subsequent years. The more negotiated the precise transition, the less radical the transitional justice process would be—not only because of a certain degree of societal reconciliation but also because elites from the previous regime would continue to be part of the political process and could tamp down impulses for transitional justice. Again, many countries corroborate this hypothesis: the Czech Republic had a very abrupt break with the former regime and also had the most decisive array of transitional justice policies, while Poland and Hungary (with their roundtable talks during the transition) opted for milder measures vis-à-vis the past.

Third, patterns of truth and justice have also been influenced by constitutional arrangements (such the role of popularly elected presidents or the power of constitutional courts) and driven by presentist politics (in certain electoral situations, institutional power games, or other instrumental political moves). In other words, irrespective of prior influences, the communist past has sometimes been a political football for different political actors, and this too has caused the process of transitional justice and memory to ebb and flow over the last three decades. This is the framework that best explains later waves of transitional justice, such as when countries decided to toughen lustration laws or expand victim benefits. It also increasingly accounts for when memory politics comes to the fore in political discourses and mobilization strategies.

All of this points to the fact that transitional justice needs to be studied not only across countries but also over time. Not only have countries differed in comparison to each other, but they have also shifted in terms of their preoccupation with these issues over the years. This makes finding a single approach to the phenomenon almost impossible. Moreover, as this chapter has shown, "transitional justice" is in reality a composite of at least three levels of policy measures, adopted in relation to either perpetrators or victims, enacted either right after a democratic transition or many years later, and aimed at redressing repressive acts committed toward the end of the former regime or going back many decades beforehand. All of these dimensions are important to map out before more specific analysis can begin.

Likewise, scholars have reflected on whether transitional justice has any kind of downstream effect on other democratic processes.[47] That is to say, apart from the moral ambitions of transitional justice (to achieve "truth" and/or "justice"), we can also ask whether transitional justice helps improve specific issues like elite political culture, respect for rule of law, trust in political institutions, or democratic values in society. Research in this area has been inconclusive, since transitional justice is unlikely to be the sole explanatory variable for these latter phenomena. For example, low or high levels of trust in political institutions may be caused by other factors, such as policy performance or levels of corruption. Nevertheless, this perspective on transitional justice is an important one, since it asks the broader question of what transitional justice is good for.

Finally, we have seen that issues of transitional justice are being increasingly blended with and perhaps even superseded by memory politics. Political contests are often about how society will remember and perceive the communist era and less about how to resolve its wrongdoings. Perspectives have begun to shift from how to deal with the past to how that past was dealt with. This does not imply that the debate will become wholly historical or academic, any more than this has happened with, say, questions of slavery and the Civil War in the United States or the Holocaust and World War II in Germany. Politics will remain a crucial element in these debates since it will influence how each nation crafts its historical identity. If communism is remembered primarily as victimhood (as many conservative parties would like), this will influence not only certain domestic political orientations but also relations with the rest of Europe in terms of a desire to continue recasting broader European historical identity. If other, more varied narratives emerge, this may relativize the place that transitional justice and memory will hold in Central and East European politics.

Study Questions

1. What is transitional justice? What forms and dimensions of transitional justice can we find in the Central and East European region?
2. What are the different temporal dimensions involved in postcommunist transitional justice?
3. What controversies have emerged with the implementation of transitional justice measures?
4. How do you think communism should be remembered in public or in the histories of the countries of Central and East Europe?
5. Who is involved in making decisions about how the past is remembered?
6. What relevance do memory stances have for today's political developments in the region? How does memory shape politics and policies?

Suggested Readings

Assmann, Aleida, and Linda Shortt, eds. *Memory and Political Change*. London: Palgrave Macmillan, 2012.

Belavusau, Uladzislau, and Aleksandra Gliszczyńska-Grabias, eds. *Law and Memory: Towards Legal Governance of History*. Cambridge: Cambridge University Press, 2017.

Blacker, Uilleam, Alexander Etkind, and Julie Fedor, eds. *Memory and Theory in Eastern Europe*. London: Palgrave Macmillan, 2013.

Lebow, Richard Ned, Wulf Kansteiner, and Claudio Fogu, eds. *The Politics of Memory in Postwar Europe*. London: Duke University Press, 2006.

Neumayer, Laure. *The Criminalisation of Communism in the European Political Space after the Cold War*. London: Routledge, 2020.

Pakier, Malgorzata, and Bo Strath, eds. *A European Memory? Contested Histories and Politics of Remembrance*. New York: Berghahn Books, 2010.

Subotić, Jelena. *Yellow Star, Red Star: Holocaust Remembrance after Communism*. Ithaca/London: Cornell University Press, 2019.

Teitel, Ruti G. "Transitional Justice Genealogy." *Harvard Human Rights Journal* 16 (2003): 69–94.

Notes

1. Because of our focus on postcommunist transitional justice, we will not cover in this chapter transitional justice processes related to the ethnic (or civil) war in many parts of former Yugoslavia. While it is true that a number of the measures that have been undertaken vis-à-vis these conflicts (such as trials against war criminals and the memorialization of victims) are similar to the measures we outline here, in many instances they have also been linked to international criminal law (the International Criminal Tribunal for the former Yugoslavia, ICTY), or they have become internationalized political issues (serving as conditionality elements for European Union accession). The type of postcommunist transitional justice that we examine here (that is, in relation to former communist leaders and the former communist regime) has been very limited in countries such as Croatia, Serbia, North Macedonia, and Bosnia-Herzegovina.

2. Ruti G. Teitel, *Transitional Justice* (Oxford: Oxford University Press, 2000).

3. In Slovenia, too, resurgent center-right parties tried to pass different transitional justice measures in the late 1990s, but each time they failed to get a requisite majority in parliament.

4. For a more detailed conceptualization of this time dimension, see Eva-Clarita Pettai and Vello Pettai, *Transitional and Retrospective Justice in the Baltic States* (Cambridge: Cambridge University Press, 2015), 14–43.

5. Claus Offe, "Coming to Terms with Past Injustices," *European Journal of Sociology* 33, no. 1 (1992): 195–201; Neil J. Kritz, "The Dilemmas of Transitional Justice," in *Transitional Justice: How Emerging Democracies Reckon with Former Regimes*, ed. Neil J. Kritz, vol. 1, *General Considerations*, xix–xxx (Washington, DC: US Institute of Peace Press, 1995); Noel Calhoun, *Dilemmas of Justice in Eastern Europe's Democratic Transitions* (New York: Palgrave Macmillan, 2004); Brian K. Grodsky, *The Costs of Justice: How New Leaders Respond to Previous Rights Abuses* (Notre Dame, IN: University of Notre Dame Press, 2011).

6. Jon Elster, *Closing the Books: Transitional Justice in Historical Perspective* (Cambridge: Cambridge University Press, 2004); Muriel Blaive, "The Czechs and Their Communism, Past and Present," in *IWM Junior Visiting Fellows' Conferences*, vol. 17, ed. D. Gard et al. (Vienna: IWM, 2005).

7. Frigyes Kahler, "Communist Terror in 1956 and the Rule of Law," *Hungarian Review* 4, no. 1 (2013): 49–62.

8. Raluca Grosescu, "The Trials of the Romanian Revolution," Cultures of History Forum, January 17, 2019, https://doi.org/10.25626/0093.

9. See Roman David, "From Prague to Baghdad: Lustration Systems and Their Political Effects," *Government and Opposition* 41, no. 3 (2006): 347–72. For an explanatory model of lustration based on institutional rules and strategic interaction, see Monika Nalepa, "The Institutional Context of Transitional Justice," in *Routledge Handbook of Comparative Political Institutions*, ed. Jennifer Gandhi and Ruben Ruiz-Rufino, 389–403 (Oxon: Routledge, 2015).

10. Mark S. Ellis, "Purging the Past: The Current State of Lustration Laws in the Former Communist Bloc," *Law and Contemporary Problems* 59, no. 4 (1997): 181–96; Robert C. Austin and Jonathan Ellison, "Albania," in *Transitional Justice in Eastern Europe and the Former Soviet Union: Reckoning with the Communist Past*, ed. Lavinia Stan, 176–99 (London: Routledge, 2009).

11. For accounts regarding the Polish case, see Matt Killingsworth, "Lustration after Totalitarianism: Poland's Attempt to Reconcile with Its Communist Past," *Communist and Post-Communist Studies* 43, no. 3 (2010): 275–84.

12. Cynthia Horne, "'Silent Lustration': Public Disclosures as Informal Lustration Mechanisms in Bulgaria and Romania," *Problems of Post-Communism* 62, no. 3 (2015): 131–44.

13. Lavinia Stan, "The Băsescu Case: Romania's Lustration Debate Revisited," Cultures of History Forum, December 13, 2019, https://doi.org/10.25626/0106.

14. Cynthia Horne, "Late Lustration Programmes in Romania and Poland: Supporting or Undermining Democratic Transitions?," *Demokratization* 16, no. 2 (2009): 344–76; Kieran Williams et al., "Explaining Lustration in Central Europe: A 'Post-Communist Politics' Approach," *Democratization* 12, no. 1 (2005): 22–43.

15. Roman David and Susanne Y. P. Choi, "Victims on Transitional Justice: Lessons from the Reparation of Human Rights Abuses in the Czech Republic," *Human Rights Quarterly* 27, no. 2 (2005): 392–435; Lavinia Stan, *Transitional Justice in Post-Communist Romania* (Cambridge: Cambridge University Press, 2013).

16. The issue of reparations for Soviet-era damages remains a highly contentious issue in Baltic-Russian relations. Both Latvia and Lithuania have put together detailed compensation claims to the Russian Federation, something that Moscow has dismissed outright.

17. Csilla Kiss, "Hungary," in *Encyclopedia of Transitional Justice*, ed. Lavinia Stan and Nadya Nedelsky, 230–36 (Cambridge: Cambridge University Press, 2013).

18. Mark Blacksell and Karl Martin Born, "Private Property Restitution: The Geographical Consequences of Official Government Policies in Central and Eastern Europe," *Geographical Journal* 168, no. 2 (2002): 178–90; Lynn M. Fisher and Austin J. Jaffe, "Restitution in Transition Countries," *Journal of Housing and the Built Environment* 15, no. 3 (2000): 233–48; Csongor Kuti, *Post-Communist Restitution and the Rule of Law* (Budapest: Central European University Press, 2009).

19. In this subsection we will concentrate on declarations that specifically condemn a country's former Communist Party or ruling elite as opposed to communism as an ideology or social system. Given the distinction we are seeking to make between transitional justice and memory, we see the denunciation of former rulers as part of the former and the censure of communism as the latter.

20. Full text in Neil J. Kritz, *Transitional Justice: How Emerging Democracies Reckon with Former Regimes*, vol. 3, *Laws, Rulings, and Reports* (Washington, DC: US Institute of Peace Press, 1995), 428–31.

21. Nadya Nedelsky, "Czechoslovakia, and the Czech and Slovak Republics," in *Transitional Justice in Eastern Europe and the Former Soviet Union: Reckoning with the Communist Past*, ed. Lavinia Stan, 37–75 (London: Routledge, 2009); National Assembly of Bulgaria, "Law on Declaring the Criminal Nature of the Communist Regime in Bulgaria," May 5, 2000.

22. Tamara Kotar, "Slovenia," in *Transitional Justice in Eastern Europe and the Former Soviet Union: Reckoning with the Communist Past*, ed. Lavinia Stan, 200–221 (London: Routledge, 2009).

23. Latvijas Republikas Saeima, "Deklarācija 'Par Latvijas Okupāciju,'" August 22, 1996.

24. Timothy Garton Ash, "Trials, Purges and History Lessons: Treating a Difficult Past in Post-Communist Europe," in *Memory and Power in Post-War Europe: Studies in the Presence of the Past*, ed. Jan-Werner Müller, 265–82 (Cambridge: Cambridge University Press, 2002).

25. Lavinia Stan, "Truth Commissions in Post-Communism: The Overlooked Solution?," *Open Political Science Journal* 2 (2009): 1–13.

26. Vello Pettai, "State Commission for the Examination of Repressive Policies Carried Out during the Occupations," in *Encyclopedia of Transitional Justice*, ed. Lavinia Stan and Nadya Nadelsky, 161–67 (Cambridge: Cambridge University Press, 2013).

27. Eva-Clarita Pettai, "Negotiating History for Reconciliation: A Comparative Evaluation of the Baltic Presidential Commissions," *Europe-Asia Studies* 67, no. 7 (2015): 1079–101.

28. Monica Ciobanu, "Criminalising the Past and Reconstructing Collective Memory: The Romanian Truth Commission," *Europe-Asia Studies* 61, no. 2 (2009): 313–36; Alina Hogea, "Coming to Terms with the Communist Past in Romania: An Analysis of the Political and Media Discourse concerning the Tismăneanu Report," *Studies of Transition States and Societies* 2, no. 2 (2010): 16–30.

29. Eva-Clarita Pettai, "Delayed Truth: Latvia's Struggle with the Legacies of the KGB," Cultures of History Forum, July 22, 2019, http://doi.org/10.25626/0101.

30. Georges Mink, "Institutions of National Memory in Post-Communist Europe: From Transitional Justice to Political Uses of Biographies (1989–2010)," in *History, Memory and Politics in Central and Eastern Europe: Memory Games*, ed. Georges Mink and Laure Neumayer, 155–70 (Basingstoke; New York: Palgrave Macmillan, 2013).

31. James Krapfl and Andrew Kloiber, "The Revolution Continues: Memories of 1989 and the Defence of Democracy in Germany, the Czech Republic, and Slovakia," Cultures of History Forum, May 28, 2020, https://cultures-of-history.uni-jena.de/debates/slovakia/the-revolution-continues-memories-of-1989-and-the-defence-of-democracy-in-germany-the-czech-republic-and-slovakia.

32. Ilana R. Bet-El, "Unimagined Communities: The Power of Memory and the Conflict in Former Yugoslavia in Memory and Power," in *Post-War Europe: Studies in the Presence of the Past*, ed. Jan-Werner Müller, 206–22 (Cambridge: Cambridge University Press, 2002); see also Ljiljana

Radonić, "Commemorating Bleiburg—Croatia's Struggle with Historical Revisionism," *Cultures of History Forum*, June 11, 2019, http://doi.org/10.25626/0100.

33. For a detailed overview of the evolution of "memory laws" in Europe, see Nikolay Koposov, *Memory Laws, Memory Wars: The Politics of the Past in Europe and Russia* (Cambridge: Cambridge University Press, 2017).

34. Marta Bucholc, "Commemorative Lawmaking: Memory Frames of the Democratic Backsliding in Poland after 2015," *Hague Journal on the Rule of Law* 11 (2019): 85–110.

35. Jan Kubik and Michael Bernhard, "A Theory of the Politics of Memory," in *Twenty Years after Communism: The Politics of Memory and Commemoration*, ed. M. Bernhard and J. Kubik, 7–35 (Oxford: Oxford University Press, 2014).

36. *Anti-Communist Congress and Proceedings of the International Public Tribunal in Vilnius "Evaluation of the Crimes of Communism" 2000* (Vilnius: Ramona, 2002); Lavinia Stan, *Transitional Justice in Post-Communist Romania* (Cambridge: Cambridge University Press, 2013).

37. Jan T. Gross, *Neighbors: The Destruction of the Jewish Community in Jedwabne, Poland* (Princeton, NJ: Princeton University Press, 2001).

38. Alexander Etkind et al., *Remembering Katyn* (Cambridge: Polity Press, 2013); Claus Leggewie, "Battlefield Europe: Transnational Memory and European Identity," *Eurozine* 28 (2009); Aleida Assmann, "Transnational Memories," *European Review* 22, no. 4 (2014): 546–56.

39. Mink, "Institutions of National Memory in Post-Communist Europe"; Laure Neumayer, "Integrating the Central European Past into a Common Narrative: The Mobilizations around the 'Crimes of Communism' in the European Parliament," *Journal of Contemporary European Studies* 23, no. 3 (2015): 344–63.

40. While all of the Central and East European members of the EU have adopted this day onto their national calendars, only Sweden and Finland have taken the date on board among Western European countries.

41. Zoltan Dujisin speaks in this context about an emerging "field of transnational anticommunism"; see Zoltan Dujisin, "A History of Post-Communist Remembrance: From Memory Politics to the Emergence of a Field of Anticommunism," *Theory and Society*, July 8, 2020, online first, https://doi.org/10.1007/s11186-020-09401-5.

42. European Parliament, "19 September 2019 (2019/2819[RSP])," P9_TA (2019)0021, https://www.europarl.europa.eu/doceo/document/TA-9-2019-0021_EN.pdf.

43. Mitja Velikonja, "Lost in Transition: Nostalgia for Socialism in Post-Socialist Countries," *East European Politics & Societies* 23, no. 4 (2009): 535–51; see also Joakim Ekman and Jonas Linde, "Communist Nostalgia and the Consolidation of Democracy in Central and Eastern Europe," *Journal of Communist Studies and Transition Politics* 21, no. 3 (2005): 354–74; Maria Nikolaeva Todorova and Zsuzsa Gille, *Post-Communist Nostalgia* (New York: Berghahn Books, 2010).

44. Michael Bernhard and Jan Kubik, eds., *Twenty Years after Communism: The Politics of Memory and Commemoration* (Oxford: Oxford University Press, 2014).

45. Ivan Krastev and Steven Holmes, *The Light That Failed: The Reckoning* (London: Penguin, 2019).

46. For a good overview of explanatory models for transitional justice, see Vello Pettai and Eva-Clarita Pettai, "Dealing with the Past: Post-Communist Transitional Justice," in *Routledge Handbook of East European Politics*, ed. Adam Fagan and Petr Kopecky, 281–94 (London: Routledge, 2017).

47. Cynthia M. Horne, "Assessing the Impact of Lustration on Trust in Public Institutions and National Government in Central and Eastern Europe," *Comparative Political Studies* 45, no. 4 (2012): 412–46; see also the chapters by Lynch and Marchesi and by David in *Post-Communist Transitional Justice: Lessons from Twenty-Five Years of Experience*, ed. Lavinia Stan and Nadya Nedelsky (New York: Cambridge University Press, 2015).

CHAPTER 8

Gender Regimes

Éva Fodor

In 2011, the Council of Europe adopted the Istanbul Convention, a human rights treaty designed to prevent violence against women. Within the next few years, the treaty was ratified by thirty-four council members. Surprisingly, nine of the eleven members who refused to adopt the convention have been postcommunist countries from Central and East Europe. In a show of open defiance, Hungary explicitly declared that the parliament would not be going forward with ratification, and a few months later, in the summer of 2020, Poland also announced plans to rescind its signature. Siding with extreme conservative voices, both countries objected to the term *gender* used in the text of the treaty, specifically to the suggestion that people's sex is anything other than natural, biological, or divinely ordained. How did we get here after decades of communist emancipation campaigns, social policy seeking to grant women financial independence and political voice, and several years of European Union–mandated gender equality action plans?

This chapter describes this trajectory in broad strokes: it explores changes in the gender regimes of Central and East European (CEE) societies, starting the story after World War II and ending in the present in 2020. The historical horizon is important, as is the socioeconomic and geopolitical context, which together shape, and are shaped by, local gender regimes. The chapter will focus primarily on Central European countries, specifically on Poland, the Czech Republic, and Hungary, but will bring examples from beyond this circle as well.

The chapter begins after World War II and discusses the ways in which communist gender ideologues and state socialist regimes reshaped gender relations between 1949 and 1989. Next is a closer look at how the collapse of state socialism and the multiple paths to marketization transformed gender relations in the region and, concurrently, how this transformation was conditioned on specific conceptualizations of masculinity and femininity, as well as on men's and women's different positions in society. The final section of this chapter examines recent developments: the reconceptualization of gender relations in support of illiberal political rule, as well as the politicization of the concept of "gender" itself in two countries, Hungary and Poland. It ends with a brief look at the possible impact of the COVID-19 pandemic on gender relations.

State Socialist Gender Regimes and Their Collapse

The American National Exhibition of 1959 in Moscow was designed to showcase the progress of the US economy, technology, and culture in the midst of the Cold War.[1] One of its most famous moments came when US vice president Richard Nixon and Soviet premier Nikita Khrushchev toured a model family kitchen presented by the American exhibitors. Showing off the most "high-tech" labor-saving devices on display Nixon explained to his Soviet counterpart that these were designed to "make life more easy for our housewives." Soviet Premier Khrushchev responded with a memorable, if unfriendly line: "Your capitalistic attitude toward women does not occur under Communism."[2]

Indeed, the concept of the housewife was eliminated from the policy vocabulary of the communist parties, which came to power in Central and East Europe after World War II. In the media and in party propaganda materials the trope of the fashionably dressed, leisurely "bourgeois housewife" featured only as reference to the inevitable decay of Western civilization.[3] Instead, Communist Party ideologues, from Khrushchev to his counterparts in CEE countries, set out to "emancipate" women by integrating them into the paid labor force and into party politics. In sharp contrast to securing modern kitchen appliances for individual housewives, early communist policy makers believed that reproductive work should be socialized and communal kitchens and eating spaces, cheap laundry, and child-care facilities, rather than labor-saving devices, would ease women's burden.

This women's emancipation agenda had ideological antecedents in the writings of Engels, Bebel, and the Marxist feminists of the 1920s, who argued that women must join the international proletariat, as their liberation was only possible once they escaped the confines of the bourgeois household and actively contributed to the elimination of capitalism.[4] Beyond this ideological mandate, after World War II women's labor was desperately needed as postwar countries embarked on rebuilding their economies, sought to catch up with their Western neighbors, and repositioned themselves in the postwar geopolitical world order.[5] As part of this modernization project,[6] newly state socialist Central and East European governments had to radically increase the size of their labor force as they initiated more and more ambitious plans to build new factories, military weapons, and mines and to rebuild roads, railways, and bridges. Before World War II, about 30 to 35 percent of women were involved in paid work in CEE countries,[7] so policy makers saw a vast pool of underutilized labor that could be mobilized.

Just when the trope of the middle-class housewife became fashionable in the 1950s in Western Europe and the United States (as Nixon's claim above attests), women in state socialist countries left their households to start careers in the paid labor force. Working-age women were encouraged, indeed required, to participate in paid work, education, and political life.[8] Not surprisingly, this turned out to be rather shocking for urban middle-class housewives, who had been raised not expecting to be working anywhere beyond their households. Many had significant cultural capital, spoke foreign languages, could type, and were well versed in logistics and communication skills given their experience running often sizeable households. In some cases, these skills were put to good use in state socialist offices, and a number of women enjoyed their newfound careers. Others, however, struggled to find work, experienced class-based discrimination from communist supervisors, and were forced to toil in jobs well below their qualifications (author's interviews in Hungary in 1992). Yet most women had little choice but to try to join the paid labor force. Social policies were redesigned in a way that access to numerous provisions was possible only through employment, rather than through spousal or widows' rights.[9]

Factories and work institutions themselves took over the role of distributing social provisions, from child care to access to low-cost vacations. In addition, political pressure, in the early 1950s direct political surveillance, supported the new policy, which required that all women of working age find waged work.[10] Indeed, by the early 1980s, most able-bodied women in the region had paid employment—with the notable exception of women of the largest ethnic minority in the region, the Roma, who were more likely than non-Roma women to face discrimination and joblessness. Nevertheless, the vast majority of generations born after World War II in CEE countries were no longer familiar with the concept of the "stay-at-home mother" or housewife.

The actual percentage of women of peak working age in the labor market varied across countries and ranged between 70 and 90 percent by the end of the 1980s.[11] Overall, this percentage was significantly higher than women's participation rates in comparable Organisation for Economic Co-operation and Development (OECD) countries, and in contrast to the otherwise more comparable Scandinavia, women in state socialist societies worked full time and expected to do so all through their adult lives. The percentages may have been similar in Sweden and the Czech Republic, but the very experience and meaning of paid work came to be gendered differently in state socialist and Western capitalist societies.

Although state socialist countries declared and legislated women's equal rights in the 1950s, not all jobs were open to women. In the early 1950s, communist parties in Central and East Europe made concerted, ideology-driven efforts at integrating women into male-dominated jobs in heavy industry and agricultural work.[12] But this campaign was short-lived partly because it met with serious political resistance from outside and even inside party circles. Gradually, policies and propaganda material were modified, and women's integration proceeded on the assumption that women would do work in the "nonproductive" sectors, that is, in the services and in state bureaucracies. As the name suggests, the "nonproductive" sector had lower prestige, lower pay, and fewer benefits, so this strategy resulted in the solidification of already existing patterns of job segregation, which propelled women toward areas such as teaching, clerical work, and retail. One obvious consequence of job segregation soon became apparent: an increasing wage gap between men and women. Several sources estimate the average gender wage gap at close to 30 percent in CEE countries during the early 1980s.[13]

Married women and mothers were also required to work for wages. In all CEE countries until the mid-1960s, mothers were expected to return to work soon after childbirth and, if required, were granted twenty-minute breast-feeding breaks every three hours, during which time they could visit their babies in their company's nursery.[14] But building and maintaining acceptable quality nurseries proved more expensive than women's unpaid domestic work.[15] In addition, the problem of labor shortages eased by the 1960s; in fact, unemployment became a concern, and party officials noted with dismay that postwar birthrates had started to decline. As a solution to what today would be called a "work-life

Photo 8.1. A 1920 Soviet propaganda poster about opportunities the October Revolution created for women. Some inscriptions on the buildings read "library," "kindergarten," "school for adults." (Nikolai Kupreyanov, Wikimedia Commons)

balance" problem and to encourage childbirth, most Central and East European countries instituted maternity leave policies in the 1960s and early 1970s. The actual policies varied in generosity and scope. In Estonia, for example, the Work Code of 1972 guaranteed an eighteen-month unpaid leave after the birth of a child, which was only later extended to a paid, lengthier leave. At the other extreme, in Hungary, as in Czechoslovakia already in 1966, women could take a three-year leave and receive a flat-rate allowance. In every country, however, parental leave was initially granted to women only, reinforcing the gender division of child-care labor and constructing women as mothers first and paid laborers only second. This arrangement was only eased in the 1980s.[16]

Communist Party leaders sought other aspects of women's emancipation as well. At the end of World War II, women were vastly underrepresented at all levels of education. This began to change slowly, and by the late 1970s the proportion of female college students had caught up with men's in the region.[17] Women tended to specialize in fields that were understood as appropriate given their assigned place in the nonproductive sectors, a pattern that exacerbated occupational segregation at every level. Nevertheless, a higher-than-ever number of women could aspire—with their new credentials—to white-collar professional work. Research focusing on Austria and Hungary has shown that women in state socialist Hungary had significantly better chances of moving up to middle-level leadership positions than comparably situated women in Austria until well into the 1990s.[18]

High-level leadership, however, was restricted to men only. Although by the mid-1980s close to a third of members of parliament and central committees were women in most CEE countries, the top ranks of leadership were reserved for men, with a single token woman typically featuring as a member of the Politburo, the most powerful organ of the Communist Party in each country. Women's representation was compartmentalized: each Communist Party had a women's section. It was the job of the women's organization to deal with what were considered "women's issues," often separate from the more important, mainstream social agenda. There is a lively debate in the literature about the extent to which these organizations could or could not represent women's true interests against the mandates of the all-powerful communist parties:[19] some argue that they did indeed have a voice both domestically and internationally, even one that could be labeled "feminist." Others point out that these organizations were under the thumb of their respective parent communist parties, and only limited divergence from the centrally set agenda was possible. The pattern of women's underrepresentation repeated itself in opposition politics too. Women's participation was limited and often invisible amid the imagery of the heroic shipyard worker and the dissident urban intellectual.[20]

In sum, the great experiment at "women's emancipation" in CEE countries produced a new gender regime[21] that was flexibly shaped by the needs of the ever-changing economic and political goals of a centralized planned economy and state socialist political system. The new regime offered important new educational, career, and family-focused opportunities to different groups of women, yet did so in a way that was limited by both the authoritarian nature of the state socialist system and policy makers' reluctance to renegotiate the division of care work within the household. And it left large groups of women, as well as men, behind. The main pillars of the state socialist labor force—an abundance of paid work, manageable work hours, low productivity, company vacation homes, and free kindergartens—disappeared overnight as the regime collapsed in 1989.

After 1989: From Crisis to Crisis

Women themselves remained largely invisible in the deliberative processes that took place in 1989–1990, and calls to direct attention to women's issues were typically dismissed as low priority when the main principles of democracy had to be negotiated. Yet some questions about reproduction and reproductive rights landed immediately on the political agenda. Gal and Kligman[22] show that after the execution of Romanian Communist Party leader Nicolae Ceaușescu and the collapse of his infamous regime, one of the first pieces of legislation passed was one directly affecting women's mental and physical health: it lifted the coercive ban on abortions introduced in 1966. For many, Romania's strict antiabortion laws and oppressively pro-natalist policies signified the illegitimacy of the regime. Rescinding this legislation was the perfect symbol for the dawn of the new era. As in the Kitchen Debate between Nixon and Khrushchev, women's rights and social roles were used to claim legitimacy, superiority, and moral authority for a new political rule.

All over CEE, the collapse of the state socialist regimes found women firmly entrenched in the paid labor market, albeit in typically segregated jobs, which accrued lower wages than male-dominated ones. In addition, unpaid care work, such as raising children, caring for the elderly in the context of extremely low-quality and inaccessible public health-care institutions, and procuring goods in a shortage economy to feed families was also understood as primarily women's responsibility. According to time budget surveys, women spent roughly two and a half times more time on these care tasks than men even when simultaneously working full time, which resulted in a sizeable leisure gap between men and women.[23] In this context, the image of the middle-class stay-at-home housewife, who does not have to juggle paid and unpaid work, seemed rather attractive to overworked and exhausted women in the region.[24] It is thus no surprise that, when the state socialist political regimes were brought down and unemployment became rampant in the ensuing economic crisis, women's engagement in paid work came to be questioned immediately.

Unlike in Western countries, where women's struggle to gain a foothold in the labor market had just started to bear fruit in the early 1990s, women in Central and East European countries did not experience compulsory work in state-owned enterprises as emancipatory, especially if followed by a second shift of domestic work. Much to the chagrin of Western feminists who enthusiastically promoted women's continued paid employment, many women active before 1989 understood the "public" sector itself as a site of domination and unfreedom, where one had to be careful about expressing one's views openly and could be reported to the authorities if identified with ideas contrary to the doctrines of the Communist Party. Work in the household, political debates held in private family spaces, family life—all shielded from state surveillance—seemed the most important sources of liberation for all.[25]

In addition, conservative parties emerged on the political scene in each post–state socialist country, and their representatives—male and female alike—argued that women had been "overemancipated" under state socialism and should return to the domestic sphere as their natural environment.[26] Some even blamed women as the undeserving beneficiaries of the state socialist system who had unfairly claimed the rewards of affirmative action policies, as well as many of the social benefits targeting families. This resonated well in the context of rising joblessness and a widespread identity crisis that destabilized existing tropes of masculinity and femininity. Indeed, public opinion polls on women's desired role in society show that in 1994 over 70 percent of Hungarians, 65 percent of Poles, 73 percent of Bulgarians, close to 60 percent of Czechs, but only 44 percent of Austrians, 35 percent of West Germans, and 30 percent of the Dutch agreed with the statement that "working for wages is fine but what women really want is a family."[27] In several countries, women's reproductive rights were also challenged during this transformation process, although only Poland introduced major restrictions.

Economic recession of long-unseen intensity ravaged CEE countries after 1990. Job loss varied from about 30 percent of paid positions disappearing practically overnight in Hungary to a less than 10 percent decline in some of the other countries, such as Poland or the Baltic states. The volume of job loss notwithstanding, labor markets were profoundly transformed everywhere. The state socialist period was characterized by labor shortages, where workers could find employment with relative ease, with the notable exception of a handful of marginalized groups, such as, for example, the rural Roma population. Within two years after the economic collapse, unemployment, joblessness, early retirement, and withdrawal due to hopelessness affected a large segment of the population. Rapid marketization meant that state-owned companies were privatized by domestic investors who transformed the conditions of employment in search of quick profits. International capital also sought to invest in the region: transnational companies and factories moved in to make use of the skilled yet cheap and docile labor force. As a result, and given rather lax state regulations, job shortages, and a dearth of social protection measures, labor conditions deteriorated, and workers' vulnerability increased. The timing and severity of this process was different in each country, but the impact was visible in all.[28] Given that women were typically considered more marginal to the labor market than men and the fact that they were primarily responsible for raising children, researchers feared that women's employment positions would be especially threatened.[29]

Indeed, women in most countries turned out to be somewhat more vulnerable than men to employment loss.[30] Yet in a few significant areas they competed successfully with men. After all, a large number of women did acquire a sizeable volume of human capital under state socialism: women's level of general education was higher than men's, and they also had a great deal of work experience in the service sector along with training in languages. These resources may have been fairly useless in a context that valued physical work more, but they became revalued as centrally planned economies gave way to global capitalist ones. Labor market demands shifted rapidly and measurably: fewer workers were needed in agriculture or in jobs in the heavy industries and more in tourism, banking, finance, and real estate. Transnational companies required the services of white-collar professionals with language and communications skills. After the collapse of state socialism, there were more women who qualified for these jobs given the segregated patterns of education and employment practices under state socialism.[31] As a result, there were groups of women who benefited from the changes in the 1990s and managed to secure a reasonable income, in contrast to men of similar educational levels who had been working in the heavy industries or in agriculture. Older women, less educated women, women in distant rural areas, and women belonging to the Roma minority were not so lucky.

In addition, a large group of women started to experience discrimination on a surprising scale: women with children.[32]

The *motherhood penalty*—the disadvantage that women with children encountered in the post-socialist labor market—was partly due to the cost that employers perceived hiring women of childbearing age accrued: since most of these countries had lengthy parental leave policies in place, women were expected to drop out of work after childbirth and not return for several years. As a result, employers viewed them as temporary and unreliable workers. Employers in sectors where labor supply was abundant were especially likely to charge a motherhood penalty, not hire women, screen out those who exhibited a vague interest in having a family, or keep women in marginal positions within their companies.[33]

As in the labor market, in national-level politics too, women practically disappeared after 1989: men dominated the democratic transition. In the new democratically elected parliaments of CEE countries, women received nowhere more than 15 percent of the seats, and only about 9 percent in Poland, 7 percent in Hungary, and 13.5 percent in Czechoslovakia in the first elections.[34] Over time, this proportion increased to 20 to 25 percent in several countries, but some, such as Hungary and Romania, still lag behind. In both of these countries the proportion of women MPs has hovered around 10 percent during the past thirty years. Multiple factors, including explicit discrimination, a political institutional context that is extremely family unfriendly, male-biased electoral systems, and women's lack of experience in lower-level politics and more limited access to useful political networks, may explain the decline.[35]

While women's participation in formal political institutions, especially at the national level, decreased, newly formed feminist/women's groups emerged all over the region. With the possible exception of the more extensive Polish feminist movement (fueled by the region's vilest backlash against women's reproductive rights), most newly formed feminist/women's groups were small, issue focused, or transient. Yet they played an important role by highlighting issues left out of the lofty discussions carried out within parliament: reproductive rights, rights to home birth, domestic violence, care work, rights of sexual minorities, and so forth. Their success varied, as did their ability to find domestic funding and their engagement with and dependence on funding and guidance from international NGOs.[36]

In the more economically developed Central European countries, the post–state socialist economic recovery started in the late 1990s, which in combination with preparations for European Union (EU) membership brought about a gradual increase in women's employment opportunities in the region as well as some attention to discrimination and work-life balance problems. As members of the EU after 2004, CEE countries had to establish equal opportunity commissions, units within their administration that oversaw EU-mandated equality policies, action plans, and road maps to meet transnational targets for women's employment rates and child care. The success of these endeavors is debatable, but they certainly directed more attention to gender issues, especially those related to the labor market, educated women's career advancement, discrimination, and what came to be called "reconciliation policies."

In 2004, women's activity rates exceeded the EU average in the majority of CEE countries (except for Bulgaria, Poland, Romania, and Hungary), while men's activity rates were lower than the EU average everywhere in CEE. As a result, the gender gap in labor force participation rates was smaller in Central and East Europe than the EU average. Figure 8.1 shows changes in this activity gap by country. As the figure demonstrates, the gap ranged between 8 and 15 percent in the post-socialist region in 2000, and this level remained fairly stable until the economic crisis of 2008 hit the region. (The average EU-15 gap in 2000 was 18.4 percent.)

Women's labor force participation, risk of living in poverty, and general well-being are correlated more closely than men's with the generosity of state redistribution. State socialist countries had strong welfare states and an extensive system of redistribution, occasionally channeled through state-owned companies and their trade unions. Parental leave policies, for example, were designed to support women's dual role as mothers and workers within the context of a centrally planned economy, where returning to work after several years away was common. This special context, however, changed radically. Initially, important parts of the social policy regime remained in effect, but by the middle of the 1990s, modifications could not be avoided in several areas, including the pension system and the protection of the most vulnerable, for example, the unemployed. The guiding principles chosen by new leaders for the emerging welfare states had important consequences for women's lives and gender inequality. Pension systems, for example, are one of the key determinants of the poverty rate of older men and women. Since there are significantly more women than men among the elderly, pension systems also affect gender inequality in poverty. This gender gap is smaller in Hungary, the Czech Republic, Slovenia, and Poland, where, due to the transformation of the pension system and efforts

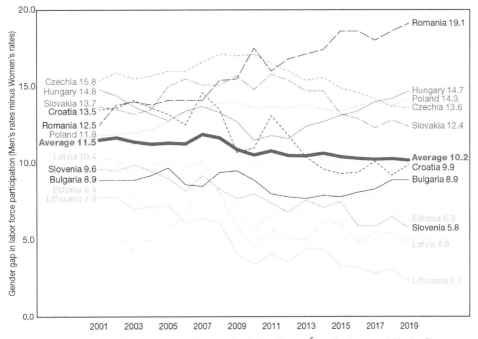

Figure 8.1. Gender Gap in Labor Force Participation. (Éva Fodor and Kevin Deegan-Krause). *Data Source:* Eurostat/Labor Force Survey 2020.

to keep the value of pensions level with wages, the poverty rate of elderly pensioners is below 20 percent, as compared to Bulgaria, Estonia, Latvia, and Lithuania, where it hovers at over 40 percent.[37]

Other aspects of the social policy regimes influence the division of paid and domestic labor via the allocation of benefits to parents. These include maternity, paternity, and parental leaves; payments or tax credits related to these and to the cost of raising children; and state-provided and subsidized child care. In this regard, too, CEE countries introduced a wide range of new policies and renewed old ones that took on different significance under the logic of neoliberal capitalism. Arguably, a common feature of these policies was their *familialist* tendencies, that is, the move to relegate care work to families, or specifically to mothers, and frame the provision of care work as the responsibility of women within private households. But even within this broad frame, different versions of familialism are possible depending on whether or not women's paid work is encouraged in addition to motherhood, on the role (if any) allocated to men, on the responsibilities retained by the state, and so forth.

Szelewa and Polakowski[38] identify four different forms of familialism,[39] each with somewhat different consequences for women's labor force participation and the domestic division of labor. The variation across countries is explained by their state socialist legacies, which proved significant even after three decades of democratization; the speed and principles of the transition process and the resulting relationship between citizens and the state; the length of left-wing party rule after 1989; and the presence of the Roma minority and the degree of racism they must endure. In most countries, policies favored the middle classes and offered more financial benefits and options to those who were already in a better social position (see more on this later, since this tendency is especially visible under certain types of illiberal regimes). In the early years of the transition, family allowances, especially those allocated on a universal basis, had poverty-alleviating impacts, but this faded away as governments allowed these benefits to be devalued and stigmatized.[40]

The gender regime that emerged in CEE countries after 1989 varied considerably, but it was typically characterized by a contraction in women's labor market participation, accompanied by shrinking state support to various vulnerable groups, including working mothers. Divisions among women widened. Younger and better-educated women enjoyed the new opportunities the globally oriented capitalist economies offered. By contrast, older, less educated, more marginalized women; single mothers; and the elderly suffered the negative consequences of the region's quick adoption of neoliberal economic policies. They were also more likely to have lost access to state services due to the retrenchment and reorganization of the welfare state, which characterized the turn of the millennium.

The economic crises of 2008 hit CEE countries hard, with significant contractions and employment loss. As elsewhere, the crisis affected men and women somewhat differently.[41] Researchers have noted that in recent economic recessions women in several countries of the European Union have been less likely to lose their jobs and their livelihood because they were typically working in economic sectors, and within sectors in specific occupations, that were less vulnerable to contractions.[42] The temporary closure of the gap in labor force participation rates visible in figure 8.1 during the years 2009–2010 shows that this was also true for CEE countries: women were less likely to drop out of the labor market than men. As the figure also shows, however, the impact was temporary. After a few short years, as economic recovery started to pick up, the gap between men and women increased again to men's advantage. Then, from 2010 onward, a new type of gender regime started to emerge in parts of the post-socialist region.

The Gender of Illiberalism(s)

Job segregation offered women a small degree of protection during the 2008 economic crisis,[43] but the second major recession within twenty years in the region made it abundantly clear that neoliberal economic policies and state austerity have exacerbated precarity for the majority of the population. A gradual but accelerating process of democratic backsliding followed, which is described in depth elsewhere in this volume (see especially chapters 4, 11, and 13) and beyond. Here the focus will be on the ways in which the newly emerging "illiberal" populist regimes used not only gender relations but the concept of gender itself to cement their rule and how they endeavored to reshape these in turn. The precise meaning of the concept of *illiberalism* is much debated even as politicians themselves are beginning to employ it to describe their rule. Certainly, variations of illiberalism abound. A rather loose definition is used for the purposes of this chapter. Illiberal regimes are those that ignore or openly reject, fully or partially, the principles of the rule of law, liberal open democracies, and civil liberties.[44] In turn, the gender regimes created in societies that we would designate as illiberal also vary significantly. The two Central European forerunners in this regard are Hungary and Poland, and they will be the main sources of information for this chapter.

The pages that follow identify three key features of the emerging gender regimes in Hungary and Poland, emphasizing their internal logic and similarities but also pointing out the differences: first, the use of "anti-gender" rhetoric in the postcrisis reconstruction of femininity; second, the introduction of pro-natalist policies to solve what has been perceived as a "demographic crisis"; and third, the continued push toward women's labor market participation. These three features are related. Arguably, illiberal regimes are built on the exacerbated exploitation of women, who are carefully constructed in political discourse and policy making as embodying two roles. They are expected to act as heroic mothers who give birth and raise an increasing number of children. Simultaneously, they are supposed to function as "naturally" dedicated and selfless, if secondary, workers who—just as in their households—are willing to exert themselves in their specific support roles for minimal remuneration.

The Use of Anti-Gender Rhetoric: A Reconstruction of Femininity

The illiberal regimes of Hungary and Poland aligned themselves easily with the transnational anti-gender movement, which started in the late 1990s. Following the politicization of the term *gender* and its use in the documents of the 1995 UN World Conference on Women, a wave of what came to be called "anti-gender" protests started in Western Europe and soon spread to Latin America and Central and East Europe. The protests and related media and popular literature accounts addressed a wide range of issues, including sex education in schools, gay marriage, policies against domestic violence, gender studies programs, abortion rights, and transsexuality. The topics varied, but the shared underlying political agenda was the denial of the socially constructed nature of gender, indeed of the term *gender* itself.[45]

Anti-gender rhetoric became visible in CEE countries as it merged into the concept of illiberalism as a form of governance.[46] Anti-gender principles have been readily translated into policy measures, including threats against abortion rights, the exacerbation of gender stereotypes in school textbooks and kindergarten curricula, the elimination of degree programs in gender studies, the legalization of the ban on sex change, and justifications for states' withdrawal from the Istanbul Convention. Kováts and Pető argue that "anti-genderism" serves to construct a political enemy for authoritarian rulers and brings together a diverse set of political actors and themes well beyond the concept of gender.[47] Korolczuk and Graf further point out that anti-gender discourses help place the blame for all social ills on external forces, such as on "Brussels," the European Union, or the Hungarian-born millionaire and philanthropist George Soros and liberal international NGOs.[48]

Photo 8.2. A protest in October 2020 in the Polish city of Wrocław after Poland's top court accepted a law banning abortions. The young woman pictured holds a poster with the text, "This is war." (Lena Ivanova, Shutterstock)

Anti-gender discourse is transnational and present in several countries. But as an official government policy it has only been adopted by illiberal leaders in Hungary and Poland. This rhetoric elevates a specific kind of femininity into the mainstream: a femininity predicated on motherhood, on the compulsory nature of care work, on sacrifice, and on a supportive role within the household and in society. In a 2019 publication celebrating International Women's Day pointedly titled "Women's Soul through Men's Eyes," ninety Hungarian male politicians and public figures described their relationship to and admiration for women.[49] As colleagues, women were extensively praised for being excellent peacemakers, compromise seekers, and detail managers. Here is an example from a deputy state secretary in the Ministry of Finance: "I am glad that I have numerous female colleagues, who, purely because of their personalities, style, and intuition for compromise, can help us end debates with good compromises. . . . I owe thanks to my female colleagues because they ensure the possibility of harmony and agreement not only in the family but also in the workplace."[50] Note the quick analogy between women's role in the household and at work, the reference to natural "intuitions," and the important yet supportive role assigned to women in government offices. The minister of finance added the following as way of appreciation: "The lion's share of invisible work is done by women. They do this out of the kindness of their hearts, without expecting anything in return, simply because they feel that it is the right thing to do."[51] These claims are much less innocent than the bouquet of flowers women typically receive on March 8, the International Day of Women, widely celebrated in CEE. In these quotes, as in numerous others included in this government-funded and endorsed publication, women are being described, indeed constructed, as devoted workers who are ready to sacrifice themselves for their families and willing to do a vast amount of work without compensation. The anti-gender rhetoric is extremely helpful here: women's behavior is linked to their "true nature," and femininity itself is preconditioned on loving self-exploitation, which in this way can remain unchallenged. At the other end, as Csányi argues, anti-gender ideologies seek to enforce male privileges in a socioeconomic context where these are perceived to be threatened by the recent experience of economic recessions, increasing job loss, and in-work poverty.[52]

Selective Pro-natalism and Labor Market Participation

The specter of a demographic crisis has been haunting politicians in CEE countries since the birthrate started to fall precipitously in the region in the 1960s. In the countries where fertility rates fell below what was required for natural replacement, the vision of national extinction due to women's irresponsible fertility behavior was regularly raised. Most notably in 1966, the Romanian communist regime instituted a set of coercive pro-natalist measures that came to symbolize the authoritarian nature of communist rule and which, in addition, proved largely ineffective and extremely detrimental to women's health.[53]

The problem of population decline surfaced again in the twenty-first century, this time seconded by EU policy makers who voiced concern about the dwindling labor supply and its impact on productivity and social insurance funds. After the transition, the birthrate of most CEE countries fell to all-time lows: the Czech Republic recorded a total fertility rate of 1.13 in 1999, Hungary bottomed out at 1.23 in 2011, and Catholic Poland fell to 1.22 a few years earlier. While immigrant labor, including that from Central and East European countries, may have solved labor shortages in West European countries, the illiberal governments of Hungary after 2010 and Poland after 2015 ruled out the possibility of inviting migrants into the country, and in fact started to wage an international war against immigration itself. Both Hungary and Poland reached for a different solution: they introduced a range of pro-natalist policies designed to encourage population growth. These included tax cuts for families with children, direct cash transfers upon childbirth, and family support schemes, as well as subsidized loans and mortgages to large families and the promise of new kindergartens and nurseries, along with enhanced parental leave schemes. The new policies helped boost the political popularity of the illiberal rulers in both countries but so far have contributed little to raising the birthrate.[54]

It is important to note the difference between the approaches toward pro-natalism in Hungary and Poland. The main pillar of Poland's pro-natalist policy, the "Family 500+" program introduced in 2016, guarantees 500 zloty per month (about 12 percent of the average wage) to families for each child they raise. This is a universal benefit to which children in every Polish family are entitled. As a result, even though it has not been particularly successful at increasing the birthrate, the policy did meet its secondary goal: a reduction in child poverty.[55]

Hungary's pro-natalist approach is quite different. Heterosexual families are given center stage in no less uncertain terms than in Poland, but family benefits, in the shape of earned income tax credits, pronouncedly favor the more privileged. This is so because less affluent parents whose income from the formal job market does not reach a specific threshold cannot claim the full sum. Similarly, subsidized housing loans are only available to those who are legally married, in formal employment, and considered creditworthy. These eligibility requirements rule out a large number of people whose main income comes from the informal labor market and who work without registration. This is not merely a class bias: Hungary's largest ethnic minority, the Roma, are disproportionately among the poor and are thus unable to utilize this form of family benefit. Widespread prejudice against the Roma creates legitimacy for these exclusionary family benefits in Hungary and simultaneously reproduces racial inequalities.

Two similarities in Hungary's and Poland's pro-natalist policies should be mentioned. First, neither country has sought to mobilize fathers to participate in caring for children, no matter how strong the emphasis on family values has been. In the first radio interview after his reelection victory in 2018, Hungarian prime minister Viktor Orbán proposed a "pact with women": an agreement that they would be having more children if the government provided sufficient financial support. Note that the prime minister singled out women, not families, couples, or would-be parents: he implied that making decisions about having children, as well as birthing and raising them, is solely women's responsibility. Not surprisingly, Hungary has one of the lengthiest parental leave policies in Europe, utilized almost exclusively by mothers, and one of the shortest leaves that only fathers can take upon childbirth (five days). Similarly, Poland guarantees a mere two weeks' paid parental leave to new fathers.

Second, both sets of pro-natalist policies retained familialist overtones well known from earlier periods: the state may have provided resources, but the work of child care remained primarily the job of families, specifically women. Although both the Hungarian and the Polish governments promised to build more nurseries for small children, these efforts have lagged behind cash transfers and tax breaks.

Hungarian policy makers further introduced special measures to encourage women to return to work after childbirth. This was not the case in Poland, where the "500+ program" resulted in incentives for lower-paid women to withdraw from the labor market and women's employment rates declined as a result since its introduction. In Hungary, those who return to work soon after childbirth can collect both wages and a parental allowance, and they can even choose to work part time. Grandparents, too, are allowed to take parental leave to allow the younger generations to return to work. This is thus no "back to the kitchen" ideology. Not only are women encouraged to have at least three children (when the largest state benefits kick in), but they are also expected to work for wages. Given that companies, even public sector ones, are reluctant to offer family-friendly work conditions, the success of these pro-natalist policies is dubious,[56] and the motherhood penalty is high. These inequalities, however, are easily explained away by the anti-gender/anti-feminist rhetoric characteristic of illiberal governments.

The Impact of the COVID-19 Pandemic

The struggle over gender equality is in large part a struggle over the unequal division of care work. Not only do women bear the brunt of unpaid reproductive labor, but care work is typically low prestige, underpaid, and invisible. As suggested above, illiberal policy makers in Hungary and Poland often make discursive efforts at hiding the true nature and extent of care work by arguing that women are naturally suited for it and will provide it out of love and dedication as a natural expression of who they are.

Nowhere did this become more explicitly problematic than during the first wave of the COVID-19 pandemic in the spring of 2020. As countries in Central and East Europe started to close kindergartens and schools and asked elderly grandparents to stay home, parents of school-age children found themselves in a particularly difficult situation. Children needed full-time care, while parents had to make a living. Schools moved to online education, but most children relied on the support of parents to use electronic devices and follow the instructions, or to stay motivated and figure out the digital maze through which teachers communicated their requirements. The volume of care work needed within households, especially in households with school-age children, multiplied.

While anecdotal evidence in the news suggested that women were especially heavily impacted by the work burden of the pandemic, few studies so far have been able to assess the extent to which the lockdowns altered the division of labor within households and the groups of women especially affected. With a Hungarian team of researchers, we managed to conduct a representative survey of the population in early May, the week after the lockdown ended in the country. Contrary to expectations, we have found that both fathers and mothers increased the amount of time they dedicated to child care during the pandemic, and both did so by about 35 percent. But given that mothers' regular time contributions were significantly larger in absolute terms, women's work hours increased much more than men's did.[57]

Furthermore, it was primarily middle-class, highly educated women who tended to take on the excessive extra burden of care work: they were more likely to work from home, were more likely to have lost the child-care contributions of grandparents, and were possibly the most conscious of their responsibility in preventing their children from falling behind developmentally. Interestingly, when both parents could work from home, the gender gap in time dedicated to child care did not decrease: proximity just barely increased fathers' predilection to step in. It was primarily mothers who had to find the gaps between child care to meet work demands and the gaps between work demands to look after household needs and children.[58] The gender patterns of a different kind of care work, elder care, were also altered but in a different way. In this respect, men increased their contributions, while women decreased them. We hypothesize that this is because of the type of work newly required: instead of having to tend to bodies and keeping the elderly company, actual physical tasks, such as shopping or fixing things, were needed, and this may have made it easier for men to step into the role of care provider.

The pandemic had yet another gendered impact in Central and East Europe. Because of the specific state socialist pattern of educational and job segregation, the medical profession is significantly more feminized in CEE than elsewhere in the world. Women outnumber men not just among nurses but also among doctors: Estonia has the highest rate of female doctors in the world, closely followed by most other post-socialist countries.[59]

Photo 8.3. A woman doctor tests an elderly patient for COVID-19 outside a hospital in Galati, Romania. (Pazargic Liviu, Shutterstock)

The same is true for teachers at all levels of state education below university. Workers in these—otherwise extremely underpaid—sectors had to work extraordinary hours and have been exposed to health risks at a rate higher than those working in other segments of the economy. Although the data on the impact of the pandemic is still limited, it suggests that the pandemic exacerbated women's care burden and the care gap between men and women, especially among middle- and upper-middle-class groups. In addition, women's work was required not only as mothers but also as those working at the front lines of the struggle against the pandemic.

Conclusion

This chapter described some of the key patterns of gender relations—especially the division of paid and unpaid labor and access to political participation—as well as changes in this important domain in Central and East Europe since World War II. Although the countries in this region differ greatly in their trajectories, this chapter highlighted key similarities while also acknowledging divergences in gender regimes.

Gender relations profoundly shape all aspects of political, economic, and social life—including production systems, the ways in which political rule is legitimated, and the ideas, opportunities, and everyday life choices of citizens. Central and East Europe offer countless illustrations for the centrality of gender regimes. The division of domestic labor, the number of children women had, and the participation of women in paid work and education have all been used to strengthen and legitimate state socialist and post–state socialist political rule to make specific political and economic visions possible. In turn, these economic, political, and cultural processes have shaped gender relations themselves and prescribed the ways in which masculinity and femininity can be experienced. It is this recursive relationship this chapter sought to highlight.

The pattern of gender relations in Central and East European countries was often quite different from that observed in some of the most developed countries in Western Europe. While women were returning to the domestic sphere after World War II in the West, women in state socialist Central and East Europe had to embark on full-time careers at work and go back to school. As women's labor force participation rates started a rapid climb in Western Europe after 1990, those of women in post-socialist countries declined. And as the European Union instituted international regulations to encourage gender equality—limited in ambitions as these may have been—illiberal politicians in several post-socialist societies started to argue that women's natural calling was motherhood while their paid work engagement, though necessary, was simply meant to support this.

The COVID-19 pandemic raised the possibility of a convergence and a reconsideration of the division of paid and unpaid work, as well as the hours people are expected to dedicate to it. The experience of the lockdown period forced employers in CEE countries, as elsewhere, to contemplate flexibilization of the workplace and work hours. Women certainly expressed a desire to continue working flexibly—from home, at irregular hours—as long as child-care institutions are open and available. The pandemic made care work visible and highlighted its value, it showed novel ways in which it can be combined with other types of work, and it opened up space for men to participate even while staying within the confines of hegemonic masculinity. Whether the changes observed during the pandemic will last beyond its immediate aftermath and how the experience of the pandemic will impact the generation of adults who managed it and the children who endured it remains to be seen.

Study Questions

1. How would you characterize the typical state socialist gender regime?
2. What were the legacies of state socialism that influenced gender inequality after the collapse of state socialist regimes in 1990?
3. Care work is crucially important for gender equality. How was the division of care work and state regulations regarding care work different in state socialist societies, and how did these change after 1990? What about during the pandemic?
4. What were the most important changes that the post-2010 conservative (or illiberal) turn brought in CEE countries in terms of gender ideology and policies related to gender inequality?
5. How are pro-natalist policies in Hungary and Poland different, and what could explain these differences? How does the conservative turn in gender ideology in CEE fit into global trends?

Suggested Readings

Fodor, Éva. *Working Difference: Women's Working Lives in Hungary and Austria, 1945–1995.* Durham, NC: Duke University Press, 2003.

Haney, Lynne. *Inventing the Needy: Gender and the Politics of Welfare in Hungary.* Berkeley: University of California Press, 2003.

Korolczuk, Elżbieta, and Agnieszka Graff. "Gender as 'Ebola from Brussels': The Anticolonial Frame and the Rise of Illiberal Populism." *Signs: Journal of Women in Culture and Society* 43, no. 4 (2018): 797–821. https://doi.org/10.1086/696691.

Krizsan, Andrea, and Connie Roggeband. *The Gender Politics of Domestic Violence: Feminists Engaging the State in Central and Eastern Europe.* New York: Routledge, 2018.

Szelewa, Dorota, and Michal P. Polakowski. "Who Cares? Changing Patterns of Childcare in Central and Eastern Europe." *Journal of European Social Policy* 18, no. 2 (2008): 115–31.

Websites

Inter-Parliamentary Union's gender equality site: https://www.ipu.org/our-impact/gender-equality

International IDEA's Gender Quotas Database: https://www.idea.int/data-tools/data/gender-quotas

Organisation for Economic Co-operation and Development (OECD) Gender Initiative: https://www.oecd.org/gender

UN Development Programme's Gender Inequality Index: http://hdr.undp.org/en/content/gender-inequality-index-gii

Notes

1. https://www.history.com/this-day-in-history/nixon-and-khrushchev-have-a-kitchen-debate.

2. https://www.cia.gov/library/readingroom/docs/1959-07-24.pdf.

3. Susan E. Reid, "Cold War in the Kitchen: Gender and the De-Stalinization of Consumer Taste in the Soviet Union under Khrushchev," *Slavic Review* 61, no. 2 (2002): 211–52, https://doi.org/10.2307/2697116.

4. Hana Hašková and Zuzana Uhde, eds., *Women and Social Citizenship in Czech Society: Continuity and Change* (Prague: Institute of Sociology, Academy of Sciences of the Czech Republic, 2009); Susan Zimmermann, "Gender Regime and Gender Struggle in Hungarian State Socialism," *Aspasia: International Yearbook for Women's and Gender History of Central, Eastern and South Eastern Europe* 4, no. 1 (2010): 1–24; Lynne Haney, *Inventing the Needy: Gender and the Politics of Welfare in Hungary* (Berkeley: University of California Press, 2002), https://books.google.com/books?hl=en&lr=&id=uYZLb_JZHZ4C&oi=fnd&pg=PR7&ots=u7vnSCzhpg&sig=bYbCHN9T5Gx9BpmGaewI9zrrd2w; Barbara Lobodzinska, *Family, Women, and Employment in Central-Eastern Europe* (Westport, CT: Praeger, 1995); Sharon Wolchik, "The Status of Women in a Socialist Order: Czechoslovakia, 1948–1978," *Slavic Review* 38 (December 1979): 583–602.

5. Zimmermann, "Gender Regime."

6. Joanna Goven, "Gender and Modernism in a Stalinist State," *Social Politics* 9, no. 1 (2002): 3–28.

7. Gabor Gyani, "Női Munka És Család Magyarországon (1900–1930)," *Történelmi Szemle* 88, no. 3 (1987): 366–79; Malgorzata Fidelis, "Equality through Protection: The Politics of Women's Employment in Postwar Poland, 1945–1956," *Slavic Review* 63, no. 2 (2004): 301–24, https://doi.org/10.2307/3185730.

8. Kristen Ghodsee and Julia Mead, "What Has Socialism Ever Done for Women?," *Catalyst* 2, no. 2 (2018), https://catalyst-journal.com/vol2/no2/what-has-socialism-ever-done-for-women; Éva Fodor, *Working Difference: Women's Working Lives in Hungary and Austria, 1945–1995* (Durham, NC: Duke University Press, 2003); Lynne Haney, "'But We Are Still Mothers': Gender and the Construction of Need in Post-Socialist Hungary," *Social Politics* 4 (1997): 208–44; Mike Ingham, Hilary Ingham, and Henrik Domanski, *Women in the Polish Labor Market* (Budapest, Hungary: CEU Press, 2001).

9. Haney, *Inventing the Needy*.

10. Fidelis, "Equality through Protection"; Natalia Jarska, "Female Breadwinners in State Socialism: The Value of Women's Work for Wages in Post-Stalinist Poland," *Contemporary European History* 28, no. 4 (2019): 469–83, https://doi.org/10.1017/S0960777319000201.

11. Barbara Einhorn, *Cinderella Goes to Market: Citizenship, Gender and Women's Movements in East Central Europe* (London: Verso, 1993); Anna Pollert, "Gender, Transformation and Employment in Central Eastern Europe," *European Journal of Industrial Relations* 11, no. 2 (2005): 213–30, https://doi.org/10.1177/0959680105053964.

12. Fidelis, "Equality through Protection"; Éva Fodor, "Smiling Women and Fighting Men: The Gender of the Communist Subject in State Socialist Hungary," *Gender & Society* 16, no. 2 (2002): 240–63; Wolchik, "The Status of Women."

13. Jarska, "Female Breadwinners"; Zimmermann, "Gender Regime"; Gergely Csányi, "Genderrezsim És 'Nőpolitika' Magyarországon, 2008–18," *Fordulat*, no. 26 (2019); Ingham, Ingham, and Domanski, *Women in the Polish Labour Market*.

14. Marre Karu and Katrev Pall, "Estonia: Halfway from the Soviet Union to the Nordic Countries," in *The Politics of Parental Leave Policies: Children, Parenting, Gender and the Labour Market*, ed. Sheila B. Kammerman and Peter Moss, 69–86 (Bristol, UK: Policy Press, 2009).

15. Jarska, "Female Breadwinners"; Fodor, *Working Difference*; Csányi, "Genderrezsim És 'Nőpolitika' Magyarországon."

16. Dorota Szelewa, "Three Faces of Familialism: Comparing Family Policies in the Czech Republic, Hungary and Poland," in RC19 Annual Academic Conference: Social Policy in a Globalizing World: Developing a North-South Dialogue, 2006, https://www.dsps.unifi.it/upload/sub/szelewapaper.pdf; Haney, *Inventing the Needy*; Steven Saxonberg, *Gendering Family Policies in Post-Communist Europe: A Historical-Institutional Analysis* (London: Palgrave Macmillan, 2014).

17. Szoja Szelenyi, *Equality by Design: The Grand Experiment in Destratification in Socialist Hungary* (Stanford, CA: Stanford University Press, 1999); Ingham, Ingham, and Domanski, *Women in the Polish Labour Market*.

18. Fodor, *Working Difference*.

19. Nanette Funk, "A Very Tangled Knot: Official State Socialist Women's Organizations, Women's Agency and Feminism in Eastern European State Socialism," *European Journal of Women's Studies* 21, no. 4 (2014); Francisca De Haan, "Continuing Cold War Paradigms in the Western Historiography of Transnational Women's Organisations: The Case of the Women's International Democratic Federation (WIDF)," *Women's History Review* 19, no. 4 (2010): 547–73; Kristen Ghodsee, "Rethinking State Socialist Mass Women's Organisations: The Committee of the Bulgarian Women's Movement and the United Nations Decade for Women, 1975–1985," *Journal of Women's History* 24, no. 4 (2012): 49–73.

20. Padraic Kenney, "The Gender of Resistance in Communist Poland," *American Historical Review* 104, no. 2 (1999): 399–425; Joanna Goven, "Gender Politics in Hungary: Autonomy and Antifeminism," in *Gender Politics and Post-Communism: Reflections from Eastern Europe and the Former Soviet Union*, ed. Nanette Funk and Magda Mueller, 224–40 (New York: Routledge, 1993).

21. I use the term *gender regime* to describe the more or less coherent and interrelated patterns of gender relations that characterize social institutions. See Sylvia Walby, "Varieties of Gender Regimes," *Social Politics: International Studies in Gender, State & Society* 27, no. 3 (2020): 414–31, https://doi.org/10.1093/sp/jxaa018.

22. Susan Gal and Gail Kligman, *The Politics of Gender after Socialism* (Princeton, NJ: Princeton University Press, 2000).

23. KSH 2012, "Időmérleg, 2009/10 [Time budget survey of 2009–10]," Központi Statisztikai Hivatal, Budapest, 2012.

24. Einhorn, *Cinderella Goes to Market*; Nanette Funk and Magda Mueller, eds., *Gender Politics and Post-Communism: Reflections from Eastern Europe and the Former Soviet Union* (New York: Routledge, 1993).

25. Goven, *Gender Politics and Post-Communism*.

26. Marilyn Rueschemeyer, ed., *Women in the Politics of Postcommunist Eastern Europe* (Armonk, NY: M. E. Sharpe, 1998).

27. "Family and Changing Gender Roles II" (ZA No. 2620, International Social Survey Programme, 1994), data file, author's calculations, https://www.gesis.org/en/issp/modules/issp-modules-by-topic/family-and-changing-gender-roles/1994.

28. Dorothee Bohle and Bela Greskovits, *Capitalist Diversity on Europe's Periphery* (Ithaca, NY: Cornell University Press, 2012).

29. Susan Gal and Gail Kligman, *Reproducing Gender: Politics, Publics and Everyday Life after Socialism* (Princeton, NJ: Princeton University Press, 2000); Funk and Mueller, *Gender Politics and Post-Communism*; Einhorn, *Cinderella Goes to Market*; Elaine Weiner, *Market Dreams: Gender, Class, and Capitalism in the Czech Republic* (Ann Arbor: University of Michigan Press, 2009).

30. Sonja Avlijaš, "Growth Models and Female Labor in Post-Socialist Eastern Europe," *Social Politics: International Studies in Gender, State & Society* 27, no. 3 (2020): 534–61, https://doi.org/10.1093/sp/jxz012.

31. Éva Fodor, "Gender in Transition: Unemployment in Hungary, Poland, and Slovakia," *East European Politics and Societies* 11, no. 3 (1997): 470–500; Kristen Ghodsee, *The Red Riviera: Gender, Tourism, and Postsocialism on the Black Sea* (Durham, NC: Duke University Press, 2005); Abigail Gregory and Susan Milner, "Work-Life Balance: A Matter of Choice?," *Gender, Work and Organization* 16, no. 1 (2009): 1–13.

32. Christy M. Glass, "Gender and Work during Transition: Job Loss in Bulgaria, Hungary, Poland and Russia," *East European Politics & Societies* 22, no. 4 (2008): 757–83, https://doi.org /10.1177/0888325408316530.

33. Christy M. Glass and Éva Fodor, "Public Maternalism Goes to Market: Recruitment, Hiring and Promotion in Postsocialist Hungary," *Gender & Society* 25 (2011).

34. Rueschemeyer, *Women in the Politics of Postcommunist Eastern Europe*.

35. Richard Matland and Kathleen Montgomery, *Women's Access to Political Power in Post-Communist Europe* (Oxford: Oxford University Press, 2003).

36. Funk and Mueller, *Gender Politics and Post-Communism*; Krassimira Daskalova, "The Women's Movement in Bulgaria after Communism," in *Transitions, Environments, Translations: Feminisms in International Politics*, ed. Joan W. Scott, Cora Kaplan, and Debra Keates, 162–75 (London: Routledge, 2019); Katalin Fábián, "Against Domestic Violence: The Interaction of Global Networks with Local Activism in Central Europe," *Contemporary Studies in Economic and Financial Analysis* 88 (2006): 111–152; Katalin Fábián, *Contemporary Women's Movements in Hungary: Globalization, Democracy, and Gender Equality* (Washington, DC: Woodrow Wilson Center Press, 2009), https://books.google.com/books?hl=en&lr=&id=o6go_57tRJsC&oi=fnd&p g=PA280&ots=Z6ARnyMW8t&sig=ZFB6aytmobV_XfBxdAWtExvoa-s; Andrea Krizsan and Connie Roggeband, *The Gender Politics of Domestic Violence: Feminists Engaging the State in Central and Eastern Europe* (New York: Routledge, 2018); Alena Heitlinger, "Framing Feminism in Post-Communist Czech Republic," *Communist and Post-Communist Studies* 29, no. 1 (1996): 77–93, https://doi.org/10.1016/S0967-067X(96)80013-4.

37. Calculated from Eurostat data on "People at Risk of Poverty or Social Exclusion by Age and Gender," accessed January 12, 2021, https://ec.europa.eu/eurostat/databrowser/view/ilc_peps01/ default/table?lang=en.

38. Dorota Szelewa and Michal P. Polakowski, "Who Cares? Changing Patterns of Childcare in Central and Eastern Europe," *Journal of European Social Policy* 18, no. 2 (2008): 115–31.

39. See also Jana Javornik, "Measuring State De-Familialism: Contesting Post-Socialist Exceptionalism," *Journal of European Social Policy* 24, no. 3 (2014): 240–57, https://doi.org /10.1177/0958928714525815; Cristina Rat and Dorottya Szikra, "Family Policies and Social Inequalities in Central and Eastern Europe: A Comparative Analysis of Hungary, Poland and Romania between 2005 and 2015," in *Handbook of Family Policy*, ed. Guðný B. Eydal and Tine Rostgaard, 223–35 (Cheltenham, UK: Edward Elgar, 2018); Tomasz Inglot, Dorottya Szikra, and Cristina Rat, "Reforming Post-Communist Welfare States: Family Policy in Poland, Hungary, and Romania since 2000," *Problems of Post-Communism* 59 (2012): 27–49.

40. Rat and Szikra, "Family Policies"; Inglot, Szikra, and Rat, "Reforming Post-Communist Welfare States"; Elaine Fultz, Markus Ruck, and Silke Steinhilbert, eds., *The Gender Dimensions of Social Security Reform in Central and Eastern Europe: Case Studies of the Czech Republic, Hungary and Poland* (Budapest: ILO, 2003).

41. Mark Smith and Paola Villa, "The Long Tail of the Great Recession," *Revue de l'OFCE* 133, no. 2 (2014): 85–119; Francesca Bettio, Marcella Corsi, Carlo D'Ippoliti, Antigone Lyberaki, Manuela Samek Lodovici, and Alina Verashchagina, *The Impact of the Economic Crisis on the Situation of Women and Men and on Gender Equality Policies* (Brussels: European Commission, 2020), http://www.eif.gov.cy/mlsi/dl/genderequality.nsf/All/F7B0CF0F70F22D33C2257A 770040E7D0/$file/crisis_report__dec_2012_en.pdf.

42. Jill Rubery, *Women and Recession* (New York: Routledge, 1988).

43. Bettio et al., *The Impact of the Economic Crisis*; Éva Fodor and Beáta Nagy, "An Ebbing Tide Lowers All Boats," *Revue de l'OFCE*, no. 2 (2014): 121–51.

44. Fareed Zakaria, "The Rise of Illiberal Democracy," *Foreign Affairs* 76, no. 6 (1997): 22–43.

45. Roman Kuhar and David Paternotte, eds., *Anti-Gender Campaigns in Europe: Mobilizing against Equality* (London: Rowman & Littlefield, 2017).

46. Eszter Kováts, "Post-Socialist Conditions and the Orbán Government's Gender Politics between 2010 and 2019 in Hungary," in *Right-Wing Populism and Gender: European Perspectives and Beyond*, ed. Gabriele Dietz and Julia Roth, 75–100 (Bielefeld: Transcript, 2020), https://doi.org/10.14361/9783839449806-005; Eszter Kováts and Andrea Pető, "Anti-Gender Discourse in Hungary: A Discourse without a Movement?," in *Anti-Gender Campaigns in Europe: Mobilizing against Equality*, 117–31 (Lanham, MD: Rowman & Littlefield, 2017); Elżbieta Korolczuk and Agnieszka Graff, "Gender as 'Ebola from Brussels': The Anticolonial Frame and the Rise of Illiberal Populism," *Signs: Journal of Women in Culture and Society* 43, no. 4 (2018): 797–821, https://doi.org/10.1086/696691; Weronika Grzebalska and Andrea Pető, "The Gendered Modus Operandi of the Illiberal Transformation in Hungary and Poland," *Women's Studies International Forum* 68 (2018): 164–72, https://doi.org/10.1016/j.wsif.2017.12.001.

47. Kováts and Pető, "Anti-Gender Discourse in Hungary."

48. Korolczuk and Graf, "Gender as 'Ebola from Brussels.'"

49. FICSAK, "Női Lélek Férfiszemmel" [Women's soul through men's eyes], 2019, http://www.kiralynora.hu/2018/03/01/noi-lelek-ferfi-szemmel.

50. FICSAK, "Női Lélek Férfiszemmel," 2019.

51. FICSAK, "Női Lélek Férfiszemmel," 2019.

52. Csányi, "Genderrezsim És 'Nőpolitika' Magyarországon."

53. Gail Kligman, *The Politics of Duplicity: Controlling Reproduction in Ceausescu's Romania* (Berkeley: University of California Press, 1998).

54. Rat and Szikra, "Family Policies and Social Inequalities"; Kováts, "Post-Socialist Conditions."

55. Rat and Szikra, "Family Policies and Social Inequalities"; Kováts, "Post-Socialist Conditions."

56. Anikó Gregor and Eszter Kováts, "Work-Life: Balance? Tensions between Care and Paid Work in the Lives of Hungarian Women," special issue, *Social Science Review* 7 (2019): 91–115.

57. Éva Fodor, Anikó Gregor, Júlia Koltai, and Eszter Kováts, "The Impact of COVID-19 on the Gender Division of Childcare Work in Hungary," *European Societies*, September 1–16, 2020, https://doi.org/10.1080/14616696.2020.1817522.

58. Fodor et al., "The Impact of COVID-19."

59. "Women Make up Most of the Health Sector Workers but They Are Under-represented in High-skilled Jobs," Organisation for Economic Co-operation and Development, March 2017, https://www.oecd.org/gender/data/women-make-up-most-of-the-health-sector-workers-but-they-are-under-represented-in-high-skilled-jobs.htm.

CHAPTER 9

The EU and Its Newer Members

FORGING TIES IN TURBULENT TIMES

Ronald H. Linden

In 2019, the leaders and people of Europe celebrated the thirtieth anniversary of the overthrow of communist dictatorships in Central and East Europe (CEE). In 2020, they marked fifteen years since eight of those states joined a newly powerful European Union (EU), taking a huge step to creating a "Europe Whole and Free." The unprecedented expansion of an already unique transnational organization institutionalized one of the most profound transformations in European history. The changes brought about by this enlargement affected the states and societies of Central and East Europe as well as the form, function, and prospects of the European Union that welcomed them in from the cold. This chapter will review the process of CEE membership in the EU and analyze the nature of the challenges posed by the domestic and international dynamics of the EU's most recent adherents. The chapter ends with questions raised by these developments for students of political science.

After the extraordinary changes of 1989, virtually all of the newly democratizing states of Central and East Europe made overtures to join the three major organizations of what was generally referred to as "Europe": the Council of Europe,[1] the North Atlantic Treaty Organization (NATO),[2] and the European Union (see table 9.1). They wanted to do so for a number of reasons. Some were practical: to allow the people of the region to partake of the prosperity and security that the EU and NATO, respectively, had afforded the West European states since the end of World War II. Some were psychological and symbolic: to heal the division of Europe and return to where they would have been had the Cold War not cut them off, and to be included among the world's democracies. Publics inside the fifteen existing EU member states were not enthusiastic about this enlargement. A multiple simultaneous enlargement like this had never been attempted before. Though remarkably successful, the "big bang" membership expansion has had powerful and continuing consequences for the people and states of contemporary Europe and the organization itself. This chapter considers those but begins with background on the region's international environment before 1989 and the process undertaken by the CEE states to join the EU.

Table 9.1. Membership in European Organizations

| Country | Date of joining or status with organization | | | |
	Council of Europe	European Union	Eurozone	NATO
Albania	7/13/1995	Candidate		4/1/2009
Bosnia-Herzegovina	4/24/2002	Potential candidate		MAP[e] 2010
Bulgaria	7/5/1992	1/1/2007		3/29/2004
Croatia	11/6/1996	7/1/2013		4/1/2009
Czech Republic	6/30/1993	5/1/2004		3/16/1999
Hungary	11/6/1990	5/1/2004		3/16/1999
Kosovo	Partial cooperation[b]	Potential candidate		KFOR[f]
North Macedonia[a]	11/9/1995	Candidate		3/27/2020
Montenegro	5/11/2007	Candidate		7/5/2017
Poland	11/26/1991	5/1/2004		3/16/1999
Romania	10/7/1993	1/1/2007		3/29/2004
Serbia	6/3/2006[c]	Candidate		Partnership for Peace[g]
Slovakia	6/30/1993	5/1/2004	2009	3/29/2004
Slovenia	5/14/1993	5/1/2004	2007	3/29/2004
Ukraine	11/9/1995	Association agreement[d]		Enhanced opportunities partner[h]

Sources: Council of Europe, https://www.coe.int/en/web/portal; Kushtrim Istrefi, "Kosovo's Quest for Council of Europe Membership," *Review of Central and East European Law* 43 (2018): 255–73; European Union, http://europa.eu; Eurozone, https://europa.eu/european-union/about-eu/euro/which-countri es-use-euro_en; European Council, "EU Relations with Ukraine," http://www.consilium.europa.eu/en/ policies/eastern-partnership/ukraine; NATO, http://www.nato.int; Atlantic Council, "NATO Upgrades Ukraine," June 16, 2020, https://www.atlanticcouncil.org/blogs/ukrainealert/nato-upgrades-ukraine.

[a] In accordance with an agreement between Greece and Macedonia in 2018, the country was renamed the Republic of North Macedonia, effective in 2019.

[b] Though not a member of the Council of Europe, in 2014 Kosovo began cooperation with two of its rule of law commissions.

[c] Continued membership of the state of Serbia and Montenegro, dating from April 3, 2003.

[d] A "new generation" agreement providing for political association and economic integration, including a free trade area but not membership, was signed in 2014 and came into effect in 2017.

[e] Membership Action Plan; a consultation process with NATO aimed at evaluation for membership, https ://www.nato.int/cps/en/natolive/topics_37356.htm.

[f] A NATO-led security force, KFOR, has been in place since fighting ended in Kosovo in 1999. However, as four NATO members (Greece, Romania, Spain, and Slovakia) do not recognize Kosovo, NATO member- ship and participation in NATO's Partnership for Peace (see below), to which Kosovo applied in 2012, is blocked.

[g] Partnership for Peace; a NATO program established in 1994 that allows for individual countries' coopera- tion with NATO; as of 2020, twenty countries are members, https://www.nato.int/cps/en/natolive/top ics_50349.htm.

[h] Enhanced Opportunities Partnerships were created by NATO in 2014 after Russia's annexation of Crimea to encourage greater cooperation among a small group (currently six) of NATO's nonmember partners, https://www.nato.int/cps/en/natohq/topics_132726.htm.

Eastern and Western Europe before 1989

After World War II, the two parts of Europe moved in different directions economi- cally and politically. After being prevented by Joseph Stalin from participating in the US-funded Marshall Plan to rebuild Europe, Central and East Europe was absorbed

Table 9.2. Reorientation of Trade: Share of Central and East Europe's Trade with Western Europe by Period

Country	Imports				Exports			
	Pre-WWII	Last year under communism	Postcommunism		Pre-WWII	Last year under communism	Postcommunism	
	1928	1989	1995	2002	1928	1989	1995	2002
Bulgaria	61.6	13.7	38.4	51.3	64.5	7.8	38.6	55.6
CZ/SL	54.8	15.4	45.4	62.0	43.9	16.5	45.7	64.2
Hungary	32.4	30.9	61.5	57.5	25.0	24.2	62.8	73.5
Poland	54.5	27.7	64.7	67.5	55.9	30.5	70.1	67.3
Romania	50.2	7.8	50.9	63.9	53.9	17.5	54.5	68.0

Sources: For 1928 and 1989, Susan M. Collins and Dani Rodrik, *Eastern Europe and the Soviet Union in the World Economy* (Washington, DC: Institute for International Economics, 1991), 39, 40. For 1995 and 2002, European Bank for Reconstruction and Development, *Transition Report 2003* (London: EBRD, 2003), 86. Data for 1928 and 1989 reflect trade with European countries that became or were members of the European Community; data for 1995 and 2002 reflect trade with members of the European Union. For 1995 and 2002, the average for the Czech Republic and Slovakia is used.

into the Soviet-dominated economic and political system and its organizations. All of the states in this region (except Yugoslavia) became members of the Council for Mutual Economic Assistance (CMEA), founded in 1949, and the Warsaw Pact, the Soviet-dominated military alliance established in 1955. Most importantly, they were bound by bilateral economic, political, and military ties to the Soviet Union. Trade was sharply curtailed with the West and reoriented toward the Soviet Union (see table 9.2). Five-year plans approved by the respective communist parties ruled the region's economies, and private economic activity was reduced to insignificance or eliminated altogether.

As a result, during the 1960s and early 1970s, while Western Europe regained economic vitality, established convertible currencies, and began to participate actively in global trade and investment, Central and East Europe did not. The states of the region recovered from the war and made progress in providing basic goods and services for most of their populations, especially in comparison to the low level of economic development that had characterized most of the region (except for the Czech Lands) before the war. But the region was cut off from the stimulant of international trade competition, was not open to Western investment, and was in fact obliged to render economic support to the USSR, providing an estimated $20 billion worth of technology, machinery, skills, and manufactured goods in the first fifteen years after the war.[3]

The region remained a marginal global economic actor for the entire period of the Cold War, providing only 4.5 percent of the world's exports—or equal to about one-third of the amount West Germany alone provided. The typical Central and East European state received from the USSR nearly 40 percent of its imports and sent to the USSR more than one-third of its exports.[4] None of the region's currencies were convertible, even in transactions among themselves. On the other hand, the region was shielded from sharp jumps in the price of commodities like oil because these were provided to the region at the CMEA "friendship price" (a fraction of the global price). Thus, the region's socialist economies avoided sharp recessions and had little price inflation, but by the late

1970s and 1980s, they also began to show little or no growth. The states of the region also received a substantial trade subsidy from the Soviet Union because they were able to purchase energy and other resources at lower than world prices in exchange for "soft" goods (i.e., those not salable in the West).[5] When Mikhail Gorbachev became the leader of the Soviet Union in 1985, he moved to change this "international division of labor" to adjust to economic realities. The revolutions of 1989 intervened, and the Central and East European states found themselves thrown onto the harsh playing field of the global economy without the experience or economic mechanisms to compete.

The Courtship of the EU: Toward the "Big Bang"

What is today an organization of twenty-seven countries with nearly 450 million people began in the aftermath of World War II as a limited attempt to link key parts of the economies of former enemies France and Germany. In 1951, the European Coal and Steel Community (ECSC) was founded by those two countries, plus Italy, Belgium, the Netherlands, and Luxembourg. In the landmark Treaty of Rome of 1957, the European Economic Community was created to complement the ECSC and a new European Atomic Agency. These three were combined in 1965 into the European Community (EC). The members created a parliament and modified other parts of the organization, but over the next two decades, the organization grew slowly in terms of both number of members (adding the United Kingdom, Ireland, and Denmark in 1973, Greece in 1981, and Spain and Portugal in 1986) and areas of policy responsibility. By the time the Berlin Wall fell in 1989, the EC still had only twelve members, but it had committed itself (through the Single European Act of 1986) to creating the mechanisms for a single European economy. The Treaty on European Union, referred to as the Maastricht Treaty after the Dutch town in which it was signed in 1992, renamed the organization the EU and began to move the members toward more unified economic functioning as well as stronger common political institutions. Austria, Finland, and Sweden joined in 1995, bringing the number of members to fifteen. In 2002, the common European currency, the euro, was introduced in eleven of the member states.

After the overthrow of communism, the Central and East European states moved to try to join the EU as soon as possible. Hungary and Poland formally applied in 1994; Romania, Slovakia, and Bulgaria in 1995; and the Czech Republic and Slovenia in 1996. By that time, all had held at least one set of open elections deemed free and fair by international observers; had created conditions for the exercise of citizens' rights of expression, assembly, and participation; and were seeing the birth—in some cases, explosion—of political parties and interest groups. The states of the region rejected the idea of recreating the Soviet-era economic and political alliances in favor of joining the most successful and attractive international organization in history, the EU. For the organization itself, enlargement posed a huge challenge, even beyond making such a large simultaneous expansion. In previous enlargements, the candidates for membership were not only functioning democracies but had also established capitalist and Western-oriented economic systems. In Central and East Europe, by contrast, the countries seeking membership were only just starting the process of creating such systems, were much more numerous, and, most importantly, were significantly poorer than even the poorest EU member. Among potential candidates, for example, the gross domestic product (GDP) per capita of Poland (the largest) was just over two-thirds that of Greece, the poorest EU member, and only 40 percent of the average of all EU members (see table 9.3).

The EU moved somewhat slowly to establish and implement standard procedures for bringing the Central and East European states into the organization. Along with financial assistance to help these states reform their economies, the EU signed a series of association agreements, called the Europe Agreements, to govern trade with the Central and East European states. At the 1992 European Council at Lisbon, the organization for the first time pledged to help the Central and East European states not just to reform their

Table 9.3. Gross Domestic Product per Capita of New and Old EU Members, GDP in PPS per Inhabitant, 2001 (EU-15 = 100)

Luxembourg	190
Ireland	118
Netherlands	115
Denmark	115
Austria	111
Belgium	109
Finland	104
Italy	103
France	103
Germany	103
Sweden	102
United Kingdom	101
Spain	84
Cyprus	74
Slovenia	70
Portugal	69
Greece	65
Czech Republic	59
Hungary	53
Slovakia	48
Poland	41
Estonia	40
Lithuania	39
Latvia	33
Bulgaria	25
Romania	24
Turkey	23

Source: Eurostat, *Towards an Enlarged European Union* (Brussels: European Commission, n.d.).

Note: In this chart, gross domestic product per capita is calculated on the basis of purchasing power standard (PPS), which takes into account differences in prices across countries.

economies but ultimately to become members of the organization. At the Copenhagen Council in 1993, the EU set forth the basic criteria that the new members would have to meet to be admitted. These "Copenhagen criteria" include stability of institutions guaranteeing democracy, the rule of law, human rights, and respect for and protection of minorities; the existence of a functioning market economy as well as the capacity to cope with competitive pressure and market forces within the union; and the ability to take on the obligations of membership, including adherence to the aims of political, economic, and monetary union.[6]

To fulfill these criteria, applicants were obliged to accept and pass into legislation the codes, practices, and laws in place in the EU, referred to as the *acquis communautaire*. Starting in 1998, all of the applicant countries were evaluated annually to assess their progress toward establishing democratic practices, including the rule of law, the exercise of political rights by the population, and the protection of minority rights. Economic assessments judged the countries' movement toward establishing a market economy, including privatization, fiscal and monetary control, and openness to foreign investment. Each applicant's ability to undertake the "obligations of membership" was assessed by measuring the adoption of measures laid out in the *acquis*, covering, for example, agriculture, transportation, environmental policy, and justice and home affairs (e.g., the country's legal systems, including courts, police, rights of accused, and use of the death penalty).[7] In all, there were thirty-one chapters of standards by which these countries were judged, and only when all chapters had been "closed," or judged satisfactory by the European Commission, were invitations for membership issued. That happened for eight Central and East European states in 2002, leading to their simultaneous admission (the "big bang") in May 2004.[8] For Romania and Bulgaria, however, there were thirty-five chapters, and these two countries were subject to "enhanced monitoring" by the commission. They were permitted to join as of January 1, 2007, but under an unprecedented "Cooperation and Verification Mechanism" that obliged them to report on their progress in judicial reform, the fight against corruption, and, in Bulgaria's case, the fight against organized crime.[9] In 2005, Croatia began formal negotiations and in July 2013 became the twenty-eighth member (at the time) of the EU.

The Costs of Joining

For most Central and East European states, making the transition to democratic practices with regard to individual freedoms, elections, political institutions, and parties was challenging after four decades of Communist Party rule. Not all of the states moved equally quickly. In some cases, communist-era practices—and people—remained powerful, for example, in Slovakia and Romania. It took electoral defeats in the 1990s to improve the EU's opinion and these countries' chances for joining the organization.

For Central and East European governments, adapting their countries' political and legal processes to European norms involved making adjustments in a variety of policy arenas. Elimination of the death penalty and laws against homosexuality, for example, was required. Improvements in the legal system, including the formation of independent judges and constitutional courts, were needed in most cases. One of the most common areas of pressure lay in the EU's criticism of the countries' treatment of their Roma minorities. Numbering over four million and scattered throughout the region,[10] Roma minorities suffered both legal and economic discrimination, exclusion from employment and political power, and, in some cases, actual physical harassment.[11]

The EU's involvement in minority issues in the region produced some skepticism even as it provided an opportunity for domestic minority groups and nongovernmental organizations to utilize EU influence on their behalf to secure better treatment from their governments. For example, the EU insisted that the candidate states implement full recognition and guarantees of minority rights that in some cases did not apply in member states.[12]

Setting up appropriate Western-style parliamentary and electoral institutions and getting them running in forms that the EU would approve were relatively simple tasks compared to the process of wrenching the economies into line with EU expectations. These states were not as economically developed, had not traded in a competitive world market, and did not have the resources to make the economic transition without substantial pain. The Central and East European economies were more agricultural, were less productive, used more energy and human resources to produce the same number of goods as the West, and, for the most part, produced goods that were not competitive on the world market. To make matters worse, the goods these states could potentially sell globally were precisely those that the EU specialized in—farm products, steel, and textiles—and the EU was at first not eager to open its markets. Within a few years, however, tariff and quota restrictions on Central and East European exports to Western Europe were removed and trade shifted sharply from East to West (see table 9.2). Still, given the uncompetitive nature of these economies, it took several years before any could achieve significant positive trade balances.

Production in most of the Central and East European states declined dramatically after the revolutions, and it took nearly ten years for most of them to reach the economic levels of 1989 and even longer for Romania and Bulgaria.[13] Unemployment, which had not officially existed under socialism, soared, reaching more than 12 percent of the workforce on average throughout the region. Part of the adjustment to EU economic policies involved improving the environment for competition, eliminating government support of industries, ending price controls, and allowing bankruptcies. The EU also exerted pressure to allow foreign investment on a nondiscriminatory basis, meaning that experienced, successful West European companies would be free to buy up valuable assets in these states, now available at bargain basement prices. After 1989 and through the year 2004, the region attracted more than $170 billion in foreign direct investment (FDI), with the bulk going to the three Central European states, Poland, Hungary, and the Czech Republic. While proceeding slowly on formal admission, the EU did move to provide the region with substantial economic aid through its PHARE program.[14] Other programs were added for agriculture, rural development, and other areas. Together, more than €20 billion ($23.39 billion) was allocated to new members in what was termed "pre-accession aid," though some continued even after they became members.

Perhaps the major challenge to the accession process involved agriculture. Since its formation, the EU has supported farmers by controlling imports, supporting prices, and providing direct payments through the Common Agricultural Policy (CAP).[15] CAP payments constitute the single largest item in the EU budget. With seven million new farmers (and 40 percent more agricultural land) added by CEE accession to the six million already in the EU, the organization realized that it could not afford to extend to the new members the generous agricultural subsidies it had been providing to farmers in the EU-15 states. Moreover, in global trade negotiations, the EU had pledged to reduce the level of its subsidies. Hence, as part of these states' accession, direct payments to Central and East Europe's farmers were at first a fraction of those paid to farmers in Western Europe and were increased gradually.[16]

The Politics of Membership

When the EU was founded, the driving idea was to link continental Europe's major economic powers, France and Germany, so inextricably as to make future wars between them impossible. As other functions became part of common responsibility, such as control of nuclear energy, control of agricultural production, and external trade ties, the organization not only grew in complexity but also added members. Great Britain's membership had been vetoed by France in 1963 and was delayed for ten years, but adding democratic Portugal, Spain, and Greece in the 1980s and the relatively rich, capitalist Austria, Sweden, and Finland in 1995 was not controversial. However, adding eight or ten economically weak states that had operated as one-party dictatorships and state-run economies was not popular.[17] Despite public ambivalence, movement toward membership proceeded. This reinforced the idea among some that the organization operates with a "democratic deficit"—that is, that decisions are made by distant elites who are not responsible to anyone and reflect bureaucratic imperatives in Brussels more than the desires of their constituents.[18]

In Central and East Europe, though, accession to the EU was generally very popular. Central and East European populations trusted the EU and saw joining as the right thing to do for their country.[19] Support was not equally high throughout the region, however, as the costs of adjustment and the uneven distribution of such costs among the population became evident. In a 2003 survey, for example, less than 40 percent of Estonians and Latvians thought that membership would be "a good thing," while nearly three-quarters of Romanians and Bulgarians thought so. In most cases, as countries moved closer to joining the EU, public support for doing so fell off somewhat before rebounding.[20] Referenda on joining were held in each of the Central and East European countries due to join in 2004 and produced positive—though in some cases, close—votes.[21] In the Croatian referendum in 2012, two-thirds of those voting supported accession, but the turnout (43 percent of eligible voters) was the lowest of any new member state.[22] By 2011, among the new member states, public views of the benefits of EU membership were similar to those held in countries with longer membership, but there was somewhat more uncertainty in the new members than in the older member states as to whether EU membership was "a good thing."[23]

Apart from accommodating legal, political, and economic systems to the demands of the *acquis*, for several of the new members, certain issues provided a possible challenge to the depth of their commitment to join. Many worried that their inexperienced and weaker economies, especially the agricultural sector, would not be able to compete with rich, subsidized EU enterprises. There was concern that West Europeans would buy up their countries' low-priced assets and land, leaving local people unemployed and without property. For their part, some politicians in the EU feared that economic dislocation and the attraction of the more prosperous West would produce a vast labor migration once borders were erased and full EU citizenship, including the right to live anywhere, was extended eastward. In the end, several countries were granted transition periods in the accession treaties, during which they could retain control over agricultural land purchase. But the "free movement of persons" was also limited for new members, with restrictions remaining in place for not less than two and possibly up to seven years.[24]

Border issues were complicated for some new members. All the new members were obliged to move toward adopting the provisions of the Schengen Treaty (1985) that allows for free movement of citizens within the EU but mandates strict enforcement and guarding of the EU's external borders.[25] With that border now pushed eastward, Poles and Hungarians living in Ukraine, for example, found visiting their ethnic kin in new EU member states more difficult and expensive than it had been before. The need for visas suggested a second-class status and depressed the substantial cross-border economic activity that had grown up. Gradually, the EU approved visa-free travel for citizens of the Western Balkans and noncandidate countries like Moldova, Georgia, and Ukraine.[26] But a major challenge to coherent border policies occurred in 2015 when hundreds of thousands of refugees began to travel through the region as they fled wars and upheaval in the Middle East and North Africa, and again in 2020 when the outbreak of the COVID-19 virus led to multiple national-level travel restrictions (see below).

Most of the new members also faced serious issues in terms of compliance with environmental regulations. This chapter of the *acquis* includes extensive regulations affecting power generation (especially nuclear power), water, air cleanliness, and the burning of fossil fuels. Accommodating EU standards has been enormously expensive for these states and, in some cases, has obliged them to close down some power plants altogether. To ensure their entry, for example, Lithuania and Bulgaria agreed to close their nuclear reactors, which had the effect of increasing their dependence on Russian sources of energy.

Croatia, the EU's newest member, faced the most comprehensive and exacting scrutiny by the commission due in part to criticisms of the poor performance of Romania and Bulgaria, which joined in 2007. As with those states, the issue of action against corruption slowed negotiations, which lasted six years. Evidence of the EU's persuasive power was the fact that Croatia arrested and tried its own former prime minister, Ivo Sanader, on corruption charges in 2010. But legacy issues from the state's time as part of Yugoslavia remained. Most difficult politically was Croatia's obligation—as part of its adherence to the Copenhagen criteria—to arrest and extradite those alleged to have committed war crimes during the wars with Serbia or in Bosnia. As the Croatian government acted on these demands and former military leaders were arrested and extradited, progress toward membership resumed (see chapter 18 on former Yugoslavia).[27]

For all of the Central and East European states, the period of EU accession represented a wrenching shift in both real and symbolic terms. These states had been part of the Soviet Union's external empire for the four decades after World War II, and Moscow had used political, economic, and organizational ties to maintain control. In Hungary in

1956 and in Czechoslovakia in 1968, the USSR had been willing to use force to keep the countries subordinate. Only in 1989 did the USSR, under Mikhail Gorbachev, refrain from intervening to prevent democratic transformation and the return of full sovereignty to the states of this region. The irony is that, having finally achieved full control over their own affairs, the leaders of the newly democratic CEE states, with their populations' agreement, moved relatively quickly to surrender key parts of that sovereignty to a different power center, the European Union. All were willing to remake virtually all of their institutions and practices to conform to standards set by Brussels. Finally, fifteen years after the revolutions that toppled dictatorships in Central and East Europe, and only after the EU was satisfied that national laws and institutions accorded with its norms, virtually all of the eastern and western parts of Europe were formally reunited.

The EU and the Region: Achievements and Challenges

Changing the Institution and the Setting

The enlargement of the EU to the east obliged the organization to adapt its governing structure. Voting mechanisms in the European Council and the number of representatives in the European Parliament were adjusted, but the organization did not change the size of the European Commission (all member states still nominate one commissioner).[28] Though the EU grew dramatically in size and power after the end of the Cold War, eastern expansion turned out to be one indicator of a high watermark in the growth of both dimensions. In 2005, a proposed European Constitution was defeated in referenda in Holland and France. A new, less ambitious Reform Treaty (referred to as the Lisbon Treaty) was drafted and finally ratified in 2009. The new treaty reflects Europe's emergence as an international actor, providing for the new political posts of president of the European Council and high representative for foreign affairs and security policy. It also reflects a desire to improve decision making and reduce the democratic deficit by strengthening the ability of the European Parliament to affect decisions.[29]

In terms of changes in the states, the gains from EU enlargement were multiple and substantial: durable security was established in a region known for conflict, the Central and East European countries were bound together and to Western Europe economically and politically, and the painstaking creation of democratic institutions and societies was initiated and supported.

For the first time in modern history, the possibility of military conflict in the heart of Europe was rendered nonexistent. All of the Central and East European states joined those in Western Europe as full members of both the EU and NATO. In the Balkans, Albania and almost all parts of what was once Yugoslavia have joined or aspire to join these organizations (see table 9.1).[30] Across the membership area, international warfare of the type seen in the last century seems as unlikely as war between France and Germany. The significance of the organization's success on this dimension was thrown into sharp relief by the occurrence of military action just outside the EU domain in Georgia in 2008 and in Ukraine in 2014. Economically, the region's trade and investment are overwhelmingly tied to fellow members (see below), and by 2015, the single-currency Eurozone had grown to nineteen members and included five CEE states (Slovakia, Slovenia, Estonia, Latvia, and Lithuania).

In addition, the EU's aim of promoting democratic institutions and practices in the region has been broadly successful. Table 9.4 shows the effect of EU involvement. A measurement of democracy developed by Freedom House (with 7 indicating the most democratic and 1 the least)[31] shows improvement in virtually all of the CEE states preparing to join the EU. Though some of these states began with certain historical or geographic advantages, substantial symbolic and concrete EU involvement ensured that the entire first "graduating class" of EU joiners from the region were considered "consolidated democracies"[32] by 2005. The impact can also be seen in the differences among non-EU joiners. In the Balkans, where membership has been at least a possibility (see below), the average democracy score showed measurable improvement in the first five years of the new century. No such improvement—and even regression—is evident in the scores for the former Soviet states.

Preserving Democracy

Building enduring foundations for democracy anywhere in the world is a formidable task. It is subject to political and social challenges and movement "backward," as recent assessments have shown.[33] Central and East Europe is no exception, and the leaders of the EU recognize that their work is not finished. In 2019, recalling the fall of the Berlin Wall, German chancellor Angela Merkel said, "The values on which Europe is founded—freedom, democracy, equality, rule of law, human rights—they are anything but self-evident and they have to be revitalized and defended time and time again."[34] Preserving the gains of democracy is especially arduous in a region with precious little democratic history, and even more so in times of crisis. The slow, often unwieldy processes of democracy often test the public's patience, and those seeking greater power are willing to exploit grievances and threats (real or imagined) to weaken democratic institutions. A powerful regional actor like the EU can be a motivator and guide, but once the chief prize, membership, has been achieved, momentum can shift in the other direction. In the last decade, significant "democratic backsliding" has occurred in Central and East Europe, as seen in the decline in table 9.4 of the average score in new EU members from 5.55 in 2008 to 5.13 by 2020. Figure 9.1 illustrates that the decline has been dramatic in some cases.

As these indicators demonstrate, EU membership has not prevented the erosion of democracy in several CEE states. Hungary and Poland represent the greatest challenge to the EU's much-lauded "soft power" (i.e., its ability of motivate other countries to cooperate based on their values and examples).[35] In Hungary in 2010, the conservative Alliance of Young Democrats (Fidesz), in coalition with the Christian Democratic People's Party, won a two-thirds majority in parliament. After temporarily losing its two-thirds supermajority in parliament in 2014, the government of Prime Minister Viktor Orbán exploited Europe's refugee crisis, joined with the right-wing Jobbik party, and regained dominance in the 2018 elections (see chapter 13 on Hungary). In creating its self-styled "illiberal democracy," the Orbán government has enacted many measures, including a new constitution, that strengthen the hand of the ruling party, weaken electoral opposition, and

Photo 9.1. A demonstration in Budapest after the parliamentary elections of 2018 secured continuation of Prime Minister Viktor Orbán's ruling coalition. (Balodann, Shutterstock)

Table 9.4. Democracy Scores for Central and East Europe, the Balkans, and States of the Former Soviet Union

Country	1999–2000	2002	2004	2005	2008	2013	2017	2020
New EU Members								
Bulgaria	4.42	4.67	4.75	4.82	5.14	4.82	4.64	4.54
Croatia	3.54	4.46	4.17	4.25	4.36	4.39	4.29	4.25
Czech Republic	5.92	5.54	5.67	5.71	5.86	5.86	5.75	5.64
Estonia	5.75	6.00	6.08	6.04	6.07	6.04	6.07	6.07
Hungary	6.12	5.87	6.04	6.04	5.86	5.11	4.46	3.96
Latvia	5.71	5.75	5.83	5.86	5.93	5.93	5.96	5.79
Lithuania	5.71	5.79	5.87	5.79	5.75	5.68	5.68	5.64
Poland	6.42	6.37	6.25	6.00	5.61	5.82	5.43	4.93
Romania	4.46	4.29	4.42	4.61	4.64	4.50	4.61	4.43
Slovakia	5.29	5.83	5.92	6.00	5.71	5.43	5.39	5.29
Slovenia	6.12	6.17	6.25	6.32	6.14	6.11	5.96	5.93
Average	5.41	5.52	5.57	5.59	5.55	5.43	5.29	5.13
The Balkans								
Albania	3.25	3.75	3.87	3.96	4.18	3.75	3.86	3.82
Bosnia	2.58	3.17	3.71	3.82	3.89	3.61	3.46	3.32
Macedonia	4.17	3.54	4.00	4.11	4.14	4.07	3.57	3.75
Yugoslavia	2.33	4.00	—	—	—	—	—	—
Serbia	—	—	4.17	4.25	4.21	4.36	4.18	3.96
Montenegro	—	—	4.17	4.21	4.21	4.18	4.11	3.86
Kosovo	—	—	2.50	2.68	2.79	2.75	3.04	3.18
Average	3.08	3.62	3.74	3.84	3.90	3.79	3.70	3.65
Non-Baltic Former Soviet States								
Armenia	3.21	3.17	3.00	2.82	2.79	2.64	2.61	3.00
Azerbaijan	2.42	2.46	2.37	2.14	2.00	1.36	1.07	1.14
Belarus	1.75	1.62	1.46	1.36	1.29	1.29	1.39	1.39
Georgia	3.83	3.42	3.17	3.04	3.21	3.25	3.39	3.25
Kazakhstan	2.50	2.04	1.75	1.71	1.61	1.43	1.36	1.32
Kyrgyzstan	2.92	2.54	2.33	2.36	2.07	2.04	2.00	1.96
Moldova	3.75	3.50	3.12	2.93	3.00	3.18	3.07	3.11
Russia	3.42	3.00	2.75	2.39	2.04	1.79	1.43	1.39
Tajikistan	2.25	2.37	2.29	2.21	1.93	1.75	1.36	1.18
Turkmenistan	1.25	1.17	1.12	1.07	1.07	1.07	1.04	1.00
Ukraine	3.37	3.08	3.12	3.50	3.75	3.14	3.39	3.39
Uzbekistan	1.62	1.54	1.54	1.57	1.14	1.07	1.04	1.14
Average	2.69	2.49	2.34	2.26	2.16	2.00	1.93	1.94

Source: Compiled by the author with data for 1997–2013 from Freedom House, Washington, DC, and data for 2005–2020 from "Nations in Transit" (Washington, DC: Freedom House), https://freedomhouse.org/report/nations-transit.

Note: The democracy score ranges from the highest level, 7, to the lowest level, 1, and is an average of ratings for electoral process (EP), civil society (CS), independent media (IM), national democratic governance (NGO\1), local democratic governance (LGO\1), judicial framework and independence (JFI), and corruption (CO). See "Nations in Transit Methodology," https://freedomhouse.org/reports/nations-transit/nations-transit-methodology.

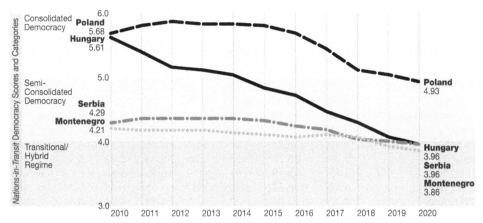

Figure 9.1.   Democratic Backsliding in Central and East Europe (Kevin Deegan-Krause). *Data Source:* Freedom House, *Nations in Transit,* 2020.

erode the independence of the media, judiciary, universities, and central bank. These and other actions have drawn judgments of violations by the European Court of Justice (ECJ) and criticism from the Council of Europe, the European Commission, and especially the European Parliament (EP). In September 2018, the European Parliament, for the first time in its history, voted to ask the European Council to determine if Hungary's actions were in violation of the EU's founding principles. The author of a critical EP report was very blunt: "Now it is up to the European leaders to take their responsibility and stop watching from the sidelines as the rule of law is destroyed in Hungary."[36]

The EU also faces a challenge to its ability to protect democracy in Poland, where the government of the PiS (Law and Justice) party, in power since 2015, has adopted similar measures. Lacking enough votes in the Sejm (parliament) to change the constitution, the government has taken several steps to try to ensure PiS control of the staffing and behavior of the country's judiciary, including the Constitutional Tribunal and Supreme Court (see chapter 11 on Poland). In this case, both the European Commission and the European Court of Justice have taken action to reject the validity of the Polish government's actions and warn them of the consequences of these infringements on a fundamental aspect of the rule of law.[37]

For both Hungary and Poland, one possible consequence could be the first use of Article 7 of the Treaty on European Union that allows penalties—including suspension of certain voting rights—in cases of "clear risk of a serious breach" of European values.[38] The struggle to preserve democracy and protect its institutions and individual rights is central to the EU's mission. Its articulation of and support for human and democratic rights are one of the most important pillars of its soft power. But the EU's capacity to act is cumbersome. Actions against noncompliance with ECJ judgments require additional procedures, and sanctions by the council under Article 7 need unanimity—which is unlikely to occur.[39] In 2020, the lethal spread of COVID-19 sharpened further the contrast between Europe's professed democratic values and the allure of autocratic practices.

The underlying foundation of democratic attitudes can also erode, as the demands of economic and party competition and the forces of global change test public commitment to the still-new systems. Surveys have shown a dissatisfaction with the way democracy operates in the region and a lack of trust in political parties and democratic institutions, such as presidents and parliaments.[40] In 2009, a Pew survey showed that support for the multiparty system had steeply declined in Bulgaria, Lithuania, and Hungary, while staying flat, or nearly flat, in Poland, the Czech Republic, and Slovakia.[41] A survey in 2017 (table 9.5) found disturbingly weak support for democracy, with only Romania, Croatia, and Lithuania among the CEE EU members showing majority preference for democracy compared to other systems. Equally troubling, the survey shows a strong minority embracing a political indifference that makes them vulnerable to populist, all-purpose solutions proposed by nationalist parties and actors hostile to democracy.[42] More fundamentally, a kind of cultural humiliation is prevalent in the region, in the face of what Ivan Krastev and Stephen Holmes call the "imitation imperative" to copy the West. Such sentiments, articulated and exploited by populist politicians, have fueled a backlash against the West, the EU, and the "uphill struggle to become, at best, an inferior copy of a superior model."[43]

The EU is the most prominent manifestation of that model, and if it cannot provide real solutions for pressing issues in the region, the democratic approach to government

Table 9.5. Support for Democracy in Central and East Europe

Most countries lack majority support for democracy as best form of government		
Percentage who say . . .		
	Democracy is preferable to any other kind of government	In some circumstances, a nondemocratic government can be preferable	For someone like me, it doesn't matter what kind of government we have
Greece	77	15	6
Lithuania	64	15	17
Georgia	55	19	21
Croatia	54	19	23
Armenia	53	13	32
Romania	52	28	17
Czech Republic	49	27	22
Hungary	48	26	21
Poland	47	26	18
Bosnia	46	22	26
Estonia	46	29	20
Bulgaria	39	34	23
Belarus	38	35	17
Ukraine	36	31	23
Latvia	34	30	26
Russia	31	41	20
Moldova	26	44	19
Serbia	25	28	43

Source: "Democracy, Nationalism and Pluralism," *Religious Belief and National Belonging in Central and Eastern Europe,* Pew Research Center, May 10, 2017. Survey conducted June 2015–July 2016 in eighteen countries. "Don't know/refused" responses are not shown. Available at http://www.pewforum.org/2017/05/10/democracy-nationalism-and-pluralism; see appendix A, "Methodology," for details.

will be tarnished and imperiled. The last decade has provided an ample stock of concrete problems that continue to test the values and practices of the union.

Economic Struggles

The CEE states are poorer members of the EU. The six most populous CEE states (Poland, Romania, the Czech Republic, Hungary, Bulgaria, and Slovakia) have an average GDP per capita of $32,600, while the EU average is $44,500.[44] But since joining the organization, the CEE states have narrowed the gap, showing higher growth rates, for example, than longtime EU members. As noted, five CEE states have joined the Eurozone so far, but the two largest East European economies, Poland and Romania, have not. In this subset of EU members, a single currency operates, and states' fiscal (budget) autonomy is limited. Still, all of the new Central and East European EU members have become tightly entwined with the economic dynamics of their European partners. EU countries are the principal source of FDI, and EU partners account for anywhere from three-fifths to more than three-quarters of Central and East European trade.[45]

Thus, when an international economic crisis hit Europe in 2008, begun by a deep recession in the United States, both new and old Europe felt the impact. With both investment funds and the market for exports sharply reduced, poorer EU states that had counted on cheap credit began instead to borrow, at first to cover domestic needs and then—at much less attractive rates—to cover earlier borrowing. With unsustainable debt building in Greece, Ireland, Spain, and Portugal, the EU was obliged to act. It did so at the behest of richer "paymaster countries," Germany, the Netherlands, and Finland, and imposed severe austerity programs in return for aid.

At the same time, new centrally controlled institutions of the EU were created, like the European Stability Mechanism and a "European Fiscal Compact,"[46] while existing institutions, like the European Central Bank, began providing long-term, low-interest loans to banks. The combined effect of these actions did work to make the annual budget situation in Italy, Portugal, and Spain somewhat more manageable, and modest growth returned to the Eurozone in 2014. As a result of this global downturn, deep recessions occurred in Central and East Europe. Only Poland was able to maintain growth. In many new member countries, economic crisis led to political change. Governments in Croatia, the Czech Republic, and Eurozone members Slovenia and Slovakia succumbed to early collapse. Hostility to costly bailouts was also evident in the region. When successive bailouts for Greece were being considered in 2015, Slovak prime minister Robert Fico said, "Let no one ask Slovaks who earn €550 to €600 [per month] and get pensions of €250 to €300 to put money together and send out €1 billion."[47]

The Central and East European states did rebound quickly, in fact outpacing Western Europe—at least until the effects of the pandemic hit in 2020. While public opinion in the East, like that across most of Europe, had shown fading faith in the EU, by 2019 trust in the EU had rebounded throughout Europe, including CEE. Here majorities indicated their trust in the EU, even in states that challenged Brussels directly, like Poland and Hungary.[48] Nevertheless, loss of population, economic dissatisfaction, corruption, and opposition to EU directives, especially on migration and democratic practice, helped strengthen support for nationalist parties across the region.[49] Fear of migrants and, more recently, the coronavirus has boosted the stock of political forces that blame globalization and the EU and offer more "homegrown" solutions. This has increased the pressure on the EU to make sure the organization can demonstrate value in return for the transfer of sovereignty it requires from members.

Responses to Migration

The collapse of the Arab Spring movement for democracy after 2011 and especially the worsening of the civil war in Syria produced a migration flow to Europe of unprecedented proportions. At the end of 2014, just over fifty thousand people had fled war, poverty, and hopelessness in the Middle East and North Africa to seek asylum in Europe. By the end of 2015, that number exceeded 1.3 million. In the East, the refugees came through Turkey in an attempt to reach the richer countries of Europe, especially Germany. To do so, they had to traverse some CEE states, notably Serbia and EU member Hungary. By the end of 2015, more than 177,000 refugees were camped in Hungary, the highest number per capita in Europe. Despite their commitments to the EU, several Central and East European members rejected the idea of taking in refugees and challenged the EU's right to make such policy.

Anti-immigrant and anti-Muslim fears were exploited by populist parties in each of these countries, but the problem was exacerbated by the EU's inability to construct an effective and equitable solution. On the western route, thousands were dying in the Mediterranean as they tried to reach Europe, and the burden of rescue and settlement fell disproportionately on Greece and Italy. EU interior ministers, in an unusual majority vote, adopted a plan in 2015 to distribute by quota some 120,000 arriving refugees (plus 40,000 previously agreed to).[50] Despite these meager numbers compared to the overall surge and the fact that less than 10 percent would be settled in Central and East Europe, Hungary, Slovakia, the Czech Republic, and Romania voted and acted against the plan. Hungary built barriers on its borders (in violation of Schengen Treaty principles) and later, along with Slovakia, sued the EU in the European Court of Justice, unsuccessfully, to try to block the plan. With the quota plan producing weak results (just over eighteen thousand resettlements by spring 2017), the EU itself took legal action against the Czech Republic, Hungary, and Poland and in 2020 secured a judgment that these members had failed to honor their obligations.[51] Aside from building a case against the CEE members, the ruling has little practical effect, as the EU signed an agreement with Turkey in 2016 that sharply cut the number of refugees coming from that direction, in return for €6 billion in refugee aid. While most of these funds have been disbursed, other provisions, including visa-free travel for Turks, have not been enacted, leading to repeated threats from Turkey's leader, Recep Tayip Erdoğan, to cancel the pact.[52] A fresh attempt by the EU to create an overall plan to handle refugees—a goal made even more difficult by the coronavirus crisis—was put forth in September 2020.[53]

The CEE states are not the only EU members to resist the distribution of migrants, but this very public resistance by newer members represents a clear rejection of both the values and ideals of the EU. At the same time, it provides a powerful focus for those domestic nationalist and populist forces willing to demonize both "the other" and external actors like the EU for political gain.[54]

Dealing with Russia

Another dimension of the EU's international role became decidedly more complicated after the admission of eleven Central and East European states, three of which were once part of the Soviet Union and virtually all of which have diverging histories with, and views of, Russia. Russia and the EU are active economic partners; for example, the EU is the largest investor in Russia, accounting for three-fourths of all FDI. Russia ranks fifth among EU trade partners, and the EU is first among Russia's partners. In large part this is because Russia is the leading supplier of Europe's oil (28 percent of its non-EU imports) and natural gas (44 percent of its imports from outside the bloc). Dependence on Russian energy is not evenly distributed, with the proportion being much higher among some of the Central and East European states who import more than 75 percent of their oil or natural gas from Russia.[55]

These differences, plus historical paths that have included both liberation from the Nazis and occupation by the communists, produce a range of attitudes toward Putin's Russia. The Baltic states, Poland, and Romania, for example, prefer that the EU take a tough stand on sanctions imposed on Moscow after its seizure of the Crimean Peninsula from Ukraine in 2014 and its support of rebels in the eastern part of that country. These states tend to see a more imminent threat to their hard-won sovereignty. Others, notably the Czech Republic and especially Hungary as its government feuds with the EU, are more willing to seek greater cooperation with and prefer fewer penalties on Russia. Still, the EU has been able to maintain and extend its sanctions against Russia for its actions against Ukraine.[56]

Foreign policy has always been the weakest policy area of EU coordination. Adding so many states with a range of attitudes toward Russia, plus high levels of energy dependence, produces a complex map of possible responses to Russia. Germany, for example, is already the major terminus of Nord Stream, a pipeline for Russian gas, and has supported construction of a second pipeline, Nord Stream 2, to be owned 100 percent by Gazprom, Russia's state gas company (see map 9.1). As these pipelines bring gas directly into Europe without passing through Ukraine, CEE members like Poland and the Baltic states sharply criticized the project, arguing that both European dependence and their own vulnerability will increase because Russia can cut off energy to Ukraine and to them without jeopardizing its sales to West Europe. In this fight, they have the support of the United States, which has applied sanctions in an unsuccessful attempt to block the Nord Stream 2 pipeline.[57]

New Kid on the Block: China and CEE

Following a period of rapid growth after the turn of the twenty-first century, China's economy began a prolonged slide, provoking its leaders to look for new markets, new resources, and foreign economic partners. At first directed toward less-developed but resource-rich countries, Chinese overseas FDI took off in Europe in 2014, producing more than €130 billion in total investment in five years. Chinese investment in Europe has slowed in recent years but remains concentrated in the richer EU members like

Map 9.1. Gazprom's Nord Stream Pipelines

Germany, the UK (at the time), and Italy.[58] Such involvement is part of the global Belt and Road Initiative designed to link Chinese producers with rich markets and investment opportunities. Most EU countries welcomed access to the Chinese market and the flow of investment, especially after the effects of the 2008 worldwide economic recession spread. Mutual interest made China into the EU's number two trade partner and the leading supplier of its imports.

The Central East European countries have also seen a rising presence of Chinese officials and some investment. In 2012, the "16+1" group (now 17 + 1) was initiated by Beijing to facilitate bilateral links between China and the countries of the region, including eleven CEE EU members.[59] Along with investment came many soft-power institutions, including media outlets and Confucius Institutes to teach Chinese culture and language.[60] With massive support from the state, China was able to offer CEE funds without EU restrictions. Investment grew rapidly at first, for example in Serbia and Hungary. Eventually Chinese involvement across Europe caused concern in Brussels, and in 2019 the EU declared China to be a "systemic rival." In the same year, the EU adopted for the first time a system of monitoring all foreign investment throughout the bloc. In CEE, some high-profile projects, such a Chinese-financed Budapest–Belgrade highway, faced EU opposition because of a lack of open bidding. After many Chinese promises went unfulfilled or produced outsized debt obligations, poor payoffs, and fears of political influence, CEE ardor seemed to cool, and Chinese investment in the CEE states, following global trends, declined.[61]

Managing the Pandemic

The outbreak in 2020 of the global coronavirus (COVID-19) pandemic infected more than 127 million people and killed nearly 3 million worldwide. It did not spare Europe. As of April 2021, the EU had seen more than 26 million cases, coming in several murderous waves, with France, Italy, Spain, and Germany accounting for more than half of the cases and deaths from the disease.[62] The states of Central and East Europe at first fared somewhat better, but by early 2021 they had COVID death rates that were the highest in the world.[63]

In responding to the spread of the disease, individual states took actions that ran counter to years of EU progress toward open borders and seamless protection of citizens' rights. Seventeen of the twenty-two members of the Schengen free-travel area introduced border restrictions in 2020 in an effort to stem the spread of the disease. The entire Schengen Area was closed to non-EU citizens in March 2020 and began to reopen in midsummer, but several states reimposed restrictions in 2021 in response to renewed waves of infections.

Taking effective action against the virus and its social and economic consequences poses an existential challenge to the EU. The EU's ability to coordinate action in a crisis is crucial to sustaining faith in the organization in Europe and globally. As Rosa Balfour, the director of Carnegie Europe, put it, the pandemic has been European leaders' "Armageddon."[64] As with migration and debt management, in this health crisis Brussels ultimately must rely on cooperation from member states. And the EU's weak performance on COVID-19 vaccination—inadequate supply, national squabbles, and a rate well behind that of the United States—demonstrates how difficult effective coordination can be.[65]

As the EU's executive agency, the European Commission is the most visible, most "hands-on" of the EU's institutions, and it has taken the lead from the beginning in coordinating the EU's response to the coronavirus. Measures included recommendations on travel and information flows, provision of personal protective and medical equipment, and some funds provided directly to various countries supporting research and health care systems.[66] In May 2020, commission president Ursula von der Leyen proposed the creation of a plan, costing more than €750 billion ($825 billion), in which Brussels would collect and redistribute funds to help members cope with the effects of the virus.[67] Such action—like the financial rescue plans of 2015—can represent a step toward a more "federal" Europe, but wary CEE EU members (e.g., Hungary and Poland) were nevertheless inclined to support such steps, as they are in line to receive billions of euros. At the same time, leaders of these states were eager to blunt attempts by the EU to link coronavirus aid to the application of strict "rule of law" criteria. This complicated negotiations, delaying a deal until December 2020.[68]

As in many other regions,[69] the attack on democratic governance in CEE was exacerbated by the health crisis. In Hungary, which had relatively few coronavirus cases, the Fidesz-controlled parliament passed legislation allowing the government to rule by decree. This extraordinary suspension of democratic rule came in for sharp criticism from the European Parliament and the commission, as numerous measures that had little to do with COVID-19 were passed during the declared "Time of Danger." The parliament formally ended this period in June 2020, but observers of Hungarian democracy remained wary as many of the emergency measures were adopted into law.[70]

A Weakened European Union

In addition to these ongoing challenges, the EU faces two unprecedented blows to its standing and threats to both its hard and soft power. If the organization cannot rise to meet them, these challenges will damage societies and systems in both old and newer members.

With Friends Like This . . .

Almost from the beginning of his administration, US president Donald Trump demonstrated a willingness to disparage and demean America's most important European allies and even threaten them with trade wars. At the same time, he praised—and at times defended—the world's autocrats, like Vladimir Putin. Under Trump, the United States pulled out of several major treaties and negotiations that had included the EU and its members as partners, including the Transatlantic Trade and Investment Partnership, the Joint Comprehensive Plan of Action designed to restrain Iran's nuclear weapons program, and the Treaty on Climate Change. In addition, Washington pulled out of one of the longest-running and most comprehensive arms control treaties with Russia, the Treaty on Intermediate Range Nuclear Forces, which had kept Russia from deploying multistage nuclear missiles that could threaten Europe.

These actions, accompanied by a steady barrage of anti-Europe tweets, threats, and attacks by the Trump administration, amounted, in the view of some observers, to a "wrecking-ball approach to the post–World War II order that the U.S. and Europe built."[71] While US actions and statements drove favorable views of Washington to an all-time low among traditional allies, the president's appeal remained very strong among leaders and the public in CEE.[72] But for the EU as a regional and global actor, the corrosion of US-European solidarity was ominous. "For the past 70 years," writes Ivan Krastev, "Europeans have known that, no matter who occupies the White House, America's foreign policy and strategic priorities will be consistent. Today, all bets are off."[73] The election of Joseph Biden in 2020 seemed to offer prospects for repairing US-European ties, but for the EU—and especially its CEE members—uncertainty and worry are compounded by the disappearance from the EU of the UK.

Brexit

On January 31, 2020, for the first time in the history of the EU, a member left the community. And not just any member, but its third-largest in terms of population and economy and its most militarily capable member. The EU now faces powerful adversaries like Russia and China with reduced economic clout and even less hard-power capacity than before. Members' trade and investment ties with the United Kingdom will have to be negotiated along with many other specifics, including the status of EU citizens in the United Kingdom and vice versa.

For the CEE member states, the ramifications are many. Great Britain had been one of the strongest proponents of enlargement to the East as well as the EU member most firm in its critical attitude toward Russia. Thus, countries like Poland, Romania, and the Baltic states will lose a critical ally in those policy debates within the EU. At the same time, the UK's "special relationship" with the United States gave strongly pro-US countries like Poland an organic connection to Washington within the EU that will now be gone.

On a societal level, more than one and a quarter million people had left to live and work in the United Kingdom after accession, increasing the connection between East and West and sending valuable remittances back home. After the UK referendum vote in

2016, overall immigration to the UK slowed, and the inflow of Poles, Lithuanians, and others from CEE dropped dramatically.[74] With the UK no longer a member, Central and East Europeans, like all EU citizens, will have to apply for legal residence there, a process likely to become more uncertain as a result of the economic slowdown engendered by coronavirus restrictions.[75]

A Future EU

Further Enlargement

Is the EU at its most effective size? Has the process of building a united Europe ended, with some European states permanently left out? Can the EU successfully exert pressure on future members, and other states, to build democracy and open economies and thus strengthen Europe as a whole? During the accession of postcommunist Central and East Europe, Brussels saw itself as helping to extend the benefits of democracy and economic vibrancy to a region cut off for decades by the Cold War. This enlargement was generally welcomed by the leaderships and populations of the CEE states and was, overall, successful. Can it be duplicated and the map "finished" in the Balkans?

In 2003, the EU committed itself to continuing enlargement to include all of the states in what is referred to as "the Western Balkans."[76] Slovenia joined the organization in the first wave of enlargement in 2004, and Croatia did so in 2013. Currently, Montenegro, Serbia, Albania, and North Macedonia are all officially "candidate members" (like Turkey), but negotiations for accession have proven uneven. Formal talks, which typically take years, began with Montenegro in 2012 and Serbia in 2014, but German and especially French concerns over the enlargement process halted forward movement in 2019. Macedonian progress toward membership had previously been blocked by Greek objections to the country's name, but this was resolved by the Prespa Agreement of 2018.[77] In 2020, the EU restructured the enlargement process in an effort to make it more coherent by grouping key chapters of the *acquis* together, but also "reversible," meaning that backsliding in a candidate state could, in theory, result in movement away from membership. The council agreed to start negotiations with both Albania and Macedonia, the latter under the country's new name, the Republic of North Macedonia.[78]

Two other Western Balkan states face special obstacles to membership. Bosnia-Herzegovina, one of two "potential candidates," needs constitutional reform that would strengthen the country's ability to act as a unified entity, but domestic politics has stalled this (see chapter 18 on former Yugoslavia). Kosovo declared independence from Serbia in 2008, but despite general global acceptance, is not recognized by five EU members (nor by candidate member Serbia). Still, EU pressure has helped to secure some steps toward normal Kosovar-Serbian trade relations and in 2013 succeeded in brokering a power-sharing agreement that affects the northern part of the new country where most members of the Serb minority live.[79] While far from full recognition, movement toward normalization of relations is a product of the desire of both sides to enhance their prospects for EU membership, an important positive result of the EU's Western Balkans policy.

The Western Balkans represent a crucial test for the EU's economic power and the attractiveness of the European democratic model of governance in the face of weariness, skepticism about eventual membership, and the rise of populist autocrats.[80] Nor is further enlargement popular across the union, with support stronger in the new CEE members and weakest in West Europe.[81] As the organization struggles for influence against other interested powers like Russia, China, and Turkey, these challenges and new ones, like the coronavirus, have prompted a somewhat more vigorous provision of both rhetorical and concrete economic support from Brussels.[82]

Other states on the eastern periphery of Europe—Moldova, Armenia, Azerbaijan, Belarus, Georgia, and Ukraine—have not been offered a "membership perspective." Instead, the EU tries to exercise influence—and movement toward democracy and an open economy—by offering association agreements and stronger economic ties through its "Eastern Partnership" program. Launched in 2009, this initiative was refocused with an emphasis on "tangible results" in 2020.[83] The record of EU involvement in this region has been mixed, with emblematic setbacks and achievements in the largest of the European post-Soviet states, Ukraine.

Ukraine

Ukraine is multiethnic and has only a brief history as a separate country (see chapter 19 on Ukraine). Since the collapse of the USSR, the EU, and especially some members like Poland, have been eager to push the country toward democratization; a more open, better-run economy; and a stronger relationship with the EU.

During the contested presidential elections at the end of 2004 (the Orange Revolution), the EU did not accept the election of Viktor Yanukovych and pushed strongly for new elections. These made Viktor Yushchenko president. Ukraine was granted the status of "functioning market economy" and was considered a "priority partner country." EU-Ukrainian relations were governed at first (1998) by a partnership and cooperation agreement, and the EU became the country's largest trading partner and the largest donor of technical assistance. As with other Eastern Partnership countries, Brussels pushed for an association agreement, and long negotiations did eventually produce an accord in 2012, ironically with Viktor Yanukovych as president. This agreement, the first of its kind for partnership countries, was to provide for a stronger form of "political association" with the EU, including domestic reforms, and deeper economic ties, including the establishment of a free trade area.

Those very ties, however, alarmed Russia, which saw this as further Western incursion into a region in which it claims "privileged interests."[84] During 2013, a combination of political pressure and economic incentives (such as a lower price for natural gas) persuaded President Yanukovych to suspend plans to sign the association agreement. As a result of this action and accumulated frustrations with corrupt and ineffective government, huge demonstrations erupted in central Kyiv (labeled the "Euromaidan") that culminated in Yanukovych's fleeing the country to Russia in February 2014.

When a new interim government was formed, Russia continued to warn it against signing the agreement with the EU. At the same time, Moscow took advantage of upheaval in the country and secessionist sentiment in the Crimean Peninsula to forcibly wrest that territory from Ukraine. The EU, along with the United States, condemned the military and political intervention and applied targeted sanctions against Russian and pro-Russian Ukrainian elites. Nonetheless, Crimea was annexed to Russia on March 21, 2014. The same day, the Ukrainian government signed the political provisions of the association agreement with the EU, which immediately began to implement free trade measures as part of a package of economic and political support measures designed to bolster Ukraine's economy and sovereignty.[85]

Even while a full-scale rebellion erupted in the eastern part of the country, led by forces opposed to the Kyiv government and supported by Russia, newly elected president Petro Poroshenko in June 2014 signed the full association agreement with the EU. This included provisions for a "Deep and Comprehensive Free Trade Agreement." The agreement came into effect in 2017, and by the next year the EU accounted for 42 percent of Ukraine's total trade. In addition, financial aid during the period between 2014 and 2019 amounted to more than €15 billion.[86]

The EU and the United States have applied an ever-widening package of sanctions against actors and sectors in the Russian economy because of their "illegal annexation of territory and deliberate destabilization of a neighboring sovereign country."[87] In mid-2016, these became linked to the implementation of the Minsk Agreements signed by Russia, Ukraine, Germany, and France in 2015 to try to resolve the conflict. As full implementation has not occurred and Russian occupation of Crimea and assistance to eastern rebels has continued, sanctions have been repeatedly extended.[88]

Despite the fact that the EU is Russia's largest export partner and leading investor, its leverage is blunted by its own members' dependence on Russian energy and by divisions among them over how best to deal with Moscow. Sanctions have not prevented the construction of the second Nord Stream gas pipeline nor arrangements by some EU members, like Hungary, to sign their own deals with Russia's Gazprom.[89] Still, despite considerable cost to some exporting countries, the EU has held firm and even expanded the scope of the sanctions.[90] And Ukraine has been a vigorous actor in and beneficiary of the organization's Eastern Partnership program.[91]

Implications for the EU and for Political Science

A combination of political, economic, and human challenges has brought the European Union to a crucial point in its history. From its limited beginnings, the transnational organization expanded and grew into an influential economic and policy actor with a huge European and global impact. After a creative and forceful response to the end of the Cold War that included adding eleven new CEE members, the unique supranational organization now finds its actions—and inactions—questioned by its members, political parties across the region, and many of its nearly 450 million people. This is true within newer CEE members, in states still in the accession process, and among those outside the EU for whom membership is not "on offer." At the same time, nationalist challenges from powerful allies (the UK, the United States) and adversaries (Russia, China) are testing the ability of a now reduced EU to ensure that its successes—and the values on which these are based—are not undone.

Studying this dynamic will tell us a great deal about global politics. For example, the role of soft power is a central theme of the study of international relations. As the preeminent wielder of such power, the EU showed remarkable ability to persuade newly sovereign CEE states to reorganize their domestic systems and surrender some of their newly won sovereignty, using conditionality and the power of the European model. Now that this has been achieved, analysts focus on assessing the ability of the EU to continue to exert influence on its *members*—including CEE states who are no longer applicants—on remaining applicants, and on others not even offered membership.

Viewed at the national level, the behavior of the CEE demonstrates another puzzle for our understanding of interstate relations. During the fifteen years of their early "post-communist" period, why were the newly liberated Central and East European states so willing to dance to the EU's tune? What combination of incentives or threats were applied and with what effect?[92] Students of national behavior ask: Did these states conform out of considerations of pure power (the realist point of view)? Due to the nature of their governments (the liberal point of view)? Because of genuine changes in their identity (the constructivist point of view)? Or because of the role of international institutions (the liberal institutionalist point of view)?[93]

The behavior of the Central and East European states leading up to accession to the EU provides an approximate "natural experiment" for testing these theories. In the real world, states cannot be put in laboratories with some variables held constant and others allowed to vary. But during the years after the revolutions, the states of Central and East Europe and their paths represent an observable group of outcomes that can be studied comparatively. These states, with different cultures and histories and different experiences of conflict, all became democratic and were freed from the dominant power that had ruled their region. They all had strong economic and political incentives to join the EU. Their leaders and populations all claimed to want to adhere to democratic norms, and in most cases they moved to do so, at least until after EU membership was achieved.

As political scientists, it is reasonable to ask what explains a roughly similar outcome (democratic progress) among differing actors.[94] Measurements of democracy (like those of Freedom House) and the other chapters in this volume show that, overall, EU involvement helped progress toward democratization (see table 9.4).[95] Still, as some observers note, there were differences among the CEE states in their paths and paces of democratization, which, among other factors, reflects the varying effectiveness of EU involvement.[96]

Some scholars, like Grzymala-Busse, suggest that now, more than a decade after Europe was formally reunited, divergences among CEE states are more important than those separating "East" from "West" Europe. Pointing to the rise of populism across the continent, she says, "If anything, the real divide runs between mainstream European political elites and large swaths of voters disappointed in what they perceive as the failure of their representatives to respond to their concerns."[97]

Since accession, it is clear that significant democratic backsliding has occurred among some new EU members.[98] This raises the question of whether EU influence can continue once the major prize, membership, has been achieved. As Mungiu-Pippidi has put it, "enlargement is nearly miraculous as an *incentive*, but quite sluggish and ineffective as an assistance *process*."[99]

This has stimulated scholarship that examines the conditions under which external policy levers, including those from the EU to promote democracy, might or might not continue to work.[100] In some new EU members, the strains of a working democracy and the power of those who oppose it have grown, leading many to wonder if the EU's leverage now will be strong enough to back up its values.[101] That this dynamic of "democratic deconsolidation" is not confined to Central and East Europe—or even Europe as a whole—makes the question even more intriguing and compelling.[102]

From the EU perspective, political scientists ask, how powerful is the soft-power model after all? What external influence can the EU exert—especially in its new reduced form—beyond its borders? On the international stage, has the once-dominant "soft-power" influence of the EU been defeated by the hostility of local regimes to democracy and the "hard-power" capabilities of traditional states like Russia?[103]

Focusing on the international-national nexus is a part of one of the broader, fundamental questions of our age: can democracy, once achieved, be preserved and improved, or is it destined to fade or even be destroyed? The histories of Weimar Germany and post–Cold War Russia do not suggest a happy answer. In both of these cases, along with powerful domestic dynamics hostile to democracy, there were few effective international instruments to support the process. In the case of the EU and the states of Central and East Europe, though, there have been and continue to be instruments available to the "normative hegemon" (the EU).[104] But, as the cases of Hungary and Poland show, democratic practices have been seriously weakened, and the EU has been unable to reverse that trend. The question of why democracy succeeds at all and becomes robust in some countries but fails in others is bigger than this chapter or this book, to be sure, but it is one that the recent experience of Central and East Europe and its intensive interaction with the EU can help answer.[105]

Study Questions

1. Viewing the period before accession to the EU, how do you explain the willingness of the Central and East European states to comply with the organization's comprehensive demands so soon after regaining their independence of action after the collapse of the Soviet alliance system?

2. What seems to explain the success or failures of these states to achieve democracy and an open economy? Is there a link between economic success and democratization? Is success in building democracy in Central and East Europe related to affinity for West Europe, the recent or more distant past, underlying culture, or contemporary political dynamics?

3. Why have we seen democratic backsliding in some CEE states and not in others? Some, like the Baltic states, lie very close to Russia and have only brief histories of independence, yet they rate highly in preserving democracy, while others, like Poland, have a liberal (for its time) history to draw on yet exhibit a decline in democracy.

4. How will global factors, such as the changing power relations between the United States, Russia, and China, affect the relationship between the EU and its CEE members?

5. In international politics, what strengths and weaknesses does the new, reduced EU bring to the struggle to maintain its alliance with the United States and resist pressures on Central and East Europe and the Balkans from Russia and China?

Suggested Readings

Bechev, Dimitar. *Rival Power: Russia in Southeast Europe*. New Haven, CT: Yale University Press, 2017.

Berend, Ivan T. *From the Soviet Bloc to the European Union: The Economic and Social Transformation of Central and Eastern Europe since 1973*. New York: Cambridge University Press, 2009.

Freedom House. *Nations in Transit 2020: Dropping the Democratic Façade*. Washington, DC: Freedom House, 2020.

Grabbe, Heather. *The EU's Transformative Power: Europeanization through Conditionality in Central and Eastern Europe*. New York: Palgrave Macmillan, 2006.

Jacoby, Wade. *The Enlargement of the European Union and NATO: Ordering from the Menu in Central Europe*. Cambridge: Cambridge University Press, 2004.

Krastev, Ivan, and Stephen Holmes, *The Light That Failed*. New York: Pegasus, 2019.

Pop-Eleches, Grigore, and Joshua Tucker. *Communism's Shadow: Historical Legacies and Contemporary Political Attitudes*. Princeton, NJ: Princeton University Press, 2017.

Repucci, Sarah, and Amy Slipowitz. *Freedom in the World 2021*. Washington, DC: Freedom House, 2021.

Schimmelfennig, Frank, and Ulrich Sedelmeier. *The Europeanization of Central and Eastern Europe*. Ithaca, NY: Cornell University Press, 2005.

Vachudova, Milada. *Europe Undivided: Democracy, Leverage, and Integration after Communism*. Oxford: Oxford University Press, 2005.

Websites

Archive of European Integration, University of Pittsburgh: http://aei.pitt.edu/view/euar

European Bank for Reconstruction and Development: http://www.ebrd.com/pages/homepage.shtml

European Center for Disease Prevention and Control: https://qap.ecdc.europa.eu/public/extensions/COVID-19/COVID-19.html.

European Union: http://europa.eu/index_en.htm

European Union, European Commission, Enlargement: https://ec.europa.eu/info/policies/eu-enlargement_en

Freedom House: https://freedomhouse.org

Nations in Transit: https://freedomhouse.org/report-types/nations-transit

New Eastern Europe: https://neweasterneurope.eu

Transitions Online: http://www.tol.org

Visegrad Group: http://www.visegradgroup.eu

Notes

I would like to thank Shane Killian, Kristen Flanagan, and Isabel Ranner for their research on this chapter and Michael Meltzer of Freedom House for his provision of and assistance with democracy scores. I am very grateful to Paula Pickering for her careful editing and suggestions on this chapter.

   1. On the Council of Europe's enlargement, see Wojciech Sadurski, "Enlargement of the Council of Europe and Constitutionalization of the European Court of Human Rights,"

in *Constitutionalism and the Enlargement of Europe*, ed. Wojciech Sadurski, Oxford Scholarship Online, 2012; Karen Smith, "Western Actors and the Promotion of Democracy," in *Democratic Consolidation in Eastern Europe*, vol. 2, *International and Transnational Factors*, ed. Jan Zielonka and Alex Pravda (New York: Oxford University Press, 2001), 41–44.

2. On NATO's enlargement, see Wade Jacoby, *The Enlargement of the European Union and NATO* (Cambridge: Cambridge University Press, 2006).

3. Paul Marer, "Has Eastern Europe Become a Liability to the Soviet Union? (III) The Economic Aspect," in *The International Politics of Eastern Europe*, ed. Charles Gati (New York: Praeger, 1976), 65.

4. James L. Ellis, "Eastern Europe: Changing Trade Patterns and Perspectives," in *East European Economies: Slow Growth in the 1980s*, US Congress, Joint Economic Committee, 99th Cong., 2nd sess., March 28, 1986, 17, 24, figures are for 1980.

5. Michael Marrese and Jan Vanous, *Soviet Subsidization of Trade with Eastern Europe* (Berkeley, CA: Institute of International Studies, 1983).

6. These criteria can be seen on the website of the European Commission, https://ec.europa .eu/neighbourhood-enlargement/policy/glossary/terms/accession-criteria_en.

7. These annual reports can be found at the Archive of European Integration, University of Pittsburgh, http://aei.pitt.edu/view/euar; scroll to "External: Enlargement: Pre-accession report on . . ."

8. In case a Central or East European state failed to fulfill its commitments in certain areas (internal market, justice, and home affairs) after accession, "safeguard clauses" were included in the Accession Treaty, allowing for "appropriate measures" to be taken by the European Commission. The full text of the Accession Treaty can be seen on the Eur-Lex website: https://eur-lex.europa.eu/ legal-content/EN/TXT/?uri=OJ:L:2003:236:TOC.

9. For background on this process and the reports, see "Cooperation and Verification Mechanism for Bulgaria and Romania," European Commission, https://ec.europa.eu/info/poli cies/justice-and-fundamental-rights/upholding-rule-law/rule-law/assistance-bulgaria-and-romania -under-cvm/cooperation-and-verification-mechanism-bulgaria-and-romania_en.

10. Estimates and censuses vary widely on the number of Roma. For a comparative assessment at the turn of the twenty-first century, see Zoltan Barany, *The East European Gypsies* (New York: Cambridge University Press, 2001), 157–64.

11. Dena Ringold, *Roma and the Transition in Central and Eastern Europe: Trends and Challenges* (Washington, DC: World Bank, 2000).

12. Michael Johns, "Do as I Say, Not as I Do: The European Union, Eastern Europe and Minority Rights," *East European Politics and Societies* 17, no. 4 (Fall 2003): 682–99.

13. Economic data can be found in the annual transition reports published by the European Bank for Reconstruction and Development: http://www.ebrd.com/news/publications/transition-r eport/transition-report-201617.html.

14. The term "PHARE" was derived from the French title for the assistance program origi-nally designed for Hungary and Poland and later expanded to all the Central and East European countries.

15. For background on the CAP, see "The Common Agricultural Policy (CAP) and Agriculture in Europe—Frequently Asked Questions," European Union, http://europa.eu/rapid/ press-release_MEMO-13-631_en.htm.

16. "Enlargement and Agriculture: An Integration Strategy for the EU's New Member States," European Union, http://europa.eu/rapid/pressReleasesAction.do?reference=IP/02/176&fo rmat=HTML&aged=1&language=EN&guiLanguage=en.

17. A Eurobarometer survey in 2000, for example, showed that an average of 38 percent of the people in the EU at that time (15 members) supported enlargement of all applicants.

None of the CEE candidate states received a favorable majority opinion. European Commission, Eurobarometer, Report No. 53, October 2000, https://ec.europa.eu/commfrontoffice/publicop inion/archives/eb/eb53/eb53_en.pdf.

18. See Peter Mair, "Popular Democracy and EU Enlargement," *East European Politics and Societies* 17, no. 1 (Winter 2003): 58–63.

19. Public opinion polls for the Central and East European states during the 1990s can be found at https://ec.europa.eu/commfrontoffice/publicopinion/archives/ceeb_en.htm.

20. European Commission, *Eurobarometer 2003.2: Public Opinion in the Candidate Countries* (Brussels: European Commission, 2003), https://ec.europa.eu/commfrontoffice/publicopinion/ archives/cceb/2003/2003.2_full_report_final.pdf.

21. Referenda results for states joining in 2004 can be seen in Györgi Szondi, "The Eastern European Referendum Campaigns on the Accession to the European Union—A Critical Analysis," *Journal of Public Affairs* 7 (2007): 55–69, 59.

22. Andrea Čović, "Referendum Briefing No 18 Croatia's EU Accession Referendum, 22 January 2012," European Parties Elections and Referendums Network, http://www.sussex.ac.uk/s ei/documents/epern-ref-no18.pdf.

23. Eurobarometer surveys can be retrieved from https://www.gesis.org/eurobarometer-data-service/home.

24. "Report on Results of the Negotiations on the Accession of Cyprus, Malta, Hungary, Poland, the Slovak Republic, Latvia, Estonia, Lithuania, the Czech Republic and Slovenia to the European Union," European Commission, https://ec.europa.eu/neighbourhood-enlargement/sites/ near/files/archives/pdf/enlargement_process/future_prospects/negotiations/eu10_bulgaria_roma nia/negotiations_report_to_ep_en.pdf.

25. Background on the Schengen Treaty can be found at https://www.schengenvisainfo.com/ schengen-agreement.

26. Yan Matusevich, "Terms and Conditions Apply: Georgia and Ukraine's Visa-Free Victory," *Open Democracy Russia*, June 2, 2017.

27. For a timeline of Croatia's accession, see https://ec.europa.eu/neighbourhood-enlargemen t/countries/detailed-country-information/croatia_en.

28. The website of the European Commission is https://ec.europa.eu/info/index_en. A 2019 study found significant underrepresentation of Central and East Europe in EU leadership bodies. See Louis Drounau, "East-West Divide in EU Leadership," European Democracy, November 14, 2019; https://eudemocracy.eu/east-west-divide-in-eu-leadership.

29. For a summary and explanation of the Lisbon Treaty, see http://europa.eu/rapid/pr ess-release_MEMO-09-531_en.htm?locale=en. On key changes, see "The 'Treaty of Lisbon,'" EurActiv.com, http://www.euractiv.com/future-eu/treaty-lisbon/article-163412.

30. Serbia has not applied to join NATO.

31. For a discussion of Freedom House methodology, see "Nations in Transit Methodology," https://freedomhouse.org/reports/nations-transit/nations-transit-methodology.

32. For a discussion of EU measures, see Ronald H. Linden, "After the Fall: Postcommunist Dynamics in Central and Eastern Europe and Their Implications for Cuba," in *Paths for Cuba: Reforming Communism in Comparative Perspective*, ed. Scott Morgenstern, 271–95 (Pittsburgh, PA: University of Pittsburgh Press, 2018).

33. Sarah Repucci and Amy Slipowitz, *Freedom in the World 2021* (Washington, DC: Freedom House, 2021), https://freedomhouse.org/report/freedom-world/2021/democracy-under -siege.

34. Quoted in "Berlin Wall Anniversary: Merkel Warns Democracy Is Not 'Self-Evident,'" BBC News, November 9, 2019.

35. On the difference in types of power, see Joseph S. Nye Jr., "Hard Power, Soft Power and the 'War on Terrorism,'" in *American Power in the Twenty-First Century*, ed. David Held and Mathias Koenig-Archibugi, 114–33 (Cambridge, UK: Polity Press, 2004).

36. European Parliament, News, "Rule of Law in Hungary: Parliament Calls on the EU to Act," September 12, 2018, https://www.europarl.europa.eu/news/en/press-room/20180906IP R12104/rule-of-law-in-hungary-parliament-calls-on-the-eu-to-act.

37. European Commission, "Rule of Law: European Commission Launches Infringement Procedure to Protect Judges in Poland from Political Control," April 9, 2019, https://ec.europa .eu/commission/presscorner/detail/hr/IP_19_1957; Marc Santora and Joanna Berendt, "Poland Ordered to Reverse Purge of Supreme Court," *New York Times*, October 19, 2018.

38. The text of Article 7 can be seen at https://eur-lex.europa.eu/legal-content/EN/TXT/?ur i=celex%3A12012M007. See also Alice Cuddy, "What Is 'Article 7' and Why Was It Triggered against Poland?," *Euronews*, December 20, 2017.

39. Eszter Zalan, "EU Legal Threat to Hungary over Failure to Obey ECJ," EUObserver, February 19, 2021, https://euobserver.com/political/150984; Eszter Zalan, "EU Action on Hungary and Poland Drowns in Procedure," EUObserver, November 13, 2018, https://euob server.com/political/143359.

40. Richard Rose, *Understanding Post-Communist Transformation* (London: Routledge, 2009).

41. *Two Decades after the Wall's Fall: End of Communism Cheered but Now with More Reservations* (Washington, DC: Pew Global Attitudes Project, 2009).

42. Holly Case, "Shape-Shifting Illiberalism in East-Central Europe," *Current History*, March 2017, 112–15; Michael Minkenberg, *The Radical Right in Eastern Europe: Democracy under Siege?* (New York: Palgrave Macmillan, 2017).

43. Ivan Krastev and Stephen Holmes, *The Light That Failed* (New York: Pegasus, 2019), quote is from p. 22.

44. GDP per capita as measured by purchasing power parity (PPP), http://statisticstimes.com/ economy/european-union-countries-by-gdp-per-capita.php.

45. Eurostat, "Extra and Intra EU-27 Trade in Goods, 2019," https://ec.europa.eu/eurostat/ statistics-explained/index.php?title=File:Extra_and_intra_EU-27_trade_in_goods,_2019.png&ol did=491106.

46. Andrew Walker, "What Is the European Stability Mechanism?," BBC News, July 7, 2015. For the text of the "Fiscal Compact," see http://europa.eu/rapid/press-release_DOC-12-2_en.htm.

47. Lucia Virostkova, "Slovakia Takes Hard Look at Greek Talks," *EUObserver*, June 12, 2015.

48. European Commission, "Spring 2019 Standard Eurobarometer: Europeans Upbeat about the State of the European Union—Best Results in 5 Years," https://ec.europa.eu/commission/pre sscorner/detail/en/IP_19_4969.

49. Krastev and Holmes, *The Light That Failed*; Milada Anna Vachudova, "Ethnopopulism and Democratic Backsliding in Central Europe," *East European Politics* 36, no. 3 (2020): 318–40.

50. Allocation of refugees was based on a state's GDP, population, unemployment rate, and asylum applications already processed. "Migrant Crisis: EU's Juncker Announces Refugee Quota Plan," BBC News, September 9, 2015.

51. Matina Stevis-Gridneff and Monika Pronczuk, "E.U. Court Rules 3 Countries Violated Deal on Refugee Quotas," *New York Times*, April 2, 2020.

52. "Turkey Threatens EU on Migrant Deal as Erdogan Blasts 'Spirit of Fascism,'" *Euractiv*, March 16, 2017.

53. European Commission, "New Pact on Migration and Asylum: Questions and Answers," September 23, 2020, https://ec.europa.eu/commission/presscorner/detail/en/qanda_20_1707. For an analysis, see Lauren Chadwick and Lillo Monella, "What Is the EU's New Migration Pact and

How Has It Been Received," *Euronews*, August, 10, 2020, https://www.euronews.com/2020/09 /24/what-is-the-eu-s-new-migration-pact-and-how-has-it-been-received.

54. "The East European Response to the 2015 Migration Crisis," special issue, *Slavic Review* 76, no. 2 (Summer 2017).

55. Eurostat, "EU Imports of Energy Products—Recent Developments," November 2019.

56. Martin Banks, "Sanctions against Russia Extended," *EU Political Report*, September 11, 2020, https://www.eupoliticalreport.eu/sanctions-against-russia-extended.

57. Anthony J. Blinken, "Nord Stream 2 and Potential Sanctionable Activity," US Department of State, March 18, 2021, https://www.state.gov/nord-stream-2-and-potential-sanct ionable-activity; Paul Belkin, Michael Ratner, and Cory Welt, "Russia's Nord Stream 2 Pipeline: Running in Place," Congressional Research Service, September 28, 2020.

58. Agatha Kratz, Mikko Huotari, Thilo Hanemann, and Rebecca Arcesati, "Chinese FDI in Europe: 2019 Update," *Papers on China* (Berlin: Rhodium Group and Mercator Institute for China Studies, April 8, 2020).

59. In April 2019, Greece was added, making it the "17+1" Group, with twelve EU members.

60. Plamen Tonchev, *China's Soft Power in Southeast Europe* (Sarajevo: Friedrich-Ebert-Stiftung Dialogue Southeast Europe, 2020); Ivana Karásková et al., *China's Sticks and Carrots in Central Europe: The Logic and Power of Chinese Influence* (Prague, Czech Republic: Association for International Affairs, 2020).

61. Stuart Lau, "China's Eastern Europe Strategy Gets the Cold Shoulder," *Politico*, February 9, 2021, https://www.politico.eu/article/china-xi-jinping-eastern-europe-trade-agriculture-strategy-gets-the-cold-shoulder; Bartosz Kowalski, *All Quiet on the Eastern Front: Chinese Investments in Central Europe Are Still Marginal*, Central European Institute of Asian Studies, 2019, https://ceias .eu/all-quiet-on-the-eastern-front-chinese-investments-in-central-europe-are-still-marginal.

62. Data from European Center for Disease Prevention and Control cover the EU/EEA area, which includes non-EU members Norway, Iceland, and Lichtenstein, https://www.ecdc.europa.eu/ en/cases-2019-ncov-eueea.

63. Piotr Skolimowski and Zoltan Simon, "The Nations with the Worst Covid Death Rates Are in One Region," Bloomberg, March 25, 2021, https://www.bloomberg.com/news/articles/ 2021-03-25/poland-tightens-restrictions-as-covid-infections-spike-to-record.

64. Rosa Balfour, "European Leaders Are Facing Their Armageddon," Carnegie Europe, March 25, 2021, https://carnegieeurope.eu/strategiceurope/84166.

65. "Why the EUs Covid-19 Vaccination Programme Went Wrong," *Economist*, March 31, 2021, https://www.economist.com/briefing/2021/03/31/why-the-eus-covid-19-vaccination -programme-went-wrong; European Centre for Disease Prevention and Control, "Rollout of COVID-19 Vaccines in the EU/EEA: Challenges and Good Practice," March 29, 2021, https:// www.ecdc.europa.eu/en/publications-data/rollout-covid-19-vaccines-eueea-challenges-and-good-practice.

66. European Commission, "Overview of the Commission's Response," June 3, 2020, https://ec.europa.eu/info/live-work-travel-eu/health/coronavirus-response/overview-commissions-response_en.

67. European Commission, "Speech by President von der Leyen at the European Parliament Plenary on the EU Recovery package," May 27, 2020, https://ec.europa.eu/commission/press-corner/detail/en/speech_20_941; European Council, "Conclusions," July 21, 2020, https://www .consilium.europa.eu/media/45109/210720-euco-final-conclusions-en.pdf.

68. Lily Bayer, "EU Leaders Back Deal to End Budget Blockade by Hungary and Poland," *Politico*, December 10, 2020, https://www.politico.eu/article/deal-reached-to-unblock-eu-budget -and-recovery-fund.

69. International IDEA, "Global Monitor Tracks Impact of COVID-19's Impact on Democracy and Human Rights," July 7, 2020, https://www.idea.int/news-media/news/new-global-monitor-tracks-impact-covid-19-democracy-and-human-rights.

70. Shaun Walker, "Hungarian Government to End Orbán's Rule-by-Decree Legislation," *Guardian*, May 26, 2020.

71. Aileen Torres-Bennett and Anna Gawel, "Trump's Transactional Realpolitik Alienates America's European Allies," *Washington Diplomat*, June 29, 2018.

72. Richard Wike, Jacob Poushter, Janell Feterrolf, and Shannon Schumacher, "Trump Ratings Remain Low around Globe, While Views of U.S. Stay Mostly Favorable," Pew Research Center, January 8, 2020; Bill Wirtz, "There's Plenty of Love for Trump in Europe," *Real Clear World*, February 1, 2018.

73. Ivan Krastev, "Will Europe Ever Trust America Again?," *New York Times*, December 3, 2019.

74. Christopher Hope, "Net Migration from Eastern Europe to Britain Slows to a Trickle after Brexit Vote," *Telegraph*, May 25, 2017.

75. Madeleine Sumption, *Not Settled Yet? Understanding the EU Settlement Scheme Using the Available Data* (Oxford: Migration Observatory, April 16, 2020).

76. See the "Presidency Conclusions" of the Thessaloniki European Council, Council of the European Union, June 19 and 20, 2003, http://www.consilium.europa.eu/uedocs/cms_data/docs/pressdata/en/ec/76279.pdf.

77. For background on this dispute, see Matthew Nimetz, "The Macedonian 'Name' Dispute: The Macedonian Question—Resolved?," *Nationalities Papers* 48, no. 2 (2020): 205–14.

78. Svjetlana Ramic Markovic, "New Enlargement Strategy of the EU: A New Chance for the Balkans," *New Eastern Europe*, March 31, 2020; European Council, "Council Conclusions on Enlargement and Stabilisation and Association Process: Albania and the Republic of North Macedonia," Brussels, European Council, March 25, 2020, https://www.consilium.europa.eu/en/press/press-releases/2020/03/25/council-conclusions-on-enlargement-and-stabilisation-and-association-process. Last-minute objections raised by Bulgaria show the fragility of the membership process: "Bulgaria's Block on North Macedonia's Bid to Join EU 'Massively Endangers Europe's Security,'" *Euronews*, August 12, 2020, https://www.euronews.com/2020/12/08/bulgaria-s-block-on-north-macedonia-s-bid-to-join-eu-massively-endangers-europe-s-security.

79. Fatos Bytyci, "Kosovo Removes Trade Barriers on Serbia to Allow Talks," Reuters, June 6, 2020; Dan Bilefsky, "Serbia and Kosovo Reach Agreement on Power-Sharing," *New York Times*, April 19, 2013.

80. Austin Doehler, "The European Union's Shot at Redemption in the Balkans," *War on the Rocks*, July 10, 2020, https://warontherocks.com/2020/07/the-european-unions-shot-at-redemption-in-the-balkans.

81. Polish Robert Schuman Foundation, "Attitude of EU Citizens towards the Enlargement," EnlargeEUrope, September 27, 2019.

82. Dušan Reljic, "The Influencers' Futile Toils: Russia and Turkey in the Balkans," IEMed Mediterranean Yearbook 2019 (Barcelona: European Institute of the Mediterranean, 2019), 187–91; Aliénor Cameron and Michael Leigh, "Has COVID-19 Dented the EU's Credibility in the Balkans?" (blog post, June 15, 2020), https://www.bruegel.org/2020/06/has-covid-19-dented-the-eus-credibility-in-the-balkans; "EU Aims to Reassure Balkans with Virus Aid, Economic Support," Associated Press, May 6, 2020, https://www.usnews.com/news/business/articles/2020-05-06/eu-balkans-leaders-to-reaffirm-ties-amid-virus-crisis.

83. European Commission, "Eastern Partnership," https://ec.europa.eu/neighbourhood-enlargement/neighbourhood/eastern-partnership_en; European Commission, "Eastern Partnership Policy beyond 2020," https://ec.europa.eu/neighbourhood-enlargement/sites/near/files/joint_communication_on_the_eap_policy_beyond_2020.pdf.

84. Andrew Kramer, "Russia Claims Its Sphere of Influence in the World," *New York Times*, August 31, 2008.

85. For a text of the agreement, see "Association Agreement," https://eur-lex.europa.eu/legal-content/EN/TXT/PDF/?uri=CELEX:22014A0529(01)&from=EN.

86. Delegation of the European Union to Ukraine, "Ukraine and the EU," https://eeas.europa.eu/delegations/ukraine/1937/ukraine-and-eu_en.

87. "Statement by President Barroso and President Van Rompuy in the Name of the European Union on the Agreed Additional Restrictive Measures against Russia European Commission—STATEMENT/14/244 29/07/2014," https://ec.europa.eu/commission/presscorner/detail/en/STATEMENT_14_244.

88. European Council, "Timeline—EU Restrictive Measures in Response to the Crisis in Ukraine," https://www.consilium.europa.eu/en/policies/sanctions/ukraine-crisis/history-ukraine-crisis.

89. Gabriella Lovas and Zoltan Simon, "Hungary Commits to Russia Gas Route as Poland Looks to U.S.," *Bloomberg*, July 7, 2017.

90. Rikard Jozwiak, "EU Expands Russia Sanctions List Linked to Aggression toward Ukraine," Radio Free Europe/Radio Liberty, January 28, 2020. For a study of the impact of the sanctions on trade, see European Parliament, *Russia's and the EU's Sanctions: Economic and Trade Effects, Compliance and the Way Forward* (Brussels: European Union, 2017).

91. Hanna Bazhenova and Tomasz Stępniewski, "Zelenskyy's Ukraine and the Eastern Partnership," *New Eastern Europe* 5 (September 4, 2020).

92. See, e.g., the discussion in Milada Vachudova, *Europe Undivided: Democracy, Leverage, and Integration after Communism* (Oxford: Oxford University Press, 2005); Tim Haughton, "When Does the EU Make a Difference? Conditionality and the Accession Process in Central and Eastern Europe," *Political Studies Review* 5 (2007): 233–46.

93. See James E. Dougherty and Robert L. Pfaltzgraff Jr., *Contending Theories of International Relations* (New York: Addison Wesley Longman, 2001), for a review of international relations theories.

94. For a discussion of factors underlying variation in democratization, see Linden, "After the Fall." Among those who see the postcommunist region as providing a "natural experiment," see Fernando Casal Bértoa, "Parties, Regime and Cleavages: Explaining Party System Institutionalisation in East Central Europe," *East European Politics* 28, no. 4 (2012): 452–72.

95. Ulrich Sedelmeier, "The European Union and Democratization in Central and Southeastern Europe since 1989," in *Central and Southeast European Politics since 1989*, ed. Sabrina Ramet and Christine Hassenstab, 539–62 (Cambridge, UK: Cambridge University Press, 2019).

96. Alina Mungiu-Pippidi, "Is East-Central Europe Backsliding? EU Accession Is No 'End of History,'" *Journal of Democracy* 18, no. 4 (October 2007): 8–16.

97. Anna Grzymala-Busse, "An East-West Split in the EU?," *Current History*, March 2016, 89–94, 92.

98. Elisabeth Bakke and Nick Sitter, "The EU's Enfants Terribles: Democratic Backsliding in Central Europe since 2010," *Perspectives on Politics*, July 24, 2020, 1–16, https://www.cambridge.org/core/journals/perspectives-on-politics/article/eus-enfants-terribles-democratic-backsliding-in-central-europe-since-2010/10CE615BAD56E79125E828D321641C0A#.

99. Mungiu-Pippidi, "Is East-Central Europe Backsliding?," 14.

100. Ulrich Sedelmeier, "Is Europeanisation through Conditionality Sustainable? Lock-in of Institutional Change after EU Accession," *West European Politics* 35, no. 1 (2019): 20–38.

101. Ulrich Sedelmeier, "Political Safeguards against Democratic Backsliding in the EU: The Limits of Material Sanctions and the Scope of Social Pressure," *Journal of European Public Policy* 24, no. 3 (March 2017): 337–51.

102.   Roberto Stefan Foa and Yascha Mounk, "The Signs of Deconsolidation," *Journal of Democracy*, January 2017, 5–15.

103.   Karen E. Smith, "The European Union in an Illiberal World," *Current History*, March 2017, 83–87.

104.   Thomas Diez, "Normative Power as Hegemony," *Cooperation & Conflict* 48, no. 2 (June 2013): 194–210.

105.   For a review of "democratic regression" worldwide, see Larry Diamond, "Democratic Regression in Comparative Perspective: Scope, Methods, and Causes," *Democratization*, September 2020.

CHAPTER 10

Russia Rising

SOFT AND HARD POWER CHALLENGES TO SECURITY

Jennie L. Schulze

On March 18, 2014, Russian and Crimean officials signed the Treaty of Accession of the Republic of Crimea to Russia. The referendum that was held two days earlier to legitimize Russia's annexation of the peninsula was illegal under Ukrainian law and lacked credible international observers. The move, which constitutes the biggest land grab in Europe since World War II, has damaged Europe's post–Cold War security order.[1] Russia's support for Russian separatists in the ongoing war in eastern Ukraine involves hybrid tactics that include a campaign of fake news, hostile Twitter bots, and encouraged protests.[2] In 2008, Russia intervened militarily in Georgia on the basis of claims that it was protecting Russian citizens in South Ossetia from aggression by the Georgian government. Russia's increasingly assertive and aggressive foreign policy raises concerns about Russia's threat to regional security and complicates relations between Russia and the West.

Russia's actions in Georgia and Ukraine have raised security concerns in other former Soviet republics (FSRs), particularly those with high concentrations of Russian-speakers, such as Estonia and Latvia. The collapse of the Soviet Union and the creation of new borders left twenty-five million ethnic Russians and thirty-six million Russian-speakers who identify Russian as their mother tongue stranded outside of Russia.[3] In a speech to the Federal Assembly in 2005, Russian president Vladimir Putin famously described the collapse of the Soviet Union, which resulted in the division of the Russian nation, as a major geopolitical disaster.[4] The protection of its Russian diaspora emerged as a central feature of Russia's foreign policy in the early 1990s, and in 1992, President Boris Yeltsin issued the decree "On the Protection of the Rights and Interests of Russian Citizens outside the Russian Federation." Throughout the 1990s, Russia's policy toward Russian-speakers evolved, culminating in the adoption of an official compatriot policy in 1999. During that process, Russia widened its circle of protection and, by implication, its potential to meddle in other countries.[5] As James Sherr observes, "the federal law on compatriots defines the term so permissibly as to enable Russia to claim as its own virtually any people whose past ties them to Russia or the former USSR."[6] According to the policy, "*sootechestvenniki* (compatriots) who reside abroad are entitled to support from the Russian Federation in the realization of their civil, political, social, economic, and cultural rights,"[7] including diplomatic and financial support.

The emergence of Russia as an active kin-state on behalf of its co-nationals in neighboring countries is hardly surprising considering Russia's rapid decline as a great power, as well as the need to define a new foreign policy character and to consolidate power domestically. Russia's compatriot policy serves to legitimize Russia's status as a global leader and supports the narrative that Russia is needed and welcomed outside its borders.[8] Russia uses a variety of "harder" and "softer" mechanisms against FSRs in the name of ostensibly defending Russian-speakers living there. In doing so, Russia often links the situation of Russian-speakers to other political and economic issues, including trade, energy, citizenship and visa policies, the settlement of borders, and the admission of countries to NATO and the EU. In some countries, such as the Baltic states of Estonia, Latvia, and Lithuania, the nationalizing approach to state building adopted in the early 1990s, which conceived of the state as belonging to the ethnic majority, provided the pretext for Russia's intervention. Such interventions have brought Russia into political conflict with those states and with Western institutions. The dynamic interplay between Russian-speakers, their resident states, European institutions, and Russia is the focus of much scholarship on nationalism and minority rights in Central and East Europe.[9]

Russia also uses economic ties, such as dependency on Russian oil and gas, as well as information campaigns in the Russian media, to encourage other Central and East European (CEE) countries to adopt policies that serve Russia's interests. Russia's ability to influence neighboring states depends on a variety of factors, including the political situation, historical legacies, economic ties, energy dependence, and the relationship of those countries with the West.

The chapter begins with an overview of the hard- and soft-power resources that Russia uses to influence other countries in the region and then proceeds with a discussion of how Russia has applied those tools in specific cases. The case study examples are not intended to be exhaustive but rather to highlight how Russia seeks to influence Central and East European countries through military and economic pressures, cyberattacks, information campaigns, and support for particular political parties. The chapter concludes with a discussion of the West as an alternative center of power and the challenges CEE countries face at the crossroads of Russian and European influence.

Tools of Influence: Hard Power, Soft Power, and Public Diplomacy

Russia's influence campaigns aim broadly at maximizing the economic benefits of its relationships in the region, weakening the credibility and moral authority of the EU and NATO, and elevating its own model of governance as an attractive alternative to the liberal democratic West.[10] Russia began to focus more on developing its soft-power resources after the color revolutions that swept through the region in the early 2000s. However, Russia has also modernized its hard-power arsenal and typically deploys hard and soft power simultaneously in target states.

Hard power refers to the coercive use of economic or military pressure to influence state behavior and implies the use of inducements ("carrots") or threats ("sticks").[11] Despite

Russia's success in pushing Georgian forces out of Abkhazia and South Ossetia in the 2008 Russia-Georgia war, the conflict revealed weaknesses in Russia's military forces, particularly its outdated equipment and inadequate training.[12] After the war, Russia began a massive modernization of its armed forces and is currently ranked eleventh in the world in terms of defense spending.[13] The Russian military has also gained valuable on-the-ground experience in Syria. The modernization of the Russian military has been on display during Russia's annual military exercises, which have been growing in scale and drawing considerable attention from Western observers.[14] Combined with its nuclear arsenal, which is the largest in the world, and intercontinental ballistic missile capabilities, Russia presents a formidable military force. Russia is considered by some to be second only to the United States in terms of military strength.[15] Comparatively, Poland is ranked twenty-third, the highest rank among the countries of Central and East Europe.[16] Russia also possesses other security resources, such as direction of one of the Global Navigation Satellite Systems (GLONASS), a skilled intelligence apparatus, and considerable cyberwarfare capabilities.

States with higher national incomes are better equipped to maintain large armed forces and to put economic pressure on other states.[17] Russia ranks sixth in the world for gross domestic product (GDP), adjusted for purchasing power parity. Poland, the highest-ranked CEE country, is in the twentieth spot.[18] While the United States leads the world in oil production, producing approximately 19 percent of the world's oil, Russia is third, producing 11 percent.[19] Russia also has the largest natural gas reserves and leads the world in natural gas exports.[20]

Photo 10.1. While Russia has lost considerable global power since the collapse of the Soviet Union in 1991, it continues to be a formidable military power in its region. Russia controls the largest nuclear arsenal in the world. (Free Wind 2014, Shutterstock)

Russia also has a seat at the table in the most important security and economic organizations. It inherited the Soviet Union's permanent seat on the UN Security Council and therefore has important veto power over decisions within the organization. Russia became a member of the World Trade Organization (WTO) in 2012 and is a member of the G20. It was included in the Group of Eight (G8) in 1998, an intergovernmental forum that includes the major industrialized powers that meet annually to discuss climate change, security, and the economy. Russia's membership was suspended following the annexation of Crimea in 2014, and Russia officially withdrew from the organization in 2017. The G7 has remained committed to sanctions against Russia and has tied relations between Russia and the group to a reversal of Russia's actions in Ukraine.[21] While Russia is not a member of the Organization of Petroleum Exporting Countries (OPEC), it formalized its relationship with the group through the OPEC+ structure in 2019.[22]

Russia uses its hard-power resources to pressure Central and East European countries into adopting policy positions favorable to Russian interests. In addition to using military force, as in the case of Ukraine, Russia also threatens to use military force, as it did repeatedly in its attempts to dissuade the Baltic states from joining NATO. Russia uses its business ties in other countries to influence policies to its advantage, and the dependency of much of the region on Russia for energy provides Russia with a powerful lever to influence politics in the region.

Russia's interest in developing soft-power resources increased in the wake of the color revolutions that toppled entrenched regimes and brought to power reform-minded governments in Georgia ("Rose," 2003), Ukraine ("Orange," 2004), and Kyrgyzstan ("Tulip," 2005). These events were a wake-up call for Russian elites, who recognized the need to increase Russia's influence in the post-Soviet region through the media, cultural initiatives, and coordination with nongovernmental organizations (NGOs).[23] The entrance of some Central and East European countries into NATO in 1999 and 2004 also focused Russia's attention on the cultivation of soft-power resources and public diplomacy in the region. Inherent in *soft power* is "an act of persuasion," whereby states make culture, values, or foreign policies appear more attractive to other states in order to induce favorable behavior.[24] Public diplomacy is the means of cultivating and projecting soft power by sending messages to the "people" of another country.[25]

Soft power emerged as a key component of the 2007 Russian foreign policy review, where it was described as a "tool to influence the behavior of foreign countries through the use of the attractiveness of Russian culture and civilization, foreign policy and other factors, as well as through the use of the country's public diplomacy network."[26] Soft power has been reaffirmed as an important foreign policy tool, for example in 2016.[27] While Russia's conceptualization of soft power shares similarities with Western notions, Russia's application of soft power through public diplomacy differs from Western practices. Russia's usage is based far less on notions of "win-win" strategies and persuasion inherent in the original concept and far more on antagonism and manipulation, especially in former Soviet republics.[28] This is evident in the use of disinformation campaigns and the "manufacturing of enemy images" in target countries,[29] with the goal of refuting negative images of Russia and creating a network of allies that can be used to achieve specific foreign policy goals.[30]

Russia has developed several institutions of public diplomacy to support its soft-power agenda. In 2007, Russia established the Russkiy Mir (Russian World) Foundation, an NGO under the Ministry of Foreign Affairs. With an operating budget of approximately $20 million annually, the foundation has established centers to promote Russian language and culture throughout the region and has provided grants to individuals and NGOs in target countries.[31] Russkiy Mir works closely with Rossotrudnichestvo (the Federal Agency for the Commonwealth of Independent States, Compatriots Living Abroad, and International Humanitarian Cooperation), founded in 2008 to "create a circle of friends of Russia abroad" through the coordination of cultural and scientific centers.[32] The Gorchakov Public Diplomacy Foundation and the Russian Council on International Affairs were created in 2010 to coordinate research and events aimed at improving Russia's image among Western audiences.[33] The Russian Orthodox Church builds connections to other Orthodox churches in the region[34] and promotes the concept of the "Russian world" as an alternative to Western values.[35] Russia coordinates its activities and the allocation of funding to minority NGOs in target countries through Coordination Councils of Russian Compatriots, whose leadership is run through Russian embassies.[36]

The Russian media is an important resource for influencing public opinion abroad and for encouraging support for Russia's foreign policy domestically. The Russian government directly controls state media and exercises significant influence over the Russian business elite that controls private media outlets.[37] In addition to outlets like Sputnik and RT, which are aimed at foreign audiences and broadcast in several languages, Russian media is also directly available to Russian-speakers in other states. While the most popular media among older generations of Russian-speakers is television, social media is an increasingly important source of information for younger generations and therefore is an important tool of public diplomacy.[38] The extensive use of social media by Russian protestors in 2011, who organized in opposition to widespread fraud in Russia's parliamentary elections, raised the government's awareness of the need to monitor and control social media and messaging.[39] Russia's social media campaigns aim to influence audiences through a combination of "news tweets, non-attributed comments on web pages, troll and bot social media accounts, and fake hashtag and Twitter campaigns."[40] Russia's social media campaigns cannot be entirely separated from its traditional media operations, because traditional news stories are disseminated online through social media.

These media campaigns have multiple objectives that include sowing discord, promoting politicians and groups that support Russia's political agenda, creating alternative narratives supportive of that agenda, and eroding trust in Western democratic institutions.[41] In "near abroad" countries, Russia targets Russian-speaking populations, drawing on themes related to a shared legacy as post-Soviet states; the failure of the West to deliver prosperity; traditional conservative values relating to family, gender roles, and Orthodoxy; fear of violent revolutions; and discrimination against Russian-speakers.[42] While the technology for spreading the Kremlin's narratives is new, propaganda campaigns have a long history in Soviet "active measures," which involved the manipulative use of slogans, arguments, disinformation, and carefully selected true information to influence the attitudes and actions of foreign publics and governments.[43]

Hard power is associated with coercion and soft power with persuasion; however, the lines between hard and soft power are often blurry. For example, a strong economy may provide for the more efficient use of economic sanctions, while also serving as a source of attractiveness to other states. Furthermore, the exercise of hard power may have reputational effects.[44] The annexation of Ukraine in 2014, and Russia's ongoing support for separatists in the war in eastern Ukraine, both executed with hard-power resources, has affected Russia's soft power. At the end of 2019, Russia's soft-power ranking had fallen to thirty, its lowest ranking since 2015, according to the Soft Power 30 index. While Russia has significant soft-power resources, particularly cultural and diplomatic networks, Russia is viewed with skepticism in many parts of the world due to its actions in Ukraine, opportunism in the Middle East, and interference in Western elections.[45] Finally, it is important to recognize that Russia has been employing hard- and soft-power mechanisms simultaneously to influence the region since the early 1990s. For example, the use of "hybrid" tactics, which combine military force with information campaigns designed to confuse and misinform the adversary, were on full display in Russia's recent aggressions in Ukraine.[46]

The examples in the following sections are not intended to be exhaustive but to illustrate the various ways that Russia uses its hard- and soft-power resources to influence politics in CEE. The cases of Ukraine and the Baltic states deserve special attention, as they have been the primary targets of Russia's hard- and soft-power campaigns. Russia's actions in Ukraine reawakened existential security concerns in the Baltic states and prompted an assessment of strategic vulnerabilities in the northeastern Ida-Virumaa region of Estonia and the southeastern Latgale region of Latvia, both of which border Russia and have high concentrations of Russian-speakers (81 percent and 55 percent, respectively).[47] As a result, Russia's aggressions in the region have had a substantial impact on both security and minority policies in the Baltic states.[48]

Military Pressure: Ukraine and the Baltic States

Russia used military force to annex Crimea in 2014, and as this chapter goes to press, Russia continues to provide military support to separatists in the war in eastern Ukraine. On the morning of February 27, 2014, heavily armed men in unmarked green uniforms stormed the parliament building in Simferopol, the capital of the Crimean Peninsula, and raised the Russian flag over the building.[49] The seizure came days after the ousted Ukrainian president Viktor Yanukovych fled Kyiv in the wake of Ukraine's Maidan Revolution, which broke out after President Yanukovych rejected a deal for greater economic integration with the European Union (EU). Over the course of the following weeks, masked troops seized Ukrainian military and strategic buildings, as well as the airport in Simferopol. On March 6, the Crimean Supreme Council voted to ask to accede to Russia. On March 16, a referendum was held giving voters two choices: accede to Russia or remain part of Ukraine under the rules of the 1992 constitution, which gave the area greater autonomy. There was no choice for maintaining the status quo. The referendum, which took place without credible international observers, was reported to have resulted in an overwhelming 96.7 percent supporting accession to Russia, amid high voter turnout (83 percent). These results were treated with skepticism by the international community, considering the ethnic composition of Crimea, which includes both ethnic Ukrainians and Crimean Tatars.[50] On March 18, Crimean and Russian officials signed the Treaty of Accession of the Republic of Crimea to Russia.

Two months later, separatists in the Luhansk and Donetsk regions of eastern Ukraine held referenda to declare independence from Ukraine. The violence that erupted in eastern Ukraine between Russian-backed separatists and Ukrainian forces has resulted in over ten thousand civilian casualties and over one million internally displaced persons.[51] The July 2014 downing of Malaysian Airlines flight 17 over Ukrainian territory resulted in international condemnation against Russia when it was determined that a Russian-built surface-to-air missile brought down the flight, killing all 298 onboard. Since February 2015, France, Germany, Russia, and Ukraine have attempted unsuccessfully to broker a cessation of violence through the Minsk Accords, which include agreements on a cease-fire as well as Ukrainian control throughout the disputed territory.[52] Russia has voiced preferences for the federalization of Ukraine, or at least a special status for the Luhansk and Donetsk regions.[53] The recent cease-fire that was negotiated between Ukrainian forces and Russian separatists in July 2020 had broken down by February 2021. At the time of this writing, both sides are concerned that the escalation could trigger a major regional conflict. Divergent interests among authorities in Kyiv, Moscow, and the Donbas have made it difficult to use the Minsk Accords as a road map to peace.[54]

In Ukraine, Russia has used a mixture of hard- and soft-power tools, including disinformation strategies, to achieve its objectives. Russia's use of military force to annex the Crimean Peninsula caught the West by surprise and prompted a reassessment of military strategy in the region. The arrival of Russian troops in uniforms without any insignia, which Russia described as "local defense units," allowed Russia plausible deniability about its involvement in Crimea.[55] Only after the referendum and the signing of the treaty of annexation did Russia abandon its pretense of noninvolvement in Crimea.[56] Russia gradually increased the number of Russian troops in Ukraine, including the introduction of military officers and specialists into rebel units in eastern Ukraine,[57] while continuing to deny involvement in the Donbas.[58] As a result, Russia is not identified as a belligerent in the Minsk agreement but as an outside observer, thereby placing the burden of implementation on Ukraine.[59] The massing of troops on Ukraine's border, support for rebel groups in eastern Ukraine, the escalation of violence prior to negotiations with Ukraine, and repeated military threats, including the use of nuclear weapons, are tactics intended to intimidate Ukraine and to deter intervention by Western powers.[60] President Putin justified these moves by claiming the need to protect locals in Russian-speaking regions from alleged repression by the Ukrainian nationalist government.[61]

The historical context is important for understanding Russia's connections to the region.[62] Russia colonized Crimea under Catherine the Great and founded Sevastopol, the main port and base for Russia's Black Sea Fleet. In 1954, Crimea was transferred to Ukraine from the Russian Soviet Federative Socialist Republic. Ukraine is a storied place in Russia's national narrative and a popular vacation spot for Russians. While some scholars have interpreted Russia's moves as a geopolitical reaction to NATO's expansion eastward,[63] domestic politics also provides motivation for Russia's actions in Ukraine. The annexation proved popular with the Russian public and shored up President Putin's approval ratings in the wake of domestic protests over election fraud.[64]

The existential security threat that Russia poses to the Baltic countries diminished immediately following their accession to NATO in 2004. However, Russia's military interventions in Georgia in 2008 and in Ukraine in 2014 reawakened fears of Russian aggression toward the Baltic states. In fact, Russia has likened the situation that led to action in Ukraine to the situation that exists in the Baltics.[65] Baltic scholars argue that Russian-speakers concentrated in the cities of Narva (Estonia) and Daugavpils (Latvia) are different from Russian-speakers in the Donbas and that Baltic membership in NATO and the EU make a Ukraine scenario unlikely.[66] It is nevertheless understandable that Baltic elites might feel nervous despite assurances of NATO protection under Article 5 (NATO's collective defense clause), due to reports highlighting NATO's unpreparedness in the event of a Russian invasion of the Baltic states and Russia's aggressive military maneuvers involving Baltic contingencies.[67] These fears were amplified by reports that it would take Russia only three days to overrun the Baltic states.[68] In response to Russia's actions in Ukraine and grim reports about NATO's preparedness on its eastern flank, the three countries have pursued strategies of deterrence by hosting NATO forces in their territories, increasing their defense budgets, and incorporating strategies of total defense into their military doctrines.[69] NATO has deployed four battalions to Eastern Europe, rotating troops through Estonia, Latvia, Lithuania, and Poland to deter Russian aggression. In September 2017, these battalions were joined by two US Army tank brigades deployed in Poland to bolster the alliance's deterrent posture.[70] Despite having the largest military and economic potential in the region, security concerns are also high in Poland. Its shared borders with both the militarized Kaliningrad oblast and Ukraine, along with difficult historical legacies involving Russian aggression, have contributed to strong Polish support for NATO deterrence and economic sanctions against Russia.

Concerns over Russia have always been high on the Baltic security agenda, and all three states have been on the receiving end of military threats from Russia since they regained independence in 1991. In the early 1990s, Estonia and Latvia passed alien and citizenship policies that politically disenfranchised the vast majority of Russian-speakers by rendering over half a million persons stateless in each country. In response, Russia linked Soviet troop withdrawal to the situation of retired Soviet military personnel, imposed economic sanctions, and halted the supply of natural gas. The delay of troop withdrawal was particularly sensitive for Baltic elites because they considered the Soviet military to be an occupying force.[71] Throughout the postindependence period, military pressure has involved threats of military force, military exercises involving Baltic contingencies, and frequent flyovers through Baltic airspace, all intended to intimidate Baltic elites and to bring policy more in line with Russian interests.[72] The transit of weaponry across Lithuania to the Kaliningrad enclave is also a reminder to Baltic and Polish elites of Russia's military capabilities.

Russia's aggression in Ukraine has also raised warning flags for other countries in the region. Romania, for example, has a complicated historical relationship with Russia and has been a strong proponent of Moldova's accession to European institutions, putting it at odds with Russia, which would prefer to maintain the "frozen" status quo in Transnistria.

In response to Russia's actions in Ukraine, Romania raised its defense spending, tried to deepen ties with its Black Sea partners Georgia and Ukraine, and acknowledged the security threat that Russia poses to both the region and its own interests.[73]

The Growing Sophistication of Cyberattacks: Estonia, Ukraine, and the Western Balkans

Russia has become increasingly assertive in cyberspace, engaging in a number of cyberattacks against Central and East European countries. Attacks designed to sabotage physical infrastructure were carried out in Georgia, Estonia, Ukraine, and Montenegro, highlighting the increasing sophistication of Russia's cyberwarfare. In spring 2007, Russia launched a series of cyberattacks against the Estonian government and commercial websites in a well-coordinated "denial of service" attack. While the first wave of attacks on April 29 and 30 crippled Estonia's largely paperless government, the attacks continued throughout May 2007, targeting banks, newspapers, schools, and other institutions.[74] The cyberattacks followed the controversial decision of the Estonian government to relocate the Bronze Soldier, a Soviet-era World War II memorial from downtown Tallinn to a military cemetery on the outskirts of town. The statue's removal sparked riots in Tallinn and in northeastern Estonia. Russian political leaders denounced the decision to relocate the monument, equating it with fascism and the glorification of Nazism.[75] The Estonian government was quick to accuse Russia of the cyberattacks, given Russia's outspoken opposition to the relocation of the monument, the numerous instructions on the internet detailing in Russian how to inflict damage on Estonian cyberspace,[76] and the successful tracing of one of the cyberattacks to a computer in the Russian government.[77] Moscow officials denied involvement and refused to cooperate in the investigation to find the perpetrators.[78]

Estonia appealed to NATO and tried to link the cyberattack to Article 5. While other NATO members rejected the appeal, top military commanders from seven NATO countries and the Allied Command Transformation signed an agreement on May 15, 2008, to create a new Centre of Excellence for Cyber Defense in Tallinn. The Bronze Soldier crisis and aftermath resulted in a marked downturn in relations between Estonia and Russia and heightened unease among Baltic leaders regarding Russia's intentions in the region.[79] Russia's military intervention in Georgia the following year confirmed their wariness. In 2013, at the Wales summit, NATO adopted the principle that Article 5 of the Washington Treaty also applies in cyberspace and that a cyberattack against one is considered a cyberattack against all.[80]

Ukraine has been subjected to numerous Russian cyberattacks since the conflict began in eastern Ukraine in 2014. These have included attacks against media, state institutions, banks, utility companies, and power grids.[81] In addition to denial-of-service attacks and spreading propaganda through hacked email and SMS accounts, businesses and government systems have also been hit with malware attacks. The "NotPetya" malware attack, which spread to computer systems worldwide, caused billions of dollars in damage.[82] Several countries have attributed that attack to Russia.

The Western Balkan countries have also been the targets of several cyberattacks. For example, cyberattacks with a Russian fingerprint escalated alongside Montenegro's

Photo 10.2. The Estonian government's 2007 relocation of a Soviet war memorial in the capital city of Tallinn allegedly resulted in a massive cyberattack by Russia on Estonian government and commercial websites. Russia exercises power in the region in a wide variety of ways. (Atovot, Shutterstock)

NATO accession process.[83] These included denial-of-service attacks against network infrastructure, pro-EU and pro-NATO parties, and election monitors on the day of the 2016 parliamentary elections, as well as a spear phishing campaign directed against the Ministry of Defense. Cybersecurity firms determined that APT28 (Advanced Persistent Threats), a hacking group directed by Russian Military Intelligence (GRU), was responsible; the same group (APT29) hacked the Democratic National Committee's emails prior to the 2016 US elections.[84]

Economics, Energy, and Corruption: Bulgaria, Serbia, and Hungary

Russia has established a substantial economic footprint in Central and East Europe, which it can utilize to manipulate target governments. In Bulgaria, businesses support pro-Russian politicians, who in turn support policies favorable to Russian business.[85] In Serbia, pro-Russian politicians emphasize the benefits of economic ties with Russia, even as Serbia becomes more dependent on Russian gas and has lost money on pipeline ventures with Russia.[86] While Russia's penetration into CEE in the early 2000s was mostly opportunistic, after the global recession in 2008, Russia pursued strategic investment to create structural dependencies in key industries in order to achieve greater leverage in the region.[87]

Russia's extensive financial networks throughout the region have allowed Russia to become a significant player in several strategic sectors, including media, real estate, transportation, arms, finance, and industry. However, because Central and East Europe is disproportionately reliant on Russia's oil and natural gas, the energy sector is Russia's primary economic lever of influence.[88] Russia's price determination model rests more upon the reliance of a country on Russian energy and the role of a single company in the market than on the domestic or regional energy demand. For example, due to Bulgaria's dependence on Russia's Gazprom, Bulgaria has paid much more for energy than Germany. This is a trend that holds across the region to greater or lesser degrees.[89] While the Czech Republic receives most of its gas from Russia despite policies of energy diversification and pays more than the EU average,[90] Romania is less dependent on energy from Russia due to its own domestic fossil fuel supplies.[91]

Russia uses energy dependence as a political tool in Central and East Europe.[92] For example, Russia froze natural gas deliveries to Estonia in 1993 after Estonia passed a controversial and exclusionary Aliens Law that required all noncitizens to apply for a residence permit within one year and to reapply every five years.[93] The official justification for stopping shipments was the backlog of unpaid debts; however, the commercial director cited the treatment of Russian-speakers as the reason for the sanctions.[94] In 1998, when the nationalist Latvian government violently broke up a demonstration of pensioners, Moscow responded with harsh criticism and imposed economic sanctions. The sanctions involved cutting oil deliveries; imposing a 20 percent transportation surcharge on most goods shipped to, from, or through Latvia; and reducing the use of Latvian ports.[95] Russia also imposed economic sanctions on Estonia following the "Bronze Night," which included reducing passenger rail services and oil transit through Estonia and encouraging Russians to boycott the purchase of Estonian products.[96]

The European Union has maintained solidarity in response to Russia's use of energy levers in Ukraine. Even governments with pro-Russian sympathies, such as Slovakia and Hungary, have reversed energy flows to Ukraine in response to Russia cutting gas supplies to the country after 2014. Critics of Russia's Nord Stream 2 pipeline, which travels under the Baltic seabed, have argued that the pipeline would allow Russia to bypass Ukrainian pipelines when delivering gas to Europe, placing additional political and economic pressure on Ukraine. Ukraine's pipelines supply gas to CEE countries and provide lucrative transit fees to Ukraine's economy.[97] Bulgaria is also vulnerable to energy levers because it has been unable to diversify its energy supply away from Russian gas, which enters the country through Ukraine.[98] As a result, the price of gas has been linked to Bulgarian support for Russian projects, such as the South Stream pipeline.[99] In recognition of the significant threats to energy security in the region, NATO created the Energy Security Centre of Excellence in Vilnius to provide expertise and support to allied countries. Lithuania constructed the "Independence," a floating liquid natural gas terminal in 2014, in response to the threat of being energy dependent on Russia. The terminal enables Lithuania to receive shipments from global sellers, thereby reducing its near-complete dependence on Russian pipeline fuel.[100]

Corruption in politics greases the wheels of Russia's economic influence. Numerous politicians that are associated with pro-Russia parties, businesses, and NGOs have been implicated in graft, bribery, and public procurement scandals.[101] Here, Latvia provides a positive example for the region. Russia's economic footprint in Latvia has increased over time, making Latvia vulnerable to Russian pressure, particularly in the energy and transportation sectors. However, Latvia has also increased its anticorruption efforts through the Corruption Prevention and Combating Bureau (KNAB). These efforts have exposed high-ranking politicians and businessmen, such as the famous "Oligarch's Case" involving the former minister of transportation Ainārs Šlesers; the mayor of Ventspils, Aivars Lembergs; and former prime minister Andris Šķēle.[102] Journalists released transcripts of recorded conversations to the public that revealed schemes to control democratic institutions, including the media, and to use power to promote their business interests. The men periodically referenced Russia as a model for such practices. While no official charges were filed, protests broke out, and the parties of the three oligarchs suffered defeats in subsequent elections.[103] Latvia does not rank as well as its Baltic neighbors on corruption indices.[104] However, reigning in corruption is important for limiting "unvirtuous cycles" of Russian economic and political influence,[105] as well as for maintaining its commitments to the EU and NATO, including support for sanctions against Russia and a NATO Forward Presence in Latvia. In 2019, Ukraine, a country that has been plagued by corruption, elected Volodymyr Zelenskyy as president, a former comedian who campaigned on an anticorruption platform. It remains to be seen if Zelenskyy's administration will be able to deliver on its platform, but his election could be interpreted as the Ukrainian public's weariness with the political establishment and with politics as usual.[106]

Hungary provides an example of a more worrisome trend. Since the election of Prime Minister Viktor Orbán in 2010, corruption has risen in Hungary. According to Transparency International, Hungary is now tied with Romania as the second most corrupt country in the EU, after Bulgaria. Hungary's growing corruption provides more avenues for Russian influence, especially when combined with a government that has adopted pro-Russia policy stances.[107] Bulgaria, however, has demonstrated some resilience to Russian pressure despite Russia's economic influence and high levels of corruption. Bulgaria remains committed to membership in Western institutions and its consequent obligations, even while decisions on business contracts often favor Russia. For example, Bulgaria complied with the US request not to permit Russian military overflights over Bulgaria in 2015, despite significant political pressure.[108]

Serbia also continues to pursue membership in the European Union, now a candidate country, despite its significant economic ties with Russia and its history of political support from Russia both prior to World War I and after the collapse of Yugoslavia.[109] Russia has supported Serbia politically by vetoing a UN Security Council resolution labeling the massacre of Bosnian Muslims by Serb forces at Srebrenica during the Balkan Wars a genocide[110] and has refused to recognize Kosovo as an independent state after it seceded from Serbia in 2008. Serbia, for its part, has refused to participate in the European sanctions regime against Russia. Balancing pro-Europe and pro-Russia positions could become difficult for Serbia in the future, as the normalization of relations between Serbia and Kosovo is a requirement for accession to the EU. In June 2020, Serbian president Aleksandar Vučić stated that Serbia expected concessions in exchange for recognizing Kosovo and that doing so would not be possible without Russia's consent.[111] In September 2020, Serbia and Kosovo agreed to take steps toward economic cooperation, but Serbia still refused to recognize Kosovo's independence.[112]

Propaganda and Disinformation Campaigns: Strategies across the Region

Russia's soft-power strategies include the use of Russian media to influence public opinion. The popularity of Russian media in the near abroad creates opportunities for Russia to disseminate disinformation, which is then amplified through social media by both trolls and everyday users of Russian social media networks.[113] These tactics have raised considerable concerns among Central and East European elites, particularly in the Baltic states and Ukraine because they have large Russian-speaking populations and considerable access to Russian media.[114] In order to educate leaders and policy makers about the threat of disinformation, NATO established a Strategic Communications Centre of Excellence (StratCom) in Riga.

The annexation of Crimea was accompanied by a storm of propaganda and disinformation. Through a mix of traditional media and modern technologies, Russia sought to shape public opinion about the situation in Ukraine. For example, in July 2014, Russia propagated multiple explanations for the downing of Malaysian Airlines flight 17 over eastern Ukraine.[115] RT posted stories that quoted a supposed air-traffic controller who had tweeted that Ukrainian fighter jets were following the plane, as well as other stories including a supposed leaked RAND report advising Ukraine on how to carry out an ethnic genocide in the East.[116] Russian media have repeatedly presented the Ukrainian government as "Banderites," a reference to the pro-Nazi World War II Ukrainian movement leader Stepan Bandera, and have proliferated false stories of atrocities committed by Ukrainian forces.[117] Social media groups, moderated by Moscow, spread disinformation as a means to undermine the morale of Ukrainian troops and to discredit the military leadership, as well as to mobilize protests against the Ukrainian government.[118] Bots posting automatic complaints to social media sites have also succeeded in blocking pro-Ukraine user accounts, thereby limiting the proliferation of alternative narratives.[119]

Russia has increasingly favored "softer" mechanisms of influence in the Baltic states after they joined the EU and NATO in 2004.[120] Russia's propaganda and disinformation campaigns are a particular concern in Estonia and Latvia, where approximately a third of the population are Russian-speakers.[121] Lithuania is also a prominent target of Russia's disinformation campaigns, despite its considerably smaller Russian-speaking population (approximately 7 percent). In the Baltic states, there are two information spheres that feature different content, one in the Russian language and the other in the state language. Media in the Russian language is available from media registered in the Baltic states and from the Russian media. Russian media, particularly television, is popular among older generations, while social media is more important to young people.[122] Though ethnic majority populations strongly favor local-language media, a substantial portion may regularly consume Russian media for its entertainment value. Consequently, these societies are susceptible to the propaganda and disinformation that Russia proliferates through the media.

Russia's narratives portray the Baltic states, particularly Estonia and Latvia, as "neo-fascist" countries.[123] This narrative is more prominent surrounding days of commemoration, such as May 9, which marks the capitulation of Nazi Germany to the Soviet Union at the end of World War II, and March 16, which honors the Fifteenth and Nineteenth Waffen Grenadier Divisions of the SS that fought alongside Nazi forces in Latvia. These days symbolize different social memories for Russian-speaking and ethnic majority communities.[124] While May 9 is a day of pride for many Russian-speakers and their families, for ethnic majority populations the date is a painful reminder of the illegal Soviet occupation of the Baltic states.[125] Russia's failure to recognize the Soviet occupation of the Baltic states remains a source of tension. Recently, the foreign ministries of all three Baltic states condemned a legislative initiative in the Russian State Duma that would revoke a December 24, 1989, resolution by the Soviet Union's Supreme Council condemning the nonaggression pact (the Molotov-Ribbentrop Pact) between Nazi Germany and the Soviet Union that paved the way for the Soviet occupation of the Baltic countries.[126] Poland has been mired in similar historical disputes with Russia, recently in response to Russia's accusations that Poland was responsible for the outbreak of World War II.[127] The Russian media also promotes narratives that present the Baltic countries as "failed states," in both economic and political terms, by highlighting poor socioeconomic conditions and discrimination against Russian-speakers.[128] Finally, false stories of transgressions by NATO personnel in the Baltic countries are intended to weaken public support for a NATO Forward Presence.[129]

Russian narratives have also entered the media landscape of Central and East European countries that do not have large Russian-speaking populations. These narratives focus on the failure of the Western liberal democratic model and US leadership, as well as the corruption of Western elites.[130] In Serbia, Russia's messaging focuses on EU membership as an unattractive alternative to stronger relations with Russia, which provides a more natural cultural fit. These narratives are transmitted through outlets like Sputnik Srbija and Russia Beyond the Headlines, and are republished in Serbian, Bosnian, and Montenegrin outlets.[131] False stores proclaiming support for Russian policy stances have also proliferated in Romania through platforms such as Sputnik and through social media.[132] In the Czech Republic and Slovakia, which have small Russian minorities and only a few Russian media outlets, Russian narratives nevertheless make their way into social discourse through pro-Russian public personalities and NGOs, whose messaging is amplified on social media.[133] In other countries, like Poland, where the population is generally skeptical about Russian media, narratives find their way into the discourse via independent internet media platforms and Russian trolls.[134]

Political Parties and Illiberal Trends

Russia supports particular parties, politicians, and policy positions in Central and East European countries through both the media and funding.[135] In the Baltic states, parties that represent Russian-speakers, such as the Centre Party in Estonia and Harmony Centre in Latvia, signed association agreements with Russian president Vladimir Putin's United Russia Party. Investigative journalism revealed several organizations, well-known pro-Russian politicians, and activists in these countries that have received funding from Russkiy Mir.[136]

Russia has also supported policy positions and protests in Estonia and Latvia that run counter to state policy. In Latvia, the transition of all state-funded secondary schools to teaching at least 60 percent of their curriculum in the national language sparked mass protests in 2003–2004.[137] Russian media encouraged the protests,[138] and sources in Russia provided financial support to the "Headquarters for the Defense of Russian-Language Schools."[139] Russia also supports NGOs linked to the leadership of the Latvian Russian Union (LKS), a pro-Russian political party in Latvia, which has organized demonstrations against the most recent education reforms that require a complete transition to teaching in Latvian.[140] Russkiy Mir also funded the Human Rights Information Center's fight against increased Estonian-language instruction in Russian schools.[141] In 2012, Russian-speakers in Latvia organized a constitutional referendum to make Russian a second official language. The Russkiy Mir Foundation provided funding to the organizers of the referendum,[142] and the First Baltic Channel (PBK), a popular and trusted Russian-language station, devoted significant airtime to the signature-gathering campaign that was necessary for launching the referendum.[143] While the referendum did not pass, the events contributed to a further political polarization between ethnic Latvian- and Russian-speaking parties and reenergized the debate about Russia's influence in Latvia.[144]

In other parts of Central and East Europe, Russia has built connections with political parties and politicians who are Euroskeptical, sympathetic to Russia, and/or have autocratic tendencies.[145] Examples include Hungary's Jobbik, Bulgaria's Ataka, the Slovak National Party, and the Serbian Radical Party, all of which are far right, nationalist, Euroskeptic parties. Other parties in these countries have also adopted pro-Russia policy stances, particularly regarding Russia's actions in Ukraine and in the energy sector.[146] Political influence translates into economic influence, as politicians facilitate infrastructure projects and energy deals with Russia. Businessmen can then pressure politicians, creating an "unvirtuous cycle" of Russian influence.[147] Because these parties tend to be obstructionist, in addition to favoring Russian policy positions they also produce paralysis in national parliaments, which further undermines public faith in the democratic model.[148]

The Kremlin's authoritarianism and emphasis on "sovereign democracy" serves as an attractive alternative to liberal democracy in some countries. Hungary, a democratic front-runner in the region leading up to EU and NATO accession, turned down an illiberal path after Prime Minister Viktor Orbán rose to power in 2010. Orbán, an admirer of Russia's illiberal democracy, pushed through constitutional reforms that threaten the independence of democratic institutions like the Constitutional Court.[149] The passage of media laws that regulate TV, newspaper, radio, and the internet have prompted Western commentators to accuse Hungary of being "in league with Russia and Belarus on press freedom."[150] Prime Minister Orbán has advocated for Russian economic ventures in the energy sector and has expressed opposition to EU economic sanctions against Russia following the annexation of Crimea.[151] Former prime minister

Robert Fico (2012–2018) of Slovakia reportedly espoused similar aspirations to emulate Putin's style of governance.[152]

Poland's populist and Euroskeptic Law and Justice party has also orchestrated a democratic backslide that challenges European norms regarding rule of law, putting the country at odds with other EU member states. In many ways, the party is closer to Russia ideologically with respect to conservatism, sovereignty, and the rejection of liberal democracy than it is to the West. However, both the leader of the party, Jarosław Kaczyński, and the party's electorate are hostile toward Russia.[153] Consequently, Poland has remained committed to deterring Russian aggression through a NATO Forward Presence in the country and has been supportive of Ukraine's integration into European structures.[154]

Russia's Impact on Public Attitudes and Policies

While Russia's propaganda and disinformation campaigns have been fairly well documented, assessing the influence of those campaigns on public attitudes is difficult. Media consumption does not necessarily translate into influence, and both media literacy and trust in various media sources are important mitigating factors. In Ukraine, studies have reported that Ukrainians (outside Crimea) remain skeptical about the information presented by Russian media. In the Baltic states, Russian-speakers evaluate Russian media as an important and trustworthy source of information, while ethnic majority populations have greater trust in the local-language media.[155] Nevertheless, there is some evidence that Russia's information campaigns influence public attitudes. One survey study conducted in Russia, Ukraine, Moldova, and Kyrgyzstan in 2016 concluded that more frequent consumption of Russian media was associated with a greater tendency to accept the Russian narrative that the United States was responsible for the conflict in Ukraine.[156] In the Baltic context, several studies have revealed that Russian-speakers living in a predominately Russian information sphere have different worldviews and a weaker identification with their country of residence compared with those who consume state-language media.[157] StratCom found that comments by Russian trolls are associated with an increase in comments from nontrolls in a variety of Russian-, Latvian-, Estonian-, Lithuanian-, and Polish-language internet portals. Thus, to some extent, Russia is shaping public discussion.[158] Russia's public messaging campaign in Serbia, which focuses on presenting Russia as a more attractive option than the European Union, may have affected public opinion on foreign policy. Public opinion polls demonstrate that Russia is viewed more favorably than the European Union, despite the fact that the EU contributes more to the region. Support for EU membership has also been lower in Serbia than in other Western Balkan countries.[159]

The Bronze Night events that unfolded in Estonia in spring 2007 provide another example of Russia's ability to stoke ethnic tensions through Russian-language media.[160] It remains the only incident of large-scale violence in postindependence Estonia. While some ethnic Estonians did join in the rioting, the majority of the rioters were young Russian-speakers. Rumors circulated that the Russian embassy paid protestors. Both during and after the crisis, the Russian media focused almost entirely on police brutality and accused the Estonian government of cutting the statue into pieces in order to relocate it. Estonian authorities responded by accusing Russia of stoking ethnic divisions through its biased coverage of the events in the media.[161] Russian politicians denied any involvement and called for the resignation of the Estonian government for its failure to protect the rights of Russian-speakers and to ensure interethnic peace.[162]

Studies conducted in the wake of the crisis reveal a sharpening of ethnic divides between Estonians and Russian-speakers, as well as a generalized feeling of alienation from Estonian society and distrust of the government among Russian-speakers.[163] There was also a significant increase in Russian citizenship applications between August 2007 and March 2008 compared with the same period the previous year. According to Russian embassy officials, applicants reported "losing confidence" in Estonian democracy.[164] Russia has used the incident, both in the media and in international organizations, to mount more frequent attacks against Estonia for falsifying history and glorifying Nazism.[165] The Bronze Night also sparked discussions about emphasizing Estonian language proficiency as the key to minority integration. While Russia cannot be held entirely responsible for the events of spring 2007, as the government's decision to relocate the monument and its handling of that decision are also to blame, Russia clearly played a role in mobilizing and exacerbating ethnic tensions.

In the Baltic countries, studies have shown that Russia's use of hard- and soft-power levers affects policy making toward Russian-speakers. While some scholars argue that Russia's activism produces defensive reactions by policy makers, ultimately working against the liberalization of minority policies,[166] others find that Russia's activism has been both an accelerator and a brake on reform in Estonia and Latvia. Russia's kin-state activism provides strategic opportunities for policy makers to frame their policy preferences in new and convincing ways, ultimately influencing the path and form of policies. These processes contributed to both inclusionary and exclusionary policy reforms before and after EU accession.[167] These examples demonstrate that despite Russia's considerable resources and leverage, its influence on policy making depends on both the agency and configuration of domestic actors.

Russia's efforts to attract Russian-speakers have been less successful. In Ukraine, Russia's information campaigns have failed to translate into majority support for Russian actions in any region outside Crimea.[168] In the Baltic states, Russia's inability to reorient Russian-speakers away from a primary sense of belonging to their resident state, or to mobilize large numbers of Russian-speakers around compatriot initiatives or support for separatism in border regions,[169] has led some to declare Russia's soft-power agenda a "failure" in the Baltic states.[170] Surveys commissioned by ministries of defense after the annexation of Crimea reveal that a significant portion of Russian-speakers are willing to actively defend the state in the case of an armed attack.[171] Consequently, while the Russian media presents a strategic vulnerability, there is consensus that Russia has failed to "win over" Russian-speakers en masse and that they do not pose a significant security threat to the Baltic states.[172]

Nevertheless, the conflict in Ukraine demonstrates that the mobilization of a relatively small number of activists can have serious security implications. Consequently, Central and East European countries are taking Russia's hard- and soft-power strategies seriously. Concerns over Russia's media influence led the Estonian government to launch a new Russian-language television station in 2015 (ETV+).[173] In the wake of the coronavirus pandemic, ETV+ viewership has tripled, owing to the fact that Russian-speakers need information about Estonian policies that are not available in the Russian media. While Russian-speakers are still consuming more Russian media, the increase in ETV+ viewership, in combination with opinion polling data that shows ETV+ is considered more trustworthy than Russian media outlets, is a positive development toward the creation of a common information sphere.[174] Latvia and Lithuania have allocated more funding to state-owned bilingual stations and have imposed temporary bans on Russian-owned media for knowingly disseminating false information.[175] In 2017, the Lithuanian parliament passed a law restricting media content produced in Russia on Lithuanian TV. At least 90 percent of television content must now be produced in the EU and broadcast in official EU languages.[176] Despite such measures, Russian narratives can still work their way into public discourse through pro-Russian media outlets in the European Union or via social media. Here, Baltic "elves," who consist of thousands of volunteer journalists, IT professionals, businesspeople, students, and scientists aiming to expose and counter the narratives of Russian trolls, are an important defense.[177]

Ukraine created a Ministry of Information Policy whose mission is to protect Ukraine's informational sovereignty. In 2014, the government began shutting down broadcasts from Moscow-controlled television, extending the ban to at least seventy-three stations by 2016. The state has also extended the ban to social media, blocking the popular Russian social media site VK. Combined with language quotas for radio and television, the result has been a real reduction in the consumption of Russian television.[178] The Ministry of Information Policy also launched a new channel (UA/TV) that broadcasts in five languages on its own website, YouTube, European cable networks, and three satellite stations.[179] Following the escalation of violence in February 2021, President Volodymyr Zelenskyy took three pro-Russian television stations connected to the pro-Russian Opposition Platform—For Life party off the air. The leader of the pro-Russian opposition, Viktor Medvedchuk, was also sanctioned for financing Donbas separatists.[180] Volunteer journalists and students have also developed initiatives to identify and counter Russian propaganda and disinformation on the internet.[181] Experts in Ukraine and the Baltics have recognized that the best way to combat Russia's information campaigns is to increase media literacy in target populations so that people are able to identify Russian propaganda and disinformation.[182]

The EU East Strategic Communications Task Force is also raising awareness about Russia's information campaigns, disseminating information on EU policies, and supporting independent media in the region.[183] Countering Russia's influence in the region will require the EU and NATO to project their own clear messages about the advantages of membership in these organizations, as well as the purpose of NATOs Enhanced Forward Presence in the Baltic countries and Poland.[184] These efforts of course have their limits, as countercampaigns cannot stop Russia's information campaigns from reaching targeted audiences.[185]

Russia and the West as Alternative Centers of Power

Russia's relationship with Western countries and Western organizations is crucial for understanding and contextualizing Russia's influence in Central and East Europe. In

February 2007, President Vladimir Putin gave his famous Munich speech, where he "asserted that Russia would no longer accept the US-led uni-polar order of international relations, and that Russia would implement its own independent foreign policy in pursuit of its geopolitical interests."[186] At the same time, Russia recognized the leverage that soft power has given Western democracies and sought to cultivate its own soft-power resources. In doing so, Russia portrays its own political values and culture, which are rooted in national identity, Christian values, traditional gender roles, and value-free cooperation as fundamentally different from Western values centered on democracy, human rights, and the rule of law.[187] Russia accuses Western countries of using soft power as a cover for hostile and manipulative actions, including the color revolutions and the Arab Spring, and presents its own use of the media and public diplomacy networks as a defense against the West.[188]

Russia and the West represent alternative poles of soft power, and CEE countries are at the crossroads of both Russian and Western influence. The attraction of Europe as a countervailing weight provides an explanation for why Russia's soft-power agenda has not been more successful in the region.[189] Membership in the EU not only presents favorable economic opportunities compared with Russia, but NATO membership, along with the presence of NATO multinational battle groups as a deterrent force in all three Baltic states and Poland, provides important reminders of Western commitments to regional security.[190] These factors make it highly unlikely that Russian-speakers in these states would mobilize violently against the state or that a "Ukraine scenario," which depended on the ambiguity surrounding local support, could play out elsewhere.[191]

In order to destabilize Western societies and weaken the appeal of the Western liberal democratic model, Russia also targets Western countries with propaganda and disinformation campaigns. Russia employs tactics of "reflexive control," supplying adversaries with false information in order to influence their policy responses.[192] Russia's support for right-wing anti-EU political parties and politicians in Western Europe whose political agendas align with Russian objectives increases possibilities for reflexive control because Russia's narratives are likely to find traction within such groups.[193]

These campaigns have political, social, and financial aspects. The political content aims "to tarnish democratic leaders or undermine institutions" through "allegations of voter fraud, election rigging, and political corruption."[194] For example, the Central Intelligence Agency (CIA), Federal Bureau of Investigation (FBI), and National Security Agency (NSA) determined that Russia undertook an extensive operation in the United States to influence the 2016 election by using a mixture of information operations backed by social media.[195] Financial narratives are intended to erode citizen and investor confidence in markets by stoking fears over national debt and discrediting Western business experts and leaders. Finally, Russia attempts to undermine the social fabric of Western societies by leveraging social tensions over various issues.[196] For example, RT continued to run a story about a Russian schoolgirl in Berlin who had been abducted and raped by Middle Eastern men, even after the German police debunked the allegations.[197] Prior to the national referendum on the United Kingdom leaving the European Union, which was a very divisive issue, Russian media heavily favored a pro-Brexit stance.[198] More recently, concerns in several countries center on Russia's ability to spread disinformation regarding the COVID-19 pandemic and the Western response.[199] While many Russian narratives are easily proven false, they still proliferate. Western media outlets may present Russian narratives out of the adage that there are two sides to every story, in the process helping them to reach their target audiences.[200] Russia has also carried out high-profile cyber-attacks against Western countries, including the United States, France, and the United Kingdom, prompting NATO and the EU to invest more intensively in cybersecurity.[201]

The success of Russia's strategy is evident in the delayed response of Western powers to Russia's aggression in Ukraine due to their confusion over Russia's presence there. Nevertheless, the West has maintained solidarity in not recognizing Russia's claims to Crimea and in encouraging Russia and Ukraine to resolve the ongoing conflict through the Minsk Agreement. The United States and the EU, along with Australia, Canada, and Japan, have imposed economic sanctions on Russian individuals and sectors of the Russian economy, and Russia has been suspended from the G8.[202] The United States has increased foreign aid to Ukraine and has provided training and equipment to Ukrainian forces. NATO has also engaged in military exercises with Ukraine. Russia will likely continue to "chip away" at European solidarity by courting actors from Europe's far right, such as the Front National in France, Lega in Italy, and the Freedom Party in Austria.[203] The most serious threat that Russia's influence poses to Western solidarity may be in situations that require consensus, such as meeting NATO's Article 5 commitments.[204]

At the same time, Russia uses its seat at the table in Western organizations to politicize Russian-speakers in its near abroad, not only to justify its continuing interference in

Photo 10.3.   Russia seeks to exercise hard and soft power in the states of Central and East Europe. It also uses soft-power tools like television media to influence public opinion in Western countries. RT broadcasts news and propaganda in multiple languages outside of Russia. (fifg, Shutterstock)

the region but also to tarnish the democratic reputation of these institutions.[205] Russia has raised the situation of Russian-speakers in all major international and regional forums, including the United Nations, the Organization for Security and Co-operation in Europe, and the Council of Europe, as well as in discussions with the EU and NATO.

Future Challenges

While Russia may be less potent than the Soviet Union, it is indeed a rising power with a number of hard- and soft-power resources at its disposal to influence policies and public attitudes in CEE countries. Russia has not only increased its military spending and engaged in the modernization of its armed forces but is undoubtedly a great cyber power both for its expertise and willingness to act aggressively in cyberspace. Russia's aggressive cyberattacks in its near abroad, particularly in Estonia, Georgia, and Ukraine, as well as in several Western democracies, has elevated cybersecurity on the agenda of all major powers.[206] Russia has also developed numerous tools of public diplomacy, the most significant being the strategic use of traditional Russian-language media and social media to spread propaganda and disinformation in order to destabilize societies, discredit Western institutions, and promote pro-Russian policy agendas. Russia's unpredictability presents one of the greatest challenges to Western democracies in countering Russia's influence in the region. Russia's military annexation of Crimea, widespread disinformation campaigns, and devastating cyberattacks have taken both CEE countries and Western powers by surprise.[207]

Russia is unlikely to stop projecting power in the region anytime soon. The lesson that Russia can draw from recent military conflicts in Georgia, Ukraine, and Syria is that the use of military force is valuable for achieving its strategic objectives. Absent stronger international consequences, Russia may be encouraged to pursue further military adventurism.[208] Effectively deterring Russia will require not only a significant force presence in the region but also consistent messaging that NATO will take all steps to defend its allies up to and including the use of force.[209] Combating Russia's information war will also be difficult. The goals of such campaigns are to sow confusion and doubt, make "objective" reporting suspect, and in the process undermine Western democratic institutions.[210] Russia's disinformation campaigns are not "new," but Russia has been able to harness new technologies to amplify its narratives. Nevertheless, Russia's influence must still be filtered through domestic structures, and therefore it is difficult to predict the effects of Russia's influence campaigns on target states.

Societal resilience to disinformation campaigns in CEE countries and initiatives to undercut Russia's economic influence provide instructive examples of how states can mitigate Russia's influence. There is evidence of societal resilience in the Baltic states in the volunteer armies of Baltic "elves" who seek to counter Russian narratives and the work of Russian trolls on social media. Recognition of the need to increase media literacy in society and to develop programs targeting different sectors of society provides guidance for other states in the region. In Estonia, Russian viewership of the Estonian state Russian-language television station ETV+ increased markedly in the wake of the coronavirus pandemic as Russian-speakers sought trustworthy sources of information. Lithuania's efforts to break its dependency on Russian energy, and the successful diversification of energy sources in the Czech Republic and Romania,[211] provide important lessons for other states in how to weaken Russia's ability to use energy as a political lever. Whether other countries, such as Ukraine, are able to follow Latvia's example of targeting corruption remains to be seen; however, doing so is crucial for combating Russia's economic influence.

The rise of far-right national populist parties across the European landscape has provided easy targets for Russia's influence campaigns. While some countries, such has Hungary, have adopted more explicitly pro-Russian sympathies, other countries like Poland have maintained a deterrent posture toward Russia despite democratic backsliding. Weaker economic ties between the two countries mean that Russia has less leverage to deploy. The real test may come in the ability of countries like Serbia and Bulgaria to maintain pro-European and pro-Russian orientations, particularly in the absence of energy diversification.

The countries of Central and East Europe remain at the crossroads of European and Russian influence. This presents a constant strategic challenge for states in the region, in particular for those with sizeable Russian-speaking populations. While the challenges of a rising Russia are formidable, the lasting impact of Russia's influence campaigns in the region will depend to a considerable extent on the leadership and resilience of these societies. It will also depend upon the purposeful action of Western countries and organizations in both deterring Russia's military adventurism and providing consistent alternative narratives about the benefits of liberal democracy and membership in Western organizations.

Study Questions

1. How is hard power different from soft power?
2. What hard- and soft-power resources does Russia possess, and how does it wield those resources to influence politics in Central and East Europe?
3. How has Russia's foreign policy affected countries in the region since the Soviet collapse?
4. What strategies might countries in the region adopt to mitigate Russia's influence in their societies?
5. How should Western organizations, like the EU and NATO, respond to a rising Russia and its increasingly assertive foreign policy?

Suggested Readings

Conley, Heather A., James Mina, Ruslan Stefanov, and Martin Vladimirov. *The Kremlin Playbook: Understanding Russian Influence in Central and Eastern Europe*. Lanham: Rowman & Littlefield, 2016.

Laruelle, Marlene, ed. *Eurasianism and the European Far Right*. London: Lexington Books, 2015.

Muižnieks, Nils, ed. *Manufacturing Enemy Images? Russian Media Portrayal of Latvia*. Riga: University of Latvia Academic Press, 2008.

Pelnēns, Gatis, ed. *The Humanitarian Dimension of Russian Foreign Policy toward Georgia, Moldova, Ukraine, and the Baltic States*. Riga: Centre for East European Policy Studies, 2009.

Rostoks, Toms, and Andris Sprūds. *The Different Faces of Soft Power: The Baltic States and the Eastern Neighborhood between Russia and the EU.* Riga: Latvian Institute of International Affairs, 2015.

Schulze, Jennie L. *Strategic Frames: Europe, Russia, and Minority Inclusion in Estonia and Latvia.* Pittsburgh, PA: University of Pittsburgh Press, 2018.

Sherr, James. *Hard Diplomacy and Soft Coercion: Russia's Influence Abroad.* London: Chatham House, 2013.

Toal, Gerard. *Near Abroad: Putin, the West and the Contest over Ukraine and the Caucasus.* New York: Oxford University Press, 2017.

Websites

NATO Cooperative Cyber Defense Centre of Excellence: https://ccdcoe.org/library/publications.

NATO Energy Security Centre of Excellence: https://www.enseccoe.org/en/studies-and-publications/225/journals.

NATO Strategic Communications Centre of Excellence: https://www.stratcomcoe.org.

Russkiy Mir Foundation, "What Is a Center?": https://russkiymir.ru/en/rucenter.

Notes

1. Steven Pifer, "Crimea: Six Years after Illegal Annexation," Brookings, March 17, 2020, https://www.brookings.edu/blog/order-from-chaos/2020/03/17/crimea-six-years-after-illegal-annexation.

2. Todd C. Helmus, Elizabeth Bodine-Baron, Andrew Radin, Madeline Magnuson, Joshua Mendelsohn, William Marcellino, Andriy Bega, and Zev Winkelman, "Russian Social Media Influence: Understanding Russian Propaganda in Eastern Europe," Rand Corporation, 2018, 2.

3. Gerard Toal, *Near Abroad: Putin, the West and the Contest over Ukraine and the Caucasus* (New York: Oxford University Press, 2017), 66.

4. President of Russia, "Annual Address to the Federal Assembly of the Russian Federation," April 25, 2005, http://en.kremlin.ru/events/president/transcripts/22931.

5. Gudrun Persson, "Russian Influence and Soft Power in the Baltic States: The View from Moscow," in *Tools of Destabilization: Russian Soft Power and Non-military Influence in the Baltic States*, ed. Mike Winnerstig (FOI-R-3990-SE, 2014), 22.

6. James Sherr, *Hard Diplomacy and Soft Coercion: Russia's Influence Abroad* (London: Chatham House, 2013), 87, citing Vladimir Putin, "Speech to the Congress of Compatriots Residing Abroad," October 11–12, 2001.

7. Pål Kolstø, "Beyond Russia, Becoming Local: Trajectories of Adaption to the Fall of the Soviet Union among Ethnic Russians in the Former Soviet Republics," *Journal of Eurasian Studies* 2 (2011): 159.

8. Vera Zakem, Paul Saunders, and Daniel Antoun, *Mobilizing Compatriots: Russia's Strategy, Tactics, and Influence in the Former Soviet Union*, CNA Analysis and Solutions, November 2015, https://www.cna.org/CNA_files/PDF/DOP-2015-U-011689-1Rev.pdf; Marlene Laruelle, ed., *Eurasianism and the European Far Right* (London: Lexington Books, 2015).

9. David J. Smith, "Framing the National Question in Central and Eastern Europe: A Quadratic Nexus?," *Global Review of Ethnopolitics* 2, no. 1 (2002): 3–16.

10. Heather A. Conley, James Mina, Ruslan Stefanov, and Martin Vladimirov, *The Kremlin Playbook: Understanding Russian Influence in Central and Eastern Europe* (Lanham, MD: Rowman & Littlefield, 2016), 2.

11. Joseph Nye, *Soft Power: The Means to Success in World Politics* (New York: Public Affairs, 2004), 5.

12. Keir Giles, "Russia's 'New' Tools for Confronting the West: Continuity and Innovation in Moscow's Exercise of Power," Chatham House, Russia and Eurasia Programme, March 21, 2016, 15, https://www.chathamhouse.org/publication/russias-new-tools-confronting-west; Maria Snegovaya, "Putin's Information Warfare in Ukraine: Soviet Origins of Russia's Hybrid Warfare," Institute for the Study of War, September 2015, 9.

13. Global Firepower, "Defense Spending by Country (2021)," https://www.globalfirepower.com/defense-spending-budget.php.

14. Dmitry Gorenberg, "5 Things to Know about Russia's Vostok-2018 Military Exercises," *Washington Post*, September 13, 2018, https://www.washingtonpost.com/news/monkey-cage/wp/2018/09/13/5-things-to-know-about-russias-vostok-2018-military-exercises.

15. Global Firepower, "2021 Military Strength Ranking," https://www.globalfirepower.com/countries-listing.asp.

16. Global Firepower, "2021 Military Strength Ranking."

17. Jan-Phillip N. E. Wagner, "The Effectiveness of Hard and Soft Power in Contemporary International Relations," E-International Relations, May 14, 2014, https://www.e-ir.info/2014/05/14/the-effectiveness-of-soft-hard-power-in-contemporary-international-relations.

18. Central Intelligence Agency (CIA), *The World Factbook*, https://www.cia.gov/the-world-factbook/field/real-gdp-purchasing-power-parity/country-comparison.

19. US Energy Information Association (EIA), "FAQs: What Countries Are the Largest Producers and Consumers of Oil?," https://www.eia.gov/tools/faqs/faq.php?id=709&t=6.

20. CIA, *The World Factbook: Natural Gas—Exports*, https://www.cia.gov/the-world-factbook/field/natural-gas-exports/country-comparison; CIA, *The World Factbook: Natural Gas—Proved Reserves*, https://www.cia.gov/the-world-factbook/field/natural-gas-proved-reserves/country-comparison.

21. "G7 Leaders Reject Russia's Return after Trump Invite," BBC News, June 2, 2020, https://www.bbc.com/news/world-us-canada-52885178.

22. Andrew Chatzky and Anshu Siripurapu, "OPEC in a Changing World," Council on Foreign Relations, April 9, 2020, https://www.cfr.org/backgrounder/opec-changing-world?gclid=Cj0KCQjwgJv4BRCrARIsAB17JI7ZvMehB8Uyb0gNaKV8eXy3E0VzAhC42TTEn93qkrJsWG8oOajwEzAaAm76EALw_wcB.

23. Vasif Huseynov, "Soft Power Geopolitics: How Does the Diminishing Utility of Military Power Affect the Russia-West Confrontation over the 'Common Neighborhood,'" *Eastern Journal of European Studies* 7, no. 2 (December 2016): 80; Sinikukka Saari, "Russia's Post–Orange Revolution Strategies to Increase Its Influence in Former Soviet Republics: Public Diplomacy *po russkii*," *Europe-Asia Studies* 66, no. 1 (January 2014): 51; Alexander Sergunin and Leonid Karabeshkin, "Understanding Russia's Soft Power Strategy," *Politics* 35, nos. 3–4 (2015): 349.

24. Yulia Kiseleva, "Russia's Soft Power Discourse: Identity, Status and the Attraction of Power," *Politics* 35, nos. 3–4 (2015): 318; Nye, *Soft Power*, 5.

25. Greg Simons, "Perception of Russia's Soft Power and Influence in the Baltic States," *Public Relations Review* 41 (2015): 3.

26. Andis Kudors, "Latvia between the Centers of Gravitation of Soft Power—the USA and Russia," in *Latvia and the United States: A New Chapter in the Partnership*, ed. Ivars Indāns (Riga: Centre for East European Policy Studies, 2012), 102.

27. Ministry of Foreign Affairs of the Russian Federation, "Concept of the Foreign Policy of the Russian Federation," approved by President of the Russian Federation Vladimir Putin on November 30, 2016, https://www.mid.ru/en/foreign_policy/official_documents/-/asset_publisher /CptICkB6BZ29/content/id/2542248.

28. Media Ajir and Bethany Vailliant, "Russian Information Warfare: Implications for Deterrence Theory," *Strategic Studies Quarterly* 12, no. 3 (Fall 2018): 77; Saari, "Russia's Post–Orange Revolution Strategies," 62.

29. Nils Muižnieks, ed., *Manufacturing Enemy Images? Russian Media Portrayal of Latvia* (Riga: University of Latvia Academic Press, 2008).

30. Kudors, "Latvia between the Centers of Gravitation of Soft Power," 94, 104; Persson, "Russian Influence and Soft Power," 19–24; see also Ministry of Foreign Affairs of the Russian Federation, "Concept of the Foreign Policy of the Russian Federation," approved by President of the Russian Federation Vladimir Putin on February 12, 2013, https://www.mid.ru/en/foreign_ policy/official_documents/-/asset_publisher/CptICkB6BZ29/content/id/122186.

31. Saari, "Russia's Post–Orange Revolution Strategies," 60; see also Russkiy Mir Foundation, "What Is a Center?," https://russkiymir.ru/en/rucenter.

32. Saari, "Russia's Post–Orange Revolution Strategies," 61.

33. Saari, "Russia's Post–Orange Revolution Strategies," 55–56.

34. Conley et al., *The Kremlin Playbook*, 6.

35. Persson, "Russian Influence and Soft Power," 26–27.

36. Andis Kudors, "Russian Soft Power and Non-Military Influence: The View from Latvia," in *Tools of Destabilization. Russian Soft Power and Non-military Influence in the Baltic States*, ed. Mike Winnerstig, FOI-R-3990-SE (Stockholm: Swedish Defense Agency, 2014), 81.

37. Zakem et al., *Mapping Russian Media Network*, iii.

38. Kolstø, "Beyond Russia, Becoming Local," 158.

39. Helmus et al., "Russian Social Media Influence," 1.

40. Helmus et al., "Russian Social Media Influence," ix.

41. Helmus et al., "Russian Social Media Influence," 3, 7; Kudors, "Russian Soft Power and Non-Military Influence," 89; Vera Zakem, Paul Saunders, Umida Hashimoya, and P. Kathleen Hammerberg, *Mapping Russian Media Network: Media's Role in Russian Foreign Policy and Decision-Making*, CNA Analysis and Solutions, January 2018, iii, https://www.cna.org/cna_files/ pdf/DRM-2017-U-015367-3Rev.pdf.

42. Zakem et al., *Mapping Russian Media Network*, 10.

43. Andrew Weisburd, Clint Watts, and J. M. Berger, "Trolling for Trump: How Russia Is Trying to Destroy Our Democracy," *War on the Rocks*, November 6, 2016, https://warontherock s.com/2016/11/trolling-for-trump-how-russia-is-trying-to-destroy-our-democracy.

44. Nye, *Soft Power*.

45. The Soft Power 30, https://softpower30.com/country/russian-federation.

46. Snegovaya, "Putin's Information Warfare in Ukraine," 12.

47. Population and Housing Census 2011, http://pub.stat.ee; Population and Housing Census 2011, http://data.csb.gov.lv/pxweb/en/tautassk_11/tautassk_11__tsk2011/?tablelist=true &rxid=a79839fe-11ba-4ecd-8cc3–4035692c5fc8.

48. Jennie L. Schulze, *Strategic Frames: Europe, Russia, and Minority Inclusion in Estonia and Latvia* (Pittsburgh, PA: University of Pittsburgh Press, 2018).

49. Carl Schreck, "From 'Not Us' to 'Why Hide It?': How Russia Denied Its Crimean Invasion and Then Admitted It," Radio Free Europe/Radio Liberty, February 26, 2019, https://www.rferl.org/a /from-not-us-to-why-hide-it-how-russia-denied-its-crimea-invasion-then-admitted-it/29791806.html.

50. Pifer, "Crimea: Six Years after Illegal Annexation."

51. Council on Foreign Relations, "Global Conflict Tracker: Ukraine," https://www.cfr.org/global-conflict-tracker/conflict/conflict-ukraine.

52. Council on Foreign Relations, "Global Conflict Tracker: Ukraine."

53. Snegovaya, "Putin's Information Warfare in Ukraine," 15.

54. Pavel Felgenhauer, "Russia Escalates Its Proxy War in Eastern Ukraine," *Eurasia Daily Monitor*, March 11, 2021, https://jamestown.org/program/russia-escalates-its-proxy-war-in-eastern-ukraine.

55. Schreck, "From 'Not Us' to 'Why Hide It?'"

56. Schreck, "From 'Not Us' to 'Why Hide It?'" A documentary, *Crimea: The Way Home*, which aired on Russian state television in March 2015, made clear Russia's involvement in the annexation of the Crimean Peninsula.

57. Snegovaya, "Putin's Information Warfare in Ukraine," 13.

58. Jonathan Masters, "Ukraine: Conflict at the Crossroads of Europe and Russia," Council on Foreign Relations, February 5, 2020, https://www.cfr.org/backgrounder/ukraine-conflict-crossroads-europe-and-russia.

59. Snegovaya, "Putin's Information Warfare in Ukraine," 18.

60. Snegovaya, "Putin's Information Warfare in Ukraine," 13.

61. Masters, "Ukraine: Conflict"; Schreck, "From 'Not Us' to 'Why Hide It?'"

62. Toal, *Near Abroad*.

63. John Mearsheimer, "Why the Ukraine Crisis Is the West's Fault: The Liberal Delusions That Provoked Putin," *Foreign Affairs* 93, no. 5 (September/October 2014): 77–89.

64. Michael McFaul, Stephen Sestanovich, and John J. Mearsheimer, "Faulty Powers: Who Started the Ukraine Crisis?," *Foreign Affairs* 93, no. 6 (November/December 2014): 167–78; Pifer, "Crimea: Six Years after Illegal Annexation."

65. Ian Johnston, "Russia Threatens the Use of Nuclear Force over Crimea and the Baltic States," *Independent*, April 2, 2015, https://www.independent.co.uk/news/world/europe/russia-threatens-to-use-nuclear-force-over-crimea-and-the-baltic-states-10150565.html.

66. Ieva Bērziņa, ed., *The Possibility of Societal Destabilization in Latvia: Potential National Security Threats: Executive Summary* (Riga: National Defence Academy of Latvia, 2016); Andres Kasekamp, "Why Narva Is Not Next," Estonian Foreign Policy Institute Series 21, May 2015.

67. Dan de Luce, "If Russia Started a War in the Baltics, NATO Would Lose—Quickly," *Foreign Policy*, February 3, 2016, http://foreignpolicy.com/2016/02/03/if-russia-started-a-war-in-the-baltics-nato-would-lose-quickly; Stephen Blank, "Putin's Next Potential Target: The Baltic States," Atlantic Council, January 5, 2016, https://www.atlanticcouncil.org/blogs/ukrainealert/putin-s-next-potential-target-the-baltic-states; "US Army Commander Warns of Russian Blocking of Baltic Defence," *Baltic Times*, November 9, 2015, http://www.baltictimes.com/u_s__army_commander_warns_of_russian_blocking_of_baltic_defence.

68. David A. Shlapak and Michael Johnson, "Reinforcing Deterrence on NATO's Eastern Flank," Rand Corporation, 2016, https://www.rand.org/pubs/research_reports/RR1253.html.

69. Stephen J. Flanagan, Jan Osburg, Anika Binnendijk, Marta Kepe, and Andrew Radin, "Deterring Russian Aggression in the Baltic States," Rand Corporation, 2019, 2–3, https://www.rand.org/pubs/research_reports/RR2779.html. Total defense involves a "whole of society" approach to national defense and resilience.

70. Council on Foreign Relations, "Global Conflict Tracker: Ukraine."

71. Rasma Karklins, *Ethnopolitics and Transition to Democracy: The Collapse of the USSR and Latvia* (Washington, DC: Woodrow Wilson Center Press, 1994), 121.

72. Giles, "Russia's 'New' Tools for Confronting the West," 21.

73. Kremlinwatch, "Romania," https://www.kremlinwatch.eu/countries-compared-states/r omania.

74. Nicu Popescu and Stanislav Secrieru, *Hacks, Leaks and Disruptions: Russian Cyber Strategies, Chaillot Papers* (Paris: European Union Institute for Security Studies, October 2018), 54–58.

75. For a good description of these statements, see Gatis Pelnēns, ed., *The Humanitarian Dimension of Russian Foreign Policy toward Georgia, Moldova, Ukraine, and the Baltic States* (Riga: Centre for East European Policy Studies, 2009), 60.

76. "Estonia Urges Firm EU, NATO, Response to New Form of Warfare: Cyber-Attacks," Agence France-Presse, May 16, 2007; see also "Analysis: Estonia Accuses Russia over Cyber-Attacks," *BBC Monitoring Europe—Political*, May 17, 2007.

77. "Russia Accused of Unleashing Cyberwar to Disable Estonia," *Guardian*, May 16, 2007, http://www.theguardian.com/world/2007/may/17/topstories3.russia; "Denial of Service: The Estonian Cyberwar and Its Implications for US National Security," Elliot School of International Affairs, George Washington University, http://www.iar-gwu.org/node/65.

78. "Estonia Says Russia Brushing off Cyber-Attack Probe," Agence France-Presse, July 6, 2007.

79. David J. Galbreath and Ainius Lašas, "The 'Baltic' Factor in EU-Russian Relations: In Search of Coherence and Co-operation in an Era of Complexity," *Journal of Contemporary European Studies* 19, no. 2 (2011): 265.

80. Popescu and Secrieru, *Hacks, Leaks and Disruptions*, 97.

81. Popescu and Secrieru, *Hacks, Leaks and Disruptions*, 61.

82. Council on Foreign Relations, "Global Conflict Tracker: Ukraine"; Mark Lander and Scott Shane, "US Condemns Russia for Cyberattack, Showing Split in Stance on Putin," *New York Times*, February 15, 2018, https://www.nytimes.com/2018/02/15/us/politics/russia-cyberattack.html.

83. Popescu and Secrieru, *Hacks, Leaks and Disruptions*, 86.

84. Popescu and Secrieru, *Hacks, Leaks and Disruptions*, 87–88.

85. Heather A. Conley, James Mina, Ruslan Stefanov, and Martin Vladimirov, *The Kremlin Playbook: Understanding Russian Influence in Central and Eastern Europe* (Lanham: Rowman & Littlefield, 2016), 2.

86. Conley et al., *The Kremlin Playbook*, 7, citing "EUR 30mn Spent on South Stream, and We Won't Get It Back," B92, January 13, 2016, https://www.b92.net/eng/news/business.php?yyy y=2016&mm=01&dd=13&nav_id=96688.

87. Conley et al., *The Kremlin Playbook*, xii.

88. Conley et al., *The Kremlin Playbook*, 9.

89. Conley et al., *The Kremlin Playbook*, 9.

90. Martin Jirušek and Petra Kuchyňkova, "The Conduct of Gazprom in Central and Eastern Europe: A Tool of the Kremlin or Just an Adaptable Player?," *East European Politics and Societies* 32, no. 4 (November 2018): 825.

91. Kremlinwatch, "Romania."

92. Orenstein, "Geopolitics of a Divided Europe," 538.

93. See Minorities at Risk Data, "Chronology for Russians in Estonia," June 25, 1993, http://www.mar.umd.edu/chronology.asp?groupId=36601.

94. David Galbreath, *Nation-Building and Minority Politics in Post-Socialist States: Interests, Influences, and Identities in Estonia and Latvia* (Stuttgart: Ibidem-Verlag, 2005), 215; Kelley, *Ethnic Politics*, 111.

95. "Russia Announces Sanctions against Latvia; Government Crisis in Riga," *Monitor* (Jamestown Foundation) 4, no. 69 (April 9, 1998); "On the Border: Latvia," *Monitor* 0, no. 26 (July 6, 1998); "Russia's Upper Chamber for Embargo on Latvia," *Monitor* 4, no. 32 (July 10, 1998).

96. Galbreath and Lašas, "The Baltic Factor," 265, 270.

97. Masters, "Ukraine: Conflict."

98. Jirušek and Kuchyňkova, "The Conduct of Gazprom in Central and Eastern Europe," 826.

99.   Jirušek and Kuchyňkova, "The Conduct of Gazprom in Central and Eastern Europe," 828.

100.   James Kanter, "Lithuania Offers Example of How to Break Russia's Grip on Energy," *New York Times*, October 27, 2014, https://www.nytimes.com/2014/10/28/business/energy-envi ronment/lithuania-offers-example-of-how-to-break-russias-grip-on-energy.html.

101.   Conley et al., *The Kremlin Playbook*, 8.

102.   Una Bergmane, "The Three Little Oligarchs: Latvia's Corruption Scandal," *Foreign Policy Research Institute*, November 22, 2017, https://www.fpri.org/article/2017/11/three-little-oligarchs- latvias-corruption-scandal.

103.   Bergmane, "The Three Little Oligarchs."

104.   Transparency International, https://www.transparency.org/en/countries/latvia; "Latvia Maintains Position in Corruption Perceptions Index," Public Broadcasting of Latvia, January 29, 2019, https://eng.lsm.lv/article/society/crime/latvia-maintains-position-in-corruption-perceptions -index.a307638.

105.   Conley et al., *The Kremlin Playbook*, 29.

106.   Robyn Dixon and David L. Stern, "How Ukraine's Zelensky Lost the Anti-Corruption Movement," *Washington Post*, March 17, 2020, https://www.washingtonpost.com/world/europe/ ukraine-corruption-zelensky-ryaboshapka-venediktova-trump-biden/2020/03/17/7dcab542-6636 -11ea-912d-d98032ec8e25_story.html.

107.   "Hungary Is Listed as the Second Most Corrupt Country in the EU," *Daily News Hungary*, January 24, 2020, https://dailynewshungary.com/hungary-is-the-second-most-corrupt-c ountry-in-the-eu.

108.   Conley et al., *The Kremlin Playbook*, 46.

109.   Conley et al., *The Kremlin Playbook*, 59.

110.   UN News, "UN Officials Recall 'Horror' of Srebrenica as Security Council Fails to Adopt Measure Condemning Massacre," July 8, 2015, https://news.un.org/en/story/2015/07/503712-un -officials-recall-horror-srebrenica-security-council-fails-adopt-measure.

111.   Aleksandar Vasovic, "Serbia Ready to Sacrifice EU Membership over Kosovo Deal," Reuters, June 18, 2020, https://www.reuters.com/article/us-serbia-russia-kosovo/serbia-ready-to -sacrifice-eu-membership-over-kosovo-deal-idUSKBN23P2G0.

112.   "Serbia, Kosovo Agree to Normalize Economic Ties in Pact Signed at White House," *DW*, April 9, 2020, https://www.dw.com/en/serbia-kosovo-agree-to-normalize-economic-ties-in -pact-signed-at-white-house/a-54822694.

113.   Helmus et al., "Russian Social Media Influence," 15–16.

114.   M. Crandall, "Soft Security Threats and Small States: The Case of Estonia," *Defense Studies* 14, no. 1 (2014): 30–55.

115.   Giles, "Russia's 'New' Tools for Confronting the West," 37.

116.   Helmus et al., "Russian Social Media Influence," 15, citing Peter Pomerantsev and Michael Weiss, *The Menace of Unreality: How the Kremlin Weaponizes Information, Culture and Money; A Special Report Presented by the Interpreter, a Project of the Institute of Modern Russia* (New York: Institute of Modern Russia, 2014), https://imrussia.org/media/pdf/Research/Michael_We iss_and_Peter_Pomerantsev__The_Menace_of_Unreality.pdf.

117.   Snegovaya, "Putin's Information Warfare in Ukraine," 13–14.

118.   Helmus et al., "Russian Social Media Influence," 16, citing Lana Samokhvalova, "The Russian Organizers of a 'Third Maidan' in Ukraine," *Euromaidan Press*, February 14, 2016, http:// euromaidanpress.com/2016/02/14/the-russian-organizers-of-a-third-maidan-in-ukraine/#arvlbdata.

119.   Giles, "Russia's 'New' Tools for Confronting the West," 35.

120.   Sherr, *Hard Diplomacy and Soft Coercion*, 58.

121.   Statistics Estonia, "Population by Ethnic Nationality," https://www.stat.ee/34278; Statistics Latvia, "Characteristics of Usually Resident Population in 2018," https://www.csb.gov.lv

/en/statistics/statistics-by-theme/population/number-and-change/search-in-theme/2402-number
-population-latvia-2017.

122.   Helmus et al., "Russian Social Media Influence," 66; Ministry of Culture, "Monitoring Integration in the Estonian Society (2017): Media Use and Information Fields," https://www .kul.ee/en/integration-monitoring-estonian-society-2017; Latvijas Fakti, "Media Literacy of the Inhabitants of Latvia: A Quantitative Study," June 2017, https://www.km.gov.lv/uploads/ckedi tor/files/mediju_politika/petijumi/eng/Main%20conclusions_research_Media%20Literacy%20of %20the%20Inhabitants%20of%20Latvia_2017_ENG.pdf.

123.   For example, see Ministry of Foreign Affairs of the Federation of Russia, "Regarding the Situation with the Glorification of Nazism and the Spread of Neo-Nazism and Other Practices That Contribute to Fueling Contemporary Forms of Racism, Racial Discrimination, Xenophobia and Related Intolerance," May 6, 2019, https://www.mid.ru/en/web/guest/general_assembly/-/ asset_publisher/lrzZMhfoyRUj/content/id/3193903.

124.   Nils Muižnieks, ed., *The Geopolitics of History in Latvian-Russian Relations* (Riga: University of Latvia Academic Press, 2011); Piret Ehin and Eiki Berg, "Incompatible Identities?," in *Identity and Foreign Policy: Baltic-Russian Relations and European Integration*, ed. Eiki Berg and Piret Ehin, 1–14 (Farnham: Ashgate, 2009).

125.   For discussion of the events surrounding the Bronze Soldier crisis, see Berg and Ehin, *Identity and Foreign Policy.*

126.   "Baltic States Protest Russia's Historical Revisionism on Molotov-Ribbentrop Pact," Radio Free Europe/Radio Liberty, June 19, 2020, https://www.rferl.org/a/baltic-states-protest-russ ia-historical-revisionism-on-molotov-ribbentrop-pact/30679562.html.

127.   Anne Applebaum, "Putin's Big Lie," *Atlantic*, January 5, 2020, https://www.theatlan tic.com/ideas/archive/2020/01/putin-blames-poland-world-war-ii/604426/?gclid=CjwKCAjwx9 _4BRAHEiwApAt0zq8vTYHVpSKnXEtd6uNNwI85ygNbr9mbNHPBafIaLodHYb-Rp7payB oCWyMQAvD_BwE.

128.   Bērziņa, *The Possibility of Societal Destabilization in Latvia*, 15–20; Andis Kudors, "Russian World—Russia's Soft Power Approach to Compatriots Policy," *Russian Analytical Digest* 81, no. 10 (2010): 4; Ministry of Culture, "Estonian Integration Monitoring 2011: A Summary" (Tallinn: Ministry of Culture, 2011), 33, http://www.kul.ee/webeditor/files/integratsioon/Integratsiooni _monitooring_2011_ENG_lyhiversioon.pdf; Pelnēns, *The Humanitarian Dimension*, 182; Inga Springe, Sallija Benfelde, and Miks Salu, "The Unknown Oligarch," *Re:Baltica The Baltic Center for Investigative Journalism*, April 11, 2012, www.rebaltica.lv/en/investigations/money_from_russ ia/a/686/the_unknown_oligarch.html.

129.   Julian E. Barnes and David E. Sanger, "Russian Intelligence Agencies Push Disinformation on the Pandemic," *New York Times*, July 28, 2020, https://www.nytimes.com/2020/07/28/us/po litics/russia-disinformation-coronavirus.html.

130.   Ivana Smoleňová, "The Pro-Russia Disinformation Campaign in the Czech Republic and Slovakia," special edition, *Per Concordiam: Journal of European Security and Defense Issues*, 2016, 26, file:///C:/Users/schulzej/AppData/Local/Temp/pc_v7_specialedition_en.pdf.

131.   Popescu and Secrieru, *Hacks, Leaks and Disruptions*, 88–89.

132.   "Russia Wants to Divide Romanian Society," *Romania Monitor: Warsaw Institute*, December 27, 2019, https://warsawinstitute.org/russia-wants-divide-romanian-society; Kremlinwatch, "Romania."

133.   Smoleňová, "The Pro-Russia Disinformation Campaign," 26–27.

134.   Piotr Buras and Adam Belcer, "An Unpredictable Russia: The Impact on Poland," European Council on Foreign Relations, July 15, 2016, https://www.ecfr.eu/article/commentary_a n_unpredictable_russia_the_impact_on_poland.

135. Conley et al., *The Kremlin Playbook*, 6; Kudors, "Russian Soft Power and Non-Military Influence," 89.

136. Anna Bulakh, Julian Tupay, Karel Kaas, Emmet Tuohy, Kristiina Visnapuu, and Juhan Kivirähk, "Russian Soft Power and Non-Military Influence: The View from Estonia," in Winnerstig, *Tools of Destabilization*, 51; Kudors, "Russian Soft Power," 89; Nils Muižnieks, ed., *Latvian-Russian Relations: Domestic and International Dimensions* (Riga: University of Latvia, 2006), 22, 32; Salu and Springe, "Who Is the Puppet and Who Is the Master?"; "Spreading Democracy in Latvia, Kremlin Style," March 19, 2012, *Re: Baltica*, The Center for Investigative Journalism, http://www.rebaltica.lv/en/investigations/money_from_russia/a/606/spreading_demo cracy_in_latvia_kremlin_style.html; "Money from Russia: Kremlin's Millions," August 27, 2015, *Re: Baltica*, The Center for Investigative Journalism, https://en.rebaltica.lv/2015/08/kremlins -millions.

137. Open Society Institute, "Monitoring the EU Accession Process: Minority Protection in Latvia," 327, citing Baltic Institute of Social Sciences, Canadian International Development Agency, OSCE, Soros Foundation Latvia, *Analysis of the Implementation of Bilingual Education*, 20.

138. "7000 Opponents of Latvia's Minority Education Reform Gather in Mass Protest," Baltic News Service, May 23, 2003.

139. Muižnieks, *Latvian-Russian Relations*, 127.

140. "Money from Russia: Kremlin's Millions." The Latvian Center for Human Rights, a major recipient of funds, was founded by Tatjana Zdanoka, who is a leading politician for the Latvian Russian Union, a pro-Russian political party in Latvia.

141. "Moscow's Spin Machine in Estonia," *Baltic Times*, March 21, 2012, http://www.balt ictimes.com/news/articles/30854.

142. "Spreading Democracy in Latvia, Kremlin Style." One of the beneficiaries was Aleksander Gaponenko, one of the initiators of the referendum.

143. Kudors, "Russian Soft Power and Non-Military Influence, 91.

144. Daunis Auers, *Comparative Politics and Government of the Baltic States: Estonia, Latvia, and Lithuania in the 21st Century* (New York: Palgrave Macmillan, 2015), 93.

145. Conley et al., *The Kremlin Playbook*, 2.

146. Conley et al., *The Kremlin Playbook*, 43–44, 55, 61. The Bulgarian Socialist Party (BSP) has called for lifting sanctions against Russia, and the Movement for Rights and Freedom (MRF) and Alternative for Bulgaria (AVB) have supported Russia in the energy sector. The ultranationalist "The People's Party–Our Slovakia" has supported Russian foreign policy positions and is critical of Slovakia's membership in the EU and NATO. The Serbian Socialist Party defends Serbia's close relationship with Russia.

147. Conley et al., *The Kremlin Playbook*, 2.

148. Conley et al., *The Kremlin Playbook*, 6.

149. "The Fundamental Law of Hungary," 2011, Act CLI, http://www.kormany.hu/download /e/02/00000/The%20New%20Fundamental%20Law%20of%20Hungary.pdf.

150. "The Putinization of Hungary," *Washington Post*, December 26, 2010, http://www.wash ingtonpost.com/wp-dyn/content/article/2010/12/26/AR2010122601791.html.

151. Conley et al., *The Kremlin Playbook*, 39.

152. Conley et al., *The Kremlin Playbook*, 7, 55.

153. Buras and Belcer, "An Unpredictable Russia."

154. Anne Applebaum, "Putin's Big Lie."

155. Ministry of Culture, "Monitoring Integration in the Estonian Society"; Latvijas Fakti, "Media Literacy of the Inhabitants of Latvia."

156. Theodore P. Gerber and Jane Zavisca, "Does Russian Propaganda Work?," *Washington Quarterly* 39, no. 2 (Summer 2016): 79–98.

157.   Bērziņa, *The Possibility of Societal Destabilization in Latvia*, 15–20; Ministry of Culture, "Estonian Integration Monitoring," 2011, 2015, 2017; Muižnieks, *Manufacturing Enemy Images?*; Pelnēns, *The Humanitarian Dimension*.

158.   Robert Szwed, *Framing of the Ukraine-Russia Conflict in Online and Social Media* (Riga, Latvia: North Atlantic Treaty Organization Strategic Communications Centre of Excellence, May 2016), http://www.stratcomcoe.org/framing-ukraine-russia-conflict-online-and-social-media.

159.   Conley et al., *The Kremlin Playbook*, 63. See also "Western Balkans between East and West: Public Opinion Research in Bosnia-Herzegovina, Macedonia, Montenegro, Serbia," National Democratic Institute, November 2018, https://www.ndi.org/sites/default/files/Downl oad%20Report_0.pdf; Popescu and Secrieru, *Hacks, Leaks and Disruptions*, 89–90.

160.   "The Security Policies of the Republic of Estonia," *Annual Review*, 2007, 13, https://ww w.kapo.ee/en/content/annual-reviews.html.

161.   "Estonia Moves Soviet War Monument, Sparking Russian Fury," Agence France-Presse, April 27, 2007, quoting parliamentarian Krstiina Ojuland and President Toomas Ilves; "Claims of Russia's Part in Clashes in Estonia Unfounded—MP," *RIA Novosti*, April 29, 2007, quoting Foreign Minister Urmas Paet.

162.   "Russian MPs in Tallinn Criticize Human Rights Violation," *BBC Monitoring Former Soviet Union—Political*, May 1, 2007, source Channel One, Moscow; "Russian Delegation Alleges Torture in Estonia Row," Agence France-Presse, May 1, 2007.

163.   Martin Ehala, "The Bronze Soldier: Identity Threat and Maintenance in Estonian Society," *Journal of Baltic Studies* 40, no. 1 (2009): 139–58; Külliki Korts, "Interethnic Attitudes and Contacts between Ethnic Groups in Estonia," *Journal of Baltic Studies* 40, no. 1 (2009): 121–37; Jennie L. Schulze, "Shattering the Glass Ceiling: Russian Perspectives on Integration in Estonia," in *Nation-Building in the Context of Post-Communist Transformation and Globalization*, ed. Raivo Vetik, 283–318 (Frankfurt: Peter Lang, 2012).

164.   Priit Järve and Vadim Poleshchuk, "Country Report: Estonia," *EUDO Citizenship Observatory, Robert Schuman Centre for Advanced Studies*, 2013, 14, http://eudo-citizenship.eu/doc s/CountryReports/Estonia.pdf.

165.   For discussion, see Pelnēns, *The Humanitarian Dimension*, 50–62.

166.   Dovile Budryte, *Taming Nationalism? Political Community Building in the Post-Soviet Baltic States* (Aldershot: Ashgate, 2005); Muižnieks, *Latvian-Russian Relations*; Jennie L. Schulze, "Estonia Caught between East and West: EU Conditionality, Russia's Activism, and Minority Integration," *Nationalities Papers* 38, no. 3 (2010): 361–92.

167.   Schulze, *Strategic Frames*; Jennie L. Schulze "Reframing Russian Soft Power in Estonia and Latvia: The Cases of Naturalization and Education Reforms," *Eurasian Geography and Economics*, published online December 19, 2020, https://www.tandfonline.com/doi/abs/10.1080/15387216 .2020.1855997.

168.   Snegovaya, "Putin's Information Warfare in Ukraine," 19.

169.   Bērziņa, *The Possibility for Societal Destabilization in Latvia*; Kristina Kallas, "Claiming the Diaspora: Russia's Compatriot Policy and Its Reception by Estonian-Russian Population," *Journal on Ethnopolitics and Minority Issues in Europe* 15, no. 3 (2016): 1–25; Muižnieks, *Manufacturing Enemy Images?*; Pelnēns, *The Humanitarian Dimension*,

170.   Kristian Nielson and Heiko Paabo, "How Russian Soft Power Fails in Estonia: Or, Why the Russophone Minorities Remain Quiescent," *Journal of Baltic Studies* 1, no. 2 (2015): 125–57.

171.   "Public Opinion on National Defense: Latvian Resident Survey," SKDS, November 2015. Twenty-eight percent of Russian-speakers in Latvia were willing to participate in defense. Comparatively, 42 percent of Russian-speakers in Estonia indicated their willingness. Juhan Kivirähk, "Public Opinion and National Defense," Estonian Ministry of Defense, October 2016.

172. Conley et al., *The Kremlin Playbook*, 51.

173. Rachel Nielson, "Estonia Launches New Channel to Win Over Its Russians," *Moscow Times*, September 27, 2015, https://www.themoscowtimes.com/2015/09/27/estonia-launches-n ew-channel-to-win-over-its-russians-a49854.

174. Erkki Bohavsky, "First Steps toward the Estonian Media Space," *International Center for Defense and Security*, April 2, 2020, https://icds.ee/first-steps-towards-the-estonian-media-space; "Interest in ETV+ Russian Programs Has Increased Significantly," *ERR*, April 3, 2020, https://ne ws.err.ee/1072568/interest-in-etv-programs-in-russian-has-increased-significantly.

175. Tom Rostoks and Nora Vanaga, "Latvia's Security and Defense Post-2014," *Journal on Baltic Security* 2, no. 2 (2016): 71–108, 88.

176. Matthew Thomas, "Defeating Disinformation Threats," Foreign Policy Research Institute, February 19, 2020, https://www.fpri.org/article/2020/02/defeating-disinformation-threats.

177. Michael Peel, "Fake News: How Lithuania's Elves Take on Russia's Trolls," *Financial Times*, February 4, 2019.

178. Helmus et al., "Russian Social Media Influence," 70.

179. Helmus et al., "Russian Social Media Influence," 87.

180. Felgenhauer, "Russia Escalates Its Proxy War in Eastern Ukraine."

181. Helmus et al., "Russian Social Media Influence," 75.

182. Giles, "Russia's 'New' Tools for Confronting the West," 51; Helmus et al., "Russian Social Media Influence," 79.

183. Helmus et al., "Russian Social Media Influence," 76.

184. Helmus et al., "Russian Social Media Influence," 91.

185. Helmus et al., "Russian Social Media Influence," 77.

186. Snegovaya, "Putin's Information Warfare in Ukraine."

187. Huseynov, "Soft Power Geopolitics"; Kiseleva, "Russia's Soft Power Discourse"; Sherr, *Hard Diplomacy and Soft Coercion*; Mitchell A. Orenstein, "Geopolitics of a Divided Europe," *East European Politics and Societies* 29, no. 2 (May 2015): 533.

188. Ajir and Vailliant, "Russian Information Warfare," 71.

189. Nielson and Paabo, "How Russian Soft Power Fails in Estonia," 128; Sergunin and Karabeshkin, "Understanding Russia's Soft Power Strategy," 357.

190. Simons, "Perceptions of Russia's Soft Power," 11.

191. Kasekamp, "Why Narva Is Not Next."

192. Giles, "Russia's 'New' Tools for Confronting the West," 41; Snegovaya, "Putin's Information Warfare in Ukraine."

193. Elena Servattaz, "Putin's Far-Right Friends in Europe," Institute of Modern Russia, January 16, 2014, https://imrussia.org/en/russia-and-the-world/645-putins-far-right-friends-i n-europe; Andrew Weiss, "With Friends Like These: The Kremlin's Far-Right and Populist Connections in Italy and Austria," Carnegie Endowment for International Peace, February 27, 2020, https://carnegieendowment.org/2020/02/27/with-friends-like-these-kremlin-s-far-right-and -populist-connections-in-italy-and-austria-pub-81100; see also Laruelle, *Eurasianism and the European Far Right*.

194. Weisburd et al., "Trolling for Trump."

195. Office of the Director of National Intelligence, National Intelligence Council, *Assessing Russian Activities and Intentions in Recent US Elections*, Intelligence Community Assessment 2017-01D, January 6, 2017, https://www.dni.gov/files/documents/ICA_2017_01.pdf.

196. Weisburd et al., "Trolling for Trump."

197. Helmus et al., "Russian Social Media Influence," 22.

198. Helmus et al., "Russian Social Media Influence," 21.

199. Barnes and Sanger, "Russian Intelligence Agencies Push Disinformation."

200. Giles, "Russia's 'New' Tools for Confronting the West," 33.

201. Popescu and Secrieru, *Hacks, Leaks and Disruptions*, 7.

202. Masters, "Ukraine: Conflict."

203. Weiss, "With Friends Like These."

204. Giles, "Russia's 'New' Tools for Confronting the West," 43.

205. For discussion, see Pelnēns, *The Humanitarian Dimension*, 50–62, 140–53.

206. Popescu and Secrieru, *Hacks, Leaks and Disruptions*, 118.

207. Giles, "Russia's 'New' Tools for Confronting the West," 3.

208. Giles, "Russia's 'New' Tools for Confronting the West," 4.

209. Giles, "Russia's 'New' Tools for Confronting the West," 65.

210. Giles, "Russia's 'New' Tools for Confronting the West," 38.

211. Martin Jirušek and Petra Kuchyňkova, "The Conduct of Gazprom in Central and Eastern Europe," 835.

Part III

CASE STUDIES

Map 11.0. Poland

CHAPTER 11

Poland

Jane L. Curry

Poland was the first and one of the most successful transitions from communism to Western-style democracy in 1989 when the Central and East European transitions began. After a difficult beginning, its economy not only transformed very quickly into a capitalist economy, but, even during the European economic crisis beginning in 2008, it had one of the highest growth rates in the European Union (EU). It was also the leading Central and East European state in the EU and a strong advocate for aid to and inclusion of countries to its east. Poland's politics changed with the 2015 presidential and parliamentary elections when Law and Justice, a populist right-wing party, won enough seats to control the presidency and both houses of the parliament. In the ensuing years, its leaders have consolidated power and transformed Poland into an illiberal democracy.

They began by taking control of the courts, media, and educational system and imposing nationalist and populist policies as well as policies on issues, such as barring abortions, long demanded by the Catholic Church. At the same time, they increased (or promised to) social welfare benefits for their core supporters, most of whom felt they had lost out in the economic transformation and then not been heard by the prior Civic Platform (PO) government. As a result, the opposition is increasingly powerless to do anything more than demonstrate against government policies in the streets.

The story of how Poland became both the leader in the democratization process in Central and Eastern Europe and one of the first states to have its democratic institutions dramatically weakened by populism began long before 2015. Its history set the stage both for the relative liberalism of Poland's communism and its establishment of an "illiberal democracy" in which the institutions of democracy function but the power of any opposition in the system is severely limited at best.

Political History

This was not the first dramatic change in Poland's history. In his definitive history of Poland, Norman Davies makes the point that Poland has been the country most conquered and fought over in Europe and has undergone successive experiments and disasters.[1] It went from being the largest country in Europe, sitting as it did in the "heart of

Europe,"[2] to, by 1795, not existing. Then it was split between the Russian, German, and Austrian Empires. Only in the smaller Austrian section could Polish be used anywhere in public outside of the churches. So Catholicism became not only the religion of most Poles but also a central element of Polish national identity, the importance of which was heightened by Poles' battles to reclaim what they saw as their country and the presence of other nationalities within what became Poland after the World War I settlements.

Those boundaries drawn in the Versailles Peace Treaty at the end of World War I made Poland a multiethnic state: fully one-third of the population was not ethnically Polish. This new state was burdened by having to establish national structures, deal with a diverse population of peoples with long histories of conflict, and build an economy and infrastructure out of the pieces of the three empires. Democracy and capitalism enjoyed a brief success in the initial years of independence only to be virtually washed away by the Great Depression. From their history, Poles learned to maintain their culture and national identity, defined as it was by "being Catholic" and opposing outside oppression. At the same time, the divisions between the empires remained embedded not only in where the trains ran but also in the differences that still exist in the regional economies and political leanings of the three regions.

Poland was devastated during World War II. In September 1939, the Molotov-Ribbentrop Pact divided it between the Germans and the Soviets. Then, in 1941, the Germans turned on the Soviets, took over all of Poland, and used it as a base to attack the Soviet Union and annihilate Jews as well as a large number of ethnic Poles. Large numbers of Poles fought in a national underground (the Home Army) against the Russians and Germans, while a far smaller group tied to communism fought against the Germans and the nationalist underground. Ultimately, one-third of Poland's population perished (including almost all of its Jewish population); its capital, Warsaw, was razed to the ground; and much of its industrial base and many other cities were destroyed.

Communism

Soviet troops brought a communist regime in as a "baggage-train government" when they marched across Poland and pushed the Germans out in 1945. That new leadership was an uneasy alliance between Polish communist officials who had spent the war in the Soviet Union and communists who had fought in the small communist underground. These new rulers had to rebuild most of the country and, at the same time, impose unwelcome communist rule.

In the process, many of the factories and much of the infrastructure that had survived were taken back to the Soviet Union to rebuild its own infrastructure. To add to the complications of rebuilding, in postwar agreements the boundaries of Poland were moved far to the west into what had been Germany, and most of Poland's eastern territories were annexed by the Soviet Union. With this shift came a massive population transfer: most Germans in what became western Poland were forced out or went willingly to Germany. There were battles between Poles and Ukrainians. Many Poles who lived in what had been eastern Poland were moved or were forced west to settle the areas the Germans had vacated.

The Communist Party (the Polish United Workers' Party, PUWP) took control of the government and established state ownership of much of Poland's economy. With this came Stalinist terror, but it was more restrained than elsewhere in Central Europe because the top leaders knew the Communist Party was seen as "Russian" and unwelcome in Poland while the Catholic Church was very closely identified with "being Polish." So, the Catholic Church was allowed to function openly and run religious and secular organizations throughout the communist period. At the same time, there were many who gained from the ongoing reconstruction and industrialization when large numbers of new industries were built and young peasants moved to cities to work in factories. In the process, a whole new working class was established and educated.

With the deaths of Joseph Stalin in 1953 and Poland's Stalinist leader, Bolesław Bierut, in March 1956, fear and control decreased. In the summer of 1956, Polish workers demonstrated in the Western city of Poznań, demanding "bread and freedom" and calling out, "The press lies." Polish troops fired on the demonstrators, killing almost a hundred. Open intellectual protests spread throughout Poland. Many PUWP members demanded reforms in the party itself. The party leadership tried to end this "Polish October" by bringing back Władysław Gomułka, the party leader jailed in the Stalinist period for his independence. When he was returned to power, he started "a Polish road to socialism," allowing private farming, small private enterprises, more freedoms for the Catholic Church, and greater freedom for public discussion. From then on, Poland remained on its own "freer" road.

Revolts against communism's failings continued with student and intellectual demonstrations in 1968 and workers' strikes, and demonstrations triggered by price increases and economic failures erupted in 1970, 1976, and 1980. After each of the workers' demonstrations, the communist authorities made concessions to buy support and then failed to meet their promises. With each uprising, though, the opposition grew and became more organized. After the 1976 workers' demonstrations, the Workers' Defense Committee (KOR) formed to aid arrested workers and their families. It produced underground publications to inform people about their rights and human rights violations in Poland, as well as to encourage independent thinking. By the late 1970s and early 1980s, this opposition had flowered into a massive underground press empire, a number of human rights organizations, and a whole alternate cultural milieu, including a "Flying University" offering courses and instructors not permitted in the communist educational system.[3] It was from this opposition, in combination with the shipyard workers who had demonstrated and lost in 1970, that Solidarity would emerge a decade later.[4] After 1989, when the communists inadvertently negotiated themselves out of power, these two organizations, KOR and Solidarity, produced many of the elites of democratic Poland.

When Edward Gierek took over as head of the party after the December 1970 Gdańsk shipyard strikes, he promised Poles that their lives would improve. To jumpstart the economy and provide for a higher living standard, Poland borrowed from the West to build new factories with Western equipment and began importing Western consumer goods. The loans were supposed to pay for themselves with earnings from the export of products to the West. However, the plan did not work: much of the money was wasted, Polish goods did not sell, and Poland had to borrow more and more just to pay the interest on its debts. By the beginning of the 1980s, the shelves of Polish stores were bare, and Poland was in the midst of a debt crisis with $8.1 billion—far more than its ready cash and assets would cover—of its over $20 billion debt to the West due in 1980.

The government was so desperate in 1980 to placate Western creditors without touching off demonstrations that it imposed price increases on food staples (as required by Western creditors), region by region, with instructions to local leaders to negotiate pay increases if there were strikes or demonstrations. By August, rolling price increases on food had been imposed across the country, last of all in the seacoast towns where the 1970 riots had brought down the Gomułka regime.

In response to the price increases, workers in the Gdańsk shipyards went on strike and simply refused to negotiate pay increases. Under the leadership of dissident worker Lech Wałęsa, workers occupied the shipyards in Gdańsk and other Baltic towns, demanding not just the economic and social welfare benefits communism had promised but also the rights to have an independent trade union and to strike, as well as more media freedom so they would know what was really going on. Intellectuals joined them. Workers from other places in Poland sent messages of support, and some joined in support strikes. In August, the Polish government conceded to the workers' demands by negotiating and signing the Gdańsk Agreement. Solidarity was the first independent trade union in the communist world and became a national movement for economic and political change in Poland.

Poles were further emboldened to stand up to their leaders by the election of Karol Wojtyła, the former archbishop of Kraków, as pope in 1978 and his triumphant return to Poland as a conquering hero in June 1979. His trip was organized and run by church volunteers rather than the government, even as he was feted by communist leaders and the population alike. This gave Poles a sense that they did not need the government to organize.

The rise of Solidarity was dramatic. By the end of its first year, more than one-third of the population had joined the movement. A farmers' Solidarity and a students' union had also formed and forced the government to recognize them. Workplaces organized. Many party members joined Solidarity and sought to bring its openness into the PUWP. Independent presses and discussions appeared everywhere. Solidarity elections and a national congress were held. Solidarity, at its height in 1981, had over ten million members, easily the majority of Poland's workforce.

Popular demands on the government increased. Poland's economy did not work well enough to feed its population, much less to provide the gains promised in the Gdańsk Agreement. As the economic situation worsened, strikes and demonstrations became the order of the day. Food had to be rationed. Individuals used their connections to get the meat and other necessities they could not get with their rations.

The strikes and hardships of "real socialism" in Poland created friendship groups that helped people survive and informal professional groups that helped counter the controls in the communist system. These groups, as well as the high level of social resistance, also allowed alternative elites to establish themselves, provided the personal ties between groups that would help in the transition, and gave people organizing experience that facilitated what would be Poland's negotiated transition.

The government made more and more political concessions, even as the Soviet Union and other Soviet bloc states pressed for a crackdown. For Polish leaders and their allies, the potential for chaos and threat of contagion were all too real. Party leader and head of the Polish military, Wojciech Jaruzelski, and those around him were convinced by the end of 1981 that the Soviet Union would invade if popular actions and government concessions went any further.

On December 13, 1981, Jaruzelski declared martial law, and the freedoms Solidarity had enjoyed for fifteen months ended with a Polish military "takeover." Solidarity and other independent groups were declared illegal and shut down. Thousands of Solidarity and intellectual activists, as well as some top PUWP leaders accused of corruption and mismanagement during the Gierek era, were interned. Polish soldiers and police were on the streets. Military officers supervised factories, schools, media, and government offices for months. Media freedom and free discussion ended. Individual parishes and Catholic organizations provided havens for discussion and distributed donations of food and clothing that were provided by other Poles and, ultimately, by Western governments and organizations. Most Poles were too shocked to act. The United States and some other Western countries imposed sanctions on Poland. Martial law continued formally for a year and a half, but the last internees were released only after three years. Then, until the mid-1980s, an active underground movement functioned, and dissident publications and activities proliferated. At the same time, the difficulties of daily life amid constant shortages meant that most individuals focused on feeding and supplying their families rather than on protesting.

The weaknesses of the old communist system that made it more open than other communist systems also complicated the transition. Poland was, by 1989, over $40 billion in debt to the West[5] and still enmeshed in the Soviet bloc economic system. This meant that its options for economic reform were limited by the other Soviet bloc states and the need to satisfy its Western creditors. Its opposition, which had been the strongest in the communist world well before Solidarity's heyday in 1980–1981, had ideological divisions. From the 1970s on, most Poles had real knowledge of and very high expectations for democracy and capitalism from having been guest workers in the West, having ties to family members there, and having an elite that tried to buy them off with its openness to the West. The image of democracy and capitalism they took away from this was of prosperity, not inequality. In Poland, they learned to work around or oppose the system. They did not learn, however, how to function as citizens in a normal democratic system. In the end, the communist-era reforms left them with high hopes for democracy, little practice working within a democracy, and an economy of foreign debt, inflation, and failed factories.

Early Postcommunism

By the late 1980s, Poland's economy had failed to rebound and provide what Poles thought they had been promised. The communists' efforts to win support or even draw in some workers and intellectuals had largely failed. Much of Poland's population was alienated from both Solidarity and the communist government. Random strikes with no specific goals worried both Solidarity leaders and the communists. To deal with this alienation, communist leaders reached out to the opposition. They also tried to get the economy moving by decreasing controls on prices and forcing factories to be self-supporting. When none of these maneuvers worked, the government, with the support of the Catholic Church, sought Solidarity leaders' agreement to begin discussions on systemic change. Church leaders helped bring the two sides together and facilitated Roundtable Talks between them.

No one thought communism would end. For the rulers, the Roundtables were a way to hold on to power by getting Solidarity to share responsibility for Poland's problems and move toward a new, more open system of government over the next four years. For Solidarity's representatives, the most important goal was to force the relegalization of Solidarity as a trade union (something the government conceded on the first day of the public Roundtables). The population hoped that the Roundtable agreements would protect the economic guarantees of a social welfare state and that the freedoms of the Solidarity era would be returned. The Catholic Church wanted the Roundtables to stabilize Poland and ensure its interests and position.

After five months of private discussions and nine weeks of public discussions, the two sides agreed to defer decisions on economic reforms and move ahead with political reforms and partially free parliamentary elections designed to reassure the Soviet Union by ensuring that the Communist Party and its former allies held a majority of seats in the main house (Sejm) and that Solidarity and other nonparty people were just "junior partners." So, 65 percent of the seats in the Sejm were designated for candidates who had been in one of these communist-era parties, and 35 percent of the seats were designated for candidates who had not belonged to a party in the communist era.

The Polish political system was redesigned to have a second legislative chamber (the Senate) and a president elected by the two houses together. Finally, forty seats in the Sejm were reserved, in this first election, for the so-called National List of the regime's notables and reformers. The new Senate, as a trade-off, was elected without any constraints. A majoritarian election system, in which those who did not get a majority had to run in a second election, was used for both "party" and nonparty seats in the Sejm and new Senate as well as for those on the National List.

The results of the elections on June 4, 1989, defied all expectations. Candidates Solidarity identified as theirs won every nonparty seat in the Sejm and all but one in the Senate. Only a few of the Communist Party candidates got the requisite majority to win in the first round. Most of the "party" seats had to be decided in the second round. All but the two men whose names were at the bottom of the National List lost in the first round. Few who lost in the first round ran again in the second.[6] The presidency (elected by the Sejm and Senate) went, as had been tacitly promised, to Jaruzelski, the man who had both called for the hated martial law and championed the Roundtable Talks. His victory was the result of a political compromise Solidarity leaders engineered to placate Communist Party and military hard-liners in Poland and hard-line leaders elsewhere in the Soviet bloc.

The 65 percent majority established for the Communist Party and its old allies did not hold. The smaller parties, long Trojan horses to draw peasants and small entrepreneurs into the system, broke with the PUWP and joined Solidarity, reversing the

Photo 11.1.   A Solidarity poster, based on a Gary Cooper poster for the film *High Noon*, created for the June 1989 elections. (Grand Warszawski, Shutterstock)

percentages for the "establishment" and the "opposition" in the Sejm. People elected as PUWP members, as a result, held 35 percent of the seats, and 65 percent of the seats were held by Solidarity and its new allies from the old system.

The Soviet leaders accepted the results. But no one knew what would happen next. The platform of Solidarity's deputies had been against communism, but they had no actual plans for what would change and how. Communist-era deputies had expected to share power with nonparty members. They had no plan for what to do when they were in opposition.

A new, noncommunist government was formed in September 1989. Tadeusz Mazowiecki (longtime Catholic editor, dissident, and adviser to Solidarity leader Lech Wałęsa) was named prime minister on Wałęsa's recommendation. He formed a unity government of dissident intellectuals, experts in economics, specialists from the parties formerly aligned with the Communist Party (PUWP), and three communist ministers to manage the most important ministries for Soviet interests: the Ministry of Interior (police and spy services), the Ministry of Defense, and the Ministry of Foreign Trade. Western-educated economist Leszek Balcerowicz was named minister of finance and deputy prime minister to manage economic reform.

What had been the Solidarity monolith against the communists dissolved into many factions. Faced with minority party membership after forty years of party rule, PUWP deputies wanted as little to do with the rejected system as possible. By January 1990, PUWP had dissolved itself and passed its resources on to the new Social Democratic Party of the Polish Republic (SLDRP).

Solidarity and communist deputies all worked to cut and paste the election results and the Roundtable Accords into the communist constitution. They excised provisions like the "leading role of the party" and the promise of fealty to the Soviet Union. All national symbols dropped their communist elements. Then, under pressure from the United States and Western Europe, the Sejm passed bills instituting "shock therapy" economic reforms (the Balcerowicz Plan) for rapid privatization, foreign aid, and investment. This program—coupled with the inflation that began after the last communist government freed most food prices so that they skyrocketed with the reforms (while salaries remained stable)—triggered a drop in the purchasing power of the zloty by 40 percent at the end of the plan's first month (January 1990). It brought a rapid end to the popular euphoria over communism's end and Poland's "return to Europe."

Political Institutions

Until 2007, governance was based on the "Small Constitution" of 1992 that codified the additions and deletions made in 1990 to take "communism" out of the communist-era constitution and define the basic powers of new major institutions. It did not provide a framework to establish, coordinate, and balance what institutions could and could not do. So, until the final constitution was completed, legislators legislated powers for themselves, and whatever president or prime minister was in office simply claimed the right to act and, in the process, set a precedent. As a result, the final constitution in 1997 was a product of proposals from various political parties and also, particularly in the case of the powers of the presidency, of what the five presidents since 1990 had done and not done that had worked or angered people.

Wojciech Jaruzelski, as a remnant of the defeated regime, did only what he was asked to do by the Solidarity government and parliament. His successor, Lech Wałęsa, the former leader of Solidarity, took control by ignoring the restrictions on presidential powers. Two years into his rule, he faced a very divided parliament, public opposition to and disgust with his style of leadership, and even claims, among former supporters, that he had been a secret agent.

Aleksander Kwaśniewski, who was elected president in 1995 and again in 2000, took a very different position. Given the public attacks on the SLD (Democratic Left Alliance), which had been the SLDRP, the successor to the PUWP (the disbanded communist party), he focused on disproving stereotypes about communists. He was a by-the-book president, doing only what was constitutionally mandated. In his first term, he had an SLD and Peasant Party parliamentary majority, so legislation was passed and conflicts avoided. After the 1997 parliamentary election, he worked with the right-wing parliamentary coalition by avoiding direct conflict and presenting himself as a professional. He was able to get parliament's support for the new constitution, which he had played a key role in developing. In his presidency, he focused on international diplomacy and negotiating Poland's entrance into the North Atlantic Treaty Organization (NATO). In the process, he returned prestige and the faith of the public to the presidency.

As a result of these experiences, the 1997 constitution reined in the powers of the presidency and increased the powers of the prime minister and cabinet. The president got the right to step in and name a prime minister only if the Sejm was too divided to agree. The prime minister and his cabinet can be removed only by a vote of no confidence by the parliament. The prime minister was solely responsible for selecting his cabinet and presenting his choices to the Sejm for approval. The powers of legislation are concentrated in the Sejm. The Senate, on the other hand, is primarily a body to review and revise Sejm legislation and serve as a moderator in conflicts. In this system, the powers of the presidency are counterbalanced by those of the parliamentary bodies and the prime minister. The government also has the explicit responsibility of leading the policy-making process in domestic and foreign affairs, carrying out the laws passed by the parliament, putting forth regulations when authorized by the Sejm, and managing the state budget. Finally, the president and prime minister must cosign all laws.

A Constitutional Court was established to determine whether laws and international agreements are constitutional and also adjudicate disputes over whether the actions of individual institutions are constitutional. The fifteen justices are chosen by the Sejm for staggered nine-year terms so that no one political group can name all the justices. Lower-level courts' judges are to be selected and nominated by bodies of legal experts who judge their competence, and then be appointed by the Sejm. All this assumed that the three branches of government were not controlled by the same party and that the politicians in power respected the constitutional provisions.

Even after the 1997 constitution, elected leaders influenced the balance of power among these institutions. In 2001, SLD returned as the dominant party in parliament, balanced against a fragmented right wing. In practice, Poland moved back to a semi-presidential state, with Kwaśniewski appointing economist Marek Belka as prime minister and taking leadership in areas like foreign policy that were the constitutional purview of the presidency.

In 2005, Lech Kaczyński of the Law and Justice party was elected president. The parliamentary elections that followed resulted in his party being the largest in the Sejm. Because it did not have a majority, though, it formed a government with two small radical right-wing parties. Kaczyński named his identical twin brother, Jarosław, prime minister. The two brothers, as president and prime minister, expanded their powers by claiming that anyone who disagreed with them had been a communist or agent and should be purged. They also put into effect a review process of the old secret police files that made them public and allowed for the removal of individuals from public office based on the contents of their files. This made opposition to their government risky.

In 2007, Jarosław Kaczyński's coalition government fell apart, triggering parliamentary elections a month after the government dissolved as a result of popular disaffection with the right-wing coalition's attacks about who did what in the past. A movement spearheaded by young people to get out the vote brought the more policy-focused center-left Civic Platform to power.

The party's centrist leader, Donald Tusk, became prime minister. He worked to modernize the bureaucracy so that the government would be more responsive. He and his coalition moved Poland back to having closer relations with Germany. Tusk's positive and professional style of leadership, as well as Poland's economic health during the recession, made him a popular leader. But he faced constant attacks and vetoes of legislation by Lech Kaczyński, who essentially pushed against these shifts by using his presidential veto powers and publicly attacking his enemies as "communists."

When Lech Kaczyński began his campaign for a second term as president in 2010, public opinion polls showed that he was not popular enough to win. He escalated his rhetoric. In foreign policy, he battled with the prime minister, Donald Tusk, over who could speak for Poland. So, after Tusk represented Poland in the official Russian-Polish commemoration of the Katyn Massacre, the slaughter of Polish officers by Soviet soldiers at the start of World War II, Lech Kaczyński, as president, organized his own delegation of political leaders and families of the men slaughtered to the site in Russia. The plane carrying them crashed in Smolensk, Russia, killing all aboard and setting off a political battle, led by his twin brother as head of the Law and Justice party, with the Russian authorities over whether the accident was the result of pilot error, bad landing conditions, or a Russian attack. Jarosław Kaczyński also began a battle with Civic Platform over how to memorialize his brother that continues today with a demonstration in front of the Presidential Palace on the monthly anniversary of the crash.

In the special election in 2010 to replace his deceased brother as president, Jarosław Kaczyński, the Law and Justice candidate, lost to Civic Platform's candidate, Bronisław Komorowski. This again put both the parliament and the presidency in the hands of one party. Civic Platform remained popular and cohesive under Komorowski and Tusk. Poland continued to do well economically, although there were tax increases and demonstrations over the low incomes of professionals in health care and education.

The tide turned in 2015. Law and Justice won an early election to replace Tusk when he became the first Central and East European to be president of the European Council. Its victory over Civic Platform was triggered by revelations from a series of secret tapes of high officials from Civic Platform and the former communist SLD party talking about their foreign vacations, impatience with "Poles," and a growing disaffection among Poles outside the major cities. The votes for the moderate left Civic Platform were also splintered by the fragmentation of the old left and the appearance of new candidates, including an unknown rock musician who came in third in the first round of the presidential race in 2015 with a youthful protest vote. As a result, Komorowski lost the presidency in the second round to a relatively unknown candidate of Law and Justice, Andrzej Duda. In the parliamentary election that followed later that year, Law and Justice won a bare majority of Sejm seats.

In office and controlling both the presidency and the Sejm, Law and Justice has proved to be far from the centrist message on which it campaigned. Jarosław Kaczyński is the dominant figure in the party, even though he has no formal role other than being a deputy in the Sejm. In rapid succession, once it was in power, the party moved to put the Constitutional Court under its control by refusing to recognize the justices appointed earlier by Civic Platform and, when those justices did not step down, refusing to recognize and publish the court's decisions as is required for them to be legally binding. Then it passed legislation that effectively took control of state radio and television and put it under a new body Law and Justice developed and appointed in 2016. A year later, it moved to take control of the courts at all levels by putting them, along with the prosecutor's office, under the control of the minister of justice. These changes triggered a summer of demonstrations and then were partially blocked by a veto from the president against his own party's laws.

Photo 11.2. Protestors holding posters reading "constitution" rally in July 2017 in front of the Presidential Palace in Warsaw, Poland, after the ruling party, Law and Justice, passed legislation weakening the independence of the judiciary. (Grand Warszawski, Shutterstock)

Political Competition

After 1989, Poland not only had to develop a new political system, but it also had to develop political parties. The citizen's committees that formed in 1989 essentially had no platform other than being against the Communist Party, PUWP, and its traditional allies, the Polish Peasant Party and the Democratic Party, which represented the small-scale peasant farmers and small-scale private entrepreneurs. These parties had been allowed to function in Poland since 1956. Once the Communist Party was defeated in 1989, rather than establishing clear and stable policy options, parties and elections focused on individual battles between political leaders. The clearest divide, among voters and parties, was initially between those who saw the communist system in a positive light and those who identified with the Catholic Church. This divide was often more significant than specific economic interests in determining how people voted in the first two decades.[7] As a result, Poland has had a low level of electoral participation that is seldom more than a few points over 50 percent.

Elections have been marked by party instability and increased ideological fragmentation. Only the former communists had the resources for and tradition of party organization and offices. Newer parties ran, most often, out of leaders' homes or church buildings. This led to instability and to a real personalization of politics that made it difficult for voters to develop a connection to what were initially ephemeral parties and candidates that had no clear policy commitments.

In the long run, these irresolvable noneconomic divisions have made the battles in Polish politics more over divisive and irresolvable issues of the past and religion than over how best to deal with the economy and what the state should do for people. As a result, without alternative policies for soluble problems, political rhetoric has often focused on charges and countercharges.

After the first elections in 1989, Lech Wałęsa and his followers campaigned to force Jaruzelski's resignation and pass a law for direct popular election of the president. Jaruzelski conceded to this pressure and resigned. The law was changed, so the first presidential election was held in 1990.

Shifting loyalties and voting for someone new who seemed to promise dramatic improvement in living conditions and, on the right, condemned all opponents became the pattern in Poland. Two other long-term features of party affiliation in Poland also began at this point. One was the regional difference in party support between the prosperous west, with its big cities that supported pro-reform candidates, and the impoverished east, and other areas where factories had gone bankrupt and small-scale agriculture had failed. They supported the "right" with its promises of social welfare and condemnation of the "communists." While almost all politicians recognized the authority of the Catholic Church, it was the right that committed to Catholic social policies. The left, on the other hand, was connected, by many, with the former Communist Party. So it avoided ties with the past.

Initially, a plethora of tiny parties emerged, making coalitions difficult if not impossible after the initial free elections. In the early parliamentary elections of 1991, one hundred parties ran candidates, and twenty-nine parties were elected by proportional representation. The Senate was also fragmented after its elections. In addition to two warring Solidarity-based parties and the Solidarity trade union, there were various small right-wing parties that condemned both the former communists and Solidarity deputies for the losses "caused by" the Balcerowicz Plan in a campaign that was marked by nationalist and religious rhetoric. Only the former communists, the Social Democratic Party of the Polish Republic (in what was eventually the SLD), remained unified.

So divided was this parliament that, within two years, it was unable to make policy and turned in on itself. In the process, two new laws were passed that impacted party politics. First, to cut down on the fragmentation of the Sejm, political parties were required to win 5 percent of the national vote and coalitions 8 percent to hold seats in the Sejm. This has meant that many small parties run for election but do not get enough votes to qualify. Their votes are then distributed to parties crossing the threshold. As a result, the percentages of seats larger parties get are sometimes far more than their percentage in the actual vote. Second, the Sejm legalized a system allowing parties represented in parliament to receive national government funding for their campaigns if they won at least 3 percent in the election. The amount of this funding was proportional to the number of seats a party won in the Sejm or Senate.

In 1993, this electoral law resulted in the SLD, with only 20.41 percent of the votes, and its former allies, the renamed Polish Peasant Party, with 15.4 percent of the vote, winning 60.5 percent of Sejm seats. The nine right-wing parties that ran could not form a coalition, and none reached the 5 percent of the vote required to hold seats in parliament, so they got no seats even though, together, they polled 34.45 percent of the vote.

After the era of Communist Party rule, the very word "party" and the notion of being a party member had negative connotations, so, until the 2015 elections, most of the groups that ran for elections eschewed the word "party" and did not build structures or enroll members. Candidates, even from the most established parties, have had to invest their own money in campaigns. Only if they win seats in parliament are they at least partially reimbursed by the state. The expenses of being in parliament are paid through their party directly from the parliament's budget.

This funding did not result in political parties with permanent structures. Initially, only the former communists (SLD) had the infrastructure typical of European parties. This was because they and their subsidiary parties from the communist era, the Peasant Party and the Democratic Party for small entrepreneurs, inherited their parties' communist-era buildings, equipment, and membership lists, as well as old members who had long organized for the party. These old party workers were willing to work for the SLD and the Peasant Party, even when the parties voiced a procapitalist ideology. They did this because the other parties attacked or shunned anyone who had been in communist-era parties. By 2015, the postcommunist SLD had sold off the former buildings of the PUWP to support itself, and its former loyalists were no longer active. It collapsed.

The other political groups in Poland initially did not have the resources or desire to invest in increasingly expensive permanent infrastructures and offices. In the early years of Poland's democracy, some, mostly right-wing, parties received support and facilities from the Catholic Church in exchange for advocating strongly for its interests. But, in the years between elections, even the more successful parties remained essentially "couch parties," focused on individual leaders and existing only during political campaigns and in their formations in the Sejm and Senate. Until the reformation of Law and Justice after Kaczyński's defeat in 2010, most center and right-wing parties had no formal membership and owned no property. Leaders and parliamentary deputies only held together because they got funding, beyond their salaries, from their party in parliament. Even the dominant party between 2007 and 2015, Civic Platform, did not build a strong party organization. It basically functioned as a Western catchall party focused on its strong and popular leadership.

Parties' ideologies were unstable and confusing at best. The Democratic Left Alliance (SLD) cast off its Marxist ideology in 1989 and voted for the Balcerowicz Plan. It then shifted to advocating for "trickle-down economics," claiming that the poor would gain from excess profits in a capitalist economy. Its leader, Aleksander Kwaśniewski, in the presidential races in 1995 and again in 2000, ran as a modern, procapitalist, European leader who was above the political fray. But the SLD, once it won the 2001 parliamentary election, became known for the benefits its lower-level leaders took for themselves and, as a result, lost its popular support. Kwaśniewski's attempt to save the left by linking those from the old Solidarity who stood for workers' rights and social democracy—who had never gotten an electoral foothold—and the SLD together in a group called Left and Democrats failed in the 2007 elections. Little remains of the left except for small groups of young politicians who advocate for what are marginal issues in Poland.

The initial political center, the Freedom Union, could not disassociate itself from the losses people had suffered due to the Balcerowicz Plan it had supported as one of its first pieces of legislation in 1989. As a result, its candidates were defeated in the 1990 presidential election and the 1991 parliamentary elections and then returned to government in 1995 as an element of the Civic Platform. This center party stood against Polish nationalism and for establishing a liberal market economy, democratization, and a return to Europe. Although some of its leaders were lay Catholic opposition leaders during the communist era, it did not support giving the Catholic Church a dominant voice in legislation.

In 2001, Civic Platform won 12.7 percent of the votes, coming in second to the Democratic Left Alliance with its 41.0 percent. In 2007 and 2011, the Civic Platform won the parliamentary elections, as well as the presidential election in 2010. It has maintained a pro-European and pro–free market position and supports a strong Polish presence in the EU. Equally important to its strength for a decade was its reputation for rational and reasoned political action rather than a politics marked by strong rhetoric of charges and countercharges, seen as a negative characteristic of the right. But, in 2015, it was unable to hold on to power.

The one long-term party to hold seats in every parliament since the first free elections in 1989 has been the Polish Peasant Party, an outgrowth of the communist-era peasant party. It has been in coalitions with both sides. Initially, it focused on the interests of the agricultural sector; more recently, it has positioned itself as a moderate party supporting both economic development and a preservation of social supports. In the 2005 election, it did lose some of its peasant supporters to the radical Self-Defense Party; in 2007, however, it regained voter support as a party not involved in the ideological fights and also as the one major party that did not support the war in Iraq. It barely got enough votes to hold seats in the Sejm in 2015 when peasants were drawn by the economic promises of the Law and Justice party.

The right-wing Law and Justice (PiS) party has focused on the bitterness of Poles, particularly those in the east with its small towns and peasant areas, over what they lost in the rapid shift to capitalism. Like earlier culturally right-wing parties, it advocates for what used to be "left" social policies of social welfare and protecting workers. They rail against communist-era repression, the profits "communists" and the others have made by using their positions to buy up valuable properties during the transition, and the communists' supposed connections to Russia and the old secret police. Most of Poland's right-wing parties, including Law and Justice and, in the 2007 elections, Solidarity Action Coalition and the League of Polish Families, also, implicitly or explicitly, support Catholic religious values and church authority. In identifying themselves as Polish nationalists, most also have opposed Poland's deep involvement with both the West and the governments of the former Soviet states. As such, they did not fully support joining the EU.

The most powerful and long-standing of these parties, Law and Justice, has remained focused on the corruption of "the elite"; promises to end inequality and to punish communists and their agents by, at the least, excluding them from power; and, finally, Polish nationalism and support for the Catholic Church. Since Law and Justice emerged out of the Solidarity coalition in 2001 with Lech Kaczyński, then minister of justice, as its leader, it has won seats in the Sejm and Senate in every election. In 2005, it was able to form a coalition with the more centrist Civic Platform and have its leader, Lech

Kaczyński, elected in the presidential race. Since then, it and one of the Kaczyński twins have dominated Polish politics even after president Lech Kaczyński was killed in 2010. His brother Jarosław lost the election to replace him but has remained in control of PiS.

He initially strengthened the power of the party by working to create "local circles" of party members who were often in coordination with the right-wing Catholic organizational base that had formed around the so-called conservative Radio Maryja and its leader, Father Tadeusz Rydzyk. These local circles, its campaign as a moderate center-right party that was going to "listen" to the voters, and the fragmentation of the left into parties that were too small to meet the 5 percent threshold to enter parliament made it possible for Law and Justice to get enough votes (37.58 percent) in the 2015 election to hold a bare majority of the seats in parliament. Its win was both a result of the divisions in the left and also a general exhaustion among Poles who lived in poorer regions of Poland and felt they had not benefited from the strength of the Polish economy. Young people also supported Law and Justice as they were bitter about not being able to get their own apartments or good jobs.

Once it was in power, Law and Justice has rewarded loyal party members and its supporters in the population. Local circles have held the party members together and allowed Kaczyński to place relative unknowns, dependent on him for their positions, as candidates in various electoral districts. The local circles also reward their members with opportunities like being bused to Warsaw to see Donald Trump speak in July 2017 and events like the monthly mass and memorial for Lech Kaczyński.

These victories have given Jarosław Kaczyński enough power to control the PiS majority in parliament and Andrzej Duda's presidency even though his only office is being a PiS deputy in the Sejm. He has also been able to ensure that party loyalists hold key positions in the courts and state bureaucracies. It also has allowed the president and parliament to increase the number of members of the Supreme Court, appoint its supporters to judicial positions at all levels, and take over most of the leadership positions at all levels of the administration. These changes led to a condemnation by the European Parliament in April 2017 because of Poland's violations of European democratic norms with its moves, among others, to control the court system.

Economically, PiS has served its base and the interests of the Catholic Church by providing 500 zlotys (more than $100) monthly for every child more than one in a family. It has promised to build a million new, cheap apartments for young people. And, it also reduced the retirement age to sixty-five for men and sixty for women. In addition, PiS has changed the Polish school system and increased "patriotic" education in literature and history while decreasing science and foreign languages. Its "educational reform" also made it easier for teachers to be fired for deviating from the line. It has also taken steps to hamper the private media and NGOs by putting up barriers to their receipt of foreign support. In foreign policy, it has increasingly taken an anti-EU stance.

The success of Law and Justice in retaining its power was clear in the parliamentary elections in 2019, which drew the highest turnout of any election but the founding ones. In this 2019 election, it maintained its majority in the Sejm even though, in this election as in the preceding one, it did not get a majority in the first round. Instead, it got 43.6 percent of the vote, the highest vote of any party since the first free election in 1989. It did lose its majority in the Senate election that was held simultaneously. In the presidential election in 2020, Andrzej Duda, the Law and Justice candidate and president since 2015,

Photo 11.3. The leader of Poland's ruling party Law and Justice, Jarosław Kaczyński, attends a press conference in Warsaw in November 2018. (Grand Warszawski, Shutterstock)

was reelected in a right-left battle that pitted him against Warsaw's liberal mayor. In this election, though, he won only 51 percent of the vote. These results leave Law and Justice in the same controlling position it held after the 2015 election. It, like earlier national elections, resulted from a political split along geographical lines, with the major cities and suburbs as well as central Poland supporting the more liberal parties and the east and less urbanized areas supporting Law and Justice.

Civil Society

Unlike the rest of the postcommunist world, Poland had well-established and independent civil society groupings in the communist period. The Catholic Church, by the mid-1950s, not only held religious services but also had intellectual organizations and its own press. Informal intellectual opposition groupings as well as increasingly restive official professional associations existed as well. The various intellectual opposition groups that emerged in the mid-1970s had clear leaders known to the public, produced elaborate and regular sets of illegal publications, ran an alternative educational system, and provided legal and financial support for individuals working in the opposition or workers punished for their participation in demonstrations. Professional associations also acted more independently than their equivalents elsewhere in the Soviet bloc as they pressed for privileges and power for their members. In addition, the shortages in the economy and complications in getting things done in the system resulted in Poles being part of elaborate friendship networks that often involved personal ties between those in the regime and those in the opposition.

These institutions, after being significant forces in ending communism, rapidly lost out in the transition. The informal networks were no longer necessary. Professional groups could not work as they had earlier because there was now competition for jobs between professionals, and the state did not control workplaces. And, while established opposition groups and Solidarity retained their symbolism, they lost popular support when they had to be for something (particularly the painful economic reforms) rather than simply against communism.

The Catholic Church also saw its power shift. At its zenith in the 1980s, it was able to function in ways that were not possible for religious institutions elsewhere. It also benefited from having a Polish pope who played an active role in Polish politics. Local priests were critical as a base for independent action and then as mediators during the Gdańsk shipyard strikes and the formation of Solidarity. In the martial law years, individual churches served as havens for the opposition and also as distribution centers for donated food and clothing. Church leaders were then the intermediaries and guarantors for the Roundtable Talks and the elections that followed.

Local churches and the national hierarchy have since inserted themselves directly into politics, pressing public officials with demands to enact policies the church wanted and supporting individual candidates and parties. The Catholic Church and the parties it supports have been able to legislate policies that were not supported by large segments of the population, such as requiring religious education in all schools and imposing strict limits on abortion.

These gains have created problems for the church. Although Poland remains one of the most Catholic countries in Europe (88 percent of its citizens identify as Catholic, although only 58 percent claim to be practicing[8]), the number of births out of wedlock and the number of abortions continue to increase. While many politicians were and are wary of going against the church's wishes, increasing numbers of Poles see the church as having too much influence in politics and ignore many of its directives.[9] Liberal Catholic intellectual organizations have largely folded because they are no longer needed given the freedoms of the media and public discussion that now exist. And the church hierarchy no longer controls religious messages. The right-wing, privately owned Radio Maryja, with its xenophobia, racism, and anti-Semitism, has become so powerful and popular that the church hierarchy cannot moderate it or stop it.[10]

As the economic transition reduced the free time and resources of most people, new civil society institutions have failed to become players in politics. Initially, Western foundations created or funded civil society organizations in Poland. Most of these lasted only as long as the funding from the outside did. Other organizations appeared. Some were charities for needy groups, but most focused on providing special benefits and privileges for their members or on substituting for poor state services. They have not been significant political actors or avenues for popular participation in politics.

Economic Policies and Conditions

The economy was the Achilles' heel of Poland's leaders in the communist period and during the transition. It benefited from the foreign aid it received early on from the United States and Western Europe and then, when it was preparing to enter the EU, from the EU. Poland's economy went from being one of the most problematic in the postcommunist world to having the highest growth rate of any EU country during the recession that began in 2008. But many Poles, especially the elderly, those who live outside of the big urban agglomerations, and the less educated, saw and see themselves as losers, even when Poland's economy is strong.

When communism ended in 1989, Poland was an economic disaster. The reformers inherited a failed economy built on the Soviet model of state ownership but with small private farms as well as state farms. It was further distorted by communists' attempts to jumpstart the economy in the 1970s by borrowing heavily from the West to build new factories, raise salaries, and import Western goods to satisfy the population. This made it the third most indebted country in the world by 1990.[11] Poles were allowed to go abroad to work. They were also allowed to start their own small firms as early as the 1970s and 1980s. This meant that reformers faced a population with higher expectations than elsewhere in Central and East Europe, a crushing debt to both the West and East, and an economic system that was already partly privatized. Its population had higher expectations, and its economic reformers had less flexibility because of Poland's debt to the West and East.

Decisions about how to transform the economy depended on the approval of Western creditors because Poland needed debt reduction as well as Western aid to survive and change. As a result, economic reform began with the "shock therapy" of the Balcerowicz Plan to revive the economy by ending price controls and freezing salaries. In the process, prices rose dramatically and then fell. The Polish zloty became convertible to Western currencies. And trade barriers and government subsidies for state enterprises ended while interest rates on loans increased.

The initial results were disastrous for most individuals. By the end of January 1990, individual purchasing power was reduced to nearly half of what it had been at the end of 1989. Registered unemployment went from 0.3 percent in December 1989 to 6.5 percent a year later, jumping to 11.4 percent in December 1991 and 16.4 percent in 1993.[12] Declines in all the major economic indicators for the next two years were equally dramatic. Gross domestic product (GDP) dropped over 18 percent. In the first month of 1990 alone, industrial production dropped 30 percent, and the purchasing power of wages and salaries went down more than one-third. Peasant incomes fell by about half. Polish agricultural goods lost out on the domestic market to better-packaged and heavily subsidized Western goods that were often cheaper than their now unsubsidized Polish equivalents. Old state cooperatives and private enterprises that had survived the communist era collapsed because they could not compete with mass-produced Western goods or pay the soaring costs for rent, supplies, and salaries. At the same time, a small group of wealthy "owners and consultants" emerged. By 1993, the economy had begun an upswing that lasted into the mid-1990s, when it slowed perceptibly and economic growth hovered around 5 percent per year.

Even as the economy grew, however, there were problems. Growth happened only in specific areas where new technology brought increases in productivity and job losses. The export sector lagged behind, leaving Poland with a serious deficit. Inflation remained high. For a large percentage of Poles, the new buildings and foreign investments in the major cities were coupled with bankruptcies of the factories and other institutions that had kept smaller cities and rural regions alive. This triggered significant regional unemployment outside the major cities in what was known as "second Poland" and a slide into poverty for a majority of the population, even as a small but ever-increasing number of people grew wealthy from the changes. These had not existed, at least visibly, in the communist period. The socioeconomic divisions lasted for decades and helped create an embittered population that turned to right-wing populist parties and elected Law and Justice twice.

The solution for the government was to push privatization. New small firms, largely based on imports and street trade, blossomed. They often began by working around the existing rules, selling on the street, and paying little or no taxes. Many state stores were simply privatized by their employees. As a result, the share of employment and the national income in the private sector grew from less than one-third to more than half of the Polish economy by 1993, even though larger and weaker state firms continued on, virtually untouched by privatization.

The next step proved extremely complex and contentious. Solidarity leaders advocated moving toward employee ownership and maintaining cooperative enterprises. Leszek Balcerowicz, as deputy prime minister and minister of finance in the first post-communist government, and his supporters wanted to simply privatize state industries as quickly and completely as possible by establishing a stock market and letting weak industries go bankrupt. Only after eleven draft laws were rejected did this Margaret Thatcher–style privatization become law.

In the end, Poland's privatization was initially piecemeal, done largely through a combination of foreign investment and mass privatization. Those firms that were viable were consolidated into national investment funds. Only 512 of the 8,453 state firms were strong enough to be included in the fund. As a result, initially only about 2 percent of the total workforce was involved. Much of the money earmarked to prepare firms for privatization went to managers rather than to upgrading and reorganizing the firms. Every adult Pole got a certificate worth 180 zlotys (about $40) to invest in these funds. For most Poles, this minimal "mass privatization" was far from enticing. Rather than enlivening the market, the process caused the worth of the firms and the certificates to fall to less than half their original value.[13]

Most foreign direct investment involved government and private firms buying up state firms and Western businesses moving in to renovate or replace them or open new businesses. The bulk of new investments were in construction and the opening of huge foreign-based supermarkets and discount stores. In the end, the Polish economy, 75 percent of which was in private hands by 2000, became a "subsidiary economy" of foreign firms. At the turn of the century, after these initial investments, foreign investment a decade after the collapse of communism decreased dramatically: between 2000 and 2002, direct foreign investment dropped from $9.341 billion to $4.131 billion.[14]

There were serious political complications in both mass privatization and foreign direct investment. For most Poles, privatization seemed to hurt rather than help. Newly privatized firms were often sold or transformed to make money for their managers. Wages and work conditions in many foreign firms, particularly in the large supermarkets, were often below Polish standards. Almost 75 percent of banking services have been controlled by Western capital. Large parts of other key institutions, such as the media, some postal services, and telephone services, are owned or partly owned by outside interests. Many Poles have felt that Poland was being sold off, at bargain prices, to the West. The public's disgust at not getting the benefits it had expected from capitalism has been magnified by accusations and revelations of corruption because the selling off of Polish industries and resources to Western firms and Russian interests often involved huge tax and price breaks.

The growth in Poland's GDP during the 2008 European recession was largely the result of the funding the EU gave to prepare Poland's economy and infrastructure for accession; the comparatively small amount of its GDP invested in exports, most of which were agricultural products; the slowness of its banking sector to modernize and lower its standards for loans or make large loans in foreign currency; and the fact that Poland had not joined the Eurozone. This meant that the Polish economy was not affected by the economic problems of many West European states when the recession hit. It also meant Poland had its own funding for investment projects. Its agricultural sector, after having opposed joining the EU, found itself actually benefiting from Poland's membership. Not only did the EU provide substantial agricultural aid as Poland was joining, but Poland's small, traditional farms found a valuable niche as producers of organic foods.

For all of Poland's macroeconomic successes, these gains did not help large sectors of the population. The percentage of Poles who were unemployed grew, and the worth of most workers' earnings dropped because of increases in inflation. To keep the state sector solvent, many (mostly larger) state plants that could not easily be sold to private investors were closed down or sold off at low prices. In 2004, the unemployment rate was 19.1 percent. Because so much of Poland's industry had been concentrated in single-industry towns and regions, outside the major cities these changes created areas of mass unemployment in what came to be known as "second Poland." It resulted in what has been ongoing disaffection with the more liberal Civic Platform in Poland's small towns and less industrialized areas.

By the 2015 election, the economy again had become a political issue. And since the election, it has continued to be problematic. Poland's economic problems have grown since then. The unemployment rate has moved up and down. It has gone from a high of 6.16 percent in 2015 to 3.47 percent in 2018 and then to 5.5 percent in January 2020 and 6.1 percent in July 2020.[15]

Efforts to reduce debt by cutting state benefits have hurt the most vulnerable parts of the population. The pressure of unemployment on the economy has grown because the loss of jobs elsewhere in Europe has forced the Poles who had left to work or study abroad to return. This has increased the level of unemployment in Poland. It has been made worse, politically, because those who returned had seen how the people in the West lived and, unlike their predecessors who had worked abroad for short periods during the communist era, the money they earned abroad and brought back did not go far. Then, with the conflict in Ukraine in 2014, the already large flow of Ukrainians coming into Poland to take poorly paid jobs as guest workers exploded as large numbers of refugees from the war and economic collapse took refuge in Poland. They soaked up some of the jobs students and unqualified workers would normally have taken.

Key Social Issues

While life is better now than it was after communism fell or even in the early 2000s, the disparities between the under- and unemployed and the urban middle and upper classes anger those who feel they have lost in the last two decades. Most, as a result, support Law and Justice because it has railed against the "rich" and made clear commitments to increase social welfare supports for large segments of the population. To date, the payments to families for children and increases in welfare payments have resulted in more individual spending, but the costs of these benefits pose real problems for the economy.

There have been real gains for many in the population since 2005 when 17 percent of the population lived below the government-established social minimum (enough income to cover not only food and housing but also clothes, limited cultural events, and education) and 26 percent of children lived in poverty.[16]

Among Poland's youth, however, unemployment remains a problem, with approximately 27.3 percent registered unemployment among youth, down from 39 percent in 2004. Much of this was long-term unemployment. The cohort of young people entering the labor market has also decreased, in part because, as of 2010, nearly two million were working abroad and many others were attending universities. These gains, though, are not all permanent. By 2013, many young people going into the labor market, after working abroad or finishing their educations, found that there were no jobs for them, even though, under the Law and Justice party, the age for mandatory retirement has been decreased, taking some older workers out of the labor market.

The impact of these inequities and demographic changes was, from the beginning, aggravated by the economic reforms' negative effect on the very aspects of social welfare that were "givens" in the communist era—free education and health care and guaranteed pensions. This, coupled with EU pressures for a low budget deficit, made reforming or supporting social services and having a welfare system difficult at best.

These trends have also been aggravated by the heightened demand on and costs to the state for health care and education as well as unemployment assistance and pensions. The economic reforms increased the cost of basic necessities dramatically, even as privatization and the commitment to an exchangeable currency and meeting EU requirements decreased the money the state could spend on such services. So doctors and teachers have experienced a steady decline in their salaries, and financial support for hospitals, schools, and other social welfare institutions has dried up. This has been buffered because the wealthier segment of the population can use new private hospitals, clinics, and schools. Many professionals also shifted to the new private sector in education and health care where salaries were higher, worked multiple jobs, or left the country.

All this increased Poles' sense of the inequality in their society. The results of these social demands and the inability of the state to meet them have resulted in a number of problems. Unemployment and family support funds have been, most often, so limited that no one can live above the biological minimum level on only unemployment benefits or the family subsidies regions give out. So most of the unemployed have drifted away into the gray economy of illegal trade and crime. Particularly in rural areas and small towns, poverty became a steady state. And the divisions between the well-off and those who are less well-off seem much more dramatic.

State support for the poor has been limited at best. After 1989, Jacek Kuroń, a longtime member of the opposition and the first noncommunist minister of social welfare, fought for decent unemployment benefits and even set up his own soup kitchens as a model for private action to deal with problems for which there was no government money. Only after the 1997 election was there an attempt to create coherent public programs to reorganize the health-care and pension systems and their funding. But by 2005, neither the right-wing Solidarity Electoral Action government nor its social democratic successor had been able to implement effective reforms in these areas. Hospitals closed down for months at a time because of lack of funds. The Constitutional Court declared a health-care reform law unconstitutional in 2002, leaving the health-care system to function with no legal structure for more than a year until a new law was passed in 2004. The crisis in the public sector has decreased slightly with the passage of some health-care and education legislation, but it is far from over. Salaries for public sector employees remain a major political issue and resulted in some medical personnel going on hunger strikes in 2017. The pandemic in 2020 only exacerbated the economic problems for individuals and the state. Poland's high national debt has weakened the state's ability to deal with the demands that have been placed on its social services during the pandemic. It has also decreased the resources of both the state budget and the resources individuals have to deal with the crisis.

A contentious social issue has been how Poland deals with its past, a significant part of political discussions and battles. Its transitional justice policies have been focused on three processes: trying leaders accused of ordering attacks on major demonstrations, lustrating politicians listed as agents in secret police files, and setting up programs for recognizing and getting information out on long-ignored moments in Polish history (see chapter 7 on transitional justice). Ironically, public opinion surveys show that these processes have not been of great interest to the population; they have, however, been significant in political battles.

Because Poland's negotiated transition was begun by and included communists in the Roundtables and in the first postcommunist government, many of the leading dissidents initially were reluctant to punish the men and women of the former regime, its secret police, and its network of agents. This led to their "drawing a thick line" between the past and present. The files stayed in the police offices, and secret police officials continued to work, often supervised by the men they had monitored. The first and partial lustration law was passed only in 1996.

Before 2007, individual politicians were "lustrated" (barred from public office for having served as agents of the secret police) only if they lied in the declaration required of each candidate and some state officials about whether they had been such an agent. These declarations were posted in election district polling stations but did not deter voters from supporting strong candidates even if they admitted to having been agents. If they were challenged and a top government official was found to have lied on his forms, he was given the choice of either simply resigning from his positions or going through a trial in a special, closed court.

In the void this delay in opening the files caused, politicians on the right made accusations and claimed to have proof that their political opponents had been agents in what was "wild lustration." This forced politicians on the left to move to establish a legal process for dealing with the past, complicated as it was by the secret police files having remained in the hands of the police so they were vulnerable to being destroyed or tampered with.

In 2006, the Law and Justice party pushed through legislation expanding the requirement for lustration to legal, media, and education professions, as well as to other state offices, and opening up the police files of those who had been spied on not just to the victims but to journalists and scholars as well. That legislation was largely rejected by the courts because it violated European human rights standards. Then, in 2007, the Institute of National Memory was opened after a more developed and broader law was passed.

With the opening of files and lustration, charges of political enemies having been an agent of the secret police or the Soviet Union, as well as references to the past, remain regular parts of political discourse. To the extent that they had credibility, these attacks muddied not only political battles but also the public image of the Catholic Church and the opposition movement, both prime targets for secret police pressure. And although most of the victims and perpetrators are now dead or elderly and there is little political support for the politics of attacks, the secret police and their agents remain a popular topic in Polish film, and "who did what" is of interest to younger generations as well.

Pressure from the right also resulted in trials of Wojciech Jaruzelski, the former president of Poland, and others around him. These trials have been for the killing of workers in 1970 (although Jaruzelski did not sign the order and was not in the area when the attacks happened) and for the imposition of martial law. The trial for the 1970 killings dragged on for years. Both trials drew little public interest and ended because the defendants were too old and ill even to attend the trials. Ultimately they had no effect on public opinion: a significant part of the population saw martial law as "the lesser evil."

The Institute of National Memory has also taken an active role in historical discussions of the atrocities of World War II and events in the communist period by publishing books, sponsoring meetings, and even producing games designed to remind people of what happened, inspire them with Polish heroism, and teach youth about the problems of life in communist systems.

At the same time, new museums and monuments have been opened on issues ignored in the communist era: the Warsaw Uprising at the end of the war, the history of Jews in Poland, and repression under the communists. The content of these museums and the "telling" of much of modern Polish history has become an increasingly contentious issue under Law and Justice, with legal actions taken against people who refer to "Polish death camps" or blame Poles for killings during World War II. There were also battles over who really was the leader of Solidarity—Lech Wałęsa or Lech Kaczyński. In November 2017, this increasingly heated nationalist and anti-immigrant rhetoric helped trigger massive nationalist demonstrations against Jews and Muslims on a newly established "Independence Day." But since then, these battles over history have died down even as Poland has continued to emphasize the potential dangers of taking in refugees and others from bordering countries, including those who have come from Ukraine, Belarus, and even Russia to work as laborers for the Poles.

Emerging Challenges

The grand irony of the Polish transition has been that Poland was the furthest from Soviet-style communism (with the exception of Yugoslavia) before the transition began, had the best-developed civil society, and was the first state to begin the transition. Communist rule had been weak enough that the Catholic Church played a major political role beginning in the communist period and continuing through the transition and into current Polish politics. In the end, the weakness of Poland's communist regime and the Polish economy not only opened the door for a negotiated transition and a dramatic opening to the West but also made it difficult for the new capitalist and democratic system to satisfy most Poles.

Yet Poland and Hungary are the two countries that are now the most troubled, with the public turning to a populist right, supported by the Catholic Church in Poland, as it reflects and uses widespread popular disaffection with both the economy and politics.

Poland was the first state to democratize in Central and East Europe and went from being an economic "basket case" to having a very strong economy that rode out the 2008 recession. In spite of these gains, for many the pains of the economic transition and the gap between their expectations and reality delegitimized Poland's shift to capitalism and democracy. Most Poles did not get what they imagined would come with the end of communism and "the return to the West" and are still dissatisfied with their system.

The forces that had challenged the power of the Communist Party, the Catholic Church and the dissident movement, were unable to bring the kinds of changes Poles had hoped for. As a result, support for the Catholic Church and church attendance have dropped dramatically in the last decade. And the centrist parties that were initially formed in 1989 have lost out to the radical right. Despite popular protests, under the Law and Justice regime the church has been able to get the government to pass strict laws

Photo 11.4. Polish citizens protesting in October 2020 in Wrocław in support of the "Women's Strike" against tightening the abortion law in Poland. (Lena Ivanova, Shutterstock)

prohibiting all abortions. These have triggered massive women's marches and strikes of women against the passage of increasingly strict antiabortion laws. These strikes closed down businesses and public services that have depended on women employees.

The original reformers and the communists who became democrats lost credibility. This left Poland's political system with virtually no parties that participated in the change. At the same time, Poland's delay in dealing with the past and the secret police files on agents, who came to symbolize the evils of communism, made it possible for the past to be a political football that, even when the old leaders died and the communist system was gone, is still a part of the political rhetoric. The failures of the initial economic reforms and the power of the right's rhetoric and connections with nationalism and the Catholic Church have left Poland with weak center and left parties that have largely lost credibility in the immediate postcommunist years.

The COVID epidemic has required government restrictions in Poland as it has in many other European states. It increased popular skepticism of the national government. It also could have had political ramifications as the pandemic struck Poland at virtually the same time the presidential elections were scheduled. This limited in-person campaigning, but the election went ahead as scheduled, and in fact the turnout of 52.1 percent was higher than it had been in the preceding election. In spite of the questions that were raised about its handling of the pandemic, Law and Justice won both the parliamentary elections and the presidential election in 2019 and 2020. So it again controls both the presidency and the legislature. This increasingly authoritarian government has also weakened Poland's position in virtually all European institutions. The European Parliament even directed the European Commission to sanction Poland for its violations of EU and other European regulations. Poland's increasingly authoritarian governance garnered support from the United States under the Trump administration but has weakened Poland's position in the EU.

Study Questions

1. Why was Poland's communism less repressive and more inclined to liberalization of the economy and some aspects of society than that of other states in the region? How did this affect the transition process?
2. What were the key elements in Poland's history that made its communist rule different from other Central and East European states? What were the differences?
3. Why was Poland's transition a fully negotiated one, and how did this affect the characteristics of the initial government and the making of its critical decisions? What have been its long-term effects?
4. What are the structures of the government and the powers of the different branches of the government in postcommunist Poland? How was this system developed?
5. What has been the impact on Poland's political system of the election of Law and Justice in 2015? How has it changed the political system? What have its economic policies been? Who do they benefit?
6. Why was civil society strong in communist Poland and weak in postcommunist Poland?

Suggested Readings

Curry, Jane L., and Luba Fajfer. *Poland's Permanent Revolution*. Washington, DC: American University Press, 1995.

Davies, Norman. *The Heart of Europe: The Past in Poland's Present*. Oxford: Oxford University Press, 2001.

Garton Ash, Timothy. *The Polish Revolution: Solidarity*. New Haven, CT: Yale University Press, 2002.

Kowalik, Tadeusz. *From Solidarity to Sellout*. Translated by Eliza Lewandowska. New York: Monthly Review Press, 2012.

Websites

Center for Public Opinion Research: http://www.cbos.pl/EN/home_en/cbos_en.php

Gazeta.pl: http://www.gazeta.pl (general news website with limited English translation)

Government Central Statistical Office: http://stat.gov.pl/en

Polish Ministry of Foreign Affairs: http://www.msz.gov.pl/en/ministry_of_foreign_affairs

Warsaw Voice: http://www.warsawvoice.pl (weekly English-language publication)

Notes

God's Playground is a two-volume history of Poland by Norman Davies (New York: Columbia University Press, 1982). In the title of this definitive history of Poland, Davies makes the point that Poland has been the country most conquered and fought over in Europe and has undergone successive experiments and disasters.

1. Norman Davies, *God's Playground: A History of Poland*, 2 vols. (New York: Columbia University Press, 1982).

2. Norman Davies, *The Heart of Europe: The Past in Poland's Present* (Oxford: Oxford University Press, 2001).

3. Padraic Kenney, *Carnival of Revolution* (Princeton, NJ: Princeton University Press, 2002).

4. Jane Curry and Luba Fajfer, *Poland's Permanent Revolution* (Washington, DC: American University Press, 1995).

5. David S. Mason, "Poland," in *Developments in East European Politics*, ed. Stephen White, Judy Blatt, and Paul G. Lewis (Durham, NC: Duke University Press, 1993), 45.

6. Those two probably won only because, for the National List, voters could use a single X to mark out all the candidates on the two-column National List ballot. The names at the bottom of the two columns often fell below the X and so were not counted as being crossed out.

7. Miroslawa Grabowska, *Podzial postkomunistyczny: Spoleczne podstawy polityki w Polsce po 1989 roku* (Warsaw: Wydawnictwo naukowe Scholar, 2004).

8. CBOS, "Religinosc: 2013" (yearly report).

9. Beata Roguska and Bogna Wciorka, "Religijnosc i stosunek do kosciola," in *Nowa rzerczywistosc*, ed. Krzystof Zagorski and Michal Strzeszewski (Warsaw: Dialog, 2000).

10. Agnieszka Cybulska et al., "Demokracja w praktyce," in *Nowa rzeczywistosc*, ed. Krzystof Zagorski and Michal Strzeszewski (Warsaw: Dialog, 2000), 80–84.

11. Steven Greenhouse, "Poland Is Granted Large Cut in Debt," *New York Times*, March 16, 1991, http://www.nytimes.com/1991/03/16/business/poland-is-granted-large-cut-in-debt.html.

12. World Economy Research Institute, *Transforming the Polish Economy* (Warsaw: World Economic Research Institute, 1993), 6.

13. Barbara Blaszczyk and Richard Woodward, *Privatization and Company Restructuring in Poland*, Report No. 18 (Warsaw: CASE, 1999).

14. *Rocznik statystyczny 2004* (Warsaw: GUS, 2005), 597.

15. Trading Economics, "Poland Unemployment Rate," November 2020, http://www.macrotrends.net/countries/POL/poland/unemployment.rate.

16. Daniele Checchi, Vito Peragine, and Laura Serlenga, "Fair and Unfair Income Inequalities in Europe," DP No. 5025, IZA, June 2010, http://ftp.iza.org/dp5025.pdf.

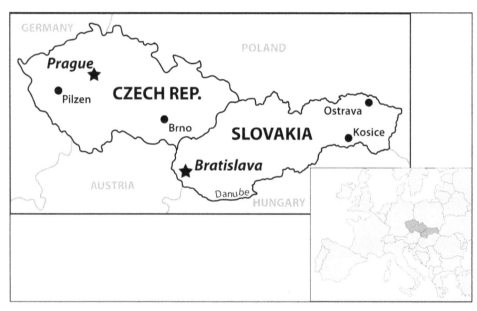

Map 12.0. The Czech and Slovak Republics

CHAPTER 12

The Czech and Slovak Republics

Sharon L. Wolchik

In February 2018 massive numbers of citizens in Slovakia took to the streets to protest the murder of journalist Ján Kuciak, who was investigating ties between the government and organized crime, and his fiancée Martina Kušnírová. Protests continued and led to the resignation not only of the interior minister but also of then–prime minister Robert Fico, although the government as a whole remained in power. The aftermath of the murder and protests also led to the election of an antigraft president and, in 2020, a new center-right government. Both were elected on anticorruption platforms.

Protestors also took to the streets in Prague and other cities in the Czech Republic in 2019 to protest the replacement of the interior minister by one more favorable to Prime Minister Andrej Babiš, whom the European Union (EU) concluded made fraudulent use of EU subsidies for his own benefit and who was about to be investigated for fraud in his own country. Demonstrators, led by the Million Moments for Democracy movement founded in 2018, did not succeed in removing Babiš, whose party remained the most popular as of August 2020. But they did succeed in reawakening popular engagement in politics, evident in the protests that continued in 2020 and came to include criticism of the government for its handling of the coronavirus crisis.

How do we account for these protests, which were the largest since those that brought about the fall of communism in 1989, in countries that commonly have been held to be among the most successful countries that have transitioned from communism? Czechoslovakia, particularly the Czech Lands, has often been seen as the exception to conditions and trends in the region. The country was also viewed as having the best preconditions for recreating and maintaining democracy due to its previous democratic experience in the interwar period, a legacy that was particularly true in the Czech Lands. To what extent are these countries still exceptional, especially in terms of the turn toward illiberalism and authoritarian government evident in many other countries in the region, most notably Poland and Hungary?

This chapter examines the actions that citizens and leaders have taken to meet the many challenges they have faced in restoring democracy, recreating a market economy, and taking their rightful place on the world stage. After a discussion of the history of both the transition from communism and the early postcommunist period, the pages to follow discuss the institutional structure of politics, important political and civil society actors and trends, and ongoing and new challenges citizens and leaders face. They conclude with a return to the question posed above that is central to understanding politics in both countries: to what extent are the Czech Republic and Slovakia exceptions today?

Political History

Prior to the peaceful separation of Czechoslovakia and the formation of two independent states, Czechs and Slovaks experienced several periods of being apart and together. As a result, there were, until fairly recently, some important differences between the two areas.

Precommunist History

Many of these differences date to the precommunist era. Before the creation of an independent Czechoslovak state in 1918, both regions were part of the Austro-Hungarian Empire. In contrast to several other ethnic groups in the region, neither Slovaks nor Czechs, after the Battle of White Mountain in 1620, had a native nobility. However, the Czech Lands were ruled by Austria, whereas Slovakia formed part of the Hungarian kingdom for nearly a thousand years. As a result, the Czechs had greater opportunities to develop a strong national movement and participate in politics. The Czech Lands also became the center of the empire's industry.

In Slovakia, however, efforts to Magyarize, or Hungarianize, the population prevented the formation of a broad-based national movement. These efforts, which were particularly

Photo 12.1. A 2019 antigovernment protest in Slovakia. (Ventura, Shutterstock)

strong after 1878, also kept Slovaks from receiving secondary or higher education in their own language. In contrast to the Czech Lands, which were among the most developed parts of the empire, Slovakia remained predominantly agrarian. Tax codes designed to preserve the political power of the landowning aristocracy in Hungary stifled industrial development, although numerous mining and other centers, largely inhabited by Germans, did develop.

A final difference between the two regions was evident in the sphere of religion. Both peoples were predominantly Roman Catholic, but the population in the Czech Lands was far more secular than that in Slovakia. There were also important differences in the relationship between Catholicism and national identity, as well as in the role of Protestantism. Although the Czech national movement that developed in the nineteenth century included Catholic figures and symbols, such as Saint Wenceslas, Protestant figures, such as Jan Hus, the fifteenth-century precursor of Martin Luther who called on the church to reform and was burned as a heretic in 1415, were equally if not more important. Catholicism played a relatively small role in the development of Czech national identity. A small Protestant minority in Slovakia also played an important role in efforts to create a national revival. However, Catholic figures and, in the interwar period, Catholic priests and the church were much more closely linked to the emerging sense of Slovak identity. Slovaks were also much more likely to attend church and turn to church ceremonies to mark major life passages.[1]

These differences came to the fore very soon after the formation of the Czechoslovak Republic in 1918. The result of efforts by leaders in exile such as Tomáš Masaryk and Milan Štefánik, as well as the need to fill the void created by the fall of the Austro-Hungarian Empire at the end of World War I, the new state, which came to include Ruthenia in 1919, brought together regions at very different levels of development, populated by peoples with very different experiences. Thus, the identification of Czechoslovakia as the exception to the rule in many areas during the interwar period applied largely to the Czech Lands. In Slovakia, conditions were much more similar to those of other countries in the region.

The impact of these differences was evident throughout the interwar period. The government in Prague was committed to closing the gap in development levels between the two parts of the country. However, very little progress was made in this respect before the Great Depression plunged Czechoslovakia, as much of the rest of the world, into economic decline. Levels of unemployment skyrocketed, and emigration increased.[2]

Other policies of the government also fed Slovak dissatisfaction. Faced with the need to staff bureaucratic positions vacated by Hungarians, the government turned to the generally better-educated Czechs. Czech administrators, as well as Czech businessmen and specialists who came to Slovakia as part of the development effort, frequently provoked resentment. The expansion of opportunities for education in the Slovak language during the interwar period led to a significant increase in the numbers of Slovaks with secondary and higher education, but there were relatively few Slovaks with these qualifications at the beginning of the period.[3] The unitary nature of the state, which was a centralized government based in Prague, also provoked dissatisfaction among many Slovaks, who came to feel that they had merely traded rule from Budapest for rule from Prague.

As a result of these factors, support for nationalist groups grew in Slovakia. Founded by Father Andrej Hlinka, the Slovak People's Party gained an increasing share of the vote in Slovakia. As Adolf Hitler gained power in Germany, many leaders and members of the party adopted the trappings of Nazism and looked to Hitler to support their goal of an independent Slovak state.

The German minority in the Czech Lands also became increasingly dissatisfied with the state. The Sudeten German Party received the overwhelming share of the vote of the Germans in the Sudetenland, and the dissatisfaction of this group provided the pretext for Hitler's demand at the September 1938 Munich Conference that Czechoslovakia cede the Sudetenland to the Third Reich. Faced with the unwillingness of his British, French, and Russian allies to come to Czechoslovakia's aid, President Eduard Beneš acceded to Hitler's demands. Beneš also agreed to autonomy for Slovakia in October 1938. These steps only temporarily spared his country, however, as the Germans invaded on March 15, 1939, and established the Protectorate of Bohemia and Moravia under German control. Slovak leaders, threatened with invasion as well if they did not comply with Hitler's demands that they declare independence, declared Slovakia an independent state on March 14, 1939. This independence was largely illusory, and the Slovak state adopted many of the policies of the Nazis, including sending most of the country's Jews to death camps.

Czechoslovakia was the only state in the region to retain democratic government until it was ended by outside forces. The interwar democratic system, which is often idealized, was certainly more successful than those in neighboring states in dealing with many of the pressing issues of the day. Progressive labor and occupational safety legislation and an extensive social welfare system succeeded in incorporating the growing working class and deflecting dissent. Elite political culture, heavily influenced by President Masaryk, also played an important role in supporting democracy, although the country in fact had a dual political culture, as evident in the large size of the legal Communist Party.[4] The dominant role of the *pětka*, the five-party coalition that ruled the country for much of this period and often set policy in discussions among party leaders outside parliament, resulted in a form of democracy dominated by a narrow group of disciplined political parties and their leaders. The interwar leadership was less successful in dealing with ethnic issues than with social problems, a weakness that eventually contributed to the end of the interwar state.

Inhabitants of the Czech Lands and Slovakia had different experiences during World War II. Both areas experienced lower levels of human and property loss than states such as Poland and Yugoslavia. Occupied by the Germans, the Czech Lands were considered a source of manufactured goods and labor for the Nazi war effort. Beneš formed an exile government in Britain, but aside from sporadic acts against German rule, there was little armed resistance, particularly after the Germans retaliated for the assassination of the Protector by burning the village of Lidice to the ground. Although it had little real autonomy, many Slovaks saw the Slovak state led by Jozef Tiso as the realization of Slovak aspirations for independence. As Hitler's ally, Slovakia was also spared heavy destruction. In August 1944, Slovak anti-Nazi opposition leaders staged what has come to be known as the Slovak National Uprising against the Germans in central Slovakia. This action came to be seen after the war as a symbol of Slovak resistance and a counter to the policies of the Slovak state.

Most Jews in both the Czech Lands and Slovakia perished in the Holocaust. Roughly ninety thousand Jews lived in the Czech Lands before the outbreak of World War II. In

1942 alone, fifty-five thousand of them were sent to Theresienstadt; many of these were later deported to Auschwitz and other death camps. An estimated eighty thousand Czech Jews, or 90 percent of the community, perished in the course of the war. In Slovakia, only fifteen thousand of the estimated ninety thousand Jews survived.[5]

The Communist Experience

With the exception of the area of western Bohemia around Plzeň, which was liberated by US troops, Czechoslovakia was liberated by the Red Army. Afterward, the country was reestablished according to its interwar boundaries with the exception of Subcarpathian Ruthenia, which became part of the newly expanded Ukrainian Soviet Socialist Republic. From 1945 until February 1948, the country experienced a modified form of pluralism. The Communist Party enjoyed certain advantages, including control of the ministries of information, the interior, and agriculture, but other political parties existed and were able to participate in political life. In the 1946 elections, generally considered free and fair although the political spectrum was truncated because several parties were banned for collaborating with the Nazis, the Communist Party emerged as the most popular party with 38.6 percent of the vote. Declining support on the eve of the scheduled 1948 elections, coupled with changes in Joseph Stalin's plans for the region in light of the beginning of the Cold War, led the party to instigate a government crisis in February 1948 over control of the police. The democratic members of the government resigned, and after President Beneš accepted their resignations, a government clearly dominated by the Communist Party took power.

After the February coup, the Czechoslovak communist leadership began implementing the Soviet model in earnest. The few political parties allowed to continue to exist were subordinated to the Communist Party, which became the only effective political party. The new government also stepped up the nationalization of industry and aggressively collectivized agriculture. A central planning board was established to set binding five-year plans based on reorienting the country's economy to focus on heavy industry, to the neglect of light industry, the consumer and service sectors, and agriculture. Efforts were also made to industrialize Slovakia, still much less developed than the Czech Lands at the outset of the communist period.

As in other states in the region, the leadership also implemented measures designed to change the social structure by improving the status of previously disadvantaged groups, such as workers and farmers, and removing the privileges of the previous elites. The associational life of the country was simplified. Most voluntary organizations were outlawed and replaced by large, unitary, mass organizations under the control of the party. The independent media were disbanded, and a system of strict censorship was established. The party also asserted its control over education, culture, and leisure. Political criteria became important for admission to higher education, and the content of education was politicized. The elites also made efforts to use culture and leisure to propagate values and behaviors consistent with Marxism-Leninism. As part of the latter effort, the regime undertook a brutal campaign against religion that resulted in the desecration of numerous churches. The party also controlled those clergy who were allowed to continue to work.

Since the changes involved in implementing the Soviet model affected almost every area of life and were not chosen by the population but rather were imposed from the top down, it is not surprising that the leadership came to rely increasingly on coercion. The purge trials in Czechoslovakia were among the harshest in the region, and numerous high party officials, including the secretary general of the party, Rudolf Slánský, were executed after highly publicized show trials.[6]

Czechoslovakia remained a model Soviet satellite throughout the 1950s and early 1960s. An uprising in Plzeň after Stalin's death in 1953 was quickly put down. The regime survived de-Stalinization, which led to the Revolution of 1956 in Hungary and popular protests and strikes in Poland in 1956, with only modest changes in personnel and lip service to the need to rout the cult of personality and restore socialist legality. By 1961, however, the country's previously dynamic economy also began to show the effects of Stalinism. After the economy registered a negative growth rate in that year, party leaders commissioned a team of loyal party economists at the Academy of Science to propose economic reforms. This step, which was followed by the formation of other commissions to examine ways to reform other areas of life, initiated a large-scale process of renewal and rethinking at the elite level. Coupled with growing demands for intellectual freedom by creative intellectuals, particularly writers, it resulted in the elaboration of a new model of socialism that its creators deemed more appropriate to a Western, developed society. The mid-1960s also saw the growth of Slovak dissatisfaction with Slovakia's position in the common state with the Czechs, as well as greater activism on the part of youth and several of the mass organizations.[7]

In late 1967, the reform process spread to the Communist Party itself, and in January 1968 Alexander Dubček replaced Antonín Novotný as head of the statewide party. Despite the persistence in the leadership of a hard-line faction, under Dubček and his supporters the reform developed an explicitly political aspect. After the end of censorship in March 1968, the movement for change spread to groups beyond the party and its loyal intellectuals. More radical in its demands than those of the reformists within and associated with the party, this mass current kept pressure on Dubček and his colleagues to continue their efforts to create "socialism with a human face," as the model they were elaborating came to be called.

The reformist communist leadership that supported Dubček wanted to pursue reforms within the system. Best expressed in the Action Programme adopted by the party in April 1968, these reforms did not include an end to the Communist Party's monopoly of power or any effort to renounce membership in the Warsaw Pact or to separate Czechoslovakia from the Soviet Union and other socialist countries.[8] However, conservative leaders in East Germany and Poland, as well as the Soviet leadership, became increasingly fearful that the reformist spirit would spread to their countries.

Dubček and his supporters were caught between the need to maintain the slowly growing trust of the population and the need to satisfy their allies that socialism was not under threat. The growth of groups outside the party, including the Club of Engaged Nonparty People (KAN) and Club 231 (a club of former political prisoners), as well as the increasingly radical demands being voiced by some intellectuals,[9] led reformist leaders to consider the use of force to rein in the reform process, even as they attempted to reassure their colleagues in other socialist states.[10] After several meetings with the Soviet leadership in the summer of 1968 failed to produce the desired results, Soviet and other Warsaw Treaty Organization forces invaded Czechoslovakia on August 21, 1968.

In April 1969, when Gustáv Husák, also a Slovak leader, replaced Dubček as the head of the party, it was clear that the reform era was over. Husák presided over the effort to restore orthodoxy in a process called "normalization." An attempt to reverse the reforms in all areas of life, "normalization" involved the reassertion of a clear monopoly of political power by the Communist Party, the restoration of censorship, and the end of economic reform. It was accompanied by a massive personnel purge that removed many of the most talented figures in areas as diverse as culture, education, the economy, and politics from their public and professional positions. The loss of these reformists, estimated to have included from two hundred thousand to five hundred thousand people, and the restoration of party control over the mass organizations and media led to an almost twenty-year period of stagnation. During this time, Czechoslovakia once again became a model satellite. All discussions of reform became taboo, and only small numbers of intellectuals, soon labeled dissidents by the regime, engaged in independent activity.

During this period, the regime relied on a combination of material incentives and coercion to ensure the population's compliance. The standard of living improved, and many families acquired summer or weekend cottages. Coercion was used primarily against dissident intellectuals who refused to accept the status quo or were active in the small number of independent groups that developed to protest the regime's disregard for human rights and to support independent activity. Charter 77, formed in response to the regime's signing of the Helsinki Accords in 1975 and the prosecution of a group of young rock musicians, the Plastic People of the Universe, in 1977, was the most important of these. Founded by Václav Havel and other intellectuals centered mainly in Prague and other large cities in Bohemia and Moravia, Charter 77 was named for the document to which these intellectuals were signatories, which circulated in samizdat (unauthorized material reproduced and circulated clandestinely). In the last years of communist rule, in particular, the group came to serve as the center of a growing community of independent activists, and many people who remained in good standing with the official world came to rely on its analyses for accurate information about problems that the regime either did not want to discuss or handled in a clearly biased way.[11] In 1989 and the years immediately following the end of communist rule, Charter 77 exerted an influence disproportionate to its numbers, as its leaders founded Civic Forum and many of its members moved into prominent positions in public life.

In Slovakia, where few intellectuals signed the charter, dissent based on religious grounds was the most prominent form of opposition. Unauthorized pilgrimages to religious shrines drew upward of five hundred thousand people in the late 1980s, and Catholic activists organized a candlelight demonstration in Bratislava in December 1988 demanding religious freedom. Some Slovak intellectuals also participated in what came to be called "islands of creative deviation"—that is, groups of people who still held positions in the official world but used approved organizations as venues for conducting unauthorized, nonconformist activities.

Early Postcommunism

On November 17, 1989, the process that came to be known as the Velvet Revolution was set in motion by police brutality during a peaceful demonstration called to commemorate the death of a student during the period of Nazi occupation. Encouraged by the fall of the Berlin Wall and changes in Hungary and Poland earlier that year, hundreds of thousands of citizens participated in mass demonstrations against the regime. As it became clear that the demonstrators were not going to give up and that the Soviet Union would not intervene to preserve communism in Czechoslovakia, leaders of the Communist Party began negotiations with Civic Forum in Prague and Public Against Violence in Bratislava—umbrella groups formed by Charter 77 and other dissidents in Prague and members of the opposition in Bratislava to coordinate the mass demonstrations. Within twenty-one days the rigid, seemingly all-powerful, repressive communist system in Czechoslovakia fell. Many of the most conservative, compromised party members were removed from the federal legislature, and new elections were scheduled for June 1990. The election of former dissident playwright Václav Havel as president of Czechoslovakia on December 31, 1989, by a parliament still dominated by Communist Party members, capped the victory of the so-called Velvet Revolution.

After the end of communism, Czech and Slovak leaders faced many of the same tasks as leaders in other postcommunist states. The top-priority goals were aptly summarized in the election slogans of almost all parties that ran candidates in the June 1990 parliamentary elections: democracy, the market, and a return to Europe. In the political realm, the country's new leaders had to come to terms with the communist past and establish new institutions or reorient the work of existing institutions so that they could function democratically. Other tasks included the recruitment of new leaders to replace the discredited old elite, the repluralization of the political landscape, both in terms of political parties and associational life, and the need to combat the legacy of communism on political values and attitudes to create a political culture suitable for a democratic polity.

In the economic realm, the new elites had to enact the legislative basis for the re-creation of private ownership and private enterprise; privatize state assets, which in Czechoslovakia accounted for over 90 percent of all economic activity at the end of communist rule; encourage the development of new private enterprises; restore economic assets to their rightful owners or their heirs; deal with rising unemployment, poverty, and inequality in a previously very egalitarian society; and address the environmental consequences of the communist pattern of industrialization. With the breakup of the Soviet Union and the Council for Mutual Economic Assistance, they were also required to reorient the country's trade, which had remained heavily centered in the socialist bloc, to the West.

In the area of foreign policy, the new leaders soon reasserted the country's status as a sovereign nation by negotiating the withdrawal of Soviet troops from its territory and began the process of reclaiming their rightful place on the European stage. After the breakup of the Soviet Union in 1991, Czech and Slovak leaders began a campaign to join the EU and NATO.

The new leadership of the country, as well as its citizens, also had to cope with the social and psychological aspects of the far-reaching changes the transition entailed. In the social realm, these included changes in social structure, as well as the emergence into the open and exacerbation of old social problems, such as juvenile delinquency, alcoholism, drug abuse, crime, and domestic abuse, as well as new issues, such as human trafficking and organized crime, that emerged with the opening of borders and the decline in police repression. The widespread dislocations, as well as, in many cases, the positive effects of the transition, including the vastly expanded choices available to people, also had negative psychological effects on many members of the population.

Very soon after the end of communism, it became evident that the transition, and particularly the shift to the market, would be more difficult in Slovakia. Because Slovakia had industrialized largely during the communist era, it had more of the "monuments of socialist industry," or very large, inefficient factories that could not compete in market conditions. Slovakia had also become the center of the country's sizable arms industry. The shift to the market, with its emphasis on profit and the ability to compete on the world market, therefore, created much greater economic disruption in Slovakia, where levels of unemployment were significantly higher than in the Czech Lands. In 1993, for example, when 3 percent of the population was unemployed in the Czech Republic, close to 15 percent was unemployed in Slovakia.

The nature of the Czechoslovak federation was another irritant to many Slovaks. Although the adoption of a federal system was one of the few changes discussed during the reform period of 1968 that was implemented in 1969, the provisions that granted Slovakia a great deal of autonomy in managing its own economic, as well as cultural and educational, affairs were soon rescinded as the country was "normalized." After 1971, the federation functioned largely as a unitary state. Growing Slovak dissatisfaction with Slovakia's position in the common state was reflected in public opinion polls conducted in the early 1990s that showed that some 80 percent of Slovaks were dissatisfied with the federation.[12] Although most Czechs and Slovaks continued to say that they did not want the state to break up, Czech and Slovak leaders were unable to agree on an acceptable division of power between the republic and federal governments. After the June 1992 parliamentary elections led to the victory of the center-right under Václav Klaus in the Czech Lands and the center-left led by Vladimír Mečiar in Slovakia, the two leaders oversaw the process of dissolving the federation. This step formally occurred on January 1, 1993, when the Czechoslovak Federative Republic, as it was called, was replaced by the Czech Republic and the Slovak Republic.

Initially, political and economic developments diverged markedly in the two independent states. Expectations that the transition would be smoother in the Czech Republic were borne out by that country's inclusion in the first round of expansion of both NATO and the EU. Vladimír Mečiar's dominance of political life in Slovakia, on the other hand, and the antidemocratic actions of his government stalled economic reform and resulted in Slovakia's exclusion from the first round of NATO expansion. The victory of Citizens' Campaign 98 (OK'98) in the 1998 parliamentary elections brought a broad coalition of parties favoring reform to office. The government of Prime Minister Mikuláš Dzurinda quickly restarted economic reforms, included representatives of the 460,000-strong Hungarian minority in the government, rescinded anti-Hungarian measures adopted by the Mečiar government, and restored the rule of law and respect for human rights and political liberties. These steps put Slovakia back on track, and the country was admitted to NATO in the second round of expansion and included in the EU's first round of expansion to the postcommunist world in 2004.

Political Institutions

The legislature elected for a two-year term in Czechoslovakia in June 1990 was to have been a constituent assembly: its main task was to revise the country's constitution and reform its legal system to be compatible with democratic government and the creation of a market economy. Although the country's new leaders made a great deal of progress in the latter area, their inability to agree on a division of power between the federal and republic governments contributed to the breakup of the state.

The two new states that replaced the federation in January 1993 were both unitary. Their constitutions, which went into effect in both countries on January 1, 1993, identify them as parliamentary democracies and include provisions guaranteeing their citizens broad political and civil liberties. The preambles of the two states differ in important ways. The Czech preamble begins, "We the citizens of the Czech Republic in Bohemia, in Moravia and in Silesia . . ." The preamble also affirms the Czech Republic's irrevocable status as a democracy and its commitment to the rule of law and refers to the UN Charter of Human Rights.[13] In Slovakia, the preamble begins with "We, the Slovak nation . . . together with members of national minorities and ethnic groups living on the territory of the Slovak Republic . . ." The constitution also includes a section, the "Rights of National Minorities and Ethnic Groups," that notes, among other provisions, the right of these groups to use their native languages as regulated by law.[14]

In both states, the government is formed based on the results of parliamentary elections and is responsible to the legislature. The Czech Republic has a bicameral legislature. The lower house consists of two hundred members elected for four-year terms on the basis of proportional representation. The upper house, the Senate, created in 1996, consists of eighty-one members elected according to the majority principle for six-year terms. One-third of senators are elected every two years. Slovakia has a unicameral legislature. Its 150 members are elected to four-year terms according to proportional representation.

In addition to governments headed by prime ministers responsible to parliament, both countries also have presidents who serve as head of state. The president is directly elected in Slovakia and, since 2013, in the Czech Republic. Previously, the Czech president was elected by parliament. Officially, the duties of the president are largely ceremonial in both countries. They also play a role in appointing governments after elections and can, in certain circumstances, dissolve the parliament. Other powers of the president, including the power to declare war and control of the military, are shared with the prime minister or, in the Czech case, the Senate. Both presidents also play a role in the appointment and recall of judges.

Although the presidents' official powers are fewer than those of the prime ministers in both countries, in both cases, the office has sometimes been used to counteract or counterbalance actions by the government in ways that go beyond its formal powers. These activities were most evident in Slovakia during the Mečiar period, when President Michal Kováč, formerly a close colleague of Prime Minister Mečiar, opposed some of his more authoritarian actions. Václav Havel, who was both the first postcommunist president of the federation and the first president of the independent Czech Republic, exercised influence that far exceeded the powers of his office due to his enormous moral authority and reputation around the world.[15]

Photo 12.2.   Václav Havel at an event commemorating the twentieth anniversary of the collapse of communism in 2009. (Marcin Kadziolka, Shutterstock)

The next Czech president, Václav Klaus, a known Euroskeptic, held up Czech ratification of the Lisbon Treaty in October 2009 by refusing to sign without certain EU guarantees. He finally signed it after the Constitutional Court rejected a challenge from the Civic Democrats, making the Czech Republic the last country to approve the treaty. His successor, Miloš Zeman, the first popularly elected president in the Czech Republic, has tried since his election in 2013 and narrow reelection in 2018 to expand the powers of the office beyond its ceremonial duties. In the 2014 presidential elections in Slovakia, Andrej Kiska, a wealthy businessman and philanthropist with no previous political experience, won an upset victory over Robert Fico, the incumbent prime minister, with 59.4 percent of the vote in the first round of the election. Fico's election, had it occurred, would have meant that both the majority in parliament and the president were from the same party, an outcome Slovak voters evidently wanted to avoid. Kiska, a moderate politically who had no affiliation with a political party while in office, often took positions at odds with those of Prime Minister Fico and the government, particularly on immigration and refugee policy.[16]

In the 2020 presidential elections in Slovakia, Zuzana Čaputová, an attorney and liberal NGO activist who only became affiliated with a political party in 2017,

Photo 12.3. Zuzana Čaputová became Slovakia's first female president in June 2019. (Jindřich Nosek [NoJin], Wikimedia Commons)

defeated a nominally independent candidate known to be close to Robert Fico's party. Campaigning on an antigraft theme, her candidacy was fueled in part by popular outrage over the February 2018 murder of Ján Kuciak and his fiancée, Martina Kušnírová. Čaputová's Western orientation, evident in her strong support of Slovakia's participation in the EU and NATO, contrasts sharply with Czech president Miloš Zeman's often favorable stance toward Russia.[17]

In both countries the highest court is the Constitutional Court. In Slovakia the thirteen judges are chosen for twelve-year terms from twenty-six candidates proposed by the legislature. There is also a Judiciary Council, whose members serve five-year terms, that plays a role in appointing judges to lower courts. Eight of its members are elected; the legislature, president, and government each choose three members.[18] The president also appoints members of the Supreme Court from a list of potential judges presented by the Judiciary Council. In the Czech Republic, the fifteen justices of the Constitutional Court who serve for ten-year terms are appointed by the president with the consent of the Senate. The president also appoints the president and vice president of the Supreme Court, which serves as the top civil and criminal court. There are also lower courts at the regional and district levels, as well as administrative and military courts in both countries.[19]

To date, the courts in Slovakia and the Czech Republic have not been the object of massive political manipulation, as has occurred in Poland and Hungary. The protests in Prague that started in February 2018 and continued through 2019, in which protestors called for Prime Minister Babiš to resign, were based in part on fears that he would try to influence judicial outcomes by replacing the justice minister with one close to President Zeman, his political ally. The change happened a day after Czech police called for Babiš to be prosecuted for fraud in connection with EU subsidies. According to Czech law, the state prosecutor, who is under the control of the justice minister, must initiate prosecutions. In December 2019, the chief prosecutor overruled a decision by his subordinate to stop the case and reopened the investigation.

Political Competition

After the end of communism, one-party rule by the Communist Party was replaced by a plethora of political parties. The most important of these, initially, were the broad umbrella groups formed in November 1989 to direct the mass demonstrations and negotiate with the government: Civic Forum in the Czech Lands and Public Against Violence in Slovakia. Almost immediately, however, other political parties began to form. These included successors to parties that had been active in the interwar period and were banned under communism, new parties with links to parties in the rest of Europe, nationalist or regional parties and movements, single-issue groups, and parties focused on new issues. Several small parties that had been allowed to exist under communism, albeit under the control of the Communist Party, began to act independently. Reformed and unreformed versions of the Communist Party also participated in politics in both regions.[20]

Although they won the June 1990 elections resoundingly, Civic Forum and Public Against Violence soon splintered into smaller groups. In the Czech Lands, then–finance minister Václav Klaus broke away from Civic Forum in April 1991 to form the Civic Democratic Party (ODS). Those who remained in Civic Forum founded the Civic Democratic Movement and the Civic Democratic Alliance, which succeeded in electing candidates to the Federal Assembly in the 1992 elections but were not viable political entities after that. In Slovakia, Vladimír Mečiar, initially part of Public Against Violence, broke away in April 1991 to found the Movement for a Democratic Slovakia, which became the most popular party in that republic. Public Against Violence was replaced by a variety of other parties on the center-right.

As table 12.1 illustrates, the number of political parties and movements that have fielded candidates has in fact increased in both the Czech Republic and Slovakia since 1990. However, many of these have been unable to obtain enough votes to pass the threshold of 3 or 5 percent of the vote required to seat deputies in parliament. As the result of the 2017 elections in the Czech Republic, nine parties earned enough votes to seat deputies in the lower house of parliament. After the 2020 parliamentary elections in Slovakia, six parties seated deputies in the legislature.

Although a relatively small and stable number of parties have seated deputies in the legislatures since 1990, the figures in table 12.1 mask an important aspect of politics in the period since 1989. As table 12.2 shows, parties continue to appear and disappear with great frequency. In 2016, twelve of twenty-three parties in the Slovak elections were newly formed, as were fourteen of the twenty-four parties that competed in the 2020 elections. Seventeen of the thirty-one parties in the Czech elections were new in 2017, a proportion exceeded only in 2002.

Table 12.1. Ratio of the Number of Parties Seating Deputies to the Number of Parties Fielding Candidates by Election

Czechoslovakia Federal Assembly (Chamber of Nations and Chamber of People)				
	Czech National Council	Czech Lands	Slovakia	Slovak National Council
1990	0.31 4/13	0.27 4/15 +0.27 4/16	0.29 5/17 +0.29 5/17	0.44 7/16
1992	0.42 8/19	0.30 6/20 +0.30 6/21	0.27 6/22 +0.23 5/22	0.22 5/23

Czech Republic Chamber of Deputies		Slovakia National Council	
1996	0.40 6/15	1994	0.41 7/17
1998	0.42 5/12	1998	0.35 6/17
2002	0.14 4/28	2002	0.28 7/25
2006	0.20 5/25	2006	0.29 6/21
2010	0.31 8/26	2010	0.33 6/18
2013	0.30 7/23	2012	0.23 6/26
2017	0.29 9/31	2016	0.35 8/23
		2020	0.25 6/24

Sources: Statistical Office of the Slovak Republic, "Elections and Referenda," http://volby.statistics.sk/index-en.html; Czech Statistical Office, http://www.volby.cz.

Analysts of politics in both countries have disagreed about how to characterize the political party system that followed the breakup of the initial umbrella organizations. By the mid-1990s, some analysts argued that the proliferation of political parties that followed the demise of these groups was coming to an end and that a simplified party system was emerging. Others argued that, although party labels continued to change, the electorate was sorting itself into two coherent, identifiable, large blocs that corresponded in a general way to the left-right division seen in many other European polities.[21] As subsequent elections demonstrated, events have not supported either view. Instead, the party system has continued to be fluid. As table 12.2 illustrates, both the number of parties and the parties themselves have tended to change from one election to another. In 2012, Tim Haughton and Kevin Deegan-Krause described the party systems in these countries, as well as others in the region, as composed of "perennials," which were long-lived and lasted from election to election, and "annuals," parties that appeared, received enough votes to seat deputies in parliament and sometimes even serve as part of a government coalition, but failed to gain enough votes to seat deputies in the next election. By 2015, they described the party systems as being in "hurricane season," a period in which even some of the "perennials" lost their representation in parliament or folded.[22]

With few exceptions, voters have tended to "throw the rascals out" at each election. The reelection of a center-right government in Slovakia and a center-left government in the Czech Republic in 2002, although both with changes in the composition of the coalition, was unusual not only in those countries but in the postcommunist region as a whole.[23] In the 2006 parliamentary elections, voters in both countries reverted to the more common pattern of defeating the incumbent government until the 2012 early elections in Slovakia in which the Smer (Direction) movement led by Robert Fico won reelection with 44.4 percent of the vote, which gave them over a majority of parliamentary seats (83 of 150) and led to a government composed solely of Smer members.[24] In the Czech Republic's 2013 elections, held after a scandal involving corruption and misuse of government resources led to the resignation of the prime minister and the appointment of a caretaker government, ODS, the dominant party in the three-party coalition formed

Table 12.2. Number of Parties Fielding Candidates and Number of New Parties in the Czech Republic and Slovakia since Independence

	Czech Republic				Slovakia		
	New Parties	Total Parties	Ratio		New Parties	Total Parties	Ratio
1996	8	15	0.53	1994	12	17	0.71
1998	5	12	0.42	1998	13	17	0.76
2002	21	28	0.75	2002	17	25	0.68
2006	13	25	0.52	2006	8	21	0.38
2010	13	26	0.50	2010	9	18	0.50
2013	10	23	0.43	2012	15	26	0.58
2017	17	31	0.55	2016	12	23	0.52
				2020	14	24	0.56

Source: Statistical Office of the Slovak Republic, "Elections and Referenda," http://volby.statistics.sk/index-en.html; Czech Statistical Office, http://www.volby.cz/.

after the 2010 elections and a constant in the Czech political party scene since its founding in 1991, barely received enough votes to seat deputies in parliament, although it has recovered somewhat since that time.

Given the multiparty nature of the party system, it is not surprising that most governments are coalitions. The one-party government led by Robert Fico from 2012 to 2016 was unusual not only in Slovakia but in the region as a whole. Fortunately for the prospects of democratic government in Slovakia, he did not win a supermajority as Viktor Orbán did in Hungary in 2010, which allowed Orbán to change the constitution and adopt other antidemocratic policies. Fico's Smer party lost its majority in the 2016 parliamentary elections in Slovakia, although it received the most votes, and was forced to form a coalition government once again.

As Tim Haughton, Darina Malová, and Kevin Deegan-Krause note, although three of the eight parties that entered the Slovak parliament in 2016 were new to that body, more voters moved from one established party to another than to new parties.[25] The most shocking result of the election was the fact that a neo-Nazi, far right-wing party, Marian Kotleba's People's Party–Our Slovakia, gained entry to parliament for the first time. Kotleba, who won election as head of one of Slovakia's regions in the 2013 regional elections, benefited from the anti-immigrant mood in the country that Fico sought to exploit, as well as the general dissatisfaction of most citizens with the government and political leaders.[26] In 2017, two of the party's members of parliament were charged with hate speech, and the attorney general has sought to ban the party for what he described as attacks on the democratic system. Kotleba's party was also defeated in the regional elections in 2017.

In the 2020 parliamentary elections in Slovakia, the Ordinary People and Independent Personalities party (OL'aNO) won the most votes (25.02 percent) and formed a coalition with three other parties on the center-right, We are Family (8.24 percent of the vote), Freedom and Solidarity (6.22 percent), and For the People, the party formed by former president Andrej Kiska (5.67 percent).[27] The defeat of the parties in the government coalition reflected popular disgust with the government previously led by Robert Fico and, after mass protests forced Fico's resignation as prime minister, Peter Pellegrini, also of Smer. The new prime minister, Igor Matovič, whose party adopted the slogan "Together Against the Mafia" in the electoral campaign, promised vigorous action against corruption. His government survived a no-confidence vote in July 2020 centered on the prime minister's admitted plagiarism.[28] Smer came in second with 18.29 percent of the vote and with Kotleba's party, which gained 7.97 percent of the vote, formed the main opposition. For the first time since 1992, there are no Hungarian parties in parliament.[29]

The election of a far-right party to the Slovak parliament in 2017 and 2020, as well as the presence in the Czech parliament elected in 2013 of the far-right party Dawn and the Freedom and Solidarity party in the parliament elected in 2017, illustrate one of the results of the current system of political parties in both countries. Most political parties in the Czech Republic and Slovakia are weak organizationally, with small memberships and poorly staffed local organizations. The unreformed Communist Party in the Czech Republic and the Christian democratic parties in both countries had larger memberships than most other parties, but their memberships are also relatively small. Levels of party identification, which in more established democracies helps simplify political choices, link citizens to the political system, and moderate conflict, have also remained low. Many citizens do not believe that parties play an essential role in a democratic state, and many continue to hold parties and party leaders in low regard.[30]

In part, these trends reflect the legacy of the communist period. In reaction to the need to be a member of the Communist Party or its youth organization if one wanted to study at university or hold many professional jobs, many people have refused to join any party. Low levels of party membership may also reflect, however, the trend in much of the rest of Europe for parties to change from being membership organizations that influence many aspects of their members' lives to electoral parties more along the lines of US political parties. The lack of willingness to become a member of a party or to take part in party-sponsored activities, as well as negative attitudes toward parties, may also reflect citizens' experiences in the postcommunist era. The tendency of parties to come and go, the similarities in the platforms of many parties, and the frequent change in the party affiliation of political figures all make it difficult and costly in terms of time and attention for citizens to affiliate with particular parties. These trends also reinforce citizens' views of parties as vehicles to advance the personal fortunes of their leaders rather than as mechanisms to aggregate interests and pursue broader policy objectives. The lack of strong partisan identification with particular political parties in turn makes voters more susceptible to mobilization by antisystem parties (see chapter 4 on political parties).

Civil Society

In contrast to the situation in Poland and Hungary, where strong civil societies independent of the government had begun to form prior to the end of communism, there were very few independent groups in Czechoslovakia prior to 1989. Due to heavy repression and the very real threat of imprisonment, removal from jobs, and other forms of retaliation, the number of independent organizations remained very small even after Mikhail Gorbachev's glasnost. Experts estimated that there were approximately fifteen hundred independent groups in Hungary in the late 1980s,[31] compared to thirty in Czechoslovakia.[32]

Following the end of communism, Czechoslovakia experienced the same resurgence of associations and voluntary organizations that occurred elsewhere in the postcommunist world. As with political parties, some of these groups had ties to groups that had been active in the interwar or immediate post–World War II periods. Some were attached to the newly emerging parties or were branches of international organizations. Still others were new groups designed to further the interests of their members, provide charitable services, or unite citizens with similar hobbies.

Most of these new nongovernmental organizations were funded in early postcommunism by outside sources, and many remained heads without bodies—that is, groups of intellectuals in the major cities with few links to ordinary citizens or members. Domestic philanthropy has increased over time, as has the number of NGOs that no longer rely on foreign funders. Similarly, citizens are more likely to participate in the work of NGOs than in that of partisan political organizations.[33]

The NGO sector was particularly well organized in Slovakia during the mid-1990s when Vladimír Mečiar dominated partisan politics. A coordinating committee known as the Gremium included representatives of the main sectors of the NGO community and sponsored an annual conference to discuss issues of importance to NGOs. The Gremium and activists who had participated in NGO campaigns formed the core of those who organized the OK'98 campaign of civic actions that increased voter turnout sufficiently to oust Mečiar as prime minister in 1998. The impact of this campaign, the first full elaboration of the electoral model of ousting semiauthoritarian leaders in the postcommunist world, was not limited to Slovak politics but served as an inspiration and model for NGO activists in other postcommunist countries.[34]

Once the new government was formed, NGO activists continued to serve as watchdogs of the government and succeeded in passing a freedom-of-information law. With the end of government harassment of NGO activists and the return of respect for democratic procedures, the unity of the sector has diminished. During the 2002 election campaign, individual NGOs sponsored election-related actions. However, there was no repetition of the large-scale NGO campaign to get out the vote that occurred in 1998. Although some NGOs continue to lobby political leaders and monitor their actions, most NGOs have returned to focusing on their particular areas of activity.[35] Others have redirected their activities toward providing assistance to NGOs seeking to promote democracy in other countries.[36] Civil society is still weaker in both the Czech Republic and Slovakia than it is in older European democracies, and many citizens do not trust NGOs, although participation in such groups has increased over time since the end of communism.[37]

Citizens have also organized protests over a variety of issues in both countries independently of NGOs, such as those that occurred in 2017 in Slovakia to protest corruption in Fico's government and efforts to combat hate speech in the Czech Republic.[38] Such protests grew in magnitude in both countries in 2018, 2019, and 2020. They had the greatest impact in Slovakia where, as noted earlier, protests beginning in February 2018 after the murder of Ján Kuciak and his fiancée led to the resignation of the prime minister and interior minister. Popular reaction to these murders also contributed to the election of antigraft crusader Čaputová as Slovakia's president in 2019 and the victory of OL'aNO and other anticorruption parties in the 2020 elections.

In the Czech Republic, demonstrations led by the Million Moments for Democracy movement have not succeeded to date in removing Babiš and his colleagues. Its leaders have argued that opposition leaders must unify to challenge Babiš at the polls and claim that they will remain civil society activists and stay out of partisan politics.[39] In both cases, these protests were started by people who had not been active in politics or organized NGOs. They also reflect the trend that Foa and Ekiert argue has become more common as an expression of civil society in other postcommunist countries, for spontaneous protests to take place outside of formal NGOs.[40]

In addition to democratically oriented civic groups, antidemocratic extreme right groups have formed in both the Czech Republic and Slovakia since the end of communism. Some of these were short-lived skinhead or extreme-right groups that were active mainly on the local level and posed little real threat to the democratic system. However, some of their members engaged in sporadic and at times deadly violence against members of the Roma and Hungarian minorities. In recent years, more organized groups have formed, including some affiliated with extreme-right political parties, such as Kotleba's

Photo 12.4.   Hundreds of thousands of citizens protest against Czech prime minister Andrej Babiš in November 2019. (Tomas Vynikal, Shutterstock)

party in Slovakia. Members of the latter, who were affiliated with Kotleba's previous political party that was banned for racist and antidemocratic speech and behavior, wore black shirts reminiscent of Nazi uniforms and were vehemently anti-Roma and anti-Jewish. More recently, anti-immigrant sentiment, stoked in part by mainstream political leaders such as former Slovak prime minister Fico as well as by extremists like Kotleba, whose party was the third-largest vote getter in the 2017 Slovak elections, led to an increase in support for extremist rallies and actions.[41] The actions of extremist groups have also led to the organization of groups and individuals that try to combat the views of extremists among youth and to publicly identify extremists online.[42]

In the Czech Republic, Ministry of the Interior reports indicate that the total number of extremist incidents decreased somewhat from 2015 to 2016. The nature of the incidents also changed. As in previous years, more episodes were organized by far-right than by far-left groups. However, in 2016, nearly all such actions reflected anti-immigrant and anti-refugee views.[43] In perhaps the most bizarre episode, Martin Konvička, who had founded a number of far-right groups, rode a camel into Prague's Old Town Square wearing an Arab headdress and robes in August 2016; he was followed by "fighters" firing mock guns in a simulated Islamic State invasion.[44] The Bloc Against Islam, which he led, however, dissolved itself in April 2016.[45] The Interior Ministry's 2020 report noted that, in addition to far-right groups, some parties, such as Freedom and Direct Democracy (SPD), whose leader is the vice chair of the lower house of parliament, are now among the main groups propagating far-right ideas and intolerance.[46]

Political Values and Attitudes

The political values and attitudes of citizens in the Czech Republic and Slovakia reflect a variety of influences, as in many other postcommunist countries. Some of these stem from the precommunist political culture, which contained both democratic and nondemocratic elements. Others derive from the communist era, and still others have developed in response to transition experiences since 1989.

The political attitudes of citizens of the Czech Republic and Slovakia differ somewhat from those of citizens in non-postcommunist members of the EU. These differences are most evident in perceptions and levels of trust in government institutions and in citizens' perceptions of their own political roles as well as in levels of political efficacy, the sense that they can make a difference at either the local or national level if their interests are threatened.[47] Surveys conducted in 2019 found somewhat contradictory attitudes concerning the functioning of the political system. Thus, somewhat over half of respondents reported satisfaction with democracy (57 percent in the Czech Republic and 52 percent in Slovakia) and 88 percent in Slovakia and 79 percent in Slovakia believed the state was run for the benefit of all (an increase of 18 and 17 percent, respectively, from 1991), the highest levels in Europe. Large percentages of people in both countries also felt that voting gives people like them a say (73 percent in the Czech Republic and 75 percent in Slovakia). At the same time, similarly large percentages in both (63 percent in Slovakia and 73 percent in the Czech Republic) did not believe that elected officials cared about what people like them think. Citizens in both gave more importance (82 percent in the Czech Republic and 70 percent in Slovakia) to a fair judiciary and free speech (70 and 61, respectively), as well as to free media and freedom for opposition parties, than to freedom for civil society (46 percent in the Czech Republic and 51 percent in Slovakia).[48]

In the early 1990s, citizens in the Czech Lands were more likely than those in Slovakia to agree that citizens should be responsible for ensuring their own well-being; they also accepted that a certain level of unemployment was part of the shift to the market. As unemployment rates grew in the Czech Republic, differences decreased. Popular resistance to fees for higher education and medical services, as well as to other measures that have decreased the government's responsibility for services and welfare, are further indications of the extent to which citizens internalized the belief common under communism that the state owes citizens a great deal of material security. By 2019, most citizens in both countries believed that success in life was determined by outside forces (61 percent in Slovakia and 37 percent in the Czech Republic), the second- and fourth-highest levels in the European countries surveyed.[49]

Early studies of tolerance found that levels of anti-Semitism were lower in the Czech Republic than in Slovakia, Poland, and Hungary. Attitudes toward Jews were favorable in 2018 in both countries, especially in the Czech Republic (65 percent positive; 58 percent in Slovakia), though just over a quarter of respondents in both expressed negative views of Jews.[50] Studies done in early postcommunism and more recently repeatedly documented very high levels of prejudice against the Roma in the Czech Republic as well as in Slovakia. In 2019, 66 percent of respondents in the Czech Republic and 76 percent of those in Slovakia held negative views of Roma.[51] Anti-Islam and anti-refugee attitudes are common in both countries. In 2018, 68 percent of respondents had negative views of Muslims; in Slovakia, 77 percent had negative views.

These studies illustrate continuing challenges in developing democratic political cultures in the two countries among ordinary citizens. As the instances of misuse of power and scandals indicate, there are also continuing problems at the elite level, where the notion that public office is largely for self-enrichment and a lack of respect for conflict-of-interest rules are common.

Economic Policies and Conditions

Shortly after the end of communism, Czechoslovakia's new elites began debating the best way to return to a market economy. Early discussions of a more gradual, or third, way were soon replaced, under the direction of the then–federal finance minister Václav Klaus, by the decision to move rapidly and decisively to the market. This decision—accompanied by the end of, or decreases in, government subsidies, a rapid increase in prices, and efforts to privatize the economy, which was almost entirely in state hands—led to a steep drop in production and an increase in unemployment, economic hardship, and poverty. The negative effects of the shift to the market were especially evident in Slovakia.

The country's new leaders used a variety of methods to privatize economic assets. These included auctions, sales to foreign investors, and, most distinctively, the use of vouchers or coupons. Under the latter system, citizens were able to buy vouchers very inexpensively, which they could then exchange for shares in privatizing companies. This system, which became a sort of parlor game at the time, was designed to compensate for the lack of domestic capital at the end of communism as well as to give most citizens a personal stake in the continuation of market reforms. However, because it was not accompanied by changes in the banking sector or even, until several years later, the adoption of a bankruptcy law, it did little to restructure the economy. As in other postcommunist countries, privatization was also accompanied by massive fraud and corruption.[52]

Political elites also adopted laws to regulate restitution, the return of property that had been seized by the state to its rightful owners or their heirs, and to stimulate the development of new private enterprises. The country's trade was also rapidly reoriented to the West.

Eventually the shift to the market created more favorable economic conditions in both the Czech Republic and Slovakia. However, in the period soon after the end of communism, policies designed to achieve this goal created greater hardship in Slovakia. They also affected different groups of the population very differently. Thus, the economic transition created both winners and losers. The former were those who had the education, contacts, and ability to benefit from the new opportunities to increase their skills and qualifications, travel abroad for study or work, practice their occupations free of ideological interference, work for a private or international corporation, or found a private business. These were primarily the young, urban, and well educated. For those lacking such skills and opportunities (those who were older, rural, and less educated, as well as families with several children and the Roma), the shift to the market and other economic changes brought primarily hardships.

Both the Czech and Slovak economies have attracted sizable amounts of foreign investment (see chapter 5). In the Slovak case, outside investors began investing in Slovakia after the victory of the liberal opposition in the 1998 elections. Both countries now play an important role in producing many products for the European market, including, most notably, automobiles. After nearly a decade of high growth rates, both countries suffered from the 2008–2009 global economic crisis. Gross domestic product contracted in 2009 by 4.1 percent in the Czech Republic and 4.7 percent in Slovakia, after 2.5 percent growth in the Czech Republic and 6.2 percent growth in Slovakia in 2008.[53] Both economies began to recover in 2010 but grew at slower rates and more unevenly than in the 1990s. As planned, Slovakia adopted the euro on January 1, 2009. Despite fears about the impact of this move on more vulnerable parts of the population, most analysts believe that it helped Slovakia weather the global crisis.

Economic performance in both countries has more recently been affected by the coronavirus pandemic. Leaders in both countries initially were among the most successful in Europe in combating the virus. Death rates in both were among the lowest in Europe through June 2020 due to early shutdowns, coherent and consistent messaging on the part of national leaders, and citizens' willingness to wear masks and adhere to other guidelines concerning social distancing and behavior. Once restrictions were lifted, however, cases in both countries rose in late July and began to surge in late October and November.[54] Death rates in late October in the Czech Republic were among the highest in the world.[55] Governments in both countries declared states of emergency and reinstituted partial lockdowns, which, with some easing of restrictions, were expected to remain in effect for much of the rest of 2020. Slovaks who received negative test results in a round of mass testing in early November were exempt from the nighttime curfew but had to carry a certificate affirming their negative status with them outside their homes.[56] In late June, the Organisation for Economic Co-operation and Development (OECD) projected an approximate 13 percent drop in GDP in the Czech Republic and an 11 percent drop in Slovakia, if, as occurred, there was a second wave of the virus.[57] Similar factors influenced these projections in both countries, including the pandemic's impact on the automotive industry and both countries' integration into European supply chains. Unemployment in the Czech Republic, which was the lowest in the OECD in 2019 at 2.0 percent, was predicted to increase to 3.8 percent in 2020, and to 9.6 percent in Slovakia that same year, up from 5.8 percent in 2019.[58]

Key Social Issues

In addition to bringing poverty and unemployment to some groups, the shift to the market and the broader transition also had a number of social consequences. First among these is growing inequality. Although inequalities in terms of lifestyles, values, and access to higher education existed under communism,[59] and the communist leadership clearly had many material privileges, Czech and Slovak societies were generally very egalitarian, and those who had greater wealth were fairly circumspect about it. With the return to the market, inequalities increased dramatically. Wage differentials, which had been among the lowest in the communist world, widened significantly, and with the expanded availability of consumer durables and goods, it suddenly became clear to many families that they were not living as well as their neighbors.

Czech and Slovak societies have once again become more complex, as the return of the market led to the emergence of new occupations and groups, particularly in the rapidly expanding service and financial sectors. Restitution and the growth of the private sector also led to the reemergence of certain previously banned social categories, such as capitalists and entrepreneurs. There were also important shifts in the status and prestige, as well as the incomes, of different occupations and groups. At the same time that these changes opened up many new opportunities for some citizens, the situation of members of other groups, such as agricultural workers, manual workers, and some members of the party's former apparatus, worsened. Negative economic trends have had a particularly noticeable impact on Roma in both countries.

The opening of the borders and decline of tight political and police control also led to the intensification of all forms of social pathology, such as alcoholism, drug use, and abuse within families, and to the emergence of new issues, such as trafficking in persons, smuggling, and HIV/AIDS. Many of these problems were intensified by the economic transition as economic hardship took its toll on families.

The end of communism also allowed certain issues, such as ethnic tensions and issues related to sexuality, to emerge into the open and get onto the political agenda. Hungarian activists in Slovakia formed their own political parties and began to make demands for greater respect for minority culture and more attention to minority rights. The positive start to forging new relationships evident in the inclusion of a Hungarian party in the first postcommunist coalition government in Slovakia was interrupted temporarily by Mečiar's government, which enacted a number of laws that, among other things, restricted the right of the Hungarian minority to use its language in official dealings, removed dual-language street signs, and required Hungarian women to add the Slavic suffix *ová* to their last names.

With the victory of the democratically oriented opposition in 1998, the by-now-single Hungarian party was once again included in governing coalitions, and the most offensive legislation of the Mečiar era was reversed. Hungarian leaders continued to press for greater recognition of minority rights but played a constructive role within the coalition government on many issues. The inclusion of the nationalist, anti-Hungarian Slovak National Party in Prime Minister Robert Fico's coalition after the 2006 elections halted the progress made in this regard. There were several isolated incidents of violence by Slovaks against ethnic Hungarians who were speaking Hungarian. The inflammatory rhetoric used by some political leaders at this time heightened tensions within Slovakia and also contributed to worsening relations between Slovakia and Hungary. Ethnic relations and Slovak-Hungarian relations took a turn for the worse in 2009 when a language law was enacted that restricted the use of Hungarian and other non-Slovak languages in official contacts in Slovakia. The government's effort to replace Hungarian geographic names with Slovak names in Hungarian-language textbooks, which Hungarian-language schools refused to use,[60] further angered ethnic Hungarians in Slovakia. The center-right government formed after the 2010 elections, which once again included representatives of a Hungarian party, worked to improve Slovak-Hungarian relations within the country and Slovakia's relations with Hungary. The formation of a political party explicitly designed to cross the ethnic divide, Most-Híd (a party whose name consists of the Slovak and Hungarian words for "bridge"), reflected the effort of some Hungarian and Slovak leaders to foster good relations among the two groups. However, Most-Híd's participation in Fico's coalition government, along with a far-right party, was one of the factors that led to its defeat in the 2020 elections. Since no other Hungarian party passed the required threshold to seat deputies, there are no representatives of the Hungarian minority in the Slovak parliament at present.

The status of the Roma community has also become an important issue. Subject to various measures to foster assimilation during the communist era, Roma continue to face widespread prejudice and discrimination in both the Czech Republic and Slovakia. Education levels among the Roma are very low, and the practice of sending Roma children to special schools for the mentally handicapped remains widespread. Unemployment rates approach 85 percent in many Roma communities. The living conditions of many Roma, who reside in "settlements" on the outskirts of towns and cities, are very poor, as many lack running water, electricity, and other public services. Violence against the Roma has also been an ongoing problem since the end of communism. Unlike the Hungarian minority, the Roma have not developed effective political organizations to raise their claims in the political arena. Both the Czech and Slovak governments have adopted programs, in part at the prodding of the EU, to improve the status of the Roma, but serious problems, including overwhelmingly negative public attitudes toward the group, remain in both countries.[61]

Gender issues have also emerged as political issues since 1989. In part because women's equality was an official goal during the communist era, and in part because the uneven pattern of change in women's roles created great stress for women and their families,[62] many Czechs and Slovaks rejected the idea of women's equality immediately after the end of communism. This backlash was reflected in the view that women should emphasize their maternal rather than economic roles, as well as in the reluctance on the part of many women to be actively involved in politics. Although most women continued to be employed, women were more likely than men to lose their jobs in the Czech Republic as a result of the transition. In both countries, they also faced increased competition from men for jobs in areas such as tourism, law, and financial services, which became more attractive under market conditions. Given the continued traditional division of labor within the home, the task of dealing with the results of declining social services, as well as the need to stretch family budgets to cover necessities, also fell most heavily on women during the early part of the transition.

Women's political representation also declined in the early postcommunist period. Many women appeared to share the view of male leaders, including some former dissidents, who argued that politics was too dirty for women or that women had more important tasks than arguing about political issues. This pattern began to change in the late 1990s as levels of women's representation increased in both the Czech Republic and Slovakia. However, women are still underrepresented in the political elite, and it is still difficult for women leaders to raise issues of particular concern for women.[63] As a result of the 2010 elections, Iveta Radičová, a former NGO activist and sociologist who has done research on gender issues, became Slovakia's first woman prime minister. She also became the first woman candidate for president to advance to the second round, although she lost to the incumbent.[64] Despite Radičová's position as head of the government, the number of women in the Slovak parliament decreased from 18 to 15.3 percent after the 2010 elections. In the Czech Republic, 22 percent of members of the lower house of parliament were women after the 2010 elections. In Slovakia, women's percentage of deputies in the legislature increased slightly to 20 percent after the 2016 elections; in the Czech Republic, women's representation was at its 2010 level of 22 percent after the 2017 elections.[65] The election of Zuzana Čaputová as Slovakia's president in 2019 and Markéta Pekarová

Adamová's election as head of the TOP party in the Czech Republic raised hopes that women would come to play a greater role in national politics.[66] However, as the OECD report on the 2020 Slovak elections noted, only 632 women were among the 2,736 registered candidates, and only two of the women, who generally comprised a quarter or less of candidates on parties' lists, were in the top ten positions. The report also noted that parties did not take any special measures to encourage women to run or vote.[67]

By the mid-1990s, the backlash against even considering or discussing issues related to women's status began to decrease. Social scientists and women's advocates succeeded in getting certain issues related to women's situations onto the political agenda. Women's groups, particularly the small number of such groups that identify themselves as feminist, have also succeeded in establishing links with a few political leaders and have provided background materials as well as position papers on issues such as same-sex partnerships and legislation prohibiting sexual harassment in the workplace. Public discussion of women's issues in the media also increased. The EU accession process accelerated these trends in both countries, as political leaders were forced to adopt nondiscrimination laws and establish government institutions to address issues related to women's status as part of that process.

Women activists in both countries continue to press for changes in a variety of areas. In the Czech Republic, Forum 50% supporters are working to increase women's share of elected officials to 50 percent. In Slovakia, women affiliated with *Aspekt*, a feminist journal, threatened to organize a protest should the conservative Christian Union, which is part of the main party in the government coalition, follow through on its plans to restrict abortion in September 2020.[68] A variety of feminist groups are active in the Czech Republic.[69]

Emerging Challenges: Exceptions or Part of a Common Pattern?

To return to the question posed at the beginning of this chapter, are the Slovak and Czech Republics exceptions to the rule in Central and East Europe? Or are retreats from democracy evident in the rest of the region, particularly in Poland and Hungary, also evident in these countries?

As the preceding pages have illustrated, both Slovakia and the Czech Republic are among the success stories in the postcommunist world. Although political and economic developments diverged in Slovakia under Mečiar, in the period since 1998, political leaders have successfully achieved many of the objectives set out after the fall of communism in 1989. Thus, both Slovakia and the Czech Republic are now among those countries classified as "free" by Freedom House and other international ranking bodies. Although important problems remain with the party system, as well as with elite and mass political culture, both are widely recognized as functioning liberal democracies. Securely anchored in European and transatlantic institutions, both Slovakia and the Czech Republic have also achieved recognition for their roles in supporting pro-democracy movements in the postcommunist world.

Both countries' economies have also been among the success stories in the region. Economic growth rates were among the highest in Europe prior to the 2008 crisis in the world economy. Privatization was successfully accomplished, and the standard of living has long surpassed its 1989 level in both countries. As with most countries in Europe and elsewhere, economic growth rates plummeted in 2020 as a result of the COVID crisis. Both also faced the continuing need to deal with the pandemic's resurgence in fall 2020 and with popular "COVID fatigue" caused by fluctuating restrictions and reopenings.

As in other postcommunist, as well as many other developed, Western countries, numerous problems remain in all of these areas. In the political realm, these include the need to develop a stable system of political parties and to increase linkages between political leaders and citizens, as well as between political leaders and the NGO sector. The inclusion of far-right parties in the parliaments of both is another worrisome trend that reflects the weaknesses in the party system as well as ongoing issues with both elite and mass political values and attitudes. As anti-Islamic demonstrations and the negative attitudes of citizens toward refugees illustrate, both countries also need to continue to foster tolerance as well as a political culture that supports democracy and includes a greater sense of citizens' responsibility to take action to resolve public problems and join with others to address common issues. The election of Andrej Babiš in the Czech Republic in 2017 and steps his government has taken to try to limit the number of people involved in policy making, as well as the elimination of press conferences after cabinet meetings, raise the possibility that the Czech Republic may also experience democratic backsliding, as does the reelection of Miloš Zeman as president. Babiš's replacement of the interior minister soon after he was about to be investigated for fraud also raised the possibility that he, like leaders in Hungary and Poland, would try to control and misuse the judiciary. In Slovakia, the government crisis that occurred in March 2021 led to Matovič's resignation as prime minister over his purchase of a Russian COVID-19 vaccine despite the opposition of certain members of the government. This crisis illustrates the problems that the need for coalitions due to the nature of the party system poses for government stability.

There is also room for improvement in dealing with corruption. Both countries have recently experienced major political scandals that have tainted political life and political elites. In Slovakia, the Gorilla corruption scandal, in which top leaders were taped discussing bribes, hampers the development of a large center-right party. More recently, the murder of Ján Kuciak highlighted the ongoing problems with corruption in Slovakia. The continued popularity of Prime Minister Babiš's party, despite the fact that he is under investigation for improper use of EU funds, is another indicator of the tolerance of corruption in the Czech Republic.

In the economic arena, both governments continue to face regional disparities and unemployment, as well as a host of problems arising from aging and declining populations. They also must address the problem of persistent poverty among certain groups, particularly the Roma, as well as other unresolved issues related to the marginal status of the Roma. Gender issues are another area requiring greater attention. As changes occur in the wage differentials relative to those in more developed EU members, which made both countries attractive to foreign investors, Czech and Slovak leaders will also need to find other incentives to attract outside capital. They must also deal with the devastating impact of the COVID-19 crisis on the economy.

In sum, political leaders and citizens face important challenges in both Slovakia and the Czech Republic. However, although these issues raise the possibility that both countries may follow in the footsteps of neighboring Poland and Hungary, to date there has not been the same degree of backsliding from democratic norms and practices as has been evident in those two countries. Recent developments in Slovakia, including the success of public protests in bringing about the resignation of both a prime minister and the interior minister and the results of recent elections, indicate a clear repudiation of corrupt practices and a desire for transparent government. Although their impact to date has not been as great, massive protests calling for the resignation of Prime Minister Babiš also indicate a desire to remove corrupt politicians from office and to maintain a strong democracy in the Czech Republic. Whether the Czech Republic and particularly Slovakia, which are not exceptional in the problems they face, will continue to be exceptional in their active resistance to gross violations of democratic practices and norms, and thus avoid backsliding, depends significantly on the actions of political leaders and citizens.

Study Questions

1. How were developments in the precommunist and communist periods reflected in the postcommunist period in the Czech Lands and Slovakia?
2. What caused the Velvet Divorce, and what were its consequences?
3. What role did NGOs play in the ouster of Vladimír Mečiar in Slovakia in 1998?
4. What trends are evident in the party systems in each country?
5. What major challenges face leaders and citizens in each country?
6. Have these countries resisted the trend toward backsliding from democracy seen in their neighbors?

Suggested Readings

Bunce, Valerie J., and Sharon L. Wolchik. *Defeating Authoritarian Leaders in Postcommunist Countries.* New York: Cambridge University Press, 2011.

Guasti, Petra. "Development of Citizen Participation in Central and Eastern Europe after the EU Enlargement and Economic Crises." *Communist and Post-Communist Studies* 49, no. 3 (September 2016): 219–31.

Leff, Carol Skalnik. *The Czech and Slovak Republics: Nation vs. State.* Boulder, CO: Westview, 1996.

Skilling, H. Gordon. *Czechoslovakia's Interrupted Revolution.* Princeton, NJ: Princeton University Press, 1976.

Stolarik, M. Mark, ed., *The Czech and Slovak Republics: Twenty Years of Independence.* Budapest: Central University Press, 2016.

Wolchik, Sharon L. *Czechoslovakia in Transition: Politics, Economics, and Society.* London: Pinter, 1991.

Websites

Czech Republic
Prague Daily Monitor: http://praguemonitor.com
Prague Post: http://www.praguepost.com

Slovakia
Slovak Spectator: http://spectator.sme.sk
Pozor Blog: http://pozorblog.com

Notes

The author is grateful to Alison Keefner, Gabriel Kelly, and the Institute for European, Russian and Eurasian Affairs at George Washington University.

1. Samuel Harrison Thomson, *Czechoslovakia in European History* (Princeton, NJ: Princeton University Press, 1953).

2. Zora Pryor, "Czechoslovak Economic Development in the Interwar Period," in *A History of the Czechoslovak Republic: 1918–1948*, ed. Victor S. Mamatey and Radomír Luza (Princeton, NJ: Princeton University Press, 1973).

3. Owen V. Johnson, *Slovakia, 1918–1938: Education and the Making of a Nation* (New York: Columbia University Press, 1985).

4. H. Gordon Skilling, "Stalinism and Czechoslovak Political Culture," in *Stalinism: Essays in Historical Interpretation*, ed. Robert C. Tucker (New York: Norton, 1977).

5. Lucy S. Dawidowicz, *The War against the Jews: 1933–1945* (New York: Bantam; Bratislava: Institute for Public Affairs, 1975), 20.

6. See Arthur Koestler, *Darkness at Noon* (New York: Macmillan, 1941), for a fictionalized account of the purges.

7. See H. Gordon Skilling, *Czechoslovakia's Interrupted Revolution* (Princeton, NJ: Princeton University Press, 1976.

8. Robin Alison Remington, ed., *Winter in Prague: Documents on Czechoslovak Communism in Crisis* (Cambridge, MA: MIT Press, 1969).

9. Ludvík Vaculík, "2,000 Words to Workers, Farmers, Scientists, Artists and Everyone," in *Winter in Prague: Documents on Czechoslovak Communism in Crisis*, ed. Robin Alison Remington (Cambridge, MA: MIT Press, 1969).

10. Kieran Williams, *The Prague Spring and Its Aftermath: Czechoslovak Politics, 1968–1970* (Cambridge: Cambridge University Press, 1997); Jaromír Navrátil, ed., *The Prague Spring '68* (Budapest: Central European University Press, 1998).

11. Sharon L. Wolchik, "Czechoslovakia," in *The Columbia History of Eastern Europe in the Twentieth Century*, ed. Joseph Held (New York: Columbia University Press, 1992).

12. Sharon L. Wolchik, "Institutional Factors in the Break-Up of Czechoslovakia," in *Irreconcilable Differences: Explaining Czechoslovakia's Dissolution*, ed. Michael Kraus and Allison Stanger (New York: Rowman & Littlefield, 2000).

13. Parliament of the Czech Republic, "The Constitution of the Czech Republic," Chamber of Deputies of the Parliament of the Czech Republic, adopted 1993, accessed August 7, 2020, https://www.psp.cz/en/docs/laws/constitution.html.

14. President of the Slovak Republic, "Constitution of the Slovak Republic," Office of the President of the Slovak Republic, accessed August 7, 2020, https://www.prezident.sk/upload-files/46422.pdf.

15. Sharon L. Wolchik, "The Czech Republic: Havel and the Evolution of the Presidency since 1989," in *Postcommunist Presidents*, ed. Ray Taras (Cambridge: Cambridge University Press, 1997).

16. See Beata Balogová, "Kiska: 'I Am Not One of Those Traditional Politicians,'" *Slovak Spectator*, March 9, 2014; "Kiska: Attitude to Migration Crisis to Define the Character of Slovakia," *Slovak Spectator*, September 7, 2015, https://spectator.sme.skc/20060149/kiska-attitude-to-migration-crisis-to-define-the-character-of-slovakia.html.

17. Nina Hrabovská Francelová, "From Attorney and Activist to President of Slovakia: Who Is Zuzana Čaputová?," *Slovak Spectator*, March 30, 2019, https://spectator.sme.sk/c/22086171/zuza na-caputova-is-the-new-slovak-president.html.

18. President of the Slovak Republic, "Constitution of the Slovak Republic."

19. President of the Slovak Republic, "Constitution of the Slovak Republic."

20. Sharon L. Wolchik, "The Repluralization of Politics in Czechoslovakia," *Communist and Post-Communist Studies* 26 (December 1993): 412–31.

21. Tomáš Kostelecký, *Political Parties after Communism: Development in East Central Europe* (Baltimore, MD: Johns Hopkins University Press, 2002).

22. Kevin Deegan-Krause and Tim Haughton, "In with the New (Again): Annuals, Perennials and the Patterns of Party Politics in Central and Eastern Europe" (conference paper prepared for the Nineteenth International Meeting of Europeanists, Council on European Studies, Boston, MA, March 22–24, 2012); Tim Haughton and Kevin Deegan-Krause, "Hurricane Season: Systems of Instability in Central and East European Party Politics," *East European Politics and Societies and Cultures* 29, no. 1 (February 2015): 61–80. See also Tim Haughton and Kevin Deegan-Krause, *The New Party Challenge: Changing Cycles of Party Birth and Death in Central Europe and Beyond* (Oxford: Oxford University Press, 2020).

23. See Martin Bútora, "New Prospects for Alternative Politics," in *Alternative Politics? The Rise of New Political Parties in Central Europe*, ed. Zora Bútorová, Olga Gyárfášová, and Grigorij Mesežnikov (Bratislava: Institute for Public Affairs, 2013), 11ff; Sarah Engler, "Corruption and Electoral Support for New Political Parties in Central and Eastern Europe," *West European Politics* 39, no. 2 (2016): 278–304; Oľga Gyárfášová, Miloslav Bahna, and Martin Slosiarik, "Sila nestálosti: volatilita voličov na Slovensku vo voľbách 2016," *Středoevropské politické studie* 19, no. 1 (2017): 1–24, https://journals.muni.cz/cepsr/article/v iew/6861/6357.

24. National Democratic Institute, "2016 Parliamentary Elections Signal a Shift to the Right in Slovakia," National Democratic Institute, April 29, 2016, https://www.ndi.org/Parliamentary -Elections-Signal-Political-Change.

25. Tim Haughton, Darina Malová, and Kevin Deegan-Krause, "Slovakia's Newly Elected Parliament Is Dramatically Different and Pretty Much the Same. Here's How," *Washington Post*, March 9, 2016, http://www.washingtonpost.com/news/monkey-cage/Slovakia's-newly-electe d-parliament-is-dramatically-different-and-pretty-much-the-same-here's-how.

26. Haughton, Malová, and Deegan-Krause, "Slovakia's Newly Elected Parliament."

27. Spectator Staff, "Final Results: Debacle for the Coalition, Great Victory for Matovič," *Slovak Spectator*, March 1, 2020, https://spectator.sme.sk/c/22338362/2020-parliamentary-elect ion-slovakia-preliminary-results-outcome.html.

28. Spectator Staff, "Matovič Survives No Confidence Vote, Remains PM," *Slovak Spectator*, July 24, 2020, https://spectator.sme.sk/c/22453355/matovic-survives-no-confidence-vote-remains-pm.html.

29. Spectator Staff, "Final Results: Debacle for the Coalition."

30. See Institute for Public Opinion Research, "Evaluation of Political Parties and Selected Institutions," June 2017, https://cvvm.soc.cas.cz/en/press-releases/political/politicians-political -institutions/4382-evaluation-of-the-activities-of-political-parties-and-selected-institutions-june -2017; see also Naděžda Čadová, "Důvěra k vybraným institucím veřejného života, březen 2017," https://cvvm.soc.cas.cz/media/com_form2content/documents/c6/a4297/f77/po170410 .pdf; Naděžda Čadová, "Názory české veřejnosti na úroveň demokracie a respektování lidských práv v ČR—únor 2017," March 28, 2017, https://cvvm.soc.cas.cz/en/press-releases/political /democracy-civic-society/4280-public-opinion-on-the-functioning-of-democracy-and-respect-to -human-rights-in-the-czech-republic-february-2017; and Robert Klobucký and Marianna Mrava, "Všeobecná dôvera v slovenskej populácii je na relatívne nízkej ale stabilizovanej úrovni: tlačová konferencia v rámci projektov APVV-14-0527, APVV-15-0653, 3.2.2017," SAV [elektronický

zdroj] (Bratislava: Sociologický ústav SAV, 2017), http://www.sociologia.sav.sk/cms/uploaded/254 3_attach_TB_Klobucky_Mrva.pdf.

31. Rudolf Tokes, "Hungary's New Political Elites: Adaptation and Change, 1989–1990," *Problems of Communism* 39 (November–December 1990): 44–65.

32. George Schopflin, Rudolf Tokes, and Ivan Volgyes, "Leadership Change and Crisis in Hungary," *Problems of Communism* 37, no. 5 (September–October 1988): 23–46.

33. Tereza Vajdová, *An Assessment of Czech Civil Society in 2004: After Fifteen Years of Development* (Prague: Civicus, 2005).

34. See Pavol Demeš, "Non-Governmental Organizations and Volunteerism," in *Global Report on Society, Slovakia 2002*, ed. Grigorij Mesežnikov, Miroslav Kollár, and Tom Nicholson (Bratislava: Institute for Public Affairs, 2002); and Valerie J. Bunce and Sharon L. Wolchik, "Favorable Conditions and Electoral Revolutions," *Journal of Democracy* 17, no. 4 (October 2006): 5–18. See also Peter Vandor, Nicole Traxler, Reinhard Millner, and Michael Meyer, eds., *Civil Society in Central and Eastern Europe: Challenges and Opportunities* (Vienna: ERSTE Foundation, 2017).

35. Jana Kadlecová and Katarina Vajdová, "Non-Governmental Organizations and Volunteerism," in *Global Report on Society, Slovakia 2003*, ed. Grigorij Mesežnikov and Miroslav Kollár (Bratislava: Institute for Public Affairs, 2004).

36. See Tsveta Petrova, *From Solidarity to Geopolitics* (New York: Cambridge University Press, 2014).

37. See Marc Morje Howard, *The Weakness of Civil Society* (New York: Cambridge University Press, 2003); and Jiří Navrátil and Miroslav Pospíšil, *Two Decades Later, Civic Advocacy in the Czech Republic* (Brno: MUNI Press, 2014).

38. Pavol Frič and Martin Vávra, "Czech Civil Sector Face-to-Face with Freelance Activism," *International Journal of Sociology and Social Policy* 36, no. 11 (2017): 774–91, http://proxygw.wrlc. org/login?url=https://search-proquest-com.proxygw.wrlc.org/docview/1832070360?accountid=11 243. See also Roberto Stefan Foa and Grzegorz Ekiert, "The Weakness of Postcommunist Civil Society Reassessed," *European Journal of Political Research* 56, no. 2 (May 2017): 419–39.

39. Hana de Goeij and Marc Santora, "In the Largest Protest in Decades, Czechs Demand Resignation of Prime Minister," *New York Times*, June 23, 2019, https://www.nytimes.com/2019 /06/23/world/europe/czech-republic-protests-andrej-Babiš.html.

40. Foa and Ekiert, "The Weakness."

41. "Kotleba Accused of Extremism, Faces Losing Mandate," *Slovak Spectator*, July 28, 2017, https://Spectator.sme.sk/c/20615664/kotleba-accused-of-extremism-faces-losing-mandate.html.

42. See http://www.protinavisti.cz and http://www.exitslovensko for examples.

43. See also Vandor et al., *Civil Society in Central and Eastern Europe*.

44. Ministerstvo vnitra České Republiky, *Report on Extremism in the Territory of the Czech Republic in 2016*, Prague, 2017.

45. http://www.radio.cz/en/sefin/news, April 25, 2016.

46. "Czech Interior Ministry Report Finds Far-Right Party Was the 'Super-Spreader' of Hate Last Year," *Prague Monitor*, July 13, 2020, http://www.romea.cz/en/news/czech/czech-interior-m inistry-report-finds-far-right-party-was-the-super-spreader-of-hate-last-year-2.

47. Richard Wike et al., "European Public Opinion Three Decades after the Fall of Communism," Pew Research Center, October 15, 2019, https://www.pewresearch.org/global/ 2019/10/15/european-public-opinion-three-decades-after-the-fall-of-communism.

48. Wike et al., "European Public Opinion."

49. Wike et al., "European Public Opinion."

50. Pew Research Center, "Eastern and Western Europeans Differ on Importance of Religion, Views of Minorities, and Key Social Issues," Pew Research Center, October 29, 2018, https://ww w.pewforum.org/2018/10/29/eastern-and-western-europeans-differ-on-importance-of-religion-v iews-of-minorities-and-key-social-issues.

51. Wike et al., "European Public Opinion."

52. Jiří Pehe, *Vytunelování demokracie* (Prague: Academia, 2002).

53. Economist Intelligence Unit, "Country Report: Czech Republic" (London: Economist Intelligence Unit, 2009), 19; Economist Intelligence Unit, "Country Report: Slovakia" (London: Economist Intelligence Unit, 2009), 18.

54. See Miroslav Beblavy, "How Slovakia Flattened the Curve," *Foreign Policy*, May 6, 2020, https://foreignpolicy.com/2020/05/06/slovakia-coronavirus-pandemic-public-trust-media; and Yasmeen Serhan, "Lessons from Slovakia—Where Leaders Wear Masks," *Atlantic*, May 13, 2020, https://www.theatlantic.com/international/archive/2020/05/slovakia-mask-coronavirus-pandemic -success/611545. See also http://worldometerws.info.

55. Rob Cameron, "COVID-19: How the Czech Republic's Response Went Wrong," BBC News, October 26, 2020, https://www.bbc.com/news/world-europe-54639351.

56. "Slovakia's Second Round of COVID Tests Draws Large Crowds," Reuters, November 7, 2020, www.voanews.com/covid-19pandemic/Slovakia.

57. OECD, "OECD Economic Outlook," Volume 2020, no. 1, 195.

58. OECD, "OECD Economic Outlook," 180, 298.

59. David Lane, *The End of Inequality? Stratification under State Socialism* (New York: Penguin, 1971).

60. Freedom House, "Slovakia," in *Nations in Transit 2009* (Washington, DC: Freedom House, 2009), 494, http://www.freedomhouse.org/report/nations-transit/2009/slovakia#.U9f8 0lYSAeI.

61. Michal Jurásková, Martina Vašečka, and Tom Nicholson, *Global Report on Roma in Slovakia* (Bratislava: Institute for Public Affairs, 2014), https://is.muni.cz/el/cus/podzim2016/CZS 13/um/lecture10/romaglob_final.pdf; Freedom House, "Slovakia," 494.

62. Jane S. Jaquette and Sharon L. Wolchik, eds., *Women and Democracy: Latin America and Central and Eastern Europe* (Baltimore, MD: Johns Hopkins University Press, 1998).

63. See also Marilyn Rueschemeyer and Sharon L. Wolchik, eds., *Women in Power in Post-Communist Parliaments* (Bloomington: Indiana University Press, 2009), for the results of interviews with women deputies in six postcommunist parliaments.

64. Sharon Wolchik, "Iveta Radičová, the First Female Prime Minister in Slovakia," in *Women Presidents and Prime Ministers in Post-Transition Democracies*, ed. Veronica Montecinos, 239–58 (New York: Palgrave Macmillan, 2017).

65. Inter-Parliamentary Union, "Women in National Parliaments," http://www.ipu.org/wmn -e/classif.htm; Czech Statistical Office, http://volby.cz.

66. Ian Willoughby, "What Chance a First Female Czech Prime Minister or President?," Prague Radio International, March 6, 2020, https://english.radio.cz/what-chance-a-first-female -czech-prime-minister-or-president-8106229.

67. OSCE, "Slovakia, Parliamentary Elections, 29 February 2020: Final Report," OSCE, May 15, 2020, 9, https://www.osce.org/files/f/documents/8/3/452377.pdf.

68. Michaela Terenzani, "Coalition Reveals Plans to Amend Abortion Laws," *Slovak Spectator*, June 19, 2020, https://spectator.sme.sk/c/22429647/coalition-reveals-plans-to-amend-abortion-la ws-including-gathering-more-information-about-women-who-request-one.html.

69. Hana Havelková and Libor Oates-Indruchová, eds., *The Politics of Gender Culture under State Socialism* (London: Routledge, 2015); Iveta Jusová and Jiřina Šiklová, eds., *Czech Feminisms: Perspective on Gender in East Central Europe* (Bloomington: Indiana University Press, 2016).

Map 13.0. Hungary

CHAPTER 13

Hungary

Federigo Argentieri and Ognen Vangelov

In the late spring of 1989, a twenty-six-year-old bearded graduate in law spoke in extremely blunt terms to a large crowd in Budapest's Heroes' Square on the occasion of the solemn reburial of Imre Nagy, the leader of the government put in place by the 1956 revolution, and his associates, who had been executed thirty-one years earlier and dumped into mass graves. The speech demanded the immediate withdrawal of Soviet troops from Hungary. This frightened many observers, on the grounds that such a request was premature and could have significant consequences. The speaker was Viktor Orbán, leader of the Alliance of Young Democrats (Fidesz), a party formed the previous year, who became the favorite politician of international public opinion supporting democratic change in the region.

Almost three decades later, on July 22, 2017, at the end of a speech, the same Viktor Orbán, prime minister of the country since 2010, stated, "27 years ago here in Central Europe we believed that Europe was our future; today we feel that we are the future of Europe."[1] Orbán made this dramatic statement in Romania, the neighbor country with the largest Hungarian minority population, at the twenty-eighth annual Bálványos Free Summer University and Student Camp. The meaning of his declaration can be understood in light of the events of the previous three years. On July 26, 2014, at the same summer event, Orbán had clearly spelled out his political views and plans for Hungary. The words that caught the attention of many domestic and international observers were, "We have to abandon liberal methods and principles of organizing a society, as well as the liberal way to look at the world." The Fidesz chief went on to explain that liberalism "holds that we are free to do anything that does not violate another person's freedom. . . . Instead the principle should be do not do to others what you would not do to yourself. And we will attempt to found a world we can call the Hungarian society on this theoretical principle, in political thinking, education, in the way we ourselves behave, in our own examples."[2]

In his 2017 speech, Orbán proudly claimed that Hungary had "defended itself—and Europe at the same time—against the migrant flow and invasion." After praising Donald Trump's July 6 speech in Warsaw, he asserted in unambiguous terms that

certain theories describe the changes now taking place in the Western world and the emergence on the stage of the US president as a struggle in the world political arena between the transnational elite—referred to as "global"—and patriotic national leaders. I believe that this is a meaningful description, and there's much truth in it. If we relate it to ourselves, we can also say that back in 2010, well before the US presidential election, we were forerunners of this approach, the new patriotic Western politics.[3]

These statements reflect what has commonly been described as democratic backsliding in Hungary, which was one of the leaders in the shift away from communism and was considered to be one of the earliest "success stories" in democratization.

Hungary's transition from communism to democracy began over three decades before 1989 with the 1956 revolution and ended in 2010, the year of the first sweeping electoral victory by Fidesz. Orbán, in his first two terms, managed the "disintegration of the Third Hungarian Republic"[4] by creating an "illiberal democracy" in what had been one of the most politically stable and—at least until 2008—economically prosperous of the postcommunist states in Central and East Europe.

Political History

Hungary's history has played a major role in its present. Reunified in 1713 under the Habsburg Empire, Hungarians had far greater autonomy than nations incorporated in the Ottoman and Russian Empires. The Age of Reforms—a set of gradual steps away from the absolute rule of the monarch, initiated in 1825 by Count István Széchenyi—triggered a revolution for freedom and independence in 1848–1849, which failed. Yet changes in the geopolitical realities of Central and East Europe subsequently resulted in 1867 in a dual Austro-Hungarian Empire in which Hungarians had separate administrations in every field but military and foreign affairs. As a result, by the end of the nineteenth century, Hungary's economy and culture had blossomed. In the cities, the workers prospered, even as the countryside remained backward and relations with most ethnic and religious minorities remained tense.

All this came to an end when the expansion of the Austro-Hungarian Empire into Bosnia-Herzegovina and its alliance with Germany brought the empire into World War I. As punishment for its defeat, large portions of what had been Hungarian land were occupied by Czechoslovakia and the Balkan states of Romania and Serbia, with the endorsement of Western powers. Meanwhile, a democratic republic was proclaimed in Hungary, which was quickly replaced by the Bolshevik Republic of Councils in the spring and summer of 1919. Bolshevism in Hungary, although it often disregarded Vladimir Lenin's instructions and had a certain cultural liveliness, was still characterized by mostly brutal and chaotic policies, which left communism with a negative image.

The Bolshevik experiment ended in a counterrevolutionary offensive by part of Hungary's new military, led by Admiral Miklós Horthy. As of August 1919, he and his forces had suppressed the Red regime and appointed a new regency government, which encouraged anti-Jewish pogroms because of an ostensible alliance between Bolshevism and Jewishness. To compound the political battles, the Trianon peace treaty, signed in 1920, resulted in Hungary losing not only the areas inhabited by other ethnic groups but also much of its own historic territory: 120,000 square miles and half its population were taken. Over three million Hungarians were cut off from Hungary.

Photo 13.1. Hungarian prime minister Viktor Orbán holds a press conference in Budapest on April 12, 2010—the day when Orbán's Fidesz party gained a two-thirds "supermajority" in the Hungarian parliament. (Northfoto, Shutterstock)

The devastation caused by the war, coupled with the debacle of the Red regime that followed, left Hungarians wary of and at odds with both the Soviets and the West. The "injustice of Trianon" became a key feature of Hungarian collective memory. During the interwar years, students began their classes by chanting, "Nem, nem, soha!" (No, no, never!), meaning that they would never accept the injustice of the Trianon treaty. In domestic politics, a semiauthoritarian system emerged that outlawed the Communist Party and limited voting rights as well as Jews' access to universities, based on the political myth that linked Jews to communism.[5] As pointed out in a classic essay by István Bibó, one of the most original political thinkers of the region and a key inspiration for the young Viktor Orbán, this policy was part of a more general problem caused by the collapse of prewar Hungary, which ended the successful gradual assimilation of most of the Jewish population into Magyar (i.e., ethnic Hungarian) society by making Jews suddenly appear responsible for all of the catastrophes that had befallen the nation.[6]

After the end of communism in Hungary, this stereotypical anti-Jewish prejudice would emerge anew, not only in the surge of parties of the far right, such as the Hungarian Justice and Life Party (Magyar Igazság és Élet Pártja, MIÉP) and the Movement for a Better Hungary (Jobbik Magyarországért Mozgalom, Jobbik) but also within pro-government circles. Prime Minister Orbán's longtime friend and the proud carrier of Fidesz party card number five, Zsolt Bayer, for instance, in an infamous article published in the daily *Magyar Hírlap* (January 4, 2011), expressed his regret at "all the Jews not having been buried to their necks at Orgovány," the site of one of the most gruesome Horthy-sponsored pogroms carried out in the fall of 1919.[7]

The impact of the global economic depression in the 1930s reinforced Hungarians' interest in scapegoating and excluding ethnic "others" and reclaiming lost territory, which drew Hungary into the orbit of Adolf Hitler's Germany. After the Munich Agreement and the 1938–1939 dismantling of Czechoslovakia, southern Slovakia and Ruthenia (an area south of the Carpathian Mountains in the Kingdom of Hungary, also called Carpathian Ruthenia) were returned to Hungary. Then, after the Molotov-Ribbentrop Pact between the USSR and Germany, Hungary regained most of Transylvania (an area with a substantial Hungarian population in Romania). In return, Hungary had to not only increase its restrictions on Jews but also participate in the 1941 invasions of Yugoslavia and the Soviet Union.

At the end of World War II, Hungary's military and political leader, Admiral Miklós Horthy, tried to switch sides. Hitler responded by occupying Hungary in March 1944 and replacing Horthy (who was arrested in October 1944) with Ferenc Szálasi, head of the Arrow Cross Party, the Hungarian equivalent of the Nazis. More than half a million Jews were deported, and most of them were murdered at the Auschwitz-Birkenau death camp. At the same time, the Soviets invaded Hungarian territory, which they occupied by April 1945, after a merciless and destructive fight.

The communist takeover of Hungary took almost three years. Winston Churchill and Joseph Stalin initially agreed in October 1944 that Hungary would be evenly split between the Soviet sphere of influence and the West. Although Hungary was occupied by the Red Army, the first parliamentary elections in November 1945 were free and fair, but subsequent events were nondemocratic.

The centrist, Christian, anticommunist Independent Smallholders Party won an absolute majority of over 57 percent of the votes, yet was unable to form a government itself, because the Allied Control Commission, dominated by the Soviets, forced it to go into a coalition with three left-of-center parties: the Social Democrats, the Communists, and the National Peasant Party. In February 1946, Smallholder Zoltán Tildy was elected president in what would prove to be democracy's last gasp.

Even as Hungary was establishing a democratic government, albeit in an awkward coalition of anticommunist centrists and left-wing parties, Mátyás Rákosi, head of the Hungarian Communist Party, was engaged in cutting democracy down through what he called "salami tactics," by using the secret police and other pressures to slice off pieces of the noncommunist parties until there was nothing left. The communists first pressured the Smallholders to expel their "right wing." Then, as soon as the Treaty of Paris was signed in 1947 and the Allied Control Commission was dissolved, the main leader of the Smallholders, Béla Kovács, was arrested for "espionage" by Soviet troops, who had remained in Hungary in order to secure connections with their contingent in Austria. Finally, Prime Minister Ferenc Nagy, who had resisted every attempt to nationalize property, was forced into exile. The social democrats were then given the choice of merging with the communists or facing serious consequences. Some accepted the unification. Others refused and were, at the least, forced out of public life. Some, such as the particularly resilient Anna Kéthly, were imprisoned. The Hungarian Workers' Party was born of this unification in June 1948, signaling clearly the communists' final victory.

Having successfully taken over the political institutions, the communists openly imposed control over all other sectors of society. The economy was transformed: agriculture was forcibly collectivized, and the rest of the economy was nationalized. A massive industrialization drive shifted the economy from an agricultural to an industrial one. These policies were accompanied by an exodus from the countryside to the cities, and millions of young people suddenly got a chance at education. Religious institutions were attacked. Not only were citizens punished for supporting religion, but also the head of the Hungarian Catholic Church, Cardinal József Mindszenty, was arrested, tried, and sentenced to life imprisonment. Terror even hit the Communist Party's own elite. The show trial and execution of Minister of the Interior László Rajk for being a Titoist agent in 1949 came to symbolize the spiral of terror that lasted until Stalin's death in 1953.

After Stalin's death, the different factions in the Kremlin manipulated Hungarian politics. Control of the state and the party was split between Rákosi, as head of the party, and Imre Nagy, the first communist minister of agriculture, as prime minister. The Soviets pressed the Hungarian leadership to shift from attempts at establishing heavy industry to greater production of consumer goods. Nagy pushed reform further to include a relaxation of the terror and an end to the permanent hunt for "traitors" that had paralyzed Hungarian life since the communist takeover. But as the balance of power shifted from liberals to conservatives in the Kremlin, Nagy was forced out, and Rákosi returned to power.

In 1956, to strengthen the accord with Yugoslavia and follow through on the denunciations of Stalin and his cult of personality, Nikita Khrushchev, the new Soviet leader, forced more change in Hungary. Rákosi, who had boasted of being "Stalin's best Hungarian disciple," was dismissed from office and went into exile in the Soviet Union. He was replaced as head of the Communist Party by the equally Stalinist Ernő Gerő. At the same time, the verdict against László Rajk was nullified, and his body was publicly reburied. This step, coupled with the example of liberalization in Poland during the Polish October, as well as the constant shifts in leadership, convinced Hungarians that change was possible.

The Hungarian Revolution began with student demonstrations on October 23, 1956.[8] Within a few hours, Soviet tanks entered Budapest and fired on the demonstrators. Three days later, a new government was brought in, with János Kádár as head of the Communist Party and Imre Nagy as prime minister. By this time, though, virtually the entire population was engaged in the struggle for freedom and the effort to create a genuine pluralist democracy. Parties abolished in 1948 resurfaced and were brought into Nagy's executive. The Hungarian Workers' Party dissolved itself and formed a new Hungarian Socialist Workers' Party (HSWP), and grassroots national committees and workers' councils mushroomed, declaring their wish to be complementary and not alternative to political parties. After briefly starting to withdraw their troops, the Soviets intervened a second time on November 4 to suppress the revolution, at which point the Hungarian government, buoyed by the increasingly loud demands of insurgents and the population throughout the country, denounced the Warsaw Pact even as Soviet troops killed thousands of demonstrators, jailed thousands more, and sent many thousands into exile. All of this remained seared in the national memory even though, officially, it was not allowed to be discussed until 1989.

Photo 13.2. The 1956 Hungarian Uprising: this photo shows a destroyed Russian tank and other vehicles in front of the Soviet Kilián Barracks in Budapest. (Everett Collection, Shutterstock)

János Kádár agreed to lead a new government with the support of the occupying Soviet troops. When Nagy refused to resign as prime minister, he and other leaders loyal to the revolution were arrested and deported to Romania. In 1958, they were secretly tried in Hungary, sentenced to death, executed the next day, and buried in unmarked graves. Much as the Rajk reburial had opened the floodgates in 1956, the memorial service for and reburial of Nagy and others who had been tried and buried with him in June 1989 triggered the end of communist control and then the dissolution of the HSWP.

The repression that accompanied the Soviet occupation and the reestablishment of a one-party system under Kádár's control lasted into the 1960s. Despite the violent repression of the revolution, however, its programs remained on the political agenda and were gradually reintroduced, albeit with many starts and stops from 1962 to 1963 onward. However, these reforms occurred only in the economic and cultural fields. Politics remained exclusively in the hands of the ruling party, but in the 1960s the Kádár regime began moving away from ruling by repression. Thus, from the mid-1960s on, Hungarians lived under a softer version of communism that later became known as "goulash communism" (referring to a popular Hungarian soup), which provided them with satisfactory supplies of food and consumer goods in exchange for the appearance of public support for the regime. Whereas other communist governments in the region actively repressed dissidents and those who questioned the system, the Hungarian regime became renowned for the mantra, "He who is not against us is with us."

In 1963, following the removal of the Hungarian case from the United Nations' agenda, some surviving freedom fighters and leaders were released from prison. The New Economic Mechanism (NEM) was introduced in 1968 and brought real improvement in the Hungarian standard of living and the availability of goods by enabling "profit" to become a motive for the economic activities of state enterprises and for open wage differentiation. The result was a consumer economy vibrant and varied enough to make Hungary "the happiest barrack in the camp" until the 1980s, when the forward and backward moves in the NEM and the aging of the economy showed in the failings of the consumer sector.

Politically, communism in Hungary from the mid-1960s was consistently less repressive than elsewhere in the bloc. This difference was due in part to the fact that the population was both satisfied with what it had economically and wary of trying for political change after the experience of 1956. After the mid-1960s, Hungary's borders were more open for its own citizens and for émigrés and tourists. Life for Hungarians became a trade-off: political silence for relative economic prosperity.

By the mid-1980s, however, the elaborate system of carrots and sticks that had held Hungarian communist rule in place was crumbling. The annual growth in gross domestic product (GDP) decreased from 4.8 percent in the 1970s to 1.8 percent between 1980 and 1985 and continued on a rapid downward trajectory.[9] For workers, tensions over wages grew more acute because the instruments being used to manage the economy did not allow employers to raise wages to improve enterprise performance.[10] Thus, Hungarians' real incomes stagnated and began declining, causing savings to decrease.

At the same time, changes in the Kremlin reduced whatever fear remained of Soviet repression. The Soviet occupation troops meant little when Mikhail Gorbachev came to power and made it clear that reform in the Soviet Union would evolve in ways the Hungarians had not dared attempt, and that the Soviet Union would no longer rein in its satellites. The rise of Poland's Solidarity movement in the early 1980s inspired Hungarian dissidents to publish journals that challenged historical taboos. Repression of dissidents was not an option: Hungary had signed the Helsinki Final Act in 1975. Perhaps more importantly, it was increasingly indebted to the International Monetary Fund (IMF) and other Western financial institutions. Its leaders could not risk the kinds of financial sanctions imposed on Poland after the imposition of martial law if they were going to try to keep their economic bargain with the Hungarian people. And dissent involved only a tiny section of the population.

In addition, Kádár himself had aged. Whereas Hungary had changed, he had not. When he did appear in public, his hands shook, and his speeches fell flat. The men who had risen up behind him in the party, Károly Grósz, Imre Pozsgay, and Miklós Németh, began to take the lead in the public eye and behind the scenes. Their postures, though, were increasingly critical of Hungary's status quo and divided over what should come next and how to deal publicly with the past and present. In 1988, Kádár was forced to retire.

Early Postcommunism

In large part, the smoothness of the 1989–1990 transition was a result of the distance Hungary had traveled in economic reforms and its limited political liberalization after the repression of the late 1950s, as well as the success of reform movements within the party and of intellectual dissent in the late 1980s. Not surprisingly, then, Hungary's transition was the product of ongoing and overlapping discussions and a series of Roundtables that involved reform communists and intellectual groups whose roots were framed by Hungarian historical debates.

As the regime's system of carrots and sticks crumbled, intellectuals in and out of the party began to meet and push the old limits. In June 1985, a significant part of Hungary's intellectual elite met at Monor to discuss the failings of the system since 1956. In these discussions, which occurred without interference from the party or police, the political divide between "people's nationalists and urbanists" (also known as the "populist-urbanist divide") that had characterized Hungarian thinking from the 1930s reemerged. The populists looked on the peasantry and Christianity as the base of the Hungarian spirit and wanted to find a "third way" between capitalism and communism. The "urbanists" were secular and oriented toward Western democracies and European integration. On the one hand, the populists pressed for Hungary to intervene to prevent the increasing repression of Hungarians abroad, particularly in Romania, where Nicolae Ceaușescu was engaged in a full-scale assault on Romania's sizable Hungarian minority. The urbanists, on the other hand, emerged as liberal democrats and defenders of human rights at home and sponsored radical pro-market economic reforms along with membership in all of the Euro-Atlantic organizations.

This initial meeting, the crumbling of the economy, and the visible decline in Soviet power or interest in its Central and East European satellites triggered the emergence of a plethora of different political groupings that shared an interest in democratization. In 1987, the Hungarian Democratic Forum (MDF) formed as a political and cultural movement based on Christian democracy and populist traditions. In 1988, a group of young lawyers founded the Alliance of Young Democrats, or Fidesz. It was far more outspoken than earlier movements and opposed both the reformist and nonreformist versions of the communist system. Months later, the Committee for an Act of Historical Justice (TIB) emerged, demanding the political, civic, and moral rehabilitation of the veterans of the 1956 revolution and pension benefits for its survivors. Then a Network of Free Democratic Initiatives appeared and pushed for a reduced role of the state and the protection of individual rights; it later transformed into the Alliance of Free Democrats (SZDSZ), the third of the key noncommunist parties in democratic Hungary.

These parties and two associations representing the intelligentsia met between March and June 1989 in what was known as the Opposition Roundtable (ORT). Their ultimate goal was to reach consensus so that they could be united in their negotiations and prevent the government from introducing reform legislation and taking control over the transition. They agreed to negotiate with the Communist Party (HSWP) only about holding free elections but not about what would follow thereafter. In the process, the ORT discussions spilled out and further challenged communist control.

As the opposition crystallized into groups and then political parties, the HSWP began to fall apart. After Kádár was forced to resign, Károly Grósz, a relative conservative, took over. But his was not the only faction in the HSWP. Younger reformers like Miklós Németh and Imre Pozsgay, in alliance with older ones such as Rezsö Nyers, struggled within the party. Grósz ordered the suppression of the demonstrations on the anniversary of Imre Nagy's execution in June 1988, which had been promoted by all the new organizations. Then the younger and more liberal leaders began to reconsider the "1956 events," met with opposition leaders, and symbolically removed the Iron Curtain in May 1989 by cutting the barbed-wire fence between Austria and Hungary. As a compromise between the two groups, a "committee of experts" made up of scholars and politicians was established in 1989 to investigate the real causes of the events of 1956. Its report created a major political stir. The Kádárist notion that the 1956 events were a "counterrevolution" was rejected, and the events were designated a "legitimate national uprising."

Preparations began for the reburial of Nagy and the other leaders of the Hungarian Revolution. Kádárist-style rule was clearly in its last days. In the spring, the party divested itself of much of its power, even shifting the responsibility for dealing with the politically explosive reburial to the state. Despite the objections of some in the HSWP and leaders in Bulgaria, Germany, Romania, and Czechoslovakia, the funeral of Imre Nagy was held as a public ceremony in Budapest's Heroes' Square. As more than 250,000 people observed in the square and millions more watched on television, the reform communists stood as honorary pallbearers. New political leaders from the new and old parties gave speeches. The leaders who had survived, including Nagy's press spokesman, Miklós Vásárhelyi, spoke of "justice, national unity, and the opportunity for 'a peaceful transition to a free and democratic society.'" As noted earlier, the young Fidesz leader Viktor Orbán explicitly demanded the withdrawal of Soviet troops.[11]

Negotiations between the ORT and the regime began on June 13, 1989 (simultaneously with the semi-free Polish elections). The HSWP agreed to focus only on establishing the rules for free elections and amendments to the communist constitution rather than trying to follow the Polish model of negotiating political, social, and economic issues as well. In exchange, the ORT parties had to agree to a triangular table, with the HSWP's voting power aided by the inclusion of the trade unions as minor players in the negotiations. On October 23, 1989, the Third Hungarian Republic was proclaimed. A week earlier, the communist HSWP had declared its transformation into the Western-style, social democratic Hungarian Socialist Party (HSP) and announced its intention to participate in the forthcoming elections.

The final battle of the transition was over whether to elect the president or the parliament first. For the ex-communists, the best scenario was to hold the presidential election first because their leader, Pozsgay, was still popular for dismantling the Communist Party and was the best-known politician. The Alliance of Free Democrats and Fidesz refused to agree to this plan and instead organized a referendum on whether to first elect the president or the parliament (whose members would then elect the president). On this issue, the ORT groups split from the Hungarian Democratic Forum, urging abstention rather than changing the Roundtable agreement to elect the president and then the parliament. In that referendum, the option of holding the parliamentary elections first won with 50.07 percent of the vote. The monolithic opposition started to divide.

Despite these divisions, the period from the end of communism to 2010 saw Hungary make significant progress in establishing a democratic political system. As the section below discusses, the institutions of democracy were created in a peaceful process, and for fifteen years after the democratic elections of 1990, political parties gravitated toward the center, and government coalitions were generally stable. Hungary also made substantial progress economically and was one of the first countries admitted to NATO in 1999 and to the European Union (EU) in 2004.

Political Institutions

The Roundtable Accords, as they were modified after the referendum, and the old parliament's vote for the president to be directly elected provided for a parliamentary system. After its election in March 1990, the initial center-right parliament revised the transitional constitution so that only a simple majority was needed to pass most laws, and the president was elected by the parliament every five years by a two-thirds majority. The single-house parliament was to be elected every four years with a mixed electoral system and was also to select the prime minister. The prime minister was responsible for picking and guiding the ministers. The president had ceremonial powers and some ability to intervene when there were problems within the system. None of these powers were decisive, however.

Árpád Göncz, elected president by the parliament, created a model for the Hungarian presidency that generated criticism but also secured his reelection in 1995. His model entitled the president, who represents the country, to work behind the scenes to reach consensus among the various political groups. Through this process, Göncz and his successors have tried to avoid identifying with one side or the other. At the same time, Göncz used the ability to approve the removal of such officials as the heads of radio and television to push the parties away from partisanship in these areas. His successor, Ferenc Mádl (elected in 2000), followed this model. László Sólyom, who was president from 2005 to 2010, however, was often criticized for an alleged bias toward Fidesz.

Elections for the first freely elected parliament since 1945 were scheduled for March 25, 1990, with a runoff on April 8. The electoral system provided for a parliament of 386 seats, of which 176 were to be elected in single-member districts with a French-type, double-ballot, majoritarian system, and 152 were to be selected from party lists for each region using a proportional system. The remaining seats (a minimum of 58) would be distributed to national party lists to compensate for "extra votes" that were over and above what a candidate needed to get elected or had been cast for losing candidates in the single-member districts. The goal of this redistribution was to keep the parliament truly representative of the overall national vote. At the same time, any party that received less than 4 percent of the vote nationally was disqualified from seating deputies in the parliament. Although the system has been responsive to changes in Hungarian public opinion, until 2010 it was also very stable, with governing coalitions shifting regularly from right to left but both sides remaining close to the center and ready to compromise over ideological divides.

The Hungarian democratic constitution after the collapse of communism was not a completely new document but was the result of amendments to the 1949 constitution that were passed after 1987 in several waves.[12] This constitution defined Hungary as a unitary parliamentary republic, with a unicameral parliament that elects the head of state (the president). The Constitutional Court had the authority to examine parliamentary and governmental legislation and thus limit governmental power. Also, legislative changes could be made by referendum. In comparison to many West European parliamentary systems, the postcommunist Hungarian system had some distinct features. Rather than a fusion of power, the parliament and the executive were made independent from each other: the executive could not dissolve the parliament, and a limitation on the vote of no confidence established a relatively independent executive. Also, the parliamentary majority, unlike in other West European constitutions, gained special veto power through the two-thirds majority principle, which applied to a relatively wide range of laws. The powers of the Constitutional Court also became the strongest among the constitutional courts in Europe.[13]

The stability of Hungary's political system was clear from the start. When MDF leader József Antall, the first postcommunist prime minister, died in office in late 1993, he was immediately replaced by another MDF leader, Péter Boross, who served six months until that parliament's term ended. After the socialists lost the 2004 European Parliament elections, the party (HSP) quickly responded to public disaffection by shifting its leadership. This allowed Ferenc Gyurcsány to become the first prime minister to serve two successive terms, until he resigned in spring 2009 to be replaced by Gordon Bajnai.

Although the cabinet changed with every election, the upper ranks of the state bureaucracy remained quite stable. As no effective legislation purged civil servants from the communist era, they could remain in their positions if they declared allegiance to the new system. Where changes occurred, they resulted from the government's efforts to make Hungary's overall bureaucracy smaller and more professional.

Dominant coalitions shifted from election to election. Until 2010, all cabinets were products of coalitions of centrist parties, and none was controlled by a single party. During the first postcommunist decade, three prime ministers (Antall, Boross, and Orbán) led conservative coalitions, and four (Horn, Medgyessy, Gyurcsány, and Bajnai) were prime ministers of socialist-led coalitions. No prime minister introduced major regime change until the 2010 Orbán government, which started a new era in Hungarian politics. A former left-leaning liberal, yet consistently anticommunist politician, Orbán had astutely moved to the right since 1993, realizing that the death of Prime Minister Antall created a major vacuum on the conservative side of the political spectrum. After his 2010 electoral triumph, Orbán became the leader of a supermajority in parliament and began imposing a shift in governing style that left little room for collegiality or balance in Hungarian politics.

Political Competition

Hungarian politics since 1990 can be roughly divided into three periods. The first was a period of stability and democratic competition that lasted from 1990 until 2006. This was followed by a four-year governing crisis, when the reelected government's legitimacy was immediately challenged by the Fidesz-led opposition, which organized antigovernment mobilization until the following parliamentary elections. The third period that began in 2010 was a period characterized by a Fidesz political monopoly and democratic backsliding. The following section provides an account of key developments during these periods.

The unquestionable winner of Hungary's first postcommunist democratic election was the MDF, whose president, József Antall, was inaugurated as prime minister in May 1990. In this election, six parties received enough votes to enter parliament. Three (MDF, SZDSZ, and Fidesz) were new parties. They won 277 seats and would become the center-pieces of Hungarian politics into the twenty-first century. A fourth party (the HSP) could be called both new and old, as it branded itself as new but consisted mostly of the reform wing of the old communist HSWP. The remaining two (the Independent Smallholders Party and the People's Christian Democrats) had existed in the precommunist period. Together, these historic parties won sixty-five seats. All six parliamentary parties agreed about the direction Hungary should take: toward Europe, democracy, and capitalism. Their differences centered on the details of Hungary's transition in that direction, and on the question of how to deal with the past. To many observers, these divisions resembled a tra-ditional Hungarian separation between "people's nationalists and urbanists" (also known as the "populist-urbanist" divide), but most significant parties represented a wide spectrum of political attitudes and were led by groups of intellectuals. As Bill Lomax observed in 1997,

> Hungarian parties are, almost without exception, elite groups of intellectuals, often long-standing personal friends more like political clubs than representative institutions. Many of Antall's government ministers went to the same school with him. Most of the Free Democrats were together in the democratic opposition. Several of [Fidesz]'s leaders studied law together. . . . The political identities and cleavages they do represent are based neither on social interests, nor political programmes, nor structured belief systems. In fact, to the extent that such cleavages do exist in Hungarian politics, they are found to cut across the parties almost equally—each party has its liberals, its nationalists, its conservatives, its social-democrats, its populists, its radicals.[14]

Initially, the leaders of all major parties except Fidesz were intellectuals from academia and the arts. The leaders and members of Fidesz, or the Young Democrats, were different. They and their constituents were young people. Most of the party's leaders had studied law together in the 1980s. As a result, until 1993, they were less bound by ideology and more West European in their thinking and presentation.

In 1994, the HSP was the first successor to an old ruling Communist Party of Central and East Europe to be reelected and returned to power with an absolute majority of seats. Yet, in the first of a series of unlikely coalitions, the HSP joined with the Alliance of Free Democrats. Their gains were a reaction to people's initial disappointment with what the transition had brought and also to the weakness in the Hungarian Democratic Forum brought to a head by József Antall's death and the splintering effect of the Hungarian Truth and Life Party led by István Csurka. Like the Polish social democrats, leaders of the HSP talked not of returning to the old communist system but of modernization, eco-nomic and political reform, and joining Europe. The Alliance of Free Democrats actually lost votes in 1994, but the Hungarian Democratic Forum lost far more, and the Alliance of Free Democrats was—despite its history of opposition to communism—the largest and most viable partner for the HSP.

In 1998, there was a shift in all the major players' positions and strengths. The Hungarian Democratic Forum had essentially collapsed by 1998. Most of the precommunist parties could no longer get enough votes to seat deputies in parliament. In the aftermath of Antall's death and the partnership of the Alliance of Free Democrats and HSP (confirmed by their signing of the Democratic Charter in 1991), Fidesz moved to the right. Its leaders were able, despite the simultaneous success of the extreme-rightist Hungarian Truth and Life Party, to present themselves as the legitimate successors of the declining MDF. The party leader, Viktor Orbán, when he became prime minister, openly claimed Antall's legacy. Their coalition was made up of the Smallholders and the remnants of the MDF. To further their popularity, they also added "Hungarian Civic Party" to their name (it later became "Hungarian Civic Alliance").

Toward the end of the legislature, in late February 2002, Orbán signaled his intentions to profoundly revise recent Hungarian history as told in the communist and post-communist versions. He inaugurated a statue to Béla Kovács on the fifty-fifth anniversary of his arrest and deportation, as well as Budapest's Terror House Museum, a controversial yet interesting institution intended to equate the Hungarian experiences of Nazism and communism and the crimes committed by their proponents. While nobody took issue with the first decision, the second was seriously questioned for its portrayal of historical events. Equating the crimes of Nazism and communism remains a deeply divisive aspect of memory politics across CEE, and this museum in Budapest accords more attention to crimes committed under communism than to Nazi crimes.[15]

A few weeks later, the balance shifted back to the coalition of the socialists and the Alliance of Free Democrats after a close race with the Young Democrats and the Democratic Forum Alliance. The two parties were able to govern with a razor-thin majority. However, when the coalition lost in its first elections to the European Parliament and right-wing and Euroskeptic candidates took a number of districts, Péter Medgyessy (who had been a member of the HSWP, a banker in France, and a leader in the private sector in Hungary) resigned. He was replaced by Ferenc Gyurcsány, who had risen from the Communist Youth Organization to become one of the wealthiest businessmen in Hungary. Under his leadership, the Socialist–Free Democratic Alliance was the first coalition to win two successive elections. This made Gyurcsány the first Hungarian prime minister to serve more than one term, as he led the party to a much clearer victory in 2006.

The Political Crisis after 2006 and Orbán's Ascent

After the parliamentary elections in 2006, when Gyurcsány and his Socialist Party won a second consecutive mandate, several critical events led to a political crisis that profoundly altered the political landscape in Hungary. Prime Minister Gyurcsány gave a speech at a closed meeting in Balatonőszöd for his Hungarian Socialist Party (MSZP) National Assembly members, only a month after his coalition won 210 of the 386 parliamentary seats.[16] During the speech, later dubbed the Őszöd speech, Gyurcsány said that his government had "lied in the morning, lied in the evening" in order to win the April 2006 election.[17] The speech was leaked and later broadcast on Hungarian radio. Gyurcsány also reportedly said, "You cannot quote any significant government measure we can be proud of, other than at the end we managed to bring the government back from the brink. Nothing. If we have to give account to the country about what we did for four years, then what do we say?"[18]

The leaked Őszöd speech presented an opportunity for the opposition party Fidesz to mobilize mass protests in Budapest, which turned violent. In fact, after the 2002 general election, which Gyurcsány had also won, Fidesz president Viktor Orbán vigorously pursued the creation and organization of a "Civic Circles Movement," which became "militant in pursuing its agendas, middle-class based in terms of social stratification, dominantly metropolitan and urban on the spatial dimension, and massive in terms of membership and activities."[19] This movement, moreover, reorganized and extended right-wing grassroots networks, associations, and media; leading activists in this movement (among them, professors, professionals, pundits, etc.) offered new frames and practices for Hungarians to feel, think, and act as members of the nation.[20] With the strong grassroots networks already energized, Fidesz and Orbán were able to present Gyurcsány's speech as the ultimate betrayal of the nation and to mobilize adherents to protest and possibly oust the government.

The protests were reminiscent of the 1956 Hungarian Uprising against communist rule, during which students captured the main radio station in Budapest to demand that their grievances be aired.[21] They continued leading up to the local elections that were held on October 1, with Fidesz coming out as an absolute winner, carrying eighteen out of nineteen counties and nineteen out of twenty-three cities.[22] On October 23, 2006, during commemorations of the fiftieth anniversary of Hungary's uprising against Soviet rule, Fidesz attracted more than one hundred thousand people to a protest event to continue demanding Gyurcsány's resignation. More than twenty people were injured during the protests, demonstrators and police officers alike, when protestors captured an old Soviet T-34 tank, which had been displayed for the commemorations, and drove it at the police.[23]

Gyurcsány's political survival after the Őszöd speech and the turmoil that followed faced new obstacles in 2007, when his government put in place austerity measures to reduce the state's budget deficit of 9 percent of GDP to under 3 percent in order to meet the requirements for joining the euro currency.[24] The austerity measures involved higher taxes and extensive reforms in the public sector, which reduced wages, increased inflation, and slowed economic growth.[25] The impact was immediately reflected in public attitudes in Hungary. According to a continent-wide Eurobarometer poll in 2007, Hungarians were the only respondents who expected their life to worsen over the next twelve months, and Hungary was the only country on the continent where there were more negative than positive responses to poll questions.[26]

The dismal situation for Gyurcsány's government was exacerbated by the world financial crisis of 2008. Hungary was hit hardest among EU newcomers, since most of its government debt was foreign owned, which resulted in rapid devaluation of the national currency.[27] The financial crisis forced Hungary to ask the IMF for financial help, but under the IMF conditions that Hungary had to increase its austerity measures, reducing costs and aiming at a 2.6 percent budget deficit for 2009 despite its already shrinking economy.[28] In the wake of an already strict fiscal austerity plan, the new economic measures further weakened trust in Gyurcsány's government and weakened Hungarians' overall confidence in their future prospects. In a 2009 Pew survey, Hungarians were the only respondents among the new EU member states that expressed high dissatisfaction with their personal standing. For instance, only 15 percent of Hungarians expressed satisfaction with their life in Hungary, and 32 percent were highly dissatisfied. In contrast, 44 percent of Poles, 49 percent of Czechs, 43 percent of Slovaks, 35 percent of Lithuanians, 26 percent of Ukrainians, and 35 percent of Russians were highly satisfied, and dissatisfaction was expressed by single-digit percentages of respondents in these countries.[29] Additionally, 91 percent of Hungarians were dissatisfied with the direction their country was taking, compared to 59 percent of Poles, 70 percent of Czechs, and 56 percent of Slovaks. The same situation was reflected in the trust of Prime Minister Gyurcsány, where only 17 percent approved of his work and 71 percent disapproved. In contrast, regarding approval or disapproval of their respective prime ministers, Poles responded at rates of 48 percent approving and 42 percent disapproving; Czechs at 59 percent and 24 percent, respectively; and Slovaks at 49 percent and 40 percent.[30]

In such circumstances, the opposition parties gained momentum, especially the conservative Fidesz party, but also the far-right Jobbik party. In the midst of anti-Gyurcsány sentiment in 2007, a subsidiary of the far-right Jobbik party called the "Magyar Gárda" (Hungarian Guard) was formed. The founding ceremony for this new Hungarian neofascist group attracted around three thousand people in Budapest in August 2007, swearing in fifty-six members with uniforms showing Nazi-era symbols, a number chosen to commemorate the 1956 revolution.[31] According to Gábor Vona, a cofounder of the Guard, it "has been set up in order to carry out the real change of regime (from communism) and to rescue Hungarians" from the continuous injustices it has suffered ever since the Trianon treaty.[32] Although Jobbik had no deputies in parliament at the time, it did have representatives in dozens of city councils across the country. In December 2007, around three hundred members of the Guard dressed in black uniforms marched in military formation through a Hungarian village, protesting what they called "Roma [Gypsy] delinquency" and demanding that Roma be segregated from mainstream society.[33]

The sharp decline in trust toward Gyurcsány's government after 2006 was also evident during elections for the European Parliament (EP) on June 7, 2009. Although only 36 percent of voters turned out for the EP elections, the largest opposition party, Fidesz, won the majority of seats (fourteen out of twenty-two) and 56 percent of the vote. The far-right party Jobbik won a surprising 15 percent of the vote, sending three representatives to the EP. The Socialists (MSZP) won only a slightly higher number of votes (17 percent) than Jobbik, earning four seats in the EP. In a postelection speech, Viktor Orbán claimed that "Hungarians will have a significant presence in Brussels representing the Carpathian basin,"[34] signaling his intention to be viewed as a leader of all Hungarians, regardless of state borders. Results of the Hungarian parliamentary elections in April 2010 were no surprise to the Socialists, given the slippery slope they found themselves on after the Őszöd speech by Gyurcsány in 2006. The opposition Fidesz won an overwhelming majority with 263 of the 386 mandates in parliament (68.14 percent of the vote), while the MSZP garnered only 59 mandates (15.28 percent of the vote), with an electoral turnout of 64 percent.[35] Jobbik now established itself as the third-largest party in the country; in eastern Hungary, they even beat the formerly governing Socialist Party to second place.[36]

As a result, right-wing nationalism and populism enjoyed a strong revival, reminiscent of the pre–World War II era. Although Hungary has a relatively low immigration rate and a relatively low number of ethnic minorities, among which the Roma people constitute a large part (with varied estimates of up to eight hundred thousand people in a population of nearly ten million), the Roma population has been subject to prejudice and segregation. The Jobbik party was the main proponent of the nationalist anti-Semitic and anti-Roma agenda. Jobbik created an ideology that combined traditional irredentist and ethnic nationalism, xenophobia, racism, and anti-Semitism. This strategy aimed at appealing to parts of the Hungarian population, such as the youth and people living in the countryside. Jobbik managed to appeal to this segment as the representative of the "true Hungarians." The creation of the Hungarian Guard in 2007 was a crucial step in this process, as it created "a 'grassroots' element to the movement and well-organized volunteer-militia ready to be called on for action for the common 'Hungarian cause.'"[37] Group identity had been constructed by acting against the Roma, Jews, and other minorities (who had been perceived as hostile to the "Hungarian cause"), and such identity was reinforced with every march of the Hungarian Guard. In addition, the sense of impunity for violence against Roma had been growing, since the police appeared ineffective in charging perpetrators. Indicative of the police's reluctance to fight anti-Roma crime was the fact that its 5,300-member trade union announced a formal alliance with Jobbik.[38]

These critical events leading up to the overwhelming victory of the right-wing populist party Fidesz, accompanied by the rapid rise of the far-right party Jobbik, marked a profound structural change in Hungarian politics, the core of which was right-wing

Photo 13.3.   Far-right demonstrators in Budapest on March 15, 2012. March 15 is one of Hungary's major national holidays. It commemorates the (lost) Hungarian Revolution of 1848. (Klara Z, Shutterstock)

populism and exclusive ethnonationalism. Such a landscape opened the door to changes (both institutional and extra-institutional) that later led to the disintegration of Hungary's democracy and its transition into an authoritarian model of governance.

Hungary's Democratic Backsliding since 2010

Soon after Prime Minister Viktor Orbán returned to power in 2010, he used his position to dominate virtually all institutional processes in the country by constructing a single-pyramid system of power. In many state institutions, such as government ministries and agencies, strong linkages of clientelism were established. Party loyalists were appointed, and often the prime minister was directly involved in the selection of loyalists. These linkages became deeply entrenched in state institutions, media, and businesses and began functioning as parallel informal institutions governed directly from the top of the pyramidal system of power. Once the system began transforming into a single-pyramid system of power, the country's important businesspeople had a strong incentive to support Orbán by proactively working in his interests. In a fairly short period of time, most politically and economically powerful elites became part of the prime minister's pyramid, while the opposition faced serious hurdles in rallying supporters. The process disrupted the reasonably level playing field that had existed between incumbents and opposition before 2010, without which it is impossible to maintain democratic government.[39]

At the beginning, in 2010, Prime Minister Viktor Orbán and Fidesz targeted the Constitutional Court. The court was the most powerful checks-and-balances institution in Hungary, as it could perform an effective check on legislative and executive powers. In early 2011, Fidesz passed a new constitution and a new law on the Constitutional Court, which drastically narrowed the competences of the court. It eliminated the *actio popularis* procedures for ex post review; it abolished the court's powers to review all budget-related legislation; and it repealed all court decisions made before January 1, 2012, when the new constitution entered into force.[40] The latter meant that any precedents of the court could not be invoked in new cases based on the new constitution.[41] The new law increased the number of justices from eleven to fifteen, allowing the government to nominate and elect seven new judges. It also eliminated the requirement for a parliamentary consensus on the election of justices. Within a few months after the adoption of the new constitution and the Law on the Constitutional Court, all of the justices were government loyalists, two of them former members of Orbán's first government, while several others were appointed directly from parliament to the court.[42] The new legislation allowed for indefinite tenure for justices if, by the time an individual justice's term ended, the parliament could not come to an agreement to elect a new justice (as the requirement to elect a justice is a two-thirds majority of the MPs).[43] Such provisions ensured that Orbán's and Fidesz's loyalists in the Constitutional Court would remain in place, since even if their party lost its two-thirds majority in the next election, or if it lost power altogether, the prospects of another party winning a two-thirds majority in the near future (with a capacity to reverse the changes) was very unlikely.

In order to ensure the complete subservience of the prosecutorial branch, Orbán's government adopted amendments to the Code on Criminal Procedure in July 2011 that authorized prosecutors to pick courts where they would press charges after the public prosecutor made his or her decision.[44] Although the Constitutional Court found the amendment unconstitutional, parliament included the procedure in the new constitution's transitory provisions adopted in December 2011, which could not be challenged by the Constitutional Court.[45] Also, similar to the constitutional provisions referring to the courts, the public prosecutor's mandate was extended from six to nine years, and the office was to be neither responsible to government nor parliament: his or her only duty was to report to parliamentarians once a year, but the right for his/her interpellation was abolished.[46]

The single-pyramid structure of power extended into the civil and business sectors. Within a few months of coming to power, Orbán's government passed two media laws that prompted Western commentators to warn that Hungary was "in a league with Russia and Belarus on press freedom."[47] According to the initial reports, one law essentially put the state television and all other public media under Fidesz's control, while the other created a powerful Media Council with the task of regulating newspapers, television, radio, and the internet.[48] These new media laws completely changed the finance structure of public media, merging all public broadcasters into one body, the Media Services and Support Trust Fund.[49] Orbán's plan to incorporate the media system of the country into the single-pyramid system of power seems to have been successfully carried out. By the end of his second term, the mainstream media landscape was largely under his personal influence. Once ranked in twelfth position in the world for press freedom in the Reporters Without Borders index, Hungary plummeted to eighty-ninth place in 2020.[50]

As with the media, Orbán used similar strategies in the country's economy and business sector. He put in place an elaborate plan to build a "national bourgeoisie." He authorized the Ministry of National Development to steer the development of a Hungarian "capitalist class." The process of the "Fideszization" of business and the creation of a Hungarian national bourgeoisie was set in motion with his close friend, oligarch Lajos Simicska, whom Orbán considered a financial genius.[51] Simicska was surrounded by other businessmen who became associated with the Ministry of National Development, many of whom came from the town of Szolnok, the birthplace of Orbán's wife. The whole top echelon of the ministry became in one way or another associated with Orbán confidants.[52] The head of the ministry was Zsuzsanna Németh, who also came from the circle of Orbán's friends. Before her appointment as the head of the Ministry of National Development, immediately after the elections of 2010, she had been placed in a high position of the Magyar Fejlesztési Bank, a state-owned investment bank used as a wealth fund for the Fidesz government, despite reportedly lacking a university degree.[53] The Ministry of National Development was in charge of all EU subsidies, at the time amounting to approximately 1,200 billion HUF.

Along with enriching and enlarging the businesses owned by his confidants, Orbán also engaged in more overt government takeovers of private enterprises through the purchase of shares. By 2013, Orbán's government had spent more than 3 trillion HUF in acquiring private companies.[54] Orbán's regime has focused on building its own support base in sectors such as tourism, retail, agriculture, media, and some infrastructure projects, at the same time appeasing big foreign investors. Building his domestic business coalition by entrenching his family's and friends' economic power, and simultaneously preserving budgetary and macroeconomic stability, Orbán thought to have found the key to economic success.[55] Therefore, his single-power pyramid system in the economy was successfully consolidated in economic sectors that would ensure his unchallenged dominance by garnering and maintaining enough votes to win unfair elections with a relatively low turnout and Fidesz's core of around two million votes.[56]

By the end of 2017, polls showed that Viktor Orbán and his Fidesz party, together with the far-right Jobbik, held nearly 80 percent of popular support, so his third electoral victory in April 2018 came as no surprise. Orbán again won the elections with a landslide victory, winning 133 of 199 seats in the Hungarian parliament, acquiring a supermajority on his own.[57] He even improved his score in the popular vote, winning 49 percent of the vote compared to 44 percent in 2014.[58] The far-right Jobbik party, which since 2014 had become the second-largest party in the Hungarian parliament, won twenty-six seats, also improving its score from the previous election by three seats.[59] The once-ruling Socialist party came in third with only twenty seats, in coalition with a small liberal group.[60] Soon after retaking power, Orbán's government took steps to tighten its grip on civil society. In May 2018, a few days before his swearing in as a prime minister, Orbán stated in an interview that his task in the third term would be to "preserve Hungary's security and Christian culture."[61]

Finally, at the beginning of the COVID-19 pandemic, the Hungarian parliament voted to give Orbán sweeping powers to rule by decree, without a term limit.[62] Critics feared that such a decision would further deepen Orbán's authoritarian rule, with consequences for human rights and freedom of speech. Although the rule by decree was ended on June 16, 2020, NGOs critical of Orbán's government jointly argued that ending the rule by decree was only an "optical illusion" and that the government still kept much more power than before the crisis.[63]

Civil Society

The roots of civil society in Hungary can be traced both to domestic traditions of civic organization and intellectuals' ideas about civil society in Central and East Europe in the 1980s. Historically, the concept of civil society in Hungary had been linked to bourgeois society (*polgári társadalom*), but when democratization began, the notions of civil society (*civil társadalom*) and later civil organization (*civil szervezet*) were popularized by the Soros Foundation.[64]

As in other countries of the Visegrad Group (the four-member Central European alliance including the Czech Republic, Hungary, Poland, and Slovakia), civil society actors actively opposed the communist regime in the late 1980s. But unlike in Poland, where civil society groups were unified under the umbrella of the Solidarity movement, in Hungary civil society actors began dividing along ideological lines early on. Moreover, between 1987 and 1990, civil society organizations opposing the communist regime were competing with each other to dismantle the regime.[65] The early ideological differences among civil society groups ultimately led to the development of civil society organizations that were roughly divided into the left-liberal camp and conservative-right to far-right camp.

The number of nonprofit organizations in Hungary grew from about four hundred in 1989 to about twenty-three thousand by 2011.[66] During Hungary's first postcommunist decade of difficult economic and social reforms, social grievances were mostly channeled through formal political institutions rather than protest.

In the 1990s and early 2000s, legislation was adopted by liberal-left governments that regulated and promoted the civil society sector in Hungary. A 1996 law allowed citizens to support a civil organization of their choice by donating 1 percent of their personal income tax. The 1997 law on public interest allowed civic actors to become owners of facilities important for their operation that had previously been owned by the state. Laws enacted in 2003 and 2007 on the National Civil Based Program extended the scope of resources that were made available to civil organizations in terms of funding.[67]

On the other side of the political spectrum, Fidesz leaders (having lost their bid for power in 2002 and 2006) helped organize and encourage right-wing actors to oppose the socialist-led government through the Civic Circles Movement, an umbrella organization encompassing up to sixteen thousand local units.[68] This movement mobilized large numbers of the public by organizing thousands of events in all spheres of life—political, cultural, patriotic, religious, musical entertainment, recreational, charitable, and so forth.[69] The aim of this movement was to nurture Hungarian conservative and right-wing ideology and prepare the political landscape for the defeat of the liberal-left. Beginning in 2003, civil society groups on the right rapidly proliferated and gained substantial strength, while far-right groups also became prominent. For example, Gábor Vona, who later became the leader of the far-right party Jobbik, began his activism in the youth civic movements, rallying supporters around anti-Semitic and anti-Roma agendas. These movements included even paramilitary organizations like the Hungarian Guard.[70]

Fidesz-led governments have been less tolerant of liberal-left-leaning civil society organizations. It was during the first Fidesz period of rule (1998–2002) that the government restricted the operations of civil society organizations by amending the Labor Code to limit the influence of labor unions.[71] The atmosphere for civil society organizations began to deteriorate again soon after Fidesz came to power in 2010, especially given Jobbik's entry into parliament and its hostility toward civil society organizations dealing with human rights. In 2013, Jobbik, which itself was a product of prior civil society movements, promoted a bill on "foreign agents" as an attempt to restrict freedom of association. Since Fidesz was concerned that Jobbik could capitalize on the sentiments against the liberal-left and their civil society organizations, as soon as Viktor Orbán won his second consecutive term in 2014, he pursued restrictions on the freedom of NGOs dealing with human rights and gender issues and those receiving foreign funds.[72]

Eventually, after winning his third consecutive term, Orbán announced that one of the first laws that his government would pass would be a bill called "Stop Soros," which would impose a 25 percent tax on foreign-funded NGOs that support migration, clearly targeting George Soros's foundations.[73] And indeed, within days after this statement, the Soros-founded Open Society Foundations in Hungary announced that it would close its offices, after nearly thirty-five years of operations in the country. The Open Society Foundations stated that, "over the past two years, the Hungarian government has spent more than 100 million euros in public funds on a campaign to spread lies about the Foundations and their partners."[74] According to the foundation, Orbán's hate campaign had included propaganda with anti-Semitic imagery from World War II and a "national consultation" attacking George Soros, the founder and chair of the Open Society Foundations.[75]

Soros, a native of Budapest who survived the Holocaust, immigrated in 1947 to the United Kingdom and later to the United States, where he amassed a fortune in finance. Committed to the idea of an open society, he gained permission from the country's reformed communist regime to establish the Soros Foundation in 1984 in Hungary. As regime change approached, the Soros Foundation began generously subsidizing various cultural and social groups and individuals, including almost the entire leadership of Fidesz. Viktor Orbán himself was awarded a scholarship by Soros for postgraduate work at Oxford University between 1988 and 1989. Soros established the Central European University (CEU) in 1995 as a US-accredited institution for graduate studies, awarding degrees that were also recognized in Hungary, along with other research institutes. Additionally, Soros established and funded a number of NGOs in Hungary and elsewhere in the former communist region. Those in Hungary clashed openly with the Hungarian government during the 2015 summer crisis, activism that was all the more evident as the center-left opposition was unable to offer serious alternatives to the government's position.

In April 2017, parliament passed an amendment to Hungary's higher-education law that decreed that any non-European university wishing to award degrees in Hungary needed to have a campus in its place of origin, and "set an impossibly tight deadline for establishing an American campus, ensuring that the CEU would no longer be able to accept new students by the beginning of 2018."[76] Despite several mass demonstrations involving up to eighty thousand participants, and protests from academics and universities from all over the world, the amendment was signed into law by President János Áder. Soros reacted in a Brussels speech on June 1 by echoing the title of an academic book published by the CEU Press, calling Hungary "a Mafia State."[77] The next day, Orbán asserted that "Soros' network . . . operates in a mafia style."[78] The tug-of-war between illiberal and liberal forces is ongoing.

Economic Policies and Conditions

Economic weakness has been the Achilles' heel of Hungarian politics. In the last decade of communism, borrowing money from abroad was the regime's only way to sustain the living standards of its population and maintain power. Even with the infusion of foreign loan money, Hungary's post-1990 transformation was marked by economic stagnation and double-digit inflation.

Hungary avoided the Polish "shock therapy" model. Instead, it began by creating a "social market economy" that moved toward private ownership in industries producing consumer goods and providing services. Although legislation allowed for beginning bankruptcy actions against failing enterprises, very few large-scale industries were closed. Instead, foreign investment and ownership were used as tools to get the economy going.

The economic transformation was complicated by Hungary's high debt to the West, the collapse of the Soviet market, and the end of cheap Soviet oil and natural gas supplies. Between 1989 and 1992, Hungary's GDP had fallen by 18 percent, "a decline comparable only to the worst of the Great Depression of the 1930s."[79] Only in March 1995 was the Bokros Plan for serious economic reform implemented. This reform program encouraged privatization with monetary incentives and openness to foreign investment. At the same time, state enterprises were allowed to survive, and new private enterprises were established alongside them. By 2005, 80 percent of the Hungarian economy was in private hands. Foreign ownership went from about 4 percent in 1990 to 52.1 percent in 1997.

The reforms appeared to be successful in the first decade. The population was satisfied. By 1997, the economy had begun to grow by 4 to 5 percent annually. However, the gains came with real hidden costs; many difficult economic reforms were avoided, and the economy depended instead on its Kádár-era base and foreign investment. Keeping costly social welfare programs and encouraging foreign investment by allowing profits to go abroad meant that the apparent upward course was far from secure. Government accounting only hid the problem. The promised tax reduction was not to be; taxes actually had to go up to pay for increases in government spending and inflation and to placate foreign investors. The plan for Hungary to adopt the euro in 2010 (which required a deficit below 3 percent) was also called into question as wishful thinking and turned out to be utterly unrealistic.

On winning the elections in 2010, Orbán set the country on a path characterized by strong anti–foreign capital rhetoric (and deeds) and various measures ostensibly aimed at enhancing domestic resources, as opposed to leaving a peripheral Hungary at the mercy of the global market. According to the pronouncements of Fidesz, only in this context can the necessary budget cuts be implemented and economic growth encouraged. By late 2013, the results were encouraging on both accounts, which was one of the key factors leading to the 2014 Fidesz victory.[80] A similar scenario has continued since the 2018 elections.

Key Social Issues

The challenges that Hungarian society faced during the political and economic transformation after 1990 were similar to those in other countries in the region. The Hungarian economy faced significant challenges in 1989, yet Hungarians had high expectations for economic welfare because they were accustomed to living better than most people in the Soviet bloc. As Prime Minister Antall warned after the 1990 elections, the country faced declining health and falling living standards. Indeed, the limited economic reforms the government undertook at the start of the 1990s left 1 million of Hungary's population of 10.6 million living below the subsistence level and 2 million living at the officially defined social minimum. Those hardest hit were pensioners, families with more than two children, and the unemployed. Homelessness also appeared because factories closed workers' hostels, citizens were unable to pay the increases in their rent, and people came to Budapest in search of jobs. Roma and illegal aliens—largely ethnic Romanians or Hungarians who had "escaped" the more disastrous Romanian economy—added to the numbers of homeless.[81]

In the decade and a half that followed, Hungary's living standards continued to fall. Hungarians, accustomed to rising consumption, have proved less willing than Poles to tolerate a considerable drop in living standards. While some had prospered during the 1980s, those lacking the skills needed to access the wealth from the "second economy" and those reliant on state incomes did relatively badly. Job opportunities for unskilled or uneducated people diminished throughout this time as a result of a continuing decrease in the number of vacant jobs and the shift in labor demand toward skilled workers.

Along the way, Hungary became steadily more polarized. The country's ethnic minorities, particularly Roma and undocumented migrants, were disadvantaged by economic reforms. While in 1971 Roma workers had been regularly employed, from the late 1980s onward, they were systematically pushed out of the labor market.[82] By 1993, this trend resulted in shockingly high unemployment figures for Roma. Less than half of this unemployment rate could be explained by factors such as lower educational levels and a disadvantageous distribution of labor power among Roma. The rest was due to discrimination by employers. Although they make up only 5 percent of the total population, approximately 25 percent of Hungary's roughly two million poor are Roma. Moreover, Roma face discrimination not only by employers but also by state or state-controlled institutions, including the public system, the National Health Service, the police, and the courts.[83]

In their struggle to maintain economic growth and manage the budget deficit, Hungary's governments have ignored the need to reform the country's social services. According to the Organisation for Economic Co-operation and Development country survey for 2005, Hungary needed to take strong measures to prevent "failure in the welfare regime change."[84] Yet neither the political left nor the right has championed the needs of Hungary's poor. Instead, they have talked about "trickle-down economics." In the early years of the transition, the government gave in when faced with demonstrations by those who had suffered from the economic reforms. The most famous of these demonstrations was a massive taxi strike in 1990, when taxi drivers and others blocked the streets of Budapest and roads around the country. The protest was triggered by the government's sudden decision to raise the price of gasoline by 66 percent overnight—a policy announced as a way to deal with shortages caused by decreases in sales by the Soviet Union. In the end, the government backed down.

Until the 2006 demonstrations, other responses to social problems were far smaller and more subdued. Groups have, when they could, taken matters into their own hands. Some self-help and advocacy groups have been organized, and many, like the homeless, have broken the law to provide for themselves.

Emerging Challenges

Most of the political challenges that Hungarians face in the coming years are associated with the country's shift to "illiberal democracy" after 2010. The extent of this change is best illustrated in the tense relations that the Hungarian government has developed with European institutions. Just days after Orbán's third consecutive electoral victory in 2018, the European Parliament drafted a report calling for the triggering of proceedings against Hungary for violating the union's core values. The text raised concerns about the independence of the judiciary, corruption, freedom of expression, the rights of the Roma and

Jewish minorities, refugees, and other issues. Prime Minister Orbán responded by accusing the European parliamentarian who drafted the report of being part of a conspiracy network run by George Soros. Hungary's foreign minister, Péter Szijjártó, dismissed the EP's investigation as "theater," whereas the government's official spokesperson took to calling the document the "Soros report."[85] Under Article 7 of the Lisbon Treaty, a member state can be sanctioned for breaching the European Union's core values, but all member states (except for the state under scrutiny) must agree to the imposition of such sanctions.[86] The European Parliament itself noted in January 2020 that the situation in Hungary has in fact become worse since Article 7 was triggered and called on the EU Commission, to little avail, "to use all tools at its disposal to prevent a serious breach of common values."[87]

The deep tensions characterizing Hungary's EU membership in 2020 stand in sharp contrast with the way this relationship began in the late 1980s, when Hungary was a leader in the region regarding the move toward Europe. It was the first member of the Soviet bloc to become a member of the Council of Europe. On June 4, 1990, the new and free Hungarian parliament marked the seventieth anniversary of the Trianon peace treaty by adopting a resolution that reiterated the acceptance of its existing borders. Together with the three other members of the Visegrad Group (Czechia, Poland, and Slovakia), Hungary remained in the forefront of European integration for decades, marching resolutely toward membership in NATO (1999) and the EU (2004), despite the tensions underlying its relations with neighboring states that had large ethnic Hungarian minority populations.

Since 2010, however, and especially after Fidesz's double electoral victory in 2014 (in both Hungarian and European elections), the party's leaders have rather consistently and openly challenged several major EU directives, especially in the domain of refugee policy. The so-called Dublin agreement (whereby refugees coming into the EU had to remain in the first member country they reached) was declared obsolete in mid-2015, and the EU designed a policy to distribute refugees across member states according to each country's characteristics (such as size and economic capacities). Hungary, however, along with the other three Visegrad countries, rejected this approach and stated that it would not accept any refugee resettlement policy decided outside of its domestic legislative body (in other words, by the Fidesz's supermajority in the Hungarian parliament).

The Hungarian regime's war on institutions of liberal democracy has continued despite increasing discontent expressed by European officials. The attacks on institutions that represent and stand up for liberal democratic values—such as the Central European University, the Helsinki Committee and other civil society institutions, the opposition media, and so on—have generated massive peaceful demonstrations by the regime's opposition and have also received broad international attention over the years. These incidents have been part of a larger governmental strategy that aims to control not only the institutions most directly relevant for political power but also educational and cultural institutions, including theaters and the arts. Prime Minister Orbán announced his intention to focus on these domains after winning his third (post-2010) term in 2018, when he stated, "We must embed the political system in a cultural era."[88] As part of this strategy, the government adopted a law in December 2019 that severely limited state funding for theaters, shifting responsibility for the funding of these institutions to municipal governments, while maintaining central control over the appointment of institution directors. Analysts have seen this policy change as an attempt to place pressure on local authorities, especially in the capital city of Budapest, which has a high concentration of theaters and cultural institutions, and where the opposition won the mayoral election earlier that year.

With its emphasis on ethnic nationhood and limitations on pluralism and individual freedoms, "illiberal democracy" also generates divisions by fueling anti-immigrant sentiment, racism, and xenophobia and by creating an environment hostile to gender rights and the legal protection of sexual minorities (see chapter 8 on gender regimes). Orbán's government has been critiqued as an active instigator of xenophobia and racism both through its public discourse and its policies.[89] The Council of Europe's European Commission against Racism and Intolerance (ECRI) published a report in 2015 accusing Orbán's government of rampant racism and xenophobia.[90] In follow-up conclusions from 2018, the ECRI reaffirmed its accusations by concluding that Orbán's government has not sufficiently acted upon ECRI's recommendations from its 2015 report.[91] Orbán scored a success in July 2017 by hosting an official visit by Israeli prime minister Benjamin Netanyahu and by making a solemn promise to protect the country's Jewish population.[92] Meanwhile, the economic marginalization of Roma continues. Women continue to bear the burden of the primary responsibility for parenting (and are called on to have more children in exchange for financial support), as well as care work, while they are simultaneously expected to maintain full employment. In the name of the same illiberal political ideology, sexual minority members face increasing threats.

Another consequence of illiberal ideology is the potential for a deterioration of relations with neighboring states that incorporate large ethnic Hungarian minority populations that ended up in those states through the border changes that occurred in the region during the last hundred years. Most of these neighbors are EU member states, and the European framework has helped to channel potential conflicts into peaceful cross-border relations. In the case of neighboring countries that are outside the EU, however, tensions over the Hungarian government's kin-state activism can take a different direction. The 2020 escalation of tensions with Ukraine provides a useful illustration. Against the backdrop of the Ukrainian government's ongoing difficulties in stabilizing its control over the country, the involvement of the Hungarian foreign minister in local elections (by appearing in a social media campaign on behalf of a Hungarian minority political organization) triggered a Ukrainian government ban on the entry of Hungarian high officials into the country. The Hungarian government, in turn, threatened to undermine Ukraine's Euro-Atlantic integration. The EU Commission distanced itself from the conflict by declaring the problem between Hungary and Ukraine "bilateral" and vowing to continue its "very close cooperation with Ukraine."[93]

The Hungarian government's challenges to the EU continued into 2020, amid the coronavirus crisis, when the EU proposed a financial relief stimulus package to deal with the consequences of the pandemic. Specifically, in November 2020 the EU decided to tie access to the long-term EU budget to mechanisms binding member states to uphold the rule of law and democratic standards.[94] Orbán found a staunch ally in Poland in opposing this policy by vetoing the approval of the EU budget. Eventually, both Poland and Hungary settled the issue with the EU, but the tensions continue.

Conclusion

Hungarians displayed remarkable unity in 1956 and in 1989 in their desire to achieve political freedoms. The political competition unfolding since the collapse of the communist regime has revealed significant divisions. Yet, in a region undergoing major shifts in state borders and regional realignments, the first fifteen years of Hungarian politics after 1990 were characterized by democratic pluralism and stability. The liabilities of the economic reforms introduced by Hungary's pre-1989 government (during the period of "goulash communism"), and the failures of the consecutive post-1989 governments (especially their inability to prevent socioeconomic disadvantage and marginalization among significant segments of the population), became evident only later. Still, the popular upheaval that began in 2006 over revelations about the economy's true problems was more about being misled by the Socialist-liberal government than about the government's policies. The notion of being misled, however, created deep mistrust in that government, and it made Hungarian society vulnerable to the populist nationalist political discourse that helped the Fidesz-led opposition obtain a supermajority in parliament after the 2010 elections. This supermajority, in turn, engineered the "illiberal" shift in Hungarian politics under the leadership of Prime Minister Viktor Orbán's regime.

For Hungary, joining the EU has been a clear benefit, and there is no apparent interest among the major Hungarian political actors in reversing Hungary's European integration. Yet the Orbán government's actions since 2010, while taking full advantage of the benefits of membership, have repeatedly challenged several EU norms and institutions, particularly regarding civil liberties. The government has received numerous warnings and admonishments from European institutions but has not yet faced any substantial consequences. EU rules make it extremely difficult for European officials to hold member states accountable for their policies, and European-level party politics further complicate any desires to implement European norms against defiant governments. Fidesz is a member of the European People's Party (EPP)—the EU's coalition of conservative and Christian democratic parties; and the EPP's most influential leader, German chancellor Angela Merkel, has pursued a cautious policy to avoid alienating Fidesz. Given this combination of domestic and European political conditions, "illiberal democracy" appears strong in Hungary after a decade of major changes introduced in 2010.

Study Questions

1. What legacies of Hungary's precommunist history feature prominently in contemporary Hungarian politics?
2. How did Hungary's communist-era experience shape the early opposition movement? How has it shaped the postcommunist political and economic environments?
3. How are questions about minorities, including Roma and Jews, relevant in contemporary Hungarian politics? What commonalities does Hungary share with neighboring states in this respect? What distinguishes the Hungarian case?
4. What key factors explain the mass support enjoyed by Orbán? What are sources of his appeal to Hungarian voters? What are sources of opposition?

5. What are key characteristics of Hungary's democratic backsliding? What have been its sources? What are its main manifestations? What are its identifiable consequences?

Suggested Readings

Antal, Attila. *The Rise of Hungarian Populism: State Autocracy and the Orbán Regime*. Bingley, UK: Emerald Publishing, 2019.

Borhi, László. *Dealing with Dictators: The United States, Hungary, and East Central Europe, 1942–1989*. Bloomington: Indiana University Press, 2016.

Klimó, Árpád von. *Hungary since 1945*. New York: Routledge, 2018.

Körösényi, András. *Government and Politics in Hungary*. Budapest: Central European University Press, 2000.

Magyar, Bálint. *Post-Communist Mafia State: The Case of Hungary*. Budapest: Central European University Press, 2016.

Pap, András. *Democratic Decline in Hungary: Law and Society in an Illiberal Democracy*. New York: Routledge, 2018.

Ranki, Vera. *The Politics of Inclusion and Exclusion: Jews and Nationalism in Hungary*. New York: Holmes & Meier, 1999.

Tokes, Rudolf. *Hungary's Negotiated Revolution: Economic Reform, Social Change, and Political Succession*. Cambridge: Cambridge University Press, 1996.

Websites

Politics.hu: http://www.politics.hu
Hungarian Spectrum: http://hungarianspectrum.wordpress.com
National Széchényi Library, 1956 Institute and Oral History Archive: http://www.rev.hu

Notes

1. "Full Speech of V. Orbán: Will Europe Belong to Europeans?," *Visegrad Post*, July 24, 2017, https://visegradpost.com/en/2017/07/24/full-speech-of-v-orban-will-europe-belong-to-europeans.

2. Csaba Tóth, "Full Text of Viktor Orbán's Speech at Băile Tuşnad (Tusnádfürdő) of 26 July 2014," *Budapest Beacon*, July 29, 2014, https://budapestbeacon.com/full-text-of-viktor-orbans-speech-at-baile-tusnad-tusnadfurdo-of-26-july-2014.

3. Quoted in Ingeborg van der Geest, Henrike Jansen, and Bart van Klink, eds., *Vox Populi: Populism as a Rhetorical and Democratic Challenge* (Cheltenham, UK: Edward Elgar, 2020), 169.

4. Bálint Magyar, *Post-Communist Mafia State: The Case of Hungary* (Budapest: Central European University Press, 2016), 15–16; the First Republic is considered to have been the period between late October 1918 and late March 1919; the second was proclaimed in February 1946, ending in August 1947 or May 1949, depending on points of view; the third was inaugurated on October 23, 1989.

5. Andrew Janos, *The Politics of Backwardness in Hungary: 1825–1945* (Princeton, NJ: Princeton University Press, 1982), 176–82.

6. István Bibó, *Democracy, Revolution, Self-Determination*, trans. András Boros-Kazai (Highland Lakes, NY: Atlantic Research, 1991), 155–322; see also Paul Lendvai's observations in *Hungary: Between Democracy and Authoritarianism* (London: Hurst, 2012), 53–65.

7. See a rough translation in Eva S. Balogh, "Zsolt Bayer Vents against Hungarian Jews and the Foreign Press," *Hungarian Spectrum*, last modified January 5, 2011, https://hungarianspectrum .wordpress.com/2011/01/05/zsolt_bayer_vents_against_hungarian_jews_and_the_foreign_press. Orbán and other Fidesz officials never publicly distanced themselves from Bayer on this occasion, or when he dismissed Imre Kertész, the 2002 Nobel laureate in literature, as a "non-Hungarian author." In late June 2013, the Constitutional Court, despite its reputation as a government tool, ruled that the accusations of anti-Semitism made by the liberal Klubrádió against Bayer (see https ://theorangefiles.hu/the-same-stench, accessed January 14, 2021), following which the latter had filed a libel suit, were legitimate. It is difficult not to see a deliberate "stick-and-carrot" approach by the Orbán government, which is trying to appease Jobbik, the center-left opposition, and international public opinion.

8. For a database of the Hungarian Revolution and all the actors involved, see "The 1956 Revolution," 1956 Institute and Oral History Archive, accessed January 14, 2021, http://www.rev. hu/history_of_56/naviga/index.htm.

9. Iván T. Berend, *The Hungarian Economic Reforms, 1953–1988* (Cambridge: Cambridge University Press, 1990), 246–58.

10. Berend, *Hungarian Economic Reforms*, 246–58.

11. Rudolf Tokes, *Hungary's Negotiated Revolution* (Cambridge: Cambridge University Press, 1996), 330.

12. András Körösényi, *Government and Politics in Hungary* (Budapest: Central European University Press, 1999), 158.

13. Körösényi, *Government and Politics*, 162–69.

14. Bill Lomax, "From Death to Resurrection: The Metamorphosis of Power in Eastern Europe," *Critique* 25, no. 1 (1997): 68.

15. Béla Kovács (1908–1959) had been, in 1930, one of the founders of the Independent Smallholders Party, a political force characterized by a strong pro–land reform and antidictatorial stand. He led it to the November 1945 electoral triumph (57 percent of the votes), only to be arrested and deported to a forced labor camp in the USSR, where he remained until after the Twentieth Congress of the Communist Party of the Soviet Union in 1956. During the revolution later that year, he briefly resumed his position and stated that "the land and the factories shouldn't be turned back to their old owners," a position unpopular with Fidesz, eager to emphasize solely his anticommunist relevance. As for the Terror House Museum, established in the infamous building on Andrássy Avenue that played an important role under both the Nazi and Stalinist regimes, several observers pointed to the fact that only one hall is devoted to Nazism and the Arrow Cross, and many more treat the communist regime in all its variants, which is acceptable in terms of years in power but not victims. However, Socialist-led executives from 2002 to 2010 did not alter the structure of the museum, which has since become one of the cultural attractions of Budapest.

16. "We Lied to Win, Says Hungary PM," BBC, September 18, 2006, http://news.bbc.co.uk /2/hi/europe/5354972.stm.

17. Daniel McLaughlin, "150 Injured as Hungarians Riot over PM's Lies," *Guardian*, September 19, 2006, http://www.theguardian.com/world/2006/sep/19/1.

18. McLaughlin, "150 Injured."

19. Béla Greskovits, "Rebuilding the Hungarian Right through Civil Organization and Contention: The Civic Circles Movement" (Working Paper EUI RSCAS 2017/37, Robert Schuman Centre for Advanced Studies, 2017), 5, http://hdl.handle.net/1814/47245.

20. Greskovits, "Rebuilding the Hungarian Right," 15.

21. Greskovits, "Rebuilding the Hungarian Right," 15.

22. "Socialists Defeated in Hungary's Local Elections, Gyurcsany Defiant," *Novinite: Sofia News Agency*, October 2, 2006.

23. "Hungarian Police Clamp down on Anti-Government Protests," *Guardian*, October 23, 2006, https://www.theguardian.com/world/2006/oct/23/1.

24. "Hungary Freedom House Report 2008," Freedom House, last modified 2008.

25. "Hungary Freedom House Report 2008."

26. "Public Opinion Analysis: Standard Eurobarometer 67," European Commission, last modified 2007.

27. Zsolt Darvas, "The Rise and Fall of Hungary," *Guardian*, October 29, 2008, http://www.theguardian.com/business/blog/2008/oct/29/hungary-imf.

28. Darvas, "The Rise and Fall of Hungary."

29. "Pew Global Attitudes: 2009 Pulse of Europe Report," Pew Global Attitudes, accessed July 11, 2018, http://assets.pewresearch.org/wp-content/uploads/sites/2/2009/11/Pew-Global-Attitudes-2009-Pulse-of-Europe-Report-Topline.pdf.

30. "Pew Global Attitudes."

31. Siobhán Dowling, "The World from Berlin: Neo-Fascist Magyar Garda Is 'Hungary's Shame,'" *Spiegel Online*, August 27, 2007, http://www.spiegel.de/international/germany/the-world-from-berlin-neo-fascist-magyar-garda-is-hungary-s-shame-a-502184.html; Adam LeBor, "Marching Back to the Future: Magyar Garda and the Resurgence of the Right in Hungary," *Dissent Magazine*, July 11, 2018, https://www.dissentmagazine.org/article/marching-back-to-the-future-magyar-garda-and-the-resurgence-of-the-right-in-hungary.

32. Dowling, "The World from Berlin."

33. LeBor, "Marching Back to the Future."

34. "Extremists Exceed Expectations in EP Elections," WikiLeaks, last modified June 8, 2009, https://wikileaks.org/plusd/cables/09BUDAPEST410_a.html.

35. Agnes Batory, "Kin-State Identity in the European Context: Citizenship, Nationalism and Constitutionalism in Hungary," *Nations and Nationalism* 16, no. 1 (2010): 31–48.

36. Batory, "Kin-State Identity."

37. Katalin Halasz, "The Rise of the Radical Right in Europe and the Case of Hungary: 'Gypsy Crime' Defines National Identity?," *Development* 52, no. 4 (2009): 490–94.

38. Halasz, "The Rise of the Radical Right."

39. For more on single-pyramid structures of power, see Henry Hale, *Patronal Politics: Eurasian Regime Dynamics in Comparative Perspective* (Cambridge: Cambridge University Press, 2015).

40. András L. Pap, *Democratic Decline in Hungary: Law and Society in an Illiberal Democracy* (New York: Routledge, 2018), 20.

41. Pap, *Democratic Decline in Hungary*, 20.

42. Pap, *Democratic Decline in Hungary*, 20.

43. Pap, *Democratic Decline in Hungary*, 20.

44. Pap, *Democratic Decline in Hungary*, 21.

45. Pap, *Democratic Decline in Hungary*, 21.

46. Pap, *Democratic Decline in Hungary*, 21.

47. "The Putinization of Hungary," *Washington Post*, December 26, 2010, http://www.washingtonpost.com/wp-dyn/content/article/2010/12/26/AR2010122601791.html.

48. "The Putinization of Hungary."

49. Zselyke Csaky, "How Orban Redrew Hungary's Media Map to Solidify His Power," *World Politics Review*, last modified March 7, 2017.

50. "2020 World Press Freedom Index," Reporters Without Borders, accessed December 22, 2020, https://rsf.org/en/ranking.

51. Eva S. Balogh, "The Ministry of National Development and the Building of a 'National Bourgeoisie,'" *Hungarian Spectrum*, last modified December 26, 2011, http://hungarianspectrum. org/2011/12/26/the-ministry-of-national-development-and-the-building-of-a-national-bourgeoisie.

52. Balogh, "The Ministry of National Development."

53. Balogh, "The Ministry of National Development."

54. Eva S. Balogh, "Nationalization Hungarian Style," *Hungarian Spectrum*, last modified June 27, 2013, http://hungarianspectrum.org/2013/06/27/nationalization-hungarian-style.

55. Mihaly Koltai, "The Economics of 'Orbánism,'" LeftEast, last modified April 2, 2018, http://www.criticatac.ro/lefteast/the-economics-of-orbanism.

56. Koltai, "The Economics of 'Orbánism.'"

57. Lily Bayer, "Orbán Wins Landslide to Secure Third Straight Term," *Politico*, April 8, 2018, https://www.politico.eu/article/hungary-election-2018-viktor-orban-fidesz-jobbik.

58. Bayer, "Orbán Wins Landslide."

59. Bayer, "Orbán Wins Landslide."

60. Bayer, "Orbán Wins Landslide."

61. Aleksandra Wróbel, "Orbán Pledges to Keep Hungary Safe and Christian," *Politico*, July 5, 2018, https://www.politico.eu/article/orban-christian-migrants-pledges-to-keep-hungary-safe.

62. Nick Thorpe, "Coronavirus: Hungary Government Gets Sweeping Powers," BBC, March 30, 2020, https://www.bbc.com/news/world-europe-52095500.

63. "Coronavirus: Hungary Votes to End Viktor Orban Emergency Powers," BBC, June 16, 2020, https://www.bbc.com/news/world-europe-53062177.

64. Chris Hann, "In Search of Civil Society: From Peasant Populism to Postpeasant Illiberalism in Provincial Hungary," *Social Science Information* 59, no. 3 (2020): 467.

65. Andras Bozoki and Eszter Simon, "Hungary since 1990," in *Central and Southeast European Politics since 1989*, ed. Sabrina P. Ramet (Cambridge: Cambridge University Press, 2010), 210.

66. Jason Wittenberg and Bela Greskovits, "Civil Society and Democratic Consolidation in Hungary in the 1990s and 2000s" (paper presented at the Council for European Studies' Twentieth International Conference of Europeanists, Amsterdam, 25–27 June 2013), 10.

67. Wittenberg and Greskovits, "Civil Society," 12.

68. Wittenberg and Greskovits, "Civil Society," 22.

69. Wittenberg and Greskovits, "Civil Society," 22.

70. Wittenberg and Greskovits, "Civil Society," 23.

71. "The European Union Has an Obligation to Protect Civil Society in Hungary," London School of Economics, last modified April 11, 2017, https://blogs.lse.ac.uk/europpblog/2017/04 /11/the-european-union-has-an-obligation-to-protect-civil-society-in-hungary.

72. "The European Union Has an Obligation."

73. "The European Union Has an Obligation."

74. "The Open Society Foundations to Close International Operations in Budapest," Open Society Foundations, last modified May 15, 2018, https://www.opensocietyfoundations.org/press-releases/open-society-foundations-close-international-operations-budapest.

75. "Open Society Foundations to Close"; Lily Bayer, "George Soros–Backed Foundation Leaving Hungary," *Politico*, May 15, 2018, https://www.politico.eu/article/soros-open-society -foundations-leaving-hungary.

76. Jan-Werner Müller, "Hungary: The War on Education," *New York Review*, May 20, 2017.

77. Jennifer Rankin, "George Soros Attacks Hungarian Prime Minister for Building a 'Mafia State,'" *Guardian*, June 1, 2017, https://www.theguardian.com/world/2017/jun/01/george-soros -attacks-hungarian-president-building-mafia-state.

78. "PM Orbán: The Only Network Which 'Operates Like a Mafia' in Hungary Is Run by George Soros," About Hungary, last modified June 2, 2017, http://abouthungary.hu/news-in-brie f/pm-orban-the-only-network-which-operates-like-a-mafia-in-hungary-is-run-by-george-soros.

79. Eva Ehrlich and Gabor Revesz, "Coming in from the Cold: Hungary's Economy in the 20th Century," *Hungarian Quarterly* 41, no. 157 (Spring 2000): 18.

80. "Economic Survey of Hungary 2014," OECD, accessed January 14, 2021, https://www.oec d-ilibrary.org/economics/oecd-economic-surveys-hungary-2014_eco_surveys-hun-2014-en.

81. Paul Marer, "Economic Transformation, 1990–1998," in *Dilemmas of Transition: The Hungarian Experience*, ed. Aurel Braun and Zoltan Barany (Lanham, MD: Rowman & Littlefield, 1998), 165–68.

82. Project on Ethnic Relations, *Roma in Hungary: Government Policies, Minority Expectations, and the International Community* (Princeton, NJ: Project on Ethnic Relations, 2000), 16.

83. Angéla Koczé, "Political Empowerment or Political Incarceration of Romani? The Hungarian Version of the Politics of Dispossession," in *The Hungarian Patient: Social Opposition to an Illiberal Democracy*, ed. Péter Krasztev and Jon Van Til (Budapest: Central European University Press, 2015).

84. Tibor Gazsó and István Stumpf, eds., *Jóléti rendszerváltás csődje: Gyurcsány- kormány első éve* [The failure of welfare regime change: Gyurcsány's government's first year] (Budapest: Századvég, 2005). This is the third volume of a yearbook on the activity of the executive, sponsored by Fidesz.

85. Lili Bayer and Maia De La Baume, "European Parliament Report Calls for Sanctions Procedure against Hungary," *Politico*, April 12, 2018, https://www.politico.eu/article/viktor-o rban-european-parliament-report-judith-sargentini-calls-for-sanctions-procedure-against-hungary.

86. Yasmeen Serhan, "The EU Watches as Hungary Kills Democracy," *Atlantic*, April 2, 2020, https://www.theatlantic.com/international/archive/2020/04/europe-hungary-viktor-orban-coro navirus-covid19-democracy/609313.

87. "Rule of Law in Poland and Hungary Has Worsened," European Parliament, last modified January 16, 2020, https://www.europarl.europa.eu/news/en/press-room/20200109IPR69907/rule -of-law-in-poland-and-hungary-has-worsened.

88. Palko Karasz, "Theaters in Hungary Feel the Chill of Viktor Orban's Culture War," *New York Times*, December 13, 2019.

89. Pap, *Democratic Decline in Hungary*.

90. "ECRI Report on Hungary (Fifth Monitoring Cycle)," Council of Europe, last modified June 9, 2015, https://rm.coe.int/fifth-report-on-hungary/16808b57e8.

91. "ECRI Conclusions on the Implementation of the Recommendations in Respect of Hungary's Subject to Interim Follow-Up," Council of Europe, May 15, 2018, https://rm.coe.int /interim-follow-up-conclusions-on-hungary-5th-monitoring-cycle/16808b57f9.

92. "Hungary: Jewish Group Let Down by Israel's Take on Soros Ads," July 17, 2017, https:// www.seattletimes.com/nation-world/hungary-jewish-group-let-down-by-israels-take-on-soros-ads; see also Herb Keinon, "Analysis: Why Do the Hungarians and Netanyahu Want Each Other?," *Jerusalem Post*, July 18, 2017, https://www.jpost.com/israel-news/politics-and-diplomacy/why-do -the-hungarians-and-netanyahu-want-each-other-499996.

93. Vlagyiszlav Makszimov, "EU Commission to Stay Out of Ukraine-Hungary Row," *Euractiv*, October 27, 2020, https://www.euractiv.com/section/all/news/eu-commission-to-stay-o ut-of-ukraine-hungary-row.

94. "EU Agrees to Link Rule of Law to Budget Fund Access," DW, May 11, 2020, https://p .dw.com/p/3kvHj.

Map 14.0.   The Baltic Countries

CHAPTER 14

The Baltic Countries

Daunis Auers

On August 13, 2020, peaceful crowds of Estonians, Latvians, and Lithuanians gathered outside the Belarusian embassies in their respective capitals, protesting against electoral fraud and widespread police violence during the previous weekend's presidential election in neighboring Belarus. Thirty years previously, all four countries were republics of the Soviet Union, with similar levels of economic development and a common deep disenchantment with the Soviet system. Belarus, however, failed to transition to democracy or to establish a fully functioning market economy and has remained in the gray zone of post-Soviet countries in Russia's sphere of influence.

In contrast, the three Baltic countries of Estonia, Latvia, and Lithuania undertook successful political and economic transformations. All three are members of the European Union (EU) and the North Atlantic Treaty Organization (NATO), have adopted the euro currency, and most recently joined the Organisation for Co-operation and Development (OECD), known as the developed nations' think tank. Their gross domestic product per capita is approximately double that of Belarus.[1] The Baltic countries have never been wealthier, safer, and more democratic than they are today.

Estonia, Latvia, and Lithuania share a common history, and with a combined population of approximately six million people in 2020, they are comparatively small. Much to the frustration of Baltic politicians and diplomats, this means that the three are typically bundled together as a common region rather than individual states. Indeed, they are grouped together in this chapter, and in April 2018, US president Donald Trump marked the Baltic centenaries by hosting the Baltic presidents to a common roundtable, luncheon, and chaotic press conference that was lampooned in a *Saturday Night Live* cold open a few days later.[2]

This masks significant differences in the region. Across the Baltic Sea, the citizens of the Scandinavian states of Denmark, Norway, and Sweden can communicate with each other because the three languages share similar roots. This is not the case for the Baltic states, where there are significant differences between the languages and older Balts share a common knowledge of Russian, while those under forty prefer to communicate with their neighbors in English. Estonia has close relations with Finland, with which it shares common national and linguistic roots. Lithuania's history is more closely intertwined with Poland than Latvia or Estonia. The Baltic states are competitors as much as partners, although the continuing security threat of Russia has promoted and enhanced defense cooperation.

This chapter compares and contrasts the contemporary Baltic countries. It begins with an overview of key historical moments in Baltic political history. The next section looks at the early years of postcommunism. On the one hand, these years reshaped the Baltic political and economic systems. On the other hand, there was a great deal of economic uncertainty as inflation and currency reform wiped out savings, corporate restructurings led to unemployment, and many residents were thrown into social crisis. Nevertheless, the Baltic countries navigated the tumultuous 1990s without changing the Western trajectory of their reforms. The following sections compare political institutions, political competition, and civil society in the region. The final parts of the chapter compare the Baltic economies and societies before considering the continuing challenges of demographic decline, economic growth, and threats from Russia.

Political History

The eastern littoral of the Baltic Sea was first settled around 11,000 BC. The peoples of the region were at the distant fringes of European civilization, largely isolated from the religious, military, political, economic, and cultural trends in the southern and western half of the continent. This changed in the early thirteenth century when Christian crusaders turned their attention to the last pagans in Europe in the lands that now make up Estonia and Latvia. The following centuries saw the region colonized by Germanic crusaders, followed by successive Danish, Swedish, Polish, and Russian monarchies, each leaving its own mark on the region. Throughout these changes of regime, ethnic Germans remained the local, governing nobility right up until the aftermath of World War I. The Estonians, Latvians, and Lithuanians (as well as minority Litvaks, Jews, Russian Old Believers, and Roma) largely lived as serfs in impoverished rural communities, with only small urban centers, until the tsarist reforms of the nineteenth century led to greater educational and economic opportunities that allowed for social and territorial mobility and the emergence of titular elites.

These new elites led the first national "awakenings" in the nineteenth century, in the same way that similarly "slumbering" nations, as nationalists have framed it, in Central Europe had been roused just a few decades earlier. The concept of awakening (*ärkamisaeg* in Estonian, *atmoda* in Latvian, and *atgimimas* in Lithuanian) describes three key periods in the Baltic nations' battle for sovereign autonomy. The first awakening in the nineteenth century reflects the three Baltic nations' rediscovery of their allegedly ancient national identities that had lain dormant during their many centuries of foreign subjugation. The second awakening at the end of World War I saw the three nations battle to form independent and sovereign national states. The third awakening came in the 1980s as the Baltic nations broke away from the Soviet Union. Contemporary nationalists even talk of a fourth awakening as an alternative to contemporary political and economic globalization that, they allege, has stripped the Baltic nations of their unique, sovereign identities.

The start of the twentieth century saw a flowering of Baltic cultures, civic organizations, and eventually even political activism, all of which laid the base for the independence movements. There was a first turn toward political activism in the revolutionary year of 1905 when, as one Latvian historian put it, the Latvian nation became a "living political organism," as a variety of mostly left-leaning groups organized Latvians (and Estonians) to rise up against the oppression of the German nobility.[3] A crackdown against the more radical activists of 1905 saw them dispersed into exile around Europe, but other more moderate Baltic leaders gained valuable political experience from participating in democratizing elections in the following years. These organizations and activists, both those in the Baltics and those returning from exile, came to prominence when the Russian and German Empires collapsed in 1917. This created a power vacuum as White (pro-tsarist) forces, the Red Army, German mercenaries, and Baltic nationalist forces (eight different competing armies in total) battled for control of the region.[4] Skillful political maneuvering saw Baltic political leaders establish provisional governments and declare sovereign independent states in 1918. Fighting continued for several more years, and foreign assistance from the British in particular was required, until the three states signed peace treaties with Soviet Russia in 1920 and economic reconstruction and state building began. In this period, Lithuania's capital city of Vilnius was seized by Poland. It would remain in Polish hands until World War II.

While military leaders and diplomats were settling territorial disputes, drawing up borders, and working on international recognition, politicians were debating the constitutional outlines of the new states. There was a broad cross-party consensus that the Baltic countries would be democratic republics, but the details would be negotiated in the constitutional assemblies that were elected in all three countries. Estonia adopted a permanent constitution at the end of 1920, with Latvia and Lithuania following in 1922. Largely because of the negative experience of tsarist autocracy, as well as being inspired by political trends in Western Europe, all three assemblies adopted parliamentary systems with relatively weak presidential offices. The office was especially insubstantial in Estonia, where the head of state was known as the state elder (*riigivanem*) and was combined with the office of the prime minister. Parliaments were unicameral, and representatives were elected by proportional representation from party lists. Low thresholds meant that the legislatures suffered from extreme multipartyism. For instance, fifty-seven *different* party lists won seats in the one-hundred-deputy Latvian parliament in just four elections (1922, 1925, 1928, and 1931). Party systems in the three countries were broadly similar, with strong social democratic parties on the left, large conservative agrarian parties on the right, and a wide array of small liberal, ethnic minority, single-issue, and splinter parties clustered around the middle. This contributed to unstable and short-lived government coalitions. Between 1919 and 1933, the average duration of an Estonian government was eight months. Political corruption was widespread as the smaller parties, often made up of one or two deputies, offered up votes for sale. There was widespread distrust of the political establishment and of political parties in particular, and there was little public opposition as the democratic experiments floundered. Similar to other new states in Central Europe, Lithuania slipped into authoritarian rule in 1926, followed by Latvia and Estonia in 1934.

Each Baltic country had but one authoritarian leader in the interwar years. The leaders themselves were quite similar. They were men in late middle age, and Estonia's Konstantin Päts, Latvia's Kārlis Ulmanis, and Lithuania's Antanas Smetona had all been central to their national independence movements. Smetona came to power first, having been invited to take up the presidential office by a directorate of political insurgents who seized control of the political system. In contrast, Päts and Ulmanis, in collaboration with military and security forces, seized power while already holding the highest elected executive office. All three authoritarian regimes were nationalist (reducing, for example, the role of ethnic minorities and foreigners in the economy), but avoided entanglements with extremist groups to the right or left. Politically, Lithuania maintained a parliament and allowed some political parties. Päts constructed a national movement—Isamaalit (Fatherland League)—that essentially functioned as a single dominant party, but Ulmanis avoided creating a party to prop up his regime, focusing instead on civic organizations loyal to the regime. Päts allowed some level of liberalization in 1938 when a new Estonian constitution was adopted, but he remained firmly in charge.

The economic stability of the late 1930s greatly contributed to the stability of the regimes. The first years of the independent states saw immense economic reconstruction. The Latvian capital city of Riga provides a good example. On the eve of World War I, Riga was an international hub with a population of 482,000 (100,000 people more than Stockholm at that time) and was second only to St. Petersburg in size and influence in the Baltic Sea region.[5] The city was home to the Russian-Baltic Wagon Company, which designed and built passenger and commercial cars as well as airplanes, and the Provodnik factory, which employed 13,500 people and was the world's second-largest producer of car tires. However, these big industrial enterprises were evacuated eastward to Russian territory at the outbreak of World War I and, following independence, never returned. The closed borders of the communist Soviet Union to the east destroyed the Baltic states' established export markets, while new trade barriers in Western Europe excluded the Baltic countries from these lucrative markets.

During the interwar years, the Baltic economies became distinctly more agrarian. Radical land reforms saw rural property owned by Baltic Germans in Estonia and Latvia confiscated, pooled, and then made available to ethnic Estonians and Latvians, especially war veterans, to become smallholders. The reforms created a more equitable rural society and fashioned a new class of independent farmers with a stake in the newly sovereign countries.

The Baltic economies began to grow steadily from the middle of the 1920s after internal restructuring, as well as the recovery of international markets. This brief period of prosperity ended when the great global depression reached Northern Europe in 1930. Exports fell and unemployment rose, contributing to increased public distrust of politicians and parties. The new dictators in Estonia and Latvia undertook more economic restructuring. Private enterprises had to compete with new national enterprises producing subsidized goods. For example, in the later years of his regime in Latvia, President Ulmanis authorized both a government-owned shoe factory and a government-owned brick-making enterprise (although there was no shortage of either good in Latvia at that time). The motivation for both enterprises appears to have been the wish to further drive out foreign capital from Latvia.[6] Similar corporatist policies were adopted in the two other Baltic countries as nationalism increasingly shaped economic policy. The comparative success of these policies is still debated by scholars in the Baltic region. One volume on the economic history of Europe claims that the GDP per capita of Estonia and Latvia (Lithuanian data was unavailable) in 1938 had overtaken that of Finland, Austria, Italy, and Ireland, countries that had a far higher level of economic development in 1991 when the Baltic states exited the Soviet Union.[7] Whatever the economic data might show, it is clear that public perceptions both then and now are shaped by the horrors of war and brutal occupation that followed the stability of the "golden era" late 1930s.

These relatively peaceful years were shattered by the Molotov-Ribbentrop Pact, signed by Germany and the Soviet Union in August 1939, and which contained a "secret protocol" (the existence of which the Soviets denied until the glasnost era) that divided the Baltic countries (as well as Poland, Romania, and Finland) into spheres of influence. Latvia and Estonia were ceded to the USSR, Lithuania to Germany (though later Lithuania would be claimed back by the Soviets). Notably, even today, Russia, the USSR's legal successor state, denies that an occupation took place, arguing that the Baltics voluntarily joined the USSR in 1940. This issue has salience in Estonia and Latvia, where the large Russian-speaking minority groups still celebrate the end of World War II on May 9, with many seeing it as a liberation of the Baltic states, while titular Balts see this as a day of mourning when the Baltics came under the smothering influence of the Soviet Union. Between September and October 1939, Estonia, Latvia, and Lithuania were forced to accept the terms of mutual assistance treaties with the USSR. The treaties permitted the stationing of Soviet troops on the Baltic countries' territories, and tanks rolled across their borders with no resistance: this capitulation in the face of the Soviet threat remains an object of historical debate, as many have wondered if resistance (as in the case of Finland) could have prevented the half-century-long occupation.

The three wartime occupations left a heavy shadow on the Baltic states and were marked by the violent repression of various ethnic groups. Titular Balts were repressed and deported to Siberia during the years of Soviet dominance that bookmarked World War II. The German occupation, which began in the summer of 1941, saw the Holocaust reach the Baltic countries, where both Jews and Roma were victims of horrific atrocities. In addition to deportations and the Holocaust, the later years of the war saw hundreds of thousands of Balts, fearing further Soviet repressions, follow the retreating German army westward.

At the end of the war, the Baltic lands were severely depopulated, with a particular shortage of professionals, as it was the Baltic elite who most feared Soviet repressions and had the means and wherewithal to craft an exit route to the West. For example, 70 percent of the teaching staff of the two leading universities in Latvia, the University of Latvia and the Latvian Agricultural University, emigrated westward.[8] Following the war, this led to a swift Russification of the Baltic region, particularly the more heavily industrialized parts of Estonia and Latvia, as Soviet citizens rushed to live in the Baltic republics, which were known to have better living and working conditions than other regions of the Soviet Union.

Demographic change was only one part of the rapid Sovietization of the region. Erwin Oberlander has identified the key seven elements of "Sovietization" in the Baltic

Photo 14.1. Fearing the reoccupation of their countries by the Soviet army, thousands of Balts fled westward near the end of World War II. Many spent years in Displaced Persons camps after the war. The photo shows refugee children from the Baltics in the Munich-Lohengrin camp primary school in 1947. (Lithuanian Cultural Institute in Germany [LKI])

states during both Soviet occupations. All seven phases were carried out between 1940 and 1941 to some extent, but absolutely, and swiftly, after 1944: (1) military occupation, (2) control of the political system through rigged elections, (3) the Communist Party became the only legal political organization, (4) an in-migration of Soviet cadres (often of ethnic Latvian origin in the case of Latvia), (5) nationalization of the economy, (6) expropriation and collectivization of agriculture, and (7) control of education and culture.[9] Russian became the language of government and commerce, although media, culture, and, to some extent, education continued to operate in the native languages, ensuring that the titular Baltic nations would not lose their unique cultural identities during the long occupation.

The severity of Soviet control slackened in the decades after the death of Stalin in 1956. At the same time, ever-weaker economic growth, as the Soviet Union and its satellite states in Central and East Europe visibly fell behind the living standards of the West, saw the legitimacy of the regime, always low among titular Balts, decline further. Anti-Soviet activities—"forest brother" partisans at the end of World War II, intellectual dissidents, and from the 1970s cultural and environmental protection groups that indirectly critiqued the industrial policies of the regime—were a feature of the Baltic republics throughout the Soviet era. As a result, the Baltic countries were well positioned to activate well-organized opposition movements when Soviet leader Mikhail Gorbachev's reforms made this possible. The dire state of the Soviet economy by the mid-1980s and the accompanying social crisis that most ordinary people experienced through housing shortages, poor health care, and rampant alcoholism also meant that many Russian-speakers were ready to join, or at a minimum not oppose, the new Baltic movements calling for renewed independence.

It took just half a decade to unravel Soviet power in the Baltic countries. The first small, unofficial opposition organizations appeared in the mid-1980s and were largely driven by a sense of historical injustice. "Calendar demonstrations" mobilized Balts to ever-larger public protests on historically significant days, such as August 23 (marking the signing of the Molotov-Ribbentrop Pact). Smaller groups merged into large, moderate "popular front" umbrella organizations, which became the public faces of the independence movements. Estonia and Latvia also had more radical nationalist groups, known as Citizens Congresses, which advocated "deoccupying" the region by sending Russian migrants and their families back to Russia. Support for the Soviet regime was provided by Interfront (International Working People's Front), which were led by reactionary wings of the Baltic communist parties and received most of their support from Russian-speakers in the region.

By the late 1980s, the Baltic region was a vibrant hub of political activism. The 1989 elections to the All-Union Congress of People's Deputies, the first democratic Soviet elections, followed by elections to the Baltic SSR Supreme Councils in 1990, revealed the depth of public support for independence. These legislatures, dominated by pro-independence deputies, passed important laws renewing crucial independent institutions and reforms—such as independent central banks and kick-starting privatization—that

Photo 14.2. As many Balts pushed for independence from the USSR, there were fears that Soviet authorities would try to shut down the movement. In late January 1991, thousands of people erected and guarded barricades to protect objects of national and strategic importance. This photo shows some of the barricades set up to protect the parliament building in Riga. (Apdency, Wikimedia Commons)

laid the path to independence. In 1990, the Supreme Councils voted to de jure renew the independence of the Baltic states, although they remained de facto republics of the Soviet Union.

The confrontation between the pro-independence Baltic governments and legislatures and the repressive Soviet institutions stepped up, and there were occasional outbreaks of armed violence across the region. Events came to a boil in August 1991 when the failed August coup against Soviet general secretary Mikhail Gorbachev by communist hard-liners in Moscow opened a window of opportunity for the pro-independence governments to declare independence, which was swiftly recognized by Iceland and, most importantly, just a few days later by Boris Yeltsin's Russian Republic, with the rest of the international community rapidly following. The Baltic countries joined the United Nations in September 1991. After more than fifty years of occupation, the Baltic states had regained their sovereign independence, but they now faced the daunting challenge of democratization and economic reconstruction.

Early Postcommunism

The Baltic countries in 1991 were in a slightly better situation than that in which they found themselves in 1918. First, although the economies were similarly devastated, this time after years of failed Soviet planning, there were at least some communist-era investments, such as the rail and port transit infrastructure, that added value to the economy. Second, democracy and state building would prove more straightforward thanks to the alphabet soup of international organizations, operating in a generally more favorable international environment, ready to guide the Baltic countries toward joining the club of Western-oriented capitalist democracies. However, there were also two crucial differences that would make the post-1991 transformation substantially more complicated. First, there were significant security concerns raised by the more than one hundred thousand serving Soviet (then Russian) military personnel still based in the region. Second, there were large Russian-speaking minorities in Estonia and Latvia, having arrived during the Soviet occupation, who were seeking both citizenship and cultural rights, especially in terms of language policy.

The leaders of the Baltic countries shared a relatively clear common conception of aspiring to create states similar to neighboring Nordic social welfare states. There was some optimism that this could be achieved quite quickly. After all, the Baltic countries had multitiered education systems and skilled human capital, particularly a large number of engineers and other STEM (science, technology, engineering, and mathematics) professionals. These professionals worked in what at first glance appeared to be advanced industrial economies that, for example, designed, engineered, and constructed vehicles (vans and minibuses produced at the Riga Autobus Factory, RAF), refrigerators and furniture (Lithuania), and exported energy (Estonian oil shale). The Baltic countries also had extensive road and rail links and substantial ice-free ports on the Baltic Sea. However, there was public consternation that the economic transformation proved to be far more protracted, complicated, and painful than expected.

The fundamentals of the Baltic economies were less promising than originally hoped. The education systems had suffered from years of underinvestment, politicization, and insularity. The higher-education sector was particularly uncompetitive in terms of research output and teaching quality. The curricula of law and economics programs had to be completely overhauled (although there was little change in the lecturing staff), while new social science, business, and other degree programs, not taught in the Soviet era, needed to be developed from scratch. Road networks were extensive, but the quality of the road coverings was poor and there were few stretches of broad motorway. There were no national airlines, and the airports, which had served a merely regional function in the Soviet era, were in states of disrepair, with first-time visitors to the region experiencing bumpy landings, dilapidated terminals, and shady taxi drivers hustling for business. The structure of the Baltic economies was heavily distorted through the dominance of heavy industries that were tied into production chains in other Soviet republics. There was little production of consumer goods (which were in any case uncompetitive with their Western-produced counterparts) and almost no service industry.

As a result, the early years of the economic transformation were turbulent. Economic output in all three countries fell by over 50 percent, with inflation peaking in 1992 at an annual rate of around 1,000 percent. Deep recessions marked the early 1990s before the economies returned to growth as economic reforms began to kick in, privatization started, and the first major wave of foreign investment began. Baltic governments undertook fundamental economic reforms, albeit at different speeds. Estonia's youthful, Thatcherite right-wing governments adopted speedy "shock therapy" reforms, while Lithuania, with a larger left-leaning social democratic party, took a more gradualist reform path. Latvia's pace was typically between the two. For example, Estonia set up a privatization agency in 1992, Latvia in 1994, and Lithuania in 1995. In terms of strategy, Estonia adopted the liberal approach of favoring the sale of large enterprises to outsiders, Lithuania was more protectionist and tended to favor domestic investors over international ones, while Latvia adopted both approaches. Currency reform is another example of differing reform approaches. All three states wanted to rapidly move away from using the Soviet ruble, with Estonia's *kroon* being pegged to the German DM (at a rate of 8:1), Lithuania's *lit* to the US dollar at a 4:1 rate, and the Latvian *lat* to a basket of currencies.

Economic instability inevitably impacted society. Unemployment was a particularly traumatic experience to societies that had experienced full employment since the 1940s, and falling government revenues led to smaller benefits and pensions, as well as under-funding of education and health care. Some voted with their feet, and for the first time since World War II, the Baltic region experienced emigration rather than immigration. It is perhaps a reflection of the illegitimacy and deep unpopularity of the Soviet regime in the Baltic countries that this economic and social strife did not lead Baltic politicians to veer away from their Western trajectory.

Political Institutions

Major political reforms were swiftly undertaken in the first few years of the transforma-tion. A sixty-member constituent assembly in Estonia adapted, merged, and modernized the 1920 and 1938 constitutions, which was then approved by 91.2 percent of voters in a June 1992 referendum. Lithuania's new constitution was written by the transitional

Supreme Council and supported by 75.3 percent of voters in a referendum on October 25, 1992. In contrast, Latvia's politicians delayed by insisting that only a legitimately elected Latvian Saeima (parliament) could make this constitutional decision, with the parliamentary vote on renewing the 1922 constitution only taken in the summer of 1993 after legislative elections. The decision to renew the rather outdated 1922 constitution (which had failed to prevent the authoritarian takeover in 1934) was largely driven by Latvian politicians' concerns over a perilous demographic position: the 1989 Soviet census found that ethnic Latvians made up just 52 percent of the population of the Soviet Republic of Latvia. By bringing the interwar constitution back into force, parliament created a legal basis for limiting Latvian citizenship to pre-1940 citizens and their descendants, thus ensuring an ethnic Latvian majority, and support for Western-facing policies, in the critical early post-Soviet parliamentary elections.

Defining the nation was no easy task for Estonia and Latvia. The situation was more straightforward in Lithuania, where Russian-speakers made up just 12 percent and titular Lithuanians 80 percent of the population, according to the 1989 Soviet census. The Lithuanian government swiftly passed a so-called zero-option citizenship law that granted Lithuanian citizenship to all legal permanent residents, excluding military and other former Soviet security forces temporarily based in the country. In contrast, the proportion of Russian-speakers to Estonians was 35 percent to 61 percent, and in Latvia, the proportion of Russian-speakers to titular Latvians was 42 percent to 52 percent.[10]

The more complicated demographic situation in the other two Baltic countries led to a protracted debate, where language policy and citizenship were central to the discussion. Estonian and Latvian policy makers were concerned that a zero-option citizenship law could potentially tilt their countries away from a Western-oriented transition (as they feared Russian-speakers might favor closer political, economic, and cultural links with Russia and other former Soviet countries). Legal scholars fretted that giving citizenship to Soviet-era migrants would legitimate the Soviet occupation. On the other hand, both Russia and the major Western powers, including international organizations such as the Organization for Security and Co-operation in Europe (OSCE) and the Council of Europe, pushed for inclusive citizenship laws and liberal language legislation. However, both Estonia and Latvia chose to naturalize Soviet-era migrants rather than provide automatic citizenship. In 1993, Estonia passed a law offering a route to citizenship based on competence in the Estonian language and knowledge of the country's history and culture. Latvia adopted a far more restrictive naturalization law a year later that created "windows" that only allowed a gradual naturalization, with individuals classified according to whether they had been born in Latvia and how long they had lived there, as well as tests on language and culture. With few people taking this naturalization route, and with Latvian governments coming under international pressure, subsequent amendments saw the "windows" removed and the rate of naturalization picked up. By 2019 there were still 199,000 noncitizen permanent residents in Estonia and 276,000 in Latvia, the overwhelming majority of whom are migrants (and their descendants) from the Soviet era.[11] There are three reasons why both countries still have large Russian-speaking noncitizen populations. First, many Russian-speakers opted for Russian, rather than Estonian or Latvian, citizenship. Second, resident noncitizens have essentially the same social and economic rights as citizens (and can even vote in local elections in Estonia). Third, non-citizenship does not have a great impact on their mobility and rights within the EU. As a result, significant noncitizen populations in Estonia and Latvia remain, although they shrink every year.

The place of the Russian language in the Baltic countries was also being discussed at this time. Russian had become the language of government and commerce through the half century of Soviet domination. Balts learned Russian at school, and fluency was a pre-requisite for career progression. At the same time, Russian-speaking migrants in the Baltic countries could get along without knowledge of the titular languages. This changed after August 1991. The Baltic countries introduced professional minimum language fluency for multiple categories of public and private sector employees and controlled language use in the public sphere. This continues to be a sore point between the titular and Russian-speaking communities, particularly in Latvia, where Russian-speaking parties gathered enough signatures to force a polarizing yet unsuccessful referendum on recognizing Russian as a second official language in 2012. In more recent years, Russian-speakers in Latvia have battled against the introduction of more core teaching in the Latvian language in state-funded Russian-language schools. Nationalist politicians in Latvia and Estonia continue to back policies that enshrine their language's place in those countries. They do so from a position of greater strength in numbers. In 2019, ethnic Estonians made up 68 percent of the population of Estonia and Latvians 62 percent of Latvia (and Lithuanians 86 percent of Lithuania).

The Baltic judicial systems also underwent major reform in the 1990s as part of the transition to democracy and capitalism, and again in the early 2000s in the run-up to accession to the EU. In the communist system, courts and judges largely legitimized decisions taken at a higher political level. Post-1991, courts, judges, prosecutors, and lawyers needed to adapt to the restructuring of the legal system. The Baltic countries followed the postwar European trend of creating constitutional courts that check the power of the executive and legislative branches. Estonia's Constitutional Court is combined with a Supreme Court, while Latvia and Lithuania established independent constitutional courts. In addition, Estonia's legal chancellor (a post that does not exist in Latvia or Lithuania) has constitutional review functions and refers cases to the Constitutional Review Chamber of the Supreme Court.

The electoral systems in all three states are broadly similar, with regular parliamentary, local government, and European Parliament elections. In addition, Lithuania has a presidential election every five years. All three systems have elements of preferential voting (which give voters the opportunity to support or reject individual candidates within political party lists), parliamentary elections in Estonia and Latvia have a 5 percent threshold (in 2019 Lithuania lowered this to 3 percent for parties and 5 percent for party alliances), and the term of all three legislatures is four years. Only political parties and party alliances can stand for election in Latvia and Lithuania, but Estonia also allows independent candidates. Citizens may vote from age eighteen, except in local government elections, where Estonia has followed the recent international trend of lowering the voting age to sixteen. Estonia and Latvia have proportional representation models of seat distribution, while Lithuania has a mixed ballot for parliamentary elections, with seventy proportional representation seats in the legislature and seventy-one single-member districts.

Estonia remains distinct as the only country in the world that allows internet voting in all elections. It was tested in the October 2005 municipal election and used by just 1.9 percent of voters, but by the 2019 parliamentary election, 43.8 percent of the electorate cast their votes online. However, internet voting has not stopped Estonia from joining Latvia and Lithuania in experiencing a drop in electoral turnout since the first post-Soviet elections in the early 1990s, with a pronounced lower turnout in local government and particularly European Parliament elections (although turnout can be higher when the European Parliament elections are held on the same day as other elections, such as presidential elections in Lithuania in 2004 and 2014).

Important political decisions have been approved by the public, beginning with consultative referenda on the declarations of independence in 1991, before the fall of the Soviet Union; continuing with referenda on the new Estonian and Lithuanian constitutions; and the 2003 referenda on accession to the European Union. The Estonian constitution has no clause foreseeing citizen initiatives, but they are a feature of the Latvian and Lithuanian political systems. Latvia is home to a particularly innovative grassroots citizens' initiative platform, Mana Balss (My Voice), which was launched in 2011 as a website where citizens could submit legal initiatives and attempt to collect the ten thousand signatures needed to hand in the legal initiative to parliament. In the first nine years of operation, thirty-eight initiatives were submitted to parliament, and twenty-six passed into law.[12]

The unicameral Baltic legislatures are located in the capital cities (Tallinn, Riga, and Vilnius), which also function as the national centers of commerce. Parliamentary work is structured by political groups (also known as fractions in the Latvian Saeima and factions in the Estonian Riigikogu) that are formed by political parties that have passed the electoral threshold. Membership in a political group gives parliamentary deputies access to additional administrative and financial resources as well as senior office, such as chairing parliamentary committees.

The major difference between the Baltic parliaments is in the strength of their autonomous analytical capacity to effectively perform oversight and lawmaking functions and stand up to the executive. The Latvian parliament is much weaker than its neighbors. A recent evaluation of the analytical capacity (ex ante and ex post evaluations as well as briefing and research materials for parliamentarians) of the Latvian parliament found that "the *Saeima* has a grossly inferior analytical capacity compared with the executive. . . . It causes concern regarding the *Saeima*'s ability to screen executive policy initiatives critically and fully carry out parliamentary oversight regarding the government."[13] The Latvian Saeima's Analytical Service only began operating in 2017 and in 2020 employed just four people, with limited funds to pay for external expertise. In contrast, the Estonian Riigikogu has two analytical research units (a Legal and Analytical Department and a "Foresight Centre" that functions as a think tank analyzing long-term social and economic trends) with a combined full-time staff of eighteen, as well as extensive funds to engage external experts. The Research Unit in the Lithuanian parliament employs eleven researchers. Thus, while the constitutions grant Baltic legislatures considerable powers of lawmaking and oversight, real access to resources means that political power is tilted toward the executive, especially in the case of Latvia. For example, an analysis on the origins of new legislative acts found that roughly half to two-thirds of legislative acts in Baltic countries in the 1990s were initiated by the executives, rising to over 80 percent of all Estonian and Latvian legislation in the mid-2000s. Lithuania's executive is weaker—with just half of legislative acts originating from the cabinet at that time—largely because of the influence of the directly elected president as well as the greater independent streak of the parliamentary deputies representing the single-member districts.[14]

Executive power is held by prime ministers and their cabinets. Prime ministers are nominated by the state presidents, following consultations with all elected parties, and are then subject to a parliamentary vote. However, while the appointment procedures are similar, Estonian and Lithuanian governments tend to stay in office longer than their Latvian counterparts. Between 1993 and 2020, the Latvian parliament has elected twenty different governments compared to fifteen in Estonia and twelve in Lithuania. Estonia has experienced much greater political stability in recent years, with just three different prime ministers between 2005 and 2020, while Latvia has had six and Lithuania five.

State presidents are the most important checks on the power of the Baltic countries' executives, not least because they tend to be far more popular than the politicians in parliament or the executive. In 2011, then-president of Latvia Valdis Zatlers called a referendum on the recall of parliament, claiming that it was illicitly controlled by a small group of Latvian oligarchs. Fully 94 percent of voters in the referendum supported the recall of parliament. The presidents hold similar powers, although they are elected by different procedures. Lithuania has a popularly elected president, Latvia's president is elected by parliament, and Estonia's president is elected by either parliament or, if parliament fails

Photo 14.3.   Dalia Grybauskaitė was president of Lithuania from 2009 to 2019. Both Latvia and Estonia have had or currently have women presidents. Latvia's Vaira Vīķe-Freiberga was the first woman president in the Central and East European region. (Birute Vijeikiene, Shutterstock)

to rally around a candidate, an Electoral College that brings together parliamentarians and local government leaders.

Baltic presidents hold similar powers. The Latvian and Lithuanian presidents can submit laws for parliamentary scrutiny, and all three have the power of suspensive veto (to reject and return laws to parliament), a power most frequently used by Lithuania's popularly elected president, where the president rejected 175 laws between 1992 and 2010, compared to 59 times in Estonia and just 35 times in Latvia.[15] Presidents also choose the candidate for prime minister who is then voted on by parliament.

The presidents are broadly understood to be key symbols of the state. As a result, the early presidential votes appeared to be battles for the soul, or at least the political direction, of the newly independent states. These elections saw dour, communist-era officials vie with Western émigrés or ex-dissidents for the presidential office. In Estonia, the first election (the first round of which was a public vote) was between the eventual winner, Lennart Meri, an intellectual writer and filmmaker, and Arnold Rüütel, a senior communist-era official who eventually joined the independence movement (and was finally elected president in 2001). In Latvia, the first parliamentary presidential vote was between Gunārs Meierovics, the son of Latvia's most famous interwar foreign minister (who died young in a car accident in 1925), who had been a senior figure in the Latvian émigré community, and the winner, Guntis Ulmanis, an ex–public utilities manager who had only resigned from the Latvian Communist Party in 1989 and was elected to the post largely on the strength of his surname (his uncle, to whom he bore an uncanny resemblance, was Latvia's interwar dictator, Kārlis Ulmanis). In Lithuania Algirdas Brazauskas, a former first secretary of the Lithuanian Communist Party, beat Stasys Lozoraitis, the scion of a Lithuanian émigré diplomat's family. Émigré candidates experienced more success in a later wave of presidential elections around the time of the accessions to the EU and NATO, when fluent English-speaking leaders, who had spent most of their lives in North America, assumed the positions (Toomas Hendrik Ilves, an Ivy League–educated diplomat; Vaira Vīķe-Freiberga, a retired Canadian-Latvian professor of psychology; and Valdas Adamkus, a senior US Environmental Protection Agency official). Lithuania remains the only European nation to have impeached a president, Rolandas Paksas in 2004, following an investigation by the Constitutional Court that indicted him for illegally granting Lithuanian citizenship to a campaign sponsor, leaking confidential wiretapping information, and applying pressure on business owners to sell their businesses to friends of the president.

Local governments have played an important role in government since the fall of the Soviet Union. The communist system centralized the political system in order to maximize control over society and the economy. Decentralization was a political priority after independence as all three states sought to give local authorities more sovereign decision-making mechanisms. However, the significant post-1991 demographic decline and urbanization trends have seen Baltic governments move to partially reverse the decentralization of the early 1990s through merging of local governments in order to make them more sustainable and better capable of delivering key services such as K–12 education. Estonia has settled on a two-tier local government system with fifteen counties (Maakonad) overseen by government-appointed governors who hold five-year terms of office. A 2017 local government administrative reform cut the number of local governments from 213 to 79. A similar reform in Latvia in 2020 merged 119 local governments (*pašvaldības*) into 42 (and this followed a 2009 reform that had cut the number of local governments from 548 to 119). Similar to Estonia, Lithuania also has a two-tier system, with ten counties (*apskritys*) serving as territorial and statistical units as the sixty municipalities deliver key services.

Political Competition

All three Baltic countries have multiparty political systems that have taken several decades to reach some level of stability and consolidation, although the Latvian and Lithuanian party systems remain quite volatile. After renewing independence in 1991, there were three major political blocs in each of the Baltic countries, each of which spawned a number of successor parties. On the far right, the nationalist Congress movements in Estonia and Latvia spun off a number of parties that fought for the political supremacy of the titular nations. The more moderate nationalists of the popular fronts produced a large number of mostly small, liberal, center-right conservative or center-left social democratic parties. The communist successor Interfront parties created pro-Russian-speaking minority parties that have proven to be particularly strong in rallying Russian-speakers in Latvia.

The first post-Soviet democratic "founding elections" occurred in 1992 in Estonia and Lithuania, and a year later in Latvia. They set the basic course of the transformations that followed. The electorate at that time was quite fractured and perhaps even bemused by the multitudes of new political parties vying for their vote. In Estonia, only 13 percent of the population identified with one of the more than twenty parties contesting the September 1992 election.[16] Nevertheless, from this confusion, pro-reform parties came to power in both Estonia and Latvia and set a path of economic reform and integration with the West. The next few decades would see liberal, center-right, and nationalist/radical right parties dominate government, although left-leaning parties have become more influential in Estonia over the last decade. In contrast, the founding elections in Lithuania were won by moderate former communists of the Lithuanian Democratic Labor Party (Lietuvos Demokratinė Darbo Partija, LDDP) who promised a more modest and gradual, although still Western-oriented, reform agenda.

Throughout the 1990s, the political pendulum in Lithuania swung between the LDDP on the left and the Sajudis bloc of center-right parties on the right. This made Lithuania's party system appear settled in a left-right cleavage, mirroring the postwar party systems of Western Europe, in contrast to the more volatile systems in Estonia and Latvia. Estonia's party system settled into a pattern of stable competition in the twenty-first century, while Latvia's system has remained volatile throughout the three decades since 1991. This volatility can be largely explained by the higher costs of and barriers to new party entry in Estonia and Lithuania. Estonia long had legislation requiring one thousand people to register a party (subsequently cut to five hundred), as well as generous state funding for existing parties based on their share of the vote. Lithuania increased its minimum required membership to one thousand in 2004 and then doubled it to two thousand in 2015, in addition to having a system of public financing for parties since 1999. Latvia still requires just two hundred people to register a party (although five hundred members are needed to participate in national elections), and in late 2019 it was the last Baltic country to finally adopt a generous party financing law that raised funding for parties sevenfold and further cut the amount of money that private individuals could donate to parties, effectively squeezing private money from the party system.

These legislative arrangements have also resulted in Estonia and Lithuania having far larger memberships of their political parties than Latvia. In 2016, 6.4 percent of Estonia's electorate were registered as party members, 4.6 percent of Lithuania's, but just 1.3 percent of Latvia's (well below the European average of 4.6 percent).[17] A comparison of the biggest parties in the region in 2016 revealed that there were four parties in Lithuania with over ten thousand members, two in Estonia, but none in Latvia. The biggest parties are those with the clearest ideological orientation. Social democratic parties were the largest, with the Centre Party in Estonia (Eesti Keskerakond, EK) having a registered membership of almost 15,000, Harmony Social Democracy in Latvia (Saskaņa Social Demokratija) claiming 4,470, and Lithuania's Labour Party (Darbo Partija) having over 20,000 members.

The party systems in Estonia and Latvia were less settled in the 1990s, perhaps because numerous small parties emerged from the moderate popular fronts and the nationalist Congress movements. Social democratic ideas were only weakly represented, and the small centrist and radical titular nationalist parties tended to be less ideologically rooted and weaker programmatically than the left and the center-right in Lithuania, and as a result more volatile. Parties representing ethnic minority interests have been marginalized from political power in Latvia, although they have been occasional government coalition partners in Estonia.

The cordon sanitaire isolating ethnic minorities from government reflects the strength of far-right parties in Latvia throughout the modern independence era. The far-right parties of the 1990s had grown from the Latvian Citizens Congress movements and initially advanced a three Ds policy of deoccupation, decolonization, and debolshevization, although this was moderated over the course of the decade. Over the last few decades, the far-right Latvian parties have merged into an electoral alliance under the National Alliance (Nacionālā Apvienība, NA) banner, which has been in every government coalition since 2011.

Far-right nationalism was a feature of the Estonian party system in the early 1990s, then faded from view in the early 2000s before returning to national politics in the 2010s. The Estonian National Independence Party (Eesti Rahvuslik Sõltumatuse Partei, ERSP), which supported exclusionary citizenship policies, and the more virulently nationalist Estonian Citizen party (Eesti Kodanik), led by bombastic retired US colonel Jüri Toomepuu, won parliamentary seats in the 1992 election but then faded from view and remained small, argumentative, and fragmented until 2012 when the Estonian National Movement (Eesti Rahvuslik Liikumine, ERL) and the Estonian Peoples' Union (Eestimaa Rahvaliit, ER) merged to create the Conservative People's Party of Estonia (Eesti Konservatiivne Rahvaerakond, EKRE). Building on the populist radical right party model that had helped grow similar parties in northern and western Europe, EKRE adopted a populist rhetoric that hinted at the corruption of the mainstream governing political parties and argued that liberal European immigration and social policies were a threat to the future of the Estonian nation. The party was elected to parliament in 2015 and then in 2019 entered government. EKRE has attracted international controversy, with its new ministers showing a white power symbol—forming a circle with the thumb and index finger while holding the other three fingers outstretched—when taking their oaths of office.[18] Just a few months later, an EKRE parliamentary deputy, Ruuben Kaalep, persuaded France's influential National Rally party leader, Marine Le Pen, who was visiting Estonia as a part of campaigning for the European Parliament elections, to take a joint selfie with the same pose, attracting more international attention to EKRE and harsh criticism from Estonia's moderate president, Kersti Kaljulaid.[19]

In contrast, far-right parties have had little success in Lithuania, largely because of the more homogenous nature of Lithuanian society. However, similarly to Latvia and, to a lesser extent, Estonia, populism—understood here as a "thin" ideology that focuses on the political conflict between *us* (the people) and *them* (powerful political and economic elites who are portrayed as corrupt and out of touch)—has long been a feature of the Baltic political landscape. Populism has been used as a tool for new political party entry to the party system and has fed on the high levels of distrust that Lithuanians and especially Latvians hold toward the political system. Populist narratives focus on the corruption of domestic and international elites, with international banker and philanthropist George Soros being a particular target of populist ire in the region.

Two particularly interesting populist parties emerged in the 2010s in Lithuania and Latvia. In October 2012, a curious new single-issue populist party (the Path of Courage), based on a controversial alleged pedophilia case, won almost 8 percent of the proportional vote in Lithuania's parliamentary election, feeding on widespread antielite feeling in Lithuania as well as support for conspiracy theories that tend to be critical of the elite. In Latvia, the October 2018 parliamentary election saw KPV (an acronym for Who Owns the State?) finish second with a 14 percent share of the vote (and sixteen of parliament's one hundred seats). The party was founded by Artuss Kaimiņš, an actor who became famous through his shock-jock talk show where he confronted and berated politicians. He was elected to the Latvian parliament from the Regional Alliance (Reģionu Apvienība, RA) party list in 2014, although he swiftly left the party and founded KPV as his own personal party vehicle. Although he had few, if any, legislative accomplishments in the parliament, he kept himself in the limelight with a pocket-sized camera with which he filmed candid encounters with other politicians. KPV continued this theme with an antagonistic antiestablishment campaign, accusing the mainstream parties of corruption and incompetence. This narrative in both Latvia and Lithuania feeds into a deep-rooted distrust of political parties and politicians that Eurobarometer public opinion polls indicate is well above the EU average (while Estonian distrust is lower than the EU average).[20]

Civil Society

Some of this distrust is also directed toward Baltic civil society. The broadly supported and lively civil societies of the late communist era dissipated in the 1990s as the steep economic downturn and accompanying social crisis saw people withdraw from civic life to focus on their own immediate needs. The last few decades have seen falling political participation in elections, with only antigovernment or nationalist protests being able to muster people onto the streets.

Part of the general distrust has been caused by regular attacks on the character and aims of the American billionaire George Soros and his Open Society Foundations, which was the most generous and visible supporter of civil society and NGOs in the Baltics up to accession to the EU in 2004. Critics in the media, particularly in Latvia and Lithuania, have claimed that Soros has bought control over parts of the government and civil society through different grants and scholarships given to talented young Balts in the 1990s, a number of whom have assumed prominent positions in government and business. In Lithuania in 2005, a group of prominent politicians argued that NGOs linked to Soros should be thoroughly investigated by prosecutors and the security services.[21] These attacks have weakened the legitimacy and fund-raising capacity of these individuals and organizations, particularly those battling corruption, such as Delna, the Latvian branch of Transparency International, as well as civil society as a whole.

Partly as a result of these attacks, the most influential Baltic NGOs represent economic interests rather than being driven by values or the public good. Trade unions have recovered from a legitimacy crisis in the 1990s, when they were initially discredited as being too closely related to the communist regimes, to grow ever more influential. Trade unions representing public workers—especially teachers and health staff—are far more significant than trade unions representing workers in private businesses. Employers and business associations, such as chambers of commerce, have grown to assume great influence in the Baltic states, using both the formal representation of tripartite councils (representing employers, trade unions, and governments) and private lobbying to influence politics. Thanks to the deep pockets of the businesses they represent, they have access to far greater resources than trade unions or other public NGOs.

Although civil society is underfunded and small, it partially makes up for this through innovation. Digital platforms have been created to ease donations to NGOs (in Latvia, the *Mobilly* application allows individuals to donate money to a favorite NGO while also paying for city parking). All three states have also adopted the Nordic practice of organizing "democracy" festivals (Arvamusfestival in Estonia, Sarunu festivāls LAMPA in Latvia, and Diskusijų festivalis "Būtent!" in Lithuania), which bring together people of different ages and political convictions to publicly debate various contemporary issues over a few days. Younger generations appear to be more ready to engage civil society than the 1990s generation.

Public demonstrations in the Baltic region are, for the most part, infrequent, sparsely attended, and peaceful. There have only been a handful of violent demonstrations since 1991. The decision to relocate the Soviet-era "Bronze Soldier," a monument to Soviet soldiers, triggered two days of rioting by Russian-speakers in Tallinn in 2007. Two years later there was disorder on the streets of Riga when an antigovernment rally in the Old Town of Riga ended with a few hundred people throwing bricks and bottles at the parliament. This was followed by a minor antigovernment riot in Vilnius a week later. There are smaller flashpoints when anti-LGBTQ protesters, typically connected to evangelical churches, attempt to stop gay pride marches in the Baltic capitals or when pro-Russia "antifascists" confront Latvian nationalists by the Freedom Monument every March 16, when some Latvian veterans and their supporters mark the Remembrance Day of the Waffen SS Latvian legionnaires.

The media in all three states is diverse and vibrant, but increasingly impoverished. In the 1990s and 2000s, the Latvian and Lithuanian media became extremely politicized as newspapers were purchased by powerful "oligarchs" (although the ownership was often hidden through offshore companies). A leaked 2007 report from the US embassy in Lithuania recounted how two major Lithuanian newspapers—*Respublika* and *Lietuvos Rytas*—extorted politicians and business leaders into paying bribes for positive stories. However, these expensive media acquisitions lost their luster, and a lot of money for their owners, as Balts have increasingly started getting their news from the popular free internet news portals that over the last decade have killed off much of the printed newspaper industry. Television stations have also shed viewers, and the number of independent media television channels is in decline. The economic crash of 2008–2010, followed by the steep reduction of advertising revenue after the COVID-19 pandemic hit the Baltic countries in 2020, has seen Baltic governments increasingly step up to provide public funds to maintain both public and private media. This trend is likely to continue into the future, with little prospect of an upturn in paying readers for printed or electronic media.

Economic Policies and Conditions

The long-term economic decline of the Soviet economy from the 1970s onward meant that there was broad support, among both the titular nationalities and the substantial Russian-speaking minorities, for fundamental restructuring of the Baltic economies. The first economic reforms, such as setting up independent central banks, were undertaken in the later years of the Soviet regime. However, substantial change only took place after August 1991. There was little discussion about the direction of economic reform—a Western-oriented market economy—but more debate about the pace of reform. The lack of discussion on the direction of reform reflects a paucity of alternative economic voices (communist economists were largely discredited in the debate on the economic future of the region), as the international community of experts, consultants, and advisers that descended on the region largely supported the reform approach known as the "Washington Consensus," which urged an initial focus on macroeconomic stability, currency reform, trade and price liberalization, privatization, and strict budgetary discipline. Assistance programs such as the Pew Economic Freedom Fellows Program (PEFFP) at Georgetown University, which trained twenty mid-level policy makers with a theoretical background in market-oriented economics every year in the 1990s, produced a generation of pro–Washington Consensus political leaders. The Latvian government in 1994 contained three graduates of the PEFFP—the deputy prime minister in charge of economics (Ojārs Kehris), the minister of finance (Uldis Osis), and a deputy in the Finance Ministry in charge of revenues (Jānis Platais)—who were collectively known as the "Georgetown Gang."[22]

Although the steps taken in all three states were quite similar, Estonia quickly established itself as the reform leader. In the economic parlance of the time, Estonia adopted a "shock therapy" approach to reform. Latvia, and especially Lithuania, took more time in adopting essentially the same reforms. Privatization is an instructive case. Soviet-era enterprises were uncompetitive, and after independence they required a significant infusion of capital and know-how that could only be achieved through privatization. All three countries established specialized privatization agencies that used different approaches to privatize medium- and large-sized enterprises. Estonia favored sales to outsiders (the secondary approach in Latvia and very much rarer in Lithuania), while Latvia and Lithuania initially used vouchers followed by management-employee buyouts. The privatization programs brought in significant revenues to the governments but also created controversy and led to charges of political corruption in Latvia and Lithuania where both the three-time Latvian prime minister Andris Šķēle and Lithuanian prime minister Bronislovas Lubys were embroiled in allegations of insider privatization.

Estonia has managed to significantly eradicate corruption from political life while corruption and the prosecution of public officeholders remain relevant in both Latvian and Lithuanian politics. The two new parties that finished second and third in the October 2018 parliamentary election in Latvia (KPV and the New Conservative Party [JKP]) made corruption central to their respective election campaigns, while in Lithuania the Green/Farmers, who won the election and led the new government, made the fight against corruption a key part of their 2016 parliamentary electoral campaign. These elections, and the salience of corruption discourse, are typical rather than exceptions. In Latvia, the corruption narrative was long focused around three powerful "oligarchs"—former prime minister Andris Šķēle, former minister of economics and minister of transport Ainārs Šlesers, and thirty-year veteran mayor of the oil transit port of Ventspils Aivars Lembergs—who were wealthy, allegedly controlled media, and were claimed to exert influence over certain political parties. Their alleged undue influence led the then president of Latvia, Valdis Zatlers, to call a referendum in 2011 on the recall of parliament. The resulting September 2011 election saw support collapse for the political parties of two of the three oligarchs (Ainārs Šlesers and Andris Šķēle), who subsequently stepped away from public life. Aivars Lembergs remained active in both national politics and the municipality of Ventspils, where he has controlled the mayor's office since the 1980s, even though he was technically suspended from the post in 2012 and has been battling a court case (for corruption and influence peddling) since 2009. In December 2019, the US Department of the Treasury Office of Foreign Asset Control (OFAC) sanctioned Lembergs, based on the Magnitsky Act, arguing that he was an oligarch with a track record of buying and selling influence and power.[23] Lithuania has not had a comparable class of oligarchs but has experienced a steady flow of high-level political corruption cases. In 2018, for example, courts in Lithuania began reviewing two major cases of political corruption, one concerning the acceptance of bribes by senior politicians, including a former parliamentary party leader and a deputy speaker of parliament, and the other concerning a corrupt relationship between former (impeached) president Rolandas Paksas and the publisher of a major Lithuanian daily newspaper.

The macroeconomic environment in the Baltic countries stabilized in the mid-1990s, and modest growth began in the second half of the decade and then accelerated in the first decade of the twentieth century, as foreign investment and Nordic bank-financed cheap credit arrived in the region in anticipation of accession to the European Union. The post-accession years saw further economic booms, with the countries now frequently called the "Baltic Tigers," with average GDP growth rates between 2004 and 2007 hitting a remarkable 10.3 percent in Latvia, 8.5 percent in Estonia, and 8.2 percent in Lithuania.[24] However, these years of extremely high economic growth were fueled by a credit boom rather than productivity gains and proved unsustainable in the long term. The economies crashed in 2008 as the global financial crisis spread to Northern Europe. The following Baltic recessions were comparatively short but severe. In 2009, GDP fell by 14.3 percent in Estonia, 17.7 percent in Latvia, and 14.8 percent in Lithuania. Latvia was hit particularly hard because it had experienced the largest credit boom and had the initial expense of bailing out the domestically owned, and systemically important, Parex Bank. Latvia experienced a near one-quarter fall in output over a period of less than two years. Mass unemployment inevitably followed, with rates tripling in all three countries between 2007 and 2009.[25]

All three countries responded with controversial austerity policies. Estonia was in a slightly better situation than its neighbors because recent budget surpluses had created a "rainy-day fund" that the government could draw on to cover the costs of rising unemployment and provide some stimulus to the economy. Latvia and Lithuania, however, had run deficit budgets during the years of high growth. Latvia was granted a €7.5 billion loan facility through a combination of the IMF, the European Commission, and individual European states. The issue of devaluation proved particularly controversial. Some prominent economists, including the Nobel prize–winning scholar and *New York Times* columnist Paul Krugman, argued in favor of a swift currency devaluation.[26] However, all three center-right Baltic governments at that time preferred to prioritize the long-term goal of accession to the Eurozone, with its political and economic benefits, and feared that a currency devaluation would derail this process. In addition, most loans had been taken out in international currencies, especially the euro, and it was feared that devaluation would lead to more defaults.

Instead, the three Baltic countries undertook an internal devaluation of large procyclical cuts in government spending accompanied by tax increases. Estonia focused on lowering public sector wages, cutting pension contributions, and limiting sickness benefits. Between 2008 and 2011, Latvia's cumulative fiscal adjustment was estimated at 17 percent of GDP, which involved 6.8 percent on the revenue side but cuts of 10.2 percent on the expenditure side.[27] This was achieved by reducing the average size of government ministries by one-third as well as cutting public salaries and even pensions (although a later court ruling declared the cuts to pensions illegal). Lithuania cut public sector wages and benefits but also cut the rate of income tax from 24 percent to 15 percent. There was surprisingly little public opposition to austerity. Baltic political and economic elites were entirely unified in their support for internal devaluation, and while other approaches were discussed by international experts and commentators, they were not treated as serious options by Baltic decision makers.

These harsh measures did, however, have the consequence of launching a new and accelerated wave of migration away from the region. This was not a new experience, as the Baltic countries have experienced emigration and declining (and aging) populations since 1991. In the early 1990s, the first wave of emigrants were Russian-speakers returning to Russia or other post-Soviet countries. The second wave began in the twenty-first century as the Baltic countries prepared for accession to the EU and economic migrants moved to

Western Europe, particularly the UK and Ireland with their open labor market policies, seeking greater economic opportunities. Budget airlines provided cheap and extensive travel connections between the Baltic states and Western Europe, while the internet and mobile connections allowed migrants to maintain close contacts with their families and home countries, and growing émigré communities made it easier for new migrants to settle and find jobs.

The recession and accompanying austerity measures greatly accelerated migration.[28] Latvia lost 10 percent of its active workforce (120,000 people) between 2009 and 2011, similar to total migration between 2000 and 2008. In total this amounts to 9 percent of Latvia's 2000 population. Similarly, Lithuania saw 728,000 people leave the country between 1990 and 2011, with the majority exiting in the twenty-first century. Estonia has experienced the lowest rates of migration. Since 2004, just 30,000 people have left Estonia, largely heading for Finland due to geographic proximity, as well as language similarities.

All three Baltic states have developed "diaspora" policies aimed at maintaining links with the migrant communities and eventually enticing the migrants back to the Baltic region. Estonia's "Our People Foundation" operates under the Ministry of Culture and pays out up to €2,000 to aid return migration. Latvia's "diaspora program" focuses on maintaining cultural links with émigré communities, such as encouraging Latvian-language teaching for diaspora children. The 2011–2019 Global Lithuania plan explicitly encouraged the return of migrants, albeit without the cash inducement offered by Estonia. All three countries also utilize diaspora communities as lobbying assets in the United States, where the three communities often join forces through the Joint Baltic American National Committee (JBANC).

The structure of the Baltic economies has significantly changed over the last three decades. The agricultural sector has declined in size and economic importance. In Latvia, for example, the share of GDP accounted for by agriculture declined from around 25 percent in 1990 to only 4 percent in 2018. The number of farms also declined as larger, more commercial units, better able to take advantage of the EU's Common Agricultural Policy, pushed aside smaller farms. The manufacturing sector also declined across the region. In Latvia, the manufacturing sector accounted for 44 percent of GDP in 1991, but only 12 percent in 2019. Moreover, manufacturing firms are now smaller in size and typically occupy small niches in global value chains. The biggest growth has been in the services sector, which accounted for less than one-third of GDP in the Baltics in 1991 but grew to account for three-quarters of GDP by 2019.

The three states have developed different economic profiles. Estonia has advanced as a well-regarded center of information technology (IT) innovation. The Estonian e-governance system ensures that 99 percent of government services are accessed online. It also has several unique features, including the world's only electoral system with internet voting in all—national, local, and European—elections (in the 2019 national parliamentary elections, 44 percent of votes were cast online), an e-residency that allows the citizen of any country to establish a virtual residency and set up an enterprise in Estonia (there were sixty thousand such residents and ten thousand enterprises in 2019), and the world's first "data embassy" in Luxembourg, which aims to protect all government data in case of a physical or cyberattack on the country. Three Estonians, with funding from Danish and Swedish investors, created Skype, an achievement so central to Estonian identity that the first display visitors see on entering a new national museum in the university town of Tartu is a chair and desk used by the inventors of the technology. Estonia is so famous as a global center of IT and innovation that former US president Barack Obama once reflected, "I should have called the Estonians when we were setting up our health care website," thus avoiding the myriad technological challenges that plagued the early years of the HealthCare.gov website.[29]

Lithuania's recent development has focused on attracting business service centers that provide "back-office" professional skills, such as IT, accounting, and procurement, with a particular focus on developing financial technology (fintech) investments that saw fDI Intelligence (an analytics service belonging to the *Financial Times*) place Vilnius first in a 2019 Tech Start-Up FDI Attraction Index, ranking above established financial centers like London and Singapore.

In contrast, Latvia has a more diverse profile. The idea of Latvia as a "bridge" between East and West, much as Riga had been in the decades leading up to World War I, has been a contested idea with staunch supporters and opponents. There are two key elements to the "bridge" concept. First, that Riga could serve as a regional financial center. A financial services industry serving post-Soviet markets did indeed quickly emerge after the collapse of the Soviet Union, and by 1993 there were more than sixty commercial banks registered in Latvia, including Parex Bank (which spectacularly imploded during the 2008 global financial crisis), which advertised its services to Russian clients by claiming that Latvia was "closer than Switzerland." Despite regular banking crises in the 1990s and the entry of major Nordic banks into retail banking, a "nonresident" banking sector established itself in Riga and even flourished until 2018, when the US Treasury's Financial Crimes Enforcement Network (FinCEN) announced sanctions against ABLV, at that time Latvia's largest domestically owned "nonresident" bank, accusing it of money laundering and threatening to ban it from opening or maintaining a correspondence account in the United States. ABLV swiftly went into liquidation, and tougher regulation has squeezed the once lucrative nonresident banking sector out of Latvia. The second element of the "bridge" was the rail and port transit corridor between Russia and the Riga, Ventspils, and Liepāja ports. In 2019, 70 percent of the Riga Free Port's cargo turnover was made up of transit cargo trade to and from the post-Soviet Commonwealth of Independent States (CIS) countries, although flows are shrinking quickly as Russia redirects cargoes toward its own recently constructed ports.

By 2020, when the coronavirus pandemic slowed the global economy, the Baltic states had reached a historically unparalleled level of economic development. However, Latvia continues to lag behind Estonia and Lithuania in terms of its comparative GDP per capita adjusted for purchasing power standards. In 2019, Estonia had 84 percent of the EU-27's average GDP per capita, Lithuania had 82 percent, and Latvia had just 69 percent, the same as Romania and closer to Croatia (65 percent) than its Baltic neighbors.[30] In an economic sense, Latvia is more Balkan than Baltic. Economists have struggled to explain the causes of this divergence. Latvia inherited far larger industrial enterprises than Estonia and Lithuania, and these proved to be much harder to reform or privatize. Latvia also had a higher proportion of Russian-speakers in management and innovation positions, and these enterprises were further weakened by the post-1991 brain drain as these Russian-speakers emigrated east. High levels of perceived corruption may have scared foreign investors away from Latvia, a particularly popular argument among politicians and political parties, especially in the run-up to elections, as parties can claim that they will crack down on corruption when elected to office and that this will bring swift benefits to the economy. Latvia also consistently spends less on education, innovation, research, and development than Estonia or Lithuania. The 2018 PISA international student assessment for fifteen-year-olds saw Estonia as the highest-placed European country, with Latvia nineteenth and Lithuania twenty-second.[31] In 2017, research and development expenditure in Latvia was just 0.51 percent of GDP, the second lowest in the EU after Romania and significantly less than Lithuania (0.8 percent of GDP) and especially Estonia (1.4 percent of GDP).[32]

Key Social Issues

Baltic societies felt the impact of the economic transformation in the 1990s as the unsustainable and extensive social safety net and very low rates of unemployment of the Soviet era were replaced by rising unemployment and the loss of job security, while high inflation destroyed savings and the comparative value of pensions, which were financed on a pay-as-you-go basis and not linked to previous salaries.

The Baltic countries remain relatively low spenders on welfare. In 2016, the only EU state to spend less on social protection benefits as a share of GDP than Latvia (15.1 percent) and Lithuania (15.4 percent) was Romania. With a GDP share of 16.6 percent, Estonia also lagged well behind the EU average of 28 percent.[33] As a result, Estonia, Latvia, and Lithuania inevitably have some of the highest rates of inequality in Europe. In 2018, the EU average Gini coefficient, a statistical measure of income distribution used to gauge inequality, was 30.8, but in Latvia it was 35.6, and in Lithuania 36.9. However, Estonia's recently slightly higher rate of spending as well as a series of targeted policies since 2016 has seen the Gini coefficient fall from a peak of 35.6 in 2014 (the highest Gini score among the Baltic states that year) to just 30.6, below the EU average, in 2018.[34] Inequality also has a strong regional dimension, with the capital city regions of Tallinn, Riga, and Vilnius being far wealthier than the Baltic countries' rural regions, which also have higher rates of unemployment, poverty, and social problems such as alcoholism.

Civil rights for sexual minorities became a polarizing political issue in the twentieth century as the small LBGTQ communities in the Baltic countries became more active, principally through the organization of pride marches in the capital cities. The early marchers faced virulent anti-LBQTQ activists, largely organized by conservative churches, which typically started with court challenges to the legality of the marches and continued with streams of abuse and even human excrement thrown at marchers, who initially had precious little protection from the police. Since 2009, the Baltic LGBTQ communities have united under the banner of common annual Baltic pride marches rotated among the three states. The marches have grown much larger and gained greater public legitimacy as North American and European diplomats and multinational companies, such as Accenture, have started participating in the marches. Opposition has become more muted, although same-sex marriage or registered partnerships are still banned in Latvia and Lithuania. Estonia has recognized same-sex partnerships since 2016. In the

2020 ILGA Rainbow European index (which reflects the legal and policy human rights situation of LGBTQ people in Europe), Latvia ranks only above Poland among EU member states, with Lithuania additionally ranking above Romania and Bulgaria.[35]

All three Baltic countries fare rather better in studies of gender equality. The World Economic Forum's 2020 *Global Gender Gap Report* placed Latvia eleventh, Estonia twenty-sixth, and Lithuania thirty-third among the 153 countries in the index. Men have a much shorter life expectancy than women in the region, and women make up a bigger part of the population—53 percent in Estonia and 54 percent in Latvia and Lithuania—and are more economically active. Gender inequality does exist in the Baltic region. There is a gender earnings gap, with women consistently earning less than men. For example, there is no economic sector in Estonia where women on average earn more than men, and the difference in earnings is particularly pronounced in the finance and insurance sectors (where the gender pay gap is 32 percent). Women are also underrepresented in the political sphere. While all three countries have had one female president since 1991, Lithuania has had two female prime ministers, Latvia and Estonia one. In 2019, only 21 percent of parliamentary deputies in Lithuania were women, 29 percent in Estonia, and 31 percent in Latvia. Women were also underrepresented in government (two out of fifteen ministers in Estonia, three of fourteen in Latvia, and just one of fourteen in Lithuania in 2019). The situation in local governments was slightly better: 34 percent of local government deputies in Latvia were women, and 29 percent in both Estonia and Lithuania. Nevertheless, despite the gender pay gap and underrepresentation in the political system, women in the Baltic countries make up about 60 percent of all higher-education graduates.

Emerging Challenges

The three Baltic countries face the same interconnected and persistent key challenges over the next few years. First, a rapidly shrinking, aging, and urbanizing population presents profound economic and social challenges. Second, gradually slowing economic growth will see the Baltic countries struggle to escape the "middle-income trap" and converge with the older and wealthier EU member states. Third, while the nature of the security risks posed by Russia have changed over the last thirty years, the Baltic states' eastern neighbor remains a major threat to their sovereignty and integration with the West.

As discussed earlier in this chapter, all three Baltic countries have experienced a severe demographic decline since the restoration of sovereignty. Between 1993 and 2019, the population in Estonia declined by 12.3 percent, in Latvia by 25.7 percent, and in Lithuania by 24.4 percent.[36] In recent years Estonia has managed to halt the decline, but Latvia and Lithuania still have declining populations. Demographic projections made by the United Nations Department of Economic and Social Affairs in 2019 point to continuing demographic decline in the twenty-first century, with median projections for 2100 putting the Estonian population at just over 800,000 people, Latvia at 1.15 million people, and Lithuania at 1.5 million people.[37] The three-decade-long population decline, caused by a low birthrate and high levels of emigration, as well as projections of demographic apocalypse, have led the Baltic countries to develop generous "family policies," such as maternity and child benefits, but they have had little impact on demographic trends. Public debate has increasingly addressed the issue of increasing immigration to the Baltic countries, but this has proved very controversial, and anti-immigration platforms have been fruitful vote winners for radical right political parties such as EKRE in Estonia. However, these polarizing debates will continue into the foreseeable future as populations simultaneously shrink and age.

If unchecked, these negative demographic trends will inevitably have an impact on economic development in the region, with taxes needing to rise as an ever-smaller working part of the population funds the pensions and health care of the elderly. This will make the Baltic countries a less attractive destination for foreign direct investment and contribute to the threat of them being caught in a middle-income trap of modest growth and slow, or even nonexistent, convergence with Western EU states and, particularly, the neighboring Nordic states. Even if the demographic issue can be tackled, Baltic governments face the severe policy challenges of raising investment on innovation, research (especially design), and education (human capital) in order to move up the value chain and compete with other high-income countries.

Government finances for economic restructuring will compete with spending on defense and security as Russia continues to present an existential threat to the independence of the Baltic countries. A steadily growing Russian military threat since the occupation of Crimea in 2014 has seen NATO troops deployed to the region and rapid increases in domestic military spending, particularly in Latvia and Lithuania. All three countries spend the NATO-required minimum of 2 percent of GDP on defense. The Baltic countries have also tackled Russian misinformation campaigns by banning some Russian state-sponsored media channels and developing their own Russian-language programming for their Russian-speaking minorities. The Baltic countries have also moved to reduce the presence of Russian influence over their economies by, for example, modernizing electricity links with Northern and Western Europe and constructing new sources of domestic energy generation, including a liquefied natural gas (LNG) terminal in Lithuania.

Conclusion

The Baltic countries have undergone a deep political and economic revolution over the last thirty years. The transformation can be seen in the modern, increasingly cosmopolitan capital cities with their international airports, shopping malls, bustling roads, and tourist-packed old towns, as well as in the rural towns and villages that have been regenerated by EU funds. They are now free, democratic, and deeply integrated into Western political institutions and global value chains. Estonia, Latvia, and Lithuania have developed a network of mutual cooperation institutions, particularly in the military sphere, and are part of an increasingly influential political bloc of Northern European EU member states (together with Denmark, Sweden, and Finland) known as the Nordic-Baltic Six (NB6). While differences have emerged between the three—Estonia has steadier governments and is a global leader in IT innovation, Latvia is poorer and more corrupt, while Lithuania is more assertive in its foreign policy—shared historical experiences bind them closely together. When Belarusians rose up against their president, Aleksander Lukashenko, following flawed presidential elections in August 2020, it was the three Baltic prime ministers that were the first to react and call for fresh, free, and fair elections.

Having undergone their own roller-coaster transitions, they are now in a position to help other countries move toward democracy and integration with the West.

Study Questions

1. Why have the three Baltic countries emerged as the only consolidated democracies from the fifteen successor states of the Soviet Union? What key factors may explain their divergence from other post-Soviet states?
2. What impact did the Soviet occupation have on the Baltic countries? What are the legacies of the occupation today?
3. What are the main political cleavages in the Baltic countries? How do they differ between the three countries?
4. Why has the Latvian economy lagged behind Estonia and Lithuania?
5. What are the major challenges facing the three Baltic countries over the next decade?

Suggested Readings

Auers, Daunis. *Comparative Politics and Government of the Baltic States: Estonia, Latvia and Lithuania in the 21st Century*. New York: Palgrave Macmillan, 2015.

Duvold, Kjetil, Sten Berglund, and Joakim Ekman. *Political Culture in the Baltic States: Between National and European Integration*. New York: Palgrave Macmillan, 2019.

Eksteins, Modris. *Walking since Daybreak: A Story of Eastern Europe, World War II, and the Heart of Our Century*. New York: Houghton Mifflin, 1999.

Kasekamp, Andres. *A History of the Baltic States*. 2nd ed. Basingstoke: Palgrave Macmillan, 2017.

Lieven, Anatol. *The Baltic Revolution: Estonia, Latvia, Lithuania and the Path to Independence*. 2nd ed. New Haven, CT: Yale University Press, 1994.

Purs, Aldis. *Baltic Facades*. London: Reaktion Books, 2012.

Verzemnieks, Inara. *Among the Living and the Dead: A Tale of Exile and Homecoming*. New York: Norton, 2017.

Websites

Baltic Times, English-language newspaper: https://www.baltictimes.comEstonian Public Broadcasting, English News Service: https://news.err.ee

Latvian Public Media, English News Service: https://eng.lsm.lv

Lithuanian Public Television, English News Service: https://www.lrt.lt/en/news-in -english

Notes

1. World Bank, *GDP per Capita, PPP, Current International $*, Washington, DC, 2020, https://data.worldbank.org/indicator/NY.GDP.PCAP.PP.CD.

2. Saturday Night Live, "Donald Trump Baltic States Cold Open," video, April 8, 2018, https://www.youtube.com/watch?v=1iCm8tYX-Vw.

3. Ādolfs Šilde, *Latvijas Vēsture: 1914–1940* (Stockholm: Daugava, 1976).

4. Walter C. Clemens, *Baltic Independence and Russian Empire* (New York: St. Martin's, 1991).

5. Valdis Bērziņš, *20. gadsimta Latvijas Vēsture: I Latvija no gadsimta sākuma līdz neatkarības pasludināšanai 1900–1918* (Rīga: Latvijas Vēstures Institūta Apgāds, 2000), 446.

6. Aivars Stranga, *Kārļa Ulmaņa autoritārā režīma saimnieciskā politika 1934–1940* (Riga: LU Apgāds, 2017).

7. Joan R. Roses and Nikolaus Wolf, "Aggregate Growth, 1913–1950," in *The Cambridge Economic History of Modern Europe*, ed. Stephen Broadberry and Kevin O'Rourke, vol. 2, *1870 to the Present* (New York: Cambridge University Press, 2010), 190.

8. Arnolds Spekke, *Latvia and the Baltic Problem* (London: Latvian Information Bureau, 1952), 87.

9. Ervins Oberlenders, "Instruments of Sovietization in 1939/40 and after 1944/45," in *The Soviet Occupation Regime in the Baltic States 1944–1959: Policies and Their Consequences* (Riga: Latvian History Institute Press, 2003).

10. Maire Ansaar and Vlada Stankuniene, "Population Changes, Life Expectancy and Health," in *Estonian Human Development Report 2010/2011: Baltic Way(s) of Human Development: Twenty Years On* (Tallinn: Eesti Ajalehed), 45.

11. Statistics Estonia, *Population by Citizenship—Foreigners* (Tallinn: Statistics Estonia, 2020), https://www.stat.ee/57209.

12. Mana Balss. "Paveiktais," 2020, https://manabalss.lv.

13. Valts Kalniņš, *The Use of Research-Based Evidence in the Latvian Parliament: The Case of Demography and Migration Policies* (Riga: University of Latvia, 2019), https://www.izm.gov.lv/images/zinatne/SMP_study.PDF.

14. Vello Pettai, Daunis Auers, and Aine Ramonaite, "Political Development," in *Estonian Human Development Report 2010/2011: Baltic Way(s) of Human Development; Twenty Years On* (Tallinn: Eesti Ajalehed, 2011), 144–64.

15. P. Koker, "Presidential Activism in Central and Eastern Europe (CEE): A Statistical Analysis of the Use of Presidential Vetoes in the CEE EU Member States, 1990–2010," in *63rd Political Studies Association Annual International Conference*, Cardiff, UK, http://www.psa.ac.uk/sites/default/files/52_30.pdf.

16. David J. Smith, *Estonia: Independence and European Integration* (London: Routledge, 2002), 80.

17. Daunis Auers, "Populism and Political Party Institutionalisation in the Three Baltic States of Estonia, Latvia and Lithuania," *Fudan Journal of the Humanities and Social Sciences* 11 (2018): 341–55.

18. Palko Karasz, "Estonia Ministers' Gesture Raises Fear of Support for White Supremacy," *New York Times*, May 1, 2019, https://www.nytimes.com/2019/05/01/world/europe/ok-gesture-white-power-estonia.html.

19. "When Is the 'OK' Gesture not OK?," BBC News, May 16, 2019, https://www.bbc.com/news/world-europe-48293817.

20. European Commission, Standard Eurobarometer (Brussels: European Commission), https://ec.europa.eu/commfrontoffice/publicopinion/index.cfm/Survey/index#p=1&instruments=STANDARD.

21. Daunis Auers, *Comparative Politics and Government of the Baltic States: Estonia, Latvia and Lithuania in the 21st Century* (New York: Palgrave Macmillan, 2015).

22. Juris Viksnins, "The Georgetown University Syndrome and Latvian Economic Reform," in *Latvia and the USA: From Captive Nation to Strategic Partner*, ed. Daunis Auers, 109–18 (Riga: University of Latvia Academic Press, 2008).

23. United States Department of the Treasury, "Treasury Sanctions Corruption and Material Supports Network," December 9, 2019, https://home.treasury.gov/news/press-releases/sm849.

24. Rainer Kattel and Ringa Raudla, "The Baltic Republics and the Crisis of 2008–2011," *Europe-Asia Studies* 65, no. 3 (2013): 426–49.

25. Jaan Masso and Kerly Krillo, "Labour Markets in the Baltic States during the Crisis 2008–2009: The Effect on Different Labour Market Groups" (University of Tartu—Faculty of Economics and Business Administration Working Paper Series, no. 79, 2011).

26. Paul Krugman, "Latvia Is the New Argentina," *New York Times*, December 23, 2008, https://krugman.blogs.nytimes.com/2008/12/23/latvia-is-the-new-argentina-slightly-wonkish/?_php=true&_type=blogs&_r=0.

27. European Commission, *Convergence Programme of the Republic of Latvia, 2012–2015*, 2012.

28. Mihails Hazans, "Migration Experience of the Baltic Countries in the Context of Economic Crisis," in *Labor Migration, EU Enlargement, and the Great Recession*, ed. Martin Kahanec and Klaus F. Zimmerman (Berlin: Springer, 2016).

29. Julian Hattem, "President: Estonians Should Have Built Healthcare.gov," *The Hill*, March 9, 2014, https://thehill.com/policy/technology/216478-obama-estonians-should-have-built-health caregov.

30. Eurostat, *GDP per Capita in PPS 2019* (Brussels: Eurostat), https://ec.europa.eu/eurostat/tgm/table.do?tab=table&init=1&language=en&pcode=tec00114&plugin=1.

31. OECD, "PISA 2018 Insights and Interpretations," 2019, https://www.oecd.org/pisa/PISA %202018%20Insights%20and%20Interpretations%20FINAL%20PDF.pdf.

32. Eurostat, "R&D Expenditure in the EU Increased Slightly to 2.07% of GDP in 2017," 2019, https://ec.europa.eu/eurostat/documents/2995521/9483597/9-10012019-AP-EN.pdf/856 ce1d3-b8a8-4fa6-bf00-a8ded6dd1cc1.

33. Eurostat, "Social Protection Expenditure, 2016, % of GDP," 2020, https://ec.euro pa.eu/eurostat/statistics-explained/index.php/Social_protection_statistics_-_net_expenditure_on _benefits.

34. Eurostat, "Gini Coefficient of Equivalised Disposable Income: EU-SILC Survey," 2020, http://appsso.eurostat.ec.europa.eu/nui/show.do?lang=en&dataset=ilc_di12.

35. ILGA Europe, *Rainbow Map 2020*, https://www.ilga-europe.org/rainboweurope/2020.

36. Central Statistical Bureau of Latvia, *Women and Men in the Baltics* (Riga: CSB, 2019), https://osp.maps.arcgis.com/apps/MapSeries/index.html?appid=fa20eb678fe3495e89788d000bfec641.

37. United Nations Department of Economic and Social Affairs, "World Population Prospects 2019," 2019, https://population.un.org/wpp/Graphs/Probabilistic/POP/440.

Map 15.0.   Bulgaria

CHAPTER 15

Bulgaria

Janusz Bugajski and Margarita Assenova

In the last three decades, Bulgaria successfully conducted two historic transformations: from a centrally controlled communist system to a pluralistic market-oriented democracy and from the closest ally of the Soviet Union in the former Warsaw Pact to a full member of the North Atlantic Treaty Organization (NATO) and the European Union (EU). This dual transformation was neither consistent nor predictable. For much of the early and mid-1990s, the postcommunist Bulgarian socialists ruled. They resisted full-blown capitalism and a close alliance with the West largely in an effort to preserve their political and economic positions and maintain their traditional ties with Moscow. Sofia's turn toward Western institutions and economic models accelerated after 1998, when a reformist coalition government was elected. Bulgaria became a member of NATO in 2004 and the EU in 2007.

Political History

Bulgaria emerged from the Ottoman Empire as an independent state in several stages. In 1878, following the Russo-Turkish War, the Treaty of San Stefano created a large Bulgarian state stretching from the Danube to the Aegean and including most of present-day Macedonia. The Treaty of Berlin in July 1878 reduced this territory at the insistence of the great powers because of fears of Russian dominance across the Balkans. Bulgaria subsequently included the region between the Danube and the Balkan Mountains. The area between the Balkan Mountains in the north and the Rhodope Mountains in the south formed the autonomous Ottoman province of Eastern Rumelia. These border readjustments and Bulgaria's reversion to a semiautonomous Ottoman principality under a German ruler created widespread resentment. However, in 1879, Bulgaria adopted the progressive Tarnovo Constitution that guaranteed individual rights, and in the following two decades, a number of political parties were established, including the National Liberal Party and the Bulgarian Agrarian Union.

On September 6, 1885, a popular revolt in Plovdiv resulted in the unification of Eastern Rumelia with the principality of Bulgaria, an act supported by Bulgaria's ruler Alexander Battenberg, but opposed by all great powers at the time. The country proclaimed its full independence from Turkey in 1908 after several popular revolts, including the Ilinden Uprising in August 1903, centered in the Macedonian and Thracian regions. Bulgaria's territorial claims contributed to fueling two Balkan wars in 1912 and 1913. In the first, the new Balkan states combined their forces to drive the Ottoman armies out of the region. In the second, Bulgaria was unsuccessful in its military campaign against Serbia and Greece and once again lost territories in Macedonia and Thrace to its neighbors. The result left a lasting sense of injustice in Bulgaria with regard to its rightful frontiers. Bulgaria retained only a small slice of Pirin Macedonia and a sector of the Thracian coastline. During World War I, Bulgaria allied itself with Germany and Austria, but with the defeat of the Central powers, it was forced to accept a harsh peace treaty at Neuilly in November 1919 and lost all access to the Aegean Sea.

For most of the interwar period, Bulgaria experienced political turmoil and economic crisis, particularly after the overthrow of the Agrarian government led by Aleksandar Stamboliyski in 1923. Following a military coup d'état supported by political rivals and nationalist Macedonian activists, Stamboliyski and other Agrarian leaders were murdered. After a decade of political instability and conflict, another coup in May 1934 led by military officers resulted in the formation of a personalistic regime under King Boris III. During World War II, the government in Sofia imposed a royal dictatorship and capitalized on Nazi Germany's occupation of Yugoslavia and Greece to forge an alliance with Berlin to regain parts of Macedonia and Thrace. Bulgaria also repossessed the region of southern Dobruja from Romania. King Boris died in August 1943. For the rest of the war, the country was ruled by a regency, as Boris's successor, Simeon, was only six years old. Bulgaria's territorial advances, including access to the Aegean coastline, were again reversed at the close of World War II, as Sofia found itself once more on the losing side.

Communist forces, with Soviet military and political assistance, seized power in Bulgaria in September 1944 during the closing stages of World War II. At the end of 1947, they eliminated all organized political and social opposition and held falsified elections to legitimize their assumption of absolute power. Former Moscow-directed Communist International (Comintern) agent Georgi Dimitrov returned to Bulgaria from exile and assumed leadership of the Communist Party and the state. A new Stalinist "Dimitrov" constitution was passed in December 1947 that replicated the Soviet prototype. The communist regime, under Soviet supervision, placed tight restrictions on cultural and political life, conducted a full-scale drive toward state control over the economy, and pursued agricultural collectivization among the peasantry.

Dimitrov died in July 1949 and was replaced as party leader by Valko Chervenkov, another hard-line Stalinist. Chervenkov, in turn, was replaced by Todor Zhivkov in April 1956 during the slow process of de-Stalinization. Zhivkov and his Communist Party maintained tight control over the country for the next thirty-three years, until the collapse of the centralized system. Zhivkov's absolute loyalty to Moscow and his ability to thwart any organized domestic opposition to Leninist rule earned him the complete support of the Soviet leadership. There is even evidence that the Bulgarian regime sought to join the USSR as the sixteenth republic. Bulgaria was thus considered to be Moscow's closest and most loyal ally in the Soviet bloc.

Early Postcommunism

Following a wave of public protests and increasing political pressures against the communist regime, on November 10, 1989, the Central Committee of the Bulgarian Communist Party (BCP) announced the resignation of Todor Zhivkov as secretary general and his replacement by foreign minister Petar Mladenov. The new leader promised sweeping political and economic changes to transform Bulgaria into a "modern democratic state." This "palace coup d'état" marked the beginning of the end of communism in Bulgaria, but its real goal was to avoid a popular revolution, whether a velvet one or a violent one, and to preserve the political and economic power of the communist *nomenklatura*. On the one hand, this internal party maneuver allowed for Bulgaria's peaceful transition to political pluralism, but on the other, it enabled the new BCP leadership to seek legitimacy and play a critical role in Bulgaria's transition.

The BCP organized pro-Mladenov rallies, depicting itself as the initiator of progressive reforms, scapegoating the Zhivkov leadership for the country's maladies, and trying to deny the reformist initiative to the emerging, but still embryonic, democratic opposition movement.

As head of the BCP, Mladenov held meetings with dissident activists in mid-November 1989 and pledged to implement substantive democratic reforms and to legalize all types of independent groups and activities. The BCP's subordinate bodies, including the Komsomol youth association, were allowed to be more critical in an attempt to deflate some of the opposition's demands. Reshuffles were conducted in the BCP's governing Politburo and Central Committee, and Mladenov declared himself in favor of free general elections. Following massive public protests in Sofia, the regime dropped the BCP's "guiding force" role from the constitution and promised to curtail the repressive role of the security services. These steps paved the way for the creation of a multiparty system. While the BCP endeavored to maintain its political initiative, dozens of new political groups were forming during this time.

Some reform communists demanded the resignation of the entire BCP Central Committee as divisions deepened with the emergence of the Alternative Socialist Association as a faction within the party. In early December 1989, a preparatory meeting was held between BCP officials and representatives of some independent groups. Mladenov promised that the authorities would hold a constructive dialogue with all groups "supporting socialism." In order to incorporate leading opposition elements into some workable coalition and prevent destructive splits within the party, the BCP initiated roundtable negotiations with officially sponsored organizations and some of the newly formed opposition groups in January 1990.[1]

One of the urgent problems for the new BCP leadership was restoring the rights of the Bulgarian Turks, who had been subjected to forceful assimilation by the Zhivkov regime since 1984. The assimilation campaign included imposing Bulgarian names on the Turkish population, forbidding them to practice Islam, and banning the use of the Turkish language in public, among other human rights violations. Ten years earlier, the regime had executed a similar operation targeting other minorities. The campaign against the Bulgarian Turks generated significant international criticism of Bulgaria, which Mladenov had to defend as foreign minister at the time. After peaceful protests in Sofia, the BCP's Central Committee issued a decree on restoring the birth names of Bulgarian Turks. Although the decision was generally supported by the public, Bulgarian nationalists in areas with mixed populations staged demonstrations and subsequently organized a nationalist movement. Simultaneously, Bulgaria's ethnic Turks established the Movement for Rights and Freedoms (MRF) to represent the Turkish minority and other Muslim groups, an organization often called the Turkish Party.

The regime continued to be treated with mistrust by most of the opposition, which refused to enter the Government of National Consensus proposed by the communists. At its Extraordinary Congress, held in early February 1990, the BCP selected Alexander Lilov as its new secretary general and replaced the Central Committee with a smaller Supreme Party Council and the ruling Politburo with a new presidency. BCP leaders also initiated steps to separate the party from the state (which they had fully controlled), and the party itself was renamed the Bulgarian Socialist Party (BSP) to distance it from its totalitarian past.

The National Assembly (parliament), controlled by the BSP, elected Andrey Lukanov as the new prime minister. Lukanov attempted to form a broad-based coalition government, but the initiative was rejected by the Union of Democratic Forces (UDF), which had grown into the chief democratic opposition alliance. The new cabinet became an all-communist body as the BSP's former communist-era coalition partner, the Agrarian People's Union, refused to join the Lukanov government and purged itself of compromised older leaders. In addition, reformist BSP intellectuals established an Alternative Socialist Party and cast serious doubts on the BSP's ability to democratize. Meanwhile, the UDF organized public demonstrations to protest the slow progress in negotiations with the BSP and the limitations on democratic transition.

By mid-March 1990, the BSP and UDF had reached an agreement on the transition to a democratic system and the scheduling of competitive national elections. The BSP won the parliamentary elections held on June 10 and 17, 1990, with 47 percent of the vote, giving the party 211 of the 400 parliamentary seats. The UDF earned a disappointing 36 percent (144 seats). The Agrarian People's Union took 8 percent (16 seats), and the Turkish party, the MRF, garnered 6 percent of the vote (23 seats). The UDF accused the regime of ballot rigging and maintaining a monopoly over the media. The opposition had insufficient time to organize an effective election campaign and scored particularly poorly in rural areas where the communist-socialist apparatus remained largely intact. The Socialist Party's victory in the first democratic election determined the pace of transition to a democratic system in Bulgaria, as former communist leaders managed to retain political and economic power for most of the critical first decade of postcommunism.

In April 1990, parliament formally created the office of the president but limited its authority to security matters and ceremonial functions by giving the president no veto power over parliamentary legislation. On July 6, 1990, Mladenov resigned as acting president amid public protests after a film was released in which he called for military intervention to quell peaceful protests. Parliament elected dissident philosopher and leader of the opposition Zhelyu Zhelev as the country's new head of state.

The short-lived Lukanov government left a legacy of corruption, high inflation, and civil unrest caused by enormous food and consumer goods shortages and power cuts.

This period is remembered as "the winter of Lukanov," a synonym for extreme hardship. Eventually, large demonstrations and a general strike in December brought the government down. The parliament appointed a coalition technocratic government headed by Prime Minister Dimitar Popov that included the BSP, the UDF, the Agrarians, and independents. The government's two main tasks were to launch the monetary part of economic reform by liberalizing commodity prices and to prepare and hold the next local and parliamentary elections.

Political Institutions

The unicameral National Assembly also became a constitutional assembly that drafted Bulgaria's new democratic constitution. The document defined Bulgaria as a parliamentary democracy and a unitary state and prohibited any form of territorial autonomy or the creation of political parties founded on an "ethnic, racial, or religious" basis. Parliament was given legislative supremacy; the president had the right to veto legislation passed by the National Assembly. This constitution was eventually adopted in July 1991 despite opposition from some UDF factions.

The National Assembly, composed of 240 seats, is elected every four years by a popular ballot, and the majority party is given a mandate by the president to form the new government. If none of the political parties wins a parliamentary majority, the plurality winner is given a mandate to form a governing coalition. The president of Bulgaria is elected in a general election every five years. According to the constitution, his or her role is more ceremonial and symbolic than substantive in terms of decision making, but the president serves as commander in chief in times of war. Any amendments to the constitution require a two-thirds majority in parliament. However, a completely new constitution would need to be adopted by a newly elected Grand National Assembly.

The constitution establishes the Constitutional Court as a mechanism for judicial review, interpreting laws and international treaties. This court is separate from the judiciary. It has twelve members: one-third of the constitutional judges are elected by the National Assembly, one-third are appointed by the president, and the rest are elected by a joint meeting of the judges of the two high courts—the Supreme Court of Cassation and the Supreme Administrative Court.

The Bulgarian judiciary is composed of three separate systems of law-enforcing or law-protecting authorities: the system of courts, the system of public prosecution, and the system of investigation offices. While the Ministry of Justice is responsible for the budget and some administrative functions, the Supreme Judicial Council is the administrative body running the judiciary. According to Article 129, paragraph 1, of the constitution, "Judges, public prosecutors and investigating magistrates are appointed, promoted, reduced in rank, moved and discharged from office by the Supreme Judicial Council."

Although the judiciary is established as an independent system of government, in reality it is still susceptible to political and business corruption. Slow and insufficient judicial reform has impacted Bulgaria's ability to deal with organized crime and corruption, earning it the unfavorable reputation as the most corrupt member of the EU.[2]

Bulgaria's local government consists of twenty-eight provinces named after the provincial capitals, with the national capital itself forming a separate province. The provinces are further subdivided into a total of 264 municipalities, which are the main units of local government. Elections for municipal councils and mayors are held every four years, while regional governors are appointed by the cabinet.

In April 2005, Bulgaria signed an accession treaty with the EU; it became a full EU member on January 1, 2007. The government had successfully completed the implementation of all thirty-one chapters of the EU's voluminous *acquis communautaire*, which stipulated the reforms that needed to be enacted in various areas of the economy and administrative structure for Bulgaria to meet EU standards. Brussels also included a clause in the treaty that could have led to a delay in Bulgaria's entry if the remaining reforms in the judicial system and in combating corruption were not implemented.

EU membership itself closed an important chapter in Bulgaria's post–Cold War history, as it signaled that the country had successfully completed its transformation from a communist dictatorship to a capitalist democracy. However, the EU established a special Cooperation and Verification Mechanism (CVM) to monitor Bulgaria's progress in several critical areas, such as implementing judicial reforms and countering organized crime and corruption. After twelve years, the European Commission's CVM report in October 2019 stated that Bulgaria had made sufficient progress in judicial reform and anticorruption, satisfying the commitments made by the country at the time of accession. The commission considered lifting the monitoring mechanism, but as of December 2020 this had not happened.[3]

Political Competition

Although the opposition narrowly won the October 1991 elections, splits within UDF just before the election signaled that the coalition of sixteen parties and organizations could not reconcile different ideologies and meet each group's political aspirations. UDF's largest coalition partners, the Social Democratic Party and the Agrarian National Union "Nikola Petkov," were refused a more prominent voice on the UDF Council or a greater number of candidates on the UDF electoral list. In addition, it was divided between advocates of a moderate line toward the BSP (the "light blues") and a majority demanding far-reaching decommunization and a settling of scores with the repressive communist leadership (the "dark blues"). The light blues withdrew from the union and formed the UDF-Liberals. The dark blues became known as the UDF-Movement and inherited the coalition's organizational network and media outlets. This was the beginning of a long process of division and disagreement among the democratic opposition that eventually destroyed the UDF.

In the October 1991 elections, the UDF-Movement narrowly won a plurality of votes despite declining support for the BSP. The UDF received 110 of 240 parliamentary seats, and the BSP gained 106 seats. The only other party to clear the 4 percent threshold and gain parliamentary seats was the Turkish party, MRF. Not surprisingly, the parliament became highly polarized, and the UDF had to form a coalition government with the

MRF, headed by Prime Minister Filip Dimitrov, who was installed in office in November 1991.

A top priority of the UDF-MRF administration was decommunization in all public institutions and the elimination of subversive activities by secret service officers who were trying to obstruct market reform. This task proved difficult because of entrenched interests that pervaded most state bodies and enterprises. The National Assembly passed a law to confiscate communist property. The prosecution of former communist officials was intensified. About fifty prominent figures, including Todor Zhivkov, were indicted for crimes committed during the communist regime, ranging from embezzlement to masterminding and executing the forcible assimilation of minorities.

The Dimitrov government gave qualified support for Zhelyu Zhelev in the first direct presidential ballot in January 1992. Zhelev was a sociologist who had been expelled from the Communist Party in the late 1980s for organizing a group to support political reform. There was incessant hostility between the UDF administration and President Zhelev, who represented a more moderate policy line toward the socialists. Both the government and parliament criticized Zhelev for appointing ex-communists, and both institutions tried to further undercut the president's powers.

By the summer of 1992, the Dimitrov government faced internal splits over the restitution of agricultural land and the pace of economic reform. The MRF was particularly disturbed: the decline in the economy seriously affected the Turkish rural population since land reforms implemented favored former Bulgarian owners, and the state was slow to redistribute property to minorities from the state land fund. MRF leader Ahmed Dogan called for a change of policy, but when this failed in October 1992, the MRF parliamentary delegation joined with the BSP in a vote of no confidence in the UDF government. This motion was supported by Zhelev, who accused Dimitrov of undermining the presidency and alienating the population.

Prime Minister Dimitrov resigned on October 28, 1992. His cabinet was replaced by an "expert" government headed by the socialist Lyuben Berov that survived until September 2, 1994. It was criticized for rampant corruption and ties to clandestine business interests. It was replaced by a caretaker administration under Reneta Indzhova on October 17, 1994, that was to hold power until early general elections were held.

The BSP returned to power in the elections of December 18, 1994, winning 125 parliamentary seats. Five parties were able to cross the 4 percent threshold to gain parliamentary representation. BSP leader Zhan Videnov, known as a hard-liner and an anti-reformer, became the new prime minister.[4] The popular swing toward the BSP was confirmed during local elections in October 1994.

Following their defeat, the UDF leadership resigned en masse. In early 1995, Ivan Kostov, a liberal reformer and former professor at Sofia Technical University, was elected to replace Filip Dimitrov as UDF leader. He moved to better coordinate the UDF, undercut the independence of its constituent parties and factions, and improve relations with the MRF and other opposition formations.

In just two years in office, the Socialist administration under Videnov's leadership brought the country's economy and financial system to ruin. The government was accused of maintaining secret connections with business conglomerates that siphoned off state funds for the benefit of the old communist apparatus. Reluctance to follow through on reform measures led to a rapid downturn of the economy that seriously affected living standards. The problems reached crisis proportions by the mid-1990s. Meanwhile, the UDF gradually began to regain its popular support by promoting a pro-reform and pro-Western agenda. The UDF had several splits, but it remained the most credible center-right force in Bulgarian politics throughout the 1990s. It operated as a broad anti-communist movement from its inception, with support drawn mostly from among the young, educated, entrepreneurial, and urban populations.

The year 1996 proved to be a watershed in Bulgaria. The country experienced serious economic difficulties caused by the absence of systematic market reforms, widespread corruption, and even outright theft by government officials. Pressures increased for an early parliamentary ballot that could dislodge the former communists from power. However, the BSP and its coalition partners maintained a secure parliamentary majority despite growing pressures from the major opposition bloc, the UDF. The political scene remained polarized between these two formations. Their ideological differences were evident in all major issues affecting Bulgarian society. The socialists were determined to maintain the economic status quo and stalled the privatization program, leading to further economic decline. Moreover, the government was opposed to NATO membership and strengthened its relations with Russia, despite criticism from the opposition.

Rifts were also evident within the Socialist Party between the harder-line members linked to Prime Minister Zhan Videnov and reformist elements critical of government policy. These divisions widened after the assassination of former prime minister Andrey Lukanov at the beginning of October 1996. Lukanov had become an outspoken critic of official resistance to reform. Allegedly, he also possessed information on corruption at the highest levels of government that he reportedly planned to make public.[5] Observers contended that Lukanov himself was deeply involved in corruption, and his killing resembled a gangland assassination.

The presidential elections further undermined the socialist administration. UDF candidate Petar Stoyanov, nominated through the first primary election in Bulgaria, gained an overwhelming percentage of votes (44 percent) over the socialist Ivan Marazov (27 percent) in the first round of voting on October 27, 1996. Stoyanov was elected president in the second-round runoff on November 3, 1996, with 59 percent of the vote to Marazov's 40 percent.[6] Although the post of president was primarily ceremonial, the result emboldened the opposition to push for a no-confidence vote in the socialist government.

During 1996, Bulgaria faced a major financial crisis. Hard currency reserves plummeted, and there were growing doubts that Sofia could meet its critical foreign debt payments. The Videnov government continued to prop up obsolete and uncompetitive state-owned industries. Moreover, the former communist apparatus still controlled and exploited much of the economy through shady "economic groups," in which corruption was believed to be rampant. An ambitious mass-privatization program remained stalled in parliament because of powerful vested interests. As the financial crisis deepened and the currency collapsed, prices soared dramatically. Bread shortages were reported in various parts of the country, and analysts warned of severe food and fuel shortages during the winter months. Bulgaria was in the midst of a banking crisis and entered a period of hyperinflation, which surpassed 2,000 percent on an annual basis in March 1997.[7]

Large sectors of the public were angry about the rapid decline in their living standards and reports of widespread corruption among government officials. Following several months of protests and public demonstrations, the increasingly isolated socialist government of Prime Minister Videnov resigned in December 1996. The newly inaugurated President Stoyanov called for early parliamentary elections in April 1997 and appointed the mayor of Sofia, Stefan Sofianski, as caretaker prime minister.

As in the presidential elections, the UDF participated in the April 1997 parliamentary elections as part of a broader coalition. Its chief allies in the coalition included the Democratic Party and the Agrarian People's Union, which formed the People's Union alliance. The Agrarian People's Union, originally a founder of the UDF in 1989 under the name Agrarian People's Union "Nikola Petkov," was one of about twenty groups claiming to be the successors of the precommunist Agrarians. Most of them were right-of-center formations.

The UDF won the April 1997 election overwhelmingly with 52 percent of the vote, gaining 137 of 240 parliamentary seats; the BSP only got 22 percent of the vote and 58 seats. Ivan Kostov, the UDF leader and former finance minister in Dimitar Popov's grand-coalition government, was appointed prime minister. The composition of his cabinet reflected Bulgaria's commitment to intensive economic and political reforms and included pro-Western liberal reformers. The new administration benefited from broad public support even though the impact of the planned economic reforms was painful for workers in state industries.

The key priorities of the UDF-led coalition government were stabilizing the economy, combating crime and corruption, and pursuing Euro-Atlantic integration. The UDF-dominated legislature passed a number of important measures to root out the corruption that had become endemic among state officials and industrial managers. A new law passed in September 1997 prohibited members of the former communist apparatus from obtaining high positions in the civil service for a period of five years. Parliament also approved the opening of secret police files to determine which top officials had collaborated with the communist-era security services and engaged in repressive acts. This move indicated that the authorities favored openness and transparency in government operations. Investigations into large-scale corruption were also initiated since some former socialist officials were believed to have embezzled millions of dollars from state funds.

The authorities were determined to pursue a radical economic reform program to avert a major financial crisis. In consultation with the International Monetary Fund (IMF), the Bulgarian government launched a far-reaching "stabilization program" that lifted most price controls, pegged the national currency to the German mark, and established a currency board to control government spending. As a result, the inflation rate decreased dramatically. Parliament also approved a new budget that cut state spending and reduced subsidies on unprofitable industries. An extensive privatization program was launched that had an impact on the majority of state-owned enterprises. The possibility for social unrest remained, however, since living standards declined sharply as a result of the government's austerity measures and budgetary discipline.

The new government was also determined to pursue Bulgaria's integration into various Euro-Atlantic institutions. President Stoyanov declared that Bulgaria was seeking membership in NATO and was willing to undertake the necessary reforms of its military structure. The previous socialist administration had been ambiguous about alliance membership and preferred a policy of neutrality and close relations with Russia. The new pro-NATO policy dismayed Bulgaria's traditional ally, Russia. Relations between Sofia and Moscow grew tense. Bulgaria's interior minister also accused Moscow of racketeering because of its manipulation of gas prices and control over Bulgarian energy supplies.

The parliamentary majority held by the UDF ensured that the socialist opposition did not seriously challenge the reform program. President Stoyanov remained very popular despite the painful austerity program imposed by UDF authorities. However, local elections in October 1999 were a setback for the UDF, which only narrowly defeated the socialists in a majority of Bulgarian municipalities. Growing public frustration with layoffs and state spending cuts resulted in a decreased voter turnout of some 50 percent. However, the UDF retained control of the two major cities, Sofia and Plovdiv. Despite the progress achieved by the UDF in securing macroeconomic stability and fulfilling the criteria for international loans, the living standards of the majority of citizens stagnated or fell after the elections, especially among pensioners, rural workers, and blue-collar employees, angering the population.

The Bulgarian political scene changed dramatically in April 2001 with the return of the exiled King Simeon II. The ex-monarch, deposed by the communists after World War II, formed his own political group, styled as the National Movement Simeon II (NMS). This center-right organization drew support away from both the UDF and the opposition socialists. In the parliamentary elections held on June 17, 2001, the NMS scored a landslide victory, gaining 43 percent of the vote and 120 seats in the 240-seat legislature. The UDF finished a distant second with 18 percent and 51 seats. Two other parties passed the electoral threshold: the Socialist Party captured 17 percent of the vote and 48 seats; the Turkish minority-based MRF garnered 8 percent and 21 seats.

Simeon II thus became the first monarch to return to power in postcommunist Central and East Europe, although he made no attempt to recreate the monarchy. His party captured the protest vote of impoverished elements of the Bulgarian population, and his selection of young Western-educated professionals as parliamentarians and ministers increased public support for him and his party. The king did not run in the elections and at first did not even put himself forward as prime minister. He also denied that there were any plans to restore the monarchy and pointed out that the country had far more pressing issues to contend with, such as unemployment, poverty, and corruption.

Critics charged that the NMS message was too populist and insufficiently specific on economic policies. NMS leaders countered that they would continue with the reform program launched by the UDF while paying more attention to combating corruption, attracting foreign investment, reforming the judicial system, and creating new employment opportunities. Moreover, Simeon underscored his government's commitment to EU and NATO integration.

The NMS triumph jettisoned what had essentially become a two-party system. However, the victors indicated that they were intent on creating a coalition government to achieve broader political consensus and to ensure effective government during a difficult reform process. The Bulgarian public seemed to reject the continued polarization of public life by voting for this movement that pledged to unify the nation. The MRF was the first party to offer its cooperation, indicating a valuable opportunity for involving the sizable Turkish population in the governing process. In mid-July 2001, Simeon agreed to assume the post of prime minister and formed a new cabinet.

The NMS electoral base proved diverse. The party's ministers were a mixture of young bankers with Western experience, older Bulgarian lawyers, and representatives of local business groups. However, the NMS government's failure to meet unrealistic popular expectations led to a progressive drop in support for the government and its programs, as well as increasing divisions within the NMS. By late 2003, eleven members of parliament (MPs) had defected from the NMS's initial parliamentary contingent of 120; ten of them formed the National Ideal of Unity faction to the left of the NMS. The New Time group of twenty-two MPs on the NMS's right also became largely independent. NMS candidates performed poorly in local elections in October 2003, especially as the movement lacked any significant local structures. Although it declared its intention to transform itself into a political party, the NMS lacked cohesion and was principally based on the personality of its leader.

Following its defeat in the 2001 parliamentary elections, the UDF disintegrated. The party also lost the presidential elections in October 2001 when incumbent President Petar Stoyanov was defeated by the Socialist leader Georgi Parvanov. Parvanov ran on a platform of economic reform, social democracy, and pro-Westernism, including support for NATO membership. The UDF's performance in the local elections in October 2003 was also disappointing for the party. By 2004 the center-right had splintered into several rival formations, most with weak organizational structures but with charismatic leaders. Some activists were concerned that this development would exclude them from parliament or enable the socialists to form a workable governing coalition. Mayor of Sofia and former caretaker prime minister Stefan Sofianski broke away from the UDF in late 2001 after failing to persuade his colleagues to form a coalition with the NMS. He founded a separate party, the Union of Free Democrats. Although the party was small, Sofianski benefited from high ratings on a national level. Ivan Kostov resigned as the UDF's leader and created the Democrats for a Strong Bulgaria (DSB) in May 2004, pulling some supporters away from the UDF. Other center-right groupings included the Bulgarian Agrarian People's Union, the St. George's Day Movement (Gergyovden), and the New Time.[8]

In 2005, the Bulgarian electorate followed its pattern of always voting out the ruling coalition. This time it was motivated by disappointment that the NMS had not managed to transform the economy enough to benefit the older and less educated part of the population, and it had not achieved its promises to control corruption and organized crime. Beyond this, the "kingmaker" MRF gained from the emergence of a far-right, anticommunist, xenophobic party, Ataka, which ultimately got 8.75 percent of the vote. Its attacks stimulated MRF voters to go to the polls, allowing the MRF to do far better than had been expected.

This time, both the UDF and the NMS lost to the Coalition for Bulgaria, which centered on the BSP, the successor to the BCP. Its victory was marginal; with only 34 percent of the vote for the BSP and 14 percent for the MRF, the two could not form a majority coalition. The BSP, therefore, had to reach out to the NMS (which had garnered just under 23 percent of the vote) to join forces for a three-party center-left coalition. This process was facilitated by the BSP's campaign commitment to continuing the economic

Photo 15.1.   Members of the extreme nationalist party Ataka demonstrate against using loudspeakers to call Muslims to prayer by a mosque in the capital city of Sofia. (Nadya Kotseva, Sofia Photo Agency)

reforms and maintaining a centrist posture to keep Bulgaria turned toward the West. The resulting government included men and women in their thirties and forties, with the BSP leader, Sergey Stanishev, thirty-nine years old at the time, as prime minister. The three deputy prime ministers represented the three coalition partners.

Most of the BSP social base consisted of pensioners, peasants, some of the technical intelligentsia, and Bulgarians in ethnically mixed areas who leaned toward nationalism. The party incorporated a spectrum of political trends, from Marxist dogmatists to social democrats. The more market-oriented social democrats began to prevail in the late 1990s after the party's credibility was undermined by the 1996–1997 economic collapse. Georgi Parvanov, elected BSP leader in 1996, pursued a policy of economic reform, social democracy, and pro-Westernism, including support for NATO membership. His position was buttressed by his victory on the presidential ballot in 2001. Perceived as a young reformist at the time, Sergey Stanishev was elected to be his successor as Socialist Party leader in December 2001.

Bulgaria had come a long way in its transformation process, as demonstrated by its accession into NATO in 2004 and the EU in 2007. However, economic development, structural reform, judicial effectiveness, and public trust continued to be undermined by official corruption and organized cross-border criminality.[9] Political corruption deepened under the three-party coalition cabinet of Sergei Stanishev in 2008 and 2009, involving cases bordering on state capture, flagrant instances of conflict of interest, and the use of public resources for personal benefit. Although corruption among businesses was estimated to have decreased by 50 percent after Bulgaria's EU accession, procurement of public funds, and particularly EU funding for a number of development projects, became the new target for corruption schemes. As a result, the European Commission withdrew millions of euros allocated to agriculture and administrative modernization in Bulgaria. The impunity of high-level corruption and organized crime earned Bulgaria the label of "the most corrupt EU country."[10]

Bulgarian parliamentary elections on July 5, 2009, revolved around tackling official corruption and controlling the economic recession. Because of widespread dissatisfaction with the ruling socialists and public outrage over misappropriation of EU funds, the elections were comfortably won by the newly established center-right Citizens for the European Development of Bulgaria (GERB), which gained 116 out of 240 parliamentary seats. The BSP won only 40 seats; the Turkish MRF, 38; the ultranationalist Ataka, 21; the center-right Blue Coalition (led by the UDF), 15; and the rightist Order, Lawfulness, and Justice (RZS), 10. Boyko Borisov, a former chief secretary of the Interior Ministry and former mayor of Sofia, became prime minister on July 27, 2009.

The GERB government undertook measures to combat corruption and organized crime and to restore confidence in Bulgaria's ability to manage EU funds. Shortly after taking office, Borisov's government adopted a fifty-seven-point plan to implement the EU's recommendations to reform law enforcement and the judiciary. The EU unblocked €156 million in pre-accession agriculture funds due to the new government's initial efforts to implement the EU recommendations. Specialized police operations against organized criminal groups eliminated the most notorious ones, and a number of high-profile criminal bosses were imprisoned. However, little improvement was observed in reform of the judicial system. Media freedom also declined, with the few remaining independent news outlets subjected to political pressure. Concentrated media ownership by interrelated oligarchic structures raised EU criticism.[11]

In the midst of Europe's financial crisis, the Borisov government managed to maintain financial stability and largely preserve the country's fiscal reserves. Austerity measures helped keep the budget deficit low—it was 0.8 percent of gross domestic product (GDP) in 2012.

In October 2011, GERB won the presidential election when Rosen Plevneliev, minister of regional development and public works, defeated the BSP candidate, Ivaylo Kalfin.

The government revised three major Russian energy projects signed by the previous socialist-led coalition: the Burgas–Alexandroupoli oil pipeline with a 51 percent Russian share, the second nuclear power plant at Belene with Russian-built reactors, and the South Stream natural gas pipeline with 50 percent Russian ownership. The government scrapped the first two projects, backing only South Stream. The GERB-controlled parliament adopted an indefinite moratorium on shale gas exploration and extraction under pressure from green groups and lobbyists for Russian energy interests in Bulgaria.[12]

Increased electricity prices provoked massive public protests in January and February 2013, forcing the government to resign. President Rosen Plevneliev appointed a caretaker government headed by career diplomat Marin Raykov. Parliamentary elections took place on May 12, 2013, with only four political parties passing the threshold. GERB won the plurality vote, gaining 97 of the 240 seats in parliament, but was unable to form a government without a coalition partner. The elections produced a hung parliament, with BSP and its junior partner, MRF, together gaining exactly half the seats in the National Assembly. The ultranationalist Ataka, with 23 parliamentary seats, eventually sided with the Socialist-led coalition and helped it form a government. For the first time, none of the traditional center-right parties instrumental in Bulgaria's democratic transition made it to parliament, including the UDF and DSB.

In May, the Socialist Party, in coalition with the ethnic Turkish MRF, formed a government supported by Ataka. Two weeks later, parliament provoked public outrage with the appointment of controversial media mogul Delyan Peevski, an MP from the Turkish party, as chairman of the State Agency for National Security. Peevski's name has been linked to corruption and shady business interests.[13] Daily demonstrations took place in Sofia during the summer and fall of 2013, even after Peevski's appointment was revoked, as Bulgaria entered a period of political turmoil with a government that had little credibility. An October 2013 opinion poll showed that only 23 percent of citizens trusted the government, and 76 percent wanted early elections.[14]

President Plevneliev expressed support for the protestors and called for early elections, but the government survived for another year.

When Russia invaded Ukraine in early 2014, security concerns preoccupied the public and political elites, along with preparations for the May 2014 elections for the European Parliament. The MRF nominated Delyan Peevski as its leading candidate, sparking new controversies and strengthening calls for early elections.[15] GERB gained six seats in the Bulgarian delegation of seventeen members in the European Parliament, followed by the leftist Coalition for Bulgaria with four seats, the MRF and the new populist formation "Bulgaria without Censorship" each with two seats, and the center-right Reformist Bloc remaining with only one seat. Delyan Peevski was elected as a member of the European Parliament but quit his mandate under public pressure over allegations of corruption.[16] This, however, did not end the controversy surrounding the failed appointment of Peevski as national security agency chief the year before. His name came up again in dealings surrounding the collapse of the Corporate Commercial Bank in mid-2014, which had caused the biggest financial crisis in Bulgaria since 1996, costing clients and the state over €2 billion in losses.[17]

The following three years saw support for individual political parties fragment. Public frustration grew, and so did Russian interference in politics—through trolling, propaganda, promulgation of fake news, and various methods of political influence. The public protests that started in May 2013 continued for months. People demanded change because the government of Plamen Oresharski was not working to end the culture of corruption in Bulgarian politics. The cabinet's attempt to push the Russian-led South Stream natural gas project through, over EU objections and despite the sanctions against Russia for its aggression in Ukraine, also caused the withdrawal of support from coalition member MRF. The Turkish party refused to support an amendment to the Energy Act to exempt Bulgarian territorial waters from the requirements of EU's Third Energy Package. The split was exacerbated when it became public that Gazprom operatives had been the ones who concocted the draft amendment.

In August 2014, President Rosen Plevneliev appointed a caretaker government led by Georgi Bliznashki. He then organized a snap parliamentary election in October 2014.

Eight parties gained seats in parliament, but none had a majority. The National Assembly was fragmented to the extent that any new government had to depend on some unstable coalition.[18] The election result was inconclusive and disappointing for all major players, but it demonstrated the level of public confusion and disillusionment with the political establishment.

After a month of negotiations, GERB reached a deal with the center-right Reformist Bloc (RB), the nationalist Patriotic Front (PF), and the small new center-left ABV party to form the next Bulgarian cabinet. GERB and the RB sealed the coalition agreement when the PF committed to support their alliance and ABV sent former foreign minister Ivaylo Kalfin to the cabinet, thereby ensuring the support of another eleven MPs. This meant the government was able to count on a parliamentary majority of 137 (out of 240) lawmakers.[19]

One of the major decisions the new government was supposed to make was whether to continue with the Russia-led South Stream gas pipeline project or risk further "infringement procedures" and the loss of $12 billion assistance from the EU between 2014 and 2020. The choice was clear, but before Borisov made any official statement, Russian president Vladimir Putin canceled the project in December 2014. He announced a new undertaking—the TurkStream project from Russia to Turkey, supposedly connecting through Greece to Italy and bypassing Bulgaria. This plan was later changed to a route running through Bulgaria, Serbia, and Hungary to Austria.

Bulgaria's president, Rosen Plevneliev (January 2012–January 2017), was particularly critical of Russia's annexation of Crimea, its actions in eastern Ukraine, and the "hybrid war" launched on Bulgaria and the Balkans.[20] He spoke openly about the security challenges to Bulgaria stemming from Russia's assertive behavior in the region. As a result, he was often criticized by Russian politicians and subjected to numerous media attacks.[21] The GERB leadership was concerned that his candidacy for a second mandate might not receive enough public support because of the fierce opposition of pro-Russian circles in the country. Former GERB prime minister Boyko Borisov was also courting various Russophile organizations and nationalist formations, associations of former military officers (some armed and functioning as a militia), the Bulgarian Orthodox Church, the sizable Russian energy lobby, and politicians with business links to Moscow. In 2016, President Plevneliev announced that he would not run for reelection. GERB nominated the speaker of the parliament, Tsetska Tsacheva, but she lost to the candidate of the Socialist Party, Rumen Radev, former air force commander, in the second round of elections on November 13, 2016. Radev has expressed aspirations to develop closer relations with Moscow and opposed EU sanctions against Russia for the annexation of Crimea and the proxy war in Donbas.[22] Once in office, he lobbied Brussels for the removal of those sanctions.[23]

During the presidential election campaign, Borisov indicated that he would resign if his party's candidate did not win. Tensions were already threatening coalition unity as one of the main parties in the RB—Democrats for a Strong Bulgaria—split from RB and left the government in early 2016. Subsequently, ABV also departed from the ruling coalition, as its leader was preparing to run in the upcoming presidential election in November.[24] Eventually, Borisov resigned and another parliamentary election was scheduled that would bring the seventh government to power since the beginning of 2013.

Photo 15.2. Rumen Radev was elected president of Bulgaria in 2016. (Belish, Shutterstock)

The election held on March 26, 2017, produced a result that signaled further governmental and parliamentary instability. GERB reaffirmed its dominant position by gaining 95 out of 240 seats, and its leader, Boyko Borisov, formed a third cabinet since 2009. The opposition BSP recovered its support after a catastrophic electoral performance in 2014. For the first time, Bulgarian nationalists surpassed the Turkish party, and also for the first time they were included in the governing coalition. None of the traditional center-right parties made it to parliament, as they remained divided and ran separately. The center-right, which had played a major role in the 1990s, had fragmented to the point of becoming irrelevant to voters. A new populist formation, Volya, gained twelve seats (4 percent) in the National Assembly. Borisov formed a coalition with the three nationalist parties comprising the UP and the external support of Volya. The UP is a loose coalition of three nationalist parties: Ataka, VMRO-Bulgarian National Movement (a party denying the existence of Macedonian identity), and the National Front for the Salvation of Bulgaria (NFSB). They express anti-Turkish, anti-Roma, pro-Russian, Euroskeptic, and anti-NATO views and hold an anti-immigration stance. At the same time, they demand increased social spending. As a junior partner in the governing coalition, UP received four ministerial portfolios. A prominent representative of the nationalist coalition, Krasimir Karakachanov, leader of the Internal Macedonian Revolutionary Organization–Bulgarian National Movement (IMRO-BNM), was appointed as defense minister.[25] Later, he was the main driver behind Bulgaria's decision to veto the start of North Macedonia's EU accession negotiations because of disagreements between the two countries over history and Macedonian identity and language.[26]

In 2019, the ruling party, GERB, reaffirmed its hold on power in elections to the European Parliament in May and in the local elections in October, but signs of voter frustration resulted in the loss of several mayoral positions to the BSP.

GERB suffered internal divisions after Borisov's closest ally, Tzvetan Tzvetanov, head of GERB's parliamentary group, resigned amid corruption scandals. The justice minister, Tsetska Tsacheva, and the head of the country's anticorruption body, Plamen Georgiev, also resigned. Tzvetanov subsequently established a new political party, Republicans for Bulgaria, which attempted to recruit support from GERB's regional base and plans to compete with the ruling party in the next elections.[27] There were splits in the governing coalition as well when UP expelled Ataka's Volen Siderov, but this did not affect support for GERB in parliament.

BSP also faced internal confrontation between party leader Kornelya Ninova and the leader of the Party of European Socialists (PES), Sergei Stanishev, former prime minister and BSP leader. Tensions within the BSP escalated in the summer of 2020 when the party's leadership and the president ignited an antigovernment protest. The traditional center-right tried to reestablish itself in the political space by forming a new coalition called "Democratic Bulgaria," which uncharacteristically united environmental activists and conservatives.

Three factors determined the political dynamics in the country since Borisov formed his third government in 2017: first, the cabinet struggled to achieve consensus on policy matters between coalition partners with divergent political platforms; second, confrontation between GERB and BSP increased, especially after BSP gained control of the presidency; and third, Russian influence and disinformation operations reached a higher level of interference. President Radev's clearly pro-Russia policy emboldened Russian intelligence and political subversion operations in Bulgaria. Russian espionage operations penetrated the defense ministry's military intelligence department with the purpose of collecting classified information on NATO and the EU, presenting the biggest Russian espionage case in the country since the end of the Cold War.[28] In addition, the government's attempts to comply with the EU's demand that it address corruption sparked a chain of events—corrupt business and political actors tried to discredit the government while political opponents were critical of Borisov for not doing enough to deal with some of Bulgaria's most notorious opaque businesses.

However, corruption became the main driving force of the widespread protests in the summer of 2020 that demanded the resignation of the government and the prosecutor general. The protests resulted from the deepening conflict between President Rumen Radev and Prime Minister Boyko Borisov. An anticorruption action by the center-right Democratic Bulgaria exposed the unlawful blocking of a Black Sea public beach by MRF founder Ahmed Dogan and his guards. It also turned out that Dogan's security detail was paid by taxpayers. Over the last two decades, Dogan has accumulated immense personal wealth and real estate while serving as a public official. Analysts believe that he became the main conduit of Russian economic interests in the country, including cooperating with Gazprom to promote its interests in Bulgaria and secure natural gas for his thermo-power plant in Varna. Although the government initiated legal proceedings against other corrupt businessmen, Dogan and his protégé Delyan Peevski have always been out of reach, as fears of Russian retaliation have haunted Borisov since he was forced to resign in 2013.

The president leveled criticism at Borisov's cabinet, stating that the National Protection Service (NSO) should stop guarding individuals like Dogan who no longer hold public office. However, the NSO is a specialized military state service for the president of Bulgaria and is under his control. The same day, heavily armed law enforcement officers arrested two members of the presidential administration for providing classified information to private businesses. Radev, supported by BSP leaders, immediately demanded the resignation of the government and the prosecutor general. This put two rivals, the center-right Democratic Bulgaria and BSP, on the same side protesting against the government. They were soon joined by various organized and spontaneous groups, former GERB and UDF members, and youth activists to demand an end to corruption.

While the Bulgarian people are frustrated with corrupt politicians and businesspeople, the initiators of the protest had different interests. President Radev and his supporters were banking on establishing an interim government that would have a major impact on critical national security decisions, such as the purchase of military equipment, participation in NATO's Black Sea protection plans, voting on new EU sanctions against Russia for the poisoning of Kremlin critic Alexei Navalny, and compliance with EU regulations regarding the TurkStream 2 pipeline through Bulgaria. It became evident that domestic politics, including the antigovernment protests, were directly related to attempts by the BSP to change Bulgaria's geopolitical orientation.

Pro- and anti-Russian attitudes have defined political discourse and policy making for several years. Deep divisions have accompanied the purchase of F-16 fighter aircraft, support for Ukraine against Russia's invasion, and commemoration of historic events such as the seventy-fifth anniversary of the communist coup, promoted as "liberation from fascism" by the Russian embassy in Sofia. Furthermore, the large number of Russian sympathizers in the country, which resulted in the establishment of three Russophile parties during the 2020 antigovernment protests, illustrated the public's lack of consensus on Bulgaria's geostrategic orientations. BSP political leaders have called for Bulgaria to leave the EU.

Borisov and GERB have maintained a consistent Euro-Atlantic position since 2009 when the party first came to power. Borisov reaffirmed his country's Western orientation during his meeting with President Donald Trump in Washington in November 2019. However, his support for Russian energy projects, such as TurkStream and the prospective second Bulgarian nuclear power plant in Belene, demonstrated that he could not ignore Moscow's pressure on Sofia.

Economic Transition

By the end of the 1990s, Bulgaria had made steady progress in stabilizing its economy under the center-right government of UDF elected in 1997. UDF came to power after a devastating financial collapse in 1996, caused to a large extent by the previous governments' gradual approach to privatization that focused on restructuring unprofitable companies before selling them. The UDF administration focused instead on privatizing major state-owned enterprises and proved successful in steadying the banking sector and reforming social security, health care, and the pension system. Major economic reforms were implemented largely under the auspices of the IMF. These included price liberalization, reduction of tariffs, a balanced state budget, liquidation of unprofitable companies, privatization, removal of state subsidies, a simple taxation system, and deregulation of the energy and telecommunications sectors.

At the macroeconomic level, the UDF government introduced an effective currency board system to control state spending. This currency board was still in place as of 2020 and will end when Bulgaria joins the eurozone, potentially in 2023.

When the NMS government came to power in 2001, it maintained its commitment to privatization, economic growth, and attracting foreign investment. The country registered a steady GDP growth rate of about 5 percent on average. Agriculture steadily declined in terms of overall economic growth, from just under 17 percent of GDP in 1999 to 9.3 percent in 2005. The service sector contributed some 58 percent of GDP and industry about 29 percent. Fruits, livestock, tobacco, vegetables, and wine continued to be among Bulgaria's chief exports, while imports mainly included machinery, equipment, technology, mineral fuels, and processed goods. Bulgaria's national debt continued to climb and stood at $13.7 billion in 2003 and $17.5 billion at the close of 2005, an indication that the economy continued to be at least partially reliant on borrowing from overseas sources. Nevertheless, the government was able to meet its debt repayment requirements on schedule.

During the 1990s, Bulgaria diversified its trade and became less reliant on the former Soviet bloc. Trade with the EU increased steadily, especially with Italy, Germany, and Greece. As Bulgaria wanted to join the EU, it increasingly geared its economy toward compatibility with the European market and sought investments from Western countries.

The rate of foreign direct investment (FDI) steadily increased under the governing of center-right governments after 1997 as Western businesses felt more confident in Bulgaria's institutional, fiscal, and social stability. Anticorruption measures were implemented, although Western businesses and the EU pressured Sofia to pursue more comprehensive judicial and administrative reform to increase investor confidence. According to data from the Bulgarian National Bank (BNB), between 2000 and 2003, Bulgaria attracted around $3 billion in direct business investment from abroad, which was about half of the total investment attracted for the previous eleven years. In 2003 alone, foreign investment was estimated to be $1.32 billion, or 7 percent of the country's GDP. FDI inflows in 2005 reached $3 billion and continued to climb until the global economic downturn in 2008.

Most of the measures adopted by the NMS government after it came to power in 2001 were aimed at supporting specific business sectors. These measures involved the introduction of tax preferences and concessions in public procurement, as well as increased subsidies for agriculture, tobacco growing, and certain state-owned enterprises. At the same time, in order to maintain fiscal discipline, public spending in 2002 was reduced to 39 percent of GDP, compared to 44 percent in 2000. The percentage rose after 2007 as Bulgaria began to make its first contributions to the EU budget.[29]

The privatization process accelerated starting in 2003, when just over half of state-owned assets were privatized. It included a number of large enterprises, including the Bulgarian Telecommunications Company, the tobacco-industrial complex Bulgartabac, seven electric-power distribution companies, and thirty-six hydroelectric power plants.

The privatization program was implemented in three ways: capital market offerings, centralized public auctions, and cash privatization. Among the bigger enterprises offered for sale were the Pleven oil and gas prospecting company, the Energoremont companies for power facility repairs, and the Maritsa 3 thermal power plant in Dimitrovgrad.

The restitution of land and other assets to property owners or their relatives dispossessed by communist nationalization and collectivization proved complicated. Many of the private holdings acquired by farmers after 1990 were small and required owners to band together in some form of cooperative in order to afford mechanized equipment or irrigation. The government issued compensation notes and vouchers to owners who, for a variety of reasons, could not recover their property.

Although the Bulgarian economy continued to grow until 2008, income distribution remained a serious problem. Several parts of the population had not felt any improvement in their living standards, including those who live in rural communities, ethnic minorities, and unemployed citizens. Large sectors of the population continued to experience low standards of living, long-term unemployment, and low salaries, while the extent of foreign investment has been limited compared to that in other postcommunist states such as Poland and Hungary.[30] The unemployment rate remained high throughout the transition. It stood at 16.3 percent of the total workforce by the end of the 1990s and climbed to 17.6 percent in 2002 before falling to 10 percent in 2005 and rising again during the economic recession in 2008 and 2009. The reasons were common for most postcommunist states: the closure of old loss-making enterprises, an unstable business environment in a fragile market economy, and slow development of new businesses, most of which are small or medium sized. In 2009, the booming construction market in Bulgaria collapsed, seriously impacting unemployment rates. The labor market was also relatively rigid; bureaucratic restraints made hiring and firing very costly. In addition, privatization, enterprise restructuring, and military downsizing left many people jobless.

Faced with the challenge of high unemployment, the government implemented various reforms aimed at removing some bureaucratic restraints, encouraging labor market flexibility, and funding a variety of retraining programs for job seekers. These reforms proved relatively successful and, coupled with significant infrastructure spending after Bulgaria joined the EU, notably decreased jobless rates. Unemployment fluctuated between 9 and 13.3 percent in the period from 2010 to 2014 but started to steadily decline in 2015, reaching 7.6 percent in April 2017.

Labor migration, mostly to the EU after accession in 2007, has played a role in reducing unemployment in times of economic hardship, but its detrimental effect on Bulgaria's economy has been much greater, as it has led to shortages of skilled workers and highly educated professionals.[31] For example, the shortages of health-care professionals during the COVID-19 pandemic were catastrophic for many hospitals and patients.[32]

Bulgaria's unemployment rate jumped by almost 3 percent at the onset of the COVID-19 pandemic in early 2020, from 6.2 in February to 9 percent in May. It declined to under 7 percent in October.[33] With the second wave of the pandemic in the fall, coronavirus cases increased sevenfold within two months, from 21,587 cases on October 5 to 155,193 cases on December 4, 2020. Deaths have spiked from 814 in the beginning of October to 4,503 two months later, or 645 deaths per million population. By March 2021, due to consistent public downplaying and politicization of the pandemic, Bulgaria had one of the highest death rates in the world at 2,032 per million population.[34]

According to a report by the National Statistical Institute (NSI) released in June 2004, the total average personal income in April 2004 reached 157 *leva* ($96.86) per month, while the average income per household per month totaled 406.47 *leva* ($250.60). Average personal income increased steadily during the 2000s and kept pace with the inflation rate until the global recession began to impact the Bulgarian economy at the end of the decade. In 2017, the average monthly salary in Bulgaria reached 1,009 *leva* ($589), with the highest salaries of 1,956 *leva* ($1,162) in the IT sector. Income for people living in regions away from the three biggest cities was about $348.89. Despite the average income increase, the poverty level has also increased, with 22 percent living below the poverty line in 2018 compared to 18.4 percent in 2005.[35]

Between 2017 and 2020, average income increased by 34 percent, reaching 1,355 *leva* ($816) per month.[36] Pensions remained very low, however, with the average pension in 2019 at 386 *leva* ($232) a month.[37] Many older retirees have been left to survive on about 200 *leva* ($117) a month. Bulgaria has 2.2 million pensioners, almost a third of its population. Many of them feel victimized by the economic transition and express nostalgia for the social protections under communism. Retirees in Bulgaria play a critical role in elections and often support the BSP and nationalist parties.

The IMF registered an 11.7 percent fall in Bulgaria's GDP in 2009, bringing it to -5.5 percent. GDP growth returned to barely positive levels in 2010 (0.4 percent) and remained insignificant in 2011 (1.6 percent) and 2012 (0.2 percent). However, economists and EU governments applauded the fiscal restraint shown by the government of Prime Minister Borisov, elected in 2009 on a promise to combat corruption, a problem that led the EU to freeze $1.56 billion (€1.34 billion) in aid to Bulgaria in 2008. Under his administration, Bulgaria's economy avoided emergency financing and the double-digit economic contractions seen in Latvia, Lithuania, and Estonia.

After 2012, the economy started slowly growing again by 1.3 percent in 2013, 2.4 percent in 2014, and 4.0 percent in 2016.[38] Economic growth slightly exceeded the European Commission's prediction for the next three years, with real GDP reaching 3.5 percent in 2017 and marginally declining to 3.1 percent in 2018. Bulgaria fared well, with modest GDP growth of over 3.5 percent in 2019 and a budget deficit below the EU's 3 percent limit. The country's credit rating remained positive for most of 2019 and until February 2020, but dropped to stable with the spread of the coronavirus.[39]

The COVID-19 pandemic undercut expectations for continuing economic growth. GDP contracted at a record-breaking pace in the second quarter of 2020 as the economy was severely impacted by the health crisis. The downturn was largely driven by plunging fixed investment amid depressed business confidence. At the same time, falling exports reflected weak European demand and disrupted global supply chains. The third quarter showed improved confidence in the services and retail trade sectors. Bulgaria sought a €511 million loan under the EU's SURE scheme to help cover the costs of unemployment spending. The IMF projected that Bulgaria's GDP growth would drop to -4 percent.[40] GDP declined 5.2 percent year-on-year in the third quarter, a softer drop than the second quarter's 8.6 percent slump, as some containment measures were lifted in the summer. But new restrictions due to COVID-19's rapid spread in the fall led to further economic contraction. Nevertheless, economists expect the economy to rebound in 2021 from its coronavirus-induced contraction.[41]

Civil Society

A host of independent groups appeared in the early 1990s, ranging from environmental movements to consumer organizations and public policy institutes.[42] A new nongovernmental organization (NGO) law adopted in 2000 introduced the concept of public benefit organizations. This legislation created special financial and tax incentives for NGOs because they were seen as complementary to the state in dealing with important social issues. Parliament also formed the Civil Society Committee, a special standing committee to promote the development of civil society. It provides NGOs with an opportunity to publicly present their issues. However, because of the diversity of civil society, not all of its members' important issues are presented at this forum. To increase its legitimacy, the Civil Society Committee has created its own consultative body, the Public Council, with NGO representatives from different fields of expertise and diverse geographic regions to promote its agenda more effectively in parliament.

In some areas, the NGO-government partnership has developed fruitfully, especially in terms of providing social services at the local level. Often, municipalities contract with NGOs to be independent providers of social services. NGOs are allowed to perform a few health activities in the areas of mental health and health education.

In September 2013, after a summer of massive public protests, President Rosen Plevneliev established a Civil Society Forum. He stated at the opening of the forum, "Civil society came on stage, attracted the spotlight, and now sets the agenda of the institutions." It had, as he noted, drawn attention to issues such as corruption, the mafia, monopolies, oligarchs, an inefficient judicial system, and an unfair state. While the young people who joined the Protest Network in the summer of 2013 boosted the political role of civil society in Bulgaria, NGOs now have fewer sources of funding than they did in the 1990s. Despite the marked activation of citizen's groups, especially in promoting judicial reform and rejecting corruption, Bulgaria's ranking on civil society by Freedom House has been slightly downgraded, citing vigilante group attacks on refugees in 2016 and the endorsement they received from some politicians and media outlets.[43]

Civil society organizations have continued to participate in various protests, although they have been subject to verbal attacks by politicians. In 2019, protests were organized by doctors' and nurses' organizations, police associations, transportation workers, mothers of children with disabilities, and others advocating for social policy changes, better pay, and equal rights.[44] In 2020, civil society organizations joined antigovernment protests, while others protested against the president for stirring conflict between government institutions.

However, not all civil society organizations are working for charitable causes and democratic progress. Nationalist groups, for example, have tried to limit funding for NGOs working on justice reform.[45] In 2019, they openly attacked the Bulgarian Helsinki Committee for advocating for due process in the case of an Australian citizen convicted of murder.

Photo 15.3. Antigovernment protests took place in Sofia in the summer of 2020. This protestor's sign reads, "I am here to bring you down! #Resignation." A target of the protest was the prosecutor general of the country, who is blamed for not dealing with corruption. (Ju1978, Shutterstock)

In 2020, a number of groups taking part in antigovernment protests openly promoted the political interests of the Socialist Party and the president. A former BSP member of three parliamentary assemblies, Maya Manolova, used her civic platform "Stand Up Bulgaria" to call for the resignation of the government. The pro-Russian Vazrazhdane (Revival) party joined these calls, also advocating for the convening of "fair elections" and a "change of the political system." The party is highly critical of the EU and NATO and never criticizes Russia.[46]

Russian intelligence has penetrated and finances some civil society organizations in Bulgaria with the purpose of enlisting them as advocates for better relations with Russia and the Eurasian Economic Union, closer relations with the Russian Orthodox Church, and support for Russian energy projects. They also serve as opponents of new sanctions against Moscow for the war in Ukraine and as critics of NATO and the EU. Among them are environmental groups, sports associations, church groups, and friendship societies. A Russophile group in Bulgaria, which the government accused of spying for Moscow in 2019, announced the establishment of a Russophile party in the midst of the antigovernment protests.[47]

Key Social Issues

Among the key social problems of Bulgaria are steady poverty levels impacting one-fifth of the population; low wages of working-class people; demographic decline due to low birthrates, high death rates, and emigration; a struggling health-care system with shortages of doctors and nurses; a high share of the retired population with very low pensions; and insufficient state funds to assist socially vulnerable populations.

In an attempt to bridge the poverty gap, the government undertook a series of initiatives and social welfare programs. It increased subsidies for agriculture, tobacco growing, and state-owned enterprises. The ratio of subsidies as a portion of GDP increased from 2.1 percent in 1998 to 2.4 percent in 2002; social and welfare spending increased from 11 percent of GDP in 1998 to 14.6 percent in 2002.[48] However, under IMF requirements, Bulgaria simultaneously needed to balance the state budget. Doing so was difficult without increasing the tax burden on besieged small and medium enterprises, which make up the majority of the economy. Instead of increasing such taxes, the authorities have tried to broaden the tax base and make tax collection more effective. Although the government faced difficulties in meeting the IMF's budgetary targets in some years, in 2003 it registered a budgetary surplus, which remained in place until 2009, when a budgetary deficit of -0.9 percent was registered.[49]

An ongoing problem for Bulgaria, as for several other Central and East European countries, is a steady decline in the population, especially as many of the most economically productive, skilled, and educated younger generation have emigrated to find more lucrative employment in Western Europe and the United States. Officials estimate that approximately fifty thousand citizens have emigrated annually since 1995; according to official data, some 850,000 people have left Bulgaria since the early 1990s. Out of a population of almost 9 million in 1989, the total declined to 6.9 million by 2020, when the annual growth rate stood at -0.7 percent. Birthrates have remained around nine births per thousand population, lower than the average in Eastern Europe, while death rates at sixteen per thousand are the highest in the world, according to the Population Reference Bureau.[50]

About 85 percent of Bulgaria's population of approximately 6.9 million is Bulgarian. The country's three largest minorities are the Turks, at about 9 percent of the population; the Roma, estimated at around 4 percent; and the Pomaks, or Slavic Muslims, who make up less than 1 percent of the population. Under the communist regime, during the 1980s, there was a policy of forced assimilation directed primarily at the ethnic Turkish minority, which led to a mass exodus to neighboring Turkey. Since the collapse of communism, Bulgaria has not experienced any significant ethnic conflicts. After Todor Zhivkov's ouster, Bulgarian officials made strenuous efforts to improve the country's minority policies and repair the damage suffered by ethnic Turks during the repressive government campaigns of the 1980s. During Zhivkov's assimilation campaign, for instance, Turks had to "Bulgarize" by adopting Slavic names—typically a Slavic suffix was added to a Muslim name, and after 1984, the Turks were forced to choose an entirely new name from a list of acceptable Bulgarian names—and giving up many of their national customs. Over three hundred thousand Turks fled the country, fearing even more severe repression. Their properties were confiscated by the state or sold at low prices to Bulgarians. About half this number of Turks returned to Bulgaria after the democratic changes, but many faced problems in reclaiming their houses and other possessions. In the following decade, many emigrated to Turkey for economic reasons. But when Bulgaria joined the EU in 2007, the country became attractive for younger generations of Bulgarian Turks living in Turkey to return, start businesses, and take advantage of the expanded trade opportunities with Europe.

During the summer of 1989, at the height of the Turkish exodus from Bulgaria to Turkey, the bulk of the Pomak (Slavic Muslim) population opposed efforts at forcible integration, and some sought to emigrate. The Pomaks, ethnic Bulgarians who had converted to Islam during the Ottoman occupation, are a small group estimated to be anywhere between seventy thousand and four hundred thousand people. Most of them do not self-identify as Bulgarian Muslims or Pomaks. The authorities were reluctant to allow them to leave the country and denied passports to people residing in predominantly Pomak regions. These policies resulted in several substantial Pomak protests. Pomak regions suffered steep economic decline with the closure of local industries. Observers feared that economic problems would intensify political tensions. Bulgarian officials warned that unemployment and economic deprivations in regions with ethnically and religiously mixed groups were alarmingly high, and minorities complained about increasing discrimination in employment. After 1989, many Pomaks adopted a Turkish identity or demanded Turkish-language education, viewing it as advantageous to associate with a more influential minority.

The ethnic repression of its communist regime was one of the first parts of its past that Bulgaria jettisoned. In December 1989, the BSP (then still named the BCP) renounced forcible assimilation, allowing Muslims the freedom to choose their own names, practice Islam, observe traditional customs, and speak their native language. In January 1990, the National Assembly recommended the adoption of a special statute for minority rights. With Sofia's policy reversal, thousands of ethnic Turks returned to Bulgaria and faced new problems of adjustment. Most had lost their jobs and sold their houses for less than their true value. On their return, they demanded appropriate reparations. Ahmed Dogan, the political leader of Bulgaria's Turks, demanded a legal resolution that would restore property to victims of the exodus. Turkish deputies in parliament eventually introduced a law that was adopted in July 1992. It stipulated that all Turks were to be given back their property by April 1993 for the low price at which it had been sold. Those who were unable to buy back their former homes would be given low-interest loans toward the purchase of alternative housing.[51]

In March 1990, the country's major political forces agreed to pass a Bulgarian Citizens' Names Law that allowed all victims of forcible assimilation to return to their old names. New birth certificates were issued, and the process of changing names was simplified from a judicial process to a simple administrative measure. The process was complicated and costly only for those Muslims who did not act before December 31, 1990.[52]

The issue of minority rights, particularly language use, education, and access to the mass media, generated some controversy. According to the 1991 constitution, Bulgarian was to be the sole official language. Under the Zhivkov regime, ethnic Turks were forbidden to use their mother tongue officially. The legacy of language discrimination persisted in a variety of forms. For example, parliament was reluctant to implement Turkish-language programs in secondary schools for fear of ultranationalist reactions.[53] The problem was solved in 1991 with the adoption of the new Bulgarian constitution, which guaranteed ethnic minorities the right to study and use their language. The Bulgarian parliament promised to implement a state-controlled Turkish program in all public schools with a significant minority enrollment. Bulgaria's nationalist opposition claimed that these programs were unconstitutional, so parliament issued assurances that they would not jeopardize the "unity of the Bulgarian nation."[54]

The Bulgarian constitution adopted in 1991 prohibits the creation of political parties based on "ethnic, racial, or religious lines" and organizations that "seek the violent usurpation of power."[55] Although intended to protect the state, these stipulations were frequently cited in efforts by nationalists to undermine the rights of minorities. Nationalist organizations capitalized on Bulgarian fears of alleged Turkish subversion and applied pressure on government organs to outlaw ethnic-based associations on the grounds that they were politically motivated and therefore "antistate."

Even with the regime's repudiation of the old communist-era ways, the Turks have had a hard time advocating for themselves. The main Turkish organization, the MRF, was singled out for attention. In August 1991, the Sofia City Court decided that a political party formed by the MRF was unconstitutional because it was ethnically based. As a result, it could not participate in any elections. The MRF, in turn, claimed that it was not an entirely ethnic party and harbored no separatist ambitions. In September 1991, the Supreme Court barred the Rights and Freedoms Party (the political wing of the MRF) from participation in general elections on the grounds that it propounded an exclusivist ethnic and religious platform.[56] Nonetheless, the MRF and various Turkish cultural and social organizations were not prohibited from functioning, and the MRF legally competed in the second general elections in October 1991. It gained twenty-four parliamentary seats, with 7.55 percent of the popular vote, making it the third-strongest party in Bulgaria and a coalition partner for the UDF. On April 21, 1992, the Constitutional Court rejected a petition by ninety-three MPs, mostly associated with BSP, to declare the MRF unconstitutional, opening the way for modern politics in Bulgaria.[57] For almost two decades, the MRF would play the role of a "balancer of power" in virtually all Bulgarian parliaments and governments, until 2009 when Bulgarian nationalist movements started assuming that role. By that time, corruption scandals and controversial appointments had discredited the party, but it still retained a measure of voter support and a parliamentary presence.

In some respects, Macedonian groups have been more persecuted than either Turks or Pomaks. The Bulgarian government, together with most Bulgarian political parties, has refused to accept Macedonians as a legitimate minority. Instead, they have defined them as Slavic Bulgarians with the same language and history as the rest of the country. They persist in this policy even though the Council of Europe and some human rights groups have criticized Sofia for its alleged political discrimination against the Macedonian minority.[58] For instance, according to Bulgarian leaders, a Macedonian minority did not exist in the Pirin region in western Bulgaria despite the activities of local radicals who wanted some form of regional autonomy or even unification with the independent state of Macedonia. An openly Macedonian organization, called "Ilinden" after the 1903 uprising against the Ottoman Empire, was established in the Pirin area and applied for official registration, only to be turned down in July 1990 by a district court.

Protests by Ilinden supporters were suppressed, and Bulgaria's Supreme Court ruled that Ilinden violated the unity of the Bulgarian nation. Ilinden's statutes promoted the recognition of a sovereign Macedonian minority, a fact that evidently served as evidence that the organization intended to achieve "a united Macedonian state." Ilinden was ordered to disband but persisted in a covert fashion, claiming that the decisions of the Bulgarian courts were in violation of international law.[59] In November 1998, the local court in Blagoevgrad reversed its earlier decision and allowed the registration of a Macedonian organization, OMO "Ilinden"–Pirin, with its headquarters in Blagoevgrad.[60]

Nationalist pro-Macedonian groupings were active in Bulgaria in the 1990s and called for closer social, economic, and political links with Macedonia that they hoped would culminate in eventual reabsorption of this former Yugoslav republic by Bulgaria. At the same time, some autonomist Macedonian organizations became active in western Bulgaria, amid suspicions that they were funded by Belgrade and by some militant groups in the Republic of Macedonia to sow discord within Bulgaria and press for the separation of the Pirin region from the Bulgarian state.

Although Bulgaria addressed its most pervasive ethnic problems during the 1990s and early 2000s, the treatment and status of the large Roma minority remains a problem. Bulgarian officials claim their policies have been guided by the Human Rights Charter and the Bulgarian constitution. Clearly they were in part a response to the tragic treatment of the Turkish population at the end of the communist period. Just as clearly, outside pressures and aid by international human rights organizations and the European institutions Bulgaria wished to join have influenced the Bulgarian government to develop legislation that balances concerns over national security and state integrity with respect for minority rights and ethnic aspirations.

The social and economic position of the large Roma minority and the persistent prejudice and discrimination against it remain major problems. The Roma themselves are split on what they want and need. Unlike Turks in Bulgaria, whose leaders perceived the gravest threat as coming from forcible assimilation, Romani leaders have been particularly opposed to the segregation and marginalization of the Roma population. Many representatives of the Roma have opposed separate schooling for Roma children because it results in inferior education, insufficient exposure to the Bulgarian language, and stymied career advancement. On the other side, some Roma leaders are pressing for a revival of Romani culture, education, and ethnic identity, fearing gradual assimilation by either the Bulgarian or Turkish communities. In addition, the law on political parties, which prohibited the registration of organizations established according to ethnic or religious criteria, worked to the detriment of Romani self-organization. After all, even though the Roma clearly do not represent a threat to Bulgaria's "territorial integrity" and the "unity of the nation" or "incite national, ethnic, and religious hostilities," they are barred from forming electoral associations.[61]

A few populist and nationalist groupings have been formed to advocate for "Bulgarian" national interests. Shortly after it was established, Ataka managed to win twenty-one seats in the June 2005 parliamentary elections and tried to mobilize anti-Roma sentiment in Bulgarian society. The party gained twenty-three seats during the 2013 parliamentary elections and supported the Socialist-led coalition with the MRF, although it did not formally join the government. Its program has been opposed by the majority of parliamentary deputies, but as the "kingmaker" in the government coalition, it had a significant impact on official policy.

For two decades after the fall of communism, the Bulgarian nationalist formations were not significant political players—including the Nationwide Committee for the Defense of National Interests and various parties working together as the Internal Macedonian Revolutionary Organization (IMRO). IMRO has campaigned for Bulgarian "national interests" on issues such as the rights of Bulgarian minorities abroad. It has attracted some support in a few regions and posts in local government but rarely won seats in parliament. IMRO and Gergyovden stood together for parliament in 2001, narrowly missing the 4 percent threshold. However, that changed with the start of the European migrant crisis in 2014, when the influx of refugees from the Middle East was met with xenophobia that gave impetus to Bulgarian nationalism. As a result, Bulgarian nationalist organizations became part of the government for the first time. While Bulgaria avoided serious interethnic clashes in the early 1990s by including the Turkish party, the MRF, in mainstream politics, the country faced the prospect of rising nationalist sentiment and populist attitudes as a result of identity politics.[62]

Emerging Challenges

It will take many years for Bulgaria to achieve the economic level of its West European partners, but EU membership also means access to the union's structural funds, which has helped to develop the country's economy. This turned out to be a critical factor at the time of the pandemic, which presented a grave danger to the poorest EU member states. The government will seek to rebuild the economy and raise GDP growth to the level of 2019. Attracting greater Western investment may be difficult for the next two years while the world is dealing with a global economic downturn. Many students and professionals returned from Western Europe during the pandemic, but their return was temporary. Reversing the outflow of the most educated segments of society will remain a key goal as the country recovers from the simultaneous health crisis and political crisis. Bulgaria also needs to address unfinished judicial reforms and the public's anticorruption demands before becoming attractive for educated Bulgarians making careers abroad.

Bulgaria's position is complicated by the fact that the EU itself has been undergoing major challenges deriving from the pandemic, Brexit, the rise of populist and nationalist parties, and Russian interference in elections, security structures, and internal politics. These problems are feeding into emerging Euroskepticism and anti-NATO sentiment in Bulgaria. Although Sofia maintains close relations with the United States and tries to meet its EU and NATO commitments, the rise of pro-Russian attitudes in the country presents a serious challenge to Bulgaria's Euro-Atlantic future. Increasing Russian intelligence operations, including involvement of Russian military intelligence (GRU) operatives in the assassination attempt of a Bulgarian arms dealer in 2015, Moscow's emboldened espionage operations, its economic penetration through energy projects and real estate holdings, and its support for local pro-Russian organizations and political parties signify greater interference in Bulgarian politics and undermine Sofia's position in the EU and NATO.

Relations with Russia became extremely divisive after Moscow's illegal annexation of Crimea and its attack on eastern Ukraine. Officially, Sofia endorsed the EU sanctions against Moscow, but Russian influence within society grew through penetration of the mass information space. Bulgarian society was torn between loyalty to the EU and NATO on the one hand and a historic affinity for Russia reinforced by dependence on Russian energy sources. As the government took a strong stand supporting the territorial integrity of Ukraine, some nationalist parties with close ties to Moscow called for a veto of the sanctions and recognition of the disputed March 2014 referendum in Crimea. The public debate about events in Ukraine has raised questions concerning the extent to which Bulgaria remains a reliable EU and NATO member.[63]

Bulgaria's relations with Russia adjust according to the ideology of the ruling party. Previous president Rosen Plevneliev (2011–2016), who came from the center-right GERB party, has stated on numerous occasions that Russia remains a threat to Bulgarian security. The report prepared for the NATO summit at Wales in September 2014 stated that Moscow's ambitions to restore Russia's influence along its flanks and establish itself as a pole of power presented a serious danger to Bulgaria and to NATO's security. Among the risks stemming from Russia's behavior were listed "the new hybrid war, combining conventional methods with insurgency, cyber and informational war, as well as actions in violation of international law." The report further stated that "Russian propaganda, spread especially through Bulgarian political and economic entities, media outlets, and non-governmental organizations represents an informational war that undermines the integrity of state institutions and sovereignty, and attacks directly the national democratic values, spirit and will."[64] Although this language was subsequently softened at the request of the interim prime minister at the time, Plevneliev spoke openly on this topic to Bulgarian and foreign audiences.

President Plevneliev's staunch opposition to Russia's "hybrid war" in Bulgaria has been replaced by a Russia-friendly attitude by the current president, Rumen Radev, elected in November 2016 on the ticket of the Socialist Party–led coalition. Radev has spoken in favor of lifting the EU sanctions against Russia for the annexation of Crimea.[65]

The elections on April 4, 2021, produced a fragmented parliament with six political parties and no clear majority able to form a coalition government. The ruling GERB gained only 26 percent of the vote, followed by the newly established populist "There Is Such a People" party of showman Slavi Trifonov, which received almost 18 percent.[66] A potential governing coalition led by Trifonov's party with the participation of the Socialist party could ensure more extensive Russian influence in Bulgaria's domestic affairs and foreign policy and could potentially accommodate Moscow's ambition to push Bulgaria to the fringes of Euro-Atlantic institutions. Counterweights to Russia's subversive offensive seem to have been diminished. The traditional center-right parties that laid the foundations for Euro-Atlantic integration in the 1990s have been absent from parliament since 2017. They gained less than 10 percent of the vote in April 2021.

Bulgaria is facing a significant challenge with its support for TurkStream, a natural gas pipeline under the Black Sea to western Turkey. Its second string is planned to pass from Turkey to Bulgaria and then through Serbia and Hungary to Austria. The pipeline is often called South Stream Lite, as much of its route duplicates that of the now defunct Russian-led South Stream natural gas project. Similarly to South Stream, TurkStream appears to be at odds with EU energy regulations and could also fall under US sanctions, as 90 percent of the gas will originate in Russia.[67]

In November 2020, Sofia vetoed the start of North Macedonia's EU accession talks, hoping to extract concessions from Skopje. The government of Boyko Borisov demanded that Skopje acknowledge the Bulgarian roots of the Macedonian language, guarantee it will not support the recognition of a Macedonian minority in Bulgaria, and declare that the use of the term "North Macedonia" refers only to the territory of the Republic of North Macedonia.[68]

The decision was surprising as Bulgaria was the first state in the world to recognize Macedonia as an independent state immediately after the republic split from Yugoslavia in early 1992. At the same time, the Bulgarian authorities have been unwilling to recognize the existence of a separate Macedonian nation and have refused to recognize the Macedonian ethnic minority within Bulgaria. Sofia and Skopje ended a period of political deadlock concerning Bulgaria's recognition of a separate Macedonian language with the signing of a joint declaration and a number of accords in 1999. In 2017, the two neighbors signed a friendship agreement in the midst of Skopje's negotiations with Athens on changing Macedonia's name to North Macedonia in exchange for Greece lifting its veto on the country's Euro-Atlantic integration. Sofia has been using a similar method to obtain concessions from North Macedonia focused on historic disputes. The policy was mainly driven by nationalists in the governing coalition, but it gained 80 percent public support and became a useful political tool for the embattled prime minister after months of antigovernment protests.[69] Bulgaria's blockage of EU accession talks for North Macedonia has played into Moscow's hands, as the Western Balkan countries that remain outside NATO and the EU have been more vulnerable to Russian economic and political influence. It remains unclear how this challenge will be resolved.

Study Questions

1. Why did communism collapse in Bulgaria?
2. What were the key stages of Bulgaria's transition to a democratic system?
3. How have minority rights protections, including their political representation, evolved since 1989? How has Bulgarian nationalism also changed over this time?
4. Why did the traditional center-right coalition lose its place in the Bulgarian political system?
5. How has corruption impacted the political process in Bulgaria?
6. How is Russia's influence undermining Bulgaria's position in NATO and the EU?

Suggested Readings

Anguelov, Zlatko. *Communism and the Remorse of an Innocent Victimizer*. College Station: Texas A&M University Press, 2002.

Bell, John D., ed. *Bulgaria in Transition: Politics, Economics, Society, and Culture after Communism*. Boulder, CO: Westview, 1998.

Crampton, R. J. *Bulgaria*. Oxford: Oxford University Press, 2009.

Crampton, R. J. *A Concise History of Bulgaria*. New York: Cambridge University Press, 2005.

Ganev, Venelin I. *Preying on the State: The Transformation of Bulgaria after 1989*. Ithaca, NY: Cornell University Press, 2007.

Groueff, Stephane. *Crown of Thorns: The Reign of King Boris III of Bulgaria, 1918–1943*. Lanham, MD: Madison Books, 1987.

Leviev-Sawyer, Clive. *Bulgaria: Politics and Protests in the 21st Century*. Sofia: Riva, 2015.
Neuburger, Mary. *The Orient Within: Muslim Minorities and the Negotiation of Nationhood in Modern Bulgaria*. Ithaca, NY: Cornell University Press, 2004.

Websites

Balkan Insight: https://balkaninsight.com
Bulgarian News Service, English Language: http://www.bta.bg/en
The World Bank—Bulgaria: https://www.worldbank.org/en/country/bulgaria

Notes

1. For a valuable account of postcommunist Bulgaria, see John D. Bell, "Democratization and Political Participation in 'Postcommunist' Bulgaria," in *Politics, Power, and the Struggle for Democracy in South-East Europe*, ed. Karen Dawisha and Bruce Parrott, 353–402 (Cambridge: Cambridge University Press, 1997).

2. Transparency International, *Corruption Perception Index 2019*, https://ec.europa.eu/regi onal_policy/en/newsroom/news/2020/01/27-01-2020-the-corruption-perception-index-2019-the -eu-is-the-best-performer-in-the-world.

3. For more information, see "European Commission's Report on Progress in Bulgaria under the Cooperation and Verification Mechanism," October 2019, https://ec.europa.eu/info/sites/info /files/progress-report-bulgaria-2019-com-2019-498_en.pdf.

4. Stefan Krause, "Socialists at the Helm," *Transition* 1, no. 4 (March 1995): 33–36.

5. Ivo Georgiev, "Indecisive Socialist Party Stumbles into Crisis," *Transition* 2, no. 26 (December 1996): 26–28.

6. Stefan Krause, "United Opposition Triumphs in Presidential Elections," *Transition* 2, no. 26 (December 1996): 20–23.

7. Anne-Mary Gulde, "The Role of the Currency Board in Bulgaria's Stabilization," *Finance and Development Magazine*, IMF, December 1999, http://www.imf.org/external/pubs/ft/fandd /1999/09/gulde.htm.

8. For an overview of the center-right, see Dilyana Tsenova, "SDS to Have Golden Moment in 40th Parliament," *24 Chasa* (April 2004).

9. Center for the Study of Democracy, *Corruption, Contraband, and Organized Crime in Southeast Europe* (Sofia: Center for the Study of Democracy, 2003); *Corruption Assessment Report, 2003* (Sofia: Coalition, 2000, 2004); *On the Eve of EU Accession: Anti-Corruption Reforms in Bulgaria* (Sofia: Center for the Study of Democracy, 2006); *Anti-Corruption Reforms in Bulgaria: Key Results and Risks* (Sofia: Center for the Study of Democracy, 2007).

10. Center for the Study of Democracy, *Crime without Punishment: Countering Corruption and Organized Crime in Bulgaria* (Sofia: Center for the Study of Democracy, 2009).

11. "Bulgarian Media Ownership Trends Worrying, German Ambassador Says," Sofia News Agency, October 2, 2013, http://www.novinite.com/articles/154145/Bulgarian+Media+Owne rship+Trends+Worrying,+Says+German+Ambassador; "A Few Media Magnates Create 'a State within the State,'" *Dnevnik Daily*, October 2, 2013, http://www.dnevnik.bg/analizi/2013/10/02 /2152421_niakolko_mediini_magnati_si_suzdavat_durjava_v_durjava.

12. For more information, see *Eurasia Daily Monitor* reporting on Bulgaria from 2011 to 2014 by Margarita Assenova, http://www.jamestown.org/programs/edm, or articles by the author on the Jamestown Foundation website, http://www.jamestown.org/articles-by-author/?no_cache=1&tx_c ablanttnewsstaffrelation_pi1%5Bauthor%5D=651.

13. "Who Is the New Chairman of the NSC Delyan Peevski?," *Capital Daily*, June 14, 2013, http://www.capital.bg/politika_i_ikonomika/bulgaria/2013/06/14/2081416_koi_e_noviiat_preds edatel_na_dans_delian_peevski; Margarita Assenova, "Is Organized Crime Taking over the Bulgarian State?," *Jamestown Foundation Blog*, June 14, 2013, http://jamestownfoundation.blo gspot.com/2013/06/is-organized-crime-taking-over.html.

14. "Alpha Research: The Delegitimization of the Institutions and a Sense of Instability in the Beginning of the Political Season," *Dnevnik Daily*, October 2, 2013, http://www.dnevnik.bg/ana lizi/2013/10/02/2152409_alfa_risurch_delegitimaciia_na_instituciite_i/?ref=substory.

15. "DPS: Delyan Peevski Is Most Suitable for MEP," Sofia News Agency, April 9, 2014, http: //www.novinite.com/articles/159652/DPS%3A+Delyan+Peevski+Is+Most+Suitable+For+MEP.

16. "Делян Пеевски Няма да е Евродепутат" [Delyan Peevski will not be a Euro deputy], *Capital*, May 26, 2014, http://www.capital.bg/politika_i_ikonomika/bulgaria/2014/05/26/23 08123_delian_peevski_niama_da_e_evrodeputat.

17. Frances Coppola, "Bulgaria's Failed Corpbank: The Former Owner's Story," *Forbes*, October 5, 2015, https://www.forbes.com/sites/francescoppola/2015/10/05/bulgarias-failed-cor pbank-the-former-owners-story/#6d60311b50d7.

18. Bulgarian Electoral Commission, http://results.cik.bg/pi2014/rezultati/index.html.

19. "Bulgarian MPs Approve New Cabinet, Ministers Sworn In," Sofia News Agency, November 7, 2014, http://www.novinite.com/articles/164611/Bulgarian+MPs+Approve+New +Cabinet%2C+Ministers+Sworn+In.

20. Ukraine Today TV, September 26, 2014, https://www.youtube.com/watch?v=rLTdt3vxjgc.

21. "Олигарсите и Зависимите Медии Разпространяват Руска Пропаганда в Цяла Европа" [The oligarchs and dependent media spread Russian propaganda in Europe] (interview with Rosen Plevneliev for BBC, *Terminal3*, November 5, 2016), http://terminal3.bg/oliga rsite-i-zavisimite-medii-razprostranqvat-ruska-propaganda-v-evropa; "Плевнелиев: Срещу Мен Воюваха Мрежи на ДС Руски Тролове и Политици от Петата Колона" [Plevneliev: Russian trolls and politicians from the fifth column fought against me], *Dnevnik*, January 20, 2017, http:// www.dnevnik.bg/bulgaria/2017/01/20/2903699_plevneliev_sreshtu_men_vojuvaha_mreji_na_ds _ruski.

22. "Russia Is Preying on Bulgaria's Next President," *Politico*, November 5, 2016, http://www .politico.eu/article/russia-is-preying-on-bulgarias-next-president-tsetska-tsacheva-rumen-radev.

23. "Sanctions 'Hurt' Russia and the EU, Says Bulgaria President Rumen Radev," *Euronews*, February 16, 2017, http://www.euronews.com/2017/02/16/sanctions-hurt-russia-and-the-eu-says -bulgaria-president-rumen-radev.

24. "Президентска Република но с Мен за Президент" [Presidential republic, but with me as president], *Capital*, May 16, 2016, http://www.capital.bg/politika_i_ikonomika/redakcionni_ komentari/2016/05/16/2760659_prezidentska_republika_no_s_men_za_prezident.

25. Nina Barzachka, "Analysis: Bulgaria's Government Will Include Far-Right Nationalist Parties for the First Time," *Washington Post*, April 25, 2017, https://www.washingtonpost.com/ news/monkey-cage/wp/2017/04/25/bulgarias-government-will-include-nationalist-parties-on-the -far-right-heres-why-and-what-this-means.

26. Valerie Hopkins and Michael Peel, "Bulgaria Moves to Bar North Macedonia from Joining EU," *Financial Times*, November 17, 2020, https://www.ft.com/content/68191f23-0230-4a71 -9c5e-437195b5d25a.

27. "Цветан Цветанов представи лицата на партията си" [Tsvetan Tsvetanov introduced the faces of his party], *Capital*, September 20, 2020, https://www.capital.bg/politika_i_ikonomika/bulgaria/2020/09/20/4116374_cvetan_cvetanov_predstavi_licata_na_partiiata_si.

28. Margarita Assenova, "Russian Espionage Scandal in Bulgaria," *Eurasia Daily Monitor* 18, no. 52 (March 31, 2021), https://jamestown.org/program/russian-espionage-scandal-in-bulgaria; Mark Kramer, "A Weak Link in NATO? Bulgaria, Russia, and the Lure of Espionage," Davis Center, Harvard University, April 1, 2021, https://daviscenter.fas.harvard.edu/insights/weak-link-nato-bulgaria-russia-and-lure-espionage.

29. For useful economic statistics, see "Economic Structure: Annual Indicators," Economist Intelligence Unit, Country Report Subscription, October 1, 2006.

30. For more details, see Institute for Regional and International Studies, *Country Report: Bulgaria, State of Democracy, Roadmap for Reforms, 2001* (Sofia: Institute for Regional and International Studies, 2002).

31. For more details, see Ivaylo Kalfin, ed., "The Impact of Labor Migration on the Bulgarian Economy," Friedrich Ebert Stiftung, November 2018, http://library.fes.de/pdf-files/bueros/sofia/15336-the_impact_of_labour_migration_on_the_bulgarian_economy.pdf.

32. Tsvetelia Tsolova and Stoyan Nenov, "Bulgarian Doctors Exhausted as COVID Deaths Hit Record," Reuters, November 30, 2020, https://www.reuters.com/article/us-health-coronavirus-bulgaria/bulgarian-doctors-exhausted-as-covid-deaths-hit-record-idUSKBN28A2J9.

33. "Bulgaria Unemployment Rate," Trading Economics, https://tradingeconomics.com/bulgaria/unemployment-rate.

34. Coronavirus Resource Center, Johns Hopkins University, https://coronavirus.jhu.edu/map.html.

35. World Bank, http://data.worldbank.org/country/bulgaria.

36. "Bulgaria Unemployment Rate."

37. "More than 2,130,000 Pensioners Will Receive an Increase of 5.7% on Their Pensions from Today," Sofia News Agency, July 1, 2019, https://www.novinite.com/articles/198217/More+than+2%2C130%2C000+Pensioners+Will+Receive+an+Increase+of+5.7+on+Their+Pensions+From+Today.

38. Bulgaria Economic Outlook, FocusEconomics, http://www.focus-economics.com/countries/bulgaria.

39. Fitch Ratings, https://www.fitchratings.com/entity/bulgaria-80442251.

40. IMF Office in Bulgaria, https://www.imf.org/en/Countries/BGR#countrydata.

41. Bulgaria Economic Outlook, FocusEconomics, http://www.focus-economics.com/countries/bulgaria.

42. For more details, see Luben Panov, "NGOs and the State in Bulgaria: Towards Greater Cooperation," *Social Economy and Law Journal* (Winter 2003–Spring 2004): 42–43.

43. "Nations in Transit 2017," Freedom House, https://freedomhouse.org/report/nations-transit/2017/bulgaria.

44. "Nations in Transit 2020," Freedom House, https://freedomhouse.org/country/bulgaria/nations-transit/2020; Ivaylo Atanasov, "Системата Ни Убива. Но Не Тази, За Която Си Мислите" [The system is killing us. But not the one you think), *Baricada*, June 26, 2018, https://baricada.org/2018/06/26/sistemata.

45. "Nations in Transit 2020."

46. Nikolai Lavchiev, "Оставка, Лустрация, Дистанционно Гласуване. Кой За Какво Се Бори, Докато Участва В Протестите" [Resignation, lustration, remote voting: Who fights for what in the protests], Radio Free Europe, July 22, 2020, https://www.svobodnaevropa.bg/a/30739550.html.

47. "Bulgaria Charges Head of Russophile Movement with Espionage for Russia," *Sofia Globe*, September 10, 2019, https://sofiaglobe.com/2019/09/10/bulgaria-charges-head-of-russop

hile-movement-with-espionage-for-russia; "Русофилите в България Ще Си Правят Партия" [Russophiles in Bulgaria will be founding a party], *Btvnovinite*, September 21, 2020, https://bt vnovinite.bg/bulgaria/rusofilite-v-balgarija-shte-si-pravjat-partija.html.

48. Krassen Stanchev, "Bulgarian Economic Policy Is Not Rightist," Institute for Market Economics, *Kapital Weekly*, July 19, 2003.

49. "Bulgaria Ends 2016 with Budget Surplus of 1.6 pct of GDP," Reuters, January 25, 2017, http://www.reuters.com/article/bulgaria-budget-idUSL5N1FF2LU.

50. Population Reference Bureau, https://www.prb.org/international/geography/bulgaria.

51. Stephen Ashley, "Migration from Bulgaria," Radio Free Europe/Radio Liberty (RFE/RL) Research Institute, *Report on Eastern Europe*, December 1, 1989; Stephen Ashley, "Ethnic Unrest during January," RFE/RL, *Report on Eastern Europe* 1, no. 6 (February 9, 1990); Kjell Engelbrekt, "The Movement for Rights and Freedoms," RFE/RL, *Report on Eastern Europe* 2, no. 22 (May 31, 1991).

52. For a discussion of cultural assimilation and the Name Change Law, see "Minority Problems Persist: Elections Set for June," in *News from Helsinki Watch*, "News from Bulgaria," March 1990. On the new law on names, see "Deep Tensions Continue in Turkish Provinces, despite Some Human Rights Improvements," in *News from Helsinki Watch*, "News from Bulgaria," August 1990.

53. Goran Ahren, "Helsinki Committee on Turkish Bulgarians: Continued Political Oppression," *Dagens Nyheter* (Stockholm), December 24, 1989, JPRS-EER-90-009, January 24, 1990.

54. Mitko Krumov, "New Deputies Yuriy Borisov and Vasil Kostov Replace Dobri Dzhurov and Georgi Velichkov Who Resigned," *Duma* (Sofia), January 10, 1991, FBIS-EEU-91-013, January 18, 1991. For a discussion of the major strikes in Kardzhali, see Bulgarian News Agency (BTA), February 26, 1991, FBIS-EEU-91-038, February 26, 1991.

55. Constitution of the Republic of Bulgaria, adopted July 12, 1991.

56. "Second Yilmaz Letter Is Unprecedented and Greatly Alarms Nationwide Committee of Defense of National Interests," *Duma* (Sofia), August 30, 1991, FBIS-EEU-91-172, September 5, 1991; and Kjell Engelbrekt, "The Movement for Rights and Freedoms to Compete in Elections," RFE/RL, *Report on Eastern Europe* 2, no. 91 (October 4, 1991).

57. Venelin I. Ganev, "History, Politics and the Constitution: Ethnic Conflict and Constitutional Adjudication in Postcommunist Bulgaria," *Slavic Review* 63, no. 1 (Spring 2004): 66–89.

58. See the January 2004 report on Bulgaria on the website of the Council of Europe's Committee against Racism and Intolerance, http://hudoc.ecri.coe.int/XMLEcri/ENGLISH/Cycle _03/03_CbC_eng/BGR-CbC-III-2004-2-ENG.pdf.

59. See Duncan M. Perry, "The Macedonian Question Revitalized," RFE/RL, *Report on Eastern Europe* 1, no. 24 (August 24, 1990); Evgeni Gavrilov, *Duma* (Sofia), November 14, 1990, FBIS-EEU-90-223, November 19, 1990; and Bulgarian News Agency (BTA), September 23, 1991, FBIS-EEU-91-185, September 24, 1991.

60. *State Gazette* (Sofia), February 23, 1999, and March 14, 1999; Bulgarian News Agency (BTA), November 3, 1998.

61. See Helsinki Watch, *Destroying Ethnic Identity: The Gypsies of Bulgaria* (New York: Human Rights Watch, 1991).

62. Mariya Cheresheva, "Bulgarian 'Migrant Hunter' Held after Anti-Roma Rally," *Balkan Insight*, July 3, 2017, https://www.balkaninsight.com/en/article/migrant-hunter-arrested-after-anti -roma-rally-in-bulgaria-07-03-2017.

63. "Bulgarian Nationalists May Topple Government over Russia Sanctions," Reuters, April 1, 2014.

64. "Defence Ministry: Bulgaria Subject to Russian Information War," Sofia News Agency, August 26, 2014, http://www.novinite.com/articles/162925/Defence+Ministry%3A+Bulgaria+S ubject+To+Russian+Information+War.

65. Tsvetelia Tsolova, "Bulgarian Vote Shows Russia Winning Hearts on EU's Eastern Flank," Reuters, November 11, 2016, http://www.reuters.com/article/us-bulgaria-election-russia-idUSKB N13611H.

66. Central Election Commission, https://results.cik.bg/pi2021/rezultati.

67. Margarita Assenova, "The Balkan Gas Hub: A European Gas Trading Platform or South Stream Lite?," *Eurasia Daily Monitor* 15, no. 172 (December 6, 2018), https://jamestown.org/pro gram/the-balkan-gas-hub-a-european-gas-trading-platform-or-south-stream-lite.

68. Goran Buldioski and Vessela Tcherneva, "How to Advance a European Solution to Bulgaria's and North Macedonia's Dispute," *European Council on Foreign Relations*, December 2, 2020, https://ecfr.eu/article/how-to-advance-a-european-solution-to-bulgarias-and-north-mac edonias-dispute.

69. Alpha Research Opinion Poll, October 2020, https://alpharesearch.bg/api/uploads/Articles %202020/Oct%20-%20North%20Macedonia/Oct20_North_Macedonia_Report.pdf.

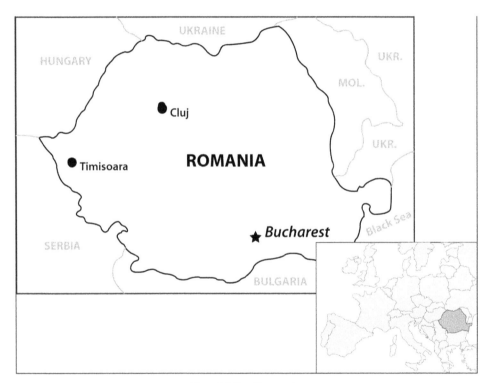

Map 16.0.　Romania

CHAPTER 16

Romania

Michelle Kelso

A man meets a friend at a bar. He asks his buddy: "Hey, what do you think of Ceaușescu?"

The friend says, "Too dangerous to talk about it here. The bar is full."

They leave and it's just the two of them outside.

The friend says, "Okay, we can talk now. I like him."

—Communist-era anecdote

Humor is one way that Romanians survived the communist repression that gripped the country for over forty years. Jokes can hide much while revealing cutting truths. The quip above illustrates how despised the regime of Nicolae Ceaușescu (1965–1989) had become. The joke plays on the notion of ears and eyes being everywhere in a country where reportedly one in five people were informing on their neighbors, colleagues, acquaintances, and family members to the Securitate, or secret police. Social control and fear rather than ideological commitment were what bound communism tightly around the nation in a political and economic system the Soviet Union had imposed on Romania after World War II.

For many today, it is difficult to grasp what life was like under communism and the lasting legacy it left. Why did Romanians despise communism? What preceded it? What replaced it after 1989?

In 1965, a young Brit traveled for the first time to Romania on an educational trip. Unfamiliar with what life was like in Romania, he heard the following from a local:

We live in socialist country, and here the state maps out your life for you from birth. You are assigned a school, you are assigned a job and you are assigned a place to live. Conformity is the rule; you do what you are told and meeting foreigners is off-limits. If your expectations are low and you don't step out of line, then you will be satisfied. And to make sure that you don't step out of line, they have the *Securitate*.[1]

In Romania, the closed political system in which the state and Communist Party functioned together exercised near-total control over daily existence.

By the 1980s, material conditions in Romania had drastically deteriorated, fueling increased dissent. Not wanting to be beholden to any power, Ceaușescu enacted draconian measures to rid the country of its international debt. Mass amounts of food were exported while imports halted, making food insecurity a norm for most Romanians. Electricity was cut across the country to save money, regularly plunging many households into darkness. Heat and hot water were also in short supply. Shortages of consumer goods from clothes to children's toys created further misery. While starving and freezing the people, Ceaușescu built a lavish palace that would become the second largest in the world after the Pentagon in Washington, DC.

One Romanian writer described the destitution he encountered traveling by train in December 1989, a week before the revolution:

> Wrinkled, gloomy faces, and worn clothes. Dirty carriages. Quiet desperation. There was nothing to remind us of the holiday spirit so cherished in the West, aside from the ragged luggage people were carrying, which looked stuffed with food and home-made wine.[2]

Referring to communism, his then-pregnant wife told him upon boarding the train, "I cannot stand it anymore."[3] She was not alone. Ceaușescu's chokehold seemed unbreakable; decades of repression and terror, and their pervasive threat, first had to be cast off to bring Romanians to the street to fight for a new system. While the Romanian revolution was among the last in Central and East Europe (CEE) in 1989, it was the bloodiest, ushering in hard-won democracy.

This chapter examines the internal and external factors that contributed to Romania's development into a democracy over the last three decades. It begins with an examination of Romanian political history. It then provides an overview of Romanian political institutions and competition before delving into economics, civil society, and present social issues.

Political History

By the nineteenth century, Romanians, like many other ethnic communities living under imperial rule, craved freedom and political and cultural autonomy. In 1848, revolutions broke out, with nations demanding their independence from empires. Romanians, who were split across three separate principalities but were increasingly aware of belonging to a single nation, agitated and revolted in the principalities of Moldova and Wallachia and united against the Turks (while in Transylvania they rose up against the Habsburgs). But their bid for independence was thwarted by the Great Powers. Nearly thirty years would pass before the dream of national self-determination was realized. In 1859, Moldova and Wallachia achieved de facto unification by choosing the same leader who ruled the unified country dubbed Romania, with Bucharest as its capital. The new country remained under the Ottoman Empire's protection, though enjoying quasi-independence as a buffer zone on the edges of three empires: the Ottomans, the Russians, and the Habsburgs.

After a series of political crises, local elites concluded that Romania needed a constitutional monarchy. They wanted a neutral king to stabilize the political environment.

The German prince Karl of Hohenzollern-Sigmaringen was chosen, who became Prince Carol of Romania in 1866. International recognition of Romania's independence came a few years later, following a new war between the Russian and Ottoman Empires in 1877, in which Romania fought on the side of the former. With Ottoman defeat, Romania's statehood was recognized by the Great Powers. Prince Carol was formally appointed king of Romania in 1881, having a key role in overseeing the modernization that turned it into a European country with contemporary political, administrative, and economic institutions.

At the outbreak of World War I, Romania remained neutral. France, Britain, and Russia bargained hard for Romania's entrance into the war, promising that Transylvania, then part of Austria-Hungary but where ethnic Romanians were the majority, would be ceded to Romania postwar.[4] In 1916, Romania allied with the Entente, declaring war on the Central powers, but hoping to fight only against Austria-Hungary, with a view to annex Transylvania.[5] Romania was to open a new front to relieve pressure on its allies. However, after initial Romanian advances in Transylvania met little resistance, the Romanian offensive had to be stopped and troops brought back to defend against a counterattack along the southern border.

After the 1917 Bolshevik revolution in Russia and their subsequent withdrawal from the war, Romania had little support. The Central powers occupied most of Romania. Romanian resistance halted further advances, and the government signed a treaty with the Central powers in April 1918. However, as the latter suffered heavier defeats on the western front, Romania denounced the treaty, reentering the war on the victors' side just before the German armistice and moving its troops into Transylvania.

Greater Romania

With the conclusion of peace treaties, the Entente powers granted Romania what they had promised. Besides the main prize—Transylvania—Romania also added the provinces of Bukovina and Banat, which had been part of Austria, as well as the eastern province of Bessarabia, which had been a part of Russia for the last century. Within a short span of time, the country doubled its territory and population, creating a much more ethnically and religiously diverse state.

In 1923, Romania adopted a new constitution, confirming the constitutional monarchy and a parliamentary regime. The two main parties that dominated the postwar years were the National Liberal Party (Partidul Național Liberal; PNL or Liberals) and the National Peasant Party (Partidul Național Țărănesc, PNȚ). The Liberals represented the growing urban, middle-class population, while the PNȚ promoted land reforms and the interests of rural populations. The governance of large Hungarian, German, Jewish, and other minority populations, comprising 30 percent of the kingdom, proved challenging for the expanded state. Each group had its own political, social, and economic interests. The nation proved ill equipped to manage the swath of interests and struggled to create a unified, inclusive national identity, which remained tightly centered on Romanian ethnicity and Orthodox Christianity. In essence, it was "the multinational state that wasn't."[6] In the following decades this led to internal discord and violence, leaving the country in a weakened position as World War II loomed.

The interwar years in Romania, plagued by the global depression and political instability, created the conditions for the rise of ultranationalistic and far-right parties. The most politically prominent was the Legion of the Archangel Michael, also known as the Iron Guard, founded in 1927 and led by Corneliu Zelea Codreanu. The party grew into a political force, advocating a return to Romanian peasant roots and adopting a fundamentalist view of Christian Orthodoxy. It promoted fervent anti-Semitism, importing fascist ideology from Italy and Germany, which they shaped into their own ideological platform. A fringe party before the mid-1930s, after the economic crisis the legion emerged as a popular movement, challenging in elections the hegemony of the traditional Liberal and Peasant parties while committing acts of political violence. Guardists carried out several high-level political assassinations, including killing two sitting prime ministers. Their antigraft message and condemnation of Romania's corrupt political class resonated with many.

Various governments failed to quell the movement. To circumvent the outlawing of the Iron Guard, Codreanu formed a political party that became the third-placing party in the 1937 elections. The party's time in parliament was short, as the king called for new elections the following year. In 1938, on the king's orders, Codreanu and several of his followers who had been imprisoned were strangled to death. The purge either drove Guardists underground or out of the country. They would reconstitute with German support and two years later formed a government in a brief yet deadly term in power. Their legacy has figured substantially in postcommunist extremist movements.

By the late 1930s, Romania's economy improved. However, Nazi Germany's rise and its political and territorial gains destabilized the region. With war looming, Carol II made a power grab in 1938, suspending the constitution and establishing a personal dictatorship. Carol attempted a regional alliance backed by Britain and France, which was meant to deter against German invasion of Romania. After Hitler invaded Czechoslovakia and Poland in 1939, Romania's troubled position was evident. Britain and France were too weak to protect the kingdom, and without support, Romanian territorial integrity was impossible. In 1940, Soviet, Hungarian, and Bulgarian territorial demands, sanctioned by Germany, rent Romania apart. The Soviet Union took the eastern provinces of Bessarabia and northern Bukovina, Hungary captured a northern part of Transylvania, and Bulgaria the southern Dobruja province.

Dictatorships

Frustration and anger mounted against Carol after the dismemberment of Greater Romania. In September 1940, Carol II was forced to abdicate in favor of his eighteen-year-old son Michael and turned over governing powers to General Ion Antonescu. Antonescu formed a government with German-backed Horia Sima of the Iron Guard, which became the only legal political party.

The partnership between Guardists and the general, however, was tenuous, lasting only five months. In January 1941, Guardists mounted a short-lived rebellion against Antonescu that he quickly quashed. The general then installed himself as military dictator, banning the Iron Guard and officially allying with the Axis powers. Romania joined the Nazi invasion of the Soviet Union in June 1941, a move that earned it a piece of the spoils—part of occupied Soviet space mainly in Ukraine. Antonescu blamed communists and their agents in Romania—a supposed "Judeo-Bolshevik" infiltration—for attacks on Romanian troops during their 1940 withdrawal from the territories taken by the Soviet Union. Under the fog of war, as his troops advanced eastward into the USSR in summer 1941, they massacred Jews in villages and enclaves in a campaign dubbed "cleansing the land."[7] For ethnic Jewish and Romani minorities, the Antonescu regime proved deadly. Expansion into Ukraine provided Antonescu the space to implement his own variant of the Final Solution. The remaining Jews in the eastern provinces and in occupied Ukraine continued being massacred and deported to a vast Romanian-run camp system. The regime then turned to Roma, deporting and interning them in camps. Over 280,000 Jews and over 11,000 Roma were killed.[8]

In August 1944 under King Michael's leadership, Antonescu was ousted in a coup, and Romania switched sides to fight against Germany. Soviet troops were already present in Romania as part of their assault against Axis forces en route to Germany. Romanian troops joined the Soviet anti-Axis campaign in Hungary and Czechoslovakia. Northern Transylvania was returned to Romania. However, Soviet troops remained. Unbeknownst to Romanians, they had been left to the Soviets when British prime minister Winston Churchill and Soviet leader Joseph Stalin met in Moscow in 1944 and divided Eastern Europe into spheres of allied influence. Churchill wanted Greece, ceding Romania to the Soviets. Romanians had no say in their future course.

Imposition of Communism

Postwar Romania entered a period of acute national suffering. Soviet-occupied and impoverished, any hope for freedom was soon dashed by peace accords. The economy, largely agrarian based, was in crisis. Massive droughts, coupled with land reforms and confiscation of grain reserves by the Soviets as part of war reparations the country owed the USSR, culminated in a two-year famine from 1946 through 1947.[9] An estimated half a million died. Coroners' reports noted that Romanian diets had completely changed, as inedibles such as wood, textiles, hay, dirt, and clay were consumed.[10] Amid the hardships, the 1947 peace agreements cemented a Soviet presence in Romania and its communist path.

In 1947, the Soviet-backed Communist Party was officially established in government after organizing fraudulent elections. King Michael was forced into exile. As elsewhere in the bloc, the Soviets installed a puppet regime that copied Stalinist policies. Land was confiscated by the government, as were private shops and factories, and dissenters were swiftly imprisoned.[11] Until Stalin's death in 1953, Romania went through a brutal Stalinistic period when Communist Party leader Gheorghe Gheorghiu-Dej implemented repressive terror tactics to subjugate the population. Prisons were designated as reeducation centers, earning brutal reputations. Sundry offenses, such as joining a literary club, could land one in prison for subversion.[12] Prisoners were "forced to stare at lightbulbs, eat feces, given electric shocks and head butt each other. They were also encouraged to inform on each other and torture fellow inmates."[13] After 1953, Romanian leaders gradually opened up relations with the West and pushed for the withdrawal of Soviet troops,[14] which departed in 1958. From 1947 to 1989, nearly two million Romanians were sent to prisons, detention centers, and even Soviet gulags, most during Dej's tenure.[15] After 1958, Romania diversified its trade away from the Soviet Union, which had earlier monopolized all exports and imports.

Photo 16.1. The interior of Râmnicu Sărat political prison is now open to visitors. (Gabriel Petrescu, Shutterstock)

In 1965, Nicolae Ceaușescu took control of the Communist Party. A former cob-bler's apprentice, Ceaușescu had earned a reputation as Dej's gritty protégé. In his early years in power, Ceaușescu accelerated the westward trend, signing economic cooperation agreements with Western countries. For example, France sold Romania a license to build Renault cars, renamed Dacia, that became the national car. Ceaușescu also developed relations with China and Israel. Ceaușescu was the "Rebel of the East" for his resistance to Soviet control. In 1968, he won Western acclaim by refusing to join the other Warsaw Pact countries in invading Czechoslovakia to remove a reformist government. Romania's economic and political prospects looked bright. Western leaders, including US presi-dents, visited Bucharest. Major economic cooperation agreements were signed, offering Romania billions of dollars in loans to speed its development.

However, by the late 1970s, it became clear that Ceaușescu had backslid on human rights, the rights of women, and those of ethnic minorities. With the introduction of a pro-natalist policy in 1966, Ceaușescu had abortion and birth control banned in an attempt to increase the country's declining birthrate.[16] Births initially increased in the first years, but so did maternal mortality rates. Romania became the deadliest place in Europe for a woman to be pregnant, as women turned to illegal and unsafe procedures to terminate pregnancies. The Ceaușescu regime also pursued repressive cultural and educational policies toward ethnic minorities, targeting particularly the large Hungarian minority concentrated in the historically contested Transylvanian region.

With each passing year, Ceaușescu's regime was becoming increasingly totalitarian, and relations with the West worsened. In the 1980s, Ceaușescu, convinced that depen-dency on foreign loans must stop, began an austerity program to pay off debts, much of which had been wasted on gigantic steelworks and infrastructure projects that had dubious benefits, such as the Black Sea–Danube canal.

Under austerity, Western imports stopped, cutting off access to technology upgrades and causing Romanian industry to become outdated. Power cuts were a daily occurrence for Romanian consumers in the name of saving energy, which was prioritized for the outdated, wasteful factories. Television offered only one program, dominated by the dictator, with his personality cult growing every year. A popular joke quipped that someone petitioned Ceaușescu to increase the programming from two to four hours daily, to which the dictator replied, "What am I to speak about for four hours?" In cities around the country, food was rationed, while Romania exported agricultural products. By 1989, Ceaușescu had paid off the national debt, but instead of relaxing conditions, he started loaning money to third-world countries in an attempt to open up new trade routes for Romanian products that no longer met the quality standards to be sold in the West.

The Revolution

In the fall of 1989, communist regimes began crumbling in CEE, while in the Soviet Union major reforms were taking place under Mikhail Gorbachev's leadership. Only Romania and Albania seemed frozen in time. Despite a domestic media blackout, many Romanians illicitly listened to Radio Free Europe or watched television stations from neighboring countries to gain information about regime changes. Rumors suggested that Ceaușescu might follow his comrades and step down. Six months prior, a letter protest by six Communist Party leaders against Ceaușescu's policies had raised hope in the West of a possible ouster. But the dictator was reelected during the November party congress[17]—amid draconian security measures, including limiting the number of people who could walk together on the streets and putting border guards under the Interior Ministry to tighten up surveillance.[18]

The revolution began in Timișoara on December 16, following a relatively minor incident: an ethnic Hungarian priest refused a transfer to another parish, and his congregation staged a protest, which amid the tense atmosphere sparked widespread unrest in the city. The military intervened, shooting dozens of protesters, but was unable to retake control. A few days later, on December 21, a defiant Ceaușescu, who failed to understand the pulse of the country, staged his own support rally in Bucharest. He blamed "hooligans" and spy agencies "from the West and from the East" for the unrest, and the crowd turned against him, chanting, "Down with Ceaușescu." The dictator later fled to the roof of the building, where a helicopter flew him to Târgoviște. There he was arrested by the military that had turned against him.

The communist regime ended when a firing squad executed Ceaușescu and his wife Elena on Christmas Day 1989. A special military tribunal set up by the new authorities sentenced the couple to death for charges that included genocide and undermining the national economy.[19] In the following days, amid sporadic shootings and competition among groups seeking to gain power, Ion Iliescu, a reformed communist who had been marginalized by Ceaușescu, consolidated his hold on power with the help of the military. Iliescu staved off challengers and set up a provisional body that he chaired, the Council of the National Salvation Front, which took control of the country and was tasked with organizing free elections.

The National Salvation Front formed its first government immediately after the shooting of the Ceauşescus, led by Petre Roman, a young professor at the Polytechnic Institute. A charismatic and multilingual figure, Roman became a darling of the Western press, giving dozens of interviews and promising radical reforms. Iliescu, however, seemed more interested in preserving a minimally reformed communist system. He appeared after Ceauşescu's death on television to reassure the Soviets that Romania was still their ally. It appeared that, despite its bloody revolution, Romania would seek a path adopted by those CEE regimes that installed reformed communists after dethroning the hard-liners. Iliescu succeeded to remain in power in the following months by controlling the only television station in the country and fomenting chaos by pitting social groups against one another. While ties with Western countries were renewed after a decade of frozen relations, Iliescu would keep Romania in the Soviet orbit until 1991, when the USSR crumbled.

Political Institutions

On December 22, 1989, Iliescu announced that a forty-member Council of National Salvation Front (CNSF) would run the country, organizing the first free elections and setting up a democracy.[20] The CNSF passed decrees allowing for the formation of political parties and nonprofit organizations, religious freedom, and free speech.[21] In January 1990, council members transformed the entity into a political party, sparking protest from civic groups and the renewed historical parties, the National Liberal Party (PNL) and the National Peasant Party (PNŢ). Opponents argued that it was unfair for the Salvation Front to organize elections in which it planned to run. Demonstrations ensued. After talks with PNL and PNŢ leaders, Iliescu announced a decision to transform the CNSF into a Provisional Council of National Union, which would have 50 percent National Salvation Front (NSF) members, while the other 50 percent of the seats would be granted to representatives of ninety newly formed parties and civic organizations. The new council would have 253 members, including representatives of the national minorities.[22] The council's main accomplishment was organizing the first free elections, which took place on May 20, 1990, when a Constitutive Assembly was elected and tasked with writing a new constitution. The NSF won a majority in the 1990 elections, dominating the Constitutive Assembly.[23]

Under the new constitution, Romania returned to prewar parliamentary bicameralism, alongside a dual executive split between a president and a prime minister. The president, directly elected by the people to a four-year term, would appoint the prime minister, represent the country, and be a mediator in society. Once elected, the president was required to resign from his or her political party. Specific powers lay with the presidency, including the appointment of top prosecutors, selecting the heads of the intelligence agencies, and signing international treaties. The bicameral parliament would be elected for four years and be responsible for passing laws and for confirming the prime minister and cabinet.

The 1991 constitution defined Romania as a national, sovereign, and unitary state; a republic that guaranteed the human rights of citizens and proclaimed the rule of law;

and a pluralist, multiparty democracy.[24] It affirmed that the country would be governed by the principle of separation of powers between executive, legislative, and judicial branches. Romania revised the constitution in 2003 in preparation to join NATO and the European Union (EU), further strengthening the rule of law, expanding democratic rights, and revising some aspects of the electoral process. The constitution banned censorship and the death penalty, and it proclaimed that international human rights conventions signed by Romania trumped domestic law. It also stated that Romania was a market economy and that the state would protect private property.

A Constitutional Court was set up. The independence of the judiciary was constitutionally guaranteed, and a Council of Magistrates was created to oversee judicial affairs. However, the government retained formal control over prosecutors, with the constitution noting that "prosecutors exercise their duties . . . under hierarchical control, under the authority of the Justice Minister." This has remained throughout the years a point of contention in discussions around judicial autonomy, particularly after high-profile prosecutions of top politicians.[25]

Over the years, Romania experienced several models of territorial organization. After the last major reform in 1981, Romania had forty-one counties, plus the capital Bucharest as its own county. As Romania began accession talks with the European Union in 1998, parliament set up eight development regions to match EU requirements and to access region-based funding.[26] Fearing Hungarian separatism in Transylvania, authorities rejected demands by ethnic Hungarians to create sixteen smaller regions, including one that would include three counties dominated by ethnic Hungarians.[27] Regional autonomy demands for the areas with a majority of ethnic Hungarians remain a thorny issue in Romania's interethnic relations.

Political Competition

Romania emerged after half a century of totalitarian regimes with only distant memories of democracy and pluralist elections. Romanians had vaguely understood democratic institutions by piecing together information while listening to foreign media like Radio Free Europe, the BBC, and Voice of America. They wanted a Western-style democracy to bring prosperity. The CNSF promised to get them there with free, multiparty elections.[28] Soon, popular interest in political competition emerged across the country. The three main pre–World War II parties—the National Liberal Party, the National Peasant Party, and the Social Democratic Party—were reborn. Tens of thousands of people lined the streets of cities around the country to register as members. Party founders were drawn from prewar members and émigrés. Some, like Corneliu Coposu, the National Peasant Party leader, had suffered in communist gulags. Émigrés returned from abroad in the days after the revolution, some taking leadership roles. In the meantime, the CNSF was also setting up branches around the country, many of them replacing Communist Party structures or local governments.

When the council morphed into a political party in January 1990, it became clear that Romania's new leaders had no intent to step down after the elections, as initially promised. Some council members resigned in protest.[29] "The Front" (as it became known), led by Iliescu, controlled the only national television and radio stations, a significant advantage in the upcoming electoral competition, as the other parties had only minuscule air time and relied for coverage only on newly appeared opposition newspapers, such as *România Liberă* (Free Romania).

Romanian society split into groups with radically different political preferences. Urban youth and university-educated people supported the opposition, while older adults, blue-collar workers, and rural dwellers supported the Front. The dividing lines were so clear that at Iliescu's rallies, workers chanted, "We work, we don't think," to differentiate themselves from the historical parties' "intellectual" supporters. That spring, opposition groups staged several large demonstrations in major cities protesting Iliescu's continued rule. Protesters accused Iliescu of trying to pursue a "human-face communist regime" instead of real democracy. Iliescu, a former communist apparatchik who fell out of favor with Ceaușescu in the 1970s after protesting his dictatorial tendencies, had long been considered as a potential reformist alternative to the dictator. In the days and months following the revolution, he presented himself as a left-wing politician who favored a Scandinavian-style social democratic system.

Romania's first postcommunist elections, based on proportional representation, were held on May 20, 1990. Over 86 percent of registered voters cast a ballot for one of the seventy-one political parties and civic organizations that competed. The Front, led by Iliescu and Roman, won 66 percent of the vote. Iliescu was elected president in a landslide, winning 85 percent of the vote. A total of fifteen parties and civic organizations, including the historical parties, won seats in the new Constitutive Assembly (whose main task was to appoint a government and draft a new constitution). The historical political parties disputed the results, claiming widespread fraud and a lack of fairness in the electoral campaign. International observers concluded that the elections were generally fair and that the Front and Iliescu had won.[30] Roman became prime minister and set up a new government.

Political Turmoil

For seven weeks, antigovernment demonstrators gathered in the center of Bucharest against Iliescu and the Front, whom they perceived as "neocommunists." Various civic leaders spoke to the crowds from the balcony of the University of Bucharest, which overlooked the city's main intersection. In a televised speech, Iliescu called demonstrators hooligans (*golani*) to delegitimize the movement. Protestors quickly adopted the moniker, proudly wearing "hooligan" badges and buttons.

On June 13, 1990, a day before the inauguration of the new government, authorities decided to clear out protesters, organizing a dawn raid and arresting protesters who were sleeping in tents in University Square. Protesters counterattacked, some armed with bottles of flaming fuel that functioned as Molotov cocktails. Protesters then occupied several government buildings and tried taking over the national television station.[31] Iliescu appealed on television to "well-meaning people" to defend his government, falsely claiming that the demonstrations were a "fascist rebellion."[32] Trains arrived in Bucharest from coal regions in southwestern Romania, carrying miners in "grubby work clothes and helmets, their faces blackened by soot" and "carrying clubs and rubber truncheons."[33] They descended on University Square prepared to inflict harm on demonstrators, with reports indicating that former Securitate officials guided them.[34] Miners indiscriminately beat residents they believed were regime opponents, singling out individuals wearing beards or glasses (seemingly intellectuals), motorists, university students, and passersby, among others. Nine people were killed and scores were injured.[35]

Iliescu's tactics temporarily quelled resistance, but it cost him support abroad. The president miscalculated how the West would perceive government-incited violence—that is, as the gross human rights violation it was. The international press covered Iliescu's role in inciting the miners' attack, which hit the front page of the *New York Times*.[36] Western leaders promptly condemned the attack, pushing Romania to the edge of diplomatic isolation.[37] The United States threatened to withhold most-favored-nation trade status.[38] Prime Minister Roman, who had fought on the Bucharest barricades against the communist regime, expended his remaining credibility reassuring Western leaders that his government was not returning to communism. He took control of the Front party and broke relations with Iliescu, calming the West and embarking on market reforms.

The Jiu Valley miners, Iliescu's former allies, went on strike in September 1991, demanding higher wages, but the cash-strapped government refused. Angered, the miners commandeered trains, coming to Bucharest to protest. This time, instead of defending the government, they came to take it down. In desperation, Iliescu ordered then transport minister Traian Băsescu, who would later become president, to destroy the train tracks. Băsescu refused, fearing that hundreds would die if the trains derailed.[39] The miners arrived, and the protest degenerated into street violence between the coal workers and riot police. The miners forcibly entered and occupied parliament and government buildings. To calm matters, Roman resigned, and Iliescu appointed the finance minister to lead an interim government. These events foreshadowed the pattern of contentious politics, involving public protest and frequent government change, that remained characteristic of politics in the state center since 1990.

With the initial, provisional two-year term of the new parliament and president ending, new elections were held in 1992. Iliescu won a four-year term, defeating a much stronger challenge this time from centrist opposition leader Emil Constantinescu, a university professor who had been among the leaders of the protests on University Square. Iliescu's new party, the Democratic National Salvation Front (which had split from the original National Salvation Front, led by former prime minister Roman), won the elections and formed a coalition with three small leftist and nationalist parties, with a cabinet led by Nicolae Văcăroiu, an economist. This government stabilized the economy, but the administration was marred by corruption scandals, overseeing the troubled emergence of a new class of Romanian "connected" capitalists, most of them former Securitate or communist officials.

Emboldened by their improved electoral performance in 1992, opposition parties consolidated their alliance. The Democratic Convention struck a deal with Roman's Democratic Party (ex–Salvation Front) and the Democratic Alliance of Hungarians in Romania to unite against Iliescu. By then, the media had diversified, with some private television stations favoring the opposition. Constantinescu, who lost the presidential elections in 1992 to Iliescu, defeated the incumbent in 1996.

The 1996 opposition victory marked a new era for Romania—often described as the real beginning of postcommunist democratization and marketization in the country. Bucharest mayor and former union leader Victor Ciorbea became the new prime minister, leading a government formed by the Democratic Convention together with Roman's Democratic Party and the Democratic Alliance of Hungarians in Romania. The government's main priority was to achieve EU and NATO membership. The inclusion of the party representing Romania's largest ethnic minority in the governing coalition sent a strong message about commitment to democratic government (see also chapter 3 on nationalism and its challenges to democracy). Hungarians constitute over 6 percent of the country's population and around 20 percent of the population in the large Transylvanian region. The umbrella political organization they created in 1989, the Democratic Alliance of Hungarians in Romania (DAHR), has been one of the most stable political parties in the country, supported by an overwhelming majority of ethnic Hungarian voters in all parliamentary elections since 1990. DAHR has participated in governing coalitions since 1997, achieving key policy changes in minority-language use and education. Hungarians face structural disadvantage especially in their ability to maintain minority institutions, but their representatives have been politically more successful than those of other minorities in the country.[40]

The new government formed in 1997 addressed the need to uncover "the truth" about the Ceauşescu dictatorship by creating a truth commission to look into the communist-era archives, allowing people to see their Securitate files and reveal collaborators of the former secret police.[41] But perpetual coalition infighting and an economic crisis plagued the centrist government for four years, making it deeply unpopular.

The 2000 elections yielded an ironic outcome: Iliescu returned to the presidency with the support of his former opposition that had joined forces to defeat him in 1996. A larger tension underlying Romanian politics, the tension between moderates and nationalist populists, helps to explain this outcome. Romania had managed to eschew political extremism in the state center until the 2000 elections. When President Constantinescu, who was broadly unpopular, did not seek reelection, a plethora of centrist candidates vied for his position. Yet the contender who arguably stole the limelight during the electoral campaign was the extreme-right leader Corneliu Vadim Tudor. Tudor was well known for his poetry, which had stoked Ceauşescu's maniacal ego. After the end of communism, he cofounded the Greater Romania Party. The ideology of this party was a mixture incorporating a nationalistic, anti-Semitic, and anti-Hungarian discourse, as well as pro-Antonescu (Romania's pro-Nazi military ruler during the war) and pro-Ceauşescu ideas. Tudor was an atypical but astute presidential candidate, among the first to employ the anticorruption theme for political success. Seizing on Romanians' dissatisfaction with public officials, he toned down the nationalist discourse and led a pointed campaign against corruption, even proposing Chinese-style public executions of corrupt officials.[42] He drove around the country in a black Mercedes wearing his signature white suit and lilac sunglasses. Surprising the political establishment, Tudor had a second-place finish in the first round, qualifying for the presidential runoffs against Iliescu. Unwilling to support Tudor's extremist politics, the centrist opposition backed Iliescu in the runoffs. Thus, Iliescu comfortably won a second term as president with 66 percent of the vote. However, riding on Tudor's (figurative) coattails, the Greater Romania party astonished many, winning 20 percent of parliamentary seats and raising its media and political profile.

The third time around, Iliescu played his cards differently. His Democratic National Salvation Front formed a minority government, with the former foreign minister Adrian Năstase as prime minister. Iliescu's party then merged with the historical Social Democratic Party, taking its name and gaining acceptance among European socialists. During his second term, he reconciled with King Michael, who was invited to relocate to Romania and regained some of his confiscated property, including the Peleş Castle. As well, Romania joined NATO and concluded most of the negotiations for joining the European Union.

Despite an improvement in living standards, entering NATO, and getting ready to join the European Union, many Romanians were unhappy with the Năstase government, perceiving it as corrupt. Anticorruption was emerging as the leading theme in Romanian politics, reinforced externally through the EU integration process. When ten other CEE countries joined the EU in 2004, corruption was European officials' key justification for delaying the accession of Bulgaria and Romania. Romanian political elites were keen on satisfying membership conditions. The opposition Liberals and Democratic Party, which had been divided four years prior and learned their lesson, formed a two-party "Justice and Truth Alliance," campaigning against official corruption. The alliance named a joint candidate for president to fight against Năstase: Traian Băsescu, a former ship captain and transportation minister, then mayor of Bucharest.

Băsescu was charismatic, with his whiskey-drinking, foul-mouthed, tough-guy persona. As mayor, he earned a no-nonsense reputation in a citywide clean-up campaign, demolishing unsightly kiosks around the capital. He also ordered the killing of tens of thousands of stray dogs that roamed the city, legacies from Ceauşescu's demolition projects that had razed older neighborhoods to the ground and replaced them with apartment buildings. Băsescu successfully sailed into the presidency. He appointed his Liberal partner, Călin Popescu-Tariceanu, as prime minister, and Romania embarked on anticorruption reforms. Monica Macovei, a former human rights lawyer, was appointed justice minister and tasked prosecutors to clean up widespread graft. The reformist government completed the remaining EU membership requirements by establishing an independent judiciary.

In 2007, Romania formally joined the European Union. The next elections, held amid the global financial crisis, resulted in a stalemate between the Social Democrats, led by Mircea Geoană and Băsescu's party. Băsescu directed his party to form a "grand coalition" with the Social Democrats to run the country during the financial crisis. A year later, the Social Democrats left the coalition just weeks before the presidential elections, with Băsescu defeating Geoană by a razor-thin margin, winning a second term. The government then embarked on austerity measures unseen since the times of Ceauşescu, fueling public protests. Simultaneously, the government struggled to manage corruption scandals and a rising opposition alliance between the Liberals and the Social Democrats. The opposition would muster enough votes in parliament to suspend an unpopular Băsescu and organize a referendum for his removal from office. Băsescu narrowly survived it due to insufficient voter turnout, but his tenure became impossible to maintain in the face of growing street protests. He was forced to make a deal with the opposition PSD, appointing their new, youthful leader, Victor Ponta, as prime minister. Ponta formed a cabinet with the Liberals and quickly restored the wages of public servants to their pre-2010 levels amid a strong economic recovery.

In another surprising turn of events, the Liberals broke up the alliance with the Social Democrats and left the government. They then backed Klaus Iohannis, an ethnic German who was mayor of the Transylvanian city of Sibiu, to run for president in 2014. Iohannis defeated Ponta and won the presidency. Iohannis had been considered an outsider, as a member of an ethnic minority and a Protestant in a country where the population is overwhelmingly Christian Orthodox. However, his record renovating the medieval city of Sibiu, as well as his calm and measured demeanor, appealed to many Romanians who wanted a change after ten tumultuous years of Băsescu's presidency.

Ponta continued to run the government until a disaster hit the capital on October 30, 2015—a fire in a nightclub that led to the death of sixty-four people. The Colectiv club fire fueled street protests, leading to the rise of a civic anticorruption movement, which turned political. The government took much of the blame for the corrupt officials who had permitted the operation of the club in an improvised building and for the botched intervention of the emergency services, and Ponta resigned. A Bucharest nongovernmental organization (NGO), the Association for Saving Bucharest, which had been fighting corrupt mayors to preserve historical buildings in the city, formed a new party called the Union for Saving Romania and competed in the parliamentary elections.[43] Those elections, held in December 2016, led to the victory of the returning Social Democrats, now led by populist leader Liviu Dragnea, who promised large increases in public wages and pensions, as well as tax cuts. Dragnea, a controversial local party official who had been convicted of voter fraud, came to power while on trial for corruption. Unable to serve as prime minister due to his criminal record, he named a little-known party official, Sorin Grindeanu, as prime minister, a decision the president accepted.

The new cabinet began a campaign to roll back anticorruption reforms, adopting almost immediately an emergency decree to decriminalize several corruption offenses, including those for which Dragnea was being tried. This drew the ire of the EU and led to mass protests, and the government canceled the measure. Under pressure from his party to issue new decrees to cancel anticorruption laws, the prime minster refused, only to be sacked by his own party after just six months on the job. A new PSD prime minister was appointed but resigned after half a year after also refusing party demands to amend anticorruption laws. Viorica Dăncilă, a close ally of Dragnea, landed the job. The new government then fired the top anticorruption prosecutor, Laura Codruţa Kövesi, generating more street protests and complaints from the EU. Romania was backsliding in the fight against corruption.

Dragnea, who by then had been sentenced to three and a half years in prison on corruption charges but was free pending an appeal to the Supreme Court, pressured the government once again to change the anticorruption legislation to avoid his own conviction. Under pressure from the EU, which threatened to suspend Romania's voting rights in the European Council and to cut off funds, the government backed down. Dragnea's trial eventually came to an end at the Supreme Court on May 27, 2019, a day after his Social Democrats were soundly defeated in the elections for the European Parliament. His appeal was rejected, and he was arrested and sent to prison. Dăncilă remained as prime minister for a few more months, announcing her candidacy for president. In the meantime, she was ousted in a no-confidence vote organized by the opposition Liberals in October 2019. Iohannis then easily defeated Dăncilă, winning a second five-year term as president.

Soon after taking office, the Liberals were faced in 2020 with the COVID-19 pandemic. The government moved swiftly to bring the virus under control, forcing a lockdown and adopting a pay-to-stay-home program for employees affected by the restrictions. It faced increasing opposition to restrictions, however, with conspiracies spreading on social media. Seemingly out of nowhere, a new party emerged, the Alliance for the Unity of Romanians (AUR). AUR organized demonstrations in front of the government against COVID-19 restrictions, disturbingly using in its manifest language similar to that of the fascist Iron Guard. In the December 2020 parliamentary elections, with the pandemic at a peak, only a third of voters turned out to vote, a historic low. AUR won nearly 10 percent of the vote, entering parliament. No party could claim a majority win. The National Liberal Party, with the participation of the Union for Saving Romania and the Democratic Alliance of Hungarians in Romania, formed a governing coalition. Florin Cîțu, a former banker and finance minister, was appointed prime minister.

Over the last thirty years, Romanian parties and governments failed to meet people's expectations and quickly lost popularity when in power, with nearly each election cycle bringing a new government to power.

Economic Policies and Conditions

In the days after the Salvation Front took over the country, the new authorities ended the decadelong austerity policies, using the money that was left in state coffers to immediately import the products that had been scarce, including coffee, oranges, and consumer goods. The government came under pressure from newly formed unions of various state industries demanding pay hikes, including the coal miners from the Jiu Valley, who received generous bonuses and became ardent, grateful supporters of the new administration led by Petre Roman and Ion Iliescu.

After winning the first elections in May 1990, Roman assembled a reformist cabinet to tackle the complicated job of remaking the Romanian economy, starting with price liberalization. One of the first issues, however, was how to decentralize a state-run economy, where a government agency had been in charge of telling each company what to produce and at what price. Another issue was that companies had been forced to hire millions more employees than needed[44] due to the communist-era policy of zero unemployment. The system inherited from Ceaușescu was incompatible with market realities. Under communism, prices and quantities were set by government bureaucrats, unrelated to market demand. Planning offices were dissolved in 1990, but no new guidance was put in place. Companies continued production as before, finding that nobody was purchasing their products, which ended up piling up in warehouses. The Berlin Wall had just been dismantled, and the Soviet-led trade bloc (the Comecon), in which Romania had participated for the past half century, was in disarray. In addition, the government had squandered the goodwill it enjoyed in the West in the months following the revolution, when it cracked down on protesters with the help of the miners, causing foreign investors to shun Romania.

Despite the challenges, market reforms continued at a high pace. For the first time in nearly half a century, the new government allowed private individuals to start a company.

While owning a business was still seen as highly risky ("what if the communists come back?"), Romanians started nearly seven thousand new companies in 1990,[45] most of them buying and selling small items in metal kiosks and flea markets that sprang up all over the country.

They were supplied with merchandise by "backpackers," tens of thousands of Romanians who crossed the borders as far as the bazaars of Istanbul, selling any items they found demand for, including ball bearings and mechanical tools, and bringing back blue jeans, cassette tapes, and gold rings, among other things. Some of the first visible business-men were shady characters doing money exchange and selling contraband cigarettes, with the word "businessman" quickly earning a bad connotation in Romanian. Consignment and pawn shops were considered among the better established.

The first wave of foreign investors who ventured in despite the chaos of the early 1990s were Arabs, especially Palestinians who had studied in Romania and returned to start import-export businesses. Small Turkish businesses also sprang up, winning over the bakery sector with tasty breads and setting up fast-food restaurants. On the heels of close bilateral ties from the communist era, thousands of Chinese investors arrived as well, setting up a massive bazaar near Bucharest with thousands of small shops, nicknamed "Europa."

Meanwhile, the government faced almost daily strikes, ranging from power utility workers to transportation workers to the all-female staff at the large textile manufacturers, with Prime Minister Roman being asked to negotiate deals personally, usually surrounded by angry workers and giving in to their demands. Inflation skyrocketed from 0.9 percent in 1989 to 128 percent in 1990.[46] As people noticed their real incomes being reduced, they demanded salary increases, causing an inflationary spiral and eating up savings until people learned to keep them in US dollars or gold. Coal miners, who had enjoyed a large boost in their incomes after the revolution, went on strike in the fall of 1991, demanding new wage hikes. Facing the reality of empty state coffers, Roman refused, which led to a miners' revolt that took down his government. The setback came just as Romania was securing a large loan package[47] and as Western companies were finally returning, seek-ing to open factories in Romania.[48] The government's collapse discouraged investment and left Romania struggling with political chaos, a deep recession, and a state sector that needed restructuring, while the private sector was still in its infancy and largely untaxed, operating on the edges of the law.

In agriculture, the country also underwent upheaval following the restitution of land that had been confiscated under communism. The reparatory measure was popular but led to fragmentation of property and a drop in production, as many of the new own-ers lived in cities or did not have the necessary equipment to work the land.[49] In these dire conditions, the challenge to build a democracy and a market economy appeared impossible.

The Challenges of Economic Restructuring

After completing price liberalization, Romania adopted a privatization law and began a mass privatization campaign,[50] with people receiving coupons in state investment funds, which would control 30 percent of the capital of state-owned companies. A few years later the campaign expanded, and people could trade coupons for stakes in state-owned companies. The smaller and more promising state-owned companies were privatized via sales to their employees and management.

The methods chosen by the government were considered the only possibilities, given the scarcity of foreign investment. The coupon privatization failed, however, to capitalize and retool the companies and improve governance. Also, in the absence of a functional stock exchange, the coupons were being traded by street vendors at a fraction of their value.[51] The first signs of crony capitalism appeared, as the government regularly gave tariff exemptions to connected businessmen or allowed them to lease various lucrative state assets at ridiculous prices in exchange for bribes. Official corruption became a national problem, with public assets being transferred to a new class of businessmen, usually well-connected former communist or Securitate officials.

The 1990s also saw the rise of pyramid schemes, which gathered the savings of millions of Romanians while promising returns eight to sixteen times larger in a matter of months. Many politicians also invested funds in these schemes but were paid with priority in exchange for letting the scheme go on. One such scheme called Caritas (charity) had millions of subscribers and was estimated to have gathered billions of dollars from people.[52] The collapse of Caritas and dozens of smaller, similar schemes left hundreds of thousands of Romanians without their savings. Financial fraud was also rampant in the banking system, with state bankers offering preferential loans to politically connected businessmen (who never repaid them) while private banks were looted by their owners at the expense of depositors.

After years of slow reforms, following the opposition's victory in 1996, Romania changed course and adopted the so-called shock therapy, which had been implemented elsewhere in CEE. With World Bank assistance, the government began a massive restructuring program, closing dozens of inefficient coal mines and laying off thousands of workers at state companies, some of which were sold off to foreign investors, including French carmaker Renault.[53] Economic output fell again,[54] bringing Romania to the verge of bankruptcy and needing salvation from the International Monetary Fund, which in turn imposed budget austerity measures, causing mass poverty and political instability. Successive governments collapsed amid scandals related to fraudulent financial schemes and coalition disputes.

Recovery and the Road to the EU

Despite the tumult of the late 1990s, Romania progressed in restructuring its economy. In February 2000, it began negotiations to join the European Union.[55] The economy started growing again, with foreign investment beginning to flow into the cash-starved economy.[56] Privatization changed from mass coupons to sale of state companies to Western investors. Big-box European retailers entered the Romanian market, and American-style malls opened in large cities.

The status as an EU candidate country made Romania eligible for financial assistance from the bloc, with billions of euros in development funds flowing in for projects such as sanitation, schools upgrades, and infrastructure improvements.[57] After Romania's 2007 EU accession, the economy remained robust, culminating in a GDP growth of

9.3 percent in 2008. Amid a general feeling of newfound and overdue prosperity, successive governments generously increased wages and pensions by double digits almost every year to make up for the previous two decades of austerity. Western banks also arrived, expanding easy credit, and Romanians turned into some of the most avid consumers in Europe, with yearly double-digit growth in sales of new appliances, electronics, and cars.[58] In real estate, prices grew massively each year. With EU membership came visa-free travel and the right to work and study anywhere in Western Europe, and millions of Romanians made use of this new freedom. This led to labor shortages in Romania, which pushed wages higher.

This period of prosperity ended abruptly in 2009 due to the global financial crisis. The International Monetary Fund and the EU extended Romania a "seat belt" rescue package worth €20 billion,[59] but tax revenues collapsed. The center-right government enacted austerity measures, cutting public sector wages by 25 percent amid massive protests and strikes.[60] In the following years, the economy recovered strongly. By 2019 it reached a level of 70 percent of the EU average in terms of purchasing power (up from 22 percent in 2000), equal to Slovakia and surpassing four other EU countries.[61] In addition, the Romanian economy is seven times larger in terms of GDP per capita in 2019 compared to 1989.[62] While fiscal discipline has been traditionally weak, public debt remains among the lowest in Europe, at 35 percent of GDP.[63]

Romania's economy was hit hard during the 2020 pandemic, with GDP dropping by 5.2 percent,[64] tax revenues collapsing, and the budget deficit exceeding 8 percent.[65] However, EU membership proved to be an anchor once again, with Romania standing to receive €80 billion from the EU reconstruction fund, which economists believe will help generate a strong recovery in 2021.

Civil Society

One of the first measures the National Salvation Front took during the revolution was to promise democracy.[66] On December 31, 1989, the Front published new rules for registering political parties and community organizations.[67] These were excessive in requiring that associations (without differentiating from political parties) have 251 registered members. Later, a law from 1924 was resurrected to ensure registering nonprofit organizations.[68] However, the law was restrictive by contemporary standards, requiring prior government approval for registration. But it offered a good framework and reduced registration requirements to twenty members.[69] In 2000, the law was changed to require only three members to form an association.[70] Thousands of associations quickly sprang up, with many being started by or partnering with foreign charities that had earlier delivered humanitarian aid to Romania.

The plight of Romania's children was a primary focus of international humanitarian assistance. Once communism fell, three pressing issues surfaced that the regime had either covered up or ignored: the callous disregard for those with disabilities, the abuse of children warehoused in state institutions, and a raging pediatric AIDS epidemic.

Within weeks of the revolution, a group of parents of children with disabilities hospitalized in Bucharest founded one of the first domestic aid organizations, the Association for Support of Disabled Children. State policy was such that parents were often interned in hospitals with their children to provide care for them, receiving no assistance from the state. Frustrated parents started the association to lobby for recognition of disabilities and financial support for disabled children. In 1992, they succeeded when parliament passed a law granting certain rights to persons with disabilities, including benefits for them and their caretakers.

When the Ceaușescu regime attempted to combat population decline by banning abortion and contraception, one result was mass child abandonment. Under the austerity measures of the 1980s, many parents either could not afford or did not want to care for their children, some of whom were unwanted or disabled. International media flooded into Romania after the revolution, uncovering the horrors inflicted upon hundreds of thousands of children in state facilities. Images of dark-headed, emaciated, and under-developed children, many of whom were severely disabled due to their institutionalization, were broadcast around the world. The children were primarily from poor communities whose parents were encouraged by the state, and duped by propaganda that the children would be well cared for, to give over their care to responsible authorities. Abandoned in "slaughterhouse" institutions with death rates around 50 percent, children were two or more to a bed, neglected, and malnourished, as staff often stole their food rations, drugged them, and beat them. They were dying of neglect, malnutrition, and disease.[71]

Another tragedy that unfolded involved some ten thousand children who were infected with AIDS, which they had contracted through state vaccination campaigns that used shared needles or through hospital procedures such as blood transfusions. Infectious disease hospitals in Bucharest and Constanta, for instance, were overwhelmed with pediatric AIDS cases, while communist authorities did not recognize the existence of the disease in Romania. By not screening donated blood, Romania had inflicted on its children the largest pediatric outbreak of AIDS in Europe.

Western church groups and other charities organized donations and began developing local networks of activists to help distribute them. In Sweden, church groups ran a telethon and donated the proceeds to Save the Children, which then dispatched a mission to collaborate with several Romanian nonprofits, including the Association for Support of Disabled Children and the Association for Children with Mental Disability. The groups were among the first advocates for legislation for children's rights, benefiting from the support of Swedish, German, and French nonprofits transferring know-how and assisting in the development of the organizations.

Save the Children Romania, founded on April 20, 1990, by the Swedish Save the Children organization, aimed at first "to offer emergency aid to children in orphanages in a dramatic state."[72] It also founded the first services to prevent child abandonment, "to support in a family system the HIV/AIDS children, protecting street children, and supporting children who were victims of sexual abuse or human trafficking."[73]

Support from Western governments and transnational organizations was critical in setting up Romanian civil society organizations that could effectively advocate for human rights and democratic freedoms. Freedom of the press and freedom of assembly were affirmed in initial legislation enacted by the National Salvation Front. However, the lack of tradition in implementing such freedoms meant that the opposition had little access to state media. During the political violence of June 13–15, 1990, for instance, opposition newspapers and leaders were physically attacked by the miners, as were students and other antigovernment protesters. Western governments condemned the violence and sent aid to set up NGOs to advocate for human rights and freedom of the press.

Among the first transnational NGOs to arrive in Romania after the end of the Ceaușescu dictatorship were Amnesty International and Human Rights Watch, which sent in rapporteurs to monitor the human rights situation. The Organization for Security and Co-operation in Europe had set up the Helsinki Watch organizations to monitor human rights in the East. In Romania, APADOR-CH (the Association for Protection of Human Rights—the Helsinki Committee) was founded in 1990 to monitor human rights abuses and support victims in bringing their cases to court. APADOR-CH monitors conditions in prison, documents police abuse, helps victims, and lobbies the Romanian authorities to improve their human rights record. Romania joined the Council of Europe in 1993, which opened a way for Romanian citizens to have access to the protections of the European Court for Human Rights, which issues judgments that are mandatory for signatory states.

Civil society organizations were also critical for developing and protecting a free press in Romania. Two organizations emerged as particularly important in this domain—the ActiveWatch Media Monitoring Agency and the Romanian Center for Independent Journalism. Formed in 1994, ActiveWatch monitors and reports on human rights violations, media pressure, and lack of transparency of central and local government initiatives.[74] As of 2004, it is a member of the Reporters Without Borders network.[75] The Center for Independent Journalism, on the other hand, has had a formative role in training many generations of Romanian journalists. The media freedom NGOs and other human rights groups had an important role in pressing for government transparency and in obtaining legislative changes such as the Law for Access to Information of 2001, which promoted transparency in the administration.[76]

One of the key players in the development of civil society in the region was the Soros Foundation, later rebranded the Open Society Foundations (OSF), established by Hungarian-born billionaire philanthropist George Soros, who set aside over $11 billion for his foundation. The Soros Foundation was the first well-funded Western group to offer grants to Romanian NGOs, supporting their development. It reported spending $150 million in Romania before closing its branch in 2014.[77]

European state-funded associations have also played a substantial role as donors in civil society development. The European Union, through its civil society and development grants, has become the largest donor for Romanian NGOs, offering significant financing packages for human resource development and other projects. Additionally, the EEA and Norway Grants are funded by Iceland, Liechtenstein, and Norway as part of their free trade deal with the European Union. A key goal of the grants is to contribute to a more equal Europe, both socially and economically.[78] In Romania it has donated over $600 million, mostly through the Foundation for the Development of Civil Society, which was set up in 1994 with funds from the European Union to support the NGO sector.[79]

A 2004 law allowed Romania's citizens to become donors to nonprofits. The legislation, named "the 2 percent law," gave Romanians a choice whether to contribute 2 percent of their due taxes to a nonprofit cause instead of going to the government.[80] The initiative has been successful, diversifying funding streams and furthering development.

By 2015, the NGO sector employed about one hundred thousand Romanians and had revenues of about $3 billion, with one in five NGOs focusing on charity, another fifth on sports and recreation, 13 percent on education, and 12 percent each operating as cultural and professional organizations. Two-thirds of nonprofits operate in urban areas.[81]

Donations, however, do not necessarily coincide with civic participation. While nearly one-third of West Europeans join civil society associations, less than 20 percent do so in East Europe.[82] Romanians, at 9.6 percent, rank the lowest in the European Union for joining at least one association.[83] Since 2015, there has been a rise in public activism due to dramatic and overt levels of government corruption, which has brought down politicians and political parties, as will be discussed in the next section.

Key Social Issues

Key social issues in Romania overlap like concentric circles, with one flowing into another, and they are often difficult to separate. The following pages will focus on three major issues affecting the everyday lives of large segments of Romanian society: political corruption, poverty, and social exclusion. Corruption is generally seen as the most pressing issue facing the country, widely perceived as intertwined with most other problems Romanians confront. Poverty is another issue that plagues too many Romanians, limiting their capacity to enact change and causing undue suffering. Social exclusion, often fueled by prejudice and intolerance, also drags down Romanian society.

Corruption has plagued Romanian politics since the 1989 revolution. Since the 2000 elections, it has emerged as a centerpiece of political campaigns, public protests, and political power struggles. Government corruption is the abuse of power for personal gain and takes many forms, including but not limited to bribery, nepotism, cronyism, and influence peddling. Often corruption flourishes in polities that lack transparency, and it has tangible consequences. In Romania, the effects of the theft of public monies by political elites and government officials are palpable: hospitals lack supplies, schools are shorted on textbooks, criminals are found not guilty, and so forth. Although corruption itself is difficult to measure, experiences and perceptions of corruption are regularly surveyed. On corruption *perception* scales, Romania continually places poorly. In 2017, 68 percent of Romanians reported being personally affected by corruption, which ranked them at the top of all EU member states.[84] One in four reported having been asked or expected to pay a bribe to receive a public service, and nearly half felt that the problem had worsened in the three years prior to the study.[85] In 2019, Romania tied for second-to-last place with Hungary in terms of corruption levels among the EU-28.[86]

The Romanian language offers a rich vocabulary for corruption. For example, *șpagă* is slang for "bribe," while *mită* is its legal term. *Bacșiș* and *peșcheș* ("tip" and "present" in Turkish) worked their way into Romanian during Ottoman rule and can signify a bribe. During communism, public services were secured through *o atenție* (a little something) that showed one's gratitude. Givers offered hard-to-find imported products like cigarettes (preferably Kent) or coffee, or flowers and sundry items. During the postcommunist period, the practice continued, but the spectrum of goods offered expanded. Cash eventually became king when market scarcities subsided. According to the EU, corruption costs more than €38 billion annually, which equals nearly 16 percent of Romania's GDP.[87]

While graft was inherent to the Romanian system, perhaps it is most notable in public administration and medicine. Medical corruption, or "patients bearing gifts," remains widespread in former communist countries, including Hungary, Poland,[88] and Latvia, where salaries are low and "overburdened medical institutions fail to meet patients' demands for prompt care, and staff accept under-the-table payments to close some of this gap."[89] Stories abound in the Romanian press about patients dying in hospitals due to a lack of care because a bribe was not forthcoming.[90]

External entities like the European Commission have monitored Romanian corruption for nearly twenty years. In 2002, the EU insisted on the formation of a special prosecutor's office. The National Anticorruption Directorate (DNA) was set up to root out corruption. Since its inception, the DNA has successfully prosecuted hundreds of officials, including a former prime minister, party heads, parliamentarians, government advisers, and hundreds of local mayors and city officials. The majority of investigations and prosecutions are of PSD party members and their affiliates. Consequently, the agency is continuously under assault from the PSD and its supporters.

Many Romanians feel they have little power to halt graft. Trust in public institutions has continued plummeting. In 2015, just 23.8 percent reported having confidence in the government, and only 12.6 percent trusted parliament.[91] Notably, 61 percent trusted the DNA, which ranked as the fourth-most-trusted public institution, after the army, the Orthodox Church, and the gendarmerie. In the past three years, however, Romanians through collective action have stood up against corruption.

Two major incidents galvanized Romanians to engage in antigovernment protests in numbers that the country had not seen since communism fell. The first was a deadly nightclub fire that brought down a government. On October 30, 2015, a Bucharest nightclub opened for a rock concert. Some four hundred young club goers packed into Colectiv (The Collective), or four times more than the club was zoned to accommodate. One patron later said, "There wasn't room to properly flick a cigarette butt to the floor."[92] The show got underway, but within seconds of setting off fireworks, everything went horribly wrong. Flames spread quickly, trapping hundreds inside. Only one exit worked; the other was locked. Panic ensued as patrons rushed the door, causing a stampede. Twenty-seven people died, and over 140 more were badly injured. More would later succumb. Corruption had become an overt killer. The country went into mourning, blaming nightclub owners and politicians for greed and corruption. Days after the tragedy, hundreds of thousands filled the streets across the country demanding change. Protestors carried banners that read "Corruption kills," calling for the resignations of the prime minister and the district mayor. Media revealed that the club had violated safety requirements, failing a fire department inspection, a requirement to operate. Yet the district mayor issued the paperwork anyway. The fire department never returned after Colectiv opened to check whether violations had been rectified. The pyrotechnics company failed to set up within regulations. In short, an amalgamation of avarice and malfeasance culminated in a national calamity. Within a week, the government and the mayor had resigned. Prosecutors were building their cases.

The deadly confluence of corruption did not end at the inferno site; it followed the survivors through the health-care system. Plagued by chronic underfunding, poor stewardship, and corruption, Romania's health care ranks repeatedly as the worst in Europe by the Euro Health Consumer Index.[93] The country spends the least amount per capita of any EU member state on health care, while mortality for preventable diseases is the highest in the EU and life expectancy among the lowest. Bucharest hospitals were unable to treat all the medical complexities of the Colectiv patients, transferring some abroad. One severe burn victim who initially received care in Bucharest was later transferred to a UK hospital. She was in a medically induced coma for a month and had multiple complications, including lung collapse. Upon returning to Bucharest, she said doctors "took a look at the wounds, and told me I was fine. The government said there was a plan to support the victims, but none of the hospitals knew what to do."[94] Her plight was ignored, and she was left to find her own care.

Other Colectiv victims literally festered in hospitals, with inadequate medical staff to treat them and no basic supplies. One survivor recounted,

I had third degree burns and grafts on my shoulder, back, and on my left hand. At the hospital, I wasn't admitted to the intensive care unit, but they covered me in a wool blanket. The cleaning lady there wiped the dust from our heads, and she used the same mop in the hallways as in our rooms. I was washed by my mother and the mother of the girl I shared the room with. If one of my wounds would fester on a Saturday or Sunday, they couldn't do anything about it because the storage room was locked on those days. They had no supplies—no bandages, no creams.[95]

Photo 16.2. Romanian paramedics load ten Colectiv fire club victims on a NATO plane to be transported to hospitals in Great Britain and Norway on November 8, 2015. (Gabriel Petrescu, Shutterstock)

Corruption also contributes to a medical brain drain as doctors and nurses choose to practice elsewhere for better pay and working conditions. In the decade after joining the EU, over forty-three thousand physicians left, creating a deficit that reflects in patient care.[96]

Corruption continued killing over the next months as the Colectiv death toll rose to sixty-four. A team of investigative journalists uncovered a corruption scandal within the corruption scandal. They learned that a big pharma company supplying antiseptics to 350 Romanian public hospitals had diluted the disinfectant.[97] In 2016, prosecutors opened an investigation against the company. Hospital directors, who are political appointees, were accused of taking a 30 percent cut of contracts for the antiseptic.[98] Prosecutors moved relatively quickly and secured numerous prison convictions, sentencing the district mayor, club and pyrotechnic firm owners, fire department officials, and others. In 2019, a documentary that followed journalists on their quest for the truth about the Colectiv incident was released, garnering international acclaim and an Oscar nomination.[99]

In February 2017, over six hundred thousand Romanians occupied streets once again in subzero temperatures in the largest antigovernment protests in twenty-five years. The aim was to take down another corrupt PSD government. One protester explained, "We have reached an unbearable limit. The ruling party is in fact a mafia organization and they are now legalizing theft."[100] For protestors, the PSD cabinet crossed the line by passing an emergency decree in a night session that made graft punishable by prison only if the monetary losses exceeded $47,500, the equivalent of "a Mercedes for every politician."[101] An amnesty bill was in the works as well to release tens of thousands of inmates, a move the government claimed was necessary to relieve prison overcrowding—but notably freeing politicians convicted of corruption alongside violent offenders.

Protestors chanted, "Thieves," "Don't let them get away," and "Shame on you." Others held signs depicting PSD leaders in prison garb, waved Romanian flags, and blew whistles and horns. "Rezist" (Resist) became the crowd's mantra, and the movement born then became known as #Rezist. Protests continued for days. Around the square in Bucharest, light shows projected onto buildings displayed the EU and Romanian flags, interspersed with *Rezist*.

A panicked government canceled its initial decree. However, PSD leaders continued to chip away at anticorruption institutions by firing the DNA chief who had prosecuted politicians and setting up a special prosecution office to handle justice officials, which the EU deemed an attempt to intimidate judges and prosecutors. The PSD chairman, Liviu Dragnea, who engineered the campaign against the justice system in order to escape corruption charges he faced, tried to mimic Hungary's populist prime minister Viktor Orbán with more pointed anti-Western rhetoric, claiming that the EU was interfering too much in Romania's domestic affairs. In 2019, relations became tense between the ruling PSD and the EU, with the latter warning Romania that it could face sanctions such as losing funding and its voting rights in the European Council if it followed through on plans to decriminalize some corruption offenses.[102] The Romanian government backed down ahead of the EU elections in May 2019, which saw the ruling PSD heavily defeated. After the elections, the Supreme Court sentenced Dragnea to three and a half years in prison for corruption.[103]

Photo 16.3. On February 1, 2017, more than 250,000 Romanians demonstrated in Bucharest against corruption in the biggest protest since 1989. (Creative Lab, Shutterstock)

Poverty in Romania

Romania's economy developed rapidly after the country joined the European Union in 2007. While there has been economic progress, with the poverty rate dropping from 40 percent in 2006 to 15 percent in 2017,[104] poverty still permeates parts of society and certain underdeveloped regions.[105] It has dire consequences for the entire country, including brain drain through out-migration, low educational attainment levels leading to an undereducated workforce and less foreign investment, and, most importantly, untold suffering and misery for millions of Romanians. Many lack access to a quality education, adequate health-care services, and even basic amenities like potable water and sanitation.[106] While poverty is experienced differently everywhere, Romania has the largest number of poor who experience deep episodes of poverty that is generational.[107] Notably, one in four Romanians lives on less than $5.50 a day.[108]

A 2018 European Commission report squarely faulted the government for not doing better, noting that poverty was deeply entrenched in Romania due to "limited integration of employment, education and social services," preventing "disadvantaged groups from escaping poverty."[109] The European Commission stated that if Romania utilized better social welfare transfer payments, poverty could be alleviated.

Poverty figures are particularly alarming for children, rural inhabitants, and the Roma minority (the last is discussed under "Social Exclusion"). In 2018, Romanian children were at the highest risk of poverty within the EU at an astonishing 38 percent. For those living in rural areas, or slightly under half the population, the at-risk level of poverty was 70 percent.[110] This was four times higher than for city dwellers and twice as high as for those residing in towns and suburbs.[111] The World Bank predicts that the COVID-19 pandemic will worsen poverty in Romania as jobs and social exclusion widen.

Social Exclusion

Since 1997, Romanian governments have adopted a series of laws to protect individual and minority rights. But governments have also adopted policies and supported political, economic, and social institutions that exclude or subordinate those who do not belong to the dominant understanding of Romanian nationhood. Two groups on the margins experience social exclusion to extremes: ethnic Roma and members of the lesbian, gay, bisexual, trans, and intersex community (LGBTI). Both consistently rank as the least tolerated minorities in Romania, at 72 percent and 74 percent, respectively.

An estimated two million Roma live in Romania,[112] and a confluence of factors converge to make Roma the most socioeconomically and politically excluded group. While some obstacles to fuller social, economic, and political inclusion may stem from Romani traditions, most result squarely from indifferent or ineffective public policies, shaped in part by historical legacies and long-standing anti-Roma racism. Roma face inequality in employment, housing, health, and education.

Roma persecution in the Romanian territories spans centuries. Romani peoples are composed of many different groups—much like Native Americans have various tribal affiliations—and historically have self-identified through their professional status, such as coppersmiths, gold miners, or bear trainers. Roma share a common Indian heritage, their migration beginning in the ninth century, making their way to Europe through various century-long trajectories. Historians date their entrance into Romanian spaces to the fourteenth century, brought by the Turks as enslaved peoples serving the army as it advanced into the Balkans. From the fourteenth through the nineteenth centuries, Roma were enslaved by the Orthodox Church, nobility, and state institutions. After emancipation in 1855–1856, most Roma eked out marginal existences, living in abject poverty in rural areas, where many worked in agriculture as day laborers, often in the same places where their families were enslaved. During World War II, Roma were victims of the Antonescu regime, which targeted them during the Holocaust. Under communism, ethnic lines were ostensibly erased when all became "comrades" (*tovarăşi*). As a result, Roma gained access to jobs, state-granted public housing, child subsidies, and education, as authorities enforced work and school attendance. However, setbacks occurred. The state targeted more persistently nomadic Romani groups, forbidding their itinerant lifestyle and forcing them into permanent residencies. While the revolution restored significant economic, political, and social rights, Roma were infrequent beneficiaries of them. Many lost jobs, having worked largely in state-owned companies that were sold off or in agricultural collectives that dissolved. Roma remained the least educated and most marginalized. In a free market, Romani labor was devalued; discrimination was no longer held in check. Signs appeared in some shop windows, reading, "No dogs, no gypsies," while graffiti scrawled on city buildings read, "Death to gypsies." Anti-Roma racism was not confined to rhetoric. From 1990 to 1995, it became violent. In forty-two locations across the country, Roma were attacked by their non-Roma neighbors who set their houses on fire, driving Roma out of their communities, sometimes with the participation of local authorities.[113] Antidiscrimination legislation has since been put in place, and Roma benefit from Romania's membership in the EU, which monitors government actions. Nevertheless, in 2017, one in three Roma reported facing discrimination while searching for employment.[114] While activist groups continuously advocate for social justice, the country lags in promoting initiatives to assist Roma.

In Romania, as in other regional countries, Roma are the poorest of the poor, with an at-risk-of-poverty rate of 84 percent, which is three times greater than for non-Roma.[115] Only slightly over a quarter of Roma report having jobs.[116] A 2014 World Bank report on Romanian Roma found that 90 percent of Romani households experience severe material deprivation and that some 40 percent of children are undernourished, leading to lifelong cognitive and socioeconomic disadvantages.[117] An estimated half of Romani children live in overcrowded conditions, and one-third live in slums.[118] Notably, poverty rates have fluctuated very little for Roma over the past decades.[119]

Social inclusion can only be secured with government policies. The EU, the Council of Europe, and the World Bank, among others, have closely monitored the situation of Roma in Central and East Europe, providing fiscal support and guidance on policy initiatives. Additionally, nonprofit organizations like the Open Society Foundations have advocated for decades for inclusion of Roma through better government programming. Recognizing that Roma live precariously throughout Europe, in 2013 the EU launched a Roma inclusion initiative for all member states to be achieved by 2020. Each state enacted its own policies based on recommendations. With little to no representation for Roma in the Romanian parliament, their concerns are all too often pushed aside.

The LGBTI Community

Social exclusion greatly affects Romania's LGBTI communities. The rights of LBGTI people in CEE are starkly different from those of their West European counterparts, who legally marry and adopt children and face less discrimination. As one writer put it, "where an iron curtain once split Europe, a rainbow curtain now divides the continent."[120] Hungary, Poland, and Romania rank as some of the worst places in Europe for LGBTI people to live. In Romania, LGBTI persons experience more discrimination, harassment, and violence than is reported on average in the EU.[121] Moreover, the country has disappointingly lost ground in the area of LGBTI rights after making progress in the 2000s when it passed antidiscrimination laws, amended hate crime laws to include attacks on members of the LGBTI community, and decriminalized homosexuality. Romanians are among the least tolerant of the EU's citizens on LGBTI issues.[122] The majority, 54 percent, do not believe that gay, lesbian, or bisexual persons should have the same rights as heterosexual couples. In 2019, the Council of Europe's Commission on Racism and Intolerance issued a report on Romania, cautioning against widespread hate speech and discrimination, as well as "inadequate responses of the criminal justice system on hate crimes."[123]

Advocacy organizations, such as the Bucharest-based nonprofit ACCEPT, actively work to promote LGBTI equality through events such as gay pride parades, education campaigns, research, and outreach activities. Despite these efforts, violence and discrimination continue. Approximately 43 percent of LGBTI persons surveyed in Romania reported being harassed in the year prior, which was higher than the EU average of 38 percent.[124] Among trans or intersex persons, 20 percent were attacked or sexually abused in the five years prior to the survey, which was double that of what other LGBTI members experienced.

LGBTI rights have come under national scrutiny over the past two years, as political parties, jockeying for favor among conservative voters, have proposed anti-LGBTI legislation. In 2018, the PSD attempted to amend the constitution to define marriage as an act between a man and a woman and thus prohibit same-sex marriages. The referendum ultimately failed due to low voter turnout, as it was seen as an attempt by the PSD government to separate Romania from the EU. State law does not allow same-sex marriages or civil unions, making Romania one of the outliers in the EU on this issue. However, it does recognize same-sex unions from abroad, due to EU law on mutual recognition of civil documents. In June 2020, parliament passed a law banning gender identity education. Widely condemned by human rights groups, the law marked a hard conservative shift, aligning Romania with Hungary and Poland, which have also enacted anti-LGBTI platforms.[125] Romania's Constitutional Court struck down the gender identity ban, ruling it unconstitutional.

Emerging Challenges

Romania embarked on a slow but consistent path toward democracy. The evolution, however, has come in waves. The political and economic transformation of the post-Ceauşescu years was accompanied by riots and social tumult, which periodically threatened stability as the country demolished the old system and rebuilt a new foundation for its government and economy. Since 2000, with the notable exceptions of the global financial crisis and the COVID-19 pandemic, the Romanian economy expanded strongly, at times leading Europe in growth. Despite this progress, Romania still has structural challenges to resolve that could threaten its future development, including the out-migration of millions of its citizens and an aging population.

Wide rural-urban and regional divisions remain visible in politics, the economy, and educational attainment. Closing this gap and bringing equal opportunity to all of Romania's regions is another major challenge, but instruments such as EU regional development funding should help meet this goal. Romanians continue to see Western institutions as allies of the citizenry against their own political elites and remain among the most enthusiastic Europeans when it comes to continued support for EU membership and trust in EU institutions.[126] During the pandemic, Romania secured €80 billion in aid from the EU, in addition to benefiting from the EU Commission making deals for COVID-19 vaccines on behalf of its member states.

As recent years have shown, the political situation remains in flux, especially concerning anticorruption politics and the consolidation of democratic institutions. More than thirty years since the revolution, most Romanians are disappointed with their democracy and politicians. According to a 2016 poll, 90 percent reported not trusting political parties to represent their interests.[127] General dissatisfaction can enable populist, antiestablishment forces and extremist movements to present alternative models of government—some of which, such as the ultranationalist one, would be dangerous in a diverse country with large ethnic minorities.

Romanians have demonstrated significant capacity to hold governments accountable, which is a key requirement for democratic government. Yet building democracy through the work of community organizations, many of them foreign sponsored, and through weak political institutions takes time and is not a straightforward process. Moreover, aside from its internal problems with corruption and the unpredictability of contentious politics, Romania is situated at a crossroads between the EU and a resurgent Russia, which has made efforts to destabilize its neighbors, especially those it considers hostile. These conditions pose ongoing challenges for Romanian politics and society.

Study Questions

1. Why did Romanians revolt against communism in 1989?
2. What preceded the communist dictatorship? How did Romania's shifting territorial borders shape its political development?
3. What replaced communism after 1989, and what were some of the unique elements of the Romanian postcommunist transition?
4. What key variables have shaped Romania's development as a democracy?
5. What are Romania's most acute social problems?

Suggested Readings

Ciobanu, Monica. "Romania's Travails with Democracy and Accession to the European Union." *Europe-Asia Studies* 58, no. 8 (2007): 1429–50.

Deletant, Dennis. *Ceauşescu and the Securitate: Coercion and Dissent in Romania, 1965–1989.* London: Hurst, 1995.

Gallagher, Tom. *Modern Romania: The End of Communism, the Failure of Democratic Reforms and the Theft of a Nation.* New York: New York University Press, 2008.

Gross, Peter, and Vladimir Tismăneanu. "The End of Postcommunism in Romania." *Journal of Democracy* 16, no. 2 (2005): 146–62.

Ioanid, Radu. *The Destruction of Jews and Gypsies under the Antonescu Regime, 1940–1944.* Chicago: Ivan R. Dee, in association with the United States Holocaust Memorial Museum, 2000.

Kligman, Gail. "Political Demography: The Banning of Abortion in Ceausescu's Romania." In *Conceiving the New World Order: The Global Politics of Reproduction*, edited by Faye Ginsberg and Rayna Rapp, 234–55. Berkeley: University of California Press, 1995.

Livezeanu, Irina. *Cultural Politics in Greater Romania: Regionalism, Nation Building and Ethnic Struggle, 1918–1930.* Ithaca, NY: Cornell University Press, 1995.

Pasti, Vladimir. *The Challenge of Transition.* Boulder, CO: East European Monographs, 1997.

Siani-Davies, Peter. *The Romanian Revolution of 1989.* Ithaca, NY: Cornell University Press, 2007.

Websites

Balkan Insight: https://balkaninsight.com

Radio Free Europe/Radio Liberty, Romanian Service: https://www.rferl.org/Romania
Romania Insider (English-language news website): https://www.romania-insider.com
Universul (English-language version of Romanian news website): https://universul.net/
  categorie/english

Notes

1. Dennis Deletant, "In and Out of Focus: An Academic in the Sights of the Securitate 1965–1989," *UCL European Institute*, December 2, 2015, https://www.ucl.ac.uk/european-inst itute/analysis/2015-16/dennis-deletant.

2. Eugen Tomiuc, "Finally We Called It Christmas Again: My Role in Romania's Revolution," Radio Free Europe/Radio Liberty, December 20, 2009, https://www.rferl.org/a/F inally_We_Called_It_Christmas_Again_My_Role_In_Romanias_Revolution__/1908965.html.

3. Tomiuc, "Finally We Called It Christmas Again."

4. V. N. Vinogradov, "Romania in the First World War: The Years of Neutrality, 1914–1916," *International History Review* 14, no. 3 (1992): 452–61, https://www.jstor.org/stable/40106598.

5. Vinogradov, "Romania in the First World War."

6. Silvia Suteu, "The Multinational State That Wasn't: The Constitutional Definition of Romania as a National State," *Vienna Online Journal on International Constitutional Law* 11, no. 3 (2017): 413–35; Irina Livezeanu, *Cultural Politics in Greater Romania: Regionalism, Nation Building, and Ethnic Struggle, 1918–1930* (Ithaca, NY: Cornell University Press, 1995).

7. Vladimir Solonari, *Purifying the Nation* (Washington, DC: Woodrow Wilson Center Press, 2010).

8. Tuvia Friling, Radu Ioanid, and Mihail E. Ionescu, eds., *International Commission on the Holocaust in Romania: Final Report* (Bucharest: POLIROM, 2004), http://www.inshr-ew.ro/ro/file s/Raport%20Final/Final_Report.pdf.

9. Sinziana Ionescu, "How Children Survived during the Great Famine," *Constanta*, August 12, 2017, https://adevarul.ro/locale/constanta/cum-supravietuit-copiii-timpul-marii-foamete-rom ania-si-a-salvat-viitorul-trimitand-fiii-zone-mai-putin-afectate-calamitate-1_598c7f825ab6550cb 8e5a1e8/index.html.

10. Christian Alexandru Groza, "The Sovietisation of Romania, 1946–1948: The First Two Years behind the Curtain of Propaganda," *Local Cultures and Societies* 7, no. 2 (2016): 369.

11. *Final Report* (Bucharest: The Presidential Committee for Analysing the Communist Dictatorship, 2006), 160, https://www.wilsoncenter.org/sites/default/files/media/documents/artic le/RAPORT%20FINAL_%20CADCR.pdf.

12. Alison Mutler, "Buried in a Casino Wall, a Dark Secret from Romania's Past," *RFE/RL*, August 8, 2020, https://www.rferl.org/a/secret-political-prisoners-note-buried-in-casino-wall-re vives-dark-memories-of-romania-s-communist-era/30773148.html.

13. Alison Mutler, "Romania: Art Exhibit at Ex Prison Show Horrors of Communism," AP, July 21, 2017, https://apnews.com/article/ee8bc2b4cd074ce5a20489215e370d78.

14. Florin Constantiniu, "The Withdrawal of Soviet Troops from Romania—Obscure Aspects," *Historia*, https://www.historia.ro/sectiune/general/articol/retragerea-trupelor-sovietice-d in-romania-1958-aspecte-obscure.

15. Constantiniu, "The Withdrawal of Soviet Troops from Romania."

16. Gail Kligman, "Political Demography: The Banning of Abortion in Ceausescu's Romania," in *Conceiving the New World Order: The Global Politics of Reproduction*, ed. Faye Ginsberg and Rayna Rapp, 234–55 (Berkeley: University of California Press, 1995).

17. "Why Ceauşescu Would Have Wanted to Resign before the 14th Congress of the PCR," *Descopera.ro*, November 24, 2019, https://www.descopera.ro/istorie/18603031-de-ce-ar-fi-vrut-C eauşescu-sa-demisioneze-inaintea-congresului-al-xiv-lea-al-pcr.

18. "Congresul al XIV-lea a PCR, şansa ratată a lui Ceauşescu de a scăpa de plutonul de execuţie," *digi24*, December 17, 2018, https://www.digi24.ro/stiri/actualitate/congresul-al-xiv-lea -a-pcr-sansa-ratata-a-lui-Ceauşescu-de-a-scapa-de-plutonul-de-executie-1050577.

19. "Documentele care au stat la baza procesului si a executiei Ceauşestilor rechizitoriul inculpatilor," *Mediafax*, December 27, 2019, https://www.mediafax.ro/social/documentele-care-au-stat -la-baza-procesului-si-a-executiei-ceausestilor-rechizitoriul-inculpatilor-18679379.

20. "Comunicatul către ţară al consiliului fsn din 22 decembrie 1989," *Historia*, https:// www.historia.ro/sectiune/general/articol/comunicatul-catre-tara-al-consiliului-f-s-n-din-22-decem brie-1989.

21. "Decretul legii nr. 8 din 31 decembrie 1989 privind inregistrarea si functionarea partidelor politice si organizatiilor obstesti din Romania," *Camera Deputaţilor*, December 31, 1989, http:// www.cdep.ro/pls/legis/legis_pck.htp_act_text?idt=11004.

22. "Decret-Lege nr. 82 din 13 februarie 1990," *Portal Legislativ*, http://legislatie.just.ro/Publ ic/DetaliiDocument/14964.

23. "Monitorul Oficial al Romaniei, Rezultatul alegerilor din 20 mai 1990," *Autorităţii Electorale Permanente*, http://www.roaep.ro/alegeri_1990/wp-content/uploads/81-82.pdf.

24. "Constituţia din 1991.Monitorul Oficial, Partea I nr. 233 din 21 noiembrie 1991," *Indaco Lege[5]*, https://lege5.ro/Gratuit/gy3donjs/constitutia-din-1991?pid=9151162#p-9151162.

25. "Lege nr. 303 din 28 iunie 2004," *Portal Legislativ*, http://legislatie.just.ro/Public/Detalii Document/53074.

26. "Lege nr.151 din 15 iulie 1998 privind dezvoltarea regională în România," *Camera Deputaţilor*, http://www.cdep.ro/pls/legis/legis_pck.htp_act_text?idt=17411.

27. "Ziare.com—Regionalizare, varianta UDMR: Despre zona maghiara si esecul dezvoltarii," *DW*, February 5, 2013, https://www.dw.com/ro/ziarecom-regionalizare-varianta-udmr-despre -zona-maghiara-si-esecul-dezvoltarii/a-16576552.

28. "Comunicatul către ţară al consiliului fsn din 22 decembrie 1989."

29. Bianca Pădurean, "The Transformation of the National Salvation Front into a Political Party," Radio France International, January 23, 2019, https://www.rfi.ro/politica-108661-trans formarea-partid-frontului-salvarii-nationale.

30. Alexandru Radu, "Primele alegeri ale postcomunismului românesc," *Sfera Politcii*, January–March 2018, https://issuu.com/sferapoliticii/docs/sfera_195.

31. Celestine Bohlen, "Romanian Miners Invade Bucharest," *New York Times*, June 15, 1990, https://timesmachine.nytimes.com/timesmachine/1990/06/15/479190.html?pageNumber=1.

32. "Interviews with Participants and Decision Makers in the June 13–15, 1990 Events," *Digi24*, December 23, 2016, https://www.digi24.ro/stiri/actualitate/evenimente/dosarul-mineri adei-13-iunie-1990-ziua-diversiunii-637712.

33. Bohlen, "Romanian Miners Invade Bucharest."

34. Roxana Dascalu, *Chronicles from the East* (Bucharest: Vremea, 2020).

35. Bohlen, "Romanian Miners Invade Bucharest."

36. Bohlen, "Romanian Miners Invade Bucharest."

37. Bohlen, "Romanian Miners Invade Bucharest."

38. "'Vigilant Violence' Assailed," *New York Times*, June 15, 1990, 6.

39. Dascalu, *Chronicles from the East*, 66.

40. Tamás Kiss, I. G. Székely, T. Toro, B. Nándor, and I. Horváth, *Unequal Accommodation of Minority Rights: Hungarians in Transylvania* (New York: Palgrave Macmillan, 2018).

41. "HOTĂRÂRE nr. 17 din 16 mai 2000," *Portal Legislativ*, http://legislatie.just.ro/Public/DetaliiDocumentAfis/22531.

42. "Romania's Left Set to Regain Power," CNN, November 25, 2000, https://www.cnn.com/2000/WORLD/europe/11/25/romania.election.

43. Catiusa Ivanov, "Nicusor Dan a lansat partidul Uniunea Salvați Bucureştiul," *Hotnews.ro*, July 1, 2015, http://www.hotnews.ro/stiri-administratie_locala-20269592-nicusor-dan-lansat-partidul-uniunea-salvati-bucurestiul-suntem-continuarea-acestui-efort-care-dna-face-curata-administratia-publica-din-bucuresti-orasul-asta-nu-are-vizune-venim-propunem.htm.

44. Sorin Pâslaru and Iulian Anghel, "După 20 de ani. Petre Roman," *Ziarul Financiar*, November 24, 2010, https://www.zf.ro/eveniment/petre-roman-cea-mai-mare-eroare-este-ca-statul-a-ajuns-la-dispozitia-politicienilor-7746095.

45. "Romania—Total Businesses Registered," Trading Economics, January 2021, https://tradingeconomics.com/romania/total-businesses-registered-number-wb-data.html.

46. "Romania—Average Consumer Prices Inflation Rate," World Data Atlas, https://knoema.com/atlas/Romania/Inflation-rate.

47. Dascalu, *Chronicles from the East*, 59.

48. Paslaru and Anghel, "After 20 Years."

49. Andrei Jean Vasile, Mieila Mihai, and Panait Mirela, "Transformations of the Romanian Agricultural Paradigm under Domestic Economic Policy Reforms: An Analysis during 1960–2011," *Land Use Policy* 67 (2017): 288–97, https://www.sciencedirect.com/science/article/pii/S0264837717304155.

50. "Lege nr.58 din 14 august 1991 Legea privatizarii societatilor comerciale," *Camera Deputaților*, http://www.cdep.ro/pls/legis/legis_pck.htp_act_text?idt=8247.

51. "Milionari doar pe hârtie—Peste 8 milioane de români au acţiuni listate la bursă de care nu mai ştiu nimic," *digi24*, August 28, 2015, https://www.digi24.ro/special/reportaje/reportaj/special-milionari-doar-pe-hartie-peste-8-milioane-de-romani-au-actiuni-listate-la-bursa-de-care-nu-mai-stiu-nimic-432752.

52. Jane Perlez, "Pyramid Scheme, a Trap for Many Romanians," *New York Times*, November 13, 1993, https://www.nytimes.com/1993/11/13/business/pyramid-scheme-a-trap-for-many-romanians.html.

53. "Romania Foreign Direct Investment Data from 1987–2019," *Global Economy*, https://www.theglobaleconomy.com/Romania/Foreign_Direct_Investment.

54. "Romania GDP Growth Rate, 1991–2021," *Macro Trends*, https://www.macrotrends.net/countries/ROU/romania/gdp-growth-rate.

55. "Two New Members Join the EU Family," *European Commission*, December 28, 2006, https://ec.europa.eu/commission/presscorner/detail/en/IP_06_1900.

56. "Romania Foreign Direct Investment Data."

57. "Evaluation of PHARE Financial Assistance to Bulgaria, Cyprus, Czech Republic, Estonia, Hungary, Latvia, Lithuania, Malta, Poland, Romania, Slovakia, Slovenia," *Business and Strategies Europe*, January 10, 2015, 26, https://ec.europa.eu/neighbourhood-enlargement/sites/near/files/pdf/financial_assistance/phare/evaluation/2015/20150806-phare-ex-post-evaluation-final-report.pdf.

58. "Top vanzari," *Revista Piaţa*, March 26, 2008, https://www.revista-piata.ro/business/special/item/165-top-vanzari.

59. Andrew Willis, "EU, IMF Agree €20bn Rescue Loan for Romania," *EUObserver*, March 29, 2009, https://euobserver.com/economic/27852.

60. "Cutting Wages and Employment in the Public Sector: Smarter Fiscal Consolidation Strategies Needed," *Intereconomics Review of European Economic Policy* 45, no. 4 (2010): 212–19, https://www.intereconomics.eu/contents/year/2010/number/4/article/cutting-wages-and-employment-in-the-public-sector-smarter-fiscal-consolidation-strategies-needed.html.

61. "GDP per Capita in PPS," *Eurostat*, https://ec.europa.eu/eurostat/tgm/table.do?tab=table &plugin=1&language=en&pcode=tec00114.

62. "Romania's GDP per Capita Evolution 1987–2019," *Macro Trends*, https://www.mac rotrends.net/countries/ROU/romania/gdp-per-capita.

63. "Government Debt to GDP Data," Trading Economics, https://tradingeconomics.com/r omania/government-debt-to-gdp.

64. "Economic Forecast for Romania," European Commission, 2020, https://ec.europa.eu/ info/business-economy-euro/economic-performance-and-forecasts/economic-performance-countr y/romania/economic-forecast-romania_en.

65. "Romania's 11-Month Deficit Widens to 8 Percent of GDP on Coronavirus Spending," *SeeNews*, December 29, 2020, https://seenews.com/news/romanias-11-mo-budget-gap-widens-to -8gdp-on-coronavirus-spending-726190.

66. "COMUNICAT din 22 decembrie 1989 către țară al Consiliului Frontului Salvării Naționale 22, December 1989," *Portal Legislativ*, http://legislatie.just.ro/Public/DetaliiDocument /96559.

67. "DECRET - LEGE nr. 8 din 31 decembrie 1989 privind inregistrarea si functionarea partidelor politice si organizatiilor obstesti din Romania," *Camera Deputaților*, http://www.cdep .ro/pls/legis/legis_pck.htp_act_text?idt=11004.

68. "LEGE nr. 21 din 6 februarie 1924," *Portal Legislativ*, http://legislatie.just.ro/Public/De taliiDocumentAfis/8.

69. "LEGE nr. 21 din 6 februarie 1924."

70. "Guvernul României Ordonanța nr. 26/2000 cu privire la asociații și fundații," *Indaco Lege[5]*, https://lege5.ro/Gratuit/gi3tsnrt/ordonanta-nr-26-2000-cu-privire-la-asociatii-si-fun datii.

71. "Half a Million Kids Survived Romania's 'Slaughterhouses of Souls': Now They Want Justice," *PRI—The World*, December 28, 2015, https://www.pri.org/stories/2015-12-28/half-m illion-kids-survived-romanias-slaughterhouses-souls-now-they-want-justice.

72. "Salvați copiii cine suntem," *Salvați copiii*, https://www.salvaticopiii.ro/cine-suntem.

73. "Salvați copiii cine suntem."

74. "About Active Watch," *Active Watch*, https://activewatch.ro/en/about-us/about-activewatch.

75. "About Active Watch."

76. "LEGE nr. 544 din 12 octombrie 2001," *Portal Legislativ*, http://legislatie.just.ro/Public/ DetaliiDocument/31413.

77. Ionuț Ancuțescu, "Fundația lui Soros își închide porțile în România. În 25 de ani, a finanțat proiecte de 160 de milioane de dolari," *NewMoney*, February 16, 2017, https://www.new money.ro/fundatia-lui-soros-isi-inchide-portile-romania-25-de-ani-finantat-proiecte-de-160-de-m ilioane-de-dolari.

78. "About Us EEA and Norway Grants," EEA Grants, https://eeagrants.org.

79. "Fundația pentru Dezvoltarea Societății Civile (FDSC)," FDSC, http://www.fdsc.ro/ despre-fdsc.

80. "Emergency Ordinance no. 138 of 2004," *Indaco Lege[5]*, https://lege5.ro/Gratuit/gu3dg nzx/ordonanta-de-urgenta-nr-138-2004-pentru-modificarea-si-completarea-legii-nr-571-2003-p rivind-codul-fiscal.

81. "România 2017 Sectorul neguvernamental—Profil, tendințe, provocări," FDSC, https:// fondong.fdsc.ro/upload/Stiri%20generale/Romania%202017.pdf.

82. Gabriel Bădescu, Paul Sum, and Eric M. Uslaner, "Civil Society Development and Democratic Values in Romania and Moldova," *East European Politics and Societies* 18, no. 2 (2004): 316–41.

83. Bădescu, Sum, and Uslaner, "Civil Society Development."

84. "Corruption in Romania: A European Affair," *EURACTIV*, September 30, 2019, https://www.euractiv.com/section/justice-home-affairs/opinion/corruption-in-romania-a-european-affair.

85. "Corruption in Romania: A European Affair."

86. "Romania's Score in Transparency International's Corruption Index Weakens," *Romania Insider*, January 27, 2020, https://www.romania-insider.com/romania-corruption-index-2019.

87. "Corruption in Romania: A European Affair."

88. "Patients Bearing Gifts," *Economist*, March 24, 2014, https://www.economist.com/europe/2015/03/24/patients-bearing-gifts.

89. "Patients Bearing Gifts."

90. Alison Mutler and Vadim Ghirda, "Romania's Hospital Scandal: Babies Left to Die as Doctors Refuse to Work without Bribes," *Independent*, March 31, 2012, https://www.independent.co.uk/life-style/health-and-families/health-news/romania-s-hospital-scandal-babies-left-die-doctors-refuse-work-without-bribes-7606242.html.

91. "What Public Institutions Do Romanians Trust the Most?," *Romania Insider*, May 20, 2015, https://www.romania-insider.com/what-public-institutions-do-romanians-trust-the-most.

92. Dana Alecu, "We Talked to the Survivors," *Vice*, November 7, 2016, https://www.vice.com/en/article/zn8zmy/colectiv-club-survivors-876.

93. "Romania's Health-Care System, the EU's Worst, Struggles to Reform," *Economist*, November 21, 2019, https://www.economist.com/europe/2019/11/21/romanias-health-care-system-the-eus-worst-struggles-to-reform.

94. Alecu, "We Talked to the Survivors."

95. Alecu, "We Talked to the Survivors."

96. Shaun Walker, "Romanian Hospitals in Crisis as Emigration Takes Its Toll," *Guardian*, April 21, 2019, https://www.theguardian.com/world/2019/apr/21/romanian-hospitals-in-crisis-as-emigration-take-its-toll.

97. Anealla Safdar, "Diluted Disinfectant Scandal Hits Romania Hospitals," Al Jazeera, May 14, 2016, https://www.aljazeera.com/news/2016/5/14/diluted-disinfectant-scandal-hits-romania-hospitals.

98. "Romania's Health-Care System, the EUs Worst, Struggles to Reform," *Economist*, November 21, 2019, https://www.economist.com/europe/2019/11/21/romanias-health-care-system-the-eus-worst-struggles-to-reform.

99. Manohla Dargis, "'Collective' Review: When Tragedy Consumes a Nation," *New York Times*, November 19, 2020, https://www.nytimes.com/2020/11/19/movies/collective-documentary-review.html.

100. Michelle Kelso, "Anti-corruption Protests Sweep Romania," *HuffPost*, February 10, 2017, https://www.huffpost.com/entry/anti-corruption-protests-sweep-romania_b_58923ba9e4b0f009905272de.

101. Kelso, "Anti-corruption Protests."

102. Samuel Trilling, "Romanian PM 'Disappointed' with EU Threats over Corruption," Organized Crime and Corruption Reporting Project, May 16, 2010, https://www.occrp.org/en/daily/9746-romanian-pm-disappointed-with-eu-threats-over-corruption.

103. "Romania Corruption: PSD Chief Liviu Dragnea Jailed," BBC News, May 27, 2019, https://www.bbc.com/news/world-europe-48421430.

104. "Romania Poverty Rate 1989–2021," *Macro Trends*, https://www.macrotrends.net/countries/ROU/romania/poverty-rate.

105. Elisabetta Capannell, "Romania's Development and Anti-Poverty Policies: Effectiveness of National Responses in Addressing a Global Problem," World Bank, May 31, 2016, https://www.worldbank.org/en/news/speech/2016/05/31/romanias-development-and-anti-poverty-policies.

106. Donato De Rosa and Yeon Soo Kim, "Romania: Thriving Cities, Rural Poverty, and a Trust Deficit," Brookings Institute, June 5, 2018, https://www.brookings.edu/blog/future-develop ment/2018/06/05/romania-thriving-cities-rural-poverty-and-a-trust-deficit.

107. Capannell, "Romania's Development and Anti-Poverty Policies."

108. Sorin Melenciu, "Romania's Poor People Are the Poorest in the EU," *Business Review*, November 22, 2018, https://business-review.eu/news/romanias-poor-people-are-the-poorest-in -the-eu-191681.

109. "Poverty and Equity Brief: Romania," World Bank, April 2020, https://databank .worldbank.org/data/download/poverty/33EF03BB-9722-4AE2-ABC7-AA2972D68AFE/Globa l_POVEQ_ROU.pdf.

110. Ronni Winter, "Top 10 Facts about Poverty in Romania," Borgen Project, September 21, 2018, https://borgenproject.org/top-10-facts-about-poverty-in-romania.

111. "Poverty and Equity Brief."

112. "Achieving Roma Inclusion in Romania: What Does it Take?," *World Bank*, February 28, 2014, https://www.worldbank.org/content/dam/Worldbank/document/eca/romania/Summar y%20Report%20RomanianAchievingRoma%20Inclusion%20EN.pdf.

113. From 1994 to 1996, I volunteered with Romani Criss, a Roma rights NGO in Bucharest. I worked on documenting cases of ethnic violence and traveled to several communities interview- ing victims as well as attended trials.

114. "Achieving Roma Inclusion in Romania."

115. "A Persisting Concern: Anti-Gypsyism as a Barrier to Roma Inclusion," European Union Agency for Fundamental Rights, April 6, 2018, https://fra.europa.eu/en/publication/2018/persisti ng-concern-anti-gypsyism-barrier-roma-inclusion.

116. De Rosa and Kim, "Romania."

117. "Achieving Roma Inclusion in Romania."

118. "Achieving Roma Inclusion in Romania," 12.

119. "The Plight of Roma Sees Little Change," European Union Agency for Fundamental Rights, June 21, 2019, https://fra.europa.eu/en/publications-and-resources/infographics/plight -roma-sees-little-change.

120. "Life beyond Europe's Rainbow Curtain," *Economist*, November 21, 2020, https://www .economist.com/europe/2020/11/21/life-beyond-europes-rainbow-curtain.

121. "A Long Way to Go for LGBTI Equality," European Union Agency for Fundamental Rights, May 14, 2020, https://fra.europa.eu/en/publication/2020/eu-lgbti-survey-results.

122. "Eurobarometer on Discrimination 2019: The Social Acceptance of LGBTI People in the EU," *European Commission*, September 23, 2019, 15, https://ec.europa.eu/info/sites/info/files/ebs _493_data_fact_lgbti_eu_en-1.pdf.

123. "Romania: Anti-racism Commission, Concerned about Hate Speech, Hate Crimes and Discrimination against Roma and LGBT Persons," *Council of Europe*, June 5, 2019, https://www.coe .int/en/web/european-commission-against-racism-and-intolerance/-/romania-anti-racism-commi ssion-concerned-about-hate-speech-hate-crimes-and-discrimination-against-roma-and-lgbt-persons.

124. "Romania: Anti-racism Commission," 2.

125. Alice Tidey, "Romania Gender Studies Ban: Students Slam New Law as Going 'Back to the Middle Ages,'" *Euronews*, June 17, 2020, https://www.euronews.com/2020/06/17/romania-g ender-studies-ban-students-slam-new-law-as-going-back-to-the-middle-ages.

126. "Public Opinion in the European Union," *Standard Eurobarometer* 81 (Spring 2014), 97–98, https://ec.europa.eu/commfrontoffice/publicopinion/archives/eb/eb81/eb81_publ_en.pdf.

127. "Partidele politice din România—percepții și reprezentări," *Institutul Român pen- tru Evaluare și Strategie*, February 2016, https://ires.ro/articol/312/partidele-politice-din-roma nia—-perceptii-si-reprezentari.

Map 17.0.   Albania

CHAPTER 17

Albania

Arolda Elbasani and Seimir Elbasani

Albania's difficult and often uncertain path to democracy offers an emblematic case to trace the role of factors that both hold back democratic transition and keep the country on track despite significant odds. On the eve of regime change in the 1990s, the country was characterized by a dearth of factors commonly associated with successful democratic transition: lack of prior democratic experiences, a long experience under a totalitarian communist regime, a chaotic mode of transition, lack of democratic leadership with the vision and experience to pursue regime change, absence of autonomous social groups, and socioeconomic underdevelopment in general. The one-party state started giving up fragments of its power only when it had no other option but to concede to mounting pressure from outside and radicalized dissent inside. As a result, regime change came late, appeared in small increments, and was forced onto the agenda by chaotic and sometimes violent mass movements, which brought the country to the brink of collapse more than once.

The initial enthusiastic support for regime change seemed to sweep away the memories of the authoritarian past and set the country on a fast track to democratic transition. Yet the evolution of postcommunist governance showed the deep resilience of the authoritarian legacies of the past. The early transition quickly plunged into a one-man usurpation of the system of checks and balances as the regime resorted to tactics of harassment, including the use of security services, to control its critics. Economic reforms too were a façade for weak capitalism that provided fertile ground for the mushrooming of pyramid schemes, whose collapse in 1997 generated violent riots. Subsequent state collapse necessitated international intervention to patch the country together. Since the 1997 institutional collapse, the international community has emerged as an indispensable component of Albanian politics by offering financial aid, providing technical assistance, and often mediating political crises.

The adoption of the first postcommunist constitution in 1998, with the help of the international actors, helped to jump-start a new wave of institution building and instill a more balanced separation of powers. The formal separation of powers, however, has been hampered in practice by fierce political polarization and a winner-takes-all style of governance, a combination that contributes to the fragility of Albania's democracy.

Almost three decades into its democratic transition, Albanian politics and society continue to share a general consensus about the goal of democracy. Democracy, moreover, is perceived as closely related to the processes of accession into the European Union (EU) and the institutional templates that the EU promotes through enlargement conditionality. In the context of the extension of the EU enlargement policy to the Balkans, the EU has progressively taken a leading role in promoting democratic institutional change.

However, Albania remains a textbook case regarding the difficulty and challenges of making democratic institutions work in practice and moving toward democratic consolidation. Specifically, key institutions of democracy—the legislative branch, the executive, and the judiciary—are in place and reflect models promoted by various Western international actors, especially the EU. Still, the mismatch between installing formal democratic institutions and the way they work in practice is perhaps the most important distinguishing feature of Albania's weak democracy. All key institutions, like the parliament, the presidency, and the judiciary, are frequently used as political instruments that serve personal or political agendas. The gap between formal models of democracy and the way they work in practice applies not only to democratic institutions but also to the wider framework of democratic politics, including political competition, civil society, and economic policy. Weak formal institutions further foster widespread informality, entrenched political patronage, and persistent corruption. These are the most obvious symptoms of weak institutions and the key challenges to the Albanian democratic experience going forward.

Political History

Albania's political history is symptomatic of the Balkans' complex past and the imprint of the past upon the present. Both its precommunist and communist past constitute a difficult legacy for democratizing actors and institutions to surmount.

The country's history before the creation of the communist regime was characterized by consecutive long periods of foreign occupation, no democratic experience except for a few months in 1924, weak statehood, and the prevalence of authoritarian leadership. Persistent foreign occupation and interference followed each other and allowed little space for the development of independent, not to speak of democratic governing structures and experiences. Notably, the long Ottoman conquest (fourteenth through nineteenth century) prevented the development of independent governance and an economic system similar to neighboring Europe. It also shaped a specific patrimonial logic of governance characterized by a personalized exercise of power, a lack of a separation between official and private realms, officials' personal subservience to the ruler, and, more generally, a tendency to regard the state as a source of provisioning for the ruler.[1]

The conversion of the majority of the population to Islam and the lack of internal unity among various religious communities, but also regional clans, further delayed the creation of an independent national movement and eventual international recognition.[2] At the outset of independence, Albania was a Muslim majority and multireligious country including Sunni, Bektashi, Christian Catholic, and Orthodox Catholic communities, indeed, a uniquely mixed polity in the then European context.[3] Consequently, Albania became the last of the Balkan countries to proclaim independence from the Ottoman Empire in 1912. Even then, emerging political groups were preoccupied with securing the country's internal and external sovereignty more than with developing concrete projects for the organization of a modern state.

European powers who were engaged with rearranging former Ottoman territories were cautious of the country's capacities for self-governance and in 1914 appointed a German prince, Wilhelm of Wied, to provide much-needed central authority. The foreign prince could not accomplish much, as power remained de facto diffused between regionally based clans and feudal landowners. In the face of domestic opposition and the outbreak of World War I, the appointed prince abandoned his position, leaving behind a vacuum of central state authority. Afterward, the country plunged again into war and remained under the occupation of expansionist neighboring countries—Italy, Greece, Serbia, and Montenegro. The borders were finally fixed in an international conference in 1921, mostly thanks to the lack of consensus among stronger neighbors on how to partition the country rather than to a viable internal alternative to national unity.[4]

The 1920s also saw the gradual rise of certain political groupings that mildly resembled conventional political parties. The most important grouping, the Progressive Party, was led by a rising authoritarian personality, Ahmet Zogu, whose primary support came from the wealthy landowning aristocracy and conservative feudal circles. The next important grouping, the Popular Party, was led by an American-educated and progressive figure, Fan Noli, who represented the incipient social groups advocating political pluralism and much-needed land reform. Political competition between the emerging groups was fierce and unruly, with governments appearing and disappearing in rapid succession. Between July and December 1921 alone, the premiership changed hands five times. In 1924, the parliament voted for Noli's reformist project, opening the way to a short-lived democratic attempt. Noli's progressive government, however, was crushed a few months later in a coup d'état orchestrated by the conservative coalition. In November 1925, Zogu, the leader of the conservative group, was self-appointed president and, later, in 1928, king of Albania.[5]

Despite his authoritarian tendencies, Zogu is credited with creating the foundational infrastructure of an independent central government and the basis of the modern Albanian state. He succeeded in bringing a degree of order and stability to the country, which was ravaged by war as much as by internal conflicts. During his reign (1924–1939), the country made significant political and economic gains. Zogu's governing project to a great extent capitalized on the Italian quest for political supremacy in the Balkans. He promised political loyalty in exchange for substantial assistance, loans, and investments, which supplied a large part of the state's mounting deficit. Although under Zogu's rule the country became essentially an Italian economic protectorate, it maintained a degree of political independence. This lasted only until 1939, when the country was occupied by fascist forces. The expulsion of Zogu, on the same day of the occupation, left the country without a cohesive governing authority or political coalition, which might have served as a rallying point against occupation and for subsequent reconstruction.

The consecutive Italian and later German occupations (1943–1944) exacerbated the conflict between rival monarchist, anticommunist, and factional leftist groups. The leftists gained supremacy once they united under the leadership of the Communist Party, founded in 1941. The communist movement took advantage of the rivalry between the old hierarchy of power and privilege represented by the landowning class and the impoverished peasantry, as well as a new generation of youth asking for radical progressive changes. The related partisan war also capitalized on the relations with international antifascist alliances and support by the Yugoslav communists. Last but not least, the communist organization, the Party of Labour of Albania (PLA), was probably the first well-organized cohesive political organization and the first to appeal above clan interests. The communists took control of the government as soon as the foreign troops left the country in the autumn of 1944.

The communists' primary objective was to create a united country under the ethos of "the new socialist man." During this process, the regime became in its own way a modernizer, to the extent that it introduced and forcefully enforced large-scale reforms, most notably in education and social policy. It also imposed order and strengthened the power of the fragile state. It simultaneously undertook major economic restructuring around the development of heavy industry. Most of the reforms were adopted at the cost of brutal totalitarianism, which evoked the cult of the communist leader, Enver Hoxha. His maneuvers to consolidate an unlimited personal rule determined most political choices of the communist regime. This was particularly the case with periodic purges that wiped out all possible sources of dissidence and clearly distinguished the country from all other communist regimes.[6] The initial campaign against "major war criminals" in the period 1946 to 1948 led to the execution and imprisonment of actual or suspected political opponents. The nationalization of industry and the confiscation of all private property, starting in 1945, eliminated as well the fragile middle class of small business owners. The radical reform of collectivization of agriculture, in the same year, targeted big landowners, who had ruled the country since independence. Even individuals or factions within the party, who advocated for reconciliatory domestic polices and/or moderate relations with both East and West, suffered execution or long-term imprisonment as "right-wing opportunists."

The foreign policy orientation was similarly radical. Following the rift with an increasingly moderate Yugoslavia, the country pursued closer relations with the Soviet Union and remained loyal to a Stalin-style regime. It became increasingly isolated from the rest of the world and exercised a siege mentality in the domestic arena, even when the communist world denounced Stalin's crimes and his personality cult in the 1960s. Following the rift with the Soviet Union in the 1960s, Albania established close relations with China, the next most orthodox communist regime at the time.[7] Under the example of the Chinese Cultural Revolution, the one-party-state regime launched a maverick campaign of revolutionizing all aspects of life. What followed was a reign of terror against all individuals who supported, even slightly, cultural liberalism or simply did not have enough revolutionary fervor in their rejection of "foreign" influences. The elite of the country, including intellectuals and artists, were the preferred targets of party purges. The few who survived turned into cultural missionaries of the regime.

By the late 1970s, even relations with China came to an end because of its pragmatist foreign policy turn and relaxation of its conflict with the Western world. The Albanian communists decreed these as "revisionism" of the fundamental traits of the Marxist-Leninist ideology. The development of détente and the normalization of relations between NATO and the Warsaw Pact by the mid-1970s were considered a threat to Albania's dogmatic conception of the inevitable triumph of socialism. The process pushed the country toward increasing isolationism, except for limited relations with a few small developing countries.

The Albanian regime also went further than any country of the Eastern bloc in copying the Stalinist model of economic development: an extremely centralized planning system, the total elimination of private property, and emphasis on the development of heavy industry. Following the rift with China in the 1970s, Albania became the only country to adopt the principle of complete autarky as a model of economic development. Economic activity was directed toward irrational political goals such as building expensive defense works and technologies that would prove obsolete as soon as alternative external supplies became available. The infamous 180,000 bunkers built throughout the country, for example, were aimed to defend "the last castle of communism" while wiping out major economic resources. The deterioration of relations with the Soviet Union and later China further deprived the country of external sources of assistance, which were fundamental for maintaining such an unproductive system and had the final touch in ruining the economy.

The 1976 constitution formalized the totalitarian design of the communist regime. The opening line of the preamble read, "The Albanian people have hacked their way through history, sword in hand," revealing the document's Stalinist-like tone in furthering the radical class struggle, revolutionary militancy, and the enmity of the Cold War. The constitution identified Marxism-Leninism as the only official ideology, ruling out the possibility of ideological pluralism. The document also emphasized that Albania is a "state of the dictatorship of the proletariat," showing the regime's determination to pursue the class struggle against all nonconformist groups and individuals. Furthermore, it formalized the role of the Communist Party as "the sole leading force of the state and of the society," while other institutions turned into mere instruments in function of the one-party regime. In the economic sphere, too, the constitution erased the legal basis for the existence of any forms of private property to the extent that it allowed only the property of one's wage, home, and articles of personal use. The country's isolationist orientation found its way into the document through the prohibition of concessions to capitalist and revisionist states, joint economic or financial enterprises, and obtaining foreign credits.

The rigid interpretation of ideology in both foreign and domestic policy worked to consolidate Hoxha's nearly absolute power over the country. Hoxha's totalitarian construct, built on the triple cult of the absolute leader, ideology, and the security forces, survived all the crises that rocked Central and East Europe and the communist world until his death in 1984. Hoxha's selected successor, Ramiz Alia, came from a technocratic background, which raised hopes of change. Reforms initiated in cultural, economic, and foreign policy, however, were tailored to prolong rather than challenge the life of the "dictatorship of the proletariat." Even the revolution of 1989 appeared to pass by Albania. The first signs of revolt, including thousands of citizens who asked for refuge in foreign ministries in June 1990 and other thousands who seized ships to migrate to Italy a month later, were spontaneous individual acts of rebellion. They were largely without political organization or claims.

On the eve of the nascent transition to democracy, the communist regime could not control acts of dissent, but it lacked key factors necessary for a peaceful mode of regime change. In particular, it lacked an organized opposition and soft-liners within the regime who were willing to negotiate a way out. Communists started giving up bits and pieces of their total power only when they had no other choice but to concede to mounting pressure from outside and radicalized dissent inside.[8] The violent collapse of the Romanian communist regime sent a particularly clear message to the Albanian communist leaders. Meanwhile, diplomatic envoys from the Western world increased pressure on the regime to liberalize and to release political prisoners. Still, regime change came late and with significant challenges.

Early Postcommunism

It was massive student protests that erupted in December 1990 that forced the communist regime to decree political pluralism. The emergence of political pluralism, however, did not ease ongoing clashes between the regime and anti-regime groups. Nor did it improve democratic governance. This time around, it was the powerful anticommunist opposition, the Democratic Party (DP), created soon after the adoption of political pluralism, that became a key protagonist of the country's difficult transition. As an umbrella organization representing various groups unhappy with the regime, the DP included both many dissidents and groups well connected to the former regime.[9] The party's leadership went to Sali Berisha, a career communist and the personal doctor of Hoxha, who was initially chosen by the communist leadership to mediate between the regime and rebelling students. From the very beginning, moreover, the DP adopted a disruptive strategy of boycott and street protests to forcefully push forward its agenda.

The first multiparty elections of March 1991 were held amid political turmoil. The Socialist Party (SP), the former communist organization reshuffled under the image of the European left, emerged as the winner. What followed were mass protests, often instigated by the DP, to correct the verdict of the ballot box. The new government lasted only two months, while the following all-party coalition government remained paralyzed by political conflict, endemic protests, and economic destruction. The coalition government was officially dissolved in December 1991 at the request of the DP. With no party willing to take charge, many basic government services ceased to exist, and the country collapsed into the disarray of the previous winter. The crisis of governance made the country dependent on international aid to ensure even minimum food supplies and security functions.

The next free elections of March 1992, which were in fact a referendum for regime change more than normal national elections, confirmed overwhelming support for the anticommunist alternative. The DP, although still a new and incohesive political group, won an impressive 62 percent of the national vote and ninety out of one hundred single-member majority districts. The Western governments also welcomed the DP government as a force for change. In the subsequent years, Albania attracted substantial international aid ranging from $200 to $400 per capita annually, becoming one of the first aid recipients among postcommunist countries.

Enthusiastic support for regime change seemed to sweep away the memories of the authoritarian past and set the country on a fast path to democratic transition. Yet, once in power, the government faced overwhelming tasks—managing the economic breakdown, ensuring public order threatened by massive protests, strengthening state authority after the vacuum created during the last year, rebuilding state institutions almost from scratch, dealing with complex questions of transitional justice, and integrating the country into the international community after years of isolation. The DP's lack of firsthand experience with a democratic system, or even governance, as well as its lack of cohesiveness as a well-established political party also did not bode well.

The system of checks and balances was the first casualty. The 1991 constitutional amendments that changed much of the communist framework of governance envisaged a parliamentary system. The president was intended to occupy a symbolic role to serve the unity of the country and to stand above political divisions. In practice, however, all initiatives regarding domestic and foreign policy came out of the new president's office, which since 1992 was occupied by the DP leader, Berisha.[10] His strong and personalistic style of leadership provided the right push for painful reforms and kept the party and government line intact. The strong anticommunist rhetoric, pro-Western stance, and liberal economic policies in line with the Bretton Woods recommendations appealed to the international community and qualified the country as a "rising star" in Central and East Europe. Yet Berisha soon led the country toward one-man rule by usurping all state powers; that is, the executive, the legislature, and most state institutions remained independent only on paper.[11] Whenever the DP majority in parliament was not enough to ensure formal support for the president's proposals, the president would circumvent the parliament through presidential decrees.

The ruling party's tendency to usurp the system of checks and balances included the judiciary. The High Council of Justice (HCJ), headed by the president, was frequently criticized for appointing or replacing judges based on their political or personal loyalty rather than professional criteria. In September 1995, for example, the head of the Supreme Court, Zef Broci, himself a DP appointee, was fired by a presidential decree after he clashed with the president regarding replacement or dismissal of judges for political reasons. In addition, the Ministry of Justice started preparing its own lawyers through six-month courses designed to prepare assistant judges. These judges were then appointed to important legal positions, thus filling the judicial infrastructure with political loyalists who lacked education or experience for the job.

The new government exercised significant political control over the media too.[12] The director of the only state TV channel was still appointed by the president's office and was typically required to serve the governing party line. Restrictive policies to license private TV channels left Albanian citizens with one source of information closely controlled by the government. By contrast, the print media had multiplied, but journalists were frequently harassed when criticizing the government. The media law adopted in 1993 decreed that journalists could be imprisoned for publicizing state secrets or injuring the dignity of the president, ministers, or parliamentary deputies, regardless of whether the news was true.

The DP's one-man style of governance affected relations with other political forces and the broader principle of pluralism. The core opposition, the Socialist Party, became the main target of the DP's anticommunist ire and its tendency to centralize power. Key communist leaders, including those who led the post-1991 government, were sent to showy political trials, during which little evidence was provided.[13] Alia, for example, was arrested in September 1992 and convicted for "dual office holding," although the law prohibiting dual office holding was not in effect when he was in power. In general, the opposition was excluded from participation in policy debates and institutional choices. Even the drafting of a new constitution to replace the provisional amendments of 1991 was done through a government commission, which excluded both the parliament and the opposition from discussing the central law of the state.

After it lost the new constitutional referendum in 1994, the DP leadership understood that it had lost the wide popular support it enjoyed in 1992. It therefore resorted to mobilizing all political and institutional means to remain in power. In 1995, the ruling majority passed several laws that effectively disqualified from electoral competition more than one hundred prospective candidates, including leaders of the opposition.[14] Furthermore, similar to its communist predecessors, the ruling party used the state apparatus and police forces against opposition candidates and other groups unhappy with government policies. Strikes from labor unions or prewar owners and political prisoners asking for compensation were commonly treated as a "public order" problem and forcefully crushed. The secret security forces were commonly used to discourage resistance and critique.

Reforms in the economic sector were similarly deceiving.[15] The DP government adopted a "shock therapy" program in line with the advice of Bretton Woods institutions to address the dire economic situation it had inherited. Formal economic indicators—9 percent growth per year and stabilization of macroeconomic parameters in the period 1993–1996—qualified the country as a "rising star."[16] More nuanced accounts of economic development, however, showed that economic growth was due to substantial external financing via foreign assistance, huge remittances, and large-scale smuggling and money laundering activities. Meanwhile, the economic recovery lacked the foundation of fundamental economic restructuring. Industrial production never recovered to the level of 1989, the infrastructure was crumbling, market institutions remained underdeveloped, and the corrupt process of privatization did not offer compensation for the heavy burden of transition. This sort of "development" provided fertile ground for the mushrooming of pyramid schemes, enterprises that offered high interest rates ranging from 8 to 30 percent a month, by paying early investors from the funds collected by later depositors. By 1996, pyramid schemes represented an estimated one-third of the GDP and most of the savings of three-fourths of Albanian families, becoming so popular that neither the government, nor the opposition, intellectuals, nor public opinion leaders dared doubt their activity.[17] Instead, the government and even the opposition lent support to these schemes because their income-generating functions were essential to retain support in anticipation of the upcoming elections.

The 1996 elections, which according to the Organization for Security and Co-operation in Europe (OSCE) violated thirty-two out of seventy-nine articles of the electoral law, led to a communist-like victory for the DP.[18] The newly created DP government, at the insistence of the International Monetary Fund (IMF) and World Bank, started an investigation into pyramid schemes, which led to the arrest of their owners and the blocking of their assets. The measures came too late to save the invested money. The major pyramid schemes had already gone bankrupt, or the accumulated money had been sent to private accounts abroad. In January 1997, the collapse of the biggest pyramid schemes, together with the loss of most of the savings of Albania's citizens, degenerated into violent protests, particularly throughout the southern parts of the country where those schemes were most entrenched. Soon enough, the riots became political and resulted in the resignation of the cabinet. However, the DP majority ruled out negotiations until it eventually lost control of the state apparatus.

In March 1997, the OSCE mediated an all-inclusive roundtable in which the Albanian political parties agreed to create a coalition government and hold fresh elections a few months later in June 1997. By then, the country had descended into a state of anarchy. Protesters attacked army depots, security forces left the cities, many areas came under the control of armed groups, criminals escaped from prison, and another fifteen thousand Albanians emigrated to Italy.[19]

Given the collapse of the state institutions, the subsequent coalition government formed with the help of the OSCE was not able to provide even minimal food, order, security, and other necessary services for the population. Between March and July 1997, the political and social chaos led to the killing of two thousand people and the wounding of more than ten thousand others. International intervention was necessary to provide some minimal security functions and to prevent further collapse. In April 1997, the United Nations, at the urging of neighboring Italy, consented to send a multinational peacekeeping force of around seven thousand troops in order to escort humanitarian convoys, patrol government and military buildings, and protect international humanitarian personnel. The OSCE created a permanent mission to facilitate ongoing dialogue, monitor institutional reform, and provide technical and organizational support for the conduct of the early 1997 elections. Given its degree and scope of involvement after the 1997 crisis, the international community has become an indispensable component of Albanian politics. The country is often depicted as a "client" state that needs foreign intervention in order to function.

Political Institutions

After the collapse of the communist regime, and again after the 1997 crisis, Albanians have recrafted most of their political institutions in line with the goal of installing a functioning Western-style democratic system.

The 1991 Law on the Main Constitutional Provisions, which was adopted by the first multiparty parliament, institutionalized political pluralism and defined the country as a parliamentary republic. Following the 1992 elections, the DP majority initiated further revisions, including adding a new chapter on the judiciary and the protection of fundamental human rights. The initial concept of the parliamentary republic was also revised to include more elements of a presidential republic.[20] The parliament retained substantial powers, including the power of electing the president, determining the orientation of the country's domestic and foreign policies, and approving government programs. This time around, however, the Democrats claimed that the challenges of transition necessitated a strong president and granted the office additional powers to appoint the prime minister, to dissolve the legislature, to decree law, to chair meetings of the Council of Ministers, and under specific conditions to set its agenda.

The 1992 constitutional changes remained a short document that failed to elaborate on the specific competences of the different branches of power. The vagueness of these provisions permitted the first postcommunist president, Sali Berisha, to accrue substantial governing powers while eclipsing the role of the prime minister, the cabinet, and the parliament.[21] The 1994 constitutional draft attempted to formalize the features of a presidential system, but it was widely rejected in a constitutional referendum. The failure of the referendum, interpreted as a general loss of support for the DP's governing model, exacerbated the regime's authoritarian tendencies, including efforts to assume control of all branches of state power.[22] By the end of the DP's first term in power, efforts to introduce new institutions were intertwined with the de facto establishment of one-man rule, limited tolerance for debate, and suppression of political participation.

The subsequent collapse of the pyramid schemes and, to some extent, state order in 1997 demonstrated that the frail system of checks and balances and weak institutions, created during the early transition, were a recipe for institutional collapse. Following the crisis, Albania had to start transition anew, this time amid an institutional vacuum, political animosity, widespread social disorder, and economic disaster. Given the dire political situation, subsequent reforms were largely sponsored by the international community, which took a key role in mediating, assisting, and sponsoring a second transition.[23]

The winner of the 1997 elections, the SP, benefited from external intervention and abundant international assistance to advance institutional reforms. The first postcommunist constitution, adopted in 1998, was effectively sponsored by various international actors, including the EU and the United States and negotiated by the OSCE. The document aimed to establish a more balanced separation of powers and stable system of governance.[24] Accordingly, the country is a unitary, undividable state, which exercises a monopoly on the use of force over its territory. The constitution also curbs the power of the presidency by declaring the country a parliamentary republic. The assembly exercises oversight over the executive and the institutions it establishes. The president is elected by the parliament and is mostly a ceremonial position, tasked with representing the unity of the country. The judiciary is conceived as an independent body that consists of three levels: general courts, courts of appeal, and the high court, with high courts being the final instance in civil and criminal cases. The Constitutional Court decides on the conformity of laws to the constitution and resolves disputes between different branches of government and between national and local authorities.

In 2008, the two major parliamentary parties, the DP and SP, agreed on a major package of constitutional changes, which introduced new rules for electing the president, a regional proportional-representation electoral system with closed party lists, and term limits of five years instead of an unlimited term for the prosecutor general. The international community greeted these changes positively, as they displayed a rare consensus in the Albanian parliament, normally characterized by permanent political bickering and blockages. The changes, moreover, served as a ticket to NATO membership the following year.

Altogether, the constitutional provisions, including the 2008 amendments, specify the role of each institution and the relations between them, contributing to a more balanced separation of powers and limiting the opportunities for one-man authoritarian rule. Still, the formal separation and balance of powers is often victim of political polarization and a winner-takes-all style of governance. This symbiosis is the root of Albania's weak democracy and fragile institutions. Specifically, the parliament is supposed to be an institution of oversight, but it de facto functions as an arena of political conflict, blockages, and boycotts, which undermines its role and legitimacy.[25] The new parliament elected in 2017, for example, was periodically boycotted by major opposition parties. In early 2019, the opposition parties took the radical decision to relinquish their parliamentary mandates in order to force the resignation of the government and force fresh elections. Such boycotts and radicalized political methods have deprived the executive in particular and the system in general of parliamentary scrutiny. They have also delayed ongoing reforms, including a major judicial reform that has been in progress since 2016.

Similarly, the president is elected by the parliament and is formally a symbolic figure representing the country. However, the position is often used as an instrument to advance political agendas. Hence, none of Albania's postcommunist presidents have been able to live up to their role as a unifying force above party politics. The presidents elected early in the transition (1992, 1996, and 1997) were representatives of the ruling party chosen with a simple majority. The 1998 constitution imposed the requirement of 84 out of 140 parliamentary votes for the election of the president in order to shape a more independent role for the presidency. Still, the presidents elected in 2002 and 2007 were systematically attacked by the ruling majorities when they tried to assert their independence. Specifically, the 2002 compromise candidate, Alfred Moisiu, was proposed by the DP when in opposition but was repeatedly harassed by top DP officials when the party returned to power after the 2005 elections.[26] Similarly, the president elected in 2007, Bamir Topi, was the second in power of the DP leadership hierarchy when voted into office, but he too developed strained relations with the ruling Democrats.

The 2008 constitutional amendments, which enabled the election of a president with simple majority, eroded the formal requirement for a cross-party consensus candidate. The first president elected according to that formula in June 2012, Bujar Nishani, was a member of the close circle of the ruling DP and acting minister of justice just before being voted into that position by his own party. As expected, Nishani lent his office to the service of the party, particularly when it came to the nomination of "independent" state officials.[27] An independent report published in 2012 noted that the 2008 constitutional changes "paved the way for an in-depth consolidation of state control and even state capture by the ruling elite."[28] The next president voted by then-coalition partners—the SP and the smaller Socialist Movement for Integration (SMI)—in April 2017 also went to then-chairman of the SMI and then-speaker of parliament, Ilir Meta. A controversial politician known for his lavish lifestyle and for taking center stage in several public cases of corruption, Meta has also used his office to advance personal political agendas. One of his most controversial decisions was the June 2019 decree canceling local elections scheduled to take place a few weeks later.[29] Another controversial act was his February 2020 call for Albanian citizens to topple the government, arguably as a countermove against the Socialist majority's launching of an impeachment proceeding against him,[30] and also his loss of control over nominations to the judiciary.[31]

Ultimately, political control over the presidency has led to political control across key independent institutions, particularly the judiciary.[32] Members of the high court and Constitutional Court, as well as the state prosecutor, which are appointed by the president and confirmed with a simple majority in the assembly, have been historically vulnerable to political influence and control.[33] Other judges that are appointed by the president upon the proposal of the HCJ, an institution chaired by the president, are also under political pressure. The result of such overt political controls is the appointment of judges who serve politicians and organized crime.[34]

Starting in 2016, the SP majority, with the help of an EU-funded mission, initiated a large-scale reform of the judiciary, which stipulates the vetting of around eight hundred members of the judiciary system. By 2020, only about one hundred judiciary officials had been vetted, and many of the new judicial structures, including the Constitutional Court, were not yet operative. Indeed, the reform itself was obstructed at each and every step by those political and institutional actors who would lose control over the system.[35]

Political Competition

Since the fall of communism, Albania has held seven national elections: March 1991, March 1992, May 1996, June 1997, May 2001, July 2005, June 2009, June 2013, and June 2017. The next election is expected in 2021. Meanwhile, the country has tried different electoral systems—majoritarian, mixed, and proportional.[36] After an initial flirtation with the majoritarian system in 1991, the parliament agreed on a mixed electoral system that combined single-member electoral districts with proportional representation. Accordingly, out of 140 parliamentary seats, one hundred were elected by direct popular vote in districts; the remaining forty seats were allocated based on parties' shares of national votes. The threshold was set to 2.5 percent.

The 2008 constitutional amendments introduced a new electoral system, the closed-list regional proportional system. The country is divided into twelve multimember constituencies that correspond to the country's twelve administrative regions. Parties must meet a threshold of 3 percent of votes in each of the consistencies. Preelection coalitions must meet a threshold of 5 percent.

Despite the use of various electoral systems and the presence of a permanent OSCE mission installed in the country since the 1997 crisis, which focuses on electoral support and supervision, Albanian electoral processes are commonly characterized by widespread irregularities and are repeatedly contested by the losing parties. The closed party list, coupled with the politicization of the electoral management process (the electoral staff are all political appointees), introduced during the 2008 constitutional amendments, has further eroded public trust in the fairness of elections. During the 2017 election, for example, the OSCE election observation mission repeated a common finding about Albanian elections: "The continued politicization of election related bodies and institutions as well as widespread allegations of vote-buying and pressure on voters detracted from public trust in the electoral process."[37] In this case, moreover, an exceptional preelectoral agreement among major parties gave the opposition control over all the electoral management institutions. Yet the losing parties still failed to recognize the results and even opted out of the elected institutions.[38] In June 2020, a cross-party agreement on electoral reform brought the boycotting parties into the fold of institutions and electoral competition. The agreement was also largely greeted by international actors, including EU and US officials, although the "reform" seemingly excluded a key OSCE recommendation—depoliticization of the electoral institutions in order to increase trust in the process.[39]

Persistent irregularities and contestation of results that are commonly associated with Albanian electoral competition are the manifestation of a problematic party system characterized by deep mistrust and a winner-takes-all style of governance.[40] The system to some extent replicates postcommunist political and ideological cleavages. The DP, the first opposition created after the sanctioning of pluralism, represents the "right" and, for many, the anticommunist movement that brought down the communist regime. The SP, which hails from the former communist organization, represents the "left" and, for many, the legacy of the old regime. The main "third" party, the SMI, split away from the SP but shares most of its ideology and even party cadres. The two main parties have alternated in power and thus controlled the path of transition through majority governments. The Democrats governed during the early postcommunist transition, from 1992 to 1997, and returned to power in the period between 2005 and 2013; the Socialists created a short-lived government after the first pluralist elections, came to power after the explosion of the pyramid crisis in 1997 to 2005, and then did so again during the period 2013 to the present. The SMI entered into a governing coalition with both main parties—first with its ideological adversary, the DP, during the 2009–2013 term and then with the SP during 2013–2017—showing that political ideologies in Albania mean little when it comes to pursuing and retaining power.

Ultimately, simple communist and anticommunist or left-right dichotomies that are frequently used to explain Albania's conflictual style of politics are outdated. The rigid division between Democrats and Socialists, more than a simple ideological or political conflict, is an active strategy to distinguish and strengthen parties' base of support. In practice, links to the old regime are dense and cross all political families. Specifically, the DP has appropriated the fight against communism, but its key leaders, including his historical leader, Berisha, are well connected to the communist regime.[41] The SP has inherited some of the former communist organization, but its key leaders come mostly from the anticommunist student movement. Additionally, all parties have similar programs stressing the need for progress in the political and economic reforms required to consolidate democracy, catch up with the rest of Europe, and further European integration. Accession to the EU is a common political goal among all parties, although realizing the required reforms has been a chronic challenge.

Much of the explanation for why political confrontation is still a useful electoral strategy relates to historically ingrained local divisions and the related patronage system nourished by political parties. The DP leaders, coming mostly from the north, have usually stressed their anticommunist credentials, which appeal to northern regions, many of which were subject to particular repression by the communist regime. The Socialists, whose main leaders tend to come from the south, have usually found appeal in the southern regions, which was the former communist organization's primary power base. These divisions are also reflected in employment in central and local administration, with most positions being filled by fierce anticommunist northerners when the DP is in power and with southerners when the SP controls the majority. Parties' winner-takes-all approach to power facilitates accommodation of their patronage networks of loyalty and service across state infrastructure.

In this context, citizens' trust in parties and institutions is chronically low. A recent survey shows that parties, the parliament, the president, courts, and government are among the least trusted institutions.[42] Political parties, particularly, are distrusted, with 75.9 percent of respondents indicating that they have no trust in them. By contrast, citizens have more confidence in foreign institutions, such as NATO, the UN, and the EU, and prefer external actors to mediate political disputes.

Civil Society

The development and role of civil society in the processes of transformation also bears the legacies of the authoritarian past. The communist regime had outlawed all independent organizations since at least 1956 and instead created a net of party-related associations ensuring total control over society.[43] As a result, on the eve of transition, the country lacked even embryonic forms of civic organization, much less so well-organized groups with ideas and experiences regarding civic action. After communism, civil society had to be created almost from scratch while facing peoples' strong distrust of voluntary work, which in the past had been forced on them by intrusive Communist Party organizations.

In line with the structure of a traditional society, Albanians have a strong sense of traditional forms of solidarity such as family and regional or clan loyalties. These traditional forms of social capital have been precious to sustain networks of cooperation and support during difficult phases of transition and in the context of weak social welfare support. Yet they arguably undermine the creation of a more civic culture of participation and solidarity beyond narrow family or local links.

Legislation enabling freedom of association was the first step to facilitate civic action. The Albanian constitution ensures a wide range of freedoms of assembly and association (Article 46). Formally, NGOs can register freely, manage their affairs, and address all

Photo 17.1.   Albanian miners protest after being denied the right to organize in a union. (Red Duck on vacations, Wikimedia Commons)

matters of public debate without state interference or restrictions. Still, given the lack of previous experience with civic action, civil society was largely nurtured through Western donor aid policies that aimed at stimulating civic participation and socializing people to democratic values and behavior.[44] Foreign assistance and support has contributed to building up various local NGOs and enriching the public sphere. Currently, there are around twelve thousand NGOs, including associations, foundations, and centers, registered in the Tirana Court of First Instance. They engage in a wide range of activities, including advocacy work, monitoring roles, and social mobilization, particularly in sectors like the environment, human rights, social protection, and rule of law.[45]

NGOs, other organized groups, and particularly media outlets have also taken an active role in assessing the performance of the government and pushing for policy change. One such important moment was the civic movement against the proposed dismantling of Syrian chemical weapons in Albania. The movement forced the government to abandon these plans.[46] Other successful cases include student movements pushing for education reform. In general, civil society's policy input and its reception from government entities has improved. So has the framework of collaboration between the two. Since 2010, a public agency for the Support of Civil Society lends budgetary support to civic organizations. In 2016, the National Council for Civil Society (NCCS), an advisory body to the government on civil society issues, has created a regular framework for more structured government consultations with civil society organizations.

Still, many NGOs are seen as mostly donor-dependent entities that need to develop both internal capacities and voluntary networks that would make them sustainable and linked to society at large.[47] Quite often, Albanian NGOs are also closely entangled in politics. Key NGO leaders maintain implicit and sometimes explicit affiliations with political parties, parties themselves court NGO leaders with government positions, and politicians sometimes move between political and NGO positions. The 2017 government, for example, includes in its ranks many NGO representatives, particularly from the ranks of Mjaft, one of the well-funded organizations that gained international recognition for its innovative style of civic action on social and political problems facing the country.[48]

The evolution of postcommunist media and its role in society is similar to that of the NGOs. This includes expansion and development, but also a gap between the ideal of the media as an independent actor and its reality on the ground. The legal framework guarantees freedom of expression, organization of mass media, and the right to information (Articles 22 and 23). As a result, the media landscape is diverse. There are more than seventy-five television stations, over one hundred radio stations, twenty daily newspapers, and numerous online publications. Social media is expansive, with the government, political parties, civil society groups, and organizations widely using social media to disseminate their political messaging.

At the same time, media is often caught in between business interests and political control, which damages their credibility as trusted sources of information.[49] In this case, both the influence of business interests and political control are interrelated. On the one hand, most media outlets have become part of the economic portfolio of prominent businessmen, who have interests in other sectors but use editorial policies to pressure for personal benefits, including political access, specific policies, lucrative public contracts, privatization deals, state advertisement, and political favors. Politicians, on the other hand, have proven ready to court media owners with public benefits in return for favorable coverage. Many media outlets are allied with one of the political parties and are part of the political patronage system.

Economic Policies and Conditions

As mentioned above, the initial economic reforms, and the mushrooming and collapse of pyramid schemes in 1997, led to a major economic and political crisis. Afterward, the country benefited from external sources, particularly substantial international aid, large remittances, and large-scale privatization, to get back on its feet. An average of around 7 percent GDP growth in the period from 1998 to 2008 was due to remittances, FDI, and privatization of state-owned enterprises. Even today, the economy is largely dependent on remittances, FDI flows, and the privatization of public enterprises.[50] However, there is not much left to privatize, while remittances and FDI contributions rise and fall based on economic conditions in the Eurozone.

The strength, but to some extent also the weakness, of the Albanian economy is thus related to its open model of economic development pursued since the beginning of transition. Open trade has been a crucial aspect of that model. Specifically, the country removed all quantitative barriers to foreign trade beginning in 1992 and introduced a range of tariff reductions since joining the World Trade Organization in 2000. The country has one of the lowest import tariffs in the region. It also has limited nontariff barriers and various regional free trade agreements, which overall indicate high trade liberalization. The 2017 "Doing Business" report ranks the country twenty-fourth out of 190 economies for ease of trading across borders, which is largely above the regional average for Europe and Central Asia.[51]

Still, the open model of the economy has left the country vulnerable to wider international crises. The 2008 crisis particularly led to a slowdown of economic growth, which fell to 1.6 percent in 2012. Economic growth has recovered since 2013. Albania avoided the direct effects of the 2008 global crisis due to the limited integration of the country's banks in world financial markets and to the decision to convert foreign bank branches into subsidiaries, subject to local supervision, and fiscal stimulus policies. Indeed, it was the only country in Southeast Europe with growth rates over 3 percent in three subsequent years. However, economic contraction in neighboring countries resulted in the contraction of already weak demand for domestic products, a decrease in remittances, and a rise in unemployment. Countries such as Greece and Italy, in addition to being the main partners for trade, are home to more than one million Albanians, who provide a substantial share of the country's GDP.

Another important factor that helped the country escape the direct effects of the 2008 crisis was the "divorce" from the IMF in 2009, a process that led to increasing public expenses. Specifically, in January 2009, the then-Berisha government ended the country's close cooperation with the IMF under a sixth three-year monitoring program (PRGF/EFF), an arrangement that had ensured the IMF's close check on the country's fiscal and monetary policies throughout an eighteen-year period. On the occasion, the prime minister thanked the IMF for its supervision and declared "the end of economic transition," effectively gaining back freedom to increase the budget deficit. Amid a strained budget and a general economic downturn, the increased public expenses were generally financed by expensive loans from domestic banks and eurobonds. In 2010, the government also pursued large-scale privatization plans, motivated by the need to finance the country's current-account and budget deficit, already suffering from the contraction of remittances and low tax revenues. Large-scale privatization meant completing the privatization of the little that was left from the communist era, though prices for these state enterprises were low.

State involvement in the economy remains minimal, especially when considering that the state was the only economic player prior to transition. Currently, the private sector supplies 80 percent of total jobs and contributes the same percentage to the yearly GDP output of the country. State presence is significant in specific sectors like energy and management of natural resources, but these tend to be problematic sectors. For example, the renationalization of the energy power distribution company after its unsuccessful privatization in 2009 cost taxpayers over €100 million. Similar initiatives involving the state, such as the €1 billion Public-Private Partnership program adopted by the current government, are expected to increase domestic consumption but will add a heavy burden to public liabilities in the long term. The costly and often nontransparent major public works are especially a concern given that the public debt relative to GDP stands at more than 70 percent, the current-account deficit at 11.3 percent of GDP, and the informal economy is estimated to comprise more than a third of GDP.

On November 26, 2019, a major earthquake shook Albania, leaving a significant imprint on economic output and living conditions in the country. Although the data are still incomplete, it is estimated that more than 10 percent of the population lost their homes, while the economic cost is estimated to be around 7.5 percent of GDP.[52] At the beginning of 2020, a donor's conference organized by the EU and international financial institutions in Brussels pledged more than €1 billion in donations to minimize the effects of the earthquake. While the economy was still grappling with the negative impact of the earthquake, the COVID-19 pandemic worsened the already shrinking economic output and increased pressure on falling tax revenues. The government has stepped in by increasing social welfare payments in order to support households impacted by the pandemic or by issuing sovereign guarantees to domestic banks in order to increase domestic lending to affected businesses.

As a result of successive crises, the economic output decreased to 2.2 percent in 2019 as compared to 4.1 percent in 2018, mainly as a result of a 12 percent economic contraction in the fourth quarter. Another contraction of 9 percent is expected in 2020. The European Bank for Reconstruction and Development (EBRD) foresees that "the economy is likely to be strongly affected by the epidemic due to its high reliance on tourism and exports of low value-added intermediate goods to Italy's fashion industry. A likely reduction in remittances will also act as a drag on growth."[53]

The impact of the recent crisis has been rendered more acute in the context of long-term structural weaknesses that characterize economic development. Political patronage schemes, widespread corruption, and weak institutions negatively influence a functional market economy. They also undermine finding a possible solution to long-term problems, such as uncertainty over land rights. Ownership of many properties, especially those expropriated during the communist regime, remains unresolved. Such property disputes usually go through all levels of the judicial process, sometimes several times, while judgments ordering restitution of properties are often not implemented. Cases addressing the breach of the principle of due process regarding property disputes have accumulated in the European Court of Human Rights. Some of these have been won by the claimants, placing a significant burden on the state budget. Corruption and abuse in such cases are especially acute given the lucrative value of these properties and the weak position of concerned individuals. When adding widespread illegal construction, illegal occupation of public property, and sometimes corrupt legalization of illegal constructions in highly populated urban and coastal areas, lack of enforcement of property rights is a big burden on the economy and inhibits the development of important projects, including in the tourism sector. With a property registration process not completed, with issues of the expropriation of land confiscated during the communist era yet to be solved, and with weak law enforcement on occupied land, much of property rights are the subject of corruption, clientelism, and the large-scale informal economy.

Migration is another issue with major economic repercussions. As of 2019, "more than a million-and-a-half Albanians have emigrated, with those between the ages of 20 and 40 being the largest group."[54] As a result, the country has experienced a major brain drain. The migrants continue to provide substantial remittances, estimated to be close to $1 billion annually. But such a high flow of emigration has significant political, social, demographic, and economic ramifications (see chapter 6).

Key Social Issues

Albania remains one of the poorest countries in Europe. According to the World Bank, one out of three Albanians is poor. Some five hundred thousand citizens live in extreme poverty, subsisting on less than $1 per day, while 7.7 percent of citizens subsist on less than $3.20 per day (see table 17.1). The current government has begun to pay attention to policies tackling poverty and social exclusion as part of meeting its EU requirements for membership in the union. A public welfare system, including regulations over social policy and institutions, is in place. Still, the government struggles with insufficient resources to deal with the needs of vulnerable groups. The Gini index, which aims to measure the degree of income inequality in a country using a scale of 0 to 100 (low to high), has fluctuated from 12 in 1992 to 27 in 1996, 32 in 2002, and 29 in 2018.[55] The higher the index value, the higher the income inequality among individuals in a country. After its peak in 2002, the index has improved slightly in recent years due to increased efforts on fiscal and social policies.

Albania is a signatory to most international agreements on equal opportunities and has advanced national legislation on this issue. A law on gender equality is in place. The Labor Code includes provisions to prohibit discrimination in the workplace on the basis of gender or sexual orientation. A commissioner for protection against discrimination is intended to ensure that equal opportunities are systematically on the government's agenda. Beyond legal and institutional progress, ensuring equal opportunities on the

Table 17.1.   Key Indicators

Population	2.9 million
Population growth	0.2%
	(average annual growth rate)
Life expectancy	78.3 years
Urban population	60.3%
Human Development Index[a]	0.791
HDI rank	69
	(of 189)
UN Education Index	0.758
Gender Inequality Index[b]	0.234
GDP per capita	$13,326
	(purchasing power parity)
Gini index	29.0
Poverty[c]	7.7%
Aid per capita	$54.7

Source: Bertelsmann Transformation Index, Albania Country Report 2020, https://www.bti-project.org/en/reports/country-report-ALB-2020.html#pos14.

[a] The Human Development Index is a summary measure of average achievement in key dimensions of human development: a long and healthy life, being knowledgeable, and having a decent standard of living.

[b] The Gender Inequality Index reflects gender-based disadvantage in three dimensions—reproductive health, empowerment, and the labor market. It ranges from 0, where women and men fare equally, to 1, where one gender fares as poorly as possible in all measured dimensions.

[c] Percentage of population living on less than $3.20 a day at 2011 international prices.

ground is more difficult to achieve. According to the Gender Equality Index 2020,[56] gender equality in the country ranks seven points below the EU average. The index also notes "very unbalanced responsibilities regarding care for family members and unpaid household work," an indicator on which Albania scored only forty-eight out of one hundred points. Despite their education, women continue to earn lower incomes compared to their male counterparts. Women's participation in the labor market has increased steadily; however, it is not reflected sufficiently in decision-making processes, the media, political representation, or wages.

Serious offenses and domestic violence against women are a key topic of public debate, and high-profile cases surface almost daily. The government has strengthened support services for survivors of domestic violence, including national shelters, free legal aid, referral mechanisms at the municipal level, and a National Counseling Line for Victims of Domestic Violence.[57]

Minority groups such as Roma and Egyptian communities continue to suffer low employment rates and have difficulties accessing social protection services, leading to the systematic marginalization of these groups. Despite several amendments to specific legislation on protecting minority groups, further administrative capacity building and significant improvement in existing infrastructure is essential to improve the status of minorities.

Albanian governments have continuously pledged to increase public expenditure on education, but education's share in the budget remains the lowest of the region, less than 3 percent of GDP.[58] Expenditure on research and development is almost nonexistent, amounting to only 0.4 percent of GDP. Considering that most economic players in the country provide mainly low-technology, labor-intensive, and low-cost products, an immediate focus on and increased funding for education is necessary to expand skills, knowledge, and technological capacities. In addition, there is a large reported gap between labor demand and labor supply, which shows the need for educational institutions to update the quality and specific relevance of education for the job market.

Emerging Challenges

Almost three decades into its democratic transition, democracy remains the consensual end goal of the entire Albanian political spectrum, the governing actors, and the society at large. Perhaps as a result of the harsh communist dictatorship, there are no relevant social or political actors that contest the ideal of democracy. The country has also installed the necessary institutional framework, including an elaborate system of checks and balances, to advance along the path of democratization. In the Albanian context, moreover, the end goal of democracy is perceived as closely related to the processes of EU membership and the institutional templates that the EU is trying to diffuse in the postcommunist candidates via enlargement conditionality.

Much of Albania's democratic institutional framework has thus benefited from direct and indirect support from the EU and the wider international community. Especially after the 1997 crisis, when waves of migration and state collapse turned the country into a European problem, the reshuffling of the institutional framework has been closely sponsored, led, or supervised by various structures of the international community. The EU has played an increasingly significant role in the context of the EU enlargement policy in the Balkans.

Although the country has established the core institutions of democracy, which follow closely the "best" Western institutional templates, the country serves as a textbook case displaying the challenges of consolidating the institutional framework. As all sections of this chapter show, the setup of the institutional framework is only the first step of a functioning democracy. The real challenge is making the institutions work in practice. Specifically, all key institutions of democracy—the legislature, the presidency, and the judiciary—have specific formal functions in the system of checks and balances. Yet their formal functions do not work as expected and have been systematically twisted by major political actors with the power to do so. Far from a network of checks and balances, Albania's key institutions function in practice as political instruments to advance specific agendas. Hence, independent institutions like the presidency and the judiciary are particularly susceptible to personal agendas and have become major mechanisms of political control.

The result is that the functioning of the democratic institutions has turned into a permanent challenge. The parliament, for example, serves as an arena of political bickering and boycotts rather than for exercising expected supervision of the executive. The presidency is used to infiltrate political loyalists across all independent institutions rather than serving to unify the country. The judiciary, too, has fallen victim to political patronage networks and functions as the political arm of specific political parties.

The gap we note between formal templates of democracy and the way they work in practice applies not only to democratic institutions but also to the wider framework of democratic politics, including political competition and civil society. Despite political parties touting similar political goals and programs, all of them employ a winner-takes-all style of governance once in power. Hence, electoral competition produces less a peaceful rotation of power than contestation of results and fierce political conflict. Civil society and media, too, are far from the ideal independent actors that serve social goals. Instead, the activity of civil society is oriented toward donors' priorities more than society's concerns. The media is often used by owners with interests in other businesses to gain specific political benefits, becoming part of the political patronage system. The weakness of formal institutions negatively impacts economic development as well.

The mismatch between templates of democracy and the way they function in practice is a phenomenon that characterizes other cases of transition to democracy and is an inherent part of the democratic consolidation process. However, it is more extreme in cases like Albania, which faces a particular democratic deficit, including lack of prior experiences with democracy and the collapse of the institutional order during the early transition. The weight of the past and institutional weakness have complicated the process of transition and continue to hinder consolidation of democratic institutions. Here, moreover, the malfunctioning institutions and the lack of enforcement they imply tend to breed widespread informality, entrenched political patronage, and persistent corruption, indeed the most obvious symptoms of weak institutions.

Study Questions

1. How were characteristics of the precommunist and communist periods reflected in the postcommunist period in Albania?
2. What was the mode of regime change in Albania, and what have been its consequences?
3. What were the key characteristics of early transition in Albania? How are they similar to and different from those in neighboring states?
4. Why has it been difficult for rule of law to become established in Albania?
5. What are the major challenges to democratic institution building in Albania?

Suggested Readings

Abrahams, Fred. *Modern Albania: From Dictatorship to Democracy in Europe.* New York: New York University Press, 2015.

Elbasani, Arolda, and Senada Sabic. "Rule of Law, Corruption and Democratic Accountability in the Course of EU Enlargement." *Journal of European Public Policy* 25, no. 9 (2018): 1317–35.

Fischer, Bernd J. *Albania at War, 1939–1945.* West Lafayette, IN: Purdue University Press, 1999.

Mehilli, Elidor. *From Stalin to Mao: Albania and the Socialist World*. Ithaca, NY: Cornell University Press, 2017.

Peshkopia, Ridvan. *Conditioning Democratization: Institutional Reforms and EU Membership Conditionality in Albania and Macedonia*. London: Anthem Press, 2014.

Pula, Besnik. "Institutionalizing a Weak State: Law and Jurisdictional Conflict between Bureaucratic and Communal Institutions in the Albanian Highlands." *Comparative Studies in Society and History* 57, no. 3 (2015).

Vaughan-Whitehead, Daniel. *Albania in Crisis: The Predictable Fall of the Shining Star*. Cheltenham, UK: Edward Elgar, 1999.

Vickers, Miranda, and James Pettifer. *Albania: From Anarchy to a Balkan Identity*. New York: New York University Press, 2000.

Websites

Balkan Investigative Reporting Network (BIRN): https://birn.eu.com
BTI Transformation Index: https://www.bti-project.org/en/home.html?&cb=00000
Freedom House: http://www.freedomhouse.org
Newspaper Tema: http://www.gazetatema.net/eng
World Bank, "Albania": http://www.worldbank.org/en/country/albania

Notes

1. Nikiforos Diamandourous and Stephen Larrabe, "Democratisation in South-Eastern Europe: Theoretical Considerations and Evolving Trends," in *Experimenting with Democracy: Regime Change in the Balkans*, ed. Geoffrey Pridham and Tom Gallagher, 24–65 (London: Routledge, 2000).

2. Nathalie Clayer, *Aux origines du nationalisme albanais. La naissance d'une nation majoritairement musulmane en Europe* (Paris: Karthala, 2007).

3. Arolda Elbasani and Artan Puto, "Albanian-Style Laïcité: A Model for a Multi-religious European Home?," *Journal of Balkan and Near Eastern Studies* 19, no. 1 (January 2017): 53–69.

4. Elsie Robert, *Historical Dictionary of Albania* (Lanham, MD: Scarecrow Press, 2010).

5. Bernd Fischer, *King Zog and the Struggle for Stability in Albania* (Boulder, CO: East European Monographs, 1984).

6. Peter Prifti, *Remote Albania: The Politics of Isolation, Collection of Essays (1969–1986)* (Tirana: Puna, 1999).

7. Elidor Mehilli, *From Stalin to Mao: Albania and the Socialist World* (Ithaca, NY: Cornell University Press, 2017).

8. Elez Biberaj, *Albania in Transition: The Rocky Road to Democracy* (Boulder, CO: Westview, 1998).

9. Biberaj, *Albania in Transition*.

10. Biberaj, *Albania in Transition*.

11. Marshall Goldman, *Revolution and Change in Central and Eastern Europe* (New York: M. E. Sharpe, 2000).

12. Fred Abrahams, *Modern Albania: From Dictatorship to Democracy in Europe* (New York: New York University Press, 2015).

13. Ben Fowkes, *The Post-Communist Era: Change and Continuity in Easter Europe* (London: Macmillan, 1999).

14. Robert Austin and Jonathan Elisson, "Post-Communist Transitional Justice in Albania," *East European Politics and Societies* 22, no. 2 (May 2008): 373–401.

15. Daniel Vaughan-Whitehead, *Albania in Crisis: The Predictable Fall of the Shining Star* (Cheltenham, UK: Edward Elgar, 1999).

16. Vaughan-Whitehead, *Albania in Crisis.*

17. Miranda Vickers and James Pettifer, *Albania: From Anarchy to a Balkan Identity* (New York: New York University Press, 2000).

18. Vickers and Pettifer, *Albania.*

19. J. F. Brown, *The Groves of Change: Eastern Europe at the Turn of the Millennium* (Durham, NC: Duke University Press, 2001).

20. Vickers and Pettifer, *Albania.*

21. Vickers and Pettifer, *Albania.*

22. Abrahams, *Modern Albania.*

23. Arolda Elbasani, "Enlargement Instruments and Domestic Constraints: Public Administration Reform in Post-Communist Albania," *Südosteuropa. Zeitschrift für Politik und Gesellschaft,* November 2009, 70–90.

24. Ridvan Peshkopia, *Conditioning Democratization: Institutional Reforms and EU Membership Conditionality in Albania and Macedonia* (London: Anthem Press, 2014).

25. "Parliamentary Boycotts in the Western Balkans (2019)," Western Balkans Democracy Initiative, https://www.wfd.org/wp-content/uploads/2019/07/WFD-WB-Boycotts.pdf.

26. Blendi Kajsiu, "Nations in Transit—Albania (2005)," Freedom House, https://www.ref world.org/docid/473aff020.html.

27. "Albania Country Report (2014)," Bertelsmann Stiftung's Transformation Index (BTI), https://www.btiproject.org/content/en/downloads/reports/country_report_2014_ALB.pdf; "Albania Country Report (2016)," BTI, https://www.bti-project.org/content/en/downloads/r eports/country_report_2016_ALB.pdf.

28. Antoinette Primatarova and Johanna Deimel, *Bridge over Troubled Waters? The Role of the Internationals in Albania* (Sofia: Centre for Liberal Strategies, 2012), http://www.clssofia.org/u ploads/files/Bridge%20Over%20Troubled%20Waters_The%20Role%20of%20the%20Internati onals%20in%20Albania.pdf.

29. "Albanian PM Vows to Hold Elections in Face of Boycott, Protests," Radio Free Europe, last modified June 21, 2019, https://www.rferl.org/a/albania-s-rama-vows-to-hold-elections-in-face-of-boycott-protests/30013063.html.

30. "Albanian President Calls on People to Topple Government," Associated Press, February 19, 2020, https://www.voanews.com/europe/albanian-president-calls-people-topple-gover nment.

31. "President Clashes with Parliament on Constitutional Court Establishment," *Tirana Times,* November 13, 2019, https://www.tiranatimes.com/?p=143495.

32. "Albania Country Report (2016)."

33. The 2016 judiciary reform has changed the institutional setup in charge of nominations in the judiciary. The creation of the new institutions was still ongoing and incomplete during the writing of this chapter. Therefore, the analysis includes only the pre-reform setup of judiciary nominations.

34. Arolda Elbasani and Senada Šabić, "Rule of Law, Corruption and Democratic Accountability in the Course of EU Enlargement," *Journal of European Public Policy* 25, no. 9 (2018): 1317–35; Arolda Elbasani, "Judiciary as a Mechanism of State Capture: External Actors, Party Patronage and

Informality," *Perspectives: Political Analyses and Commentary* 3 (2017): 26–30, https://ba.boell.org/sites/default/files/uploads/2017/09/perspectives_-_09-2017_-_web.pdf#page=28.

35. "Albania Country Report (2018)," BTI, https://atlas.bti-project.org/COUNTRYREPORT/index_2018_URL.php?country=ALB.

36. Arolda Elbasani, "Mixed Member Electoral Systems in Transition Contexts: How Has the System Worked in Albania?," *CEU Political Science Journal* 1 (2008): 72–92.

37. OSCE/ODIHR, "Parliamentary Elections 25 June 2017," *OSCE/ODIHR Election Observation Mission Final Report*, https://www.osce.org/files/f/documents/4/d/346661.pdf.

38. "Albania Country Report (2020)," BTI, https://www.bti-project.org/en/reports/country-report-ALB-2020.html.

39. Ani Ruci, "Ani Tiranë: Konsensus i partive politike për reformën zgjedhore," *DW*, June 26, 2020, https://www.dw.com/sq/tiran%C3%AB-konsensus-i-partive-politike-p%C3%ABr-reform%C3%ABn-zgjedhore/a-53704958.

40. "Albania Country Report (2016)."

41. Austin and Elisson, *Post-Communist Transitional Justice*; Arolda Elbasani and Artur Lipinski, "Transitional Justice in Albania: Historical Burden, Weak Civil Society, and Conflicting Interests," in *Transitional Justice and Civil Society in the Balkans*, ed. Olivera Simić and Zala Volčič (New York: Springer, 2013).

42. "Trust in Governance, Opinion Poll 2019," UNDP Albania, https://www.al.undp.org/content/albania/en/home/library/democratic_governance/-trust-in-governance--opinion-poll-2019-.html.

43. Luiza Chiodi, "The Profession of Civil Society in Post-Communist Albania," *Albanian Journal of Politics* 4, no. 1 (2008): 7–40.

44. Steven Sampson, "The Social Life of Projects: Importing Civil Society to Albania," in *Civil Society: Challenging Western Models*, ed. Chris Hann and Elizabeth Dunn, 121–42 (London: Routledge, 1996).

45. "Albania Country Report (2020)."

46. "Albania Rejects US Request to Host Disposal of Syria's Chemical Weapons," *Guardian*, November 15, 2013, https://www.theguardian.com/world/2013/nov/15/albania-rejects-request-disposal-syrian-chemical-weapons.

47. "Albania Country Report (2010)."

48. Elbasani and Šabić, "Rule of Law, Corruption and Democratic Accountability."

49. Zguri Rrapo, "Relations between Media and Politics in Albania," Albanian Media Institute, 2017.

50. Vaughan-Whitehead, *Albania in Crisis*.

51. "Doing Business 2017: Equal Opportunity for All," World Bank, Washington, DC, 2017, https://www.doingbusiness.org/content/dam/doingBusiness/media/Annual-Reports/English/DB17-Report.pdf.

52. "The World Bank in Albania: Overview," World Bank, accessed August 29, 2020, https://www.worldbank.org/en/country/albania/overview#3.

53. "Albania Overview," EBRD, accessed August 30, 2020, https://www.ebrd.com/where-we-are/albania/overview.html.

54. Elez Biberaj, "Challenges of Albanian Democratic Consolidation," *Albanian Daily News*, April 7, 2019, https://albaniandailynews.com/news/30029.

55. Global Campaign for Education, *Financing Public Education in Albania* (policy paper, 2018), accessed August 22, 2020, https://www.acce.al/sites/default/files/download/research/policy_paper-financing_public_education_in_albania_2018.pdf.

56. Ministry of Health and Social Protection, "Gender Equality Index for the Republic of Albania—(Tirana, 2020)," accessed August 27, 2020, https://ec.europa.eu/neighbourhood-enlar gement/sites/near/files/20190529-albania-report.pdf.

57. "Albania Vows to Include More Women in Decision-Making and the Labour Market," UN Women, accessed August 28, 2020, https://www.unwomen.org/en/get-involved/step-it-up/comm itments/albania.

58. "Albania—Public Spending on Education, Total (% of GDP)," Trading Economics, accessed August 7, 2020, https://tradingeconomics.com/albania/public-spending-on-education -total-percent-of-gdp-wb-data.html.

Map 18.0. Former Yugoslavia and Its Successors

CHAPTER 18

Former Yugoslavia and Its Successor States

Paula M. Pickering and Jelena Subotić[1]

Yugoslavia, under various regimes and various names, lasted only seventy-three years, but its legacies remain strong in its seven successor states: Serbia, Croatia, Bosnia-Herzegovina, Slovenia, Macedonia, Montenegro, and Kosovo. A multiethnic state that was created in 1918 from the ashes of empires destroyed in World War I, Yugoslavia came out of World War II as a communist federation built on a commitment to multiculturalism and socialism. Throughout the communist period, it charted its own path: while still a one-party state organized around the cult of personality of the leader Josip Broz Tito, Yugoslavia was in many ways much different from all the other states of the communist Eastern bloc. It was not under direct control by the Soviet Union, it developed a strong and independent foreign policy and economic ties with the countries of the so-called Nonaligned Movement, and its domestic policies were more liberal in areas of freedom of movement and cultural and academic production. In many ways, Yugoslavia was a largely successful communist country, with thriving tourism, a comparatively high standard of living, and freedom for its citizens to travel and explore the world beyond its borders.

The Yugoslav experiment of "socialism with a human face," however, collapsed in catastrophe in 1991, when a series of brutal wars of Yugoslav succession led to the country's disintegration into seven new states. The wars, waged in fits and starts between 1991 and 1999, also brought horrific war crimes, crimes against humanity, and genocide back to Europe, which after the devastation of World War II now witnessed new waves of violence and destruction.

The reconstruction and rebuilding of the post-Yugoslav space has been long and difficult and has included significant international involvement and supervision. However, reconstruction was uneven. Some countries that survived the Yugoslav breakup emerged relatively unscathed (e.g., Slovenia) and managed to quickly turn around, reform their economic and political systems, and join the European Union (EU) with not that much difficulty. Others (e.g., Bosnia-Herzegovina, Kosovo) continue to suffer profoundly from the legacies of the war, ethnic nationalism, and international involvement, which, while much more intrusive than elsewhere in the region, was often uncoordinated between various international bodies and oscillated between periods of excessive and inadequate attention.

The countries that succeeded Yugoslavia, therefore, experienced postcommunist and postconflict transitions in very different ways and are facing different contemporary problems and challenges. The Yugoslav successor states faced multiple overlapping transitions. The Yugoslav states simultaneously transitioned from communism to democracy, from state socialism to free markets, and from a large multiethnic federation to smaller nation-states but also, significantly, from war to peace. It is this complexity of multiple transitions that makes the experience of Yugoslav successor states stand out from the rest of the region.

Political History

Precommunist period

Yugoslavia was a multinational federation with a population made up of a number of distinct ethnic groups of "South Slavs" (Serbs, Croats, Slovenes, Montenegrins, Macedonians, and Bosniacs, as well as non-Slavic groups such as Albanians and Hungarians) who lived in the Western Balkans for many centuries under various empires (Byzantine, Ottoman, Austro-Hungarian) and with short periods of independence and semi-independence. This diverse group of peoples over time adopted three major religious practices—Eastern Orthodox Christianity, Catholicism, and Islam; smaller minorities (Roma, Jews) were also present.

The common majority language, Serbo-Croatian, was standardized in 1850 and was an important basis for the development of a future political union. As World War I ended with the collapse of the Austro-Hungarian Empire, the newly free territories merged with the already independent Kingdom of Serbia to form the new Kingdom of Serbs, Croats, and Slovenes (the other South Slavic peoples were not considered constitutive of the new state). The new kingdom was proclaimed on December 1, 1918, and ruled by the Serbian royal dynasty of Karađorđević.

Political differences in the vision of how the new state would be internally organized were evident from the beginning. The Yugoslavia of 1919 was incredibly diverse, and in some ways this heterogeneity made it unmanageable with the tools of statecraft available to the leaders at the time. It was obviously diverse ethnically, linguistically, and religiously. It was also diverse in levels of development, industrialization, and literacy, as well as in the degree of impact from World War I in terms of, among other things, population losses.

The political organization in various parts of this new state was mostly ethnic in character, a consequence of the legacy of the Ottoman and Austro-Hungarian Empires' treatment of the various peoples they governed as religiously or ethnonationally distinct, which reinforced group identities and politicized them. What this meant in practice was that Croats voted for Croat parties, Serbs for Serb parties, and so on, which made a pan-Yugoslav supranational political unity difficult to build.

The early years of the new state were already riveted by instability and violence. Across the country there was much resentment against various attempts at Serbianization. The relations between Kosovo and Serbia had not improved: Kosovo Albanians had resented Serbian rule since Serbia's occupation of the territory in 1912, which included brutal treatment of local civilians, including forced Christianization.[2]

The 1921 constitution did not resolve these disputes and in some ways exacerbated them. The constitution was passed on June 28 with a simple majority, and with no participation from the Croat parties, which boycotted what they argued was an irregular and hasty process. The new state was organized along unitary principles and recognized three "constitutive nations": Serbs, Croats, and Slovenes. This clearly neglected the national desires of Bosnian Muslims, Montenegrins, and Macedonians, who by and large were considered by Serbia to be within their ethnic domain. The king was given expansive executive and legislative powers, including powers of war and of dissolving the parliament. There was no women's suffrage, an issue that garnered little political attention at the time but partly explains Yugoslav women's subsequent embrace of communism, which promised full gender equality. At the same time as the constitution was being negotiated, King Peter I died, leaving the throne to his son Aleksandar.

On January 6, 1929, amid the growing political crisis, King Aleksandar abolished the parliament, changed the name of the country to the Kingdom of Yugoslavia, and began to rule as a dictator. Among a series of repressive policies and arrests of political opponents, Aleksandar turned with particular force against the communists—between 1929 and 1931, 400 members of the 3,500-strong Communist Party were assassinated.[3]

The new constitution of 1931 further concentrated power in the hands of the king, basically abolished the secret vote, and dropped any pretense that Yugoslavia was committed to democracy. This radicalized extremist political movements and accelerated the political consolidation of the Croatian fascist movement, the Ustasha, as well as other radical political organizations. Croatian Ustasha began developing a political plan for an independent Croatia, while in Serbia, far-right groups started to emerge and organize politically.

The first Yugoslavia suffered from multiple problems. There was the problem of legitimacy, the lack of political will to accommodate a democratic vision of the multinational state, continuing Serbian hegemony, and a worsening international situation, including the rise of Nazi Germany and the Stalinist Soviet Union. These were challenges the inexperienced and unskilled political leadership had no capacity to meet.

On October 9, 1934, King Aleksandar was assassinated while on a visit to Marseille, France, by members of the Internal Macedonian Revolutionary Organization, who conspired with the Croatian Ustasha. Since Aleksandar's son, Regent Peter II, was too young to take the throne, the shocked country was ruled by Prince Pavle. In 1941, Pavle signed the Tripartite Pact, de facto joining the Axis powers in the misguided hope that this would prevent war. Through a combination of naive political moves, inexperience, and the overwhelming power of Nazi Germany, the Yugoslav government, like most others in Europe, failed to prevent the catastrophe of World War II. On April 6, 1941, Nazi Germany invaded and occupied Yugoslavia.

What followed were astounding levels of violence and mass death as, in addition to Axis troops (German and Italian, as well as their Hungarian and Bulgarian allies), local Axis-allied militia (Croatian Ustasha, Serbian Chetniks, Slovenian Home Guard, and others) unleashed a civil war under the broader chaos of the Axis occupation. Around 80 percent of the Yugoslav prewar Jewish population was killed in the Holocaust—in

Croatia mostly in Ustasha-run concentration camps (the largest of which was Jasenovac) and in Serbia in German shooting sprees and death camps. Thousands more were transported to death camps in Eastern Europe—mostly to Auschwitz, Treblinka, and Bergen-Belsen.[4] These local conflicts and atrocities—of Ustasha against the Serbs, Jews, and Roma; of Chetniks against the Croats and Bosnian Muslims—then became the source of intergenerational trauma that was to haunt Yugoslavia until its final destruction in 1991.

As Yugoslavia disappeared with the German invasion and dismemberment of the country in April 1941, the only sustained opposition to the occupation was from the rapidly strengthening communist partisan movement. Many partisan units from across Yugoslavia organized highly effective actions, including blowing up railroads used for German transport, disrupting radio signals, and attacking German troops.[5]

The partisans also attracted a huge number of women who served in nontraditional gender roles in the resistance, including more than one hundred thousand women fighters on the front line.[6] The heroism and the loss of life among the partisans were astonishing. Out of around 800,000 enlisted Yugoslav partisans, 250,000 were killed in the war. In its strength and spectrum of activities, it was probably the largest organized armed resistance movement in occupied Europe. With the help of the Soviet Red Army in the liberation of Belgrade in October 1944, the Yugoslav partisans defeated the Axis powers, and the Communist Party formed a government with Josip Broz Tito at the head.

Communist Period

From the very early days, even before World War II and the demise of the kingdom, the communist vision of Yugoslavia was of a federal system that would avoid national domination of particular groups and would respect the country's diversity and look at it as an asset, not a liability. One of the main ideological pillars of the new state was a commitment to the "brotherhood and unity" of Yugoslavia's various nations and national minorities—Serbs, Croats, Slovenes, Macedonians, Albanians, Muslims, Hungarians, and many others. This ideology also helped to create a real, although it turned out quite fleeting, "Yugoslav" national identity, which was attractive to many people from mixed ethnic backgrounds, or those for whom the recent experience of World War II magnified the danger of ethnic nationalism. In practice, however, "brotherhood and unity" often produced fairly rigid ethnic quotas for various political positions and resembled more a conglomeration of various national identities than a truly supranational one. Yugoslav identity, therefore, was always in tension with policies that strengthened ethnonational identities.

Because Yugoslav communist partisans managed to emerge victorious from World War II with minimal assistance from the Soviet army, postwar Yugoslavia succeeded in carving an international political space that was largely unique—it successfully resisted incorporation into either the Moscow-dominated Warsaw Treaty or the Western-dominated North American Treaty Alliance (NATO). Relations with the Soviet Union further soured in 1948 after Tito broke off the alliance with Joseph Stalin and Yugoslavia was officially no longer in Moscow's political reach. This international independence allowed Yugoslavia to pursue a fairly free foreign policy, unburdened by commitments to either the East or West. It instead charted a new path as one of the founders of the alliance of nonaligned countries.

In addition to an independent foreign policy, communist Yugoslavia also developed its own brand of socialist economic development. Instead of Soviet-style state central planning, Yugoslavia introduced a system of "worker self-management" within individual companies that attempted to decentralize decision making and give workers' cooperatives more agency.[7]

Communist Yugoslavia achieved significant economic success and extraordinary levels of modernization and urbanization in a relatively short period of time. Its liberal population movement policy also allowed more than one million citizens to live and work abroad, a policy that provided for a significant amount of economic remittances (money these workers abroad sent back home to family in Yugoslavia) to be invested back in the country. From a predominantly rural and very poor prewar society, Yugoslavia by 1970 was a middle-income country with growing levels of consumption, an envy of the rest of the communist world. It was also an increasingly popular international tourist destination for visitors from East and West.[8]

The constitution of 1974 introduced a dramatic shift in the internal organization of the federation, massively decentralized the state, and introduced a de facto confederal system, a new consensus-based system of decision making, which gave six equal federal units the right to self-determination—Serbia, Croatia, Slovenia, Bosnia-Herzegovina, Montenegro, and Macedonia—and, in a blow to Serbia, endowed two Serbian provinces (Vojvodina and Kosovo) with powers close to those of the other constitutive republics. The consequence of the new constitutional arrangement was the rise in national identities of each republic, which gradually became national and political entities with their own claims to sovereignty. This institutional arrangement paved the way to the eventual disintegration of Yugoslavia and the self-determination of each constituent republic beginning in 1991.

With Tito's death in 1980, a full-blown crisis of legitimacy of the Yugoslav state emerged. The immediate instability caused by Tito's death was compounded by the massive economic crisis that had gripped the country since 1979, and soon by Albanian demonstrations demanding that Kosovo be granted the status of a republic in 1981. The crisis was obvious and profound, and yet the party leadership was unequipped to deal with it, committed as it was to the rigid ideology of a largely state-run economy and the institutional confines of the 1974 constitution. The eventual dissolution of the country, then, was not inevitable along national and ethnic lines. It was instead the consequence of poor political choices, which provided no viable political solution and no mechanism for nonviolent resolution of disputes. It thus allowed for already developed nationalist ideologies to claim the political space.

In 1987, Slobodan Milošević took the helm of the Serbian Communist Party and quickly transformed the Serbian political agenda into one of defending the Serbian nation from annihilation, even "genocide," by its hostile neighbors.[9] As part of the proposed reforms, Milošević advocated for the dissolution of Serbia's confederal arrangement and the adoption of the "one man, one vote" electoral reform, which would guarantee an ethnic Serb as president of the republic by the simple power of the Serbian population majority.

This was soon followed by a dramatic suppression of the political autonomies of Kosovo and Vojvodina, which had enjoyed significant autonomous status based on the

1974 Yugoslav constitution. The stripping of Kosovo's autonomy had especially profound political consequences as it created a de facto apartheid state in Kosovo, where the Albanian majority was discriminated against in all facets of social life—from education to hiring to expressions of cultural and national distinctness.[10] By 1989, Serbia began preparations for war, which included illegal arms imports from the Soviet Union and the transfer of weapons to and training of Serb militias in Croatia and Bosnia-Herzegovina.[11] In June 1991, the war of Yugoslav succession claimed its first casualty in Slovenia.

Yugoslavia's Violent Collapse

The destruction of Yugoslavia was a slow-rolling disaster that began in the mid-1980s and gained momentum in 1990. Individual Yugoslav republics held elections in 1990, but nationalist leaders emerged victorious, beating more moderate opponents and foreclosing avenues for compromise. The success of nationalist parties was the result of the increasing delegitimization of the federal government as a source of authority and the strengthening of nationalism across the country as the media in various republics began to blame ethnic groups from other republics for the economic crisis and political instability. Slovenia and Croatia were the first to indicate a desire to leave the federation by organizing referenda on independence and mobilizing their local forces—so-called territorial defense—into proto-state armies.

On June 25, 1991, **Slovenia** declared independence from Yugoslavia. After initial skirmishes between the Slovenian military and the Yugoslav National Army (JNA) that lasted for several days and left five Slovenes and thirty-nine JNA soldiers dead, the JNA withdrew, and Slovenia was internationally recognized as an independent state in July 1991. The relative ease of Slovenia's withdrawal—and, perhaps more significantly, Slovenia's overwhelming ethnic homogeneity—made its transition from a Yugoslav republic into a new European state the smoothest of all former Yugoslav federal units. Slovenia was also the most economically advanced and was open to market and political reforms. It was admitted to the European Union with relative ease in the first round of the EU's Eastern Enlargement in 2004.

Croatia's independence from Yugoslavia was rocky. Low-scale violence had already begun in the summer of 1990 as groups of Croatia's Serbs, with support from Serbia and the JNA, began to block some of Croatia's roadways and Croatian troops attempted to seize the Serbs' weapons. By the end of 1990, many of Croatia's Serbs had consolidated into the so-called Serb Autonomous Region of Krajina, where they declared self-rule, outside of the confines of the Croatian authorities, but with continuing support from Serbia. The Serbs were apprehensive of Croatia's leader, Franjo Tuđman, who had made a series of anti-Serb statements that rekindled a deep sense of unease and memories of Croatia's mass atrocities against Serbs during World War II. Serbs were further alarmed by the proposed new Croatian constitution, which revoked Serbs as a constitutive people in the new Croatia.

These aggressive Croatian overtures were massively magnified by Serbian news propaganda, replayed daily on Serbian television (by then under full control of Milošević and his Socialist Party of Serbia, the SPS), which reminded its viewers that Croats had a history of fascist and anti-Serb politics and could not be trusted to protect the rights of Serbs. This mix of Croatian actions and Serbian propaganda built the perception of an inevitable war by Croatia against its Serb minority. From the Serbian perspective, then, the only means for survival was rebellion.

On May 19, 1991, Croatian authorities held a referendum on possible independence from Yugoslavia, which the Croatian Serbs boycotted. Croatia's declaration of independence from Yugoslavia on June 26, 1991, immediately followed Slovenia's. Yugoslav authorities declared the referendum illegal, and the JNA began a series of military operations to prevent parts of Croatia from seceding by force. The Milošević regime in Serbia began sending weapons to Croatian Serb strongholds in the region of Krajina and to Bosnian Serb troops, which reconstituted into an army. Among the first sites of armed conflict was the coastal region of Dalmatia, where in June 1991 the JNA began a barrage of indiscriminate shelling, including of the city of Dubrovnik, a United Nations Educational, Scientific and Cultural Organization (UNESCO) protected jewel of the Adriatic coast, and one of the most recognizable attractions in Yugoslavia. In August 1991, the front line moved to the city of Vukovar in inner Croatia. Croatian Serb rebel troops surrounded the city and kept it under siege, indiscriminately shelling both Croatian troops and civilians. A large group of Croatian civilians (around 260 people) were taken to a nearby hospital and killed, in what became known as the Ovčara massacre. The city of Vukovar was almost completely leveled, with numbers of dead in the thousands. Croatia's capital, Zagreb, also came under attack. The United Nations deployed a 13,500-strong peacekeeping United Nations Protection Force (UNPROFOR), which tried, in fits and starts, to keep the peace between Croatian troops and rebel Serbs. Violence between Croatian troops, Croatian Serb armed rebels, and the JNA continued until the summer of 1995, when the Croatian army broke Serbian rebel strongholds and retook its territory. In the process, however, almost the entire Croatian Serb population—some three hundred thousand people—were either forcibly removed from their homes or fled in fear of the Croatian army. In total, around twenty thousand people died in the war. The violence and final ethnic expulsions made Croatia a mostly ethnically homogeneous state for the first time in its history. It also created a tremendous problem of refugee resettlement, which remains unresolved to this day.

The path to **Bosnia-Herzegovina**'s independence was even more violent and deadly than Croatia's. What made Bosnia-Herzegovina's situation much more difficult and volatile than elsewhere in Yugoslavia was its multiethnic and multifaith character, as well as its neighbors' claims over parts of it. At the start of Bosnia-Herzegovina's secession, the country was about 44 percent Bosniac (Bosnian Muslim), 31 percent Serb, and 17 percent Croatian. The multinational character of Bosnia-Herzegovina ensured that any solution that would work for just one ethnic group could be rejected by the others. The absence of a genuine cross-national compromise, together with neighbors' intervention, paved the path to war.

As the war in Croatia was already in full swing, and fearing domination by a rump Yugoslavia, the Bosniac and Bosnian Croat members of the Bosnia-Herzegovinian government pushed for independence, held a referendum (which Bosnian Serbs boycotted), and on April 6, 1992, declared independence from Yugoslavia. That day, the Bosnian Serbs—who had been exerting dominance over local governments and had organized their own military troops with help from Serbia and the JNA—began shelling the capital city of Sarajevo from neighboring hills that were under Serb control. This began the horrific nearly four-year siege of Sarajevo, during which its citizens were mercilessly shelled, shot by snipers, and slowly starved as the city ran out of food. Elsewhere in Bosnia-Herzegovina, Serb troops went on campaigns of ethnic cleansing—advancing into majority Bosniac villages and towns and killing or expelling Bosniac civilians. At the same time, a localized war between Bosnian Croat troops (supported from Croatia) and the Bosnia-Herzegovinian army broke out. The carnage and devastation throughout the country, despite UNPROFOR's deployment, were enormous.

The violence culminated in the summer of 1995. The single worst atrocity of the war in Bosnia-Herzegovina, and the worst massacre on European soil since World War II, took place around the town of Srebrenica in July 1995. Srebrenica was by that time designated an international "safe haven," where thousands of Bosniac refugees who took shelter there were under official protection by a Dutch UN peacekeeping battalion. The Bosnian Serb army, however, led by General Ratko Mladić, intimidated and outmaneuvered the Dutch peacekeepers, who let the Bosnian Serbs into the compound. The Serb troops proceeded to separate men from women and took all men and boys aged sixteen to sixty to the nearby woods, shot them, and buried them in unmarked mass graves. This killing went on for several days. A total of around eight thousand men and boys were killed in what the International Criminal Tribunal for the Former Yugoslavia (ICTY) later determined was an act of genocide.

While the Bosnian government had been calling for an international intervention since the beginning of the conflict, international help was inconsistent and ineffective at changing the course of the war. The UN Security Council set up an arms embargo for all sides in the conflict, which in practice disfavored the smaller and less-well-equipped Bosnian army, putting it at a huge disadvantage against the Bosnian Serb army, which could rely on JNA weapons and machinery and continuing shipments from Serbia. None of the many separate peace plans drafted by the European Community, the United Nations, the United States, and others managed to take hold. The UN peacekeeping troops were tasked with an unclear mandate, given limited authority to use force, and hampered by lack of political will among the political leaders of the UN Security Council to authorize efforts to halt violence against civilians.

The Srebrenica genocide in July 1995 finally provoked NATO air intervention against Bosnian Serb troops in August. The fighting officially ended in November 1995, when the warring sides, together with Serbian president Slobodan Milošević, agreed to a US-brokered peace at the Wright-Patterson Air Force Base in Dayton, Ohio. The Dayton Accords ended the war, but in many ways it froze the conflict in place, allowing warring parties to keep much of the territories that were under their control at the end of the war. The cruel irony of this plan was that areas in eastern Bosnia-Herzegovina, including Srebrenica, now completely ethnically cleansed of its Bosniac population, ended up under Bosnian Serb control after the war.

The new Bosnia-Herzegovinian constitution designed at the Dayton peace conference created a complex and arcane overlapping system of governance, which recognized Bosnia-Herzegovina's three major ethnic groups—Bosniacs, Serbs, and Croats—as constitutive nations, whose political representatives would share power and regularly rotate in leading the country. Territorially, the constitution established two separate entities—the Serb-dominated "Republika Srpska" (RS) and the Bosniac-Croatian Federation, with the city of Brčko gaining independent city status. The consequence of this arrangement was that it solidified ethnic divisions and ensured that Bosnian politics was again driven by ethnic nationalism.

Around 97,100 people were killed in the war in Bosnia-Herzegovina, a vast majority of them Bosniacs.[12] The violent legacy of this war and the unwieldy and complex Dayton constitutional arrangement, as well as lengthy and intrusive international supervision and control, continue to haunt Bosnia-Herzegovina's efforts at postconflict reconstruction and rebuilding.

The end of the war in Bosnia-Herzegovina in 1995 did not end the process of Yugoslavia's disintegration. Soon after the violence subsided, a new front line opened up in **Kosovo**. While low-level tensions simmered in Kosovo throughout the 1990s, it was in 1997 that, after years of a de facto apartheid regime and severe human rights abuses inflicted upon Kosovo's majority Albanian population by the Serbian regime (including prohibiting Albanian language in schools and firing ethnic Albanians from public sector jobs), Albanians rejected the long-standing tradition of peaceful resistance, which had not achieved its desired goals. They instead began to organize into an armed insurgent group, the Kosovo Liberation Army (KLA), whose goal was no longer just securing human rights for Kosovo's Albanian majority but instead Kosovo's full independence.

Starting in December 1997, the KLA began a series of armed operations against Serbian police, which were followed by harsh Serbian reprisals and incursions into villages and towns across Kosovo. Insurgent attacks and Serbian counterinsurgency operations intensified in 1998, and in January 1999 the Serbian forces carried out a massacre of Albanian civilians in the town of Račak, where forty-five people, including children, were murdered. This event brought the Kosovo crisis to international attention. Fearing a repeat of the Srebrenica genocide and increasingly alarmed that Serbia was planning a massive campaign of ethnic cleansing of Kosovo's Albanian population, the international community, led by NATO, embarked on a three-month-long air campaign against Serbian military and police forces in Kosovo and across Serbia. On June 9, realizing it could no longer withstand NATO airpower, Serbia signed an agreement that would end the air war in exchange for Serbia relinquishing its control over Kosovo and placing it under international trusteeship.

The loss of Kosovo and the continuing domestic crisis brought on by increasingly open corruption finally led to the political demise of **Serbia**'s president Slobodan Milošević. After ruling Serbia in some capacity since the late 1980s, in 2000, Milošević tried to rig the results of elections that showed his party losing. For many citizens in Serbia, this was the last straw, and in October 2000, massive protests broke out against the Milošević regime. He was finally ousted from power by this popular revolt. The winning political coalition that managed to unite various factions from distant poles of the ideological spectrum successfully defeated Milošević. It soon extradited Milošević to The Hague to stand trial for the crimes against humanity he had orchestrated in Croatia, Bosnia-Herzegovina, and Kosovo. In the aftermath of his ouster, however, the profound differences within the coalition created a new cycle of political instability and infighting

Photo 18.1. The Srebrenica-Potočari Memorial and Cemetery honor about eight thousand largely Bosniac male victims of the 1995 genocide in Srebrenica, Bosnia-Herzegovina. (Ajdin Kamber, Shutterstock)

in Serbia, which dramatically slowed its democratization and narrowed its path to joining the European Union.

Over the next decade, the UN Mission in Kosovo (UNMIK) governed Kosovo and supervised the establishment of its political and administrative institutions. Internationally mediated negotiations on the status of Kosovo began in 2005, and a proposed settlement was put forward in 2007. These and other attempts at regulating Kosovo's status failed, and in February 2008, Kosovo declared independence. This was a polarizing move that divided the international community. While most countries in the world agreed to recognize Kosovo's independence, a number of countries—Serbia, Russia, and Spain, among others—refused to recognize the new country, fearing that this precedent would stoke the flames of their own internal secessionist movements. To date, Serbia and Kosovo have yet to sign a deal that would fully recognize Kosovo as an independent state but also—Serbia's concern—ensure substantial autonomy for Kosovo's Serb minority. It is this lack of progress regarding relations with Kosovo that has been a key roadblock in Serbia's accession negotiations with the European Union.

Macedonia and Montenegro mostly successfully avoided armed conflict as they became independent countries. Since declaring its independence in 1991, **Macedonia**[13] managed a fragile peace between ethnic Macedonians and a large (25 percent) Albanian minority by providing for a degree of political and cultural rights for Albanians, including Albanian-language education. Attempts at full political integration were not successful, despite efforts by the UN Preventive Deployment Force, the European Community, and the Organization for Security and Co-operation in Europe (OSCE). Macedonia came to the brink of a dangerous widespread conflict in 2001 when Albanian guerrillas supported by armed groups from Kosovo engaged in low-level armed skirmishes with Macedonian forces in the northwest of the country. The political breakthrough was the internationally brokered Ohrid Agreement, passed the same year, which provided a blueprint for constitutional amendments and reforms that would improve the status of Macedonian Albanians while keeping the country together. As part of the enforcement of this fragile peace, NATO provided for a limited disarmament mission, and there is a continuing international civilian presence on the ground.

Montenegro was allied with Serbia throughout the wars of Yugoslav succession, but in 2006 the alliance ran its course and Montenegro charted its own path, including pursuing its own NATO and EU membership.

There is no uniform scholarly agreement on what caused the breakup of Yugoslavia and the brutal wars that followed. While most scholars have by now rejected a crude hypothesis about supposed historical "ancient hatreds" between various ethnic groups and debunked it by pointing to the mostly successful multicultural life that most of Yugoslavia enjoyed between 1945 and 1991, there are differences as to what and who destroyed Yugoslavia. It is clear that Yugoslavia's demise is the result of a combination of factors. At the top of the list are Serbian and Croatian nationalisms and the refusal to undertake a much-needed constitutional reform that would guarantee power sharing between ethnic groups. Serbian nationalism found its leader in the fiercely ambitious Slobodan Milošević, who envisaged himself as the new Tito and desired to rule all of Yugoslavia, but from a position of Serbian dominance. Finally, Yugoslavia never resolved the political questions of its various ethnic minorities—Serbs in Croatia, Albanians in Serbia—and also did not have a power-sharing agreement that would maintain political stability and the multicultural character of Yugoslavia's most diverse region: Bosnia-Herzegovina. All of these reasons, coupled with the acute economic crisis, a massive political void left at the country's top after Tito's death in 1980, and a lack of democratic processes for peaceful conflict resolution, led the country to the path of destruction.

As the remainder of this chapter will demonstrate, the political, social, and cultural legacies of the former Yugoslavia continue to shape successor states' political development. The devastation of the Yugoslav wars and the continuing impact of war crimes and the lack of full accountability for them are profound political and personal traumas that reverberate throughout the region more than twenty years on.

Political Institutions

In addition to confronting the massive challenges of political and economic transformation experienced by their Central and East European neighbors, the former Yugoslav states also suffered violent change in their state boundaries. In all but Slovenia, the wars delayed democratization and economic liberalization. In addition, wars provided opportunities for self-interested elites across the political spectrum to undermine the development of strong formal institutions of horizontal accountability (checks and balances) and vertical accountability (elections and independent media), deepen their hold on power, and expand political machines.

The study of the political transition of the former Yugoslav states contributes to our understanding of transition in the Central and East European region by demonstrating that this process varies between states and within states over time. It is not a unidirectional process ending in a rock-solid consolidated democracy.[14] Slovenia had the smoothest transition toward a market-oriented democracy. In contrast, Croatia transitioned to a hybrid system mixing democratic and authoritarian elements that was dominated by a nationalist party and then in 2000 moved toward a market-oriented democracy. Serbia transitioned to a hybrid regime dominated by a nationalist party in the 1990s, toward a market-oriented democracy in the 2000s, and then back to a hybrid regime dominated by a "2.0" nationalist party in 2019. Macedonia initially transitioned toward a hybrid regime, moved toward democracy, slid back into a hybrid regime between 2010 and 2018, but is now inching toward democracy.

In those countries that experienced violence, the international community contributed to delayed transitions. The wartime systems facilitated alliances between external agencies and the warring parties at the expense of the citizens for whom the assistance was intended. For example, in Bosnia-Herzegovina, the warring parties took a cut of all humanitarian aid intended for civilians.[15] After peace agreements were negotiated with the wars' protagonists, "peace-building" international agencies tacitly helped to buttress the authority of corrupt leaders who were resisting democratization. They did so first by treating them as legitimate leaders and then acquiescing to their arguments that only they could maintain stability. The peace accords in Kosovo and Bosnia-Herzegovina did not settle disputes about power sharing or sovereignty. In addition, they did not provide a clear road map to effective, self-sustaining democratic institutions. The failure to facilitate the peaceful resolution of disputes—for example, the return of refugees and displaced persons, protection of individual and collective rights, transitional justice processes, and the status of Kosovo—ensured that recalcitrant leaders would selectively implement only those elements of the peace accords that suited their own narrow agendas. Finally, many important domestic functions were taken over by international officials, often with little knowledge about the region. Regimes in Bosnia-Herzegovina and Kosovo have democratic and authoritarian elements, while also sharing executive power with international officials.

Because formal political institutions influence political outcomes, domestic opposition and international forces seeking to promote democratization helped change electoral systems and alter the distribution of power between the president and the parliament in the former Yugoslav states. In 2000, Croatia jettisoned the single-member district system and adopted the more representative proportional representation (PR) system. By 2006, all former Yugoslav republics had adopted PR electoral systems. As democratic groups gained strength in Croatia and Serbia, they weakened their countries' presidencies by building up and increasing the independence of nonpresidential political institutions. All are now characterized as parliamentary systems. Yet merely adopting parliamentary systems has not ensured further democratization or democratic consolidation. Periods when representatives from one party serve as both president and prime minister[16]—the Croatian Democratic Union (HDZ) in 2015–early 2020, the Serbian Progressive Party

(SNS) between 2014 and 2021, and Macedonia's Internal Macedonian Revolutionary Organization–Democratic Party for Macedonian National Unity (VMRO-DPMNE) between 2006 and 2016—have allowed for the weakening of checks and balances and of the quality of democratic governance.

Independent judicial institutions and a professional public service, which the EU seeks to encourage through its pre-accession process, remain weak and susceptible to informal politics. Indeed, ruling parties have weakened and sometimes captured democratic institutions intended to check power and independently fight public corruption in Western Balkan countries both in the pre-accession phase (in Serbia, Montenegro, and Macedonia) and in the post-accession phase (Croatia). This generates public distrust and calls into question the extent to which the EU accession process has promoted the development of self-sustaining democratic institutions.[17]

The pull of the EU also encouraged dedicated seats for minorities in Montenegro and Slovenia, though the latter reserves seats only for its tiny indigenous minorities. Germany helped convince Croatia to reserve seats for ethnic minorities. Nationalists in Croatia and Macedonia reserved seats for representatives chosen by their diasporas.[18] Designers of the electoral systems also adopted laws on gender quotas in all former Yugoslav countries to ensure the representation of women in politics.[19]

In Bosnia-Herzegovina and Kosovo, international diplomats imposed elaborate power-sharing rules among major ethnic groups. Bosnia-Herzegovina's constitution features rigid power-sharing arrangements, which include ethnic quotas in all but the lowest level of governance, unconstrained veto rights by minorities, and extensive territorial and political decentralization to ethnically dominant entities. These rules contribute to a negative peace, or absence of war, but not to a durable, positive peace and ethnic cooperation. Quotas for representatives only for Bosniacs, Serbs, and Croats in the Collective Presidency and the national-level House of Peoples have excluded representatives of other groups (such as Jews and Roma), a fact that the European Court of Human Rights (ECHR) declared in 2009 to be in violation of the European Convention on Human Rights. Power sharing and the decentralized structure of Bosnia-Herzegovina's federation has often hampered governance. At the state level, this includes failing to reform electoral rules to comply with the ECHR decision, inability several times to form coalition governments for more than a year after elections, and delayed road construction that crosses the federation and RS borders into Europe even though it is needed for economic growth. Yet power sharing, with its quotas for representation, decentralization, and minority veto rights, at the state and federation levels has deterred autocratization. This is in contrast to Bosnia-Herzegovina's Republika Srpska, which has fewer checks and is more centralized, a structure that has allowed Milorad Dodik's Party of Independent Social Democrats to establish a more autocratic regime in the entity.[20]

Even in Kosovo, where power-sharing rules were combined with lessons learned from Bosnia-Herzegovina—more constrained veto rights and the rejection of extensive territorial decentralization—political participation by the Serb minority has occurred only at times and among particular segments. Kosovo Serb resistance to Pristina's authority was financed by the Serbian government, which paid €634 million in 2012 and 2013 alone to support parallel structures.[21] This lasted until the end of 2013, with the EU-mediated Brussels agreement on integrating parallel institutions[22] and Belgrade's endorsement of

Srpska List to represent Serbs in Kosovo's elections. In Macedonia, which experienced less extensive violence and less intrusive international intervention, post-violence institutions in the Ohrid Framework Agreement featured more informal power-sharing rules and decentralization only to municipalities. The Ohrid plan has encouraged the meaningful inclusion of Albanians in the state. However, it has not addressed ethnic polarization, inclusion of smaller minorities, or patronage, defined here as the use of resources and benefits that flow from public office in exchange for political support.[23] While domestic social, political, and economic situations, as well as neighbors' interference, vary in all of the deeply divided postconflict former Yugoslav states, Macedonia's more informal rules and modest decentralization to only local—not regional—levels seem to facilitate more effective governance.

Complicating efforts toward building self-sustaining institutions and effective governance, elected officials in postwar Bosnia-Herzegovina and Kosovo have shared power for decades with unelected international officials who exercise executive authority. The impact of internationally led state building in Bosnia-Herzegovina has been affected by its inconsistent strategy. International officials failed to act against years of ethnic cleansing during the war and against ethnic extremists in the period just after Dayton.[24] Then they employed executive powers to override Bosnia-Herzegovina's institutions to pass legislation and remove domestic officials—at a rate of nearly nine decisions per month between 1990 and 2005.[25] Since then, the international approach has endorsed "local ownership" as a recipe for encouraging good governance. Though the UN's imposition of a protectorate that delayed governance by Kosovo's citizens has been criticized, Elton Skendaj notes that the state bureaucracies the UN built, staffed according to merit, and insulated from politicization were more effective and less corrupt than others more quickly handed over to local control.[26] The West's current reliance on the increasingly remote carrot of EU accession to spur reform has failed to encourage domestic leaders to develop strong democratic institutions insulated from political pressure.

Political Competition

Drawing on comparative democratic political theory, we discuss how both the political institutions above and other key factors influence political competition and illustrate how they work in several country cases. One factor is the outcome of the first multiparty election. Valerie Bunce suggests that the victory of a liberal, anticommunist opposition in the founding election in newly formed states like those of the former Yugoslavia permits a decisive break with the authoritarian past and a launching of a liberal program. In contrast, the victory of an ethnically exclusive party, including former communist parties seeking to maintain their hold on power, hinders democratization.[27] A second factor affecting competition, particularly in Bosnia-Herzegovina, Kosovo, and what is now North Macedonia, is an ethnic party system, which international imposition of power-sharing rules has entrenched. The latter ensures that specific groups are included in governance, but this undermines parties' capacity to aggregate interests effectively and deliver good governance to citizens regardless of background. Several other factors that the former Yugoslav states share with their Central and East European neighbors include unorthodox parties based often on personalities[28] rather than on programs or democratic processes[29] and the increasingly frequent entrance of new parties, particularly antiestablishment ones (see chapter 4 on the topic of political parties). These features can facilitate patronage and populist rule antagonistic to liberal democratic institutions.

In the first multiparty elections, only **Slovenia** experienced a relatively smooth democratic transition and process of state formation. The noncommunist coalition Democratic Opposition of Slovenia (DEMOS) won the parliamentary elections, while the leader of the reformed Communist Party won the presidency. This new government enacted pluralist and market reforms and declared Slovenia's independence from Yugoslavia. After the movement-based DEMOS disintegrated, the fragmented party system appeared to consolidate into four strong parties. Broad agreement among Slovenia's elite that their future was tied to European and Euro-Atlantic institutions helped the country achieve early membership in the EU and NATO. In addition, the absence of substantial minorities allowed Slovenia's significant illiberal forces to remain relatively harmless during its march into Europe.[30] Yet the impact of the 2008 global recession, the 2011 Eurozone crisis, and domestic austerity policies generated conditions for antiestablishment sentiment. These contributed to the victory of a party with a vague, anticorruption, and pro-liberalization platform formed only the month prior to the 2014 parliamentary elections—the Miro Cerer Party, which led a five-party coalition government.[31] Signaling volatility, this coalition was ousted in 2018 by a different five-party coalition headed by an established party—the Slovenian Democratic Party—that used anti-immigrant rhetoric and whose leader had been convicted for corruption.

In contrast to developments in Slovenia, the first multiparty elections in **Croatia and Serbia** enabled parties to advance ethnic agendas rather than build consensus. These steps resulted in hybrid political systems. In Croatia, a nationalist movement-based party, the Croatian Democratic Union (HDZ), under the leadership of former Partisan general and later political dissident Franjo Tuđman, and with substantial support from the Croatian diaspora, won the founding elections for both the presidency and parliament in 1990. It did so based largely on its anticommunist expression of Croatian identity.[32] A majoritarian electoral system turned the HDZ's 46 percent of the popular vote into 67.5 percent of seats in parliament. With this political dominance and the rising power of the hard-line faction of HDZ, Croatia began building an ethnically based rather than civically based nation. Serbian leaders labeled the Croatian government as fascist and armed Croatia's Serb Democratic Party (SDS), which it radicalized. These policies created conditions for HDZ to weaken political opponents and capture state institutions for the rest of the decade.

In Serbia, Slobodan Milošević weathered several waves of anti-regime demonstrations in the 1990s and intraparty conflict and remade the League of Communists of Serbia into an authoritarian nationalist party. In the founding election in 1990, his Socialist Party of Serbia (SPS) ensured that it would dominate the parliament. The SPS's program appealed to socialist conformists, as well as to Serbians who had criticized Tito's "weakening of Serb interests" in Yugoslavia in the 1980s.[33] The party was strongest outside Belgrade and in the Serbian heartland. Milošević used existing structures to retain power, acquire wealth, distribute patronage to his family and to allies within his criminalized support structure,[34] and manage "Serb" territories outside Serbia.[35]

As long as violence continued, Tuđman's and Milošević's parties could monopolize power, delay democratization, demonize political opponents as traitors, and engage in massive corruption. After the violence ended, domestic opposition forces in 2000 brought down these hybrid political systems and launched "second" democratic transitions. With the return of all Serb-held territory in Croatia and the changes made to the electoral laws, the diverse opposition to the HDZ made significant electoral gains on platforms of good governance and political change. After President Tuđman's death in the run-up to the elections in early 2000, a moderate six-party opposition coalition headed by the reformed communist successor party, now the Social Democratic Party (SDP), won control of parliament. Its governing program included accession to the EU, cutting the purse strings of the hard-line HDZ in Bosnia-Herzegovina, and cooperation with the ICTY. In Serbia, after the end of fighting in Kosovo, ordinary Serbs increasingly attributed their worsening circumstances to the SPS's poor governance. Milošević's supporters among the criminal class had become independent of his patronage. The leaders of the liberal opposition finally set aside personal antagonism to unite, and the youth organization Otpor (Resistance) effectively led civic mobilization that defeated Milošević's plans to rig the 2000 presidential elections. They helped secure the victory of Vojislav Koštunica, who was supported by an eighteen-party opposition coalition. This opposition coalition won the December 2000 parliamentary elections, selecting the Democratic Party's (DS) Zoran Đinđić as prime minister.

Broad-based anti-regime coalitions in 2000 were better at bringing down hybrid regimes than they were at delivering good governance. This was particularly the case because they were confronted with huge domestic tasks of political and economic reform that had been hijacked under one-party dominant rule in the 1990s, faced enduring opposition by holdovers in the politicized administration and security services, and received international pressure to comply with ICTY and EU pre-accession criteria. Indeed, in 2003, members of Serbia's security services assassinated Đinđić over planned reforms. While the new democratic coalition governments took steps to build democratic institutions, they soon splintered and eventually were voted out.

Democratic reforms continued, as the victory of democratic coalitions in 2000 compelled formerly ruling parties in Croatia and Serbia to moderate their platforms and membership. All major parties in Serbia's 2012 parliamentary election supported EU membership.[36] The EU's pre-accession requirements also encouraged the formation of governments with multiethnic support. In Croatia, both SDP- and HDZ-led governments have included a minister from or been supported by the Independent Democratic Serb Party. At the same time, elections in the 2010s have allowed parties to tap into citizens' disillusionment, take advantage of the fragmentation of the opposition, and champion reform rhetorically while using the levers of power to favor the continued rule of their party. While competition is significantly more open in Croatia, which became a member of the EU in 2013, than in Serbia, the HDZ expanded its power over still-weak democratic institutions between 2015 and 2020. It then held both the parliament and the presidency and operated in the post–EU accession period, when the regional organization had fewer sticks and carrots to wield.[37] In Serbia, Aleksandar Vučić's Serbian Progressive Party's capture of both parliamentary and presidential powers and ambivalence toward EU accession has enabled it to build a new hybrid political system.

Ethnic party systems, where party membership is rooted in and seeks the support of only one ethnic group, channel competition within rather than across ethnic groups. These party systems in the Western Balkans came from a combination of historical legacy, social structure, anticommunist sentiment, and electoral rules. A 1990 court decision striking down Bosnia-Herzegovina's ban on ethnic parties, an electoral rule mandating that election results not deviate more than 15 percent from the ethnic distribution in the census, and anticommunist sentiment contributed to the victory of the ethnically based Muslim Party of Democratic Action (SDA) and Bosnian branches of the HDZ and SDS in the founding elections. In the aftermath of violence in Bosnia-Herzegovina, Kosovo, and Macedonia, external interventions imposed power-sharing rules among the largest ethnic groups in an effort to prevent one ethnic group from engaging in a tyranny of the majority. Bosnia-Herzegovina and what is now North Macedonia illustrate how ethnic parties bolstered by internationally written power-sharing rules funnel competition and complicate governance.

The postwar Dayton constitution imposed on **Bosnia-Herzegovina** features ethnic quotas throughout most levels of governance. These rules encourage ethnic parties and discourage parties from appealing to the common concerns of citizens, regardless of ethnicity, or those that cut across ethnically dominant territories or ethnic lines.[38] The first elections after violence allowed the wartime protagonists to participate in the new system, strengthen patronage networks, and increase interethnic tensions in Bosnia-Herzegovina. Since ethnically based parties rarely win votes from other ethnic groups, party leaders have strong incentives to make radical appeals, claiming to protect their own group from threats by ethnic "others," in order to ensure greater voter turnout of their own group.[39] This dynamic is further encouraged in fragmented party systems like Bosnia-Herzegovina's, where many parties compete for the vote of one ethnic group. Once in power, ethnic parties seek to extend their rule by using ethnicity to deflect from their failures in delivering good governance[40] and by using public resources to reward party loyalists, for example through awarding contracts and securing employment in state-owned enterprises or administration. This is particularly the case for the governing Party of Independent Social Democrats (SNSD) in the RS, whose more centralized system has abetted SNSD's ability to limit competition and checks on power to establish a more autocratic system in the entity than in the federation.[41] In ethnic party systems, ethnic parties with more moderate aims and a willingness to bridge ethnic divides through cooperation can be the best hope for improved governance for all citizens. Yet Social Democratic Party–led coalition governments in 2000 and in 2010 failed to improve the quality of governance. These records contributed to widespread cynicism that all politicians, regardless of party, are part of a "political class" prioritizing their own interests over those of citizens. Civic-based parties exist but remain small, rooted in urban constituencies and finding success mainly in local and regional elections in the federation.

The leading Bosniac, Croat, and Serb parties in the mid-2000s onward reaffirmed their divergent objectives, which strengthened political deadlock in national-level politics. They also scuttled initiatives for constitutional changes for the state in 2008 and 2009 and for the federation in 2013,[42] which were intended to create a more functional state and advance Bosnia-Herzegovina's accession to the EU. Major political leaders reacted coolly to the recommendations, apparently from fear of damaging their patronage networks. In the federation, parties claiming to represent Bosniacs have advocated for a more unified Bosnia-Herzegovinian state, and Croat parties continue to advocate for increased Croatian collective rights. Since 2006, the SNSD has shown little interest in the central government and instead has sought to enhance the RS's already substantial autonomy, holding a referendum on the republic's "statehood" day and threatening referenda against state judicial institutions and on secession, which is not permitted under the Dayton constitution.[43]

North Macedonia provides another example of an ethnic-based party system. While all governments in the country since 1990 have been coalitions including Macedonian and Albanian parties, these coalitions have been formed through informal rather than formal quotas, as in Bosnia-Herzegovina.[44] However, in 2001, increasing dissatisfaction from Macedonian Albanian members of parliament about their role in decision making, particularly in governments led by the nationalist Internal Macedonian Revolutionary Organization–Democratic Party for Macedonian National Unity (VMRO-DPMNE) and criminal forces from neighboring Kosovo, contributed to months of fighting ended by the EU-negotiated Ohrid Framework Agreement. Ohrid provided Macedonians with additional incentives to form inclusive, multiethnic governments and power-sharing arrangements, albeit far less rigid ones than in Bosnia-Herzegovina.

After the first postconflict election in 2002, the Social Democratic Union of Macedonia (SDSM) formed a multiethnic coalition government committed to the agreement and EU accession. However, VMRO-DPMNE won the next several national elections, forming a coalition with the most popular Albanian party after violence, the Democratic Union for Integration (DUI), entrenching itself in power for ten years (2006–2016). This extended hold over the state and an EU accession process stalled initially over Greece's objection to the country's name laid the foundation for institutionalized corruption. A political crisis developed due to the ruling parties' targeting of independent media, opposition boycotts of parliament, and use of administrative resources for the 2014 elections. It was deepened by the release of illegally wiretapped telephone conversations between top government officials, which contained suggestions of high-level crimes. In June 2015, EU and US mediators constructively brokered an agreement on an interim government that included the opposition, the resignation of Prime Minister Gruevski in January 2016, reforms for the April 2016 elections, and a special prosecutor's office to investigate criminal allegations contained in the wiretaps. Despite VMRO-DPMNE obstruction, the investigations led to indictments of former officials in late 2016.[45] After the December 2016 elections, the SDSM-led coalition formed a multiethnic coalition government excluding VMRO-DPMNE.

The VMRO-DPMNE president delayed the formation of a government for six months, alleging that Zoran Zaev "endanger[ed] the country's sovereignty" by accepting demands of Macedonian Albanian parties for inclusion in a ruling coalition that focused on greater language and economic rights for the Albanian community.[46] During this standoff, VMRO-DPMNE supporters forcibly stormed the parliament. This crisis was primarily generated by an intra- rather than interethnic Macedonian struggle for power, with the ruling VMRO-DPMNE leadership using state resources, allied social groups, and ethnically divisive rhetoric to cling to power. Macedonia's Albanian parties exacerbated interethnic tensions with demands for greater Albanian rights at a meeting with Albanian officials in Tirana.

These developments highlight the vulnerability of North Macedonia's political system to democratic backtracking and to conflict between and within ethnic groups. They also illustrate the potential for democratic political and civic forces to remove hybrid leaders. The European Commission has recommended several times that the European Council move the country to the next stage in the accession process by opening negotiations, most recently in 2019 after implementation of new reforms and a historic agreement with Greece to officially change the country's name to North Macedonia. After a delay due to a French demand that the EU accession process be revised, the European Council decided in March 2020 to open accession negotiations with North Macedonia. This decision was met by resistance from Bulgaria, which blocked further accession progress over identity and language disputes, again leaving North Macedonia in a precarious limbo.[47]

Parties oriented around personalities rather than ideologies or policy interests have endured as a feature of Western Balkan party systems since the earliest days of postcommunism. Examples in Serbia, Montenegro, and Kosovo illustrate the roots and consequences. In **Serbia**, Milošević reinvented the ideologically based Communist Party in Serbia into the Socialist Party of Serbia, ostensibly devoted to Serb interests throughout former Yugoslavia. This transformation allowed the party to dominate Serbia and use the state to reward loyalists throughout the 1990s. The fall of Milošević's rule, democratic reforms, and the EU accession process tied partly to compliance with the ICTY created conditions in 2008 for a wing to break from the Serb Radical Party to form the Serbian Progressive Party (SNS), which distinguished itself as being pro–European Union while inheriting other elements of the old nationalist platform.

During SNS's domination of both the presidency and parliament since 2014, it has undermined checks and balances, obstructed independent media, and used state resources to further weaken fractured opposition parties. SNS's leader, Aleksandar Vučić, a former ally of Milošević's, modestly proclaims to have accomplished more than Tito did and deftly courts Europe, Russia, and China. To protest unfair election conditions, the main opposition coalitions boycotted the 2020 parliamentary elections, contributing to a low turnout of 48 percent and a sweeping victory for the SNS, which gained two-thirds of the parliamentary seats.[48] Some scholars argue that the EU has abetted Vučić's hold on power by accepting his argument that he is essential for maintaining stability in the region and that alternatives are far worse, while overlooking policies that undermine the rule of law. Arguably, this strategy bolsters his legitimacy and encourages "stabilitocracies," not democracies.[49]

Montenegro provides an example of the longevity of rule by a personality-based party—the Democratic Party of Socialists (DPS). It astoundingly dominated Montenegrin politics since it emerged from the League of Communists in 1991 until August 2020. The party, led by Milo Đukanović since 1997, who like Vučić has shifted between the prime ministership and presidency, masterfully used its control over state resources, the manipulation of crises created by "enemies," and the rhetoric of EU integration to undermine mechanisms of accountability and maintain its hold on power. DPS elites allowed for the development of democratic institutions demanded by the EU that on paper could exercise accountability, while in practice maintaining nearly unrestricted influence over them.[50] This has not prevented Montenegro from progressing in the EU accession process and acceding to NATO in 2017.

In **Kosovo**, the rule of Ibrahim Rugova's Democratic League of Kosovo, which spearheaded peaceful resistance to Milošević's rule over Kosovo, was soon eclipsed in the postwar period by parties created by Kosovo Liberation Army wartime personalities. These are Hashim Thaçi's Democratic Party of Kosovo (PDK) and Ramush Haradinaj's Alliance for the Future of Kosovo (ADK), the former of whom was indicted for war crimes by the Kosovo Specialist War Crimes Chamber in 2020. These established parties have worked as "personally driven patronage networks."[51] UNMIK's decision to cooperate with these parties that supported the international administration and later the European Union Rule of Law Mission in Kosovo (EULEX) agenda of stability created conditions for public corruption to grow and flourish.[52] The dominance of PDK and ADK lasted until 2019, when Vetëvendosje, the Self-Determination Movement, headed by former youth leader Albin Kurti, won the parliamentary elections. Voters' frustration with the wartime personality-based parties' governance record of a struggling economy, corruption, and patronage, along with the stalled talks with Serbia, contributed to voting out the establishment and giving a chance to a party claiming to fight corruption, international intervention, and the domestic political elite.[53]

Turnover in power often contributes to democracy. Yet Kurti's party's willingness to use tactics such as the release of teargas in parliament to try to prevent votes on issues it opposes—ratification of a border deal with Montenegro and the establishment of an autonomous association of Serb-majority municipalities—raises questions about its commitment to the rule of law. Personality-based parties appear to thrive in postcommunist party systems in the Western Balkans by adapting their rhetoric to the shifting sentiments of the large portion of the electorate that chooses not to identify with any party and by developing powerful informal networks.

In sum, democratic political party systems across the former Yugoslavia are still in flux. The outcomes of the founding elections in 1990 jump-started Slovenia's democratic reforms while delaying democratic reforms in Serbia and Croatia for another decade. Though political competition exists across the former Yugoslav countries, no party system is wholly dominated by mainstream parties that offer clear programs that spell out how they will fix the issues citizens prioritize. Instead, parties continue to splinter, powerful personality-based and ethnically based parties endure, and new parties with grand promises and amorphous programs emerge. The inclusion of minority and sometimes regional parties in governments in Croatia, Macedonia, Serbia, Montenegro, and Kosovo is a positive sign that partly comes from EU pressure and that can enable these coalition parties to divide political power. Yet exclusivist parties also remain coalition options, such as Croatia's recently formed Homeland Movement Party, whose leaders have expressed sympathies with the fascist Ustasha. Ethnic party systems have not just exacerbated ethnic divisions; they have also generated conflict within ethnic groups over power. The success of new parties that pledge to battle the establishment and corruption in Slovenia and Kosovo reflects popular dissatisfaction with the quality of governance delivered by established parties, a dynamic hardly unique to the Western Balkans but one intensified by the region's parties' weak ties to voters.[54] Personalistic parties can act as vehicles for demagogues to prioritize their self-interests, further weaken democratic institutions, use state resources to reward loyalists, and constrain, although not eliminate, political competition.

Civil Society

The sections above focus on the influence of top-down factors—political institutions and political elite interests—on political competition and outcomes. Yet top-down factors provide only part of the story about how politics works. Citizens' values and political and civic participation also have a significant effect on politics.

The willingness of citizens to participate in voting has varied according to timing, political context, and economic situation. Citizens quickly discerned the self-serving behavior of politicians working in postcommunist political institutions, perpetuating a gap between rulers and citizens. In all countries, voter turnout declined from high rates in 1990 to stable but moderate rates two decades later. Across the region, youth have been substantially less likely than other age groups to vote.[55] Research suggests that citizens are rationally disaffected with a political system whose parties they distrust and who present them with few meaningful choices. Expressing frustration with options in their ethnic party system, just 19 percent of respondents in a nationally representative survey in Bosnia-Herzegovina believed that only monoethnic parties could protect their vital interests.[56] In Slovenia and Serbia, 63 percent and 66 percent of voters, respectively, did not feel close to any political party.[57]

In a 2016 survey, 54 percent of Croatian, 46 percent of Bosnian, but only 25 percent of Serbian respondents agreed that democracy was preferable to any other government.[58] Though Serbians are outliers, these findings of tepid support for democracy, including among youth, are consistent with opinions across postcommunist Europe. This lackluster support is likely linked to low levels of satisfaction with the way democracy works in their countries. Merely 31 percent of respondents in Slovenia and 17 percent in Croatia in 2018 expressed satisfaction with the way their democracy works.[59] When asked to identify elements of democracy they considered extremely important, citizens from Serbia, Kosovo, Croatia, Bosnia-Herzegovina, and North Macedonia all ranked "a justice system treating everybody equally," "economic prosperity," and "a government that guarantees meeting the basic economic needs of all the citizens" as their top three associations with democracy.[60] These priorities reflect concern about arbitrary rule, the limited reach of prosperity, and the prevalence of corruption. They also indicate an enduring preference for the state to provide for basic needs. Citizens regardless of ethnic background want governments to prioritize economic development. The low priority given to political elements of democracy, such as civil liberties and political pluralism, is consistent with the views of citizens in Romania and Bulgaria,[61] leaving them open to tolerance of illiberal rule.

Surveys indicate that citizens in most Yugoslav successor countries express not only low levels of trust in their political institutions (see table 18.1) but also substantially lower levels of trust in judicial intuitions than citizens of the EU. These institutions are often criticized as corrupt, unresponsive, and failing to consistently deliver benefits to ordinary citizens.[62] Data on political participation, values, and policies suggest that elites are more

Table 18.1. Levels of Trust in Political and Social Institutions in 2019 (Percentage)

Country	Political parties	Parliament	Judicial institutions	Police
Bosnia	27	35	37	51
Croatia	12	16	20	53
Kosovo	29	35	42	80
Montenegro	34	40	42	46
North Macedonia	17	24	16	42
Serbia	15	35	41	55
Slovenia	14	26	25	65
EU-28	*19*	*34*	*51*	*71*

Sources: For public opinion data in Croatia, Macedonia, Montenegro, Serbia, Slovenia, and EU-28, answers refer to those respondents who "tend to trust" the specific institutions. For judicial institutions, the specific question asks about trust in the justice/legal system. "Standard Eurobarometer 92: Public Opinion in the European Union, Data Annex," European Commission, December 2019, https://ec.europa.eu/commfrontoffice/publicopinion/index.cfm/Survey/getSurveyDetail/instruments/STANDARD/surveyKy/2255. Kosovo does not have a national army. Data on trust in parties in Bosnia: Bozo Skoko and Marko Custic, *Media Freedoms in Bosnia and Herzegovina in 2019*, Millinium Promocija; and in Kosovo: "Kosovo Ranks Its Political Parties and External Allies," *Prishtina Insight*, February 2019, https://prishtinainsight.com/kosovo-ranks-its-political-parties-and-external-allies. Data on trust in police in Kosovo and Bosnia: "Citizens in the Western Balkans at the Same Time Believe and Question the Police," PointPulse, November 2018, https://pointpulse.net/activities/citizens-in-the-western-balkans-at-the-same-time-believe-and-question-the-police. For Bosnia and Kosovo, answers on trust in judicial institutions—specifically Courts and the Judiciary—and parliament report those who tend to and absolutely trust, "Balkan Barometer 2019: Public Opinion Survey Analytical Report," Sarajevo, 2019, https://www.rcc.int/pubs/89/annual-report-of-the-secretary-general-of-the-regional-cooperation-council-2019-2020.

responsible than citizens for illiberal rule in the Western Balkans. However, disaffected citizens have abetted poor governance through their withdrawal or adaptation.

Citizens frustrated with their political systems may choose instead to participate in civil society organizations (CSOs), which produce social capital that has the potential to strengthen democratization. However, the actual impact of such organizations and social movements depends partly on the type of social capital they build and their rootedness in local society. Democratic advocacy organizations that link citizens to policy makers can help hold political leaders accountable. Those groups that disperse authority horizontally, rather than concentrate it, are best at cultivating the repeated interdependent interaction that builds interpersonal trust. Groups that look outward, beyond the interests of their own members, toward benefiting the larger community are better at solving broader social problems than those that only focus inward. Finally, those groups that link together people of different cultural backgrounds are better at helping to integrate a diverse society than those that bring together and provide social support only to those of the same cultural background.[63]

Many civil society organizations in the region are monoethnic. Voluntary associations that focus on strengthening bonds within single ethnic groups contributed to conflict in Yugoslavia's multiethnic republics. For example, many religious leaders' direct participation in exclusivist nationalist appeals in the 1990s undermined the capacity of religious organizations to facilitate reconciliation and moderation.[64] Some monoethnic local organizations, which were linked to nationalist parties, crowded out a range of moderate groups that opposed violence.[65] Other organizations have been inward looking, hierarchically structured, and willing to use violence to realize their exclusivist goals.

However, at the end of the 1990s, local CSOs advocating democracy in Croatia and Serbia mobilized citizens against ruling party abuses and brought down their repressive regimes in elections.[66] Some local, multiethnic organizations that grew out of the war produce social capital that bridges ethnic divisions. Medica Zenica, for example, is a voluntary organization formed by local women residents of all backgrounds in Zenica, Bosnia-Herzegovina, to aid female victims of the war.[67] Other groups include displaced persons, veterans, and families of missing persons. Victims' groups in Bosnia-Herzegovina and Kosovo have adopted different strategies: either to return as minorities to their homes in their places of origin or to rebuild new lives in areas where they are among the ethnic majority. Veterans associations, which are split along ethnic lines and are inward looking, resent their marginalization in the postconflict period and tend to support nationalist parties.[68]

Western agencies have assisted the CSOs that support democratization and transitional justice but have overlooked groups that emerged from local traditions of informal mutual help networks rooted in everyday life, such as in the neighborhood and the workplace.[69] Donors have favored CSOs that engage in advocacy—even where they might have shallow roots in society—and whose formation is driven largely by donors' needs. A recent study of civil society in the Western Balkans found that civic organizations remain heavily dependent on foreign donors.[70]

It is encouraging that leaders of advocacy groups, such as legal aid and human rights groups, have made progress in forming networks to monitor and influence government.[71] Some examples of CSO efforts to affect policy include the following: Bosnia-Herzegovina's CSOs ensured that Serbs, Croats, and Bosniacs are all legally constituent peoples throughout the country and successfully advocated for the adoption of a law on the direct election of mayors; Serbian CSOs contributed to the Law on Associations in Serbia; and Kosovar CSOs led a successful campaign for an open-list, proportional electoral system and have also participated in government-led initiatives related to reconciliation and the rule of law.[72] In general, however, CSOs have not been strong enough to compel elected officials to include them in discussions of politically sensitive policies.[73]

Citizens often view local CSOs as promoters of Western agendas and as sources of funding for opportunistic leaders. A nationally representative survey in 2019 in Bosnia-Herzegovina found that only 18.7 percent of the respondents reported membership in a civil society organization.[74] In an example that fuels citizens' skepticism about CSOs, a 2013 investigative report on seven years of contracts awarded by Serbia's Ministry of Youth revealed that the party controlling the ministry awarded the largest projects to organizations headed by fellow party members.[75] In Croatia, the ruling HDZ recently captured the National Foundation for Civil Society Development, steering funds to allied conservative organizations and movements.[76] A different study conducted in Serbia found that many citizens were skeptical of local CSOs because they were perceived to work on issues that are unimportant, narrowly focused, or imported, rather than on issues that resonated with citizens' priorities and values, including socioeconomic needs and community welfare.[77]

Frustration with formally organized groups has led progressive young people to be active in more informal and less hierarchical ways. For example, citizens frustrated by poor governance, corruption, and economic hardship have engaged in plenums, sit-ins, and protests (in Slovenia, Croatia, Serbia, North Macedonia, Bosnia-Herzegovina,[78] and

Kosovo); efforts to help victims of flooding in 2014 (in Bosnia-Herzegovina and Serbia); and demonstrations protesting opaque urban development projects (in Belgrade, Skopje, and Zagreb).[79] Social movement tactics have started with concrete, often local problems that symbolized more systemic issues. They have emphasized horizontal processes, participation, and dialogue. These steps have succeeded in mobilizing and giving voice to citizens, but with varying political impacts. Research has found that social movement protests in North Macedonia helped bring down the then-ruling VMRO-DPMNE due to their links to other CSOs, a relatively strong opposition party, and the EU. This is in contrast to the yearlong, weekly social mobilizations throughout 2019 among progressive youth opposed to the rule of Serbian president Vučić, who infamously declared that he would not give in to protestors' demands even if five million people were to gather. These protesters have not developed strong links to CSOs or the EU, whom they distrust, while they face a fragmented opposition.[80] These factors, together with COVID-19, have weakened their political impact, at least for now.

Economic Policies and Conditions

Political disputes over how to address socialist Yugoslavia's economic challenges contributed to the collapse of the country. Reform policies adopted during and immediately after the collapse add to some of the shared struggles and to the divergences visible in today's economies of the former Yugoslav countries. For example, countries such as Slovenia, Croatia, and Macedonia that implemented macroeconomic stabilization early on were able to bring inflation under control by the mid-1990s.[81] In contrast, countries where macroeconomic stabilization was delayed by leaders, coalitions of interests opposed to reforms, and violence—Serbia, Montenegro, Bosnia-Herzegovina, and Kosovo—suffered from inflation and the development of informal economies.

Wars in Croatia, Bosnia-Herzegovina, Serbia, and Kosovo curtailed already decreasing inter-republican trade, strengthened corruption, and inhibited foreign investment. The economies of these countries suffered physical destruction of infrastructure and productive capacity, as well as the emigration of young, highly educated, and skilled labor. Serbia suffered under sanctions throughout the 1990s for its support of the Serb war effort in Croatia and Bosnia-Herzegovina, as well as from NATO bombing for its violence in Kosovo in 1999. A Greek boycott over the name dispute and the cutoff from Yugoslav markets negatively impacted Macedonia's economy in the 1990s. The wars dramatically slowed the economic development of these successor states, particularly in the first half of the 1990s. In a period of increasing unemployment, these economies uniformly experienced high inflation and decreasing production and gross domestic product (GDP).

In addition to the wars, the incomplete structural reforms initially adopted by most of the countries of former Yugoslavia provided fertile soil for corruption and slowed economic growth (see chapter 5). Throughout the 1990s, Croatian president Tuđman ensured that the manager-employee buyouts (MEBOs) approach to privatization ended up so that the largest and most profitable enterprises were transferred to owners with HDZ connections.[82] In Serbia, Milošević monopolized the limited privatization process in the 1990s to benefit supporters of his regime. It was not until 2000 that the democratic opposition in Serbia began more radical privatization. In the 2000s, privatization in Serbia occurred through direct sale, with formerly publicly owned enterprises being sold according to auctions or public tenders. One study found that employment and sales growth after privatization were the highest in those companies that received some foreign investment.[83] Montenegro and Macedonia started privatization with MEBOs, a strategy that worked best in Slovenia, which was already well integrated into the European economy. When state funds in Montenegro were required in 1996 to sell their shares in enterprises to the public or to foreign investors, it resulted in opaque sales of prominent enterprises to foreign investors.[84] In Macedonia, MEBOs allowed the most profitable enterprises to be sold to managers at substantial discounts. Postwar Bosnia-Herzegovina's use of voucher privatization, guided by USAID, resulted in cash-strapped citizens selling vouchers, which were then accumulated by well-connected, wealthy businessmen rooted in each of the three ethnonational communities.[85] While many smaller enterprises in Bosnia-Herzegovina have been privatized, many larger industrial enterprises, particularly in the RS, have remained state owned and not restructured. Privatization in postwar Kosovo involved direct sales, many of them murky, and was then followed by vouchers, which left untouched many industrial state-owned enterprises (SOEs). Bosnia-Herzegovina and Kosovo, in particular, have not yet embarked on the process of substantial structural reform.

The European Bank for Reconstruction and Development (EBRD) argues that a key lesson from twenty-five years of economic transition is that the development of a market economy requires improving the quality of both state and market institutions.[86] The vast majority of the former Yugoslav states' transitions illustrate the damage done by weak, politicized state institutions. For example, these institutions failed to develop and enforce clear and fair rules for privatization strategies. More recently, economic growth in 2019 in all but Slovenia and to a lesser extent in Croatia was hampered by weak rule of law, politicized public administrations, and informal economies.[87] Serbia's industrial production fell in 2019. A variety of privatization strategies that politically connected, wealthy elites steered toward their benefit and a lack of restructuring and oversight of remaining SOEs have had significant political consequences. It left the "winners" with disproportionate political influence, industrial workers with few employment options, and many citizens disillusioned. Remaining SOEs are poorly governed—even in Slovenia—and are used by ruling parties to dispense patronage and maintain grips on power.[88]

In the postconflict countries, international agencies initially attempted to address pressing economic problems that extended beyond market reforms as part of larger peace accords. They have donated over $14 billion to Bosnia-Herzegovina's economy since the signing of the Dayton Accords, and donors' conferences generated substantial income for Croatia and Kosovo. Although this aid contributed initially to the repair and reconstruction of housing and infrastructure, it was unevenly distributed and was denied to Serb communities in the RS and in Kosovo that did not support implementation of the peace accords. Most importantly, it was not protected by properly functioning legal frameworks that could have facilitated broad-based growth.

Deepened political commitment to integration with the EU and investment by the EU has accelerated the economic reforms and improved the economic performance—albeit to varying degrees—of the Western Balkan states during the pre-accession period.

Yet the implementation of reforms has been uneven, and vulnerable citizens have felt left out. In addition, EU-backed austerity policies have produced hardship and resentment among the poorest and most vulnerable segments of society. The global recession that began in 2008 hampered efforts of the region's governments to attract sufficient investment to help diminish unemployment and improve standards of living. The combination of the 2008 recession, delayed restructuring of the banking sector, and the Eurozone crisis hit Slovenia particularly hard. Overall, an EBRD report argues that the Western Balkans, which suffered a decline in economic activity, weathered the crisis better than expected because of "mature policies by governments and strong financial support from international organizations, and the continued commitment of privately owned foreign companies and banks to the region."[89] The Western Balkan economies attracted foreign direct investment (FDI) and generated decent GDP growth rates in 2018 (see table 18.2), though these decelerated somewhat in 2019 due partly to the slowdown among their European trading partners.

More broad-based growth is undermined by significant corruption. Of the postcommunist states, the Western Balkans are judged to have higher levels of corruption than any countries other than the non-Baltic countries of the former Soviet Union.[90] Even among the EU members, Slovenia's prime minister in 2020 had been jailed earlier for corruption, and nine ministers in the HDZ-led Croatian government had left office by early 2020 for reasons tied to corruption.

Since 2015, Russia, China, Turkey, and the Gulf states have stepped up their economic involvement in the Western Balkans. Russia has worked to establish influence over the energy sector in the region and has presented itself as an alternative to EU investment, even though the EU investment dwarfs it. The economic strategies of China and the Gulf states have taken advantage of and exacerbated nontransparent decision making among

Table 18.2. Increasingly Divergent Economies in 2019

	GNI per capita, (current USD)	Real GDP growth rate (percentage change on previous year volume)[a]	Foreign direct investment, net inflows, (percentage of GDP)	Unemployment (as percentage of labor force)	Share of youth not in education, employment, or training (as percentage of youth)
Bosnia	6,150	3.7	2.58	15.7	21.1
Croatia	14,910	2.7	1.94	6.6	11.8
Kosovo	4,640	3.8	3.84	25.6	32.5
Montenegro	9,010	5.1	8.27	15.1	17.3
North Macedonia	5,910	2.7	3.76	17.3	18.1
Serbia	7,020	4.4	8.33	10.4	15.7
Slovenia	25,750	4.1	2.57	4.4	7.0

Sources: For gross national income (GNI) per capita, Atlas method (current USD); foreign direct investment, net inflows (as percentage of GDP); unemployment (as percentage of labor force (all countries except Kosovo); and share of youth not in employment, education, or training (NEET) (as percentage of youth fifteen to twenty-four or twenty-nine): World Bank, World Development Indicators Database, last updated July 1, 2020, https://datacatalog.worldbank.org/dataset/world-development-indicators. For real gross domestic product (GDP) growth rate (percentage change on previous year volume): European Commission, Eurostat database, https://ec.europa.eu/eurostat/data/database (accessed July 18, 2020).
[a] Data are for 2018.

Western Balkan decision makers.[91] For example, Chinese road construction projects resulted in government corruption in Macedonia's then VMRO-DPMNE–led government and significant debt in Montenegro, due to Chinese loans at high rates and the utilization of Chinese contractors, workers, and materials. Vučić's ruling SNS party played up investment by and loans from China in Serbia's infrastructure during its campaigning for parliamentary elections in May 2020.[92] However, a deal between the United Arab Emirates (UAE) and the Vučić government in Serbia for the lavish Belgrade Waterfront project, which resulted in illegal demolitions and construction, has provoked a sustained protest movement, Don't Let Belgrade D(r)own (see photo 18.2).

The COVID-19 pandemic has wreaked havoc on the economies of former Yugoslav countries. The economies of Croatia and Montenegro, which are reliant on tourism, have been particularly hard hit. Croatia, where tourist spending accounts for 20 percent of GDP, suffered a 43 percent drop in tourist arrivals in the first eight months of 2020 compared to the prior year, a decline that has significant spillover effects. In other service sectors across the region, small and medium enterprises especially felt the effects of lockdowns, while the manufacturing sectors in Bosnia-Herzegovina, North Macedonia, and Serbia suffered from the disruption of global supply chains.[93] Estimates of the economic impact of the pandemic made in September 2020, just before November's surge in COVID-19 cases, projected that the GDP of the former Yugoslav states would contract by 6.1 percent,[94] prior to rebounding somewhat in 2021.

Photo 18.2. The "Don't Let Belgrade D(r)own" movement protests the Serbian government's urban development of Belgrade's waterfront. (BalkansCat, Shutterstock)

Key Social Issues

The social consequences of long wars and difficult economic reforms that failed to lay the foundation for broad-based economic growth have been painful for many. High unemployment and underemployment, coupled with severe cutbacks in the social safety net, resulted in many citizens in Bosnia-Herzegovina, Serbia, Montenegro, and Kosovo living one day at a time. Up to one-fifth of the populations of these countries live on $5.50 a day.[95] An important indicator of economic hardship felt by young people, the share of youth "not in employment, education, or training" (NEET; as a percentage of youth aged fifteen to twenty-four) reveals intense hardship experienced by youth in Kosovo, Bosnia-Herzegovina, and North Macedonia (see table 18.2, last column). The wars and poverty have created a crisis of PTSD and other war and trauma–related mental health issues.

A dire social problem for most of the successor states (especially Bosnia-Herzegovina and Serbia, and somewhat less so in Slovenia) has been brain drain and the profound demographic loss due to out-migration to the West, much of it to the EU (see chapter 6). These demographic changes have significantly reduced previously multiethnic regions, especially in Bosnia-Herzegovina, Kosovo, and Croatia, which are now increasingly homogeneous.

As the demographic trends tilt downward with consistently low fertility rates, there is growing alarm about emigration, which exacerbates the already significant shortage of highly skilled labor across various sectors of the economy. In a 2019 poll, 19 percent of respondents in the region admitted to actively seeking opportunities to migrate,[96] with higher percentages among youth. The region's demographic trends are so staggering that recent analyses have highlighted a crisis of depopulation. For example, by 2050, Serbia is projected to have 23.8 percent and Croatia 22.4 percent fewer people than in 2020. Bosnia-Herzegovina has a total fertility rate of only 1.26, ranking among the lowest in the world.[97] It is these twin pressures—of high emigration and low fertility, coupled with negligible immigration to boost the numbers—that makes the demographic trends in the region appear so dire. Some countries, such as Croatia, have tried to deal with this problem by providing generous financial incentives to encourage couples to bear more children. So far these efforts have not made much of a difference.

Persistently high levels of deep poverty—especially in Bosnia-Herzegovina, Serbia, Montenegro, and Kosovo—have created a slew of new problems, such as political apathy and social disconnectedness, and can even be traced to emerging networks of far-right violent activism.[98] Many citizens across the region see migrants from the Middle East not as a solution to the population decline but as an existential security threat and a risk to their own economic prospects. All of this has given rise to significant Islamophobia,[99] which is often stoked by political leaders who exert influence over major media outlets.

In addition to negative and xenophobic attitudes against migrants by large—but by no means all[100]—swaths of the regional population, other issues regarding minority rights persist. For example, language rights of the Serbian minority in Croatia have been consistently violated, including removal of Serbian Cyrillic-alphabet street signs in the city of Vukovar, where Serbs comprise about 30 percent of the population.[101] In Montenegro, Albanians have been consistently discriminated against in hiring for public sector jobs.[102]

Rights of sexual minorities have also been slow to expand and in some states have even contracted. Croatia has the most advanced LGBTQ protections in the region, but even there, LGBTQ rights issues remain problematic. For example, immediately after Croatia joined the European Union in 2013, it passed a referendum banning same-sex marriage. The Life Partnership Act of 2014, however, provided civil union benefits to same-sex couples, but it did not include adoption rights. Other countries in the region lag much further behind. In Serbia, homophobic attitudes are widespread, and physical violence directed at LGBTQ people is common. Same-sex marriage is illegal, as is adoption by same-sex couples.[103] Even though the Serbian president appointed Ana Brnabić, the first openly gay person to serve in high office, as the country's prime minister in 2016, this has not translated into any improvement in LGBTQ legislation or protection. Brnabić has also been at the center of controversy as she announced the birth of her child with her partner—while at the same time supporting the continuing ban on surrogacy, in vitro fertilization treatments, and adoption by Serbian same-sex couples.[104]

Across the region, however, and mostly due to EU pressure, the countries of the region have improved their legislation regarding LGBTQ rights. The biggest accomplishments are decriminalization of same-sex relationships and prohibition of discrimination on the basis of sexual orientation. However, the enforcement of existing laws and standards has remained sporadic, with most people continuing to hide their sexual identities in fear of reprisal and abuse.[105] North Macedonia, for example, does not include sexual orientation, gender identity, or gender expression at all in its antidiscrimination law and is a regional laggard in this regard. Across the region, homophobic attitudes remain. According to a 2015 poll, 73 percent of the population in the region considers same-sex marriage "completely unacceptable."[106]

The issue of women's rights and equality protections also remains unresolved. Traditional and patriarchal views about the role of the woman in the family persist, and there is often inadequate attention paid to the access of women to maternal and reproductive health. This is especially true for the most marginalized women, such as the Roma.[107]

Another enduring social issue has been the reluctance to deal seriously with the legacies of war violence and the delayed and largely inadequate project of transitional justice. While all successor countries to various degrees engaged in a transitional justice mechanism—domestic war crimes trials, truth commissions, or cooperation with the International Criminal Tribunal for the Former Yugoslavia—there has been a lack of commitment to prosecute perpetrators of one's own ethnic group. It has also been clear to the public that governments reluctantly cooperated with the ICTY and only did so out of a direct trade regarding EU accession negotiations.[108] This is why most war crimes trials in Bosnia-Herzegovina, Croatia, Kosovo, and Serbia ended up being inadequate and focused on local prosecutions of ethnic "others"—Serbs in Croatian courts, Albanians in Serbian courts, and so forth. This is a largely disappointing outcome of a huge international investment in new courts, prisons, and training sessions for prosecutors and judges. Domestic courts were often politically controlled by the governments and were unwilling to go after their own military and police personnel. International courts—such as the ICTY but also hybrid international/domestic courts such as Bosnia-Herzegovina's War Crimes Chamber—struggled to establish political legitimacy, and domestic courts avoided investigating high-profile cases. The June 2020 indictment of Kosovo's president Hashim Thaçi by the Kosovo Specialist Chambers in The Hague thus came as a surprise and is an exception to the trend.

More broadly, transitional justice—a system of legal, political, and social mechanisms for dealing with legacies of past violence—has remained an unattained goal. The ICTY has struggled to establish legitimacy among both political elites and victims groups, as its practices of plea bargaining, relatively short sentences, and high-profile deaths in custody (including, most notoriously, of Milošević himself in 2006, and more recently of Slobodan Praljak in 2017), coupled with prosecutions of mostly low- or mid-level perpetrators, have been unpopular with the public.[109] All of this—in addition to the continuing disparaging of the court by political leaders, the media, and the education system—explains the very polarizing reaction to the ICTY's conviction in 2016 of wartime Bosnian Serb political leader Radovan Karadžić and Bosnian Serb military commander Ratko Mladić (in 2017) for genocide in Srebrenica and crimes against humanity.[110]

Emerging Challenges

Though countries in the region have come a long way since the 1990s, they continue to face many challenges. Perhaps the biggest outstanding issue is the stalled accession to the European Union—other than Slovenia and Croatia, none of the other successor states have been successful in fulfilling the many complex EU requirements. In some cases, such as that of North Macedonia, even compliance with the extremely invasive demands of some EU members (in this case, the Greek demand for the country's name change from Macedonia to North Macedonia) has not been enough to satisfy the EU. Further, whatever pressure the EU can exert on candidate states evaporates once the country becomes a member. A process of democratic backsliding has been evident in Croatia with the rise of far-right parties and social movements, attacks on academic freedom at universities, and unchecked corruption.

Serbia has made substantial progress toward fulfilling various EU requirements, but its accession has stalled over unresolved issues regarding Kosovo's independence, which Serbia refuses to acknowledge. Even more significant has been the alarming return to semiauthoritarianism under the rule of the SNS party and its leader, Aleksandar Vučić. Serbia has witnessed increased media control and repression, physical attacks on journalists, high levels of corruption and no-bid contracts, further marginalization of civil society, and profound voter apathy and lack of participation. Serbia's continuing embrace of Russia, Turkey, and China—three authoritarian regional powers—has further alienated it from some of its European friends and allies.

Bosnia-Herzegovina continues to be crippled by its unnecessarily complex governing structure and by the enduring paralyzing legacies of war and the Dayton Peace Agreement. Leaders have made little progress in meeting EU criteria for reform, despite popular interest in joining the EU. The Serb-controlled entity Republika Srpska acts in large part as an autonomous sovereign state, outside the purview of the larger state of Bosnia-Herzegovina. Its leaders, especially president Milorad Dodik, have on multiple occasions threatened to organize a referendum on RS independence, which continues to destabilize and signal to the RS population that Bosnia-Herzegovina is not their state and that they should pledge their loyalty elsewhere.

Montenegro, with its accession to NATO in 2017, for a while seemed the best positioned to join the EU. Thirty years of one-party-dominant rule has seriously hampered

Montenegro's European prospects. The ongoing dispute between the Montenegrin self-declared independent Orthodox Church and the Serbian Orthodox Church that used to control Montenegro has further soured Serbia-Montenegro relations.

Kosovo remains gripped in overlapping political crises. The instability of its government, the continuing presence of former armed combatants with questionable wartime actions in high ranks of government, the deep corruption and presence of organized crime, and the lack of a clear solution of the territorial dispute with Serbia make its European prospects seem remote. As a new generation of political leaders get their chance to shine, there is hope that some of the old ways of doing things, including recalcitrant political positions, can give way to more imaginative or pragmatic solutions. These approaches could improve the well-being of not just Kosovo but other countries in the region that also suffer from relying too much on the old political guard who benefit from the status quo. The promise of the new generation of leaders, of course, will depend on stemming the seemingly unstoppable brain drain.

More broadly, however, whatever problems Yugoslav successor states may have on their own, these are also, fundamentally, European problems. The European Union is dealing with its own internal crisis of legitimacy and a profound sense of enlargement fatigue. It is also going through a significant right-wing populist resurgence, most dramatically in Hungary and Poland, but also creeping into other countries, that has begun to slowly erode some of the fundamental democratic institutional checks and balances, such as the role of the parliament, judicial and media independence, and academic freedom. Some of the enlargement decisions the EU has been making are more reflective of domestic EU problems and challenges and speak less to the accomplishments of individual Yugoslav successor states. EU benchmarks for "success," however, have also been problematic. The EU has long favored economic and banking reforms, shrinking of the public sector, and the opening of trade, while often turning a blind eye to the more amorphous erosion of liberal norms. For example, EU progress reports on Serbia have consistently focused on economic issues and praised the government for reform while disregarding the mounting evidence of Serbia's autocratization, media control, and high corruption. Further, the unresolved Kosovo/Serbia issue has allowed Serbia's President Vučić to present himself as the only guarantor of peace and stability. This has allowed him to continue with his repressive policies, as the EU has prioritized the resolution of the Kosovo issue and regional stability over domestic democratization.

The sudden and profoundly disruptive experience of the COVID-19 pandemic will undoubtedly have long-term consequences. As in many other countries, the disruption caused by the pandemic and its effects on already strained public health systems will be felt most acutely among vulnerable populations—the poor, the elderly, the marginalized, and the Roma. As discussed, the near shutdown of the tourist season in Croatia and Montenegro will be economically devastating. It is also not clear how many of the other sectors—such as hospitality services—will be fully able to go back to pre-pandemic levels. Politically, the COVID-19 pandemic is likely to lead to many backsliding trends: further autocratization and curbing of media freedom, weakening of civil society, further political polarization, and as yet unknown degrees of demographic and social change. But here—as with many other issues—the post-Yugoslav region is hardly alone. The consequences are truly global and contingent on too many factors to be knowable.

Glossary of Political Parties in Former Yugoslavia

- ADK: Alliance for the Future of Kosovo
- DEMOS: Democratic Opposition of Slovenia
- DPMS: Homeland Movement Party
- DPS: Democratic Party of Socialists
- DS: Democratic Party
- DUI: Democratic Union for Integration
- HDZ: Croatian Democratic Union
- LDK: Democratic League of Kosovo
- PDK: Democratic Party of Kosovo
- SCP: Serbian Communist Party
- SDA: (Bosniac) Party of Democratic Action
- SDP: Slovenian Democratic Party
- SDP: Social Democratic Party
- SDS: Serb Democratic Party
- SDSS: Independent Democratic Serb Party
- SMC: Miro Cerer Party
- SNS: Serbian Progressive Party
- SNSD: Independent Social Democrats
- SNSD: Party of Independent Social Democrats
- SPS: Socialist Party of Serbia
- VMRO-DPMNE: Internal Macedonian Revolutionary Organization–Democratic Party for Macedonian National Unity

Study Questions

1. What external and internal factors contributed to the violent disintegration of Yugoslavia?
2. What external and internal factors explain differences in the timing and pace of the democratization of the governments of the Yugoslav successor states?
3. What key social, economic, and political issues face the governments of the seven Yugoslav successor states?
4. How are relationships between political elites and ordinary citizens in the former Yugoslav states similar, and how do they differ in the postsocialist period?
5. How effectively has international intervention in the countries of the former Yugoslavia promoted inclusive and stable democratization?

Suggested Readings

Baker, Catherine. *The Yugoslav Wars of the 1990s*. New York: Macmillan, 2015.

Bojicic-Dzelilovic, Vesna, James Ker-Lindsay, and Denisa Kostovicova, eds. *Civil Society and Transitions in the Western Balkans*. New Perspectives on South-East Europe. Basingstoke: Palgrave Macmillan, 2013.

Cohen, Lenard, and John Lampe. *Embracing Democracy in the Western Balkans*. Washington, DC: Woodrow Wilson Center Press, 2011.

Gagnon, V. P. *The Myth of Ethnic War: Serbia and Croatia in the 1990s*. Ithaca, NY: Cornell University Press, 2004.

Judah, Tim. *Kosovo: War and Revenge*. New Haven, CT: Yale University Press, 2000.

Kapedžić, Damir, ed. Special issue on illiberal politics in Southeastern Europe, *Southeast European and Black Sea Studies* 20, no. 1 (2020).

Lampe, John. *Yugoslavia as History: Twice There Was a Country*. 2nd ed. Cambridge: Cambridge University Press, 2000.

Ramet, Sabrina Petra. *Balkan Babel: The Disintegration of Yugoslavia from the Death of Tito to the Fall of Milošević*. 4th ed. Boulder, CO: Westview, 2002.

Subotić, Jelena. *Hijacked Justice: Dealing with the Past in the Balkans*. Ithaca, NY: Cornell University Press, 2009.

Woodward, Susan. *Balkan Tragedy*. Washington, DC: Brookings Institution, 1996.

Websites

Balkan Investigative Reporting Network (BIRN): http://birn.eu.com

International Crisis Group, "Balkans": https://www.crisisgroup.org/europe-central-asia/balkans

Organization for Security and Co-operation in Europe, https://www.osce.org

Bosnia-Herzegovina

Government: of Republika Srpska: http://www.vladars.net/eng/Pages/default.aspx; Federation of Bosnia-Herzegovina: http://www.fbihvlada.gov.ba

Office of the High Representative: http://www.ohr.int

Presidency: http://www.predsjednistvobih.ba/gov/Archive.aspx?pageIndex=1&langTag=en-US

Croatia

Government: https://vlada.gov.hr

Parliament: http://www.sabor.hr/English

Kosovo

EULEX Kosovo: https://www.eulex-kosovo.eu

Government: https://www.rks-gov.net/EN/f43/republic-of-kosovo/government

Kosovo Force (KFOR): https://jfcnaples.nato.int/kfor

Parliament: http://www.kuvendikosoves.org/eng/home

North Macedonia

Government: https://vlada.mk/?ln=en-gb

Parliament: https://www.sobranie.mk/home-en.nspx

Montenegro

Government: http://www.gov.me/en/homepage
Parliament: http://www.skupstina.me/index.php/en

Serbia

Government: https://www.srbija.gov.rs/sastav/en/10/members-of-government.php#
Parliament: http://www.parlament.gov.rs/national-assembly.467.html

Slovenia

Government: https://www.gov.si/en
Parliament: https://www.dz-rs.si/wps/portal/en/Home

Notes

1. The authors contributed equally to this chapter and are listed in alphabetical order. Paula Pickering would like to thank Mark Baskin for his collaboration on earlier versions of this chapter, which have contributed to the analysis presented in the current chapter. Jelena Subotić would like to thank Saad Khan for his research assistance.

2. Noel Malcolm, *Kosovo: A Short History* (New York: New York University Press, 1998).

3. Latinka Perović, "Separatizam kao reakcija na diktaturu od 6. januara 1929. godine," *YU Historija*, 2017, http://www.yuhistorija.com/serbian/jug_prva_txt01c3.html.

4. Jelena Subotić, *Yellow Star, Red Star: Holocaust Remembrance after Communism* (Ithaca, NY: Cornell University Press, 2019).

5. Bogdan Denitch, "Violence and Social Change in the Yugoslav Revolution," *Comparative Politics* 8, no. 3 (April 1976): 465–78.

6. Jelena Batinić, *Women and Yugoslav Partisans: A History of World War II Resistance* (New York: Cambridge University Press, 2015).

7. John R. Lampe, *Yugoslavia as History: Twice There Was a Country* (Cambridge: Cambridge University Press, 1996).

8. Patrick Hyder Patterson, *Bought & Sold: Living and Losing the Good life in Socialist Yugoslavia* (Ithaca, NY: Cornell University Press, 2011); Hannes Grandits and Karin Taylor, *Yugoslavia's Sunny Side: A History of Tourism in Socialism (1950s–1980s)* (Budapest: Central European University Press, 2010); Radina Vučetić, *Coca-Cola Socialism: Americanization of Yugoslav Culture in the Sixties* (Budapest: Central European University Press, 2017).

9. Jelena Subotic, "Building Democracy in Serbia: One Step Forward, Three Steps Back," in *Building Democracy in the Yugoslav Successor States: Accomplishments, Setbacks, Challenges since 1990*, ed. Sabrina P. Ramet, Christine Hassenstab, and Ola Listhaug (New York: Cambridge University Press, 2017).

10. Denisa Kostovicova, *Kosovo: The Politics of Identity and Space* (London: Routledge, 2005).

11. Sabrina P. Ramet, *The Three Yugoslavias: State-Building and Legitimation, 1918–2005* (Bloomington: Indiana University Press, 2006).

12. Mirsad Tokača, *Bosanske knjige mrtvih: Ljudski gubici u Bosni i Hercegovini 1991–1995* (Sarajevo: Istraživačko Dokumentacioni Centar, 2012).

13. Under a UN-negotiated settlement with Greece, the state agreed in June 2018 to change its name from Republic of Macedonia to Republic of North Macedonia. See Matthew Nimetz, "The Macedonian 'Name' Dispute: The Macedonian Question—Resolved?" *Nationalities Papers*, 48, no. 2 (2020): 205–14. We use "Macedonia" for events in the country until 2018 and "North Macedonia" for events afterward.

14. Freedom House, *Nations in Transit 2020: Dropping the Democratic Façade*, https://freedomhouse.org/report/nations-transit.

15. Mary Kaldor, *New and Old Wars: Organized Violence in a Global Era* (Palo Alto, CA: Stanford University Press, 1999).

16. Dario Čepo, "Structural Weaknesses and the Role of the Dominant Political Party: Democratic Backsliding in Croatia since EU Accession," *Southeast European and Black Sea Studies* 20, no. 1 (2020): 141–59.

17. Damir Kapidžić, "The Rise of Illiberal Politics in Southeastern Europe," *Southeast European and Black Sea Studies* 20, no. 1 (2020): 1–17.

18. Mirjana Kasapovic, "Voting Rights, Electoral Systems, and Political Representation of Diaspora in Croatia," *East European Politics and Societies and Cultures* 26, no. 4 (2012): 777–91.

19. International Institute for Democracy and Electoral Assistance, "Gender Quotas Database," http://www.idea.int/data-tools/data/gender-quotas/country-overview.

20. Damir Kapidžić, "Subnational Competitive Authoritarianism and Powersharing in Bosnia and Herzegovina," *Southeast European and Black Sea Studies* 20, no. 1 (2020): 81–101.

21. Adem Beha and Arben Hajrullahu, "Soft Competitive Authoritarianism and Negative Stability in Kosovo: Statebuilding from UNMIK to EULEX and Beyond," *Southeast European and Black Sea Studies*, no. 1 (2020): 114.

22. "The Implementation of Kosovo-Serbia Political Dialogue," Policy Paper No. 4/13, KIPRED, July 2013, http://www.kipred.org/repository/docs/THE_IMPLEMENTATION_OF_AGREEMENTS_OF_KOSOVO%E2%80%90SERBIA_POLITICAL_DIALOGUE_373680.pdf.

23. On Ohrid, see Florian Bieber, "Assessing the Ohrid Framework Agreement," in *One Decade after the Ohrid Framework Agreement: Lessons (to Be) Learned from the Macedonian Experience*, ed. Marija Risteska and Zhidas Daskalovski (Skopje: Friedrich Ebert Stiftung and Centre for Research and Policy Making in Macedonia, 2011), 22.

24. Elizabeth Cousens, "Missed Opportunities to Overcompensation: Implementing the Dayton Agreement on Bosnia," in *Ending Civil Wars: The Implementation of Peace Agreements*, ed. Stephen Stedman, Donald Rothchild, and Elizabeth M. Cousens, 531–66 (Boulder, CO: Lynne Rienner, 2002).

25. See "High Representative's Decisions by Topic," Office of the High Representative, http://www.ohr.int/decisions/archive.asp.

26. Elton Skendaj, *Creating Kosovo: International Oversight and the Making of Ethical Institutions* (Washington, DC: Woodrow Wilson Center Press; Ithaca, NY: Cornell University Press, 2014).

27. Valerie Bunce, "The Political Economy of Postsocialism," *Slavic Review* 58 (Winter 1999): 756–93; see also Vernon Bogdanov, "Founding Elections and Regime Change," *Electoral Studies* 1 (1990): 288–94.

28. Grigore Pop-Eleches, "Throwing out the Bums: Protest Voting and Unorthodox Parties after Communism," *World Politics* 62, no. 2 (2010): 221–60.

29. Center for Research and Policy Making, *Analysis of Internal Party Democracy in Macedonia* (Skopje: Konrad-Adenauer-Stiftung, 2013), http://www.crpm.org.mk; and Georgi Karasimeonov,

ed., *Organization Structures and Internal Party Democracy in South Eastern Europe* (Sofia: Goetex Press, 2005).

30. Sabrina Petra Ramet, "Democratization in Slovenia—the Second Stage," in *Politics, Power, and the Struggle for Democracy in South-East Europe*, ed. Karen Dawisha and Bruce Parrott, 189–217 (Cambridge: Cambridge University Press, 1997).

31. Alenka Krašovec and Lars Johannsen, "Recent Developments in Democracy in Slovenia," *Problems of Post-Communism* 63, nos. 5–6 (2016): 313–22, doi:10.1080/10758216.2016.1169932.

32. Ivan Šiber, "The Impact of Nationalism, Values, and Ideological Orientations on Multi-Party Elections in Croatia," in *The Tragedy of Yugoslavia: The Failure of Democratic Transformation*, ed. Jim Seroka and Vukašin Pavlović, 141–71 (Armonk, NY: M. E. Sharpe, 1992); Mirjana Kasapovic, "Demokratska konsolidacija i izborna politika u Hrvatskoj 1990–2000," in *Hrvatska politika 1990–2000*, ed. Mirjana Kasapovic, 15–40 (Zagreb: Fakultet političkih znanosti, 2001); and Paula M. Pickering and Mark Baskin, "What Is to Be Done: Succession from the League of Communists of Croatia," *Communist and Post-Communist Studies* 41 (2008): 521–40.

33. Eric Gordy, *The Culture of Power in Serbia* (University Park: Pennsylvania State University Press, 1999).

34. V. P. Gagnon, *The Myth of Ethnic War: Serbia and Croatia in the 1990s* (Ithaca, NY: Cornell University Press, 2004), 92.

35. Gagnon, *The Myth of Ethnic War*; Gordy, *The Culture of Power*.

36. Andy Konitzer, "Conditionality, Public Attitudes and Euro-Skeptic Party Change in the Western Balkans," *Europe-Asia Studies* 63, no. 10 (2011): 1853–88.

37. Čepo, "Structural Weaknesses," 144.

38. "Opinion on the Constitutional Situation in Bosnia and Herzegovina and the Powers of the High Representative," European Commission for Democracy through Law, March 2005, http://www.venice.coe.int/webforms/documents/?pdf=CDL(2005)021-e.

39. Donald L. Horowitz, *Ethnic Groups in Conflict* (Berkeley: University of California Press, 2000).

40. Beha and Hajrullahu, "Soft Competitive Authoritarianism," 113.

41. This includes the federation prime minister from SDA, who was arrested in May 2020 over a scandal involving the purchase of respirators during the pandemic; see "Uhapšen Fadil Novalić," *Oslobođenje Portal*, May 28, 2020. On SNSD, see Kapidžić, "Subnational Competitive Authoritarianism."

42. Daria Sito-Sucic, "Bosnian Experts Present U.S.-Backed Plan for Reform," Reuters, May 15, 2013.

43. See Srecko Latal, "Sabre-Rattling over Serb 'Statehood Day' Shakes Bosnia," *Balkan Insight*, January 10, 2017, http://www.balkaninsight.com/en/article/new-warmongering-shakes-bosnia-over-serb-statehood-day—01-10-2017#sthash.lileIOCi.dpuf.

44. Duncan Perry, "The Republic of Macedonia: Finding Its Way," in *Politics, Power, and the Struggle for Democracy in South-East Europe*, ed. Karen Dawisha and Bruce Parrott (Cambridge: Cambridge University Press, 1997), 235.

45. Meri Jordanovska and Sinisa Jakov Marusic, "Pro-Govt Media Inflame Nationalist Hysteria in Macedonia," *Balkan Insight*, Skopje, March 15, 2017, http://www.balkaninsight.com/en/article/macedonia-s-propaganda-war-spreads-nationalist-hysteria-03-15-2017#sthash.oSi7aIcj.dpuf.

46. Sinisa Jakov Marusic, "Zaev Wins Mandate to Form Macedonia's Next Govt," *Balkan Insight*, Skopje, May 17, 2017, http://www.balkaninsight.com/en/article/zaev-recieves-mandate-to-form-new-macedonian-govt—05-17-2017#sthash.z5tj16UR.dpuf.

47. "Bulgaria Blocks Start of North Macedonia's EU Accession Talks," Radio Free Europe/Radio Liberty Bulgaria Service, November 17, 2020.

48. Sasha Dragojlo, "'One-Party' Serbia Forces Opposition to Review Its Options," *BIRN*, June 22, 2020.

49. Marko Kmezić and Florian Bieber, eds., "The Crisis of Democracy in the Western Balkans: An Anatomy of Stabilitocracy and the Limits of EU Democracy Promotion," Balkans in Europe Policy Advisory Group, March 2017, https://biepag.eu/wp-content/uploads/2017/05/final.pdf.

50. Olivera Komar, "The Elephant in the Room: Illiberal Politics in Montenegro," *Southeast European and Black Sea Studies* 20, no. 1 (2020): 61–80.

51. Beha and Hajrullahu, "Soft Competitive Authoritarianism," 108–9.

52. Christopher M. Jackson, "The EU and Rule of Law Development in Kosovo: EULEX, Domestic Spoilers, and a Two-Level Commitment Problem," *Journal of European Integration* 42, no. 7 (2020): 955–73.

53. Andy Heil, "Key Takeaways from Kosovo's Watershed Vote," Radio Free Europe/Radio Liberty Balkan Service, October 7, 2019.

54. Timothy Haughton and Kevin Deegan-Krause, *The New Party Challenge: Changing Cycles of Party Birth and Death in Central Europe and Beyond* (Oxford: Oxford University Press, 2020).

55. Data from European Bank for Reconstruction and Development, "Life in Transition Survey II: After the Crisis," 2010, data file, http://www.ebrd.com/what-we-do/economic-research-and-data/data/lits.html.

56. UNDP, *Early Warning System in Bosnia-Herzegovina*, 180.

57. European Social Survey Round 9 Data, 2018, data file edition 2.0, NSD—Norwegian Centre for Research Data, Norway—Data Archive and distributor of ESS data for ESS ERIC, https://doi.org/10.21338/NSD-ESS9-2018.

58. Kelsey Jo Starr, "Tepid Support for Democracy among Both Young and Old in Central and Eastern Europe," Pew Research, June 2017, https://www.pewresearch.org/fact-tank/2017/06/08/tepid-support-for-democracy-among-both-young-and-old-in-central-and-eastern-europe.

59. European Social Survey Round 9 Data.

60. IDEA, "Survey Results," http://archive.idea.int/balkans/survey_detailed.cfm.

61. IDEA, "Survey Results."

62. Marc Hooghe and Ellen Quintelier, "Political Participation in European Countries: The Effect of Authoritarian Rule, Corruption, Lack of Good Governance and Economic Downturn," *Comparative European Politics* 12, no. 2 (2014): 209–32.

63. Robert D. Putnam, ed., *Democracies in Flux: The Evolution of Social Capital in Contemporary Society* (New York: Oxford University Press, 2002).

64. Lenard J. Cohen, "Prelates and Politicians in Bosnia: The Role of Religion in Nationalist Mobilization," *Nationalities Papers* 25, no. 3 (1997): 481–99.

65. Anthony Oberschall, "The Manipulation of Ethnicity: From Ethnic Cooperation to Violence and War in Yugoslavia," *Ethnic and Racial Studies* 23, no. 6 (2000): 994–95.

66. Lenard J. Cohen, "Embattled Democracy: Post-Communist Croatia in Transition," in *Politics, Power, and the Struggle for Democracy in South-East Europe*, ed. Karen Dawisha and Bruce Parrott (Cambridge: Cambridge University Press, 1997), 112.

67. Cynthia Cockburn, *The Space between Us: Negotiating Gender and National Identities in Conflict* (London: Zed Books, 1998).

68. Patrizia Poggi et al., *Bosnia and Herzegovina: Local Level Institutions and Social Capital Study 1* (Washington, DC: World Bank, 2002), 83.

69. On NGOs, see Paul Stubbs, *Displaced Promises: Forced Migration, Refuge and Return in Croatia and Bosnia-Herzegovina* (Uppsala: Life and Peace Institute, 1999); on good neighborly relations, see Tone Bringa, *Being Muslim the Bosnian Way* (Princeton, NJ: Princeton University Press,

1995); on work, see Paula M. Pickering, "Generating Social Capital for Bridging Ethnic Divisions in the Balkans," *Ethnic and Racial Studies* 29, no. 1 (2006): 79–103; David Chandler, *Faking Democracy after Dayton* (London: Pluto Press, 2000); and Sevima Sali-Terzic, "Civil Society," in *Policies of International Support to South-Eastern European Countries: Lessons (Not) Learnt from Bosnia and Herzegovina*, ed. Žarko Papić, 138–59 (Sarajevo: Open Society Institute, 2001).

70. Ivana Howard, "Unfinished Business: Civil Society," in *Unfinished Business: The Western Balkans and the International Community*, ed. Vedran Džihić and Daniel Hamilton (Washington, DC: Center for Transatlantic Relations, 2012), 38–39.

71. See, for example, the Civil Society Organization, Open Parliament in Serbia, http://www .otvoreniparlament.rs.

72. For the example of Kosovo, see Skendaj, *Creating Kosovo*, chap. 5.

73. Howard, "Unfinished Business," 40.

74. IPSOS Bosnia Herzegovina, Dorota Pietrzyk-Reeves, Patrice McMahon, Paula M. Pickering, and Lisa Sundstrom, "Civic Activism Thirty Years After," datafile.

75. Aleksandar Djordjevic, "Party Ties Help NGOs Win Key Serbian Ministerial Deals," *Balkan Insight*, September 6, 2013, accessed September 14, 2013, http://www.balkaninsight.com/ en/article/party-ties-help-ngos-win-key-ministerial-deals.

76. Čepo, "Structural Weakness," 150.

77. Sladjana Danković and Paula M. Pickering, "Public Scepticism of Civil Society Organisations: Norms, Citizen Priorities, and Local Groups in Post-Socialist Serbia," *East European Politics* 33, no. 2 (2017): 210–32.

78. Elvira M. Jukić, "Plenum in Bosnian Capital Finalises Demands," *Balkan Insight*, February 29, 2014; "Završeni Protesti u bh gradovim," Al Jazeera Balkans, February 10, 2014, http://balkans.aljazeera.net/vijesti/zavrseni-protesti-u-bh-gradovima.

79. Tijana Morača, "Between Defiance and Compliance: A New Civil Society in the Post-Yugoslav Space?" *Osservatorio balcani e caucaso*, occasional paper 2, August 2016, accessed December 20, 2016, www.balcanicaucaso.org.

80. Gazela Pudar Draško, Irena Fiket, and Jelena Vasiljević, "Big Dreams and Small Steps: Comparative Perspectives on Social Movements' Struggle for Democracy in Serbia and North Macedonia," *Southeast European and Black Sea Studies* 20, no. 1 (2020): 199–219.

81. William Bartlett, *Europe's Troubled Region: Economic Development, Institutional Reform and Social Welfare in the Western Balkans* (London: Routledge, 2007).

82. Bartlett, *Europe's Troubled Region*, 66.

83. Bozidar Cerovic, ed., *Privatisation in Serbia: Evidence and Analysis* (Belgrade: Faculty of Economics, 2005), 19–48.

84. Bartlett, *Europe's Troubled Region*, 80.

85. Bartlett, *Europe's Troubled Region*, 74.

86. European Bank for Reconstruction and Development, "The EBRD and Transition," 2016, https://www.ebrd.com/our-values/transition.html.

87. European Bank for Reconstruction and Development, *Transition Report 2019–20*, November 2019.

88. Kapidžić, "Subnational Competitive Authoritarianism."

89. Peter Sanfey, "South Eastern Europe: Lessons from the Global Economic Crisis" (Working Paper No. 113, European Bank for Reconstruction and Development, February 2010), http://www.ebrd.com/downloads/research/economics/workingpapers/wp0113.pdf.

90. *Nations in Transit 2020*, Freedom House, https://freedomhouse.org/sites/default/files/ 2020-04/05062020_FH_NIT2020_vfinal.pdf. The corruption score includes a measure of government implementation of anticorruption measures, laws, and public perceptions.

91. Kurt Bassuener, "Pushing an Open Door: Foreign Authoritarian Influence in the Western Balkans" (working paper, National Endowment for Democracy, May 2019).

92. Ljudmila Cvetkovic, Maja Zivanovic, and Andy Heil, "Red Flag: Ahead of Serbian Vote, Vucic and Allies Lean on China Ties," Radio Free Europe/Radio Liberty, June 16, 2020, https://www.rferl.org/a/serbian-vote-vucic-china-ties/30674364.html.

93. "Regional Economic Prospects in the EBRD Regions: COVID-19—Early Estimates of the Damage, Uncertain Prospects," European Bank for Reconstruction and Development, September 2020, 8, 19, https://www.ebrd.com/what-we-do/economic-research-and-data/rep .html.

94. "Regional Economic Prospects in the EBRD Regions," 3.

95. "Poverty and Inequality," World Bank Development Indicators, accessed July 22, 2020, https://datatopics.worldbank.org/world-development-indicators/themes/poverty-and-inequality .html.

96. *Balkan Barometer 2019: Public Opinion Analytical Report* (Sarajevo: Regional Cooperation Council, 2020).

97. Tim Judah, "Bye-bye Balkans: A Region in Critical Demographic Decline," *Balkan Insight*, October 14, 2019, https://balkaninsight.com/2019/10/14/bye-bye-balkans-a-region-in-critical-demographic-decline.

98. Sven Milekic, Marija Ristic, Maja Zivanovic, and Denis Dzidic, "Far-Right Balkan Groups Flourish on the Net," *Balkan Insight*, May 5, 2017, https://balkaninsight.com/2017/05/0 5/far-right-balkan-groups-flourish-on-the-net-05-03-2017.

99. *Balkan Barometer 2019*.

100. Some local NGOs have offered sustained assistance and welcome to refugees. See, for example, Matthew Griffin and Haley Raphael, "Celebrants Mark World Refugee Day beside Serbian Lake," *Balkan Insight*, June 20, 2019, https://balkaninsight.com/2019/06/20/celebrants -mark-world-refugee-day-beside-serbian-lake.

101. Milivoje Pantovic, "Dispute over Cyrillic Raises Tensions between Croatia, Serbia," *Balkan Insight*, August 15, 2016, https://balkaninsight.com/2016/08/15/tensions-continue-to-ra ise-between-serbia-and-croatia-08-15-2016.

102. Samir Kajosevic, "Montenegro Albanian Official Says Discrimination Remains Rife," *Balkan Insight*, September 24, 2019, https://balkaninsight.com/2019/09/24/montenegro-albanian -official-says-discrimination-remains-rife.

103. "Serbia: LGBTI Equal Rights Association for Western Balkans and Turkey," lgbti-era.org, https://www.lgbti-era.org/content/serbia.

104. Saša Dragojlo, "Plucked from Obscurity, Serbian PM Brnabic Proves Loyalty to President," *Balkan Insight*, May 21, 2020, https://balkaninsight.com/2020/05/21/plucked-from-obscurity-serbian-pm-proves-loyalty-to-president.

105. European Parliament Policy Department for Citizens' Rights and Constitutional Affairs, *Women's Rights in Western Balkans* (Brussels: European Parliament, 2019).

106. NDI, "LGBTI Public Opinion Poll Western Balkans," 2015, http://www.lgbti-era.org/ sites/default/files/pdfdocs/LGBT%20Poll%202015%20Western%20Balkans%20NDI%20.pdf.

107. NDI, "LGBTI Public Opinion Poll Western Balkans."

108. Jelena Subotić, *Hijacked Justice: Dealing with the Past in the Balkans* (Ithaca, NY: Cornell University Press, 2009).

109. Jelena Subotić, "Legitimacy, Scope, and Conflicting Claims on the ICTY: In the Aftermath of Gotovina, Haradinaj and Perišić," *Journal of Human Rights* 13 (2014): 170–85.

110. Eric Gordy, "Was the Karadzic Verdict a Just Reckoning?," *Balkan Insight*, March 28, 2016, http://www.balkaninsight.com/en/article/q-and-a-on-the-karadzic-verdict-03-27-2016#st hash.v92ZuDNL.dpuf.

Map 19.0.   Ukraine

CHAPTER 19

Ukraine

Paul D'Anieri

Ukraine became independent in 1991 when the Soviet Union collapsed. As one of the larger states in the region, with a territory the size of France and a population of forty-five million, Ukraine is potentially an important player in Central and East European politics. Moreover, its role on the front line of the conflict between the West and Russia has given it an expanded geopolitical importance. These traits make Ukraine one of the most interesting and puzzling countries in the region. While it is one of the few post-Soviet states that have decisively rejected authoritarianism, Ukraine's democracy remains flawed and fragile. Governments have pursued economic reform halfheartedly, and so Ukraine remains relatively poor and dependent on external financial support. While the country's regional diversity makes it difficult for an authoritarian to consolidate power, it also undermines national unity, and while most Ukrainians seek closer relations with the European Union (EU), many would like to restore ties with Russia as well.

Twice, in 2004 and 2014, protests in the streets of Kyiv[1] foiled growing authoritarianism. While both episodes inspired optimism about people's ability to resist authoritarianism, both had unintended consequences. After the first, reform proved elusive, and after the second, Russia annexed the Ukrainian territory of Crimea and occupied a significant swath of eastern Ukraine. The conflict in eastern Ukraine had taken over thirteen thousand lives by 2020 and displaced over a million people. This episode showed how difficult democratization can be in a region that Russia sees as its "sphere of interest."

Political History

For all of modern history until 1991, the lands that now comprise Ukraine were ruled over by neighbors, including the Russian, Austro-Hungarian, and Ottoman Empires and Poland. *Ukraine* means "on the border," and its status as a frontier territory complicates its history in three respects.[2] First, different parts of today's Ukraine have different histories. Some regions were under Russian rule for centuries, others only from World War II to 1991. Second, the borders between the imperial powers in the region shifted repeatedly, blurring historical claims and complicating shared histories. Third, the history of

Ukraine is contested, as Russia claims much of Ukraine's history as its own. Battles over historical memory are both cause and effect of the conflict between Ukraine and Russia.

Ukraine in the Age of Empires

Russia and Ukraine both trace their origin to events in Kyiv in the latter part of the first millennium CE. The key date in this shared origin story is 988, when Prince Volodymyr (*Vladimir* in Russian) the Great had the population of Kyiv baptized en masse. At this time, Moscow was not yet a city, and Kyivan-Rus, as it was known, was the major power in a vast, sparsely populated region, connected much more to Byzantium (centered in Constantinople, present-day Istanbul) than to Western Europe. The adoption of Orthodox Christianity was an important turning point in the subsequent life of the region because it created a commonality across the region and distinguished it religiously from the Catholic (and later Protestant) lands to the west and Muslim areas to the south.

Mongol invaders from Central Asia swept westward, sacking Kyiv in 1240 and introducing a tribute system of rule in which localities were left largely on their own as long as they paid levies to the khan. Moscow rose to prominence under Mongol rule, becoming the center of an expanding empire after Mongol rule was defeated in the fifteenth century. Kyiv did not regain its former prominence, largely due to infighting, and spent the medieval period ruled by Lithuania and Poland. While this history may seem so long ago as to be irrelevant, it is the source of immense controversy today. In 2014, when Russia seized Crimea from Ukraine, Putin cited the events of 988 as showing that the territory had really been Russian all along. Similarly, Russia's claim to being the global leader of Orthodox Christianity stems from the assertion that this role passed from Constantinople to Kyiv and from Kyiv on to Moscow. While these claims rest in the realm of mythology as much as history, they shape attitudes and behavior today. The standard Ukrainian view, meanwhile, asserts a different version in which the modern Russian state emerged separately from Kyiv and has no claim to its legacy.[3]

Ukraine's history over the following centuries is largely one of the ebbing and flowing of the boundaries of four empires across its territory, punctuated by unsuccessful attempts to reestablish a Ukrainian state. The Polish-Lithuanian Commonwealth controlled much of the western part of Ukraine, losing territory through various wars to the Russian and Austrian Empires. Crimea and the north coast of the Black Sea, where the Ukrainian city of Odessa now sits, were controlled by the Crimean Tatar Khanate, under the protection of the Ottoman Empire. Russia advanced incrementally at the expense of the others. By the end of the reign of Catherine the Great (1762–1796), the Russian Empire controlled roughly two-thirds of present-day Ukraine, including Crimea. The remaining third, which today constitutes western Ukraine, was controlled by the Austro-Hungarian Empire. In contrast to Russian autocracy, which included the institution of serfdom and a ban on the Ukrainian language, these western regions were connected culturally to Vienna and experienced a less draconian form of monarchy. Today, these varied imperial legacies play out in Ukraine's regional differences, in debates about historical memory, and in claims about Ukraine's status as part of Europe or as part of a Russian-led region.

Ukraine under the Soviet Union

The twentieth century was one of repeated mass trauma in Ukraine. The eastern front in World War I was largely a contest over Ukraine. After the Bolshevik revolution, efforts to build an independent Ukrainian state splintered, and the Soviet army defeated the various pro-independence forces. The part of Ukraine that had been part of the Austro-Hungarian Empire before World War I became part of interwar Poland. These wars led to widespread famine that killed millions.

In the early 1930s, the Soviet government began a plan of rapid industrialization, which included the collectivization of agriculture—the merger of small independent farms into gigantic state-run farms. The goal was not only to modernize agriculture but also to eliminate small farmers, known as "kulaks," who were seen as resistant to Soviet power, and to stamp out Ukrainian nationalism.[4] The Soviet leadership sent activists into the Ukrainian countryside to seize grain from resistant farmers. The result was widespread famine. The best estimates are that between four and five million residents of Soviet Ukraine starved to death. Ukrainians today generally refer to this cataclysm as the Holodomor, or "famine genocide."

In 1939, after the Soviet-Nazi treaty, the Soviet Union invaded eastern Poland, occupying what is today western Ukraine. This marked the first time that most of the lands that today constitute Ukraine were controlled by one state. The Soviets embarked on a campaign of mass repression, wiping out both Poles and Ukrainians who might oppose them. This was one reason why, when Germany invaded in 1941, some Ukrainians saw the Germans as liberators. A group known as the Ukrainian Insurgent Army fought against the Soviets. They were not only anti-Soviet but in some cases anti-Jewish and anti-Polish, and they sometimes joined forces with Germany. Their legacy remains highly controversial today, and the connection between Ukrainian nationalism and collaboration with the Nazis creates a problem for Ukrainian memory politics.[5] Two million Ukrainians fought against the Nazis in the Red Army, and Ukraine's civilian population, along with that of Belarus, bore the brunt of the German invasion. Ukraine's large and vibrant Jewish community of over two million people was wiped out during the Holocaust, in some cases with local assistance.

Communism had strong support in the industrial heartland of eastern Ukraine, the area of coal mines and steel mills today known as the Donetsk Basin or "Donbas." Indeed, many important Soviet leaders hailed from what is today Ukraine, including Leon Trotsky, Nikita Khrushchev (ruled 1953–1964), and Leonid Brezhnev (ruled 1964–1982). The "Dnipropetrovsk Clan," based in the industrial city now known as Dnipro, was regarded as one of the most powerful regional factions in the Soviet Union. Ukraine was important demographically as well, being second to Russia in population and in economic output. In other words, Ukraine was at the heart of the Soviet Union.

At the same time, Ukrainian nationalism persisted despite Stalin's repression. A "thaw" under Nikita Khrushchev led to increased expression of Ukrainian culture in the 1960s, but in the 1970s a new crackdown imprisoned many Ukrainian nationalists as well as activists in the Ukrainian Helsinki Union, a human rights group, and adherents of the banned Greek Catholic Church. When Mikhail Gorbachev (ruled 1985–1991) eased limits on political expression, hoping to weaken bureaucratic resistance to reform,

Photo 19.1.   Famine victims in Kharkiv, Ukraine, in 1933 during the Holodomor. (Alexander Wienerberger, Wikimedia Commons)

those who had been repressed took advantage to speak out. In addition to speaking again of events such as the Holodomor, Ukrainians and others made new demands for greater respect for human rights and increased local economic control.

The 1986 disaster at the Chernobyl Atomic Energy Station, just north of Kyiv, shattered the passivity on which the Soviets had come to rely.[6] The government's blatant lying about the accident, and particularly the decision to hold the Kyiv May Day parade barely a week after the accident, sending thousands of children out to be exposed to radiation, badly undermined the legitimacy of the Soviet regime. While the causes of the collapse of the Soviet Union are many and complex, the impact of Chernobyl on Ukrainian opinion played an important role by broadening the appeal of demands for greater autonomy from Moscow.

Ukraine's push for more autonomy was at the heart of the process that spurred the breakup of the Soviet Union in 1991. In order to accommodate demands from Ukraine and the Baltic states, Gorbachev proposed a new "Union Treaty." Many republics signed on, but in Ukraine the "national communists" allied with the "national democrats" to push for further autonomy.[7] Conservatives, in favor of either reasserting Soviet rule or asserting Russian nationalism, opposed the new Union Treaty, believing that it gave too much control to the republics at the expense of the center. Based on historical memory as well as economics, many Soviet elites considered a Soviet Union without Ukraine an absurdity. To prevent the new treaty from being signed, a group of conservatives organized a coup against Gorbachev.

Once it was clear that the coup would fail, Leonid Kravchuk, the speaker of Ukraine's parliament, declared Ukraine's independence on August 24, 1991. He scheduled a referendum on independence to coincide with a presidential election planned for December. In that referendum, 92.3 percent voted in favor of independence. In every single region of Ukraine, including Crimea, a majority of voters supported independence. In Crimea and the naval base city of Sevastopol, the majorities were much smaller than elsewhere: 54.2 and 57.1 percent, respectively. In the eastern regions of Donetsk and Luhansk (where Russia-oriented separatism later emerged), 83.9 percent voted for independence. The Ukrainian referendum definitively established Ukraine's independence and the dissolution of the Soviet Union, but these acts raised far more questions than they answered. In the same election, Leonid Kravchuk was elected the first president of independent Ukraine.

Early Postcommunism

Rather than trying to eject the communists from power in 1991, Ukrainian nationalists joined forces with those communists who were willing to support independence. This alliance avoided the internal divisions that had undermined previous Ukrainian independence movements. It succeeded at that, but continuity had far-reaching consequences for the prospects of political transformation.

First, the existing elite were not ejected from power. Kravchuk, who became Ukraine's first president, had earlier been in charge of ideology for the Communist Party of Ukraine. Rather than holding founding parliamentary elections, as in many other postcommunist states, the existing parliament was left in place. Nor did Ukraine adopt a new constitution. Instead, piecemeal amendments to the 1977 Soviet Ukrainian constitution were made. In terms of both institutions and personnel, there was considerable continuity from the Soviet era in Ukraine to the post-Soviet era.

Second, this coalition did not prioritize economic reform. Nationalists focused on separating Ukraine and its economy from Russia. The converted communists prioritized stability and were deeply skeptical about market reforms and opening to the international economy. In contrast to Poland and Russia, which pursued variants of "shock therapy," Ukraine chose slow reform, which in many cases turned out to be nonreform.

The country faced immense challenges. It had to create a new state from scratch, reform and rebuild an economy that was running into the ground, and build a democratic political system. It also needed to forge a national identity after centuries of efforts by Russian and Soviet leaders to undermine the very idea. On top of all this, from the moment of Ukraine's independence, Russia sought to bring Ukraine back under its control and to regain control of the naval base at Sevastopol.

Ukraine's economy declined precipitously in the early post-Soviet years.[8] How much of the decline was due to conditions inherited from the Soviets and how much to the lack of reform is debatable. But this era set in motion the concentration of economic wealth and political power that continues to characterize Ukraine today. In the gray area between the state plan and the market, with weak rule of law and contradictory policies, the ruthless or well placed could gain control over economic assets worth billions. By the late 1990s, much of Ukraine's economy was controlled by a small number of "financial industrial groups" or "clans" led by people known as "oligarchs."

Street protests in eastern Ukraine and Kyiv in the fall of 1993 prompted a deal to hold new presidential and parliamentary elections in 1994. The parliamentary elections were held under the existing Soviet rules, with deputies elected in 450 single-member districts. Given the absence of a strong party system, these rules led to the election of a highly fragmented and ineffective parliament. In the presidential election, Leonid Kuchma, who had run the world's largest ballistic missile factory before becoming prime minister, defeated the incumbent, Leonid Kravchuk.

Kuchma led Ukraine from 1994 until 2004. Over this decade, some important gains were made, most notable of which was the defeat of hyperinflation and the successful introduction of a new currency in 1996. That same year, Kuchma forced through parliament a new constitution that put extensive powers in the hands of the president. While this concentration of power was justified as necessary to overcome gridlock, it paved the way for Kuchma to accumulate near-authoritarian powers.

In 1997, Ukraine and Russia signed a major "friendship" treaty in which Russia pledged to respect Ukraine's sovereignty and territorial integrity. In return, Ukraine agreed to lease Russia the naval base at Sevastopol in Crimea, where the Russian/Soviet Black Sea Fleet had traditionally been based. Kuchma pursued what he called a "multi-vector" foreign policy, seeking good relations with both Russia and the West. He pursued extensive relations with the North Atlantic Treaty Organization (NATO), which irked Russia, but he resisted the kinds of political and economic reforms that would have been needed to be more welcome in the European Union (see chapters 9 on the EU and 10 on Russia). Instead, Kuchma consolidated power by balancing among the oligarchic forces and using the power of the state to punish potential challengers. Under Kuchma, it was essentially impossible to do business without violating some law or regulation. Kuchma then went after those who did not support him, a tactic known as "selective prosecution," which has persisted.

Using these tactics, Kuchma easily won reelection in 1999 and, following the example set by Vladimir Putin in Russia, further consolidated his power. However, in September 2000, a journalist was abducted and beheaded, and leaked recordings made in the president's office implicated Kuchma in the murder as well as in other misdeeds. This sparked the process that culminated in the 2004 Orange Revolution. A new protest movement, called "Ukraine without Kuchma," emerged, and though it failed, it began a consolidation of anti-Kuchma forces behind Viktor Yushchenko, a former prime minister. As the end of Kuchma's second term approached in 2004, Yushchenko was poised to make a strong challenge.

The constitution limited the president to two terms, so Kuchma needed to either find a way around that limit, as Vladimir Putin later did, or find a suitable successor. He chose Viktor Yanukovych, the prime minister, who led the Party of Regions, a pro-Russian party with immense strength in eastern Ukraine. Vladimir Putin sent advisers to Ukraine to help the Yanukovych campaign, and both Putin and Russian media, which were widely viewed in Ukraine, overtly supported Yanukovych.

The Orange Revolution and the Revolution of Dignity

When the government announced Yanukovych's victory amid widespread evidence of fraud, hundreds of thousands of people protested in the streets of Kyiv, kicking off the Orange Revolution. After a few tense weeks, a compromise was brokered. The second round of the election would be rerun with international monitoring, and the constitution would be revised to reduce the powers of the presidency. Yushchenko easily won this rerun. Many saw this as a decisive step toward democracy and Europe and away from Russia, and while pro-European Ukrainians were overjoyed, those who had supported Yanukovych were incensed. The Russian government viewed this turn of events as a disaster.

Despite president Yushchenko's determination to turn the country westward, he accomplished much less than many hoped. Almost immediately, he and his former ally, the new prime minister, Yuliya Tymoshenko, began fighting bitterly for control of policy. Moreover, the people who entered power after the Orange Revolution appeared as eager as their predecessors to benefit financially from their positions. So, while democracy was safeguarded, corruption continued unabated, and reform was underwhelming.

In 2006, in order to avoid reappointing Tymoshenko as prime minister after parliamentary elections, Yushchenko instead appointed his former enemy, Yanukovych. Again, Ukrainian reformers had, by fighting with each other, empowered their enemies. Yushchenko was forced to reappoint Tymoshenko in 2007, but their relationship was hopeless, and Yanukovych had meanwhile been rehabilitated politically (with the assistance of US adviser Paul Manafort). The global financial crisis then hit in 2008, closing the window of opportunity opened by the Orange Revolution without much having been achieved. In the run-up to the 2010 presidential election, the recession undermined the popularity of the incumbents Yushchenko and Tymoshenko. In a development that would have been unthinkable a few years earlier, Viktor Yanukovych, who tried to steal the 2004 election, won the 2010 election freely and fairly.

Immediately upon taking power, Yanukovych began taking steps to eliminate political competition and to ensure that an increasing share of the benefits of corruption accrued to a narrow group of allies and relatives known as "the family."[9] He used promotions and bribery to get the Constitutional Court to undo the constitutional changes of 2004, thereby concentrating power in his hands. His rival Tymoshenko was imprisoned on trumped-up charges so that she could not run against him in 2015. As it had under Kuchma, Ukraine was sliding toward authoritarianism under Yanukovych.

In foreign policy, Yanukovych sought to improve relations with Russia while resisting Russia's demands for economic integration. He also sought to continue work with the European Union on an association agreement, which was popular in Ukraine and promised important economic as well as political benefits. In pursuing close ties with both Russia and the EU, Yanukovych was doing what many Ukrainians wanted, but there were two major challenges. First, the EU insisted that progress on the association agreement be accompanied by Yanukovych reversing his politicization of the justice system, as emblemized by the imprisonment of Yuliya Tymoshenko. This threatened his power, so he resisted. Second, the association agreement, which was the major goal of negotiations with the EU, was resolutely opposed by Moscow.

Photo 19.2. Pro-Europe protestors on Independence Square, or Maidan, during the "Euromaidan" or "Revolution of Dignity" in November 2013. (Mstyslav Chernov, Wikimedia Commons)

The situation came to a head in late 2013. The EU and Yanukovych appeared to reach an agreement on justice issues that would allow the association agreement to be signed in November. In response, Russian leaders threatened Yanukovych that they would take steps to devastate Ukraine's economy, making his reelection impossible. Yanukovych bowed to Russian pressure and announced that the agreement would not be signed. Again, protestors turned out in the center of Kyiv, but initially they were few in number. However, when these protestors were brutally beaten by police, hundreds of thousands turned out, igniting what became known as the "Euromaidan" (the Maidan is the square in the center of Kyiv) or the "Revolution of Dignity."[10]

In contrast to previous protests, this one turned violent, and on February 20, 2014, roughly seventy protestors were killed. This violence dramatically undermined support for Yanukovych, even among his allies. On February 22, he fled the country, and Ukraine had its second revolution in a decade. The parliament named an acting president and scheduled a new election for May.

As Ukraine was reeling from the sudden transfer of power, Russian special forces infiltrated Crimea and seized key points.[11] In three weeks, Russia seized control of the peninsula, held a sham referendum on joining Russia, and held parliamentary votes in Moscow annexing Crimea as Russian territory.

Meanwhile, militants supported by Russia occupied administrative buildings in several cities in eastern and southern Ukraine and declared their intent to establish autonomy from Ukraine or join Russia. The chaos in Kyiv, along with the failure over previous decades to reform the Ukrainian military, made it difficult for the new government to resist these forces. In some cases, local leaders and oligarchs organized forces to resist the separatists. In other areas, self-organized paramilitaries did the job. But in two regions, Donetsk and Luhansk, the Russia-supported forces held on, leading to sustained armed conflict. When Ukrainian government forces got close to defeating the insurgents in the summer of 2014, the Russian army invaded, routing the Ukrainian forces. Since

Photo 19.3. Russian special forces without insignia, known as "little green men," during the takeover of the parliament of Crimea, February 27, 2014. (Voice of America, Wikimedia Commons)

February 2015, the lines of control in eastern Ukraine have not changed much, but casualties continue to mount.

In the May 2014 presidential election, Petro Poroshenko was elected president. Ukraine, at war with Russia, turned west. The EU Association Agreement was signed and trade was reoriented, but corruption persisted. Frustration with the war and with corruption undermined Poroshenko's reelection campaign in 2019. Volodymyr Zelenskyy, a comedian with no prior political experience, defeated Poroshenko easily, winning nearly every region of Ukraine. He promised to end the war and to end corruption. Like Poroshenko, he found it hard to make progress because Russia would not budge from its demands. Each time he tried to take a step toward meeting Russia's demands, he encountered strong resistance domestically. Similarly, progress on corruption was slow, as entrenched interests, some of whom were allied with the new president, obstructed change.

Politics, History, and Memory

Russia's determination to control Ukraine today emerges from a long history of Russian domination and from intense debates about historical memory.[12] From the time Moscow emerged as a regional power in the fifteenth century, its rulers sought to bolster their legitimacy by claiming to be the heirs of early Kyiv. Thus, the claim that Russia needed to "gather" traditionally Russian lands to its west was foundational to the Russian state and remains so today. Russian historians and intellectuals cite a quotation attributed to Catherine the Great concerning Russia's seizure of Polish territory: "We only took what was ours."[13] Ukrainians and Russians today debate the meaning of a series of events spanning a thousand years, with Ukraine generally stressing the separateness of Ukraine, its democratic traditions, and the theme of Russia conquering Ukraine, while Russia stresses the commonalities of the peoples, the benefits of Russian rule, and Ukrainians' voluntary subjection to that rule. Key points of contention in the twentieth century include Ukrainian efforts to form a state at the end of World War I, the famine/genocide of the 1930s, Ukraine's role in World War II, and the circumstances surrounding the transfer of Crimea to Ukrainian control in 1954. Today, a contest is underway to define the events of 2014.

Within Ukraine, debates over some of these issues have been intense. In 2015, a series of laws on "decommunization," also known as the "memory laws," were passed.[14] Among other things, they required the renaming of thousands of streets and cities, banned Nazi and communist symbols, and gave official status to some of the most controversial World War II–era groups. While supporters saw these laws as reversing a history of foreign oppression, opponents saw them as rewriting history and limiting freedom of speech.

Political Institutions

Ukraine's political institutions were inherited from the Soviet Union, and they were modified but not overhauled in the 1996 constitution. Since then, there have been multiple tweaks to the relative powers of the president and parliament and to the rules for electing the parliament. The extent of centralization versus regional and local rule has also been a major issue, especially since 2014.

The 1996 constitution defines Ukraine as a unitary (rather than a federal) state, meaning that the central government in Kyiv has clear primacy over the twenty-seven regional governments. Many in Ukraine, especially nationalists, have insisted on maintaining this unitary structure because of the fear that a federal structure will facilitate separatism. That fear has only increased since 2014, and Russia's insistence that regional autonomy be part of the Minsk Agreements that govern the search for peace in eastern Ukraine is seen as intended to create a situation in which pro-Russian regions and politicians retain significant veto powers within Ukraine.

A reform of local government initiated in 2014 devolved many taxing and spending powers to local governments. The intent was to decentralize government without adopting a federal system. Based in part on models from the Baltic and Scandinavian countries, 60 percent of personal income tax collections are to be allocated to local authorities. This is a major change from the previous model, in which taxes were aggregated nationally and then apportioned downward to the regions and local governments. Among other things, that highly centralized model facilitated the president's ability to reward and punish politicians and voters based on how their areas voted. It also facilitated the misappropriation of funds.

Conflict over the prerogatives of the president, the unicameral parliament, and the prime minister has been endemic.[15] In contrast to the countries to Ukraine's west, most of which have adopted parliamentary systems in which the presidency is a mostly symbolic position, Ukraine and most of the post-Soviet states have adopted dual executive systems, with both a president and a prime minister. Whether this arrangement is a cause or effect of authoritarianism—or is unrelated—is debated.

In Ukraine, the key questions were whether the president or parliament appointed the prime minister and whether the prime minister or president controlled the Cabinet of

Ministers, and through it the executive branch. These conflicts were not at all theoretical. When the parliament and president disagreed over policies, especially over various aspects of reform, who would prevail? And who would control the cabinet and through them the executive branch: the president or prime minister? This was connected to who could collect the immense financial and political rewards from corruption.

The 1996 constitution was designed to concentrate power in the hands of the president in order to overcome parliamentary gridlock and resistance to reform. After the Orange Revolution, the 2004 amendments were intended to balance powers between the president and prime minister. The result was a conflict between President Yushchenko and Prime Minister Tymoshenko that threatened to turn violent. Since 2010, this conflict has been resolved in the president's favor, largely because the presidents elected since then have had more support in parliament.

Ukraine's security institutions, while playing a significant role in some respects, have not become the center of political power as they have in some other post-Soviet states. In contrast to Russia, for example, analysts do not typically refer to the "power ministries" as central actors in Ukrainian politics. Three of the most important security services are the armed forces, which were dramatically downsized but not dramatically reformed after 1991; the Interior Ministry, which controls local police across the country as well as a large paramilitary force; and the Security Service of Ukraine, successor to the Ukrainian branch of the KGB. In 2004, during the Orange Revolution, the military and Security Service sent signals that they would not use force against the protestors, which both encouraged the protestors and helped convince the government to negotiate a settlement. After Viktor Yanukovych became president in 2010, he strove to make the security institutions more politically reliable and loyal to him, but when protests emerged again in 2013, he could count on only a relatively small (five to six thousand strong) special forces unit called the Berkut to repress protestors. As protests spread around the country, there were simply not enough loyal forces to go around. As in 2004, the military stood aside.

When Russia invaded Crimea and eastern Ukraine, the armed forces were too weak to resist. They had been heavily penetrated by Russian intelligence, and entire units of the Black Sea Fleet, as well as some military leaders, went over to Russia. In sum, the weakness of the security forces is both a curse and a blessing. They have not been able to protect the country from Russia, but neither have they been easily wielded tools for aspiring autocrats. They are characterized above all by their resistance to reform and by their engagement in all sorts of corruption and organized crime.

All of Ukraine's institutional arrangements are undermined by pervasive corruption, which successive Ukrainian governments have promised to tackle but with few results. After 2014, Ukraine built a completely new and independent National Anti-Corruption Bureau, the idea being to create a new institution free from preexisting corruption. So far, however, important cases brought by the bureau have been stymied by some other branch of the Ukrainian justice system. Prosecutions for high-level corruption have been transparent efforts to punish the leadership's political rivals. The accrual and exercise of political power in Ukraine depend on patronage, corruption, and selective law enforcement, so when we talk about ending these practices, we are not talking merely about reform but about dismantling the entire system of power. Unsurprisingly, those who come to rule in that system are hesitant to undermine it. In this respect, there is a fundamental conflict of interest between Ukrainian leaders of all parties and Western donors.

Political Competition

Political competition in Ukraine is based on competition among "clans" or "oligarchs" who control patronage networks. Deeply rooted informal institutions rival formal ones in their ability to shape actors' behavior. Patronage politics, in which elites trade illicit access to state resources for the support of voters, has a deep history in Ukraine. Under the Soviet system, people often depended on patronage networks and exchanges of favors to get what they needed, including food, jobs, and administrative rulings. These informal institutions were strengthened, not weakened, by the transition from communism. When Soviet institutions broke down and were not immediately replaced, people relied even more heavily on their informal networks.

Henry Hale has conceived of politics throughout the post-Soviet region as being based on "patronalism," in which "pyramids" of patronage reach from the top of society all the way to the bottom.[16] For example, a police officer collects bribes and is expected to kick a certain portion of the money collected upward to their boss, who in turn is expected to kick a portion upward, so that those at the top can become extremely wealthy and can punish those who refuse to play along by foiling their careers. What distinguishes Ukraine from other countries in the region is that Ukraine has always been a multiple-pyramid system, with competition among clans. In Russia under Putin, in contrast, Putin has eliminated rivals so that there is only a single patronage network, with him at the top. Presidents Kuchma and Yanukovych sought to eliminate their rivals but ultimately failed. Ukraine's pluralism is not well institutionalized through laws and norms and has therefore been called "pluralism by default."[17] But it has endured despite concerted efforts to undermine it.

The weakness of Ukraine's institutions is manifested in its party system. It is difficult to locate Ukraine's parties on the conventional left-right spectrum that characterizes most modern democracies. The Communist Party and Socialist Party that emerged from the Soviet Union played important roles through the 1990s but faded after that. To a large extent, politicians and parties advance similar programs, arguing only about who will implement them better. As noted above, voting tends to break down along regional lines, implying that what matters to voters is which regional interests a party is seen as representing. In many cases, politicians and voters seem to side with whoever is expected to win in order to gain access to the benefits of patronage. The most important variations in policy have to do with embracing or rejecting Ukrainian nationalism and with the related questions of language policy and relations with Russia. In the 2019 presidential election, for example, the candidates held indistinguishable positions on major economic issues as well as on opposition to corruption. While Poroshenko ran on the slogan "Army, language, faith," Volodymyr Zelenskyy stressed anticorruption and avoided taking a position on many other issues.

Throughout Ukraine's independent history, the key cleavages that seem to shape attitudes and behavior are the overlapping factors of region, language, and national identity.[18] Which of these factors is, at the bottom, responsible for the others is the topic of extensive debate. In general, Ukraine is a country of regional rather than national parties. Attitudes toward relations with Russia, which tend to correlate with region, have long distinguished political parties. Parties that support tight relations with the West and economic liberalization tend to do better in western and central Ukraine. For this reason, it was considered exceptional when Volodymyr Zelenskyy performed well across Ukraine's regions in the 2019 presidential election, winning every region except Lviv in the second round. While many people saw Zelenskyy's cross-regional popularity as a sign of increased unity in Ukraine, regional patterns in voting were still in evidence. A key question for the future is whether the regionalization of Ukraine's vote decreases or whether Zelenskyy in 2019 turns out to have been an exception.

Since 2014, there has been some evidence of a consolidation of Ukrainian national identity, though conclusions continue to be debated. Some research indicates that Ukrainian national identity is evolving to be based less on ethnic and linguistic factors and more on citizenship.[19] In response to the conflict with Russia, more people appear to be identifying more strongly as Ukrainians. While pro-Russia parties still perform well in eastern Ukraine, their overall impact has been reduced by the fact that Russia occupied much of the territory in which their voters resided and from which much of their financial support came. Roughly 12 percent of Ukraine's pre-2014 electorate lived in territory now occupied by Russia, and they tended to vote heavily for pro-Russia parties.[20]

Many of the important parties in Ukraine at any moment are associated with a single politician and are even named for them. Even if these parties sometimes jettison their founder's name, they tend to fold once that leader ceases to be competitive. The weakness of parties makes it hard to assemble reliable majority coalitions in parliament. This increases incentives for the president to use bribery or coercion to build support for legislation. It also helps justify giving a lot of power to the president.

One of the most notable developments in recent years has been the "youth movement" that emerged in the 2019 elections. The president, Volodymyr Zelenskyy, was just forty-one when elected (born 1978), meaning that he came of age after the collapse of the Soviet Union. Similarly, the average age of the members of parliament elected in 2019 was 41, seven years younger than for the outgoing parliament. This led to widespread hope that ejection of the "old guard" of leaders who came of age under the Soviets would lead to dramatically different policies. After a year of the new leadership, it was hard to detect a fundamental change. Even if this new generation was born later, it was socialized under the system that people say they want to get rid of.

Elections

Ukraine's presidential elections take place in five-year intervals and are held in a two-round runoff system. The top two vote winners from the first round go into a runoff. The virtue of this system is that it allows a wide range of candidates to take part in the first round while ensuring that the eventual victor will have at least 50 percent of the vote. In only one election, in 1994, did the first-round winner not triumph in the second round.

The rules for Ukraine's parliamentary elections have changed several times. Some of this tweaking has been the result of sincere efforts to forge a parliament that is cohesive enough to form a working majority, while some of it seems intended to privilege some parties at the expense of others. The two major issues have been how much of the parliament will be elected in single-member districts (SMDs) versus via nationwide proportional representation (PR) and how high the threshold for entering parliament would be under PR. Most Western European parliaments are elected by some version of PR.

Ukraine's first post-Soviet parliamentary elections, in 1994, were held entirely in the SMD format held over from the communist era, with Ukraine split into 450 districts (this was roughly analogous to an election to the House of Representatives in the United States or the House of Commons in Canada or the UK). With a very weak party system, this led to a parliament with a large number of independents and very low party discipline. This hampered the ability of the parliament to pass legislation and to form an effective check on the president. To the extent that majorities were assembled to pass legislation, they tended to be onetime coalitions facilitated by inducements provided by the president. The 1998 and 2002 elections were carried out according to a mixed system, with 225 single-member districts and 225 members elected according to PR with a 4 percent threshold. In the first parliamentary elections after the Orange Revolution, in 2006, full PR was adopted, with the threshold reduced to 3 percent. Five parties received seats but none approached a majority, and the jockeying to form a majority, and hence to name the prime minister, was bitter. The ensuing morass resulted in President Yushchenko's controversial dissolution of the parliament in 2007 and the holding of new elections under the same formula. The results were essentially similar, except that the Socialist Party of Ukraine, previously an important swing party, failed to enter parliament and subsequently disappeared.

After Viktor Yanukovych became president in 2010 and gained control over parliament, apparently through a mix of bribery and coercion, the mixed system was restored for the 2012 parliamentary elections, with the threshold raised to 5 percent. The change was intended to benefit the Party of Regions, as its strong patronage networks made it extremely effective at delivering votes to win SMD seats. Because a relatively small number of votes can tip an SMD seat, the effects of patronage are disproportionate. Raising the threshold to 5 percent was intended to eliminate small parties, facilitating the formation of a working majority in parliament. This system has been retained for elections since then.

The frequent changes to the electoral rules, while providing much fodder for political scientists, have undermined the formation of an enduring party system. The party that won a majority in 2019, for example, did not exist before that year. Even so, there has been a general tendency over time toward a reduction of the number of parties represented in parliament and of the number of independents elected in the SMD portion of the mixed system.

Moreover, the formation of a reliable parliamentary majority has been elusive. In only one instance, in 2019, did one party win an outright majority in a parliamentary election. That result led to optimism that the parliamentary majority, allied with president Zelenskyy, would be able to pass needed legislation in lockstep with the president. Accountability would presumably be enhanced, as it was clear who controlled the parliament. While an early raft of measures was passed, the majority split over various issues, requiring the president to again patch together situational coalitions.

This problem with party discipline is a reflection of Ukraine's weak parties. In many countries, a parliamentarian's career would be over if they defied their party's leadership. In Ukraine, because parties come and go and party switching is frequent, individual

vicious cycle

members are "free agents," able to defect with little consequence. Moreover, the influence of oligarchs means that many parties are in part amalgamations of oligarchic factions, and the oligarchic factions pursue their own interests. Thus, in 2020, when the parliament voted on a bank reform measure that was a prerequisite for further IMF funding, a faction of the majority party defected, so that the bill passed only with the support of opposition members.

Civil Society

Civil society in Ukraine is something of an enigma. Much of the time, civil society seems weak. Labor unions are unimportant, and nongovernmental organizations have few members and are poorly funded. Some of the prominent ones rely on external support, earning them the derisive nickname "grant eaters." The government and elites often seem to ignore these groups with impunity. However, in particular cases, such as the Orange Revolution and Revolution of Dignity, citizen direct action is incredibly powerful, overthrowing aspiring autocrats who had seemed ruthless and undefeatable. Thus, Ukraine's intermediate associations are weak, but its social movements are often mighty. Citizen participation seems to be "eventful" rather than continuously influential. How do we account for this anomalous pattern?

One possible interpretation is that Ukraine does not fit the normal pattern in which strong states are accompanied by weak societies, and vice versa. Ukraine, it might be argued, has both a weak state and a weak society. The state is weak in that it struggles to coerce the society or to resist concerted public action. An example of the first is tax collection, a basic function of the state that Ukraine struggles to do successfully. An example of the second is protests: neither people themselves nor members of the state security services consider it legitimate for the state to use force against protestors. In the classic Weberian definition of the state, the monopoly on the legitimate use of force is a central characteristic that Ukraine often seems to lack.

In part because it struggles to collect taxes, the Ukrainian state struggles to provide basic services. This leaves room for other actors to step in, and oligarchs have sometimes filled that gap, building their own influence at the expense of the state. However, although Ukraine's state is weak, the society is not strong, in that it does not have reliable mechanisms for changing the state's behavior. While people can resist paying taxes, they cannot get the state to administer justice effectively or prevent officials from demanding bribes.

Though lacking effective intermediate organizations to influence the state, citizens in Ukraine have developed one powerful tactic to force their government to hear their voices: taking to the streets. The practice began in the late Soviet period, when students occupied Kyiv's Maidan to demand new parliamentary elections. Similar tactics in 1993 prompted the firing of the prime minister and the scheduling of new parliamentary and presidential elections for 1994. The 2004 Orange Revolution and 2014 Revolution of Dignity saw a similar set of tactics deployed, including occupation of the Maidan, which is roughly equivalent to New York's Times Square or the National Mall in Washington, DC; the erection of tent cities so that protestors did not need to leave; and the creation of a festival atmosphere with music performances.

These tactics do not always succeed. In some cases, protests have fizzled out. In others, the government has repressed them.[21] In 1999's "Ukraine without Kuchma" movement, for example, the government closed off the Maidan so that protestors could not occupy it. Buses bringing protestors to Kyiv were turned back, and the rallies were broken up by police. An important question, then, is why the government is willing and able to suppress some protests but not others. It would appear that one key factor is whether the security forces are willing to follow orders to repress protestors, and another is how much oligarchs choose to support the protests. In both 2004 and 2014, powerful oligarchs supported the protests because they feared that the government was becoming powerful enough to challenge the oligarchs' interests.

In the years since 2014, citizen groups have taken on some increasingly important roles. Privately organized militias played a crucial role in combating Russia-supported insurgents in eastern Ukraine. When the conflict began in 2014, the Ukrainian military struggled to respond, and paramilitary groups sprang into action. Some of these "volunteer battalions" formed from groups that had provided security during the protests in Kyiv; others were fielded by nationalist groups. Some were supported by oligarchs. These forces took on an essential role of the state: national self-defense. But while they fought valiantly, they had neither the training nor the equipment to withstand the intervention of regular Russian army forces.

As these forces were replaced with Ukrainian army units, Ukraine faced the challenge of what to do with them. On the one hand, they are popular and have weapons, so they cannot easily be disarmed and disbanded. Moreover, the state relied heavily on them to fight against Russia. On the other hand, given the weakness of government forces, there is some fear that these armed groups might intervene in domestic politics, as they have threatened in several instances where they opposed what they saw as concessions to Russia. They do not meet the definition of civil society, as they are illegal and sometimes threaten violence.

Ukraine's nongovernmental groups are playing at least three distinct roles relative to the state: influencing, undermining, and complementing. In some cases, they seek to influence policies. In other cases, they actively resist state policy. In many important ways, they do things that the state is expected to do but is not doing. For example, volunteers and donors have also provided crucial supplies to front-line troops, cared for the wounded, and helped displaced persons.

The media ideally help citizens demand accountability from the state, but in the years prior to the 2004 Orange Revolution, the government increasingly controlled Ukraine's media by coercing the companies that owned major outlets. Since 2005, Ukraine's media landscape has been vibrant and pluralistic, but several problems persist. Many outlets struggle to stay afloat, as they do all over the world. Their economic woes leave them increasingly vulnerable to offers by powerful oligarchs or politicians to reward them financially for favorable coverage. Nearly every news outlet and television station in Ukraine is owned by one of Ukraine's oligarchs. While there is a multitude of voices, there is not necessarily journalistic independence. Moreover, the Russian government uses its presence in the Ukrainian media market and social media to promote its messages and the political candidates it favors. After 2014, Ukraine banned Russian media and social media, so Russia now works indirectly, financing the purchase of Ukrainian media outlets by pro-Russian actors. Violence against journalists has increased over the years. Journalists who expose the misdeeds of powerful people have been intimidated, attacked, and killed.

Economic Policies and Conditions

By some measures, Ukraine was one of the wealthiest of the Soviet republics, but that status hid important weaknesses that have undermined both the country's economic performance and its efforts to break free from Russian influence.[22] Moreover, opposition to reform has frozen Ukraine in a "partial reform equilibrium" that benefits powerful actors but undermines growth.[23] Those who gained control of economic assets during the early phase of transition have had both the incentive and the power to block further reform.

Ukraine is known as the "breadbasket of Europe," as much of its territory is covered with some of the most fertile soil in the world, known as "black earth." The eastern areas were industrial powerhouses under the Soviet Union, mining coal and ore and turning them into steel and other products. Ukraine also had prominent aerospace, electronics, and defense sectors, and the world's largest missile plant was located in Dnipro (formerly called Dnipropetrovsk). For these reasons, many argued that Ukraine would flourish when separated from the Soviet Union, but that did not happen.

Part of the problem was that Ukraine's mix of industries was not as competitive as it appeared. Ukraine's economy was one of the most energy intensive in the world, measured in terms of how much energy went into each dollar of GDP. Both heavy industry and agriculture depended on cheap energy from Russia and the Caspian basin. In the case of agriculture, energy was needed not only to run tractors and transport produce but to make vast amounts of fertilizer. As long as the prices of that energy were artificially suppressed, the economy looked powerful. But when prices rose after 1991, Ukraine's industries were suddenly less profitable. The loss of the Soviet armed forces as a consumer of military products was a further blow.

As the Soviet Union and the Soviet economy collapsed, Ukraine's leaders faced a dilemma. If they freed prices, food and heating costs would increase dramatically, putting many people's survival at risk. But if they did not free prices, the inefficiencies and opportunities for corruption in a non-market economy would persist. In key areas, such as basic foodstuffs and natural gas, people demanded that state controls be maintained. While food prices were freed in the 1990s, the sale of agricultural land was limited, and consumers still do not pay the full market price for the natural gas they consume.

In 2020, Ukraine was still considering legislation that would allow the buying and selling of farmland. Those who work on Ukraine's farms worry that if the land they work can be sold, they will lose their livelihood. But since the land cannot be transferred, owners cannot borrow money using the land as collateral, and there is less incentive to invest in agriculture. Due largely to underinvestment in equipment and technology, Ukraine produces barely above world averages in yields per acre, despite the advantage of its exceptional soil.

A broader problem in the Ukrainian economy concerns the rule of law. For people to invest in businesses, they need confidence that their investment will be protected. Two kinds of threats persist in Ukraine. The first is extortion, in which local criminals or politicians demand payment to forestall actions (violence in the case of criminals, gratuitous law enforcement in the case of politicians). For example, if one does not continuously pay the right politicians, tax authorities or fire marshals might close one's business. The second is expropriation, in which someone demands, using threats of violence or law enforcement, that a business be sold to them. Because it is particularly hard for outsiders to navigate the murky networks that govern these activities, foreign investment is discouraged. Moreover, when one does make a significant profit, there is powerful incentive to expatriate that profit to a safe jurisdiction rather than reinvesting it in Ukraine, a phenomenon known as "capital flight."

The natural gas sector is particularly important, both to Ukraine's economy and to its relations with Russia. Nearly all the natural gas that Ukraine consumes originates either in Russia or in Turkmenistan. If Russia raises the price, Ukraine's industries are less viable, and its consumers are potentially poorer. Ukraine's government subsidizes the price of gas to Ukrainian consumers, so anytime the price goes up, so does the expense for the government.

The positioning of the Ukrainian government and various state-run energy companies in the gas market provides the opportunity for billions of dollars' worth of corruption, and Ukraine's oligarchs compete intensely over control of that source of wealth. At multiple points along the way, gas is sold for less than the world market price. At some times, Russia has sold the gas for below-market prices in order to entice Ukraine to join it economically. But even when Russia charges market price, Ukraine provides the gas to consumers (including industrial customers) at below-market prices in order to protect them. Those in the privileged position to buy gas at the subsidized price can resell it at the market price, reaping vast profits.

Ukraine's one strength in the energy markets has been the transit of gas to Western Europe. Russia depends on pipelines through Ukraine to get gas to lucrative markets in Western Europe. These contracts have generally been opaque, leading to further opportunities for corruption. Controlling these revenues not only makes one wealthy but gives one the resources to vie for further political power. It is not too much of an exaggeration to say that Ukrainian politics is about who will control the embezzlement of billions of dollars in gas and gas transit revenues.

Energy also creates a foreign policy dilemma: Ukraine is heavily dependent for energy on the country that is its biggest security threat and with which it is now at war. Russia has repeatedly used energy as a stick and a carrot, cutting deliveries when it wants to coerce Ukrainian leaders and promising increased subsidies if Ukraine will join a Russia-centered economic bloc. Ukraine has had one countermeasure: if Russia stops shipping gas to Ukraine, Ukraine can stop transshipping Russian gas to Europe. While Ukraine has not done much to create a free market for energy or to reduce its dependence on Russia, Russia has been spending billions of dollars building pipelines that circumvent Ukraine. By the time the most recent gas transit contract expires in 2025, Russia will be able to meet all or almost all of its shipments to Western Europe without going through Ukraine. At that point, Russia will be in a much stronger position to cut off Ukraine (as well as Belarus and Poland). The involvement of the European Union may mitigate some of these dangers, both by dissuading Russia from coercing Ukraine and by supplying Ukraine from Europe if needed.

Due to this array of economic problems—some inherited, some self-inflicted—Ukraine has repeatedly sought assistance from the IMF, and more recently has received significant help from the EU as well. As is typical of these programs, aid is conditioned upon Ukraine adopting reforms that the donors believe will improve the economy. Ukraine's leaders often resist implementing the measures demanded by these external donors. In some cases, such as raising consumer gas prices or privatizing farmland, reform is unpopular with voters, and the short-term harm caused may undermine politicians' reelection chances. There are genuine disagreements about the proper roles of the state and market. In other cases, such as anticorruption and justice reform, leaders resist losing important sources of power and money. Most Ukrainian leaders are supported by oligarchs whose interest in reform is quite limited.

Ukraine is a poor country, but with low inequality. Per capita GDP, measured at purchasing power parity (PPP), was $9,233 in 2018, compared to $62,795 in the United States and $27,147 in Russia. Ukraine's Gini coefficient of 0.26 is among the lowest in the world, meaning that wealth is more evenly distributed there than elsewhere.[24] In some respects, equality of poverty follows from the choices the government has made over the years—in order to protect people from the downside of the free market, economic growth has been sacrificed.

The poverty and lack of opportunity in Ukraine have led to three important demographic trends. First, and most important, many Ukrainians have emigrated to Russia or the West. At the same time, Ukraine has a great deal of immigration, primarily from Russia and other post-Soviet states, some of which is motivated by economics and some by authoritarianism or conflict. The net result has been a decline in population from 51.7 million in 1990 to 45.2 million in 2013, a decrease of 12.6 percent.[25] While Ukraine's emigration likely results in a "brain drain," there is a short-term benefit: remittances from abroad equaled 11 percent of Ukraine's GDP in 2018.[26] A second important trend has been urbanization. Population decline has been faster in rural areas, while the region around Kyiv has grown. Third, even prior to the war in eastern Ukraine, the population was declining in eastern Ukraine faster than elsewhere in the country due to economic conditions there.[27]

Following the collapse of the Soviet Union, Ukraine's first governments sought to reorient trade away from Russia and toward the European Union. This was very difficult in practice, for both economic and political reasons. Many of Ukraine's goods were uncompetitive on world markets and could compete in the former Soviet Union but not in the EU. The two areas where Ukraine has the most strength—agriculture and steel—are the two areas most protected from imports around the world and especially in the EU. Moreover, while the EU was focused on integrating new members to the west of Ukraine for much of the 1990s and 2000s, Russia was much more eager to include Ukraine in trade arrangements. Thus, the trade relationship that Ukraine could get was not the one it wanted.

Since 2014, Ukraine's trade has reoriented westward. The conflict with Russia was accompanied by a trade war, so while Russia remains an important trade partner, its role has diminished. Meanwhile, the Association Agreement with the EU, which entered force in 2017, was accompanied by a Deep and Comprehensive Free Trade Agreement (DCFTA) that reduced barriers to trade with the EU. Russia now accounts for roughly 14 percent of Ukraine's imports and 8 percent of its exports, while the EU countries, primarily Germany and Poland, account for 37 percent of its imports and 40 percent of its exports. Trade with China is also growing. Ukraine generally runs a trade deficit, which has led to a current-account deficit that on occasion has brought the state's hard currency reserves to dangerously low levels. Support for the currency, rather than direct contributions to the government budget, has been the main focus of IMF support.

After the economic shock that accompanied the revolution and outbreak of war in 2014, the Ukrainian economy grew until the COVID-19 pandemic struck. This economic growth and the reorientation of trade toward Europe have been seen as significant accomplishments. However, the cost of fighting the war is a steady drain, and Russia can easily increase the level of violence, which would be disruptive and costly. Ukraine continues to need support from abroad, and there is constant haggling over the extent of reform that will take place in return for support.

The recession that resulted from the COVID-19 outbreak hit Ukraine hard due to all the factors discussed here. With a weak economy and high rates of poverty, even a modest downturn deeply affects people's lives. Ukraine had begun a reform of its medical system, but this reform had stalled in 2019 and the system did not appear to be up to the challenge of COVID-19. As of September 2020, however, case numbers remained manageable. COVID-19 hit Ukraine later than some other countries, and the government moved quickly to put measures in place to control it. As a result, the measures were generally successful in flattening the first wave of the pandemic. The damage to the economy, however, had the government seeking additional funding from the IMF, which will eventually need to be repaid.

The reform of the health-care system is a good example of the difficulty of implementing reform in Ukraine. For years after independence, the system continued as before, inefficient and providing low-quality care. Funding was provided according to how many hospital beds were available, regardless of the number of patients treated or the quality of care. A new model was proposed to link payments to doctors and clinics to the number of patients they treated and to outcomes. While many hospitals would have received increased funding, roughly 20 percent would have seen budget cuts, and some of them would have closed. The threat of closing hospitals provoked a determined resistance. Moreover, a series of personnel changes at the top of the system, apparently made for political reasons, delayed implementation. Then COVID-19 hit.[28]

Key Social Issues

Given the low level of economic security in the country, maintenance of a social safety net is a prominent issue in Ukraine. Ukraine provides a wide variety of benefits, such as universal health care, maternity leave, and pension benefits, but the quality of provision is often quite low. Thus, while everyone has access to free health care, hospitals are understaffed and undersupplied, and because doctors are underpaid, bribes are often needed to receive care. Funds for new construction or maintenance are sometimes misappropriated, medicines disappear, and so on. These aspects of corruption infuriate citizens, though they often participate in such activities. Ukraine mandates eighteen weeks of maternity leave, as well as partially paid leave until a child reaches three years of age. Primary education is another area where nonstate groups augment the role of the state: in most schools, parents organize to collect money and materials to compensate for what the state fails to provide. Ukraine's literacy rate is 100 percent (compared with 86 percent in the United States).

Gender equality is mandated in Ukraine's constitution, but achieving it in practice has been elusive. As on many other issues, Ukraine has been better at passing legislation that meets international norms than it has been at implementing its laws. Ukrainian women face many of the challenges they face elsewhere, including underrepresentation at senior levels in all areas of government and business, pay inequalities, vulnerability to domestic violence, and widespread sexual harassment. According to the United Nations, "the root causes can be found in patriarchal attitudes and stereotypes, but also in deeply rooted systemic gaps which have not been addressed. These include weak rule of law, low capacity of the institutional mechanisms for gender equality and lack of political will."[29] The law now requires that women occupy 40 percent of the party lists in national and local proportional representation elections.

Trafficking in women is a particular problem in Ukraine. Organized crime networks recruit women in Ukraine for sex work in Europe and North America. Women are vulnerable due to the general lack of economic opportunity as well as lax law enforcement, or in many cases collaboration of law enforcement with traffickers. An additional problem is the conflict in eastern Ukraine. With the breakdown in law and order in the conflict zone, women are even more vulnerable.

While LGBTQ rights are protected by law in Ukraine, the reality is quite different. Discrimination against LGBTQ people is generally accepted, and violence is not unusual. Kyiv's annual pride parade has become a flashpoint in recent years, with anti-LGBTQ activists trying to stop the parade and law enforcement often lax in their protection of marchers. A 2018 poll by the Democratic Initiatives firm found that 47 percent of respondents supported limiting the rights of sexual minorities, while only 38 percent opposed it. The administration of Volodymyr Zelenskyy, which came to power in 2019, appeared to defend LGBTQ rights more vigorously than its predecessors, but widespread practice remains much as it has always been.

The rights of ethnic and especially linguistic minorities have been a major issue in Ukraine. While there is little discrimination on ethnic grounds, the language in which children should be educated and the establishment of "official" or "state" languages have proven controversial. Some of this controversy has deliberately been whipped up by Russia and its proxies, but the issues are real and reflect the long history in which suppression of the Ukrainian language was part of the broader Russian and Soviet effort to control Ukraine.

The tsarist and Soviet efforts to eradicate the Ukrainian language, and with it Ukrainian national identity, had some impact. As a result, after 1991, Ukrainian nationalists felt that it was necessary to promote the Ukrainian language as a way of reversing this damage. In particular, laws established only Ukrainian as the state language and promoted the use of Ukrainian in official activity and education. While many Ukrainians speak both languages, and Russian is widely heard throughout most of Ukraine, some insisted that minority languages should be given official status and should be used in education in areas where minorities predominate. Although this applied most significantly to Russian in parts of eastern and southern Ukraine, it also applied to Hungarian and Romanian in areas of far western and southwestern Ukraine.

In 2012, President Yanukovych signed an intensely controversial law that created the status of "regional languages," where at least 10 percent of the people spoke something other than Ukrainian. After Yanukovych was ousted in 2014, parliament repealed the law, and this too was controversial. Even though acting president Oleksandr Turchynov vetoed the repeal, Russia argued that the new government was limiting minority rights, and some, both inside and outside Ukraine, agreed. In 2019, the parliament adopted a new language law, which intended to strengthen the role of Ukrainian. This too was controversial, receiving intense criticism not only from Russia but from the increasingly nationalist government in Hungary as well. In spite of all this controversy, the impact of these laws on language use is not clear. Depending on the location, Russian continues to be widely spoken in Ukraine and widely used in the media. Volodymyr Zelenskyy speaks primarily Russian, but this did not prevent him from winning the presidency. Other minority languages, including Hungarian and Romanian, also continue to be used in some areas. But the issue persists as one of the most controversial within Ukraine and between Ukraine and Russia.

Religion and other aspects of ethnicity in Ukraine have been less controversial than language. In the Soviet Union, every individual had an official nationality, such as Ukrainian, Russian, or Jewish, recorded in their passport. Ukraine's 1990 declaration of sovereignty rejected this logic and established a civic definition of national identity, in which everyone who resided in Ukraine was a Ukrainian citizen. This contrasted with policies in the Baltic states, where an effort was made to define citizenship more narrowly to prevent Russians, who had immigrated in large numbers since World War II, from becoming a majority.

Ukraine also rejected the idea of an official state religion, which exists in many European states, such as England, Denmark, and Greece. Historically, one source of conflict was whether Ukraine would be Orthodox or Catholic, and the Treaty of Lublin (1569) split the difference by creating a hybrid known as "Eastern" or "Greek" Catholicism, which is under the pope but retains the rites of the Orthodox Church. The Orthodox Church in Ukraine was divided into three competing organizations: the Moscow Patriarchate, linked to the Russian Orthodox Church and supported by the Russian government; the Kyiv Patriarchate, which was founded after independence; and the Ukrainian Autocephalous Orthodox Church, which had been founded during Ukraine's brief independence in 1918. The Moscow-based church was the only one recognized by other Orthodox communities and remained highly important. It was seen by many as an agent of Russian influence in Ukraine. President Poroshenko led an intense diplomatic effort to have the entire Orthodox Church in Ukraine, including that which had been run from Moscow, made independent of Russia. The Ecumenical Patriarchate in Constantinople, head of the Orthodox Church worldwide, granted this request for "autocephaly" (independence) in 2018, angering Russia and handing a victory to Ukraine.

Historically, Ukraine had a large Jewish population as part of the "Pale of Settlement," the portion of the Russian Empire to which Jews were confined. Anti-Semitism was prominent across Europe, and in the Russian Empire this periodically erupted into pogroms against Jews. Sometimes these were sponsored by the tsarist government, while other times they were spontaneous. Pogroms at the time of the 1905 revolution in Russia led to one of the major waves of emigration of Jews from Ukraine to North America. Then, between 1939 and 1945, roughly 1.5 million of Ukraine's 2.7 million Jews were killed (most of the survivors fled eastward ahead of German forces).[30]

This legacy matters today in Ukraine for multiple reasons. As in other countries, the question of local participation in the Holocaust raises uncomfortable history. The failure of Soviet authorities to properly memorialize the sites in Ukraine is also an issue. Thus, in 2020, a major controversy broke out over plans to build a new museum at Babyn Yar in

Kyiv, where over thirty thousand of Kyiv's Jews were murdered by German troops over a few days in 1941, one of the largest mass killings of the era.

Because some of the staunchest Ukrainian nationalists of the World War II era also embraced fascism or collaborated with Germany, there remains concern today that Ukrainian nationalism embraces or at least tolerates anti-Semitism. For example, the Azov Battalion, one of the volunteer battalions that fought against Russian forces in eastern Ukraine, uses in its insignia a symbol called the "Wolfsangel" that was associated with Nazi Germany and was used by earlier, openly fascist Ukrainian parties. Therefore, the ability of independent Ukraine to overcome the region's history of anti-Semitism is seen as an important indicator of its progress toward democracy and is closely watched both inside and outside the country. For a period in 2019–2020, Ukraine was the only country in the world other than Israel to have both a Jewish president and prime minister (the prime minister was replaced in early 2020). This development does not mean that Ukraine's problems with anti-Semitism are entirely past, but it shows that to many the ethnic/religious identity of leaders is not a big issue.

As with the Jewish population, the Muslim population suffered immensely during World War II. Crimean Tatars were still numerous in Crimea until 1944, when the Soviet Union deported roughly two hundred thousand of them to Uzbekistan. Some Tatars returned to Crimea after 1991, and in 2014 many fled Crimea to avoid Russian occupation.

Ukraine is home to millions of migrants, many from Russia but also from Central Asia and Afghanistan. Migrants, especially migrants of color, often face very difficult circumstances. They lack the informal networks, built up over many years, on which Ukrainians rely to get by.[31] Even if they migrate legally, they often have less access to social services and benefits. Moreover, there is little penalty for those who abuse them. They cannot avail themselves of a functioning judicial system or an effective network of NGOs.

A more recent problem is that of people displaced by the conflict in eastern Ukraine, known as internally displaced persons (IDPs), who number 1.5 million according to the Ukrainian government. Forced from eastern Ukraine by war, they arrived in other parts of the country, often with no jobs, little money, and having lost access to many social benefits, which in Ukraine are linked to one's place of residence. Many IDPs faced a dilemma: If they retain their official residency in homes they hope to return to, they are limited in the benefits they receive in their new homes. But if they reregister as residents of other places, they might lose their claim on homes they hope to go back to, as well as to benefits available to IDPs. Similarly, if IDPs retain their right to vote in their original homes, where voting is not taking place, they cannot vote in their new homes, so they have effectively been disenfranchised. Internally displaced persons not only needed shelter, food, clothing, and jobs, but in many cases psychological and other medical services. But with all of these things already in short supply, the Ukrainian government has simply been incapable of meeting IDPs' needs. Nongovernmental groups sprang up to help, but they struggle to meet all of the needs.

Emerging Challenges

Ukraine has muddled through since 1991, but very few of its problems have been solved, and new ones have emerged. Politically, Ukraine has avoided authoritarianism but failed to consolidate liberal democracy. Economically, Ukraine reformed haltingly, and it remains poorer than most of its neighbors. In foreign policy, Ukraine has managed to retain its independence and strengthen ties with the EU, but it is involved in a war with Russia that it cannot win. For all of these reasons, Ukraine retains a long list of challenges, some of which look very similar to those it faced thirty years ago.

Ukraine's biggest problem is its relationship with Russia, and while the conflict has stabilized, the fundamental problem remains. Russian elites across almost the entire political spectrum opposed Ukraine's independence in 1991 and have continued to do so since then. Even those who do not seek to take over Ukraine's territory insist that Ukraine must remain under some form of Russian control. The events of 2014 raised the ante in two important respects. First, Russia is now occupying Ukrainian territory. While Russia's long-term intentions are opaque and perhaps not fully formed, Russia appears to be committed to retaining Crimea. Second, Ukraine is now on the front line of a new Cold War between Russia and the West.

While Russia seemed to accept Ukraine's independence and territorial integrity for a period of time after the signing of the 1997 friendship treaty, it now appears that this was due primarily to Russia's internal weakness and corresponding loss of international power. With its international power ascendant, Russia is now reasserting itself across a whole range of relationships. In many respects, Ukraine is at the heart of the conflict between Russia and the West. It is both the geographic location where the competition is focused and the major issue over which they now argue. This creates both opportunities and threats for Ukraine. The opportunity is that Ukraine is now very important to Europe and the United States. The threat is that to the extent that those actors resolve to reestablish good relations with Russia, they will have to sacrifice Ukraine's interest to do it. Ukraine's importance to the West creates another threat: because the Ukrainian leadership knows that the West does not want to cut off aid, it feels less pressure to meet demands for reform.

The major new challenge in 2020 was the COVID-19 pandemic. In contrast to Russia and Belarus, which partly or entirely obscured the extent of the pandemic, Ukraine faced the problem head-on and adopted early social distancing measures. As of November 2020, Ukraine's death rate was 26.04 per 100,000 population, compared with 37.69 in Poland, 25.38 in Russia, and 79.45 in the United States.[32] The low death rate was considered surprising, given the poor state of Ukraine's health-care system. It appears that the initial success was due to the combination of the late arrival of the disease and the early adoption of social distancing measures. As of late 2020, it is unclear whether Ukraine's success will endure through the full course of the pandemic. Moreover, as noted above, Ukraine is much more vulnerable to the economic impacts of the pandemic and the response to it.

Three related threats are materializing in the coming years. First, as Russia's new gas pipelines to the West come online, Ukraine will become much more vulnerable to a gas shutoff. Second, the war in eastern Ukraine has distracted attention from a broader array of Russian efforts to undermine Ukraine's independence, such as issuing passports to Ukrainian citizens, gaining control of Ukrainian media outlets, and interfering in Ukrainian elections. Third, political shifts in Western Europe make it increasingly likely that eventually the EU will loosen sanctions on Russia without gaining any progress on the conflict with Ukraine. In sum, Ukraine has a limited period of time to make the internal changes needed to resist Russian pressure.

Ukrainian leaders have largely treated domestic and foreign policy as disconnected, but this has never been the case, and Russia's understanding of this has worked to its advantage. Ukraine's ability to resist Russian pressure depends in large part on the health of Ukraine's economy and the strength of its domestic institutions. As it stands, the economy is weak, leaving a recurring temptation to take Russian aid in return for political concessions. Moreover, Ukraine's corrupt domestic institutions are just as easily penetrated by Russian state-owned firms and by Ukrainian oligarchs working for Russia as by pro-Ukraine oligarchs.

The weakness of the Ukrainian state and the persistence of corruption leave the country vulnerable to both domestic and international (Russian) sources of backsliding. A look to the west, at Poland and Hungary, shows how even states that appeared to have consolidated democracy can see it erode dramatically. In Ukraine, democracy is not so well consolidated. At the same time, the factors that make Ukraine so hard to govern effectively—its regional diversity, competition among oligarchs, the weakness of the state, and widespread corruption—also make it difficult to consolidate authoritarianism.

Study Questions

1. What roles do history and historical memory play in contemporary Ukrainian politics?
2. How are Ukraine's politics shaped by its location between Russia and the European Union?
3. How have efforts to build democracy shaped Ukraine's institutional design, and vice versa?
4. How do regional divisions in Ukraine shape its politics? How does regionalism in Ukraine compare to that in other countries?
5. In 2004 and again in 2014, street protests determined who would be president of Ukraine. What does that tell us about the prospects for consolidating democracy or authoritarianism?

Suggested Readings

D'Anieri, Paul. *Ukraine and Russia: From Civilized Divorce to Uncivil War.* New York: Cambridge University Press, 2019.

D'Anieri, Paul. *Understanding Ukrainian Politics: Power Politics and Institutional Design.* Armonk, NY: M. E. Sharpe, 2007.

Hale, Henry W., and Robert W. Orttung, eds. *Beyond the Euromaidan: Comparative Lessons of Reform for Ukraine.* Palo Alto, CA: Stanford University Press, 2016.

Havrylyshyn, Oleh. *The Political Economy of Independent Ukraine: Slow Starts, False Starts, and a Last Chance?* New York: Palgrave Macmillan, 2016.

Plokhy, Serhii. *The Gates of Europe: A History of Ukraine.* New York: Basic Books, 2017.

Notes

1. *Kyiv* is the transliteration of the Ukrainian name of the city, and we use it here. *Kiev* is the transliteration for the Russian spelling for the same city.

2. Kate Brown, *A Biography of No Place: From Ethnic Borderland to Soviet Heartland* (Cambridge, MA: Harvard University Press, 2006); two comprehensive and thick histories of Ukraine are Orest Subtelny, *Ukraine: A History* (Toronto: University of Toronto Press, 1988); and Paul Robert Magosci, *A History of Ukraine: The Land and Its Peoples* (Toronto: University of Toronto Press, 2010).

3. Andrew Wilson, *The Ukrainians: Unexpected Nation* (New Haven, CT: Yale University Press, 2000), 1–21; Serhii Plokhy, *Lost Kingdom: The Quest for Empire and the Making of the Russian Nation* (New York: Basic Books, 2017); Jaroslaw Pelenski, ed., *The Contest for the Legacy of Kievan Rus'* (Boulder, CO: East European Monographs, 1998).

4. Anne Appelbaum, *Red Famine: Stalin's War on Ukraine* (New York: Doubleday, 2017).

5. Yuliya Yurchuk, "Reclaiming the Past, Confronting the Past: OUN-UPA Memory Politics and Nation Building in Ukraine (1991–2016)," in *War and Memory in Russia, Ukraine and Belarus*, ed. Julie Fedor, Markku Kangaspuro, Jussi Lassila, and Tatiana Zhurzhenko, 107–40 (London: Palgrave Macmillan, 2017); Timothy Snyder, "A Fascist Hero in Democratic Kiev," *New York Review of Books*, February 24, 2010.

6. Serhii Plokhy, *Chernobyl: The History of a Nuclear Catastrophe* (New York: Basic Books, 2018); Svetlana Alexievich, *Voices from Chernobyl: The Oral History of a Nuclear Disaster* (New York: Picador, 2006).

7. This process is covered in Taras Kuzio and Andrew Wilson, *Ukraine: Perestroika to Independence* (Edmonton: Canadian Institute of Ukrainian Studies Press, 1994); and Bohdan Nahaylo, *The Ukrainian Resurgence* (Toronto: University of Toronto Press, 1999).

8. See Robert S. Kravchuk, *Ukrainian Political Economy: The First Ten Years* (New York: Palgrave Macmillan, 2002).

9. Serhiy Kudelia, "The Maidan and Beyond: The House That Yanukovych Built," *Journal of Democracy* 25, no. 3 (July 2014): 19–34.

10. On Ukraine's 2013–2014 revolution, see Marci Shore, *The Ukrainian Night: An Intimate History of Revolution* (New Haven, CT: Yale University Press, 2018); David Marples and Frederick V. Mills, eds., *Ukraine's Euromaidan: Analyses of a Civil Revolution* (Stuttgart: ibidem, 2015); David R. Marples, *Ukraine in Conflict: An Analytical Chronicle* (Bristol, UK: E-International Relations, 2017); and Andrew Wilson, *Ukraine Crisis: What It Means for the West* (New Haven, CT: Yale University Press, 2014).

11. The sources of the invasion of Crimea and the intervention in eastern Ukraine are examined in depth in Paul D'Anieri, *Ukraine and Russia: From Civilized Divorce to Uncivil War* (Cambridge: Cambridge University Press, 2019).

12. On memory politics in Ukraine, see Iryna Vushko, "Historians at War: History Politics and Memory in Ukraine," *Contemporary European History* 27, no. 1 (2018): 112–24.

13. Igor Torbakov, "Examining the Origins of Russians' Superiority Complex vis-à-vis Ukrainians: Why Does Ukraine Matter So Much in Imperial Thinking?," Eurasianet, May 26, 2020, https://eurasianet.org/perspectives-examining-the-origins-of-russians-superiority-complex-vis-a-vis-ukrainians.

14. Oxana Shevel, "Decommunization in Post-Euromaidan Ukraine: Law and Practice," PONARS Policy Memo 411, January 2016, http://www.ponarseurasia.org/memo/decommuniza tion-post-euromaidan-ukraine-law-and-practice.

15. Paul D'Anieri, *Understanding Ukrainian Politics: Power, Politics and Institutional Design* (Armonk, NY: M. E. Sharpe, 2006).

16. Henry E. Hale, *Patronal Politics: Eurasian Regime Dynamics in Comparative Perspective* (New York: Cambridge University Press, 2014).

17. Lucan Way, *Pluralism by Default: Weak Autocrats and the Rise of Competitive Politics* (Baltimore, MD: Johns Hopkins University Press, 2015).

18. The literature on these topics is massive. Good overviews and key articles include Lowell Barrington and Regina Faranda, "Reexamining Region, Ethnicity, and Language in Ukraine," *Post-Soviet Affairs* 25, no. 3 (2009): 232–56; Lowell W. Barrington, "Understanding Identity in Ukraine—and Elsewhere," *Post-Soviet Affairs* 34, nos. 2–3 (2018): 179–82; Timothy J. Colton, "An Aligning Election and the Ukrainian Political Community," *East European Politics and Societies* 25, no. 1 (2011): 4–27; Peter R. Craumer and James I. Clem. "Ukraine's Emerging Electoral Geography: A Regional Analysis of the 1998 Parliamentary Elections," *Post-Soviet Geography and Economics* 40 (1999): 1–26; and Olga Onuch, Henry E. Hale, and Gwendolyn Sasse, "Studying Identity in Ukraine," *Post-Soviet Affairs* 34, nos. 2–3 (2018): 79–83.

19. Volodymyr Kulyk, "National Identity in Ukraine: Impact of Euromaidan and the War," *Europe-Asia Studies* 68, no. 4 (2016): 588–608; Volodymyr Kulyk, "Shedding Russianness, Recasting Ukrainianness: The Post-Euromaidan Dynamics of Ethnonational Identifications in Ukraine," *Post-Soviet Affairs* 34, nos. 2–3 (2018): 119–38; Dominique Arel, "How Ukraine Has Become More Ukrainian," *Post-Soviet Affairs* 34, nos. 2–3 (2018): 186–89. See also the other articles in this special issue focusing on Ukrainian identity.

20. Paul D'Anieri, "Gerrymandering Ukraine? Electoral Consequences of Occupation," *East European Politics and Societies* 33, no. 1 (2019): 89–108.

21. Paul D'Anieri, "Explaining the Success and Failure of Post-Communist Revolutions," *Communist and Post-Communist Studies* 39, no. 3 (2006): 331–50.

22. On Ukraine's economy, see Oleh Havrylyshyn, *The Political Economy of Independent Ukraine: Slow Starts, False Starts, and a Last Chance?* (New York: Palgrave Macmillan, 2016).

23. Joel S. Hellman, "Winners Take All: The Politics of Partial Reform in Postcommunist Transitions," *World Politics* 50, no. 2 (January 1998): 203–34.

24. GINI index (World Bank estimate), https://data.worldbank.org/indicator/SI.POV.GINI ?most_recent_value_desc=false&view=map.

25. United Nations, Ukraine Migration Profiles, https://esa.un.org/miggmgprofiles/indicators/ files/Ukraine.pdf.

26. World Bank, "Personal Remittances, Received (% of GDP)—Ukraine," https://data.wo rldbank.org/indicator/BX.TRF.PWKR.DT.GD.ZS?locations=UA.

27. "Ukraine Urbanization Review," World Bank, 2015, 15–16, http://documents.worldbank.org/ curated/en/213551473856022449/pdf/ACS15060-REVISED-PUBLIC-eng-web-text-cover.pdf.

28. See "Ukraine's Ambitious Health Reform Now Hangs by a Thread," *Euromaidan Press*, May 28, 2020, http://euromaidanpress.com/2020/05/28/ukraines-health-reform-hangs-by-a-thr ead-impacted-by-ministerial-turnover.

29. "Gender Equality," United Nations Ukraine, http://www.un.org.ua/en/resident-coordin ator-system/gender-equality.

30. "The Holocaust in Ukraine," European Holocaust Research Infrastructure, https://training .ehri-project.eu/unit/3-holocaust-ukraine.

31. See Oxana Shevel, *Migration, Refugee Policy, and State Building in Postcommunist Europe* (New York: Cambridge University Press, 2011), 134–93.

32. Johns Hopkins Coronavirus Resource Center, Mortality Analysis, November 25, 2020, https://coronavirus.jhu.edu/data/mortality.

Part IV
CONCLUSION

CHAPTER 20

Changes and Challenges

THREE QUESTIONS

Zsuzsa Csergő, Daina S. Eglitis, and Paula M. Pickering

We began this text with a consideration of some of the paradoxes present in Central and East Europe today. As you have seen in the book, forces of democratic consolidation continue to make gains in some countries, while in others, democratic institutions are weakening and illiberalism is ascendant. The expansion of rights for those previously excluded from equal protections and opportunities, including women and ethnic and sexual minorities, continues in a small number of states in the region. These are important achievements even if the implementation of those rights can be uneven. Meanwhile, some of the early postcommunist adopters of democracy have sought to circumscribe or eliminate, among others, women's right to control their fertility and adoption rights for sexual minorities, or even single adults. The early post-1989 democratic euphoria that characterized the region has informed a lot of the scholarly work on Central and East Europe, which has been dedicated to tracing the "transition" from communism to democracy. However, as we have seen, this path has not been linear or homogeneous, and thirty years after the end of communism, the political shape of the future is uncertain.

The chapters of this book describe the complexities of politics in Central and East Europe—a region that has experienced some of the most challenging political and socio-economic transformations of the post–Cold War world. What lessons can we draw from these accounts, and what comes next in the politics of this fascinating region? In this final chapter, we offer an assessment through the lens of three related questions: Why does the past matter? What is the significance of nationalism today? And, finally, will democracy endure?

Why Does the Past Matter?

Legacies of the past are present in contemporary politics everywhere—in the endurance of institutions, the continuity of political actors (such as politicians or public officials who remain in positions of power after major regime change), and the historical references that actors use for justifying policy decisions and supporting a particular process of institution building. In Central and East Europe, among the most significant political legacies are those involving the creation of states and political institutions both before and after 1990 and those of early postcommunist politics on the diverse political trajectories that Central and East European states have followed in recent decades. This section of the chapter focuses on why these two aspects of the past remain consequential today.

External actors have been heavily involved in the creation of Central and East European states and political regimes. To understand the legacies of external influence, it is helpful to think of "state" and "regime" as complementary aspects of political organization, with the concept of "state" capturing the important spatial dimensions of government (its external territorial borders and internal administrative structuring and authority structure) and "regime" focusing on the political system in place within that structure (on the spectrum of democratic or authoritarian governments). From the age of empires through the states born in the wake of imperial collapse, external actors had a foundational role in both of these dimensions of political organization. State borders were drawn and redrawn in the context of great power politics at the end of three global wars (World War I, World War II, and the Cold War). The outcome was invariably a political map of some combination of ethnically diverse states that were not easily governed under the regime models imposed on or borrowed by dominant regional elites. The legacies of border shifts and reversals of ethnic fortunes are kept alive today in conflicts between the current states' "titular" majority and minority political organizations and in the politics of "divided nations"—which involves an abundance of kin-states and external minorities from the Baltics to the Balkans.[1]

The significance of external involvement on the contemporary political order was emphasized in chapter 2, where Kopstein provides an account of how political elites adopted political ideologies from the West and East, "domesticating" them in ways that could not resolve local issues but might cause significant political, economic, societal, and cultural damage (in the case of fascism and communism). Liberal democracy was also borrowed from the West and applied twice in Central and East Europe. The first effort was a failed attempt to create democratic states after World War I. The second was the postcommunist democratization of states in the region after 1990, which unfolded in the framework of the Europeanization process (described in chapter 9). This time, liberal democracy was adopted by democratically elected governments keen to satisfy the requirements of European Union (EU) membership, revising state constitutions and adopting legislation in accordance with European law. The chapters focused on countries have illustrated the achievements of this externally monitored democratization and marketization, as well as the problems, some unforeseen in the 1990s, that it caused in practice.

The developments described in the book also highlight the lasting impact of institutional legacies from the early postcommunist period. "Path dependence" is a concept commonly used to describe the way institutions created at a particular time (usually after major institutional change that creates a "critical juncture" in the course of a country's political development) sets a country on a particular trajectory that becomes difficult to change until another critical juncture occurs. The term "critical juncture" highlights the pathbreaking significance of major events, or a series of events, that create an opportunity for a fundamental shift in the existing rules of political organization, enabling actors to set up a new institutional framework.[2] A critical juncture can involve a revolution or a coup, but it can also occur peacefully. The actions of political elites in power during such a time have long-lasting consequences. Comparative evidence shows that elites in such a situation opt for an institutional structure most favorable to themselves.[3] The collapse of communism and the creation of new states and regimes in Central and East Europe is commonly considered a major critical juncture in institutional development. Yet there was significant variation across the region in the extent to which early postcommunist governments broke away from communist politics.

Where new states were created or precommunist states were recreated from dismembered ethnofederations, the mode of state collapse and state creation—whether it was peaceful or violent, and whether it was accepted by the former state center from which secession occurred—left lasting legacies for the ability of societies to create and sustain democratic government. The "Velvet Divorce" of Czechoslovakia enabled the Czech Republic and Slovakia to build independent institutions right away, democratize, and join the EU in 2004. Among post-Soviet states, the three Baltic countries were also relatively quickly enabled not only to recreate pre-Soviet states but also to join NATO and the EU in the first wave of Central and East European accessions. By contrast, the Russian state has been reluctant to allow Ukraine to choose its own path. Both state sovereignty and democracy remain weak there. The successor states of the former Yugoslavia had an even harder time, despite some significant pre-1990 advantages (not having been part of the Soviet bloc). In the aftermath of violent state collapse, democratization was derailed and EU membership was delayed, with only the exception of Slovenia (for reasons explained in chapter 18).

Arguably even more consequential are the legacies of "founding elections" that brought to power (or left in power) those who made key decisions about constitutions, electoral systems, and regional alignments (with Western democracies or Russia) and laid down some lasting patterns of political competition.[4] Where former communist elites remained dominant, in most cases they hindered the political and economic restructuring necessary for democratization and marketization. In the chapter on Ukraine (chapter 19), a country where democratic consolidation remains a challenge, D'Anieri points out that the path for weak democracy and continued Russian involvement was set in the early 1990s. The same parliament remained in place from pre-independence until 1994, when elections were held according to preexisting (Soviet) rules, and only piecemeal changes were made to the 1997 Soviet constitution. Elite continuity delayed democratization as well as EU membership in Romania (where former communists remained dominant until 1996) and Bulgaria (with elite continuity until 1997).

The founding elections also left a lasting impact in Estonia and Latvia, where large Russophone minority populations were excluded from citizenship and democratic participation. The overwhelming majority of Russophones, including those born in Estonia and Latvia, were excluded in these countries from voting for the political elites who established the structure of institutions and political competition. In Latvia, disenfranchisement occurred at all levels of government. In Estonia, noncitizen residents gained voting rights in local elections after 1993, though they could not run for office. Naturalization laws were changed slowly in piecemeal amendments achieved through divisive parliamentary battles.[5] These processes have significantly shaped the patterns of political organization among Russophones and their ability to influence decision making about minority policy in the state center.[6]

Similarly impactful are the legacies of post-1990 economic restructuring. In chapter 5, Fisher describes the magnitude of the structural changes regional economies underwent in the early 1990s. In the economic domain, postcommunist transformation was unique, different from all other examples of democratization (in Southern Europe, Latin America, and elsewhere). Only in this region did regime change involve such a fundamental reorganization of economic life. State-owned and planned economies were transformed into market economies, and the region opened up to the global market. The freedoms provided by capitalist democracy also introduced uncertainty (potential unemployment, loss of savings, deficits of affordable or subsidized housing, etc.) for people accustomed to economic safety and predictability (albeit under tightly controlled conditions). Where the conditions were favorable and governments chose policies that more effectively broke away from heavy state intervention into the economy, economies overall did better. Examples of this are the Czech Republic, Hungary, and Poland. In the post-Soviet Baltic countries, conditions were less favorable and the shift was more drastic, but there was unity and passion behind the need to shift at any cost, which made the process more successful. The Baltic states rebounded relatively quickly and have done well economically in regional comparison.

Government policies mattered. Those who implemented the "shock therapy" approach to macroeconomic stabilization, for instance, bounced back earlier and did better in the medium term. Where transitional political elites were not sufficiently committed to deep changes and Western support was weak, the transformation to capitalism was not only more difficult but also less successful in improving the lives of large segments of the population. Glaring economic inequalities and the widespread perception of insufficient opportunities for mobility have had significant political consequences. The out-migration of large numbers of young and educated people to economically stronger European democracies (discussed in chapter 6 on demography and migration) is an important indication of these failures. Right-wing populists have exploited these emotions to pursue power and, when they achieved it, to hold on to it.

The legacy of early postcommunist economic restructuring also lives on in the networks and politics of clientelism and corruption today. Although these informal practices existed during communism, postcommunist restructuring provided unprecedented opportunities for their strengthening. Where the economic institutions of the communist-controlled regimes broke down but were not replaced by well-functioning new institutions, the weakness of formal institutions enabled the strengthening of informal networks, such as the patronal networks described in D'Anieri's chapter on Ukraine. Multiple "pyramids" of patronage, where political and economic goals are pursued through the personal exchange of rewards and punishments, became predominant in Ukraine during the early postcommunist period, and it contributes to the weakness of the state today. In other countries, too, regardless of how privatization and marketization unfolded, people in power or close to power and those whose interests they served were more likely to become long-term winners of economic transformation. Those outside of the circle of power were more likely to be hit by the loss of jobs and savings, as well as other consequences of regional and global financial crises.

Thus, there are strong reasons for the emergence of the anticorruption theme as a major instrument of political mobilization in several countries of Central and East Europe. Those in political power or close to it benefited greatly, not only from privatization projects, but also from the distribution of EU restructuring funds (which were disbursed through state governments). The political class in many of these countries was transformed into the newly rich class, and the free press made it possible for ordinary people to get a glimpse into the increasing gap between those included in ruling political camps and those outside of them. In states where governments were weak and unable to provide for many basic needs of ordinary people (such as roads, school renovations, and decent health-care facilities), political corruption and the inequalities it created became even more conspicuous. EU monitors identified corruption as a major issue in Bulgaria and Romania, demanding that those governments implement anticorruption projects. Charges of political corruption became a shorthand for expressing popular discontent with governments; anticorruption protests have become a regular occurrence in Bulgaria and Romania. Along the way, the politics of corruption has also become an effective instrument for domestic political competition; prosecution for corruption has been used widely to eliminate political opponents and create a façade of governmental accountability.

Corruption has also become a major theme in Hungarian politics since EU accession. In chapter 13, Arghentieri and Vangelov discussed how Fidesz, after losing the 2006 elections, used the corruption discourse effectively to mobilize a large segment of Hungarian voters against the reelected Gyurcsány regime. Winning a parliamentary supermajority in 2010, the Fidesz government continued to rely on this corruption charge as an incumbent, blaming the previous government for any weaknesses of the Hungarian economy more than a decade after Fidesz built an unprecedented degree of control over Hungary's institutions. Anticorruption politics also strengthened elsewhere in the region, including countries that did comparatively well in democracy and economic welfare indices, such as Slovakia. In chapter 12, Wolchik explained how a new political party—the Ordinary People and Independent Personalities party (OL'aNO)—formed around the anticorruption message defeated established parties in the 2020 elections and formed a coalition government led by political "outsiders." Unlike Fidesz's victory in Hungary, Slovakia's OL'aNO victory has raised hopes that it could offer an alternative to democratic backsliding.

The surprise outcome of the 2020 Slovak elections also illustrates the massive challenge that political actors face in building party systems populated by parties capable of aggregating citizens' interests into coherent policies. This goes against the expectations of increasingly "consolidated" party systems after thirty years of democratic competition, and it reveals the depth of discontent with the "fruits" of the regimes constructed after 1990. In chapter 4, Deegan-Krause depicts significant volatility, with seemingly established parties disappearing and new parties competing in nearly every election in every country. Many parties are centered on personalities rather than ideologies—or even developed platforms—and instead of offering clear alternatives to voters, they often act as vehicles for leaders to build personal power and wealth. The result is an ongoing lack of connection between parties and citizens, with about 61 percent of respondents in a nationally representative survey of seven Central and East European countries in 2018 not affiliating with any party.[7] Those unaffiliated are susceptible to protest voting and populist appeals, which are amplified by social media.

The past in Central and East Europe is ever present in regional politics. The legacies of empires, wars, interwar independence, fascism, communism, and early postcommunism loom over political institutions and practices even today. While this book highlights contemporary politics, its contributors have also sought to provide robust historical accounts to show how the past shapes the present.

What Is the Significance of Nationalism Today?

The theme of nationalism permeates this text. As we wrap up our journey through the political history and contemporary politics of Central and East Europe, we return to this theme with the following questions: Where do we continue to see the manifestations of nationalism? What are the consequences of persisting nationalism for democratic governance in the region?

First, nationalism remains visible and powerful in the politics of the region. A defining characteristic of nationalist politics is the position that the boundaries of a national community should align with claimed territorial boundaries that the representatives of that community govern and control. A democratically governed "nation-state" is seen as an ideal model for achieving this goal. As discussed in chapter 3, however, the *ethnic* understanding of nationhood is predominant in the multiethnic states of Central and East Europe. Consequently, a key tension of the three decades following the end of communism has been the effort in many countries to build civically oriented democratic institutions and practices while still cultivating ethnocentric politics.

Nationalist strategies in politics have functioned as an instrument for political elites to cling to power. In states with large ethnic minorities, this has created major obstacles to minority integration. In Latvia, for instance, early electoral politics enabled some politicians and parties to maintain a hold on legislative power based on their claim to protect majority ethnonational interest—and they used anti-Russian sentiment to remain a preferable alternative to parties that embraced more liberal notions about Russian minority integration. The quality of parties and platforms was secondary to their commitment to maintain exclusionary politics.

In 1990s Serbia and Croatia, nationalist strategies that politicians used to cement their political power were extended beyond electoral rhetoric and domestic policy making into the use of violence, ostensibly to "protect" their nation regardless of the territorial boundaries of new states that emerged from the collapse of Yugoslavia. As an illustration of the continued salience of traditional nationalism, the ruling nationalist party in what is now North Macedonia between 2010 and 2018 used exclusive rhetoric and policies to bolster and extend their hold on power, leading the country out of democracy and into a hybrid regime. Common to these nationalist strategies are demonization of and efforts to politically marginalize not just those who are members of the "other" group or groups but also those *within* one's ethnonational group who oppose those strategies.

Significantly, in some countries, political elites have maintained their power by melding ethnic nationalism with populism in a mix of xenophobic and intolerant practices and policies. Populism emphasizes the sweeping rejection of elites on behalf of "virtuous" ordinary people.[8] Ironically, in Central and East Europe this discourse is most successfully employed by incumbent elites. Contemporary Hungary and Poland showcase acute manifestations of nationalist politics that have paved the path to illiberal governments, enabling democratic backsliding justified as a means to ensure the survival of the core nation. Paradoxically, while nationalism was a powerful force driving the effort of regional states trapped under oppressive communist regimes to seek independence, autonomy, and democracy in the 1980s, nationalism in the twenty-first century has propelled some of the most dramatic erosion of democratic practices and institutions.

Second, as we have seen in this chapter, memory politics are a significant factor in both political life and social group relations. Chapter 7, which focuses on transitional justice and memory, explores the shape and significance of this phenomenon and highlights an important point: collective narratives of history are not just stories of the past—they are also stories that legitimate claims by different ethnic groups in the region to power, territory, and status as victors or victims. In some countries, including the Baltic states and Ukraine, the roles of heroes, villains, and victims vary significantly depending on the way the story of the past—particularly the events of World War II and the Holocaust—is told. In the Baltics, for instance, the Soviet and post-Soviet (and Russian) narrative of the Second World War's end is one that is founded on the claim that the Soviet Red Army "liberated" the Baltics from Nazi occupation. The indigenous Baltic narrative is that the end of the war saw the "reoccupation" of the Baltics, as Nazi occupation was replaced by Soviet occupation, which remained in place for half a century, until 1991. In a sense, both stories of the past have factual roots, but the politics of memory are less about historical precision than about contemporary claims regarding belonging, rights, and legitimacy.

Memory politics can have an effect on international and domestic relations between groups: dramatically different renderings of the past have had an imprint on contemporary relations between, for instance, Russia and several countries of the region, including the Baltics, Ukraine, and Poland. Poland's so-called memory laws have created tensions with Western states as well: in an effort to untether itself from responsibility for the mass atrocities of the Holocaust, in 2018 Poland's legislature approved a bill that foresaw up to three years of imprisonment for "whoever accuses, publicly and against the facts, the Polish nation, or the Polish state, of being responsible or complicit in the Nazi crimes committed by the German Third Reich . . . or any other war crimes, crimes against humanity or crimes against peace."[9] While it is true that death camps like Auschwitz-Birkenau and Treblinka were German established and Poland itself was occupied by Nazi Germany, it is also true that some Poles were complicit in compromising and killing their Jewish neighbors during and even in the aftermath of the Holocaust.[10] While Poland did not implement the law due to an international outcry from allies, the effort to "legislate" history is a powerful potential tool in the arsenal of nationalist politicians.

The politics of memory can influence territorial claims, as they have done in Ukraine. They can also be catalysts for conflict—again, Ukraine is a recent example, as is the former Yugoslavia, where claims made by powerful leaders of ethnic collectivities like the Serbs about their historical dominion fostered the violence of the Balkan wars of the 1990s and continue to create tensions over space and power.

Significantly, in much of the region, the contested past focuses on the middle twentieth century and World War II in particular. With the passing of generations and the rise of younger generations of politicians with little immediate connection to the World War II past—or even the communist past—it is possible that the most acute manifestations of memory politics will fade. As well, the more global orientation and experiences of younger generations, especially those enabled by European Union membership to travel, study, and work outside of their own national territories, may contribute to building "Europeanness" that rejects narrow nationalist appeals in politics. At the same time, these globally mobile young students and workers may be creating new issues that invite the consternation of nationalists who reject European institutions and mandates, multiculturalism, and migration.

Third, nationalism is closely tied to the politics and policies that relate to demography and migration. As we saw in chapter 6, which discusses these topics, below replacement-rate fertility and population loss due to emigration have eroded population numbers in many countries, exacerbating existential fears about the survival of ethnic communities and countries. In Poland and Hungary, this has spurred legislation that amalgamates incentives, such as child payments and tax reductions, with coercive measures, including near bans on access to abortion, even in extreme cases like rape. In other countries, such as Latvia and Estonia, pro-natalist practices have been limited thus far to enticements like lengthy parental leaves and child welfare supports. Evidence on the success of these practices and policies for fostering the rise of family size is unclear, but there is little reason to believe that a reversal of population decline is imminent. On the other hand, there is growing evidence that the continuing fall in population size nurtures nationalist fears, which can translate into illiberal practices like limitations on rights of citizens, rejection of refugees seeking shelter in European states, and a conservative embrace of socially acceptable gender roles that circumscribe women's opportunities to control their own bodies and futures.

Will Democracy Endure?

Political scientists are notoriously bad at making predictions. That said, making sense of past evidence to understand the conditions under which a phenomenon of interest—in this instance, democracy—strengthens, endures, or weakens may help to anticipate possible future developments. To tackle this question, we need to reiterate what we mean by democracy. In chapter 1, we distinguished between different types of democracy: electoral and liberal democracy. *Electoral democracy* focuses on the procedural aspects of democratic government, emphasizing citizens' choice of government based on competitive, regular, free, and fair elections. *Liberal democracy* builds on electoral democracy to emphasize the importance of protecting individual and minority rights against the tyranny of the state and the tyranny of the majority. It does so by constitutionally protecting civil liberties, strong rule of law, an independent judiciary, and effective checks and balances that together limit the exercise of executive power.[11] The EU, which all the countries in this text have either voluntarily joined or aspire to join, requires adherence to liberal democratic principles and institutions. Nonetheless, as Csergő and Wittenberg (chapter 3) show, some Central and East European leaders and their supporters do not view liberal democracy as the only "game in town."

As the book's contributors have shown, all of the countries analyzed have developed more open political systems than those they experienced under communist rule. That

said, the transformation from one-party rule has been challenging, has produced varying levels of openness, and has not been a unilinear process culminating in consolidated
liberal democracy. In those countries where minimally reformed communist parties won
the first multiparty elections (Romania, Bulgaria, Serbia, Albania, and Ukraine), leaders implemented hybrid regimes that combined democratic and authoritarian elements
of rule. Over time, pro-democratic forces in these countries strengthened and aligned
with regional forces supporting democracy, particularly the EU, to democratize. What is
now North Macedonia initially transitioned toward a hybrid regime, developed electoral
democracy, slid back into a hybrid regime between 2010 and 2018, but is now inching
toward electoral democracy. In the clearest example of the erosion of democracy in the
region, Hungary after 2010 began a steep backslide, from what observers had considered a stable liberal democracy into a hybrid regime. Hungary has strikingly illustrated
that concerted policies implemented by elected parties and their leaders who question
democratic institutions that could restrain them can indeed derail democracy. Historian
Timothy Garton Ash argued on the thirtieth anniversary of the fall of the Berlin Wall
that the achievements of postcommunist governments in the first two decades outweigh
the "gathering crisis" the majority of these countries have faced in the 2010s.[12] Whether
this assessment holds up in the future depends significantly on how Central and East
European politicians, institutions, and communities respond to current challenges, which
are often the complex product of domestic, regional, and global forces.

Among significant challenges, the transformation from a state-controlled to market
economy opened opportunities for growth and prosperity, as well as corruption and a
steep rise in inequality. Some argue that the hegemony of the liberal democratic model
promoted by the EU has also resulted in inequality of respect between Western Europe
and Central and East European governments, as well as within societies (between those
who feel they have benefited and those who feel they have lost from reforms).[13] Evidence
suggests that postcommunist politicians too often have viewed parties as vehicles for
self-interest rather than as democratic vehicles to aggregate citizens' interests and have
approached government as a resource to capture rather than as an institution to be used to
protect democratic rights and develop policies to meaningfully address citizens' problems.
Liberal democratic elites have often failed to acknowledge their failures and shortcomings
in governing, particularly in listening to concerns of those who feel left out, in addressing inequalities, in learning from mistakes, and in developing bold policies to build the
foundation for a better future for all citizens. Csergő and Wittenberg (chapter 3) describe
the confluence of forces rocking liberal democracy in the region as (1) the loss of EU
interest in and ability to significantly sanction undemocratic behavior post-accession, (2)
the 2008 financial crisis that shook confidence in liberal democracy and the market, and
(3) a migrant and refugee crisis that threatened to bring thousands of "others" into their
countries. The challenges to democracy are not unique to the region, even if some take on
postcommunist characteristics stemming from the unprecedented simultaneous political
and economic transformation.

To help us assess the capacity of Central and East European leaders and populations
to address these challenges, we turn to studies of factors that contribute to and undermine
the development of democracy, as well as recent developments in the region. A combination of domestic and regional forces *contributed to democracy* after the fall of one-party

rule. These include, most importantly, the discrediting of one-party rule and the interest of key political elites and citizens in developing democratic practices and institutions, as well as the concrete support for democratic transformation provided by the EU and other Euro-Atlantic institutions.

Turning to factors that explain the *breakdown of democracy*, several studies emphasize the role played by elites. Political scientist Nancy Bermeo has demonstrated how domestic political or military elites, rather than citizens, played the most significant role in the breakdown of democracies in Europe during the interwar period.[14] A global study of the decline of democracies attributes primary responsibility to antidemocratic political elites, particularly political parties, while also noting that citizens' responses to appeals by demagogues or extremist parties may also be significant in weakening democratic norms, practices, or institutions.[15]

In recent years, illiberal political elites in the region have exploited popular frustration with public corruption, enduring gaps between elites and citizens, economic inequality and insecurity, and contested notions of national identity. Emphasizing these frustrations, illiberal leaders have used elections to gain political power and to challenge the hegemony of the postcommunist liberal state, which they argue has weakened national identity and thwarted the popular will. The front-runners in this process have been Fidesz in Hungary (since 2010) and Law and Justice in Poland (since 2015). These parties have strategically used emotion, including a politics of resentment,[16] to mobilize citizens who feel they have been left behind by postcommunist politics and economies, including those with less education, those who suffer from economic precarity, and those who hail from rural areas and small cities. They advocate politics that are culturally "right" (ethnic nationalism and social conservativism) but economically "left" (state intervention into the economy and increased social services) and appeal to those who feel marginalized. The continued volatility of parties, the outsized role played by personalities rather than programs, the sizable portion of citizens unattached to any party, and social media create opportunities for new or remade parties to obtain power with vague rhetoric promising to "clean up" corruption and restore stability. Rather than doing what political scientists Steven Levitsky and Daniel Zieblatt argue pro-democratic parties should do—that is, refuse to ally with extremists[17]—democratic parties such as those in Bulgaria, Slovakia, and Latvia have at times brought far-right parties into their coalition governments (Ataka, the Slovak National Party, and Latvia's First Party, respectively). In addition, parties have often failed to root out extremists within their ranks.

Political developments in the last decade suggest that the danger to democracy in Central and East Europe is not a full-scale assault on democracy. Instead it is illiberal politicians' use of certain elements of democracy, particularly elections, to get into office and then concertedly pursue policies, often through legal means, that undermine the checks and balances that prevent the tyranny of the majority and protect individual rights.[18]

While Hungary's government under Prime Minister Viktor Orbán rewrote Hungary's constitution and adopted other laws that dramatically attacked democracy, more often illiberal politicians (like those in Bulgaria and much of the former Yugoslavia) have taken incremental steps to weaken institutions that could check their power, particularly the judiciary, which they argue interfere with the popular will.[19] The relative immaturity of democratic institutions, the endurance of informal power that exacerbates a gap between the power of these institutions on paper and in practice, and the relatively brief period of citizens' experiences living under democratic institutions all make these institutions vulnerable to manipulation by self-interested politicians.

According to comparative research explaining the end of hybrid rule, such as the government of Serbia's Milošević in the 1990s[20] and globally,[21] a serious challenge to Fidesz's hybrid rule will require democratic political forces in favor of democracy to overcome their differences and their fragmentation to present a united democratic slate. In fact, six Hungarian opposition parties announced in December 2020 a formal agreement to coordinate in the 2022 elections on a joint candidate to oppose Fidesz in each of Hungary's electoral districts and to run on a single electoral list with a common platform.[22] Coordinating among parties with disparate goals, however, will be no easy feat.

The values and actions of ordinary people will help determine their reactions to such steps, whether democracy endures, and how governance functions. A poll on the thirtieth anniversary of the fall of the Berlin Wall of six Central and East European countries indicated that a vast majority of respondents approve of the changes to a multiparty system. However, the early postcommunist period failed to meet citizens' high expectations of bringing about a better life. Illustrating a sense of injustice, respondents from the same survey overwhelmingly believed that politicians and businesspeople benefited far more than ordinary people from the changes since the end of communism.[23] In ranking the importance of particular institutions and rights for their country, respondents in those six countries prioritized a fair judiciary, while least often considering free opposition parties or free civil society as very important. While these findings point to robust support for the rule of law, citizens frustrated with the pace and responsiveness of the democratic policy-making process can lend support to illiberal leaders who promise to "get things done."

Only in a few Central and East European countries (three out of twelve) did a majority of respondents in a 2017 poll agree that "democracy is preferable to any other kind of government" (see table 9.5 in the European Union chapter). The percentage expressing the view that in some circumstances a nondemocratic government can be preferable was just over a quarter. A strong minority indicated indifference about their country's system of governance. As Linden warns in chapter 9, those expressing indifference are susceptible to appeals by leaders who offer simple solutions and encourage voters to blame "others" for their problems, including their (understandable) dissatisfaction with the way that democracy is working and their concerns about insecurity, inequality, poverty, and isolation from power.[24] Political scientists Foa and Mounk argue that a sizable minority of citizens' loss in the belief in democratic values, attraction to authoritarian alternatives, and votes for parties that flout or reject constitutive elements of liberal democracy are signs that even liberal democracies can be "deconsolidated."[25] Increasing Central and East European citizens' faith in democratic institutions will require reform, more effective and responsive democratic policy making, and education about the value, however imperfect, of democratic institutions and norms.

What political scientist Michael Bernhard calls firewall civil society has stepped up at critical times to play an important role in defeating leaders of hybrid regimes or would-be autocrats.[26] In the electoral revolution model, in which Slovakia was an innovator, civil society initiated massive "get out the vote" and vote monitoring campaigns in 1997 in a successful effort to encourage citizens to vote out then–prime minister Mečiar's party, which was halting Slovakia's accession into the EU. About two decades later, Slovakia's civil society stepped in again, when social movements helped compel the resignation of Prime Minister Fico in 2018 after the murder of a journalist investigating the government's ties to organized crime, a move that opened space for the election in 2019 and 2020 of anticorruption politicians and parties (see chapter 12). And in 2017, social movement protests in North Macedonia allied with formal civil society organizations, a relatively strong opposition party, and the EU to bring down the incumbent party that had fostered backsliding to a hybrid regime.[27] This combination of democratic forces is far more difficult to assemble in contexts where pro-democratic parties are weaker, civil society organizations are polarized, and the EU is viewed less positively, such as Serbia. In addition, assessments of the relationship between civil society and democracy need to take seriously the elements of civil society that have allied with and been strengthened by illiberal parties, for example in Hungary and Poland.

Finally, regional forces will influence whether democracy survives. Organizations promoting democracy, particularly the EU, are weaker now than they were in the 1990s and 2000s. At the same time, Russia, China, and Turkey have stepped up to extend their influence in the region and sow distrust in democracy. For several countries, particularly Bosnia-Herzegovina, Kosovo, and Ukraine, whose independence has been violently contested by stronger neighbors, sustainable democracy and peace will be determined and shaped by domestic and neighboring actors, as well as European and Euro-Atlantic organizations. To strengthen its ability to bolster democracy in Central and East Europe, the EU will need to do a variety of things: develop policies that better address regional challenges that nondemocratic actors have exploited, including economic inequalities and the mass influx of asylum seekers and refugees; sanction member states that violate EU law; and more effectively empower pro-democratic forces in those countries still at various stages of the EU accession process.

Deegan-Krause argues in chapter 4 that strong civil society actors stepping up to support democracy and robust party competition are probably the best hope for democracy, even if they are not enough to prevent the return of autocracy. The endurance and functioning of democracy require citizens and their elected leaders to actively work to protect it, address its shortcomings, and deepen it. The American civil rights icon John Lewis wrote, "Democracy is not a state. It is an act."[28] Given the region's historical legacies, current political contexts, and the widespread endurance of socially conservative values, the outlook for liberal democracy in some parts of Central and East Europe is not bright. This includes countries that were front-runners in establishing postcommunist democracies, as well as those that were laggards. That said, illiberal rulers have not provided answers to many of the region's most significant challenges, particularly rooting out corruption and generating broad-based growth. Furthermore, the practices of hybrid regimes, particularly their continued commitment to contested elections, make them unstable and vulnerable to challenge.[29]

The prospects for the endurance of electoral democracy in most of the region are promising. There is great potential for Central and East European political leaders and communities to innovate in making reforms needed to shore up democratic institutions and practices. For example, the Baltic states have been in the forefront of tackling disinformation designed to undermine their liberal democracies, and Estonia has been a pioneer in increasing government openness. To gain more support, liberal democratic politicians will need to offer a compelling, positive vision for the future and effectively use logic *and* emotion to communicate it to a broader constituency.[30] Innovative reform and policy making will require the engagement of youth in the region, which depends on stemming their emigration west. The challenge for people in Central and East Europe is to build more broadly legitimate forms of democracy that can garner trust, build inter-ethnic solidarity while also accommodating nation-building aspirations, strengthen civil society and institutional checks that can help to hold governments accountable, and foster broader-based economic development.

Notes

1. Myra Waterbury, "Populist Nationalism and the Challenges of Divided Nationhood: The Politics of Migration, Mobility, and Demography in Post-2010 Hungary," *East European Politics and Societies* 34, no. 4 (2020): 962–83.

2. Paul Pierson, "Increasing Returns, Path Dependence, and the Study of Politics," *American Political Science Review* 94, no. 2 (2000): 251–67.

3. Kathleen Thelen, *How Institutions Evolve: The Political Economy of Skills in Germany, Britain, the United States, and Japan* (Cambridge: Cambridge University Press, 2004).

4. Valerie Bunce, "The Political Economy of Postsocialism," *Slavic Review* 58 (Winter 1999): 756–93.

5. Jennie L. Schulze, *Strategic Frames: Europe, Russia, and Minority Inclusion in Estonia and Latvia* (Pittsburgh, PA: University of Pittsburgh Press, 2018).

6. Zsuzsa Csergő and Ada-Charlotte Regelmann, "Europeanization and Collective Rationality in Minority Voting: Lessons from Central and Eastern Europe," *Problems of Post-Communism* 64, no. 5 (2017): 291–310.

7. European Social Survey Round 9 Data, 2018, data file edition 2.0. NSD—Norwegian Centre for Research Data, Norway—Data Archive and distributor of ESS data for ESS ERIC, https://doi.org/10.21338/NSD-ESS9-2018. CEE countries included were Bulgaria, the Czech Republic, Estonia, Hungary, Poland, Serbia, and Slovenia.

8. Cas Mudde and Cristobal Rovira Kaltwasser, *Populism: A Very Short Introduction* (Oxford: Oxford University Press, 2017).

9. "What's in Poland's New Memory Law?," *Economist*, February 19, 2018, https://www.economist.com/the-economist-explains/2018/02/19/whats-in-polands-new-memory-law.

10. Jan Gross, *Neighbors: The Destruction of the Jewish Community in Jedwabne, Poland* (Princeton, NJ: Princeton University Press, 2012).

11. These definitions of electoral and liberal democracy are based on the Varieties of Democracy Project, https://www.v-dem.net/en.

12. Timothy Garton Ash, "Time for a New Liberation?," *New York Review of Books*, October 24, 2019, 1–14.

13. Ash, "Time for a New Liberation?"; Ivan Krastev and Stephen Holmes, "Imitation and Its Discontents," *Journal of Democracy* 29, no. 3 (2018): 117–28.

14. Nancy Bermeo, *Ordinary People in Extraordinary Times: The Citizenry and the Breakdown of Democracy* (Princeton, NJ: Princeton University Press, 2003).

15. Steven Levitsky and Daniel Ziblatt, *How Democracies Die* (New York: Crown, 2018), 20.

16. In the US context, see Katherine J. Cramer, *The Politics of Resentment: Rural Consciousness in Wisconsin and the Rise of Scott Walker* (Chicago: University of Chicago Press 2016). In the Central

and East European context, see Jarosław Kuisz and Karolina Wigura, "The Pushback against Populism: Reclaiming the Politics of Emotion," *Journal of Democracy* 31, no. 2 (2020): 41–53.

17. Levitsky and Ziblatt, *How Democracies Die*, 26.

18. Nancy Bermeo, "On Democratic Backsliding," *Journal of Democracy* 27, no. 1 (2016): 5–19; Levitsky and Ziblatt, *How Democracies Die*.

19. Venelin I. Ganev, "'Soft Decisionism' in Bulgaria," *Journal of Democracy* 29, no. 3 (2018): 91–103; Damir Kapidžić, "The Rise of Illiberal Politics in Southeastern Europe," *Southeast European and Black Sea Studies* 20, no. 1 (2020): 1–17. Even incremental steps to undermine democracy can be dangerous as they often fly below the radar but accumulate.

20. Valerie Bunce and Sharon Wolchik, *Defeating Authoritarian Leaders in Postcommunist Countries* (Cambridge: Cambridge University Press, 2011).

21. Marc Morjé Howard and Philip Roessler, "Liberalizing Electoral Outcomes in Competitive Authoritarian Regimes," *American Journal of Political Science* 50, no. 2 (2006): 365–381.

22. Justin Spike, "6 Hungarian Parties Join Forces to Defeat Orban," Associated Press, December 21, 2020, https://apnews.com/article/primary-elections-viktor-orban-national-elections-elections-hungary-232b2bf2eadaf8dbc8f4eda28accc347.

23. The gap between perceived benefits accrued by politicians and those accrued by ordinary citizens ranged from 77 percent in Bulgaria to 21 percent in Poland. "European Public Opinion Three Decades after the Fall of Communism," Pew Research Center, October 2019, 17.

24. Anna Grzymala-Busse, "Global Populisms and Their Impact," *Slavic Review Online Forum*, no. 1 (2017): S1–2; Richard Youngs, ed., *The Mobilization of Conservative Civil Society* (New York: Carnegie Endowment for International Peace, 2018).

25. Roberto Stefan Foa and Yascha Mounk, "The Signs of Deconsolidation," *Journal of Democracy* (January 2017): 5–15.

26. Michel Bernhard, "What Do We Know about Civil Society and Regime Change Thirty Years after 1989?," *East European Politics* 36, no. 3 (2020): 1–22. Firewall civil society refers to the potential role of civil society as the last layer of accountability when antidemocratic political actors have undermined accountability mechanisms of elections and separation of powers.

27. Gazela Pudar Draško, Irena Fiket, and Jelena Vasiljević, "Big Dreams and Small Steps: Comparative Perspectives on Social Movements' Struggle for Democracy in Serbia and North Macedonia," *Southeast European and Black Sea Studies* 20, no. 1 (2020): 199–219.

28. John Lewis, "Together, You Can Redeem the Soul of Our Nation," *New York Times*, July 30, 2020.

29. Steven Levitsky and Lucan Way, *Competitive Authoritarianism: Hybrid Regimes after the Cold War* (Cambridge: Cambridge University Press, 2010).

30. Kuis and Wigura, "The Pushback against Populism," 52.

Index

Page references for figures, maps, photos, and tables are italicized.

About the Contributors

Federigo Argentieri teaches political science and international affairs at John Cabot University in Rome, Italy, and is the director of the Guarini Institute for Public Affairs. He holds degrees from the Universities of Rome (La Sapienza) and Budapest-ELTE (PhD) and attended the Harvard Ukrainian Summer Institute. He has widely published on the contemporary history and politics of Central-Eastern Europe and Italy, particularly on the Hungarian Revolution of 1956 and its Western echoes and effects, as well as on Ukraine. He teaches courses on international security and comparative politics of Europe, Latin America, and developing countries and regularly contributes to Italy's main newspaper *Corriere della Sera* and to other Italian and international media. His most recent publications include a chapter on Hungary and Suez in the book *Calendario civile europeo*, edited by Angelo Bolaffi and Guido Crainz (2019), and an article on Agnes Heller, "Metti una sera a cena nella Budapest del dopo Ottantanove," in the journal *Testimonianze* (2020).

Margarita Assenova is a senior fellow at the Jamestown Foundation in Washington, DC. She is a regular contributor to its flagship publication, *Eurasia Daily Monitor*, covering security, politics, and energy. Since 2006, she has taught area studies courses on the Balkans, the Caucasus, and Central Asia at the Foreign Service Institute, US Department of State. Assenova is a recipient of the John Knight Professional Journalism Fellowship at Stanford University for her reporting on nationalism in the Balkans. She has authored book chapters and reports published by CSIS Press, Brassey's, Freedom House, Bertelsmann Foundation Publishers, CEPA, and the Jamestown Foundation. Her recent books include *Eurasian Disunion: Russia's Vulnerable Flanks* (with Janusz Bugajski) (2016), a critical study on Russian subversion in Europe, Eurasia, and Central Asia, and *Azerbaijan and the New Energy Geopolitics of Southeastern Europe* (editor, 2015). Her reports "Nord Stream 2: Myths, Reality, and the Way Forward" (2018) and "Bulgaria's Ambitions for a Balkan Gas Hub" (2018) exposed Russian energy ambitions in Europe.

Daunis Auers (PhD, University College London) is associate professor of comparative politics at the University of Latvia, director of the Certus think tank, and president of the Association for the Advancement of Baltic Studies (AABS) between 2020 and 2022. He has been a Fulbright Scholar at the University of California–Berkeley (2005–2006) and a Baltic-American Freedom Foundation Scholar at Wayne State University in Detroit (2014). He has published widely on Europeanization, political parties, elections, and referenda, as well as on populism and the radical right in Baltic and European politics. His book *The Comparative Government and Politics of the Baltic States: Estonia, Latvia and Lithuania in the 21st Century* was published in 2015.

Janusz Bugajski is a senior fellow at the Jamestown Foundation in Washington, DC. He has authored twenty books on Europe, Russia, and trans-Atlantic relations. He is working on a new book titled *Failed State: Planning for Russia's Rupture*. His recent books include *Eurasian Disunion: Russia's Vulnerable Flanks* (with Margarita Assenova, 2016); *Conflict Zones: North Caucasus and Western Balkans Compared* (2014); *Return of the Balkans: Challenges to European Integration and U.S. Disengagement* (2013); and *Georgian Lessons: Conflicting Russian and Western Interests in the Wider Europe* (2010). Bugajski is a recipient of the Distinguished Public Service Award from the US Department of State, the US Agency for International Development, the US Information Agency, and the Arms Control and Disarmament Agency. He has testified before several US congressional committees and lectured at numerous US universities. His previous positions include senior research analyst at Radio Free Europe (1984–1985), director of New European Democracies at the Center for Strategic and International Studies (1986–2013), and senior fellow at the Center for European Policy Analysis (2014–2020).

Zsuzsa Csergő is professor of political studies at Queen's University, Canada. Her research focuses on nationalism, state-minority relations, and issues of democratic government in Central and Eastern Europe (CEE). She is the author of *Talk of the Nation: Language and Conflict in Romania and Slovakia* (2007), coeditor of *Europeanization and Minority Political Agency* (2019), and author/coauthor of numerous articles in major journals, including *Perspectives on Politics, Foreign Policy, Publius, Nations and Nationalism, Europe-Asia Studies, East European Politics and Societies*, and *Problems of Post-Communism*. She is currently writing a book about conditions for democratic minority political agency in CEE. Csergő's European research fellowships include a Fernand Braudel Senior Fellowship at the European University Institute and a Marie-Skłodowska Curie Fellowship at the University of Graz. She was president of the Association for the Study of Nationalism (ASN) from 2013 to 2019 and is director of the association's online initiative, Virtual ASN.

Jane L. Curry is professor of political science at Santa Clara University. She also has taught as a Fulbright Professor at the University of Warsaw in the political science and journalism departments and at the Studium Europy Wschodniej (Center for East European Studies) at the University of Warsaw, where she held the Fulbright Distinguished Chair in East European Studies. She now teaches regularly in their summer program. She has written *Poland's Journalists: Professionalism and Politics* and the *Black Book of Polish Censorship* and edited books on dissent and the left in Central and Eastern Europe and *Poland's Permanent Revolution*, as well as the earlier editions of *Central and East European Politics*. She has also done extensive interviews with participants at all levels in the Rose Revolution in Georgia and the Orange Revolution in Ukraine as well as in-depth interviews with Poland's former communist leaders. These are available at the Hoover Institution.

Paul D'Anieri is professor of political science and public policy at the University of California–Riverside. His most recent book is *Ukraine and Russia: From Civilized Divorce to Uncivil War* (2019). His other books include *The Sources of Russia's Great Power Politics: Ukraine and the Challenge to the European Order* (with Taras Kuzio, 2018); *Orange Revolution and Aftermath: Mobilization, Apathy, and the State in Ukraine* (editor, 2010); *Understanding Ukrainian Politics: Power, Politics and Institutional Design* (2007); and *Economic Interdependence in Ukrainian-Russian Relations* (1999). His textbook *International Politics: Power and Purpose in Global Affairs* is currently in its fifth edition. He received his PhD in government from Cornell University and his BA in international relations from Michigan State University.

Kevin Deegan-Krause is associate professor of political science at Wayne State University in Detroit, Michigan. He received a BA in economics from Georgetown University in 1990 and a PhD in government from the University of Notre Dame in 2000 and has received Truman, IREX, and Fulbright scholarships. Along with numerous articles and book chapters, his publications include *Elected Affinities: Democracy and Party Competition in Slovakia and the Czech Republic* (2006) and six years as coeditor of the *European Journal of Political Research Political Data Yearbook*, during which he oversaw development of its interactive data website (http://politicaldatayearbook.com). His ongoing research project focuses on the emergence of new political parties and the transformation of established ones, the first phase of which appears in *The New Party Challenge: Cycles of Party Birth and Death in Central Europe and Beyond* (2020), written with Dr. Tim Haughton of the University of Birmingham.

Daina S. Eglitis is associate professor of sociology and international affairs at George Washington University. She is the author of the book *Imagining the Nation: History, Modernity, and Revolution in Latvia* (2002/2004), as well as recent articles in *East European Politics and Societies, Acta Sociologica, Nationalities Papers, Europe-Asia Studies*, and the *Journal of Genocide Research*. She is a two-time Fulbright recipient and was a research fellow at the US Holocaust Memorial Museum's Center for Advanced Holocaust Studies. Dr. Eglitis has taught courses at the University of Latvia, the Latvian Academy of Culture, and Riga Stradiņš University. She is working on a manuscript about women's experiences of World War II and the Holocaust in Eastern Europe. She received an MA in Russian and East European studies and a PhD in sociology from the University of Michigan–Ann Arbor and a BA in political science from George Washington University.

Arolda Elbasani is currently academic supervisor for a project on new statehood at the Kosovo Foundation for Open Society. She has held research and teaching positions at New York University, the Robert Schuman Center for Advanced Studies in Florence, Columbia University, and the Social Sciences Research Center and the Free University in Berlin. Her articles have appeared in the *Journal of European Public Policy*, *Southeast European and Black Sea Studies, Europe-Asia Studies, Politics and Religion*, and *Democratization*. Most recently she has also edited *International-Led Statebuilding and Local Resistance* (2000) and the *Balkan and Near Eastern Studies* special issue *Governing Islam and Religious Pluralism in New Democracies* (2017). Her research interests span the fields of the EU Enlargement policy, comparative democratization, postconflict state building, and Islamic politics in the Balkans and Turkey.

Seimir Elbasani is manager of business marketing at the Commercial Bank in Albania. He has a master's of science in international and development economics from the University of Applied Sciences in Berlin (2010) and a bachelor's in economics from University Dokuz Eylul, Izmir Turkey. His research interests include institutions and policies of development, migration, informal economies, and globalization, with a focus on the transition economies in Southeastern Europe. Since 2010, he collaborates with the Bertelsmann Transformation Index (BTI) as one of the authors of the biannual report on Albania.

Sharon Fisher is economics director with IHS Markit in Washington, DC, where she heads the Emerging Europe service. In addition to overseeing the regional team, she provides economic and political analysis, risk assessment, and forecasting on a number of Central and East European countries. Previously, she worked at the RFE/RL Research Institute in Munich, the Open Media Research Institute in Prague, and the Institute for Public Affairs in Bratislava. Dr. Fisher has presented at numerous conferences and seminars in Europe and the United States, and her extensive list of publications includes the 2006 book *Political Change in Post-Communist Slovakia and Croatia: From Nationalist to Europeanist*. She has a PhD from the School of Slavonic and East European Studies at University College London, an MA from the University of Pittsburgh's Graduate School of Public and International Affairs, and a BA from the College of William & Mary.

Eva Fodor is associate professor of gender studies and codirector of the Democracy Institute at the Central European University in Budapest. She is a sociologist by training and persuasion and has written books and numerous articles on gender, state socialism, and post-state socialism, with a focus on gender inequality in the labor market, for example, *Working Difference: Women's Working Lives in Hungary and Austria, 1945–95* (2003). Currently she is working on a book that analyzes recent antiliberal transformations within the Hungarian welfare state, specifically in the system of child protection and foster parenting. She is also involved in research on changes in the domestic division of labor during the COVID-19 pandemic of 2020. She received an MA from ELTE University in Budapest and a PhD in sociology from the University of California–Los Angeles.

Michelle Kelso is assistant professor of sociology and international affairs at George Washington University. Social justice and the exploration of (in)equalities are the foundations of her research. She is particularly interested in the intersection of the Holocaust and memory, marginalization, and contemporary education policy. Her work on Romania and the Holocaust has appeared in the *Journal of Genocide Research* and *Acta Sociologica*. In 2005, Dr. Kelso released a documentary, *Hidden Sorrows*, on the fate of Romanian Roma during the Holocaust, which screened at numerous film festivals and cultural venues and on Hungarian, Romanian, and Moldovan national television channels. She has held a Boren Fellowship, three Fulbright Fellowships to Romania, and a Charles H. Revson Fellowship at the US Holocaust Memorial Museum. She received an MA in Russian, East European, and Eurasian studies at the University of Texas and a PhD in sociology from the University of Michigan.

Jeffrey S. Kopstein is professor of political science at the University of California–Irvine. In his research, Professor Kopstein focuses on political development, interethnic violence, voting patterns of minority groups, and antiliberal tendencies in civil society, paying special attention to cases within European and Russian Jewish history. These interests are central topics in his latest coauthored book, *Intimate Violence: Anti-Jewish Pogroms on the Eve of the Holocaust* (2018). His previous books include *The Politics of Economic Decline in East Germany, 1945–1989* (1997) and *Growing Apart? America and Europe in the 21st Century* (2008). He has held fellowships at Harvard University, the Hebrew University of Jerusalem, Princeton University, and the Alexander von Humboldt Foundation.

Ronald H. Linden retired in 2019 as professor of political science at the University of Pittsburgh, where he had served as director of the European Studies Center and the Center for Russian and East European Studies. During the extraordinary changes in Eastern Europe (1989–1991), Dr. Linden was director of research for Radio Free Europe. He is a contributing author to *The Berlin Wall: 20 Years Later* (2009), published by the US Department of State. His publications on Eastern Europe include special issues of *Problems of Post-Communism* on *The Meaning of 1989 and After* (2009) and *The New Populism in Central and Southeast Europe* (2008). Publications on Turkey include *Turkey in Transition* (2020) and *Turkey and Its Neighbors* (2012). Recent works on the impact of growing Chinese-European ties include "The New Sea People: China in the Mediterranean" and "The Open Door Swings Back: The Challenge of Chinese Investment" (Istituto Affari Internazionali, Rome).

Eva-Clarita Pettai is a senior research associate at the Imre Kertész Kolleg, University of Jena, Germany, and editor of the online journal *Cultures of History Forum*, which reviews current debates across Central and Eastern Europe about twentieth-century history. Her research focuses on the comparative study of memory politics, democratization, and transitional justice in the former communist region, particularly the Baltic states. She has published widely about the rewriting of history after communism; the contestation of memories in national, bilateral, and pan-European arenas; and the politics of truth and justice after extended oppressive rule. Her book *Transitional and Retrospective Justice* *in the Baltic States* (with V. Pettai, 2015) received the 2015 Baltic Assembly Prize for Literature, Arts and Science. She edited *Memory and Pluralism in the Baltic States* (2011) and authored *Democratizing History in Latvia* (in German, 2003) as well as numerous articles about historical truth commissions, postcommunist trials, and memory laws.

Vello Pettai is professor of comparative politics at the University of Tartu, Estonia, and director of the European Centre for Minority Issues in Flensburg, Germany. He has published across a wide range of topics in postcommunist political development, including ethnic politics, transitional justice, electoral studies, democratization, coalition cabinets, constitutional review mechanisms, and legislative studies. He has worked as a regional manager for the Varieties of Democracy (V-Dem) network responsible for the Baltic states. He has also served as an author and reviewer for Freedom House's Nations in Transit, the Bertelsmann Transformation Index, and the Economist Intelligence Unit. He earned his PhD in political science from Columbia University.

Paula M. Pickering is associate professor of government at William & Mary. Her research focuses on the impact of aid for peace building, local governance, and civic engagement in Southeastern Europe, as well as the link between information and local accountability in Uganda. Pickering is the author of *Peacebuilding in the Balkans* (2007). Recent coauthored articles were published in the *Proceedings of the National Academy of Sciences* and *Governance*. Her research has received support from Evidence in Politics and Governance, the US Institute of Peace, the Social Science Research Council, and Fulbright-Hays. Pickering worked as a human rights officer for the Organization for Security and Co-operation in Europe's Mission in Bosnia-Herzegovina (1996) and as an analyst on Eastern Europe at the US Department of State (1990–1994). She received a PhD in political science at the University of Michigan and a BA in international relations at Stanford University.

Jennie L. Schulze is associate professor of comparative politics and international relations at Duquesne University. Her research focuses on the influence of European institutions and kin-states on minority policies and minority integration in Central and Eastern Europe. She is the author of *Strategic Frames: Europe, Russia, and Minority Inclusion in Estonia and Latvia* (2018). The book was awarded an honorable mention for the Joseph Rothschild Prize in Nationalism and Ethnic Studies. Other scholarly articles have appeared in *Polity*, *Problems of Post-Communism*, *Nationalities Papers*, *Eurasian Geography and Economics*, the *Journal on Ethnopolitics and Minority Issues in Europe*, and *Studies of Transition States and Societies*. She has also served as an expert on Estonia and Latvia for the US Department of State and the US Department of Defense. She is currently working on a new comparative book project, *Cities of Bridges: Receiving Refugees in Times of Crisis*.

Jelena Subotić is professor in the Department of Political Science at Georgia State University. She received her PhD from the University of Wisconsin–Madison. She writes about international relations theory, memory politics, human rights, transitional justice, international ethics, state identity, and the politics of the Western Balkans. Her second book, *Yellow Star, Red Star: Holocaust Remembrance after Communism* (2019), explains how East European countries after the collapse of communism pursued new strategies of Holocaust remembrance where the memory, symbols, and imagery of the Holocaust became appropriated to represent crimes of communism. Her first book, *Hijacked Justice: Dealing with the Past in the Balkans* (2009), has been translated and published in Serbia in 2010. Her research has appeared in numerous journals, including *International Studies Quarterly*, the *European Journal of International Relations*, the *Journal of Peace Research*, and *Foreign Policy Analysis*. She is the recipient of a number of research grants, including from the National Science Foundation and USAID. She is also a frequent commentator on war crimes and the politics of the Balkans for CNN, the BBC, and other international outlets.

Ognen Vangelov holds a PhD in political studies from Queen's University, Canada, and is an assistant professor at the University American College–Skopje in North Macedonia. He is also a research fellow at the Centre for the Study of Democracy and Diversity at Queen's University in Canada. He has been a recipient of Canada's Vanier Fellowship and the US Ron Brown Fellowship. His research focuses on the drivers and mechanisms of autocratization in countries of Central and East Europe and on the politics of ethnicity and nationalism. His publications on these topics have appeared in major international academic and policy journals. His other current projects focus on the politics of complex diversity in contested cities, as well as on minority institutions and institutional domains of ethnolinguistic minorities in Central and Eastern Europe.

Jason Wittenberg received his PhD from the Massachusetts Institute of Technology and is professor of political science at the University of California–Berkeley. A former Academy Scholar at Harvard University, he has been a visiting scholar at the Helen Kellogg Institute at the University of Notre Dame, a Fulbright Scholar at the Central European University in Budapest, and a visiting professor at the University of Tokyo. Professor Wittenberg has published widely on topics including electoral behavior, ethnic and religious violence, historical legacies, and empirical research methods. His first book, *Crucibles of Political Loyalty: Church Institutions and Electoral Continuity in Hungary* (2006), won the 2009 Hubert Morken Award for the best political science book published on religion and politics. He is the coauthor, most recently, of *Intimate Violence: Anti-Jewish Pogroms on the Eve of the Holocaust* (2018), winner of the 2019 Bronislaw Malinowski Award in the Social Sciences.

Sharon L. Wolchik is professor of political science and international affairs at George Washington University's Elliott School of International Affairs, where she teaches and does research on Central and East European politics. She is author of *Defeating Authoritarian Leaders in Postcommunist Countries* (with Valerie Bunce, 2011) and *Czechoslovakia in Transition: Politics, Economics, and Society* (1992) and editor of *Central and East European Politics: From Communism to Democracy* (with Jane L. Curry, Rowman & Littlefield, 4th edition, 2018), *Women in Power in Post-Communist Parliaments* (with Marilyn Rueschemeyer, 2009), *Ukraine: The Search for a National Identity* (with Volodymyr Zviglyanich, Rowman & Littlefield, 1999), and *Women and Democracy: Latin America and Central and Eastern Europe* (with Jane S. Jaquette, 1998).

9 781538 142806